Discrete Optimization: Theory, Algorithms, and Applications

Discrete Optimization: Theory, Algorithms, and Applications

Editor

Frank Werner

 Basel • Beijing • Wuhan • Barcelona • Belgrade • Novi Sad • Cluj • Manchester

Editor
Frank Werner
Faculty of Mathematics
Otto-von-Guericke University
Magdeburg
Germany

Editorial Office
MDPI AG
Grosspeteranlage 5
4052 Basel, Switzerland

This is a reprint of articles from the Special Issue published online in the open access journal *Mathematics* (ISSN 2227-7390) (available at: https://www.mdpi.com/journal/mathematics/special_issues/discrete_optimization).

For citation purposes, cite each article independently as indicated on the article page online and as indicated below:

Lastname, A.A.; Lastname, B.B. Article Title. *Journal Name* **Year**, *Volume Number*, Page Range.

ISBN 978-3-7258-1628-6 (Hbk)
ISBN 978-3-7258-1627-9 (PDF)
doi.org/10.3390/books978-3-7258-1627-9

© 2024 by the authors. Articles in this book are Open Access and distributed under the Creative Commons Attribution (CC BY) license. The book as a whole is distributed by MDPI under the terms and conditions of the Creative Commons Attribution-NonCommercial-NoDerivs (CC BY-NC-ND) license.

Contents

About the Editor vii

Preface ix

Frank Werner
Discrete Optimization: Theory, Algorithms, and Applications
Reprinted from: *Mathematics* **2019**, *7*, 397, doi:10.3390/math7050397 1

Yuri N. Sotskov and Natalja G. Egorova
The Optimality Region for a Single-Machine Scheduling Problem with Bounded Durations of the Jobs and the Total Completion Time Objective
Reprinted from: *Mathematics* **2019**, *7*, 382, doi:10.3390/math7050382 5

Evgeny Gafarov and Frank Werner
Two-Machine Job-Shop Scheduling with Equal Processing Times on Each Machine
Reprinted from: *Mathematics* **2019**, *7*, 301, doi:10.3390/math7030301 26

Jian Lu, Shu-Bo Chen, Jia-Bao Liu, Xiang-Feng Pan and Ying-Jie Ji
Further Results on the Resistance-Harary Index of Unicyclic Graphs
Reprinted from: *Mathematics* **2019**, *7*, 201, doi:10.3390/math7020201 37

Jia-Bao Liu, Agha Kashif, Tabasam Rashid and Muhammad Javaid
Fractional Metric Dimension of Generalized Jahangir Graph
Reprinted from: *Mathematics* **2019**, *7*, 100, doi:10.3390/math7010100 50

Hassan Raza, Sakander Hayat and Xiang-Feng Pan
Fault-Tolerant Resolvability and Extremal Structures of Graphs
Reprinted from: *Mathematics* **2019**, *7*, 78, doi:10.3390/math7010078 60

Jia-Bao Liu, Mobeen Munir, Amina Yousaf, Asim Naseem and Khudaija Ayub
Distance and Adjacency Energies of Multi-Level Wheel Networks
Reprinted from: *Mathematics* **2019**, *7*, 43, doi:10.3390/math7010043 79

Kashif Elahi, Ali Ahmad and Roslan Hasni
Construction Algorithm for Zero Divisor Graphs of Finite Commutative Rings and Their Vertex-Based Eccentric Topological Indices
Reprinted from: *Mathematics* **2018**, *6*, 301, doi:10.3390/math6120301 88

Li Zhang, Jing Zhao, Jia-Bao Liu and Micheal Arockiaraj
Resistance Distance in H-Join of Graphs $G_1, G_2, \ldots, G_k$
Reprinted from: *Mathematics* **2018**, *6*, 283, doi:10.3390/math6120283 97

Fang Gao, Xiaoxin Li, Kai Zhou and Jia-Bao Liu
The Extremal Graphs of Some Topological Indices with Given Vertex k-Partiteness
Reprinted from: *Mathematics* **2018**, *6*, 271, doi:10.3390/math6110271 107

Şeyda Gür and Tamer Eren
Scheduling and Planning in Service Systems with Goal Programming: Literature Review
Reprinted from: *Mathematics* **2018**, *6*, 265, doi:10.3390/math6110265 118

Jia-Bao Liu, Zohaib Zahid, Ruby Nasir and Waqas Nazeer
Edge Version of Metric Dimension and Doubly Resolving Sets of the Necklace Graph
Reprinted from: *Mathematics* **2018**, *6*, 243, doi:10.3390/math6110243 134

Shaohui Wang, Chunxiang Wang, Lin Chen, Jia-Bao Liu and Zehui Shao
Maximizing and Minimizing Multiplicative Zagreb Indices of Graphs Subject to Given Number of Cut Edges
Reprinted from: *Mathematics* **2018**, *6*, 227, doi:10.3390/math6110227 . . . . **144**

Huiqin Jiang, Pu Wu, Zehui Shao, Yongsheng Rao and Jia-Bao Liu
The Double Roman Domination Numbers of Generalized Petersen Graphs $P(n,2)$
Reprinted from: *Mathematics* **2018**, *6*, 206, doi:10.3390/math6100206 . . . . **154**

Shahid Imran, Muhammad Kamran Siddiqui, Muhammad Imran and Muhammad Hussain
On Metric Dimensions of Symmetric Graphs Obtained by Rooted Product
Reprinted from: *Mathematics* **2018**, *6*, 191, doi:10.3390/math6100191 . . . . **165**

Hui-Chin Tang and Shen-Tai Yang
Optimizing Three-Dimensional Constrained Ordered Weighted Averaging Aggregation Problem with Bounded Variables
Reprinted from: *Mathematics* **2018**, *6*, 172, doi:10.3390/math6090172 . . . . **181**

Hong Yang, Muhammad Kamran Siddiqui, Muhammad Ibrahim, Sarfraz Ahmad and Ali Ahmad
Computing The Irregularity Strength of Planar Graphs
Reprinted from: *Mathematics* **2018**, *6*, 150, doi:10.3390/math6090150 . . . . **197**

Shahid Imran, Muhammad Kamran Siddiqui, Muhammad Imran and Muhammad Faisal Nadeem
Computing Topological Indices and Polynomials for Line Graphs
Reprinted from: *Mathematics* **2018**, *6*, 137, doi:10.3390/math6080137 . . . . **211**

Muhammad Imran, Muhammad Kamran Siddiqui, Amna A. E. Abunamous, Dana Adi, Saida Hafsa Rafique and Abdul Qudair Baig
Eccentricity Based Topological Indices of an Oxide Network
Reprinted from: *Mathematics* **2018**, *6*, 126, doi:10.3390/math6070126 . . . . **221**

About the Editor

Frank Werner

Frank Werner studied mathematics from 1975 to 1980 and graduated from the Technical University Magdeburg (Germany) with distinction. He received a Ph.D. degree (with summa cum laude) in Mathematics in 1984 and defended his habilitation thesis in 1989. From this time on, he worked at the Faculty of Mathematics of the Otto-von-Guericke University Magdeburg in Germany, becoming an extraordinary professor in 1998. In 1992, he received a grant from the Alexander von Humboldt Foundation. He was a manager of several research projects supported by the German Research Society (DFG) and the European Union (INTAS). Since 2019, he has been the editor-in-chief of *Algorithms*. He has also been an associate editor of the *International Journal of Production Research* since 2012 and of the *Journal of Scheduling* since 2014, as well a member of the editorial/advisory boards of 18 further international journals. He has been a guest editor of Special Issues in ten international journals and has served as a member of the program committee of more than 150 international conferences. Frank Werner is an author/editor of 14 books, among them the textbooks 'Mathematics of Economics and Business' and 'A Refresher Course in Mathematics'. In addition, he has co-edited three proceedings volumes of the SIMULTECH conferences and published more than 300 journal and conference papers, e.g., in the *International Journal of Production Research, Computers & Operations Research, Journal of Scheduling, Applied Mathematical Modelling*, and the *European Journal of Operational Research*. He has received Best Paper Awards from the *International Journal of Production Research* (2016) and *IISE Transactions* (2021). His main research subjects are scheduling, discrete optimization, graph theory, and mathematical problems in operations research.

Preface

This is the printed edition of a Special Issue published in *Mathematics*. This reprint contains an Editorial and 18 research papers. The subjects addressed in this reprint include graphs and networks, single- and two-machine scheduling, and goal programming, to name a few.

Finally, my thanks go to all who contributed to the great success of this issue: authors from 12 countries, many referees from all over the world, and, in particular, the staff of *Mathematics* for their invaluable support during the preparation of this issue. I hope that the readers of this reprint will find many fruitful ideas for their own future research in the field of Discrete Optimization.

Frank Werner
Editor

Editorial

Discrete Optimization: Theory, Algorithms, and Applications

Frank Werner

Fakultät für Mathematik, Otto-von-Guericke-Universität Magdeburg, PSF 4120, 39016 Magdeburg, Germany; frank.werner@ovgu.de

Received: 28 April 2019 ; Accepted: 29 April 2019; Published: 1 May 2019

Discrete optimization is an important area of applied mathematics that is at the intersection of several disciplines and covers both theoretical and practical aspects. In the call for papers for this issue, I asked for submissions presenting new theoretical results, structural investigations, new models, and algorithmic approaches, as well as new applications of discrete optimization problems. Among the possible subjects, integer programming, combinatorial optimization, optimization problems on graphs and networks, matroids, scheduling, and logistics were mentioned, to name a few.

In response to the call for papers, 51 submissions have been received, among which, finally, 18 papers have been accepted for this Special Issue, all of which are of high quality, reflecting the great interest in the area of discrete optimization. This corresponds to an acceptance rate of 35.3%. The authors of these publications come from 12 different countries: China, Pakistan, the United Arab Emirates, Saudi Arabia, Belarus, Germany, India, Malaysia, Russia, Taiwan, Turkey, and the USA, where the authors from the first four countries co-authored more than one paper in this issue. Although many different aspects of discrete optimization have been addressed by the submissions, among the accepted papers, there is a major part dealing with graphs and networks. A large part of these papers deals with topological indices and the domination of graphs. Several of these papers also emphasize the great importance of graph-theoretic works for practical applications. For this reason, I would like to draw the attention of the readers also to another future Special Issue planned for the journal Mathematics entitled "Graph-Theoretic Problems and Their New Applications" with a deadline for submissions of 31 January 2020.

All submissions have been reviewed, as a rule, by at least three experts in the discrete optimization area. Next, all published papers in this Special Issue are briefly surveyed in increasing order of their publication dates. This Special Issue contains both theoretical and practical works in the field of discrete optimization. We hope that practical operations research workers will find some interesting theoretical ideas in this Special Issue and that researchers will find new inspirations for future works.

The first accepted paper by Imran et al. [1] studies the chemical graph of an oxide network, and in particular, it deals with topological indices. The authors compute the total eccentricity, the average eccentricity, eccentricity-based Zagreb indices, the atom-bond connectivity index, and the geometric arithmetic index of such a network. In addition, arithmetically-closed formulas for these indices are given in this paper.

Imran et al [2] deal with the computation of several topological indices and polynomials for line graphs. In particular, the authors compute the first and second Zagreb indices, the hyper Zagreb index, multiple Zagreb indices, and Zagreb polynomials of the line graph of wheel and ladder graphs. To obtain their results, they used the idea of subdivision.

Yang et al. [3] deal with a problem from graph labeling that plays a role in many applications, e.g., in coding theory, radars, astronomy, or the management of databases. In particular, they discuss the total edge irregular k labeling, the total vertex irregular k labeling, and the totally irregular total k labeling of three planar graphs. The authors determine the exact value of the total irregularity strength of such graphs.

Tang and Yang [4] deal with an ordered weighted averaging aggregation problem, denoted as COWA. For the three-dimensional case, they consider two variants: the maximization variant of the COWA problem with lower bounded variables and the minimization version with upper bounded variables. They present the optimal solutions theoretically and give also empirical results. It appears that both the weights and bounds can affect the optimal solution of such three-dimensional problems. As an interesting future research subject, the authors mention the potential extension of such investigations to the case of higher dimensions.

Imran et al. [5] deal with the metric dimension of special graphs, which is defined as the minimum cardinality of a resolving set of the corresponding graph. The authors investigate the cycle, path, Harary graphs, and their rooted products, as well as their connectivity. It is shown that the metric dimension of some graphs is unbounded, while for the other investigated graphs, the metric dimension is either three or four. The paper finishes with the formulation of two open research problems.

Jiang et al. [6] investigate the double Roman domination number, which is the minimum weight of a double Roman dominating function, of so-called generalized Petersen graphs of the type $P(n,2)$. This result is obtained by using a discharging approach. As one conclusion, it turns out that the graph $P(n,2)$ is not double Roman for all $n \geq 5$, and the authors formulate that it is an interesting problem to find further Petersen graphs that are double Roman.

Wang et al. [7] deal with multiplicative Zagreb indices. For graphs with n vertices and k cut edges, the maximum and minimum multiplicative Zagreb indices are determined. In addition, the graphs with the smallest and largest first and second multiplicative Zagreb indices are provided.

Liu et al. [8] use the concept of the edge version of the metric dimension and doubly-resolving sets, which is based on the distances of the edges of a graph. The metric dimension can be used, e.g., in navigation, robotics, or chemistry. The authors apply this concept to a so-called necklace graph, which is a cubic Halin graph obtained by joining a cycle with all vertices of degree one with a caterpillar having n vertices of degree three and $n+2$ vertices of degree one.

Gür and Eran [9] give an overview on goal programming applied to scheduling and planning problems arising in service systems. They discuss 143 references from the literature. First, they give some information for which activities in service systems goal programming is typically used. Then, they explain the different types of goal programming applied in the literature. The authors also briefly discuss the methods that are integrated with the goal programming method in the literature. At the time of writing this Editorial, this is the paper of this Issue with by far the most downloads.

Gao et al. [10] consider another graph-theoretic subject, namely they deal with the extremal graphs of some topological indices of a graph G with given vertex k-partiteness, which is defined as the smallest number of vertices, the deletion of which from G yields a k-partite graph. For such graphs, they characterize the extremal values of the reformulated first Zagreb index, the multiplicative-sum Zagreb index, the general Laplacian-energy-like index, the general zeroth-order Randic index, and the modified Wiener index.

Zhang et al. [11] compute the resistance distance in the H-join G of k disjoint graphs. They use the Laplacian matrix $L(G)$ and the symmetric $\{1\}$-inverse of $L(G)$. The authors discuss also some applications of the results obtained.

Elahi et al. [12] also deal with a subject from chemical graph theory. They consider graphs containing a commutative ring, which have wide applications, e.g., in robotics, information theory, physics, or statistics. In their paper, they adopted interdisciplinary methods. They discussed vertex-based eccentric topological indices, namely the eccentric connectivity index, the total-eccentricity index, the first Zagreb eccentricity index, the connective eccentric index, the Ediz eccentric connectivity index, the eccentric connectivity polynomial, and the augmented eccentric index for zero divisor graphs of a commutative ring. These indices are useful for understanding physical structures like carbon nanostructures or those in robotics.

Liu et al. [13] consider another problem related, e.g., to chemistry. They deal with the energies of molecular graphs. In particular, they give closed forms of the distance and adjacency energies of generalized wheel networks, also known as m-level wheels. They also illustrate the dependencies of the energies on the parameters of the wheel graphs. The results can be useful both for mathematicians and chemists in industry since generalized wheels can be considered as particular cyclic structures having a common hub.

Raza et al. [14] characterize graphs having n vertices with fault-tolerant metric dimensions n, $n-1$, and two, which are the non-trivial extremal values of the fault-tolerant metric dimension. By means of a lemma for tracing a fault-tolerant resolving set from a given resolving set, an upper bound on the fault-tolerant metric dimension of a graph with a given resolving set is derived. The fault-tolerant resolvability is investigated for three infinite families of regular graphs.

Liu et al. [15] deal with the fractional metric dimension of a connected graph, which had been introduced only some years ago in 2012. In particular, they consider a generalized Jahingir graph $J_{m,k}$, the vertices of which can be classified into three categories, namely vertices of degree two (called minors), three (called majors), and m (called center), and there are km minor vertices, m major vertices, and one center vertex. They introduce the resolving neighborhood for any possible pair of vertices in a generalized Jahingir graph. As the main result, the authors determine the fractional metric dimension of a generalized Jahingir graph for $k \geq 0$ and $m = 5$.

Lu et al. [16] deal with the resistance-Harary index of connected graphs. In particular, they determine among the set of unicyclic graphs (these are graphs containing exactly one cycle) those graphs having the second-largest resistance-Harary index and, among the fully-loaded unicyclic graphs (these are unicyclic graphs such that no vertex with a degree less than three is in the unique cycle), those with the largest resistance-Harary index.

Gafarov and Werner [17] consider a two-machine job-shop scheduling problem, where each of n jobs consists of two operations and the processing times of all jobs on each machine are identical. The objective is to minimize the sum of the completion times. This problem arises also as a special single-track railway scheduling problem with three stations and constant travel times between any two adjacent stations. For this problem, the authors give a dynamic programming algorithm of complexity $O(n^5)$ and, in addition, a fast constructive heuristic of complexity $O(n^3)$. Computational results are presented for instances with up to 30 jobs.

Sotskov and Egorova [18] deal with a single-machine scheduling problem with uncertain processing times, where only lower and upper bounds on the processing times are known. The objective is to minimize the sum of the completion times. The authors investigate the properties of the optimality region. They introduce the quasi-perimeter of the optimality region and give a linear time algorithm for calculating it. Moreover, they present an algorithm for finding the job permutation with the largest quasi-perimeter of this region. Computational results are given for instances with up to 5000 jobs, which show that the constructed permutation is close to an optimal job sequence for the actual processing times of the jobs.

Acknowledgments: As the Guest Editor, I would like to thank all authors for submitting their work to this Special Issue and also all referees for their support by giving timely and insightful reports. My special thanks go to the staff of the journal Mathematics for the good and pleasant cooperation during the preparation of this issue.

Conflicts of Interest: The author declares no conflict of interest.

References

1. Imran, M.; Siddiqui, M.K.; Abunamous, A.A.E.; Adi, D.; Rafique, S.H.; Baig, A.Q. Eccentricity Based Topological Indices of an Oxide Network. *Mathematics* **2018**, *6*, 126. [CrossRef]
2. Imran, S.; Siddiqui, M.K.; Imran, M.; Nadeem, M.F. Computing Topological Indices for Line Graphs. *Mathematics* **2018**, *6*, 137. [CrossRef]
3. Yang, H.; Siddiqui, M.K.; Ibrahim, M.; Ahmad, S.; Ahmad, A. Computing the Irregularity Strength. *Mathematics* **2018**, *6*, 150. [CrossRef]

4. Tang, H.-C.; Yang, S.-T. Optimizing Three-Dimensional Constrained Ordered Weighted Averaging Aggregation Problem with Bounded Variables. *Mathematics* **2018**, *6*, 172. [CrossRef]
5. Imran, S.; Siddiqui, M.K.; Imran, M.; Hussain, M. On Metric Dimensions of Symmetric Graphs Obtained by Rooted Product. *Mathematics* **2018**, *6*, 191. [CrossRef]
6. Jiang, H.; Wu, P.; Shao, Z.; Rao, Y.; Liu, J.-B. The Double Roman Domination Numbers of Generalized Petersen Graphs $P(n,2)$. *Mathematics* **2018**, *6*, 206. [CrossRef]
7. Wang, S.; Wang, C.; Chen, L.; Liu, J.-B.; Shao, Z. Maximizing and Minimizing Multiplicative Zagreb Indices of Graphs Subject to Given Number of Cut Edges. *Mathematics* **2018**, *6*, 227. [CrossRef]
8. Liu, J.-B.; Zahid, Z.; Nasir, R.; Nazeer, W. Edge Version of Metric Dimension and Doubly Resolving Sets of the Necklace Graph. *Mathematics* **2018**, *6*, 243. [CrossRef]
9. Gür, S.; Eren, T. Scheduling and Planning in Service Systems with Goal Programming: Literature Survey. *Mathematics* **2018**, *6*, 265. [CrossRef]
10. Gao, F.; Li, X.; Zhou, K.; Liu, J.-B. The Extremal Graphs of Some Topological Indices with Given Vertex k-Partiteness. *Mathematics* **2018**, *6*, 271. [CrossRef]
11. Zhang, L.; Zhao, J.; Liu, J.-B.; Arockiaraj, M. Resistance Distance in H-Join of Graphs $G_1, G_2, \ldots, G_k$. *Mathematics* **2018**, *6*, 283. [CrossRef]
12. Elahi, K.; Ahmad, A.; Hasni, R. Construction Algorithm for Zero Divisor Graphs of Finite Commutative Rings and Their Vertex-Based Eccentric Topological Indices. *Mathematics* **2018**, *6*, 301. [CrossRef]
13. Liu, J.-B.; Munir, M.; Yousaf, A.; Naseem, A.; Ayub, K. Distance and Adjacency Energies of Multi-Level Wheel Networks. *Mathematics* **2019**, *7*, 43. [CrossRef]
14. Raza, H.; Hayat, S.; Imran, M.; Pan, X.-F. Fault-Tolerant Resolvability and Extremal Structures of Graphs. *Mathematics* **2019**, *7*, 78. [CrossRef]
15. Liu, J.-B.; Kashif, A.; Rashid, T.; Javaid, M. Fractional Metric Dimension of Generalized Jahangir Graph. *Mathematics* **2019**, *7*, 100. [CrossRef]
16. Lu, J.; Chen, S.-B.; Liu, J.-B.; Pan, X.-F.; Ji, Y.-J. Further Results on the Resistance-Harary Index of Unicyclic Graphs. *Mathematics* **2019**, *7*, 201. [CrossRef]
17. Gafarov, E.; Werner, F. Two-Machine Job-Shop Scheduling with Equal Processing Times on Each Machine. *Mathematics* **2019**, *7*, 301. [CrossRef]
18. Sotskov, Y.N.; Egorova, N.G. The Optimality Region for a Single-Machine Scheduling Problem with Bounded Durations of the Jobs and the Total Completion Time Objective. *Mathematics* **2019**, *7*, 382. [CrossRef]

© 2019 by the authors. Licensee MDPI, Basel, Switzerland. This article is an open access article distributed under the terms and conditions of the Creative Commons Attribution (CC BY) license (http://creativecommons.org/licenses/by/4.0/).

Article

The Optimality Region for a Single-Machine Scheduling Problem with Bounded Durations of the Jobs and the Total Completion Time Objective

Yuri N. Sotskov * and Natalja G. Egorova

United Institute of Informatics Problems, National Academy of Sciences of Belarus, Surganova Street 6, 220012 Minsk, Belarus; NataMog@yandex.ru
* Correspondence: sotskov48@mail.ru; Tel.: +375-17-284-2120

Received: 28 February 2019 ; Accepted: 19 April 2019; Published: 26 April 2019

Abstract: We study a single-machine scheduling problem to minimize the total completion time of the given set of jobs, which have to be processed without job preemptions. The lower and upper bounds on the job duration is the only information that is available before scheduling. Exact values of the job durations remain unknown until the completion of the jobs. We use the optimality region for the job permutation as an optimality measure of the optimal schedule. We investigate properties of the optimality region and derive $O(n)$-algorithm for calculating a quasi-perimeter of the optimality set (i.e., the sum of lengths of the optimality segments for n given jobs). We develop a fast algorithm for finding a job permutation having the largest quasi-perimeter of the optimality set. The computational results in constructing such permutations show that they are close to the optimal ones, which can be constructed for the factual durations of all given jobs.

Keywords: single-machine scheduling; uncertain job durations; total completion time objective; optimality region

1. Introduction

A lot of real-life scheduling problems involve different forms of uncertainties. For dealing with uncertain scheduling problems, several approaches have been developed in the literature. In a stochastic approach, job durations are assumed to be random variables with the specific probability distributions known before scheduling [1,2]. If there is no sufficient information to determine the probability distribution for each random duration of the given job, other approaches have to be used [3–5]. In the approach of seeking a robust schedule [3,6], a decision-maker prefers a schedule that hedges against the worst-case scenario. A fuzzy approach [7–9] allows a scheduler to find best schedules with respect to fuzzy durations of the given jobs. A stability approach [10] is based on the stability analysis of the optimal schedules to possible variations of the job durations. In this paper, we apply the stability approach to the single-machine scheduling problem with interval durations of the given jobs.

In Section 2, we present settings of the uncertain scheduling problems, the related literature and closed results. In Section 3, we investigate properties of the optimality region for the job permutation, which is used for processing given jobs. Efficient algorithms for calculating a quasi-perimeter of the optimality region are derived in Section 4. In Section 5, we show how to find a job permutation with the largest quasi-perimeter of the optimality region and develop algorithm for finding an approximate solution for the uncertain scheduling problem. In Section 6, we report on the computational results for finding solutions for the tested instances. The paper is concluded in Section 7.

2. Problem Descriptions, The Related Literature and Closed Results

There is given a set of jobs $\mathcal{J} = \{J_1, J_2, \ldots, J_n\}$ to be processed on a single machine. The duration p_i of the job $J_i \in \mathcal{J}$ can take any real value from the given segment $[p_i^L, p_i^U]$, where the inequalities $p_i^U \geq p_i^L > 0$ hold. The exact value $p_i \in [p_i^L, p_i^U]$ of the job duration remains unknown until the completion time of the job $J_i \in \mathcal{J}$.

Let R_+^n denote a set of all non-negative n-dimensional real vectors, $R_+^n \subseteq R^n$, where R^n is space of n-dimensional real vectors. The set of all vectors $(p_1, p_2, \ldots, p_n) = p \in R_+^n$ of the feasible durations is presented as the Cartesian product of the segments $[p_i^L, p_i^U]$:

$$T = [p_1^L, p_1^U] \times [p_2^L, p_2^U] \times \ldots \times [p_n^L, p_n^U] = \{p : p \in R_+^n, \ p_i^L \leq p_i \leq p_i^U, \ i \in \{1, 2, \ldots, n\}\}.$$

A vector $p \in T$ of the job durations is called a scenario. Let $S = \{\pi_1, \pi_2, \ldots, \pi_{n!}\}$ denote a set of all permutations $\pi_k = (J_{k_1}, J_{k_2}, \ldots, J_{k_n})$ of the given jobs $\mathcal{J}$.

Given a scenario $p \in T$ and a permutation $\pi_k \in S$, let $C_i = C_i(\pi_k, p)$ denote the completion time of the job J_i in the schedule determined by the permutation π_k. The criterion $\sum C_i$ denotes the minimization of the following sum of the completion times:

$$\sum_{J_i \in \mathcal{J}} C_i(\pi_t, p) = \min_{\pi_k \in S} \left\{ \sum_{J_i \in \mathcal{J}} C_i(\pi_k, p) \right\}, \tag{1}$$

where the permutation $\pi_t = (J_{t_1}, J_{t_2}, \ldots, J_{t_n}) \in S$ is optimal. From the equality (1), it follows that only semi-active schedule [11] may be optimal. Each permutation $\pi_k \in S$ determines exactly one semi-active schedule.

The above uncertain scheduling problem is denoted as $1 | p_i^L \leq p_i \leq p_i^U | \sum C_i$ using the three-field notation $\alpha | \beta | \gamma$ [12], where α denotes the processing system, β characterizes conditions for processing the jobs and γ determines the criterion.

2.1. The Related Literature

If a scenario $p \in T$ is fixed before scheduling (i.e., the equality $[p_i^L, p_i^U] = [p_i, p_i]$ holds for each job $J_i \in \mathcal{J}$), then the uncertain problem $1 | p_i^L \leq p_i \leq p_i^U | \sum C_i$ is turned into the deterministic one $1 || \sum C_i$. In what follows, we use the notation $1 | p | \sum C_i$ to indicate an instance of the deterministic problem $1 || \sum C_i$ with scenario $p \in T$. Any instance $1 | p | \sum C_i$ is solvable in $O(n \log n)$ time [13] due to the following necessary and sufficient condition for the optimality of the job permutation $\pi_k \in S$.

Theorem 1. *The job permutation $\pi_k = (J_{k_1}, J_{k_2}, \ldots, J_{k_n}) \in S$ is optimal for the instance $1 | p | \sum C_i$ if and only if the following inequalities hold:*

$$p_{k_1} \leq p_{k_2} \leq \ldots \leq p_{k_n}. \tag{2}$$

If the strict inequality $p_{k_u} < p_{k_v}$ holds, then the job J_{k_u} precedes the job J_{k_v} in any optimal job permutation π_k.

Since the scenario $p \in T$ is not fixed in the uncertain problem $1 | p_i^L \leq p_i \leq p_i^U | \sum C_i$, the completion time C_i of the job $J_i \in \mathcal{J}$ cannot be determined for the permutation $\pi_k \in S$ before completing the job J_i. Thus, the value of the objective function $\sum_{J_i \in \mathcal{J}} C_i(\pi_t, p)$ for the permutation π_k remains uncertain until all jobs $\mathcal{J}$ have been completed. Since for the uncertain problem $\alpha | p_i^L \leq p_i \leq p_i^U | \gamma$, there does not usually exist an optimal schedule for all feasible scenarios p from the set T, an additional objective or some agreements are used in the literature.

A robust schedule minimizing the worst-case regret has been developed in [3,8,14–18]. For any permutation $\pi_k \in S$ and any feasible scenario $p \in T$, the difference $\gamma_p^k - \gamma_p^t =: r(\pi_k, p)$ is called the regret for the permutation π_k. In the above notation $r(\pi_k, p)$, the objective function γ is equal to γ_p^k for the permutation π_k under scenario p and the optimal value of the objective function γ is equal to

γ_p^t for the optimal permutation π_k under scenario p. The value of $Z(\pi_k) = \max\{r(\pi_k, p) : p \in T\}$ is called the worst-case absolute regret. The value of $Z^*(\pi_k) = \max\{\frac{r(\pi_k, p)}{\gamma_p^t} : p \in T\}$ is called the worst-case relative regret.

While the deterministic problem $1||\sum C_i$ is polynomially solvable [13], finding a permutation $\pi_t \in S$ minimizing the worst-case absolute regret $Z(\pi_k)$ or the relative regret Z^* for the problem $1|p_i^L \leq p_i \leq p_i^U|\sum C_i$ are binary NP-hard even for two possible scenarios $\{p_1, p_2\}$ [3,17,19]. Discrete sets $\{p_1, p_2, \ldots, p_m\}$ of the uncertain scenarios have been investigated in [3,17,19].

The complexity of minimizing the total flow time with continues data T is characterized in [20], where it is proven that finding a permutation $\pi_t \in S$ minimizing the worst-case absolute regret $Z(\pi_k)$ for the problem $1|p_i^L \leq p_i \leq p_i^U|\sum C_i$ is binary NP-hard. For a special case of this problem, where all intervals of uncertainty have the same center, it is shown that this problem can be solved in $O(n \log n)$ time if the number of jobs is even, and remains NP-hard if the number of jobs is odd [20]. In [6], a branch-and-bound algorithm was developed for finding a permutation π_k minimizing the absolute regret for the problem $1|p_i^L \leq p_i \leq p_i^U|\sum w_i C_i$, where the jobs $J_i \in \mathcal{J}$ have different weights $w_i > 0$. The computational experiments showed that the developed algorithm is able to find such a permutation π_k for the instances with up to 40 jobs.

The fuzzy scheduling technique was used in [7–9,21] to develop a fuzzy analogue of dispatching rules or to solve mathematical programming problems to determine a schedule that minimizes a fuzzy-valued objective function.

In [22], several heuristics were developed for the problem $1|p_i^L \leq p_i \leq p_i^U|\sum w_i C_i$. The computational experiments including different probability distributions of the job durations showed that there was at least one heuristic among all performing heuristics with the error 1.1% of the optimal objective function value $\sum w_i C_i$ obtained after completing the given jobs when their factual durations became known.

In Sections 3–6, we adopt the stability approach [5,10,23–25] to the uncertain problem $1|p_i^L \leq p_i \leq p_i^U|\sum C_i$ with the additional criterion of maximizing a quasi-perimeter of the optimality region introduced in Section 3.

2.2. The Stability Approach to Single-Machine Scheduling Problems

Let M denote a subset of the set $N = \{1, 2, \ldots, n\}$. In [23,24], an optimality box for the job permutation $\pi_k \in S$ for the uncertain problem $1|p_i^L \leq p_i \leq p_i^U|\sum C_i$ is defined as follows.

Definition 1. *The maximal rectangular box $\mathcal{OB}(\pi_k, T) = \times_{k_i \in M}[l_{k_i}^*, u_{k_i}^*] \subseteq T$ is called an optimality box for the permutation $\pi_k = (J_{k_1}, J_{k_2}, \ldots, J_{k_n}) \in S$ (with respect to T), if the permutation π_k being optimal for the instance $1|p|\sum C_i$ with the scenario $p = (p_1, p_2, \ldots, p_n) \in T$ remains optimal for the instance $1|p'|\sum C_i$ with any scenario $p' \in \mathcal{OB}(\pi_k, T) \bigcup \{\times_{k_j \in N \setminus M}[p_{k_j}, p_{k_j}]\}$. If there does not exist a scenario $p \in T$ such that the permutation π_k is optimal for the instance $1|p|\sum C_i$, it is assumed that $\mathcal{OB}(\pi_k, T) = \emptyset$.*

In Section 3, we use the following remark for the definition of the optimality segment for the job $J_{k_i} \in \mathcal{J}$ in the permutation $\pi_k = (J_{k_1}, J_{k_2}, \ldots, J_{k_n}) \in S$.

Remark 1. *Any variation p'_{k_i} of the duration p_{k_i} of the job $J_{k_i} \in \mathcal{J}$ within the maximal segment $[l_{k_i}^*, u_{k_i}^*]$ indicated in Definition 1 cannot violate the optimality of the permutation $\pi_k \in S$ provided that the inclusion $p'_{k_i} \in [l_{k_i}^*, u_{k_i}^*]$ holds. The non-empty maximal segment $[l_{k_i}^*, u_{k_i}^*]$ indicated in Definition 1 with the inequality $l_{k_i}^* \leq u_{k_i}^*$ and the length $u_{k_i}^* - l_{k_i}^* \geq 0$ is called an optimality segment for the job $J_{k_i} \in \mathcal{J}$ in the permutation π_k. We denote the optimality segment as follows: $[l_{k_i}^{opt}, u_{k_i}^{opt}]$.*

If the maximal segment $[l_{k_i}^*, u_{k_i}^*]$ indicated in Definition 1 is empty for the job $J_{k_i} \in \mathcal{J}$, we say that this job has no optimality segment in the permutation π_k. It is clear that if the job J_{k_i} has no optimality segment in the permutation π_k, then the strict inequality $l_{k_i}^* > u_{k_i}^*$ holds. In [23,24], it is shown that for calculating the optimality box $\mathcal{OB}(\pi_k, T)$, one can calculate the optimality box for the modified instance $1|\hat{p}_i^L \leq p_i \leq \hat{p}_i^U| \sum w_i C_i$, where the segments $[p_i^L, p_i^U]$ for the possible job durations p_i are reduced, $[\hat{p}_i^L, \hat{p}_i^U] \subseteq [p_i^L, p_i^U]$, based on the following formulas:

$$\frac{w_i}{\hat{p}_i^L} = \min_{1 \leq j \leq i \leq n} \left\{ \frac{w_j}{p_j^L} \right\}, \quad \frac{w_i}{\hat{p}_i^U} = \max_{1 \leq i \leq j \leq n} \left\{ \frac{w_j}{p_j^U} \right\}. \tag{3}$$

The following theorem has been proven in [24].

Theorem 2. *The optimality box for the permutation $\pi_k \in S$ for the problem $1|p_i^L \leq p_i \leq p_i^U| \sum C_i$ is equal to the optimality box for the same permutation π_k for the problem $1|\hat{p}_i^L \leq p_i \leq \hat{p}_i^U| \sum C_i$ with the feasible segments $[\hat{p}_i^L, \hat{p}_i^U]$, $J_i \in \mathcal{J}$, determined in (3).*

In [23], it is shown that Theorem 2 remains correct for the problem $1|p_i^L \leq p_i \leq p_i^U| \sum w_i C_i$ with the different weights $w_i > 0$ prescribed to the jobs $J_i \in \mathcal{J}$.

Following [23,24], the notion of a block for the jobs $\mathcal{J}$ is determined for the problem $1|p_i^L \leq p_i \leq p_i^U| \sum C_i$ as follows.

Definition 2. *A maximal subset $B_r = \{J_{r_1}, J_{r_2}, \ldots, J_{r_{|B_r|}}\}$ of the set $\mathcal{J}$, for which the inequality $\max_{J_{r_i} \in B_r} p_{r_i}^L \leq \min_{J_{r_i} \in B_r} p_{r_i}^U$ holds, is called a lock. The segment $[b_r^L, b_r^U]$, where equalities $b_r^L = \max_{J_{r_i} \in B_r} p_{r_i}^L$ and $b_r^U = \min_{J_{r_i} \in B_r} p_{r_i}^U$ hold, is called a core of the block B_r.*

The following claim was proven in [23].

Lemma 1. *For the problem $1|p_i^L \leq p_i \leq p_i^U| \sum w_i C_i$, the set $B = \{B_1, B_2, \ldots, B_m\}$ of all blocks can be uniquely determined in $O(n \log n)$ time.*

If the job $J_i \in \mathcal{J}$ belongs to a single block, we say that the job J_i is fixed in this block. We say that the block B_v is virtual, if there is no fixed job in this block. We say that the job J_k is non-fixed, if the job $J_k \in \mathcal{J}$ belongs to two or more blocks and at least one of these blocks is not virtual.

Remark 2. *Any permutation $\pi_k \in S$ determines a distribution of all non-fixed jobs to the blocks. Due to such fixings of the positions of the non-fixed jobs, some virtual blocks from the set B may be destroyed for the fixed permutation π_k. Furthermore, the cores of some non-virtual blocks may be increased in the permutation π_k.*

Each block in the set B has the following properties proven in [23].

Lemma 2. *At most two jobs in the block $B_r \in B$ may have optimality segments in the permutation $\pi_k \in S$.*

Lemma 3. *If $\mathcal{OB}(\pi_k, T) \neq \emptyset$, then any two jobs $J_v \in B_r$ and $J_w \in B_s$, which are fixed in different blocks, $r < s$, must be ordered in the permutation $\pi_k \in S$ with decreasing left bounds (and right bounds as well) of the cores of their blocks, i.e., the permutation π_k looks as follows: $\pi_k = \{\ldots, J_v, \ldots, J_w, \ldots\}$, where the inequality $b_r^L < b_s^L$ holds.*

In what follows, we assume that all blocks in the set $B = \{B_1, B_2, \ldots, B_m\}$ are numbered according to decreasing left bounds of their cores, i.e., the strict inequality $b_v^L < b_u^L$ implies the strict inequality $v < u$. Due to Definition 2, each block $B_r = \{J_{r_1}, J_{r_2}, \ldots, J_{r_{|B_r|}}\}$ may include jobs of the four types as follows.

If $p_{r_i}^L = b_r^L$ and $p_{r_i}^U = b_r^U$, we say that job J_{r_i} is a core job in the block B_r. If $p_{r_i}^L < b_r^L$, we say that job J_{r_i} is a left job in the block B_r. If $p_{r_i}^U > b_r^U$, we say that job J_{r_i} is a right job in the block B_r. Let B_r^* denote the set of all core jobs. The set B_r^- (the set B_r^+) is the set of all left (right) jobs in the block B_r. Some jobs $J_{r_i} \in B_r$ may be left-right jobs in the block B_r, since it is possible that condition $B \setminus \{B_r^* \cup B_r^- \cup B_r^+\} \neq \emptyset$ holds.

The jobs J_v and J_w are identical if both equalities $p_v^L = p_w^L$ and $p_v^U = p_w^U$ hold. If the set $B_r \in B$ is a singleton, $|B_r| = 1$, then the equality $B_r = B_r^*$ holds. The following theorem was proven in [24].

Theorem 3. *For the problem $1|p_i^L \leq p_i \leq p_i^U|\sum C_i$, any permutation $\pi_k \in S$ has an empty optimality box, $\mathcal{OB}(\pi_k, T) = \emptyset$, if and only if for each block $B_r \in B$, either condition $|B_r| = |B_r^*| \geq 2$ holds or condition $B_r = B_r^- \cup B_r^+$ holds and all jobs in the set B_r^- (in the set B_r^+) are identical and both inequalities $|B_r^-| \geq 2$ and $|B_r^+| \geq 2$ hold.*

The following criterion was proven in [23].

Theorem 4. *Let all jobs from the set $\mathcal{J}$ be fixed in their blocks from the set B. Then the permutation π_k with the largest optimality box $\mathcal{OB}(\pi_k, T)$ may be constructed in $O(n \log n)$ time.*

The rest of this paper is devoted to an optimality set (it is called an optimality region), which is a superset of the optimality box $\mathcal{OB}(\pi_k, T)$ for the same permutation π_k.

3. The Optimality Region

For the permutation $\pi_k \in S$, we formally define the optimality region $\mathcal{OR}(\pi_k, T)$ such that the inclusion $\mathcal{OB}(\pi_k, T) \subseteq \mathcal{OR}(\pi_k, T)$ holds.

Definition 3. *The maximal closed subset $\mathcal{OR}(\pi_k, T) \subseteq T$ of the set R_+^n is called the optimality region for the permutation $\pi_k = (J_{k_1}, J_{k_2}, \ldots, J_{k_n}) \in S$ (with respect to T) if the permutation π_k is optimal for the instance $1|p|\sum C_i$ with any scenario $p = (p_1, p_2, \ldots, p_n) \in \mathcal{OR}(\pi_k, T)$. If there does not exist a scenario $p \in T$ such that the permutation π_k is optimal for the instance $1|p|\sum C_i$, it is assumed that $\mathcal{OR}(\pi_k, T) = \emptyset$.*

We demonstrate the above definitions and notions on the instance of the problem $1|p_i^L \leq p_i \leq p_i^U|\sum C_i$ with $n = 8$ jobs. The segments $[p_i^L, p_i^U]$ defining all possible durations of the jobs $J_i \in \mathcal{J} = \{J_1, J_2, \ldots, J_8\}$ are given in Table 1. The segments $[p_i^L, p_i^U]$ of the job durations are also represented in a coordinate system in Figure 1 for the permutation $\pi_1 = (J_1, J_2, \ldots, J_8) \in S$. The abscissa axis indicates the segments $[p_i^L, p_i^U]$ determining durations of the jobs. The ordinate axis indicates all jobs $\mathcal{J}$. There are three blocks in this instance. The jobs J_1, J_2, J_3, J_4, J_5 and J_7 belong to the block B_1. The segment $[6, 7]$ is a core of the block B_1. The jobs J_2, J_3, J_4, J_5, J_6 and J_7 belong to the block B_2. The one-point segment $[8, 8]$ is a core of the block B_2. The jobs J_4, J_5, J_6, J_7 and J_8 belong to the block B_3. The segment $[10, 11]$ is a core of the block B_3. The jobs J_2, J_3, J_4, J_5, J_6 and J_7 are non-fixed jobs. The jobs J_1 and J_8 are fixed in their blocks.

Due to the optimality criterion (2) for the permutation $\pi_k \in S$ given in Theorem 1, one can distinguish three types of segments for each job $J_{k_r} \in \mathcal{J}$, which characterize a possibility for the permutation $\pi_k = (J_{k_1}, J_{k_2}, \ldots, J_{k_n})$ to be optimal, namely:

the segment of optimality $[l_{k_r}^{opt}, u_{k_r}^{opt}] \subseteq [p_{k_r}^L, p_{k_r}^U]$;

the segment of conditional optimality $[l_{k_r}^{copt}, u_{k_r}^{copt}] \subseteq [p_{k_r}^L, p_{k_r}^U]$;

and the segment of non-optimality $[l_{k_r}^{non}, u_{k_r}^{non}] \subseteq [p_{k_r}^L, p_{k_r}^U]$.

The segment of optimality $[l_{k_r}^{opt}, u_{k_r}^{opt}]$ for the job J_{k_r} in the permutation π_k is formally determined in Definition 1 and Remark 1.

Table 1. Input data for the instance of the problem $1|p_i^L \leq p_i \leq p_i^U|\sum C_i$.

i	1	2	3	4	5	6	7	8
p_i^L	5	5	6	4	2	8	3	10
p_i^U	7	8	9	11	14	11	17	12

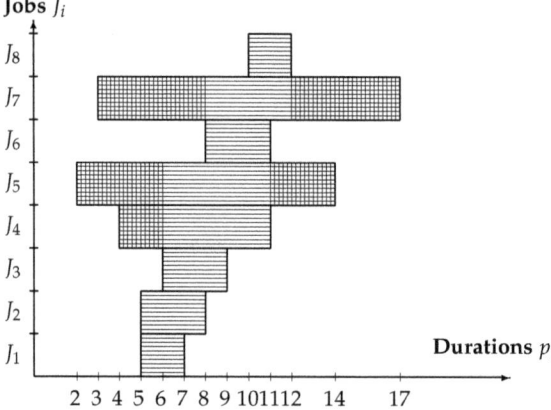

Figure 1. The segments of non-optimality (double-shaded) and the segments of conditional optimality (shaded) for the jobs $J_i \in \mathcal{J}$ in the permutation $\pi_1 = (J_1, J_2, \ldots, J_8) \in S$.

The segment of non-optimality for the job J_{k_r} in the permutation $\pi_k = (J_{k_1}, J_{k_2}, \ldots, J_{k_n}) \in S$ is a maximal (with respect to the inclusion) segment $[l_{k_r}^{non}, u_{k_r}^{non}] \subseteq [p_{k_r}^L, p_{k_r}^U]$ such that for any point $p_{k_r}^* \in (l_{k_r}^{non}, u_{k_r}^{non})$, the permutation $\pi_k = (J_{k_1}, J_{k_2}, \ldots, J_{k_n})$ cannot be optimal for an instance $1|p^*|\sum C_i$ with any scenario $p^* = (\ldots, p_{k_r}^*, \ldots) \in T$. Thus, due to the necessary and sufficient condition (2) for the permutation $\pi_k \in S$ to be optimal for the instance $1|p|\sum C_i$, we conclude that either there exists a job $J_{k_v} \in \mathcal{J}$ such that the inequality $r < v$ holds along with the following condition:

$$p_{k_v}^U = l_{k_r}^{non} < p_{k_r}^U = u_{k_r}^{non} \qquad (4)$$

or there exists a job $J_{k_w} \in \mathcal{J}$ such that $w < r$ and the following condition holds:

$$l_{k_r}^{non} = p_{k_r}^U < u_{k_r}^{non} = p_{k_w}^L. \qquad (5)$$

Furthermore, due to Definition 1, the segment $[l_{k_r}^{non}, u_{k_r}^{non}]$ of non-optimality for the job J_{k_r} in the permutation $\pi_k = (J_{k_1}, J_{k_2}, \ldots, J_{k_n})$ has no common point with the open interval $(l_{k_r}^{opt}, u_{k_r}^{opt})$ of optimality for the job J_{k_r}:

$$[l_{k_r}^{non}, u_{k_r}^{non}] \bigcap (l_{k_r}^{opt}, u_{k_r}^{opt}) = \emptyset. \qquad (6)$$

In Figure 1, the segments of non-optimality for all jobs $J_i \in \mathcal{J}$ in the permutation $\pi_1 = (J_1, J_2, \ldots, J_8)$ are double-shaded.

The segment of conditional optimality for the job J_{k_r} in the permutation $\pi_k = (J_{k_1}, J_{k_2}, \ldots, J_{k_n}) \in S$ is a maximal (with respect to the inclusion) segment $[l_{k_r}^{copt}, u_{k_r}^{copt}] \subseteq [p_{k_r}^L, p_{k_r}^U]$ such that each point $p_{k_r}^* \in [l_{k_r}^{copt}, u_{k_i}^{copt}]$ does not belong to the open interval of non-optimality, $p_{k_r}^* \notin (l_{k_r}^{non}, u_{k_r}^{non})$, and there exists a job $J_{k_d} \in \mathcal{J}, d \neq r$, with the following inclusion: $p_{k_r}^* \in [p_{k_d}^L, p_{k_d}^U]$. Thus, one can conclude that for some points $p_{k_u} \in [l_{k_r}^{copt}, u_{k_r}^{copt}]$, the permutation $\pi_k \in S$ is optimal for the instance $1|p'|\sum C_i$, where $p' = (\ldots, p_{k_u}, \ldots) \in T$, while for other points $p_{k_v} \in [l_{k_r}^{copt}, u_{k_r}^{copt}]$, the permutation $\pi_k \in S$ cannot be optimal for the instance $1|p''|\sum C_i$, where $p'' = (\ldots, p_{k_v}, \ldots) \in T$.

The segment $[l_{k_r}^{copt}, u_{k_r}^{copt}]$ of conditional optimality for the job J_{k_r} in the permutation $\pi_k = (J_{k_1}, J_{k_2}, \ldots, J_{k_n}) \in S$ has no common point with the open interval of optimality $(l_{k_r}^{opt}, u_{k_r}^{opt})$ and no common point with the open interval of non-optimality $(l_{k_r}^{non}, u_{k_r}^{non})$:

$$[l_{k_r}^{copt}, u_{k_r}^{copt}] \bigcap (l_{k_r}^{opt}, u_{k_r}^{opt}) = \emptyset; \tag{7}$$

$$[l_{k_r}^{copt}, u_{k_r}^{copt}] \bigcap (l_{k_r}^{non}, u_{k_r}^{non}) = \emptyset. \tag{8}$$

If the segment $[l_{k_r}^{copt}, u_{k_r}^{copt}]$ of conditional optimality is empty for the job $J_{k_r} \in \mathcal{J}$, we say that this job J_{k_r} has no conditional optimality in the permutation π_k.

In Figure 1, all segments of conditional optimality for the jobs $J_i \in \mathcal{J}$ in the permutation $\pi_1 = (J_1, J_2, \ldots, J_8)$ are shaded.

Remark 3. *Due to Theorem 1, for each job $J_i \in \mathcal{J}$ in the permutation $\pi_k \in S$, there may exist at most one segment of optimality, at most two segments of conditional optimality and at most two segments of non-optimality.*

In Figure 1, job J_4 has one segment $[4, 6]$ of non-optimality and one segment of conditional optimality $[6, 11]$. Job J_5 has two segments of non-optimality $[2, 6]$ and $[11, 14]$ and one segment of conditional optimality $[6, 11]$.

The following claim is based on Remark 3 and the above definitions of the segments of optimality, non-optimality and conditional optimality.

Lemma 4. *Each segment $[p_{k_r}^L, p_{k_r}^U]$ of possible durations of the job $J_{k_r} \in \mathcal{J}$ is the union of the segments of optimality, non-optimality and conditional optimality for the job J_{k_r} in the permutation $\pi_k = (J_{k_1}, J_{k_2}, \ldots J_{k_n}) \in S$.*

We next show that for constructing the optimality region $\mathcal{OR}(\pi_k, T)$ for the permutation $\pi_k = (J_{k_1}, J_{k_2}, \ldots, J_{k_n}) \in S$, it is sufficient to construct the optimality region for the instance $1|\hat{p}_i^L \le p_i \le \hat{p}_i^U| \sum C_i$ with the reduced segments of job durations: $[\hat{p}_i^L, \hat{p}_i^U] \subseteq [p_i^L, p_i^U]$. To construct the reduced segments for the permutation $\pi_k = (J_{k_1}, J_{k_2}, \ldots, J_{k_n}) \in S$, we use the equalities (9) for all jobs $J_{k_r} \in \{J_{k_1}, J_{k_2}, \ldots, J_{k_n}\} = \mathcal{J}$:

$$\hat{p}_{k_r}^L = \max_{1 \le j \le r \le n} p_{k_j}^L, \quad \hat{p}_{k_r}^U = \min_{1 \le r \le j \le n} p_{k_j}^U. \tag{9}$$

We denote $\hat{T} = [\hat{p}_1^L, \hat{p}_1^U] \times [\hat{p}_2^L, \hat{p}_2^U] \times \ldots \times [\hat{p}_n^L, \hat{p}_n^U]$. One can prove the following claim similarly to the proof of Theorem 2 proven in [24].

Theorem 5. *The optimality region for the permutation $\pi_k = (J_{k_1}, J_{k_2}, \ldots, J_{k_n}) \in S$ for the instance $1|p_i^L \le p_i \le p_i^U| \sum C_i$ is equal to the optimality region for the same permutation for the instance $1|\hat{p}_i^L \le p_i \le \hat{p}_i^U| \sum C_i$ with the reduced segments $[\hat{p}_i^L, \hat{p}_i^U]$ of the possible durations of jobs $J_i \in \mathcal{J}$ determined in (9).*

Figure 2 represents the segments of non-optimality and conditional optimality for jobs $J_i \in \mathcal{J}$ in the permutation $\pi_2 = (J_1, J_2, J_4, J_5, J_6, J_8, J_7, J_3) \in S$ for the instance $1|p_i^L \le p_i \le p_i^U| \sum C_i$ with the input data T given in Table 1.

From Definition 3 and Theorem 5, one can directly derive the following claim.

Lemma 5. *For the instance $1|\hat{p}_i^L \le p_i \le \hat{p}_i^U| \sum C_i$ with the reduced segments $[\hat{p}_i^L, \hat{p}_i^U]$, $J_i \in \mathcal{J}$, of the job durations determined in (9), the open interval of optimality $(l_{k_r}^{opt}, u_{k_r}^{opt})$ for the job J_{k_r} in the permutation $\pi_k \in S$ has no common point with the segment $[p_{k_d}^L, p_{k_d}^U]$ of possible durations of any job $J_{k_d} \in \mathcal{J}$, $d \ne r$, i.e., the following equality holds:*

$$(l_{k_r}^{opt}, u_{k_r}^{opt}) \bigcap [p_{k_d}^L, p_{k_d}^U] = \emptyset. \tag{10}$$

We next prove a criterion for the extreme case when the equality $\mathcal{OR}(\pi_k, T) = \emptyset$ holds.

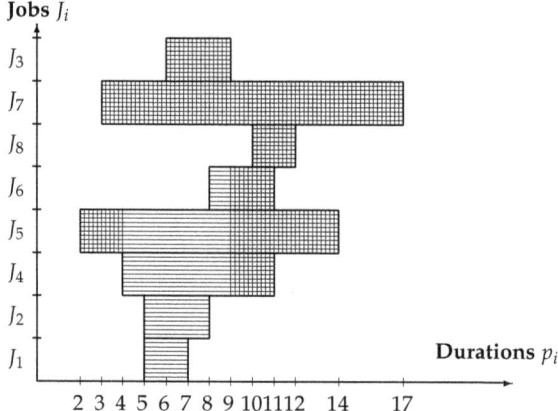

Figure 2. The segments of non-optimality (double-shaded) and the segments of conditional optimality (shaded) for the jobs $J_i \in \mathcal{J}$ in the permutation $\pi_2 = (J_1, J_2, J_4, J_5, J_6, J_8, J_7, J_3) \in S$.

Theorem 6. *The optimality region $\mathcal{OR}(\pi_k, T)$ for the permutation $\pi_k = (J_{k_1}, J_{k_2}, \ldots, J_{k_n}) \in S$ is empty, if and only if there exists at least one job $J_{k_r} \in \mathcal{J}$ with the inequality $p_{k_r}^L < p_{k_r}^U$ in the permutation π_k, which has no segment of optimality and no conditional optimality.*

Proof. Sufficiency. Let there exist a job $J_{k_r} \in \mathcal{J}$ in the permutation $\pi_k = (J_{k_1}, J_{k_2}, \ldots, J_{k_n})$, which has no segment of optimality and no conditional optimality. Due to the inequality $p_{k_r}^L < p_{k_r}^U$ and Lemma 4, the relations $[l_{k_r}^{non}, u_{k_r}^{non}] = [p_{k_r}^L, p_{k_r}^U] \neq \emptyset$ hold, and either there exists a job $J_{k_v} \in \mathcal{J}$ such that $r < v$ and the condition (4) holds or there exists a job $J_{k_w} \in \mathcal{J}$ such that $w < r$ and the condition (5) holds.

In the former case, the inequality $p_{k_v} < p_{k_r}$ holds for each duration $p_{k_r} \in [p_{k_r}^L, p_{k_r}^U]$ of the job J_{k_r} and for each duration $p_{k_v} \in [p_{k_v}^L, p_{k_v}^U]$ of the job J_{k_v}. In the latter case, the inequality $p_{k_w} > p_{k_r}$ holds for each duration $p_{k_r} \in [p_{k_r}^L, p_{k_r}^U]$ of the job J_{k_r} and for each duration $p_{k_w} \in [p_{k_w}^L, p_{k_w}^U]$ of the job J_{k_w}.

Due to Theorem 1, in both cases the permutation π_k cannot be optimal for the instance $1|p|\sum C_i$ with any scenario $p \in T$. Hence, the optimality region for the permutation $\pi_k = (J_{k_1}, J_{k_2}, \ldots, J_{k_n}) \in S$ is empty: $\mathcal{OR}(\pi_k, T) = \emptyset$. Sufficiency is proven.

Necessity. We prove necessity by a contradiction. Let the equality $\mathcal{OR}(\pi_k, T) = \emptyset$ hold. However, we assume that there is no job $J_{k_r} \in \mathcal{J}$ with the inequality $p_{k_r}^L < p_{k_r}^U$ in the permutation $\pi_k = (J_{k_1}, J_{k_2}, \ldots, J_{k_n}) \in S$, which has no segment of optimality and no conditional optimality.

Due to Definition 3, the equality $\mathcal{OR}(\pi_k, T) = \emptyset$ means that there is no scenario $p \in T$ such that the permutation π_k is optimal for the instance $1|p|\sum C_i$ with the scenario p.

However, we show next how to construct a scenario $p^* \in \widehat{T}$ with the inclusion $p^* \in \mathcal{OR}(\pi_k, \widehat{T})$. If the segment $[l_{k_i}^{opt}, u_{k_i}^{opt}]$ of optimality of the job J_{k_i} in the permutation π_k is not empty, then there exists a point $p_{k_i}^* \in [l_{k_i}^{opt}, u_{k_i}^{opt}]$. We choose the value of $p_{k_i}^*$ as the duration of the job J_{k_i}.

If the segment $[l_{k_j}^{opt}, u_{k_j}^{opt}]$ of optimality of the job J_{k_j} in the permutation π_k is empty, then due to the above assumption, the segment $[l_{k_j}^{copt}, u_{k_j}^{copt}]$ of conditional optimality for the job J_{k_j} in the permutation π_k is not empty. We choose the value of $l_{k_j}^{copt}$ as the duration of the job J_{k_j}, i.e., $p_{k_j}^* = l_{k_j}^{copt}$. Thus, we determine the scenario $p^* = (p_{k_1}^*, p_{k_2}^*, \ldots, p_{k_n}^*)$. From the equalities (7) and (8) and Lemma 5 with the equality (10), it follows that the permutation π_k is optimal for the instance $1|p^*|\sum C_i$ with the scenario p^*. Thus, $p^* \in \mathcal{OR}(\pi_k, \widehat{T})$ and the relations $\emptyset \neq \mathcal{OR}(\pi_k, \widehat{T}) = \mathcal{OR}(\pi_k, T)$ hold contradicting to our assumption that $\mathcal{OR}(\pi_k, T) = \emptyset$. The proof of Theorem 6 is completed. □

From Theorem 6, one can directly derive the following claim.

Corollary 1. *If the condition $\mathcal{OR}(\pi_k, T) \neq \emptyset$ holds, then the dimension of the optimality region $\mathcal{OR}(\pi_k, T)$ is equal to n.*

In Figure 1, there is no job $J_i \in \mathcal{J}$ in the permutation $\pi_1 = (J_1, J_2, \ldots, J_8) \in S$, which has no segment of optimality and no conditional optimality. Thus, due to Theorem 6, the optimality region for the permutation $\pi_1 \in S$ is not empty, i.e., $\mathcal{OR}(\pi_1, T) \neq \emptyset$.

In Figure 2, for the segment $[l_3^{non}, u_3^{non}] = [6, 9]$ of non-optimality for the job J_3 in the permutation $\pi_2 = (J_1, J_2, J_4, J_5, J_6, J_8, J_7, J_3)$, the following equalities $[l_3^{non}, u_3^{non}] = [6, 9] = [p_3^L, p_3^U]$ hold. Thus, there exists a job $J_3 = J_{k_r} \in \mathcal{J}$ in the permutation $\pi_2 = \pi_k = (J_{k_1}, J_{k_2}, \ldots, J_{k_n}) \in S$, which has no segment of optimality and no conditional optimality. Due to Theorem 6, one can conclude that the optimality region for the permutation $\pi_2 = (J_1, J_2, J_4, J_5, J_6, J_8, J_7, J_3) \in S$ is empty, i.e., $\mathcal{OR}(\pi_2, T) = \emptyset$.

We next prove a criterion for another extreme case for the optimality region $\mathcal{OR}(\pi_k, T)$, namely, we prove the necessary and sufficient condition for the equality $\mathcal{OR}(\pi_k, T) = T$ when the optimality region is maximally possible.

Theorem 7. *The optimality region for the permutation $\pi_k = (J_{k_1}, J_{k_2}, \ldots, J_{k_n}) \in S$ is maximally possible (i.e., the equality $\mathcal{OR}(\pi_k, T) = T$ holds), if and only if for each job $J_{k_r} \in \mathcal{J}$ in the permutation π_k the following equality holds:*

$$[l_{k_r}^{opt}, u_{k_r}^{opt}] = [p_{k_r}^L, p_{k_r}^U]. \tag{11}$$

Proof. Sufficiency. Let the equality (11) hold for each job $J_{k_r} \in \mathcal{J}$ in the permutation $\pi_k = (J_{k_1}, J_{k_2}, \ldots, J_{k_n})$.

Due to Definition 1 and Remark 1, the following equalities hold: $\mathcal{OB}(\pi_k, T) = \times_{k_r \in M} [l_{k_r}^*, u_{k_r}^*] = \times_{k_r \in M} [l_{k_r}^{opt}, u_{k_r}^{opt}] = \times_{k_r \in M} [p_{k_r}^L, p_{k_r}^U] = T$, where $M = \{1, 2, \ldots, n\}$. From Definition 1, it follows that the permutation π_k is optimal for the instance $1|p'|\sum C_i$ with any scenario $p' \in \mathcal{OB}(\pi_k, T) = T$. Thus, due to Definition 3, we obtain the desired equality $\mathcal{OR}(\pi_k, T) = T$. Sufficiency is proven.

Necessity. Let the equality $\mathcal{OR}(\pi_k, T) = T$ hold. However, we assume that there is a job $J_{k_r} \in \mathcal{J}$ in the permutation $\pi_k = (J_{k_1}, J_{k_2}, \ldots, J_{k_n}) \in \Pi$ such that the equality (11) does not hold.

Due to Lemma 4, either there exists a segment of non-optimality $[l_{k_r}^{non}, u_{k_r}^{non}] \neq \emptyset$ or a segment of conditional optimality $[l_{k_r}^{copt}, u_{k_r}^{copt}] \neq \emptyset$ for job $J_{k_r} \in \mathcal{J}$ in the permutation $\pi_k = (J_{k_1}, J_{k_2}, \ldots, J_{k_n})$. In the former case, the equality (6) holds. In the latter case, the equality (8) holds.

Thus, in both cases, there exists a scenario $p^* = (\ldots, p_{k_r}^*, \ldots) \in T$, where $p_{k_r}^* \in (l_{k_r}^{non}, u_{k_r}^{non}) \cup (l_{k_r}^{copt}, u_{k_r}^{copt}) \neq \emptyset$, such that the permutation π_k is not optimal for the instance $1|p^*|\sum C_i$ with the scenario $p^* \in T$. Hence, due to Definition 3 we obtain a contradiction $\mathcal{OR}(\pi_k, T) \neq T$ with the above assumption. This contradiction completes the proof of Theorem 7. □

In the rest of this paper, we show how to use the above results for solving the uncertain scheduling problem $1|p_i^L \leq p_i \leq p_i^U|\sum C_i$ approximately.

4. Algorithms for Calculating a Quasi-Perimeter of the Optimality Region for the Fixed Permutation

We next present Algorithm 1 for testing the equality $\mathcal{OR}(\pi_k, T) = \emptyset$. If it appears that the optimality region is not empty for the permutation π_k, i.e., $\mathcal{OR}(\pi_k, T) \neq \emptyset$, then Algorithm 1 constructs an instance $1|\hat{p}_i^L \leq p_i \leq \hat{p}_i^U|\sum C_i$ with the reduced segments $\widehat{T}$ of possible durations for the jobs $\mathcal{J}$.

Algorithm 1: Construction of the instance with the reduced segments of possible durations
---
Input: The segments $[p_i^L, p_i^U]$ for all jobs $J_i \in \mathcal{J}$;
the permutation $\pi_k = (J_{k_1}, J_{k_2}, \ldots, J_{k_n}) \in S$.
Output: The reduced segments $[\widehat{p}_i^L, \widehat{p}_i^U]$ for all jobs $J_i \in \mathcal{J}$ if $\mathcal{OR}(\pi_k, T) \neq \emptyset$.

Step 1: Set $\widehat{p}_{k_1}^L = p_{k_1}^L$, $t_L = p_{k_1}^L$, $r = 2$;
Step 2: **IF** $p_{k_r}^U \geq t_L$ **THEN GOTO** step 3 **ELSE** $[l_{k_r}^{non}, u_{k_r}^{non}] = [p_{k_r}^L, p_{k_r}^U]$;
     GOTO step 6;
Step 3: **IF** $p_{k_r}^L > t_L$ **THEN** Set $t_L = p_{k_r}^L$, $\widehat{p}_{k_r}^L = t_L$, $r := r+1$;
     ELSE Set $\widehat{p}_{k_r}^L = t_L$, $r := r+1$;
Step 4: **IF** $r \leq n$ **THEN GOTO** step 2 **ELSE** Set $\widehat{p}_{k_n}^U = p_{k_n}^U$, $t_U = p_{k_n}^U$;
Step 5: **FOR** $r = n-1$ **to** 1 **STEP** -1 **DO**
     IF $p_{k_r}^U < t_U$ **THEN** Set $t_U = p_{k_r}^U$, $\widehat{p}_{k_r}^U = t_U$ **ELSE** Set $\widehat{p}_{k_r}^U = t_U$;
     END FOR STOP
Step 6: $\mathcal{OR}(\pi_k, T) = \emptyset$ **STOP**.

In steps 1, 2, 3 and 6 of Algorithm 1, the equality $\mathcal{OR}(\pi_k, T) = \emptyset$ is tested. If $\mathcal{OR}(\pi_k, T) \neq \emptyset$, then the problem $1|\widehat{p}_i^L \leq p_i \leq \widehat{p}_i^U| \sum C_i$ with the reduced segments $\widehat{T}$ of the feasible durations of the jobs $\mathcal{J}$ is constructed in steps 2–5. It takes $O(n)$ time to realize Algorithm 1.

4.1. A Quasi-Perimeter of the Optimality Region $\mathcal{OR}(\pi_k, T)$

Due to Theorem 5, the optimality region for the permutation $\pi_k \in S$ for the problem $1|p_i^L \leq p_i \leq p_i^U| \sum C_i$ coincides with the optimality region for the same permutation π_k for the problem $1|\widehat{p}_i^L \leq p_i \leq \widehat{p}_i^U| \sum C_i$ with the reduced segments $\widehat{T}$ of the feasible durations of the jobs $\mathcal{J}$. Therefore, in what follows, we consider the problem $1|\widehat{p}_i^L \leq p_i \leq \widehat{p}_i^U| \sum C_i$ instead of the problem $1|p_i^L \leq p_i \leq p_i^U| \sum C_i$.

Definition 4. *A maximal permutation $s_v^{\pi_k} = (J_{k_v}, J_{k_{v+1}}, \ldots, J_{k_{m_v}})$, where $1 \leq v \leq m_v \leq n$ and $|s_v^{\pi_k}| = m_v$, is called a section of the permutation $\pi_k \in S$, if for each real number $d \in (\widehat{p}_{k_v}^L, \widehat{p}_{k_{m_v}}^U)$, there exists a job J_{k_i} with $i \in \{v, v+1, \ldots, m_v\}$ such that the inclusion $d \in (\widehat{p}_{k_i}^L, \widehat{p}_{k_i}^U)$ holds. The segment $[\widehat{p}_{k_v}^L, \widehat{p}_{k_{m_v}}^U]$ is called a scope of the section $s_v^{\pi_k}$. The section $s_v^{\pi_k}$ consisting of a single job, $s_v^{\pi_k} = (J_{k_v})$, is called a trivial section.*

It is clear that for each fixed permutation $\pi_k \in S$, a set of all sections $\{s_1^{\pi_k}, s_{m_1+1}^{\pi_k}, \ldots, s_w^{\pi_k}\} =: S(\pi_k)$ is uniquely determined. Note that index w in the last section $s_w^{\pi_k}$ coincides with index w of the job J_{k_w}, which is the first job in the section $s_w^{\pi_k} = (J_{k_w}, J_{k_{w+1}}, \ldots, J_{k_{m_v}})$ of the permutation π_k.

Remark 4. *Definition 4 implies that each job $J_{k_i} \in \mathcal{J}$ either belongs to a single section of the permutation π_k or this job does not belong to any section of the permutation π_k. Furthermore, if there exists at least one job $J_{k_i} \in \mathcal{J}$, which does not belong to any section from the set $S(\pi_k)$, then this job has no segment of optimality and no conditional optimality and, due to Theorem 6, the equality $\mathcal{OR}(\pi_k, T) = \emptyset$ holds.*

From Remark 4 and Theorem 6, one can derive the following claim.

Corollary 2. *The condition $\mathcal{OR}(\pi_k, T) \neq \emptyset$ holds if and only if $\pi_k = (s_1^{\pi_k}, s_{m_1+1}^{\pi_k}, \ldots, s_w^{\pi_k})$.*

If the section $s_v^{\pi_k} \in S(\pi_k)$ is trivial, i.e., the equality $s_v^{\pi_k} = (J_{k_v})$ holds, then $[\widehat{p}_{k_v}^L, \widehat{p}_{k_v}^U]$ is a scope of the section $s_v^{\pi_k}$. If the section $s_j^{\pi_k} \in S(\pi_k)$ is not trivial and $\mathcal{OR}(\pi_k, T) \neq \emptyset$, then we partition the scope

$[\hat{p}^L_{k_j}, \hat{p}^U_{k_{m_j}}]$ of the section $s_j^{\pi_k} \in S(\pi_k)$ into the maximal (with respect to the inclusion) semi-intervals of the optimality and conditional optimality:

$$[\hat{p}^L_{k_j}, \hat{p}^U_{k_{m_j}}] = [l_1^j(s_j^{\pi_k}), u_1^j(s_j^{\pi_k})) \bigcup [l_2^j(s_j^{\pi_k}), u_2^j(s_j^{\pi_k})) \bigcup \cdots \bigcup [l_{n(j)}^j(s_j^{\pi_k}), u_{n(j)}^j(s_j^{\pi_k})]. \qquad (12)$$

In the equality (12), the semi-intervals $[l_i^j(s_j^{\pi_k}), u_i^j(s_j^{\pi_k}))$ differ one from another in a way such that for different subsets $\mathcal{J}_i^j = \{J_{k_i}, J_{k_{i+1}}, \ldots, J_{k_{|\mathcal{J}_i^j|}}\}$ of the set of jobs $\{J_{k_j}, J_{k_{j+1}}, \ldots, J_{k_{m_j}}\}$, where $j \leq i \leq m_j$, the inclusion $[l_i^j(s_j^{\pi_k}), u_i^j(s_j^{\pi_k})] \subseteq [\hat{p}^L_{k_r}, \hat{p}^U_{k_r}]$ holds for each job $J_{k_r} \in \mathcal{J}_i^j$. Let $\widetilde{J}_i^j = (J_{k_i}, J_{k_{i+1}}, \ldots, J_{k_{|\mathcal{J}_i^j|}})$ denote a permutation of all jobs from the set $\mathcal{J}_i^j = \{J_{k_i}, J_{k_{i+1}}, \ldots, J_{k_{|\mathcal{J}_i^j|}}\}$. Note that the permutation $\widetilde{J}_i^j$ is a part of the permutation π_k, where index i in the permutation $\widetilde{J}_i^j$ coincides with index i of the job J_{k_i}, which is the first job in the permutation $\widetilde{J}_i^j$.

Let the condition $\mathcal{OR}(\pi_k, T) \neq \emptyset$ hold. We can calculate a quasi-perimeter of the optimality region $\mathcal{OR}(\pi_k, T)$. We define a quasi-perimeter $Per(\pi_k, T)$ of the optimality region $\mathcal{OR}(\pi_k, T)$ as a sum of all lengths (cardinalities) of the segments (sets) $OS(J_{k_r}, \pi_k)$, where jobs $J_{k_r} \in \mathcal{J}$ occupy optimal positions in the permutation π_k:

$$Per(\pi_k, T) = \sum_{r=1}^{n} OS(J_{k_r}, \pi_k). \qquad (13)$$

A sum of the lengths (of the cardinalities) $OS(J_{k_r}, \pi_k)$ for the job $J_{k_r} \in \mathcal{J}$ in the permutation π_k may be calculated as follows:

$$OS(J_{k_r}, \pi_k) = (u_{k_r}^{opt} - l_{k_r}^{opt}) + OS_{k_r}^{copt}, \qquad (14)$$

where the value of $(u_{k_r}^{opt} - l_{k_r}^{opt})$ is a length of the segment $[l_{k_r}^{opt}, u_{k_r}^{opt}]$ of the optimality for the job J_{k_r} in the permutation π_k. In the equality (14), the value of $OS_{k_r}^{copt}$ determines a cardinality of the optimality subset, which is based on a single segment $[l_{k_r}^{copt}, u_{k_r}^{copt}]$ or on both segments $[l_{k_r}^{copt}, u_{k_r}^{copt}]$ and $[l_{k_r}^{(copt)}, u_{k_r}^{(copt)}]$ (see Remark 3) of the conditional optimality of the job J_{k_r} in the permutation π_k.

To calculate the value of $OS(J_{k_r}, \pi_k) = (u_{k_r}^{opt} - l_{k_r}^{opt}) + OS_{k_r}^{copt}$, we use the partition (12) of the scope $[\hat{p}^L_{k_j}, \hat{p}^U_{k_{m_j}}]$ of the section $s_j^{\pi_k} \in S(\pi_k)$ such that the job J_{k_r} belongs to the set $\mathcal{J}_i^j = \{J_{k_i}, J_{k_{i+1}}, \ldots, J_{k_{|\mathcal{J}_i^j|}}\}$ determined for the section $s_j^{\pi_k}$, i.e., the inequalities $j \leq r \leq m_j$ hold. Because of the condition $\mathcal{OR}(\pi_k, T) \neq \emptyset$, one can conclude (due to remark 4) that there exists a single section $s_j^{\pi_k}$ containing the job J_{k_r}. The value of $OS(J_{k_r}, \pi_k)$ may be calculated as follows:

$$OS(J_{k_r}, \pi_k) = (u_{k_r}^{opt} - l_{k_r}^{opt}) + OS_{k_r}^{copt} = \sum_{[l_i^j(s_j^{\pi_k}), u_i^j(s_j^{\pi_k})] \subseteq [\hat{p}^L_{k_r}, \hat{p}^U_{k_r}]} \frac{u_i^j(s_j^{\pi_k}) - l_i^j(s_j^{\pi_k})}{|\mathcal{J}_i^j|}. \qquad (15)$$

The correctness of the equality (15) follows from the fact that the cardinality $OS(J_{k_r}, [l_i^j(s_j^{\pi_k}), u_i^j(s_j^{\pi_k})])$ of the optimality subset for the job J_{k_r}, which is based on the semi-interval $[l_i^j(s_j^{\pi_k}), u_i^j(s_j^{\pi_k}))$ of the optimality or conditional optimality for the job J_{r_r}, is equal to the following fraction:

$$OS(J_{k_r}, [l_i^j(s_j^{\pi_k}), u_i^j(s_j^{\pi_k})]) = \frac{u_i^j(s_j^{\pi_k}) - l_i^j(s_j^{\pi_k})}{|\mathcal{J}_i^j|}, \qquad (16)$$

since, due to Theorem 1, a position of the job J_{k_r} may be optimal in the permutation $\pi_k \in S$, only if the following $|\mathcal{J}_i^j|$ inequalities (17) hold:

$$\begin{cases} p_{k_r} \leq p_{k_v}, \text{ if } r < v, J_{k_v} \in \mathcal{J}_i^j; \\ p_{k_r} \geq p_{k_d}, \text{ if } d < r, J_{k_d} \in \mathcal{J}_i^j; \\ l_i^j(s_j^{\pi_k}) \leq p_{k_r} \leq u_i^j(s_j^{\pi_k}). \end{cases} \quad (17)$$

4.2. How to Calculate a Quasi-Perimeter for the Fixed Permutation

We next demonstrate the above notations and formulas on the calculation of the quasi-perimeter $Per(\pi_k, T)$ for the permutation $\pi_k = \pi_3 = (J_5, J_1, J_2, J_3, J_4, J_6, J_8, J_7) = (J_{k_1}, J_{k_2}, \ldots, J_{k_8})$ presented in Figure 3.

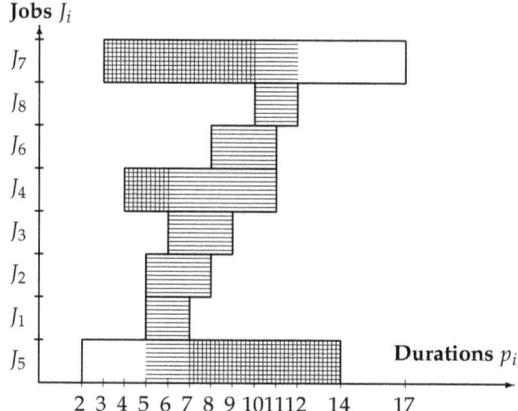

Figure 3. The segments of optimality, non-optimality (double-shaded) and conditional optimality (shaded) for the jobs $J_i \in \mathcal{J}$ in the permutation $\pi_3 = (J_5, J_1, J_2, J_3, J_4, J_6, J_8, J_7) \in S$.

For the permutation $\pi_k = \pi_3$, there exists a single section $s_1^{\pi_k} = s_1^{\pi_3} = (J_5, J_1, J_2, J_3, J_4, J_6, J_8, J_7) = \pi_3$, $S(\pi_3) = \{s_1^{\pi_3}\} = \{\pi_3\}$, with the scope $[\hat{p}_{k_1}^L, \hat{p}_{k_8}^U] = [\hat{p}_5^L, \hat{p}_7^U] = [2, 17]$. We obtain the following partition (12) of the scope $[\hat{p}_5^L, \hat{p}_7^U]$:

$$[\hat{p}_{k_1}^L, \hat{p}_{k_8}^U] = [2, 17] = [2, 5) \cup [5, 6) \cup [6, 7) \cup [7, 8) \cup [8, 9) \cup [9, 10) \cup [10, 11) \cup [11, 12) \cup [12, 17].$$

For the obtained nine semi-intervals $l_i^1(s^{\pi_3})$ in the above partition of the scope $[\hat{p}_{k_1}^L, \hat{p}_{k_8}^U]$, the following equalities hold: $\hat{J}_1^1 = (J_5)$, $\hat{J}_2^1 = (J_5, J_1, J_2)$, $\hat{J}_3^1 = (J_5, J_1, J_2, J_3, J_4)$, $\hat{J}_4^1 = (J_2, J_3, J_4)$, $\hat{J}_5^1 = (J_3, J_4, J_6)$, $\hat{J}_6^1 = (J_4, J_6)$, $\hat{J}_7^1 = (J_4, J_6, J_8, J_7)$, $\hat{J}_8^1 = (J_8, J_7)$, $\hat{J}_9^1 = (J_7)$. Using the equality (14), we calculate the optimality set $OS(J_{k_1}, \pi_k) = OS(J_5, \pi_3)$ for the job $J_{k_1} = J_5$ in the permutation $\pi_k = \pi_3$ as follows:

$$OS(J_{k_1}, \pi_k) = OS(J_5, \pi_3) = (u_5^{opt} - l_5^{opt}) + OS_5^{copt} = (5-2) + OS_5^{copt} = 3 + \frac{1}{3} + \frac{1}{5} = 3\frac{8}{15},$$

where the value of OS_5^{copt} is calculated based on the equality (15), namely: $OS_{k_1}^{copt} = \sum_{[l_i^1(s_1^{\pi_3}), u_i^1(s_1^{\pi_3})] \subseteq [\hat{p}_{k_1}^L, \hat{p}_{k_1}^U]} \frac{u_i^1(s_1^{\pi_3}) - l_i^1(s_1^{\pi_3})}{|\mathcal{J}_i^1|} = \frac{6-5}{3} + \frac{7-6}{5} = \frac{8}{15}$.

A cardinality of the optimality set OS_5^{copt} is illustrated on Figure 4, where the pyramid $\mathcal{PCO}\{J_{k_1}[l_{k_1}^1, u_{k_1}^1)]\hat{J}_1^1\} = \mathcal{PCO}\{J_5[5, 6)(J_5, J_1, J_2)\}$ of the optimality subset OS_5^{copt} for the job J_5, which is based on the semi-interval $[5, 6)$ for the permutation $\hat{J}_1^1 = (J_5, J_1, J_2)$ that is a part of the permutation

π_3. The volume of the pyramid $\mathcal{PCO}\{J_5[5,6](J_5, J_1, J_2)\}$ is determined by the system of inequalities (17), where $\pi_k = \pi_3$, $J_{k_r} = J_{3_1} = J_5$, $\widehat{\mathcal{J}}_i^j = \mathcal{J}_1^1$.

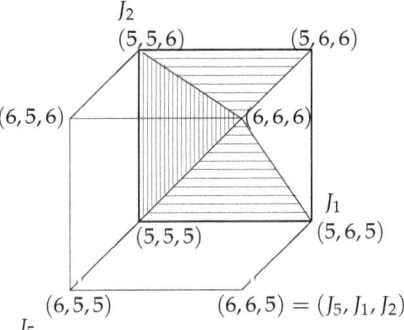

Figure 4. The pyramid $\mathcal{PCO}\{J_{k_1}[l_{k_1}^1, u_{k_1}^1)]\widehat{J}_1^1\} = \mathcal{PCO}\{J_5[5,6](J_5, J_1, J_2)\}$ of the optimality subset for the job J_5, which is based on the semi-interval $[5,6)$ for the permutation $\widehat{J}_1^1 = (J_5, J_1, J_2)$ that is a part of the permutation π_3.

Similarly, we can calculate the following values: $OS(J_{k_2}, \pi_k) = OS(J_1, \pi_3) = \frac{8}{15}$, $OS(J_{k_3}, \pi_k) = OS(J_2, \pi_3) = \frac{13}{15}$, $OS(J_{k_4}, \pi_k) = OS(J_3, \pi_3) = \frac{13}{15}$, $OS(J_{k_5}, \pi_k) = OS(J_4, \pi_3) = 1\frac{37}{60}$, $OS(J_{k_6}, \pi_k) = OS(J_6, \pi_3) = 1\frac{1}{12}$, $OS(J_{k_7}, \pi_k) = OS(J_8, \pi_3) = \frac{3}{4}$, $OS(J_{k_8}, \pi_k) = OS(J_7, \pi_3) = 5\frac{3}{4}$. Using the equality (13), we calculate the quasi-perimeter of the optimality region for the permutation π_3 as follows: $Per(\pi_3, T) = \sum_{r=1}^8 OS(J_{3_r}, \pi_3) = 3\frac{8}{15} + \frac{8}{15} + \frac{13}{15} + \frac{13}{15} + 1\frac{37}{60} + 1\frac{1}{12} + \frac{3}{4} + 5\frac{3}{4} = 15$.

It should be noted that the above quasi-perimeter $Per(\pi_3, T)$ is equal to the length $15 = 17 - 2$ of the scope $[\widehat{p}_{3_1}^L, \widehat{p}_{3_8}^U] = [2, 17]$ of the single section $s_1^{\pi_3}$ of the permutation $\pi_3 = s_1^{\pi_3}$. The following theorem shows that such an equality is not accidental.

Theorem 8. *If the condition $\mathcal{OR}(\pi_k, T) \neq \emptyset$ holds, one can calculate the quasi-perimeter $Per(\pi_k, T)$ of the optimality region for the permutation $\pi_k \in S$ as follows:*

$$Per(\pi_k, T) = \sum_{s_j^{\pi_k} \in S(\pi_k)} (\widehat{p}_{k_{m_j}}^U - \widehat{p}_{k_j}^L), \tag{18}$$

where $(\widehat{p}_{k_{m_j}}^U - \widehat{p}_{k_j}^L)$ is a length of the scope of the section $s_j^{\pi_k} \in S(\pi_k)$.

Proof. Due to Corollary 2, the above condition $\mathcal{OR}(\pi_k, T) \neq \emptyset$ implies the equality $\pi_k = (s_j^{\pi_k}, s_{m_j+1}^{\pi_k}, \ldots, s_w^{\pi_k})$. Therefore, the following equality also holds:

$$Per(\pi_k, T) = \sum_{s_j^{\pi_k} \in S(\pi_k)} Per(s_j^{\pi_k}, T), \tag{19}$$

where $Per(s_j^{\pi_k}, T)$ denotes a quasi-perimeter of the optimality region for the section $s_j^{\pi_k}$. Let $OS(\mathcal{J}_i^j, \pi_k)$ denote a quasi-perimeter of the optimality region for the permutation $\widehat{J}_i^j = (J_{k_i}, J_{k_{i+1}}, \ldots, J_{k_{|\mathcal{J}_i^j|}})$ of all jobs from the set $\mathcal{J}_i^j = \{J_{k_i}, J_{k_{i+1}}, \ldots, J_{k_{|\mathcal{J}_i^j|}}\}$.

For calculating the quasi-perimeter $Per(\pi_k, T)$ of the optimality region $\mathcal{OR}(\pi_k, T)$, we will use a summation of the values $OS(J_{k_r}, [l_i^j(s_j^{\pi_k}), u_i^j(s_j^{\pi_k})])$ through all jobs J_{k_r} in the permutation $\widehat{J}_i^j$. Thus, instead of the formulas (13)–(15), we use the equality (16) and the equalities (20) and (21):

$$Per(s_j^{\pi_k}, T) = \sum_{i=j}^{m_j} OS(\mathcal{J}_i^j, \pi_k), \tag{20}$$

$$OS(\mathcal{J}_i^j, \pi_k) = \sum_{r=i}^{|\mathcal{J}_i^j|} OS(J_{k_r}, [l_i^j(s_j^{\pi_k}), u_i^j(s_j^{\pi_k})]). \tag{21}$$

The equality (20) follows from the above definition of $Per(s_j^{\pi_k}, T)$. The equality (21) follows from the definition of $OS(\mathcal{J}_i^j, \pi_k)$. Using the equalities (16) and (21) we obtain

$$OS(\mathcal{J}_i^j, \pi_k) = \sum_{r=i}^{|\mathcal{J}_i^j|} OS(J_{k_r}, [l_i^j(s_j^{\pi_k}), u_i^j(s_j^{\pi_k})]) = |\mathcal{J}_i^j| \frac{u_i^j(s_j^{\pi_k}) - l_i^j(s_j^{\pi_k})}{|\mathcal{J}_i^j|} = u_i^j(s_j^{\pi_k}) - l_i^j(s_j^{\pi_k}). \tag{22}$$

Using the equalities (20) and (22) we obtain

$$Per(s_j^{\pi_k}, T) = \sum_{i=j}^{m_j} u_i^j(s_j^{\pi_k}) - l_i^j(s_j^{\pi_k}) = \widehat{p}_{k_{m_j}}^U - \widehat{p}_{k_j}^L. \tag{23}$$

Using the equalities (19) and (23) we obtain the desired equality (18) as follows:

$$Per(\pi_k, T) = \sum_{s_j^{\pi_k} \in S(\pi_k)} Per(s_j^{\pi_k}, T) = \sum_{s_j^{\pi_k} \in S(\pi_k)} (\widehat{p}_{k_{m_j}}^U - \widehat{p}_{k_j}^L).$$

Theorem 8 is proven. □

5. The Largest Quasi-Perimeter of the Optimality Region $\mathcal{OR}(\pi_k, T)$ for the Problem $1|\widehat{p}_i^L \leq p_i \leq \widehat{p}_i^U|\sum C_i$

We call the permutation $\pi_k \in S$ an effective permutation, if this permutation has the largest quasi-perimeter $Per(\pi_k, T)$ of the optimality region $\mathcal{OR}(\pi_k, T)$ among all permutations in the set S. The following claim follows directly from Theorem 8.

Corollary 3. *If the following equality holds:*

$$\sum_{s_j^{\pi_k} \in S(\pi_k)} (\widehat{p}_{k_{m_j}}^U - \widehat{p}_{k_j}^L) = \widehat{p}_{k_n}^U - \widehat{p}_{k_1}^L \tag{24}$$

for the permutation $\pi_k \in S$, then this permutation is effective.

Since the equality (24) holds for the permutation $\pi_3 = (J_5, J_1, J_2, J_3, J_4, J_6, J_8, J_7)$, one can conclude that this permutation is effective due to Corollary 3.

We next show how to find an effective permutation $\pi_k \in S$ in the general case of the problem $1|\widehat{p}_i^L \leq p_i \leq \widehat{p}_i^U|\sum C_i$. Similarly to the proof of Theorem 4 given in [23], we can prove the following claim.

Theorem 9. *Let all jobs from the set $\mathcal{J}$ be fixed in their blocks from the set B. Then the effective permutation $\pi_k \in S$ may be constructed in $O(n \log n)$ time.*

Thus, due to Theorem 9, the main problem, which must be solved for the construction of the effective permutation $\pi_k \in S$, is the optimal distribution of all non-fixed jobs between the effective sub-permutations of the jobs fixed in the block B_1, those fixed in the block B_2, and so on, those fixed in the block B_m. Let $\mathcal{J}^{non}$ denote a set of all non-fixed jobs of the set $\mathcal{J}$. The following lemma shows that we also need to find optimal positions for some fixed jobs of the set $\mathcal{J}$ in the desired effective permutation $\pi_k \in S$.

Theorem 10. *An effective sub-permutation of all jobs, which are fixed in the block $B_r = \{J_{r_1}, J_{r_2}, \ldots, J_{r_{|B_r|}}\} \subseteq B$, exists if and only if there is no job $J_{r_d} \in B_r$ such that the following conditions hold simultaneously:*

$$p_{r_d}^L = \min\{p_{r_i}^L : J_{r_i} \in B_r\} < \min\{p_{r_i}^L : J_{r_i} \in B_r \setminus \{J_{r_d}\}\}; \tag{25}$$

$$p_{r_d}^U = \max\{p_{r_i}^U : J_{r_i} \in B_r\} > \max\{p_{r_i}^U : J_{r_i} \in B_r \setminus \{J_{r_d}\}\}. \tag{26}$$

Proof. Sufficiency. Let there be no job $J_{r_d} \in B_r$ such that conditions (25) and (26) hold.

Hence, there exist at least two different jobs $J_{r_i} \in B_r$ and $J_{r_j} \in B_r$ such that the inequalities $p_{r_i}^L = \min\{p_{r_i}^L : J_{r_i} \in B_r\}$ and $p_{r_j}^U = \max\{p_{r_i}^U : J_{r_j} \in B_r\}$ hold. The effective sub-permutation of all jobs, which are fixed in the block $B_r = \{J_{r_1}, J_{r_2}, \ldots, J_{r_{|B_r|}}\} \subseteq B$, looks as follows $(J_{r_i}, \ldots, J_{r_j})$, where all jobs from the set $B_r \setminus \{J_{r_i}, J_{r_j}\}$ are located between jobs J_{r_i} and J_{r_j} and their order may be arbitrary.

Necessity. Let there exist a job $J_{r_d} \in B_r$ such that both conditions (25) and (26) hold.

Hence, an optimal position of the job J_{r_d} is either the first position or the last position in the effective sub-permutation of all jobs, which are fixed in the block $B_r = \{J_{r_1}, J_{r_2}, \ldots, J_{r_{|B_r|}}\}$. This choice for the job J_{r_d} depends from the positions of other such jobs in the blocks $B_l \in B \setminus \{B_r\}$ in the effective permutation π_k and from the positions of jobs from the set $\mathcal{J}^{non}$ in the effective permutation π_k. □

The following Algorithm 2 is based on Theorem 10.

Algorithm 2: Construction of the effective permutation of the jobs fixed in the block B_r

---

Input: The segments $[p_{r_i}^L, p_{r_i}^U]$ for all jobs from the set $\mathcal{J}$, which are fixed in the block $B_r = \{J_{r_1}, J_{r_2}, \ldots, J_{r_{|B_r|}}\}, i \in \{1, 2, \ldots, |B_r|\}$.
Output: The effective sub-permutation $\pi_{B_r} = (J_{r_1}, J_{r_1}, \ldots, J_{r_{|S_r|}})$ of the subset S_r of the set B_r, $S_r \subseteq B_r$, which are fixed in the block B_r.

Step 1: Find a job J_{r_i} such that $p_{r_i}^L = \min\{p_{r_j}^L : j \in \{1, 2, \ldots, |B_r|\}\}$;
Step 2: Find a job J_{r_k} such that $p_{r_k}^U = \max\{p_{r_j}^U : j \in \{1, 2, \ldots, |B_r|\} \setminus \{i\}\}$;
Step 3: **IF** $p_{r_k}^U \geq p_{r_i}^U$ **THEN** $\pi_{B_r} = (J_{r_i}, \ldots, J_{r_k})$, where jobs from the set $B_r \setminus \{J_{r_i}, J_{r_k}\}$ are ordered arbitrarily, set $S_{r_1} = \varnothing, S_{r_2} = \varnothing, S_r = B_r$
   GOTO step 11;
Step 4: Find a job J_{r_l} such that $p_{r_l}^L = \min\{p_{r_j}^L : j \in \{1, 2, \ldots, |B_r|\} \setminus \{i\}\}$;
Step 5: **IF** $p_{r_l}^L = p_{r_i}^L$ **THEN** $\pi_{B_r} = (J_{r_l}, \ldots, J_{r_i})$, where jobs from the set $B_r \setminus \{J_{r_l}, J_{r_i}\}$ are ordered arbitrarily, set $S_{r_1} = \varnothing, S_{r_2} = \varnothing, S_r = B_r$
   GOTO step 11;
Step 6: Find a job J_{r_o} such that $p_{r_o}^U = \max\{p_{r_j}^U : j \in \{1, 2, \ldots, |B_r|\} \setminus \{i, l\}\}$;
Step 7: **IF** $p_{r_o}^U \geq p_{r_i}^U$ **THEN** $\pi_{B_r} = (J_{r_l}, \ldots, J_{r_o})$, where jobs $B_r \setminus \{J_{r_l}, J_{r_o}, J_{r_i}\}$ are ordered arbitrarily, set $S_{r_1} = \{J_{r_i}\}, S_{r_2} = \varnothing, S_r = B_r \setminus \{J_{r_i}\}$ **GOTO** step 11;
Step 8: Find a job J_{r_q} such that $p_{r_q}^L = \min\{p_{r_j}^L : j \in \{1, 2, \ldots, |B_r|\} \setminus \{i, l\}\}$;
Step 9: **IF** $p_{r_q}^L = p_{r_l}^L$ **THEN** $\pi_{B_r} = (J_{r_q}, \ldots, J_{r_l})$, where jobs from the set $B_r \setminus \{J_{r_q}, J_{r_l}, J_{r_i}\}$ are ordered arbitrarily, set $S_{r_1} = \{J_{r_i}\}, S_{r_2} = \varnothing$,
   $S_r = B_r \setminus \{J_{r_i}\}$ **GOTO** step 11;
Step 10: $\pi_{B_r} = (J_{r_1}, \ldots, J_{|S_r|})$, where jobs from the set $S_r = B_r \setminus \{J_{r_i}, J_{r_l}\}$ are ordered arbitrarily, set $S_{r_1} = \{J_{r_i}\}, S_{r_2} = \{J_{r_l}\}$;
Step 11: The obtained sub-permutation π_{B_r} is effective **STOP**.

The asymptotic complexity of Algorithm 2 is equal to $O(n)$. The set S_{r_1} is either empty or contains a single job $J_{r_d} \in B_r$ for which both conditions (25) and (26) hold. The set S_{r_2} is either empty or contains a single job $J_{r_z} \in B_r$ for which both conditions $p_{r_z}^L = \min\{p_{r_i}^L : J_{r_i} \in B_r \setminus \{J_{r_d}\}\} < \min\{p_{r_i}^L : J_{r_i} \in B_r \setminus \{J_{r_d}, J_{r_z}\}\}$ and $p_{r_z}^U = \max\{p_{r_i}^U : J_{r_i} \in B_r \setminus \{J_{r_d}\}\} > \max\{p_{r_i}^U : J_{r_i} \in B_r \setminus \{J_{r_d}, J_{r_z}\}\}$ hold.

Let $\mathcal{J}^{fix}$ denote a set of all jobs $J_{r_d} \in B_r$, which are fixed in their blocks $B_r \in B$ and both conditions (25) and (26) hold. The following Algorithm 3 constructs an effective permutation $\pi_k \in S$ for the general case of the problem $1|p_i^L \leq p_i \leq p_i^U|\sum C_i$.

Algorithm 3: Construction of the effective permutation $\pi_k \in S$

Input: The segments $[p_i^L, p_i^U]$ for all jobs $J_i \in \mathcal{J}$;
the effective sub-permutations $\pi_{B_r} = (J_{r_1}, J_{r_2}, \ldots, J_{r_{|S_r|}})$, sets S_{r_1} and sets S_{r_2} for all blocks $B_r \in B$.

Output: The effective job permutation $\pi_k \in S$.

Step 1: Construct a sub-permutation $\pi_p = (\ldots, \pi_{B_1}, \ldots, \pi_{B_2}, \ldots, \pi_{B_m}, \ldots)$;
 FOR $r = 1$ to $|B|$ DO
  IF $S_{r_2} = \varnothing$ THEN $\hat{l}_r = p_{r_1}^L$, $\hat{u}_r = p_{r_{|S_r|}}^U$ ELSE
  $\hat{l}_r = p_{r_d}^L$, $\hat{u}_r = p_{r_d}^U$, $J_{r_d} \in S_{r_2}$;
 END FOR

Step 2: Construct sets of jobs $\mathcal{J}^{fix} = \cup_{r=1}^m S_{r_1}$, $\tilde{\mathcal{J}} = \mathcal{J}^{fix} \cup \mathcal{J}^{non}$, sort jobs of the set $\tilde{\mathcal{J}} = \{J_{f_1}, J_{f_2}, \ldots, J_{f_{|\tilde{\mathcal{J}}|}}\}$ by increasing of the mid-points of the segments $[p_{f_i}^L, p_{f_i}^U]$, obtain set $\tilde{\mathcal{J}} = (J_{f_1}, J_{f_2}, \ldots, J_{f_{|\tilde{\mathcal{J}}|}})$;

Step 3: Construct set $D = \cup_{i=1}^n (p_i^L \cup p_i^U)$, sort set D by increasing $D = (b_1, b_2, \ldots, b_q)$, $1 \leq q \leq 2n$, construct intervals $I_i = [b_i, b_{i+1}]$, $i \in \{1, 2, \ldots, q-1\}$;

Step 4: $S_{res} = \varnothing$, $N_{res} = \varnothing$, $sNumRes = 1$, $k = 1$,
$\hat{l}_{m+1} = \max\{p_i^U : i \in \{1, 2, \ldots, n\}\}$, $\hat{u}_{m+1} = \max\{p_i^U : i \in \{1, 2, \ldots, n\}\}$;

Step 5: IF $k \leq |\tilde{\mathcal{J}}|$ THEN $iNum = 1$, $bNum = 1$, $sNum = 1$, $S_k = \varnothing$, $N_k = \varnothing$
 ELSE GOTO step 10;

Step 6: FOR $j = 1$ to $q - 1$ DO
  IF $[b_j, b_{j+1}] \cap (p_{f_k}^L, p_{f_k}^U) \neq \varnothing$ AND $\hat{l}_{bNum} > b_j$ THEN $S_{k_{sNum}} := S_{k_{sNum}} \cup I_j$;
  IF $\hat{u}_{bNum} = b_{j+1}$ THEN $bNum := bNum + 1$;
  IF $\hat{u}_{bNum-1} = b_{j+1}$ AND $S_{k_{sNum}} \neq \varnothing$ THEN $N_{k_{sNum}} := bNum - 1$, $sNum := sNum + 1$;
 END FOR

Step 7: $s = 1$, $S_{tmp} = \varnothing$;
 FOR $i = 1$ to $sNum - 1$ DO
  FOR $j = 1$ to $sNumRes$ DO
   $S_{tmp_s} = S_{res_j} \cup S_{k_i}$, $N_{tmp_s} = (N_{res_j}, N_{k_i})$, $s := s + 1$;
  END FOR
 END FOR

Step 8: $j = 1$, $S_d = \varnothing$, $N_d = \varnothing$;
 WHILE $j < s$ DO $i = 1$;
  WHILE $i < s$ DO
   IF $S_{tmp_i} \subseteq S_{tmp_j}$ AND $i \neq j$ AND $S_{tmp_j} \notin S_d$ THEN
    $S_d := S_d \cup S_{tmp_i}$, $N_d := N_d \cup N_{tmp_i}$; $i := i + 1$;
   END $j := j + 1$;
  END $S_{nd} := S_{tmp} \setminus S_d$, $N_{nd} := N_{tmp} \setminus N_d$;

Step 9: $S_{res} = S_{nd}$, $N_{res} = N_{nd}$, $sNumRes = |S_{res}|$, $k := k + 1$ GOTO step 5;

Step 10: $maxP = 0$;
 FOR $i = 1$ to $sNumRes$ DO $P = 0$;

FOR EACH I_j IN S_{res_i} DO $P := P + b_{j+1} - b_j$ END FOR;
IF $P > maxP$ THEN $maxP = P, maxNum = i$ END FOR

Step 11: FOR $x = 1$ to $m + 1$ DO $S_x = \emptyset$ END FOR
FOR $k = 1$ to $|\mathcal{J}|$ DO $x = N_{maxNum_k}, S_x := S_x \cup J_k$; END FOR

Step 12: $\hat{u}_0 = \min\{p_i^L : i \in \{1, 2, \ldots, n\}\}$;
FOR $x = 1$ to $m + 1$ DO sort jobs of the set S_x by increasing of the
mid-points of the segments $[\max\{p_i^L, \hat{u}_{x-1}\}, \min\{p_i^U, \hat{l}_x\}]$ and obtain
sub-permutation π_{r_x};
END FOR

Step 13: FOR $x = 1$ to m DO
IF $S_{x_2} = \emptyset$ THEN $\pi_k = (\pi_k, \pi_{r_x}, \pi_{B_x})$ ELSE
IF $S_{x_1} \subseteq S_x$ THEN $\pi_k := (\pi_k, \pi_{r_x}, \pi_{B_x}, S_{x_2})$ ELSE
$\pi_k := (\pi_k, \pi_{r_x}, \hat{S}_{x_2}, \pi_{B_x})$;
END FOR
$\pi_k := (\pi_k, S_{m+1})$ STOP.

6. Computational Results

In the computational experiments, we tested six classes of hard instances $1|p_i^L \leq p_i \leq p_i^U| \sum C_i$. Algorithms 1–3 were coded in C# and tested on a PC with Intel Core (TM) 2 Quad, 2.5 GHz, 4.00 GB RAM. For all tested instances, inequalities $p_i^L < p_i^U$ hold for all jobs $J_i \in \mathcal{J}$. Table 2 presents computational results for randomly generated instances of the problem $1|p_i^L \leq p_i \leq p_i^U| \sum C_i$ with $n \in \{50, 100, 500, 1000, 5000, 10{,}000\}$.

The segments of possible durations have been randomly generated as follows. An integer center C of the segment $[p_i^L, p_i^U]$ was generated using a uniform distribution in the range $[1, 100]$. The lower bound p_i^L of the possible duration p_i was determined using the equality $p_i^L = C \cdot (1 - \frac{\delta}{100})$, where δ denotes the maximal relative error of the durations p_i due to the given segments $[p_i^L, p_i^U]$. The upper bound p_i^U was determined using the equality $p_i^U = C \cdot (1 + \frac{\delta}{100})$. For each job $J_i \in \mathcal{J}$, the point $\underline{p}_i$ was generated using a uniform distribution in the range $[p_i^L, p_i^U]$. In order to generate instances, where all jobs $\mathcal{J}$ belonged to a single block, the segments $[p_i^L, p_i^U]$ of the possible durations were modified as follows: $[\tilde{p}_i^L, \tilde{p}_i^U] = [p_i^L + \underline{p} - \underline{p}_i, p_i^U + \underline{p} - \underline{p}_i]$, where $\underline{p} = \max_{i=1}^{n} \underline{p}_i$.

Since the inclusion $\underline{p} \in [\tilde{p}_i^L, \tilde{p}_i^U]$ holds, each constructed instance contained a single block, $|B| = 1$. The maximum absolute error of the uncertain durations p_i, $J_i \in \mathcal{J}$, is equal to $\max_{i=1}^{n}(p_i^U - p_i^L)$, and the maximum relative error of the uncertain durations p_i, $J_i \in \mathcal{J}$, is not greater than $2\delta\%$. We say that these instances belong to class 1.

Three distribution laws were used in our computational experiments to determine the factual durations of the jobs. If inequality $p_i^L < p_i^U$ holds, then the factual duration of the job J_i becomes known only after completing the job J_i.

We call the uniform distribution as the distribution law with number 1, the gamma distribution with the parameters $\alpha = 9$ and $\beta = 2$ as the distribution law with number 2, and the gamma distribution with the parameters $\alpha = 4$, and $\beta = 2$ as the distribution law with number 3. In each instance of class 1, for generating the factual durations for different jobs of the set $\mathcal{J}$, the number of the distribution law was randomly chosen from the set $\{1, 2, 3\}$. We solved 15 series of the randomly generated instances from class 1. Each series contained 10 instances with the same combination of n and δ.

In the computational experiments, we answered the question of how large the obtained relative error $\Delta = \frac{\gamma_{p^*}^k - \gamma_{p^*}^t}{\gamma_{p^*}^t} \cdot 100\%$ of the value $\gamma_{p^*}^k$ of the objective function $\gamma = \sum_{i=1}^{n} C_i$ was for the effective permutation π_k with respect to the actually optimal objective function value $\gamma_{p^*}^t$ calculated for the factual durations $p^* = (p_1^*, p_2^*, \ldots, p_n^*) \in T$, which were known after completing all the jobs.

The number n of jobs in the instance is given in column 1 in Table 2. The half of the maximum possible errors δ of the random durations (in percentage) is given in column 2. Column 3 gives the average error Δ for the effective permutation π_k. Column 4 presents the average CPU-time in seconds. The smallest errors, average errors, largest errors for the tested series of the instances are presented in the last rows of Table 2.

Table 2. Computational results for randomly generated instances with a single block (class 1).

n	δ (%)	Δ	CPU-Time (s)
1	2	3	4
50	1	0.088066	0.028202
50	5	0.29217	0.028702
50	10	0.451719	0.027502
100	1	0.083836	0.040702
100	5	0.25303	0.040202
100	10	0.442234	0.038802
500	1	0.090923	0.162809
500	5	0.268353	0.160009
500	10	0.446225	0.162509
1000	1	0.09579	0.309918
1000	5	0.266479	0.310618
1000	10	0.443648	0.312518
5000	1	0.097144	1.196568
5000	5	0.264383	1.531488
5000	10	0.455035	1.556389
10,000	1	0.094943	3.103378
10,000	5	0.265045	3.073576
10,000	10	0.452539	2.993571
Minimum		0.083836	0.027502
Average		0.269454	0.837637
Maximum		0.455035	3.103378

In the second part of our computational experiments, Algorithms 1–3 were applied to randomly generated instances from other classes 2–6 of the problem $1|p_i^L \leq p_i \leq p_i^U| \sum C_i$. We randomly generated non-fixed jobs $J_1, J_2, \ldots, J_s$, which belong to blocks $B_1, B_2, \ldots, B_m$ of the randomly generated $n - s$ fixed jobs. The lower bound p_i^L and the upper bound p_i^U on the feasible values of $p_i \in R_+^1$ of the durations of the fixed jobs, $p_i \in [p_i^L, p_i^U]$, were generated as follows.

We determined a bound of blocks $[\widetilde{b}_i^L, \widetilde{b}_i^U]$ for generating the cores of the blocks $[b_i^L, b_i^U] \subseteq [\widetilde{b}_i^L, \widetilde{b}_i^U]$ and for generating the segments $[p_i^L, p_i^U]$ for the durations of $|B_i|$ jobs from all blocks B_i, $i \in \{1, 2, \ldots, m\}$, $[b_i^L, b_i^U] \subseteq [p_i^L, p_i^U] \subseteq [\widetilde{b}_i^L, \widetilde{b}_i^U]$.

Each instance in class 2 or in class 3 had a single non-fixed job J_v, whose bounds were determined as follows: $p_{J_v}^L \leq \widetilde{b}_1^L \leq \widetilde{b}_1^U < \widetilde{b}_2^L \leq \widetilde{b}_2^U < \widetilde{b}_3^L \leq \widetilde{b}_3^U \leq p_{J_v}^U$. Classes 2 and 3 of the solved instances differed one from another by the numbers of non-fixed jobs and the distribution laws used for choosing the factual durations of the jobs $\mathcal{J}$.

Each instance from classes 4 and 5 had two non-fixed jobs. In each instance from classes 2, 4, 5 and 6, for generating the factual durations for the jobs $\mathcal{J}$, the numbers of the distribution laws were randomly chosen from the set $\{1, 2, 3\}$, and they were indicated in column 4 in Table 3. In the instances of class 6, the cores of the blocks were determined in order to generate different numbers of non-fixed jobs in different instances. The numbers of non-fixed jobs were randomly chosen from the set $\{2, 3, \ldots, 8\}$.

The numbers n of the jobs are presented in column 1 in Table 3. Column 2 represents the number $|B|$ of blocks in the solved instance and column 3 the number of non-fixed jobs. The distribution laws used for determining the factual durations of the jobs are indicated in column 4 in Table 3. Column 6 presents average numbers λ of the maximal number of the variants of the non-dominated distributions of the jobs $\mathcal{J}^{fix} \cup \mathcal{J}^{non}$ in the effective permutation π_k while it was constructed on the iterations of Algorithm 3. Each solved series contained 10 instances with the same combination of n and the other parameters. The obtained smallest, average and largest values of Δ for each series of the tested instances are presented in column 5 in Table 3 at the end of series.

Table 3. Computational results for randomly generated instances from classes 2–6.

n	$|B|$	$|\mathcal{J}^{non}|$	Laws	Δ	Average λ	CPU-Time (s)
1	2	3	4	5	6	7
Class 2						
50	3	1	1,2,3	0.54205	4	0.16921
100	3	1	1,2,3	0.281253	4	0.305017
500	3	1	1,2,3	0.177597	4	0.952555
1000	3	1	1,2,3	0.121447	4	1.561289
5000	3	1	1,2,3	0.111056	4	9.481842
10,000	3	1	1,2,3	0.105322	4	18.933383
		Minimum		0.105322	4	0.16921
		Average		0.223121	4	5.233883
		Maximum		0.54205	4	18.933383
Class 3						
50	3	1	1	0.575038	4	0.098006
100	3	1	1	0.284279	4	0.334319
500	3	1	1	0.132735	4	0.647537
1000	3	1	1	0.114245	4	1.389479
5000	3	1	1	0.160372	4	9.290531
10,000	3	1	1	0.149278	4	12.189497
		Minimum		0.114245	4	0.098006
		Average		0.235991	4	3.991562
		Maximum		0.575038	4	12.189497
Class 4						
50	3	2	1,2,3	0.670408	6.5	0.408923
100	3	2	1,2,3	0.402251	6.2	0.791245
500	3	2	1,2,3	0.084687	6.2	3.866421
1000	3	2	1,2,3	0.084137	6.4	8.715098
5000	3	2	1,2,3	0.066305	6.2	35.98006
10,000	3	2	1,2,3	0.061258	6.2	78.877412
		Minimum		0.061258	6.2	0.408923
		Average		0.228174	6.3	21.43986
		Maximum		0.670408	6.5	78.877412
Class 5						
50	5	2	1,2,3	0.498197	16.2	0.969455
100	5	2	1,2,3	0.157349	15	2.035616
500	5	2	1,2,3	0.069192	15	6.832491
1000	5	2	1,2,3	0.059916	15	13.53107
5000	5	2	1,2,3	0.045986	15	86.01118
10,000	5	2	1,2,3	0.047765	15	129.1963
		Minimum		0.045986	15	0.969455
		Average		0.146401	15.2	39.762685
		Maximum		0.498197	16.2	129.1963

Table 3. Cont.

n	$|B|$	$|\mathcal{J}^{non}|$	Laws	Δ	Average λ	$\mathcal{CPU}$-Time (s)
1	2	3	4	5	6	7
			Class 6			
50	2	2–4	1,2,3	1.086983	3.9	0.496728
100	2	2–4	1,2,3	0.839207	4	0.945754
500	2	2–6	1,2,3	0.843448	3.8	4.976885
1000	2	2–8	1,2,3	0.874078	3.6	13.604478
5000	2	2–8	1,2,3	0.790634	3.7	71.244575
10,000	2	2–8	1,2,3	0.768925	3.7	153.430476
		Minimum		0.768925	3.6	0.496728
		Average		0.867212	3.8	40.783149
		Maximum		1.086983	4	153.430476

7. Concluding Remarks

The uncertain scheduling problem $1|p_i^L \leq p_i \leq p_i^U| \sum C_i$ attracts the attention of the researchers since this problem is applicable in real-life scheduling and is commonly used in many multiple-resource scheduling systems, where one of the available machines is the bottleneck and uncertain machine. The optimal scheduling decisions allow the plant to reduce the costs of productions due to a better utilization of the available machines.

In Sections 2–5, we used a notion of the optimality region of a job permutation π_k and proved useful properties of the optimality region $\mathcal{OR}(\pi_k, T)$. We investigated the permutation π_k with the largest quasi-perimeter of the optimality region. Using these properties, we derived algorithms for constructing a job permutation π_k with the largest quasi-perimeter of the optimality region $\mathcal{OR}(\pi_k, T)$.

From the computational experiments, it follows that the effective permutation π_k is close to the optimal permutation, which can be determined after completing all jobs when their durations became known. We tested classes 1–6 of the problems $1|p_i^L \leq p_i \leq p_i^U| \sum C_i$. The minimal, average and maximal errors Δ of the objective function values were 0.045986, 0.313658 and 1.086983, respectively, for the effective permutations.

An attractive direction for a further research is a generalization of the obtained results to the problem $1|p_i^L \leq p_i \leq p_i^U| \sum w_i C_i$, where the given jobs may have different weights. It is also useful to find precedence constraints on the set of jobs such that the effective job permutation may be constructed similarly to Section 5.

Author Contributions: Y.N. proved theoretical results; Y.N. and N.E. jointly conceived and designed the algorithms; N.E. performed the experiments; Y.N. and N.E. analyzed the data; Y.N. wrote the paper.

Funding: This research received no external funding.

Acknowledgments: The authors are grateful to anonymous referees for their useful remarks and suggestions.

Conflicts of Interest: The authors declare no conflict of interest.

References

1. Davis, W.J.; Jones, A.T. A real-time production scheduler for a stochastic manufacturing environment. *Int. J. Prod. Res.* **1988**, *1*, 101–112. [CrossRef]
2. Pinedo, M. *Scheduling: Theory, Algorithms, and Systems*; Prentice-Hall: Englewood Cliffs, NJ, USA, 2002.
3. Daniels, R.L.; Kouvelis, P. Robust scheduling to hedge against processing time uncertainty in single stage production. *Manag. Sci.* **1995**, *41*, 363–376. [CrossRef]
4. Sabuncuoglu, I.; Goren, S. Hedging production schedules against uncertainty in manufacturing environment with a review of robustness and stability research. *Int. J. Comput. Integr. Manuf.* **2009**, *22*, 138–157. [CrossRef]
5. Sotskov, Y.N.; Werner, F. *Sequencing and Scheduling with Inaccurate Data*; Nova Science Publishers: Hauppauge, NY, USA, 2014.

6. Pereira, J. The robust (minmax regret) single machine scheduling with interval processing times and total weighted completion time objective. *Comput. Oper. Res.* **2016**, *66*, 141–152. [CrossRef]
7. Grabot, B.; Geneste, L. Dispatching rules in scheduling: A fuzzy approach. *Int. J. Prod. Res.* **1994**, *32*, 903–915. [CrossRef]
8. Kasperski, A.; Zielinski, P. Possibilistic minmax regret sequencing problems with fuzzy parameters. *IEEE Trans. Fuzzy Syst.* **2011**, *19*, 1072–1082. [CrossRef]
9. Özelkan, E.C.; Duckstein, L. Optimal fuzzy counterparts of scheduling rules. *Eur. J. Oper. Res.* **1999**, *113*, 593–609. [CrossRef]
10. Sotskov, Y.N.; Egorova, N.M.; Lai, T.-C. Minimizing total weighted flow time of a set of jobs with interval processing times. *Math. Comput. Model.* **2009**, *50*, 556–573. [CrossRef]
11. Tanaev, V.S.; Sotskov, Y.N.; Strusevich, V.A. *Scheduling Theory: Multi-Stage Systems*; Kluwer Academic Publishers: Dordrecht, The Netherlands, 1994.
12. Graham, R.L.; Lawler, E.L.; Lenstra, J.K.; Rinnooy Kan, A.H.G. Optimization and approximation in deterministic sequencing and scheduling. *Ann. Discr. Appl. Math.* **1979**, *5*, 287–326.
13. Smith, W.E. Various optimizers for single-stage production. *Naval Res. Logist. Q.* **1956**, *3*, 59–66. [CrossRef]
14. Burdett, R.L.; Kozan, E. Techniques to effectively buffer schedules in the face of uncertainties. *Comput. Ind. Eng.* **2015**, *87*, 16–29. [CrossRef]
15. Goren, S.; Sabuncuoglu, I. Robustness and stability measures for scheduling: Single-machine environment. *IIE Trans.* **2008**, *40*, 66–83. [CrossRef]
16. Kasperski, A.; Zielinski, P. A 2-approximation algorithm for interval data minmax regret sequencing problems with total flow time criterion. *Oper. Res. Lett.* **2008**, *36*, 343–344. [CrossRef]
17. Kouvelis, P.; Yu, G. *Robust Discrete Optimization and Its Application*; Kluwer Academic Publishers: Boston, MA, USA, 1997.
18. Lu, C.-C.; Lin, S.-W.; Ying, K.-C. Robust scheduling on a single machine total flow time. *Comput. Oper. Res.* **2012**, *39*, 1682–1691. [CrossRef]
19. Yang, J.; Yu, G. On the robust single machine scheduling problem. *J. Combin. Optim.* **2002**, *6*, 17–33. [CrossRef]
20. Lebedev, V.; Averbakh, I. Complexity of minimizing the total flow time with interval data and minmax regret criterion. *Discr. Appl. Math.* **2006**, *154*, 2167–2177. [CrossRef]
21. Harikrishnan, K.K.; Ishii, H. Single machine batch scheduling problem with resource dependent setup and processing time in the presence of fuzzy due date. *Fuzzy Optim. Decis. Mak.* **2005**, *4*, 141–147. [CrossRef]
22. Allahverdi, A.; Aydilek, H.; Aydilek, A. Single machine scheduling problem with interval processing times to minimize mean weighted completion times. *Comput. Oper. Res.* **2014**, *51*, 200–207. [CrossRef]
23. Lai, T.-C.; Sotskov, Y.N.; Egorova, N.G.; Werner, F. The optimality box in uncertain data for minimising the sum of the weighted job completion times. *Int. J. Prod. Res.* **2018**, *56*, 6336–6362. [CrossRef]
24. Sotskov, Y.N.; Egorova, N.M. Single machine scheduling problem with interval processing times and total completion time objective. *Algorithms* **2018**, *75*, 66. [CrossRef]
25. Sotskov, Y.N.; Lai, T.-C. Minimizing total weighted flow time under uncertainty using dominance and a stability box. *Comput. Oper. Res.* **2012**, *39*, 1271–1289. [CrossRef]

© 2019 by the authors. Licensee MDPI, Basel, Switzerland. This article is an open access article distributed under the terms and conditions of the Creative Commons Attribution (CC BY) license (http://creativecommons.org/licenses/by/4.0/).

Article
Two-Machine Job-Shop Scheduling with Equal Processing Times on Each Machine

Evgeny Gafarov [1,*] **and Frank Werner** [2]

[1] V.A. Trapeznikov Institute of Control Sciences of the Russian Academy of Sciences, Profsoyuznaya st. 65, 117997 Moscow, Russia
[2] Fakultät für Mathematik, Otto-von-Guericke-Universität Magdeburg, PSF 4120, 39016 Magdeburg, Germany; frank.werner@mathematik.uni-magdeburg.de
* Correspondence: axel73@mail.ru; Tel.: +7-925-809-0907

Received: 23 January 2019; Accepted: 19 March 2019; Published: 25 March 2019

Abstract: In this paper, we consider a two-machine job-shop scheduling problem of minimizing total completion time subject to n jobs with two operations and equal processing times on each machine. This problem occurs e.g., as a single-track railway scheduling problem with three stations and constant travel times between any two adjacent stations. We present a polynomial dynamic programming algorithm of the complexity $O(n^5)$ and a heuristic procedure of the complexity $O(n^3)$. This settles the complexity status of the problem under consideration which was open before and extends earlier work for the two-station single-track railway scheduling problem. We also present computational results of the comparison of both algorithms. For the 30,000 instances with up to 30 jobs considered, the average relative error of the heuristic is less than 1%. In our tests, the practical running time of the dynamic programming algorithm was even bounded by $O(n^4)$.

Keywords: scheduling; total completion time; job-shop

1. Introduction

We consider a two-machine job-shop scheduling problem. Each job $j \in N = \{1, 2, \ldots, n\}$ consists of two operations, i.e., we have $n_j = 2$ according to [1]. The operation $O_{j,a}$ is processed on the machine M_a and its processing time is equal to a. The operation $O_{j,b}$ is processed on the machine M_b and its processing time is equal to b, where $a, b \in Z^+$ and $a < b$. For simplicity of the subsequent consideration, we use both notations a and M_a, where a is a descriptor in M_a and a is the processing time of any job on this machine.

Let N_{ab} be the subset of jobs j, for which operation $O_{j,a}$ precedes operation $O_{j,b}$ and let N_{ba} be the subset of jobs j, for which operation $O_{j,b}$ precedes operation $O_{j,a}$. Moreover, denote $n_{ab} = |N_{ab}|$ and $n_{ba} = |N_{ba}|$. Thus, we have $n = n_{ab} + n_{ba}$. Please note that the parameter n_j is different from n_{ab} and n_{ba}. The parameter n_j is often used in publications on job-shop scheduling to denote the number of operations of job j, and we use n_{ab}, n_{ba} to denote the numbers of jobs with the two possible technological routes. A schedule Π is uniquely determined by two permutations π_{M_a} and π_{M_b} of the operations of the set $N_{ab} \cup N_{ba}$. Let $C_{j,x}(\Pi)$ be the completion time of operation $O_{j,x}$ and $S_{j,x}(\Pi) = C_{j,x}(\Pi) - x, x \in \{a, b\}$ be the starting time of the operation in the schedule Π.

For the two-machine job-shop scheduling problem of minimizing total completion time subject to given processing times, the objective is to find an optimal schedule Π^* that minimizes the total completion time, i.e.,

$$\sum_{j \in N_{ab}} C_{j,b} + \sum_{j \in N_{ba}} C_{j,a}. \tag{1}$$

We denote this problem by $J2|n_j = 2, p_{j1} = a, p_{j2} = b| \sum C_j$ according to the traditional three-field notation $\alpha|\beta|\gamma$ for scheduling problems proposed by Graham et al. [2], where α describes the machine environment, β gives the job characteristics and further constraints, and γ describes the objective function. Please note that, without loss of generality, we can restrict to the case $a < b$ since the case $a = b$ can be trivially solved in constant time.

Our motivation to deal with this problem with an open complexity status is as follows:

- it has a theoretical significance as a special case of the classical job-shop scheduling problem with two machines with another objective function than the makespan considered by Jackson in the well-known paper from 1956 [3];
- it has also practical significance as a particular sub-problem e.g., arising in railway scheduling.

Namely, the following single-track railway scheduling problem (STRSP) can be reduced to this problem. In the STRSP, there is a single track between the stations A and C and a middle station B between stations A and C. Trains go in both directions. Each of the sub-tracks AB and BC can process only one train at a time. At the station B, a train can pass other trains, and at all stations there are enough parallel tracks to deposit trains. A single-track network can be seen as a bottleneck portion for any type of railway network topology. Furthermore, almost all national railway networks have sections, where there is a single-track between some stations. For some countries (e.g., USA, Australia), a significant part of the network is single-track. For multi-track networks such a single-track segment can be considered as a bottleneck, in which the traffic capacity is restricted.

In this paper, we present a new polynomially solvable case for the two-machine job-shop problem with minimizing total completion time based on dynamic programming [4]. At the same time, this extends an existing polynomial algorithm for the two-station single-track railway scheduling problem from [5] to the case of three stations. In addition, we present a fast polynomial heuristic of lower complexity which is able to construct near-optimal solutions.

The rest of this paper is organized as follows. A brief literature review is given in Section 2. In Section 3, some properties of the problem are presented which are the base for the dynamic programming algorithm. Polynomial exact and heuristic solution procedures for this problem are presented in Section 4. Some results of numerical experiments are presented in Section 5. Finally, concluding remarks are given in Section 6.

2. Literature Overview

The problem $J2|n_j = 2, p_{j1} = a, p_{j2} = b|C_{max}$ of minimizing the makespan (maximal completion time) can be solved in constant time by Jackson's algorithm [3]. In an optimal schedule, on the machine M_a, first all operations $O_{i,a}$, $i \in N_{ab}$, are processed and then all operations $O_{j,a}$, $j \in N_{ba}$. On the machine M_b, first all operations $O_{j,b}$, $j \in N_{ba}$, are processed and then all operations $O_{i,b}$, $i \in N_{ab}$. However, the problem $J2||C_{max}$ without the restriction to at most two operations per job and arbitrary processing times is already NP-hard [1].

Moreover, when minimizing total completion time, only very special unit-time problems can be polynomially solved (see e.g., [1]). Even the two-machine unit-time problems $J2|p_{jk} = 1, r_j \geq 0|\sum C_j$ with release dates r_j, $J2|p_{jk} = 1|\sum w_j C_j$ with job weights w_j or the three-machine problem $J3|p_{jk} = 1|\sum C_j$ are already NP-hard (see [1]). Two-machine job shop scheduling problems with unit processing times and $n_j > 2$ operations per job, where the even operations are processed on one machine and the odd operations on the other one are considered in [6,7]. The scheduling problem to minimize total completion time is considered in [8].

Some results on parallel machine and single machine scheduling problems with unit and equal processing times of the jobs are presented in [9,10]. Single machine problems are equivalent to the special case of a two-machine job shop scheduling problem with $n_j = 2, p_{j1} = a, p_{j2} = b$, where a is sufficiently small so that it can be disregarded. These problems without precedence relations are known to be polynomially solvable, except the problem $1|r_j \geq 0, p_j = p|\sum w_j T_j$ the complexity status of which is open. An additional motivation of our research is the search for an NP-hard job scheduling problem with equal processing times which is most close to single machine job scheduling problems with equal processing times without precedence relations and preemptions.

As previously mentioned, the problem under consideration is closely related to a particular single-track railway scheduling problem. Often such problems are considered in the case of maintenance of one track of a double-track line. For example, the French railway company SNCF develops such models to produce a new transport schedule in the event of an incident on one of the double-track line sections [11]. The work on single-track railway scheduling problems (STRSP) goes back to the 1970s, with the initial publication [12]. A recent literature review on the single-track railway scheduling problem can be found, e.g., in [13]. A short survey on the STRSP with several stations, where trains are able to pass each other, is presented in [14]. In [5], a single-track railway scheduling problem with two stations and several segments of the track is considered. In [15], train scheduling problems are modeled as job-shop scheduling problems with blocking constraints. Four MIP formulations are developed for the problem of minimizing total tardiness, and a computational study is made on hard instances with up to 20 jobs (trains) and 11 machines (tracks or track sections). Blocking constraints make the job-shop scheduling problem very hard from a practical point of view. In [16], a complex neighborhood for the job-shop scheduling problem with blocking and total tardiness minimization has been developed and tested on benchmark instances from the literature. Further algorithms for general railway scheduling problems have been given for instance in [17–19] and for job-shop scheduling problems with blocking in [20,21]. The blocking job-shop with rail-bound transportation has also been discussed in [22]. Please note that for a small railway network with only a few stations and enough parallel tracks at each station, the blocking constraint can be skipped as in our three-station case.

In this paper, we deal with an exact dynamic programming approach. For some further recent general approaches for the solution of different types of single and multiple criteria scheduling problems, the interested reader is referred to [23–29] which highlight the importance of developing advanced scheduling approaches. This concerns both the identification of new polynomially solvable problems as well as new MILP models and metaheuristic or hybrid algorithms.

3. Properties of the Problem $J2|n_j = 2, p_{j1} = a, p_{j2} = b| \sum C_j$

In this section, we present and prove in Lemmas 1–3 some basic properties of the problem. While Lemma 1 characterizes the structure of partial solutions, Lemmas 2 and 3 are used in the proof of the subsequent Theorem 1 which is the foundation of the dynamic programming algorithm given in Section 4.

Without loss of optimality, we can restrict to schedules, where the operations $O_{j,a}$ are processed in the same order as the operations $O_{j,b}$, $j \in N_{ab}(N_{ba})$. Then we can schedule the jobs from each subset according to increasing numbers. To distinguish the jobs from the sets N_{ab} and N_{ba}, the jobs from the set N_{ba} are overlined, i.e., we have $N_{ab} = \{1, 2, \ldots, n_{ab}\}$ and $N_{ba} = \{\bar{1}, \bar{2}, \ldots, \overline{n_{ba}}\}$.

In an active schedule, a job cannot be started earlier without violating the feasibility. Without loss of optimality, we consider active schedules only.

It is obvious that there is only a single case when an idle time on the machine M_b arises. It can be immediately before time $C_{i,a} = S_{i,b}$, $i \in N_{ab}$, i.e., when for the job $i \in N_{ab}$, the completion time of the short operation (with processing time a) is equal to the starting time of the long one (with processing time b). The same holds for an idle time on the machine M_a. An idle time can be immediately before time $C_{\bar{j},b} = S_{\bar{j},a}$, $\bar{j} \in N_{ba}$.

Lemma 1. *In any active schedule, the starting times of the operations belong to the set*

$$\Theta = \{xa + yb | x, y \in \mathbb{Z}, x, y < n_{ab} + n_{ba}\}. \tag{2}$$

Proof. We consider the possible starting time $S_{i,a}$ of operation $O_{i,a}$ in an active schedule. Let in the interval $[t_1, S_{i,a})$, x_1 operations be processed on the machine M_a without idle time and let there be an idle time immediately before t_1. Then there is a job $\overline{j_1}$ for which $C_{\overline{j_1},b} = S_{\overline{j_1},a} = t_1$. Let in the interval $[t_2, C_{\overline{j_1},b}]$, y_1 operations be processed on the machine M_b without an idle time and let there be an idle time immediately before t_2. Then there is a job i_1 for which $C_{i_1,a} = S_{i_1,b} = t_2$. For an illustration, see Figure 1.

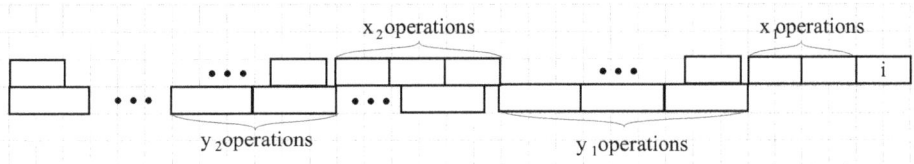

Figure 1. Illustration for the proof of Lemma 1.

By continuing this consideration, we have

$$S_{i,a} = (x_1 + x_2 + x_3 + \dots)a + (y_1 + y_2 + \dots)b. \qquad (3)$$

□

Lemma 2. *In any optimal schedule, we have $S_{1,a} = S_{\overline{1},b} = 0$, i.e., the starting times of the first operations of the first job from each subset are equal to 0.*

Proof. It is obvious that in each active schedule $S_{1,a} = 0$ for $O_{1,a} \in N_{ab}$.

Next, we show that the lemma holds for the first job $\overline{1} \in N_{ba}$. Let in a schedule Π, this does not hold. The operation sequence for machine M_a is $(O_{i_1,a}, O_{i_2,a}, \pi_1, O_{\overline{1},a}, \pi_2)$, where in the partial sequence π_1 there are k_1 operations and $i_1, i_2 \in N_{ab}$. The operation sequence for machine M_b is $(\pi_3, O_{\overline{1},b}, \pi_4)$, where in the partial sequence π_3 there are $k_2 \geq 1$ operations (see Figure 2).

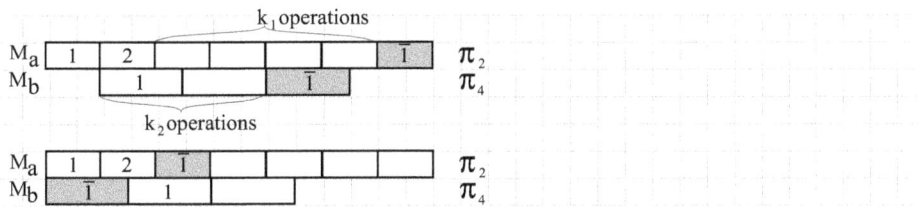

Figure 2. Illustration for the proof of Lemma 2.

Then for the schedule Π' with the operation sequence $(O_{i_1,a}, O_{i_2,a}, O_{\overline{1},b}, \pi_1, \pi_2)$ for machine M_a and the operation sequence $(O_{\overline{1},b}, \pi_3, \pi_4)$ for machine M_b, we increase the completion times for the operations $O_{i,b} \in \pi_3$ on the value $(b - a)$, and we decrease the completion time of the operation $O_{\overline{1},a}$ on the value

$$C_{\overline{1},a}(\Pi) - C_{\overline{1},a}(\Pi') = (\max\{a + (k_2+1)b, (2+k_1)a\} + a) - 3a \geq (k_2+1)b - a. \qquad (4)$$

Let $C_{i_2,a} = 2a > b$, then the completion times of the operations from π_2 and π_4 are not increased. Thus, the total completion time is decreased on a value greater than or equal to

$$(k_2+1)b - a - (b-a)k_2 \geq b. \qquad (5)$$

An analogous proof can be presented for the case $2a \leq b$. The lemma is true for the first job from the set N_{ba}. □

Lemma 3. *In any active schedule Π at each time t, where an operation $O_{i,a}, i \in N_{ab}$, is such that $t \leq C_{i,a}(\Pi)$, the number of short operations completed is greater than or equal to the number of long operations completed.*

Proof. The proof is done by induction. We consider the completion times t of the first, ..., $(k-1)$-th and k-th operations processed on the machine M_b. The lemma holds for t equal to the completion time of the first operation processed on the machine M_b, i.e., $t = C_{\overline{1},b} = b$.

Let the lemma hold for t equal to the completion time of the $(k-1)$-th operation processed on the machine M_b. Moreover, there are $l, l \geq k-1$, operations completed on the machine M_a before t. Let $\tau, \tau \leq t$, be the completion time of the last operation completed on the machine M_a before time t.

Let $t', t' \geq t+b$, be the completion time of the k-th operation processed on the machine M_b. Then, in the interval $[\tau, t']$, at least one operation can be processed on the machine M_a and thus, at time t', the number of short operations completed is greater than or equal to the number of long operations completed. □

Theorem 1. *In any optimal schedule, there is no idle time on the machine M_b before the last operation from the set N_{ba}, i.e., before the time $S_{\overline{n_{ba}},a}$.*

Proof. The proof is done by induction. First, we show that the theorem holds for the first job from the set N_{ba} and then for the next jobs $\overline{j} \in N_{ba}$. If for an operation $O_{\overline{j},b}, \overline{j} \in N_{ba}$, in a schedule Π, there is an idle time before the time $S_{\overline{j},b}(\Pi)$ on the machine M_b, then we construct a modified schedule Π', where the operations $O_{\overline{j},a}$ and $O_{\overline{j},b}$ are shifted to an earlier time so that the idle time is vanished and total completion time decreases.

If $a \leq \frac{1}{2}b$, then in any active schedule, there is no idle time on the machine M_b, since for any operation $O_{i,a}, i \in N_{ab}, i > 1$, we have $C_{i,a} < S_{i,b}$. Next, we consider the only remaining case $a > \frac{1}{2}b$.

According to Lemma 2, the theorem holds for the first job $\overline{1} \in N_{ba}$. Let the theorem hold for the job $\overline{j-1} \in N_{ba}$, and we consider the next job $\overline{j} \in N_{ba}$. Let there exist an idle time before the time $S_{\overline{j},a}$ in a schedule Π. We prove that this idle time is before the time $S_{\overline{j},b}$ as well. We do this by contradiction. Let there exist a schedule Π with $C_{\overline{j},b} < C_{i,a} = S_{i,b}$ and there is an idle time on the machine M_b in the interval $(t, S_{i,b})$. We have $C_{\overline{j},b} \leq t$ and $S_{\overline{j},a} \geq S_{i,b}$ (see Figure 3). In this case, at time t, the number $(i-1+\overline{j})$ of long operations completed is greater than the number $(i-1+\overline{j}-1)$ of short operations completed which is a contradiction to Lemma 3. So, assume that we have a schedule Π, where the operation sequences are:

$$\text{for machine } M_a: \quad (\pi_1, O_{\overline{j-1},a}, O_{i,a}, O_{i+1,a}, \pi_2, O_{\overline{j},a}, \pi_3),$$
$$\text{for machine } M_b: \quad (\pi_4, O_{i-1,b}, O_{i,b}, O_{i+1,b}, \pi_5, O_{\overline{j},b}, \pi_6),$$

(see Figure 3). In the schedule Π, the last operation completed before the idle time is $O_{i-1,b} \in N_{ab}$ according to the assumption made above that there is no idle time before operation $O_{\overline{j-1},a}$. Operation $O_{\overline{j-1},a}$ is processed immediately before operation $O_{i,a}$ since $S_{i,a} > S_{i-1,b}$.

Assume that there are k_1 short operations processed between the operations $O_{i,a}$ and $O_{\overline{j},a}$ in Π and k_2 long operations processed between the times $S_{i,b}$ and $S_{\overline{j},b}$. It is easy to show that there is no idle time between the times $S_{i,b}$ and $S_{\overline{j},b}$.

Denote $\Delta_1 = S_{i-1,b} - S_{\overline{j-1},a}$ and $\Delta_2 = C_{i-1,b} - S_{i,b}$ (see Figure 1). We have $2a = \Delta_1 + b + \Delta_2$. Then $a > \Delta_1 + \Delta_2$, otherwise

$$\Delta_1 + b + \Delta_2 \geq a + b,$$

i.e., $2a \geq a+b$ and $a \geq b$, which is false. As a consequence, we get

$$b > a > \Delta_1 + \Delta_2.$$

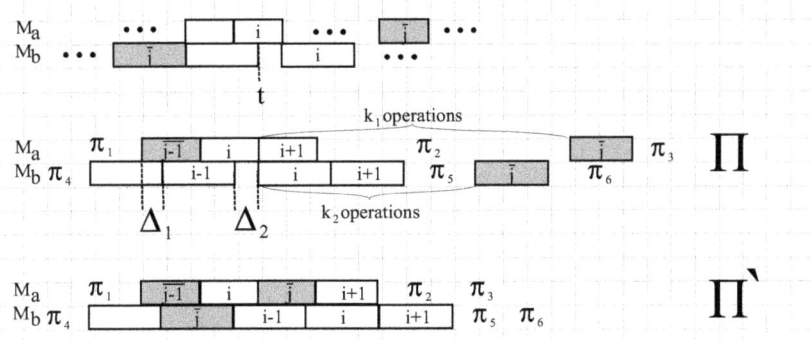

Figure 3. Illustration for the proof of Theorem 1.

Let us consider a schedule Π', where the operation sequences are

$$\text{for machine } M_a: \quad (\pi_1, O_{\overline{j-1},a}, O_{i,a}, O_{\overline{j},a}, O_{i+1,a}, \pi_2, \pi_3),$$
$$\text{for machine } M_b: \quad (\pi_4, O_{\overline{j},b}, O_{i-1,b}, O_{i,b}, O_{i+1,b}, \pi_5, \pi_6),$$

(see Figure 1).

If in the schedule Π', there is an idle time Δ_3 between the times $C_{i,b}$ and $S_{i+1,b}$, then

$$\begin{aligned}
\Delta_3 &= C_{i+1,a}(\Pi') - C_{i,b}(\Pi') \\
&= (C_{\overline{j-1},a}(\Pi) + 4a) - (C_{\overline{j-1},a}(\Pi) + \Delta_1 + 3b) \\
&= 4a - (\Delta_1 + 3b) \\
&= 2(b + \Delta_1 + \Delta_2) - (\Delta_1 + 3b) \\
&= \Delta_1 + 2\Delta_2 - b < \Delta_2.
\end{aligned}$$

It is easy to show that there is no idle time on the machine M_b between the time $C_{i+1,b}$ and the first operation in π_5 in the schedule Π'. Then for all operations in the sequences π_3 and π_6, the completion times are not increased.

Now, we increase the completion time:

$$\begin{aligned}
&\text{on } b &&\text{for operation } O_{i-1,b} \\
&\text{on } b - \Delta_2 &&\text{for operation } O_{i,b} \\
&\text{on } b - \Delta_2 + \Delta_3 &&\text{for the } k_2 - 1 \text{ operations } \{O_{i+1,b}\} \cup \pi_5
\end{aligned}$$

We decrease the completion time of the operation $O_{\overline{j},a}$ on the value

$$C_{\overline{j},a}(\Pi) - C_{\overline{j},a}(\Pi') = (C_{\overline{j-1},a}(\Pi) + 2a + \max\{k_1 a, (k_2+1)b\} + a) - (C_{\overline{j-1},a}(\Pi) + 3a) \geq (k_2+1)b.$$

Thus, we decreased the total completion time on a value greater than or equal to

$$(k_2+1)b - (b + b - \Delta_2 + (b - \Delta_2 + \Delta_3)(k_2 - 1)) = k_2 \Delta_2 - (k_2 - 1)\Delta_3 > 0.$$

So, the theorem holds for job $\overline{j}$. □

4. Solution Algorithms for the Problems $J2|n_j = 2, p_{j1} = a, p_{j2} = b| \sum C_j$

In this section, we first present a fast polynomial heuristic and then a polynomial dynamic programming algorithm which is based on Theorem 1. The problem under consideration can be solved approximately by the following polynomial heuristic, which includes 3 major steps.

Heuristic H:

1. Construct a schedule Π according to Jackson's algorithm.
2. Consider one by one the operations $O_{\bar{j},a}$ for $\bar{j} = \bar{1}, \bar{2}, \ldots, \bar{n}_{ba}$. Shift the operation $O_{\bar{j},a}$ to the earliest position in the sequence, where the total completion time is not increased in comparison to the currently best schedule obtained.
3. Consider one by one the operations $O_{i,b}$ for $i = 1, 2, \ldots, n_{ab}$. Shift the operation $O_{i,b}$ to the earliest position in the sequence, where the total completion time is not increased in comparison to the currently best schedule obtained.

Each of the steps 2 and 3 needs $O(n^3)$ operations since for each operation, we consider $O(n)$ positions and $O(n)$ operations are needed to compute the total completion time of the modified schedule. So, the running rime of the algorithm is $O(n^3)$.

Next, we present an idea of an exact dynamic programming algorithm (DP). In the first step of Algorithm DP, we construct an active schedule that contains only jobs from the set N_{ab}. Then, in each stage $\bar{j} = \bar{1}, \bar{2}, \ldots, \bar{n}_{ba}$, we compute all possible states $t = (i_a, i_b, C_{\bar{j},b}, C_{\bar{j},a})$, where

- operation $O_{\bar{j},a}, \bar{j} \in N_{ba}$, is processed between the operations $O_{i_a,a}$ and $O_{i_a+1,a}, i_a, i_a + 1 \in N_{ab}$ and after all operations $O_{\bar{j}',a}, \bar{j}' < \bar{j}, \bar{j}' \in N_{ba}$,
- operation $O_{\bar{j},b}, \bar{j} \in N_{ba}$, is processed between the operations $O_{i_b,b}$ and $O_{i_b+1,b}, i_b, i_b + 1 \in N_{ab}$ and after all operations $O_{\bar{j}',b}, \bar{j}' < \bar{j}, \bar{j}' \in N_{ba}$.

For each state t, the total completion time TCT_t of the operations $O_{i,b}, i \in \{1, 2, \ldots, i_b\}$, and the operations $O_{\bar{j}',a}, \bar{j}' \in \{\bar{1}, \bar{2}, \ldots, \bar{j}\}$, is saved.

If for two states $t = (i_a, i_b, C_{\bar{j},b}, C_{\bar{j},a})$ and $\check{t} = (i_a, i_b, \check{C}_{\bar{j},b}, \check{C}_{\bar{j},a})$, we have

$$C_{\bar{j},b} \leq \check{C}_{\bar{j},b}, \quad C_{\bar{j},a} \leq \check{C}_{\bar{j},a} \quad \text{and} \quad TCT_t \leq TCT_{\check{t}},$$

then the state $\check{t}$ can be excluded from the further considerations.

According to Theorem 1, we have $C_{\bar{j},b} = (i_b + \bar{j})b$. Thus, the state is uniquely defined by the vector $(i_a, i_b, C_{\bar{j},a})$. Please note that only states with $i_a \geq i_b$ are considered. The states obtained at stage j are used to compute the states in the next stage. After the last stage, for each state $t = (i_a, i_b, C_{\bar{j},a})$, we schedule the remaining operations $O_{i,a}, i = i_a + 1, \ldots, n_{ab}$, and $O_{i,b}, i = i_b + 1, \ldots, n_{ab}$, and add to the value TCT_t the value $\sum_{i=i_b+1}^{n_{ab}} C_{i,b}$. Then we choose the best solution.

The value $C_{\bar{j},a}$ and TCT_t can be computed in constant time. For that, in the previous stage $\bar{j} - 1$, for a state $\hat{t} = (\hat{i}_a, \hat{i}_b, \hat{C}_{\bar{j-1},a})$, we saved the value $\hat{C}_{i_b+1,a}$. Let us compute the state $t = (i_a, i_b, C_{\bar{j},a})$ from the state $\hat{t}$. For the state t, the values $C_{i_a+1,a}$ and $C_{i_a,a}$ are computed in constant time. Then the value $\sum_{i=\hat{i}_b+1}^{i_b} C_{i,b}$ can be computed in constant time according to the values $\hat{C}_{\bar{j-1},a}$ and $\hat{C}_{i_b+1,a}$. There can be only an idle time on the machine M_b before operation $O_{i_b+1,b}$ but such a state can be excluded from consideration according to Theorem 1. Then, according to $C_{i_b,b}$, the value $C_{\bar{j},b}$ can be computed in constant time. Finally, the value $C_{\bar{j},a}$ according to the times $C_{\bar{j},b}$ and $C_{i_a,a}$ and the value $C_{i_b+1,a}$ can be computed in constant time.

Theorem 2. *The problem $J2|n_j = 2, p_{j1} = a, p_{j2} = b| \sum C_j$ can be solved by Algorithm DP in $O(n^5)$ time.*

Proof. According to Lemma 1, there are no more than $O(n^2)$ possible values $C_{\bar{j},a}$. Then there are no more than $O(n^4)$ possible states $t = (i_a, i_b, C_{\bar{j},a})$ at the stage $\bar{j}$, and each state is computed in constant time. Since there are $O(n)$ stages, the running time of Algorithm DP is $O(n^5)$. □

5. Computational Results

In this section, we present some results of a numerical experiment, where we investigate the relative error of the heuristic algorithm H and the number of states considered in Algorithm DP. We generated the instances as follows. For each $n \in \{5, 10, 15, 20, 25, 30\}$, we generated 5000 instances with $b \in [3, 50], a \in [1, b-1]$, yielding in total 30000 instances. For each instance, both the exact and the heuristic algorithms were used.

In Table 1, we present the results for 30 randomly selected instances, namely five for each value $n \in \{5, 10, 15, 20, 25, 30\}$, where the main goal is to report the relative error of the heuristic presented in this paper. In columns 1–4, we present the job numbers n_{ab} and n_{ba} as well as the processing times a and b. In column 5, we give the optimal total completion time value TCT-DP obtained by Algorithm DP. In column 6, we present the maximal number MN of states remaining in the list at a stage. In column 7, we present the number $DIF = n_{ab}n_{ba}(n_{ab} + n_{ba}) - MN$, which is given to show that the maximal number of states remaining in the list is less than n^3. In column 8, we give the total completion time value TCT-H obtained by the heuristic. Finally, column 9 displays the percentage deviation PD of the heuristic from the optimal function value.

Table 1. Detailed results with Algorithm DP and Heuristic H for 30 randomly selected instances.

n_{ab}	n_{ba}	a	b	TCT-DP	MN	DIF	TCT-H	PD
1	2	3	4	5	6	7	8	9
instance data					DP		H	
2	3	13	15	264	6	24	275	4.2
2	3	34	48	822	5	25	842	2.4
3	2	9	11	188	11	19	197	4.8
3	2	24	49	783	5	25	783	0.0
1	4	16	25	439	2	18	439	0.0
5	5	10	17	985	16	234	997	1.2
2	8	39	41	2567	11	149	2604	1.4
3	7	12	19	1129	7	203	1139	0.9
8	2	40	44	2624	75	85	2752	4.9
1	9	1	24	1329	2	88	1329	0.0
4	11	17	25	3187	16	644	3214	0.8
9	6	41	43	5499	222	588	5718	4.0
12	3	31	37	4553	155	385	4808	5.6
9	6	14	17	2132	134	676	2212	3.8
13	2	3	5	606	59	331	618	2.0
2	18	6	21	4518	3	717	4518	0.0
18	2	11	16	3383	156	564	3484	3.0
1	19	2	4	878	2	378	878	0.0
12	8	26	28	6140	491	1429	6352	3.5
3	17	10	27	5840	5	1015	5840	0.0
6	19	14	16	5466	138	2712	5526	1.1
21	4	29	40	13,123	490	1610	13,476	2.7
21	4	17	20	6581	597	1503	6848	4.1
18	7	22	25	8302	798	2352	8602	3.6
12	13	39	42	14,157	671	3229	14,553	2.8
5	25	38	47	22,805	59	3691	22,921	0.5
16	14	13	21	9947	219	6501	10,022	0.8
21	9	26	30	14,208	1097	4573	14,624	2.9
4	26	19	21	10,259	82	3038	10,310	0.5
10	20	7	12	5720	59	5941	5738	0.3

In Table 2, we present some results for all 30,000 considered instances. In column 1, we give the number n of jobs. In columns 2 and 3, we present the average values MN and DIF, respectively, for Algorithm DP. For Heuristic H, we present in column 4 the average values PD and column 5 displays the percentage of instances PO solved by the heuristic optimally. We also emphasize that the average relative error over all 30,000 instances is 0.85%.

Table 2. Average results with Algorithm DP and Heuristic H for the 30,000 instances.

n	Average MN	Average DIF	Average PD	PO
1	2	3	4	5
	DP		H	
5	4.33	23.17	1.05	67.3
10	15.43	183.57	1.04	63.44
15	37.61	523.39	0.87	59.66
20	87.52	1158.48	0.85	58.14
25	156.83	2843.17	0.74	56.1
30	202.54	4834.46	0.53	58.12
Aver	84.04	1594.37	0.85	60.46

Moreover, we can state that the maximal relative error of Heuristic H among all 30,000 instances is 6.9% which has been obtained for an instance with $n_{ab} = 3, n_{ba} = 2, a = 17, b = 23$. For this instance, the optimal objective function value is 384 and the total completion time computed by the heuristic is 401. Moreover, the maximal number of states saved to the state list in a stage is 32,811 which has been obtained for an instance with $n_{ab} = 20, n_{ba} = 10, a = 47, b = 49$. In addition, if a state $\bar{t} = (\bar{i}_a, \bar{i}_b, \overline{C}_{j,a})$ has been written to the list and later a state $t = (i_a, i_b, C_{j,a})$ is computed, where $C_{j,a} \leq \overline{C}_{j,a}$ and $TCT_t \leq TCT_{\bar{t}}$, then the state $\bar{t}$ is deleted from the list. The maximal number of states in the list left after considering all states is 1743. So, there is a large difference between the number of states considered and the number of states remaining in the list.

According to the previous results, we can also present the following conjecture.

Conjecture 1. *There are only $O(n^3)$ states that have to be considered at each stage.*

As a consequence of the above conjecture, the running time of an advanced DP algorithm could be reduced to $O(n^4)$.

6. Concluding Remarks

In this paper, some properties of the scheduling problem $J2|n_j = 2, p_{j1} = a, p_{j2} = b| \sum C_j$ were considered which arises for instance in a single-track railway scheduling problem with three stations. A polynomial time solution algorithm of the complexity $O(n^5)$ and a heuristic algorithm of the complexity $O(n^3)$ were presented. In the numerical experiments with the 30000 instances, the running time of the dynamic programming algorithm was even bounded by the order $O(n^4)$. Moreover, in our tests, the average relative error of the polynomial heuristic was only 0.85%.

The two-machine job-shop problem of minimizing the makespan was considered in the pioneering work by Jackson. This result is now considered as a classical one in the scheduling theory. An interesting open question is whether there exists an NP-hard job-shop scheduling problem with equal processing times on each machine and other objective functions without precedence relations and preemptions, or whether such problems are also polynomially solvable.

Author Contributions: Investigation, E.G. and F.W.; software, E.G.; writing—original draft preparation, E.G. and F.W.

Funding: This work was funded by DAAD (Deutscher Akademischer Austauschdienst): 91695276 and by RFBR (Russian Foundation for Basic Research): 18-07-00656

Conflicts of Interest: The authors declare no conflict of interest.

References

1. Brucker, P. *Scheduling Algorithms*, 5th ed.; Springer: Berlin, Germany, 2007.
2. Graham, R.L.; Lawler, E.L.; Lenstra, J.K.; Rinnooy Kan, A.H.G. Optimization and Approximation in Deterministic Machine Scheduling: A Survey. *Ann. Discr. Math.* **1979**, *5*, 287–326.
3. Jackson, J.R. An Extension of Johnson's Results on Job Lot Scheduling. *Naval Res. Logist.* **1956**, *3*, 201–203. [CrossRef]
4. Bellman, R.E. *Dynamic Programming*; Princeton University Press: Princeton, NJ, USA, 1954.
5. Gafarov, E.R.; Dolgui, A.; Lazarev, A.A. Two-Station Single-Track Railway Scheduling Problem With Trains of Equal Speed. *Comput. Ind. Eng.* **2015**, *85*, 260–267. [CrossRef]
6. Timkovsky, V. On the Complexity of Scheduling an Arbitrary System. *Sov. J. Comput. Syst. Sci.* **1985**, *23*, 46–52.
7. Timkovsky, V. Is a Unit-Time Job Shop not Easier than Identical Parallel Machines? *Discr. Appl. Math.* **1998**, *85*, 149–162. [CrossRef]
8. Kubiak, W.; Timkovsky, V. Total Completion Time Minimization in Two-Machine Job Shops with Unit-Time Operations. *Eur. J. Oper. Res.* **1996**, *94*, 310–320. [CrossRef]
9. Baptiste, P. Scheduling Equal-Length Jobs on Identical Parallel Machines. *Discr. Appl. Math.* **2000**, *103*, 21–32. [CrossRef]
10. Kravchenko, S.A.; Werner, F. Parallel Machine Problems with Equal Processing Times: A Survey. *J. Sched.* **2011**, *14*, 435–444. [CrossRef]
11. Sourd, F. A New Tool for Reducing Delays, *Avancees*, SNCF, 1 October 2009. Available online: http://www.avancees.eu/01/index.htm (accessed on 30 November 2018).
12. Szpigel, B. Train Scheduling on a Single Track Railway. In *Proceedings of the IFORS Conference on Operational Research'72*, Dublin, Ireland, 21–25 August 1972; pp. 343–352.
13. de Oliveira, E.S. Solving Single Track Railway Scheduling Problem Using Constraint Programming. Ph.D. Thesis, School of Computing, The University of Leeds, Leeds, UK, 2001.
14. Sotskov, Y.N.; Gholami, O. Shifting Bottleneck Algorithm for Train Scheduling on a Single-Track Railway. In Proceedings of the 14th IFAC Symposium on Information Control Problems in Manufacturing, Bucharest, Romania, 23–25 May 2012; Borangiu, T., Dumitrache, I., Dolgui, A., Filip, F., Eds.; Elsevier Science: Amsterdam, The Netherlands, 2012; pp. 87–92, ISSN 1474-6670.
15. Lange, J.; Werner, F. Approaches to Modeling Train Scheduling Problems as Job Shops with Blocking Constraints. *J. Sched.* **2018**, *21*, 191–207. [CrossRef]
16. Lange, J.; Werner, F. A Permutation-Based Neighborhood for the Blocking Job-Shop Problem with Total Tardiness Minimization. In *Operations Research Proceedings*; Kliewer, N.; Ehmke, J.F.; Borndörfer, R. (eds.); Springer: Cham, Switzerland, 2018, pp. 581–586.
17. Burdett, R.L.; Kozan, E. A Disjunctive Graph Model and Framework for Constructing New Train Schedules. *Eur. J. Oper. Res.* **2010**, *200*, 85–98. [CrossRef]
18. D'Ariona, A.; Paciarelli, D.; Pranzo, M. A Branch and Bound Algorithm for Scheduling Trains in a Railway Network. *Eur. J. Oper. Res.* **2007**, *183*, 643–657. [CrossRef]
19. Zhou, X.; Zhong, M. Single-Track Train Timetabling with Guaranteed Optimality: Branch-and-Bound Algorithms with Enhanced Lower Bounds. *Transp. Res. Part B Methodol.* **2007**, *41*, 320–341. [CrossRef]
20. Liu, S.Q.; Kozan, E. Scheduling Trains as a Blocking Parallel-Machine Job-Shop Scheduling Model. *Comp. Oper. Res.* **2009**, *36*, 2840–2852. [CrossRef]
21. Liu, S.Q.; Kozan, E. Scheduling Trains with Priorities. *Transp. Sci.* **2011**, *45*, 175–198. [CrossRef]
22. Bürgy, R.; Gröflin, H. The Blocking Job-Shop with Rail-Bound Transportation. *J. Comb. Optim.* **2014**, *31*, 152–181. [CrossRef]
23. Canales-Bustos, L.; Santibanez-Gonzalez, E.; Candia-Vejar, A. A Multi-objective Optimization Model for the Design of an Effective Decarbonized Supply Chain in Mining. *Int. J. Prod. Econ.* **2017**, *193*, 449–464. [CrossRef]
24. Dulebenets, M.A. A Comprehensive Evaluation of Weak and Strong Mutation Mechanisms in Evolutionary Algorithms for Truck Scheduling at Cross-Docking Terminals. *IEEE Access* **2018**, *6*, 65635–65650. [CrossRef]
25. Peres, I.T.; Repolho, H.M.; Martinelli, R.; Monteiro, N.J. Optimization in Inventory-routing Problem with Planned Transshipment: A Case Study in the Retail Industry. *Int. J. Prod. Econ.* **2017**, *193*, 748–756. [CrossRef]

26. Dulebenets, M.A. Application of Evolutionary Computation for Berth Scheduling at Marine Container Terminals: Parameter Tuning versus Parameter Control. *IEEE Trans. Intell. Transp. Syst.* **2018**, *19*, 25–37. [CrossRef]
27. Fonseca, G.B.; Nogueira, T.H.; Ravetti, M.G. A hybrid Lagrangian metaheuristic for the cross-docking flow shop scheduling problem. *Eur. J. Oper. Res.* **2019**, *275*, 139–154. [CrossRef]
28. Dulebenets, M.A. A comprehensive multi-objective optimization model for the vessel scheduling problem in liner shipping. *Int. J. Prod. Econ.* **2018**, *196*, 293–318. [CrossRef]
29. Zulj, I.; Kramer, S.; Schneider, M. A hybrid of adaptive large neighborhood search and tabu search for the order-batching problem. *Eur. J. Oper. Res.* **2018**, *264*, 653–664. [CrossRef]

© 2019 by the authors. Licensee MDPI, Basel, Switzerland. This article is an open access article distributed under the terms and conditions of the Creative Commons Attribution (CC BY) license (http://creativecommons.org/licenses/by/4.0/).

Article

Further Results on the Resistance-Harary Index of Unicyclic Graphs

Jian Lu [1], Shu-Bo Chen [2], Jia-Bao Liu [3,*], Xiang-Feng Pan [1] and Ying-Jie Ji [1]

[1] School of Mathematical Sciences, Anhui University, Hefei 230601, China; lujianmath@163.com (J.L.); xfpan@ustc.edu (X.-F.P.); jyjgood66@163.com (Y.-J.J.)
[2] College of Mathematics, Hunan City University, Yiyang 413000, China; shuobo.chen@163.com
[3] School of Mathematics and Physics, Anhui Jianzhu University, Hefei 230601, China
* Correspondence: liujiabaoad@163.com

Received: 20 December 2018; Accepted: 14 February 2019; Published: 20 February 2019

Abstract: The Resistance-Harary index of a connected graph G is defined as $RH(G) = \sum_{\{u,v\} \subseteq V(G)} \frac{1}{r(u,v)}$, where $r(u,v)$ is the resistance distance between vertices u and v in G. A graph G is called a unicyclic graph if it contains exactly one cycle and a fully loaded unicyclic graph is a unicyclic graph that no vertex with degree less than three in its unique cycle. Let $\mathcal{U}(n)$ and $\mathfrak{U}(n)$ be the set of unicyclic graphs and fully loaded unicyclic graphs of order n, respectively. In this paper, we determine the graphs of $\mathcal{U}(n)$ with second-largest Resistance-Harary index and determine the graphs of $\mathfrak{U}(n)$ with largest Resistance-Harary index.

Keywords: Resistance-Harary Index; resistance distance; unicyclic graphs; fully loaded unicyclic graphs

1. Introduction

The topological index is the mathematical descriptor of the molecular structure, which can effectively reflect the chemical structure and properties of the material. The famous Wiener index $W(G)$ (also Wiener number) introduced by H. Wiener, is a topological index of a molecule, defined as the sum of the lengths of the shortest paths between all pairs of vertices, i.e., $W(G) = \sum_{\{u,v\} \subseteq V(G)} d(u,v)$ in the chemical graph representing the non-hydrogen atoms in the molecule. In 1993, Klein and Randić [1] defined a new distance function named resistance distance on the basis of electrical network theory replacing each edge of a simple connected graph G by a unit resistor. Let G be a simple connected graph with vertices set $V = \{v_1, v_2, \cdots, v_n\}$. The resistance distance between the vertices v_i and v_j, denoted by $r(v_i, v_j)$ (if more than one graphs are considered, we write $r_G(v_i, v_j)$ to avoid confusion), is defined to be the effective resistance between the vertices v_i and v_j in G. If the ordinary distance is replaced by resistance distance in the expression for the Wiener index, one arrives at the Kirchhoff index [1,2]

$$Kf(G) = \sum_{\{u,v\} \subseteq V(G)} r(u,v),$$

which has been widely studied [3–12].

Another distance-based graph invariant index named Harary index was introduced independently by Plavšić et al. [13] and by Ivanciuc et al. [14] in 1993 for the characterization of molecular graphs. The Harary index $H(G)$ is defined as

$$H(G) = \sum_{\{u,v\} \subseteq V(G)} \frac{1}{d(u,v)},$$

which is the sum of reciprocals of distances between all pairs of vertices of G. For more related results to Harary index, please refer to [15–22]. In 2017, Chen et al. [23,24] introduced a new graph invariant reciprocal to Kirchhoff index, named Resistance-Harary index, as

$$RH(G) = \sum_{\{u,v\} \subseteq V(G)} \frac{1}{r(u,v)}.$$

To understand the results and concepts, we introduce some definitions and notions. All of the graphs considered in this paper are connected and simple. A graph G is called a unicyclic graph if it contains exactly one cycle, simply denoted as $G = U(C_l; T_1, T_2, \cdots, T_l)$, where C_l is the unique cycle with vertices $v_1 v_2 \cdots v_l$, T_i is a tree rooted at v_i, $1 \leq i \leq l$. A fully loaded unicyclic graph is a unicyclic graph with the property that there is no vertex with degree less than three in its unique cycle. Let S_n^l denote the graph obtained from cycle C_l by adding $n - l$ pendant edges to a vertex of C_l. Let $\mathcal{U}(n;l)$ be the set of unicyclic graphs with n vertices and the unique cycle C_l and $\mathcal{U}(n)$ be the set of unicyclic graphs with n vertices. Let $\mathfrak{U}(n;l)$ be the set of all fully loaded unicyclic graphs with n vertices and the unique cycle C_l, and $\mathfrak{U}(n)$ be the set of unicyclic graphs with n vertices. Let S_n and P_n be the star and the path on n vertices, respectively.

In this paper, we improve the results of the recent paper (Chen et al. [23]) and we determine the largest Resistance-Harary index among all unicyclic graphs. Additionally, we determine the second-largest Resistance-Harary index among all unicyclic graphs and determine the largest Resistance-Harary index among all fully loaded unicyclic graphs and characterize the corresponding extremal graphs, respectively.

2. Preliminaries

In this section, we introduce some useful lemmas and two transformations. Let $R_G(u) = \sum_{u \in V(G) \setminus \{u\}} \frac{1}{r_G(u,v)}$, then $RH(G) = \frac{1}{2} \sum_{u \in V(G)} R_G(u)$. Let $C_g = v_1 v_2 \cdots v_g v_1$ be the cycle on g vertices where $g \geq 3$. By Ohm's law, for any two vertices $v_i, v_j \in V(C_g)$ with $i < j$, one has

$$r_{C_g}(v_i, v_j) = \frac{(j-i)(g+i-j)}{g}.$$

By a simple calculation, we can obtain the Resistance-Harary index of C_g, which is

$$RH(C_g) = \sum_{u \in V(C_g)} \tfrac{1}{2} R_{C_g}(v) = g \sum_{i=1}^{g-1} \tfrac{1}{i}.$$

Lemma 1 ([1]). *Let x be a cut vertex of a connected graph G and let a and b be vertices occurring in different components which arise upon deletion of x. Then,*

$$r_G(a,b) = r_G(a,x) + r_G(x,b).$$

Definition 1 ([23]). *Let v be a vertex of degree $p + 1$ in a graph G, such that $vv_1, vv_2, \ldots, vv_p$ are pendent edges incident with v, and u is the neighbor of v distinct from $v_1, v_2, \ldots, v_p$. We form a graph $G' = \sigma(G, v)$ by deleting the edges $vv_1, vv_2, \ldots, vv_p$ and adding new edges $uv_1, uv_2, \ldots, uv_p$. We say that G' is a σ-transform of the graph G (see Figure 1).*

Figure 1. The σ-transform at v.

Lemma 2 ([23]). *Let $G' = \sigma(G, v)$ be a σ-transform from the graph G, $d(u) \geq 1$ described in Figure 1. Then, $RH(G') \geq RH(G)$, with equality holds if and only if G is a star with v as its center.*

Definition 2 ([23]). *Let u, v be two vertices in a graph G, such that $u_1, u_2, \cdots, u_s$ are pendents incident with u and $v_1, v_2, \cdots, v_t$ are pendents incident with v in $G_0 \subseteq G$, respectively. G' and G'' are two graphs β transformed from G, such that $G' = G - \{vv_1, vv_2, \cdots, vv_t\} + \{uv_1, uv_2, \cdots, uv_t\}$, $G'' = G - \{vv_1, vv_2, \cdots, vv_s\} + \{uv_1, uv_2, \cdots, uv_s\}$, (see Figure 2).*

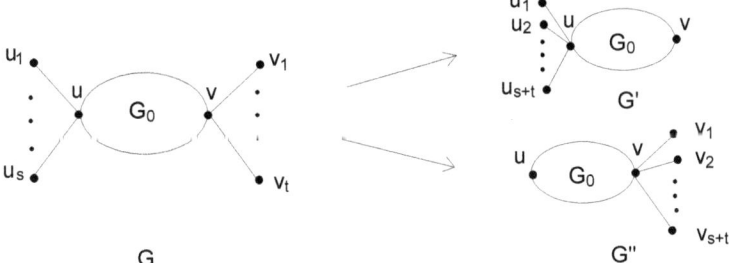

Figure 2. The β-transform.

Lemma 3 ([23]). *Let G', G'' be the graphs transformed from the graph G, $d(u) \geq 1$ described in Figure 2. Then, $RH(G) < RH(G')$, or $RH(G) < RH(G'')$.*

Corollary 1 ([23]). *Let G be a connected graph with $u, v \in V(G)$. Denote by $G(s; t)$ the graph obtained by attaching $s > 1$ pendent vertices to vertex u and $t > 1$ pendent vertices to vertex v. Then, we have $RH(G(1, s+t-1)) > RH(G)$ or $RH(G(s+t-1, 1)) > RH(G)$.*

Lemma 4. *The function $f(x) = \frac{2(k-1)}{(x+1)(k-1)-x^2} - \frac{1}{x+1} - \frac{1}{k-x} - \frac{2}{k-2}$ for $k \geq 3$ and $1 \leq x \leq \frac{k-1}{2}$ is strictly decreasing.*

Proof. By simple calculation,

$$f'(x) = \frac{2(1-k)(k-2x-1)}{(k(x+1)-x^2-x-1)^2} - \frac{1}{(k-x)^2} + \frac{1}{(x+1)^2}$$
$$= (k-2x-1)\left(\frac{2(1-k)}{(k(x+1)-x^2-x-1)^2} + \frac{(k+1)}{(x+1)^2(k-x)^2}\right),$$

Let $g(x) = \left(\frac{2(1-k)}{(k(x+1)-x^2-x-1)^2} + \frac{(k+1)}{(x+1)^2(k-x)^2}\right)$, then we have $g'(x) = \frac{2(k+1)}{(x+1)^2(k-x)^3} - \frac{2(k+1)}{(x+1)^3(k-2)^2} - \frac{4(k-1)(k-2x-1)}{(-kx+(1-k)+x^2+x)^3} < 0$ since $1 \leq x \leq \frac{k-1}{2}$ and $g(1) = \frac{2(1-k)}{4k^2-12k+9} - \frac{k+1}{4k^2-8k+4} < 0$ since $k \geq 3$. Thus, $g(x) < 0$, since $1 \leq x \leq \frac{k-1}{2}$. It follows that $f'(x) < 0$, since $1 \leq x \leq \frac{k-1}{2}$ and $k \geq 3$, thus implying the conclusion of the theorem. □

3. Main Results

By Lemmas 2 and 3, we claim that $RH(G) \leq RH(S_n^g)$ if $G \in \mathcal{U}(n; g)$. Next, we will determine the graphs in $\mathcal{U}(n)$ with the largest Resistance-Harary index and the second-largest Resistance-Harary index.

3.1. The Largest Resistance-Harary Index

Theorem 1. *If $G \in \mathcal{U}(n)$, then*

$$\max_{G \in \mathcal{U}(n)} \{RH(G)\} = \begin{cases} RH(C_n) & \text{if } n \leq 7, \\ RH(S_8^5) & \text{if } n = 8, \\ RH(S_n^4) & \text{if } 9 \leq n \leq 15, \\ RH(S_n^3) & \text{if } n \geq 16. \end{cases}$$

Proof. Let $H = G - C_g$, by the definition of Resistance-Harary index, one has,

$$\begin{aligned} RH(S_n^g) &= \sum_{\{u,v\} \subseteq V(G)} \frac{1}{r(u,v)} \\ &= \sum_{\{u,v\} \subseteq V(C_g)} \frac{1}{r(u,v)} + \sum_{\{u,v\} \subseteq V(H)} \frac{1}{r(u,v)} + \sum_{u \in V(C_g), v \in V(H)} \frac{1}{r(u,v)} \\ &= g\left(1 + \frac{1}{2} + \frac{1}{3} + \cdots + \frac{1}{g-1}\right) + \frac{1}{4}(n-g)(n+3-g) \\ &\quad + g(n-g)\left(\frac{1}{2g-1} + \frac{1}{3g-4} + \cdots + \frac{1}{g^2 - (g-1)^2}\right). \end{aligned}$$

Similarly,

$$\begin{aligned} RH(S_n^{g-1}) &= (g-1)\left(1 + \frac{1}{2} + \frac{1}{3} + \cdots + \frac{1}{g-2}\right) + \frac{1}{4}(n+1-g)(n+4-g) \\ &\quad + (g-1)(n+1-g)\left(\frac{1}{2g-3} + \frac{1}{3g-7} + \cdots + \frac{1}{(g-1)^2 - (g-2)^2}\right). \end{aligned}$$

Further, by the symmetry of C_g, one has,

$$\begin{aligned} \triangle &= RH(S_n^{g-1}) - RH(S_n^g) \\ &= (g-1)(n+1-g)\left(\frac{1}{2g-3} + \frac{1}{3g-7} + \cdots + \frac{1}{(g-1)^2 - (g-2)^2}\right) \\ &\quad + \frac{1}{2}(n-g) - g(n-g)\left(\frac{1}{2g-1} + \frac{1}{3g-4} + \cdots + \frac{1}{g^2-(g-1)^2}\right) \\ &\quad - \left(1 + \frac{1}{2} + \frac{1}{3} + \cdots + \frac{1}{g-1}\right) \\ &= (n-g)\Bigg\{\Big[\underbrace{\left(\frac{g-1}{2g-3} + \frac{g-1}{3g-7} + \cdots + \frac{g-1}{2g-3}\right)}_{g-2} + \frac{1}{2}\Big] \qquad (1) \\ &\quad - \underbrace{\left(\frac{g}{2g-1} + \frac{g}{3g-4} + \cdots + \frac{g}{2g-1}\right)}_{g-1}\Bigg\} + (g-1)\Big(\frac{1}{2g-3} + \frac{1}{3g-7} \\ &\quad + \cdots + \frac{1}{(g-1)^2 - (g-2)^2}\Big) - \left(1 + \frac{1}{2} + \frac{1}{3} + \cdots + \frac{1}{g-1}\right). \end{aligned}$$

To explore the relationship between $\triangle$ and parameters g, we first discuss the part of the first brace of Equation (1). Let

$$\Theta_1 = \left[\left(\frac{g-1}{2g-3} + \frac{g-1}{3g-7} + \cdots + \frac{g-1}{2g-3}\right) + \frac{1}{2}\right] - \left(\frac{g}{2g-1} + \frac{g}{3g-4} + \cdots + \frac{g}{2g-1}\right),$$

then
$$\Theta_1 = \begin{cases} \left(\frac{g-1}{2g-3} - \frac{g}{2g-1}\right) + \left(\frac{g-1}{3g-7} - \frac{g}{3g-4}\right) + \ldots + \left(\frac{g-1}{2g-3} - \frac{g}{2g-1}\right) \\ + \frac{1}{2} - \frac{4}{g+4} > 0, \qquad \text{if } g \geq 4 \text{ and } g \text{ is even,} \\ \left(\frac{g-1}{2g-3} - \frac{g}{2g-1}\right) + \left(\frac{g-1}{3g-7} - \frac{g}{3g-4}\right) + \ldots + \left(\frac{g-1}{2g-3} - \frac{g}{2g-1}\right) \\ + \frac{1}{2} - \frac{4g}{(g+2)^2 - 5} > 0, \qquad \text{if } g \geq 5 \text{ and } g \text{ is odd.} \end{cases}$$

Next, we consider the rest of Equation (1). Let

$$\Theta_2 = (g-1)\left(\frac{1}{2g-3} + \frac{1}{3g-7} + \ldots + \frac{1}{(g-1)^2 - (g-2)^2}\right) - \left(1 + \frac{1}{2} + \frac{1}{3} + \ldots + \frac{1}{g-1}\right).$$

(i) *If g is even, then*

$$\Theta_2 = (g-1)\sum_{i=1}^{\frac{g-2}{2}} \frac{1}{(i+1)(g-1) - i^2} - \sum_{i=1}^{g-1} \frac{1}{i}$$

$$= \sum_{i=1}^{\frac{g-2}{2}} \frac{2(g-1)}{(i+1)(g-1) - i^2} - \left(\sum_{i=1}^{\frac{g-2}{2}} \frac{1}{i+1} + 1\right)$$

$$= \sum_{i=1}^{\frac{g-2}{2}} \frac{2(g-1)}{(i+1)(g-1) - i^2} - \left[\sum_{i=1}^{\frac{g-2}{2}} \left(\frac{1}{i+1} + \frac{1}{g-i}\right) + \underbrace{\left(\frac{2}{g-2} + \frac{2}{g-2} + \ldots + \frac{2}{g-2}\right)}_{\frac{g-2}{2}}\right]$$

$$= \sum_{i=1}^{\frac{g-2}{2}} \left[\frac{2(g-1)}{(i+1)(g-1) - i^2} - \frac{1}{i+1} - \frac{1}{g-i} - \frac{2}{g-2}\right].$$

By Lemma 4, the function

$$F(x) = \frac{2(g-1)}{(x+1)(g-1) - x^2} - \frac{1}{x+1} - \frac{1}{g-x} - \frac{2}{g-2}$$

is a monotonically decreasing function on $[1, \frac{g-1}{2}]$. Thus, when $x = \frac{g-2}{2}$, $F(x)$ get the minimum value

$$F(\frac{g-2}{2}) = \frac{8(g-1)}{g^2 + 2g - 4} - \frac{2}{g-2} - \frac{2}{g} - \frac{2}{g+2},$$

since

$$g \to \infty, F(\frac{g-2}{2}) \to \frac{2}{g} > 0.$$

Actually, by simple calculation, we have $F(x) > 0$ when $g \geq 8$, it follows that $\Theta_2 > 0$ when $g \geq 8$.

(ii) Using the same argument as Equation (1), we can check that if g is an odd integer, $\Theta_2 > 0$ for all $g \geq 8$.

Comparing Θ_1 and Θ_2, it is easy to see that

$$RH(S_n^g) < RH(S_n^{g-1}),$$

since $g \geq 8$. For $g = 3, 4, \ldots, 7$, we calculate $RH(S_n^3), RH(S_n^4), RH(S_n^5), RH(S_n^6), RH(S_n^7)$ and compare the values. We have

$$RH(S_n^3) = RH(C_3) + \sum_{x,y \in V(G \setminus C_3)} \frac{1}{r(x,y)} + \sum_{x \in V(G), y \in V(C_3)} \frac{1}{r(x,y)}$$

$$= \frac{1}{20}(5n^2 + 9n + 18),$$

$$RH(S_n^4) = RH(C_4) + \sum_{x,y \in V(G \setminus C_4)} \frac{1}{r(x,y)} + \sum_{x \in V(G), y \in V(C_4)} \frac{1}{r(x,y)}$$

$$= \frac{1}{84}(21n^2 + 33n + 148).$$

Then,

$$RH(S_n^3) - RH(S_n^4) = \frac{2n}{35} - \frac{181}{210}.$$

Thus, we can get

$$\begin{cases} RH(S_n^3) < RH(S_n^4) & \text{if } n \leq 15, \\ RH(S_n^3) > RH(S_n^4) & \text{if } n \geq 16. \end{cases}$$

In a similar way, by calculating $RH(S_n^5)$, $RH(S_n^6)$, and $RH(S_n^7)$ and comparing the values, we can get the following set of inequalities,

$$\begin{cases} RH(S_n^3) < RH(S_n^4) < \cdots < RH(S_n^{n-1}) < RH(S_n^n) & \text{if } n \leq 7, \\ RH(S_n^3) < RH(S_n^7) < RH(S_n^6) < RH(S_n^4) < RH(S_n^5) & \text{if } n = 8, \\ RH(S_n^7) < RH(S_n^3) < RH(S_n^6) < RH(S_n^5) < RH(S_n^4) & \text{if } n = 9, \\ RH(S_n^7) < RH(S_n^6) < RH(S_n^3) < RH(S_n^5) < RH(S_n^4) & \text{if } n = 10, \\ RH(S_n^7) < RH(S_n^6) < RH(S_n^5) < RH(S_n^3) < RH(S_n^4) & \text{if } 11 \leq n \leq 15, \\ RH(S_n^7) < RH(S_n^6) < RH(S_n^5) < RH(S_n^4) < RH(S_n^3) & \text{if } n \geq 16. \end{cases} \quad (2)$$

To sum up, we can get $RH(C_n)$ has the largest value $\frac{343}{20}$ if $n \leq 7$, $RH(S_n^5)$ has the largest value $\frac{923}{44}$ if $n = 8$, $RH(S_n^4)$ has the largest value $\frac{1}{84}(21n^2 + 33n + 148)$ if $9 \leq n \leq 15$ and $RH(S_n^3)$ has the largest value $\frac{1}{20}(5n^2 + 9n + 18)$ if $n \geq 16$. The proof is completed. □

In [23], the unique element of $\mathcal{U}(n)$ with the largest Resistance-Harary index is determined. Herewith, we point out some minor errors in [23]. These do not affect the validity of the final result of [23] but deserve to be corrected. We list the error as follows and we give a counterexample.

Theorem 2. [23] *Let $G \in \mathcal{U}(n)$, then we have $RH(G) \leq \frac{1}{20}(n^2 + 9n + 18)$ with equality holding if and only if $G \cong S_n^3$ for $n \geq 9$ and $G \cong C_n$ for $n \leq 8$.*

Counterexample

If $n = 9$, according to Theorem 2 in [23], the largest Resistance-Harary index is $HR(S_9^3) = 25.2000$. However, $HR(S_9^4) = 25.5476$, $HR(S_9^3) < HR(S_9^4)$, is a contradiction. If $n = 8$, according to the Theorem 2 in [23], the result is $RH(C_8) = 20.7429$ has the largest value. However, $RH(S_8^5) = 20.9773$, $RH(C_8) < RH(S_8^5)$, is a contradiction. Actually, according to our Theorem 1, we have $HR(S_9^4) > HR(S_9^3)$ if $n = 9$ and $RH(S_8^5) > RH(C_8)$ if $n = 8$. Obviously, the result is consistent with our theorem.

3.2. The Second-Maximum Resistance-Harary Index

By Lemmas 2 and 3 and Equation (2) of the proof of Theorem 1, we can conclude that for $n \geq 16$ G which has the second-largest Resistance-Harary index in $\mathcal{U}(n)$ and those must be one of the graphs G_1, G_2, and $G_3(S_n^4)$, as shown in Figure 3.

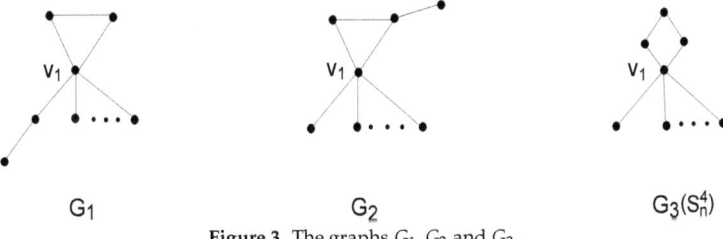

Figure 3. The graphs G_1, G_2 and G_3.

Theorem 3. *If $G \in \mathcal{U}(n)$, let $\max^*\{RH(G)\}$ denote the second-largest Resistance-Harary index of graph G, then*

$$\max_{G \in \mathcal{U}(n)}^* \{RH(G)\} = \begin{cases} RH(S_n^{n-1}) & \text{if } n \leq 7, \\ RH(S_n^4) & \text{if } n = 8, \\ RH(S_n^5) & \text{if } n = 9, 10, \\ RH(S_n^3) & \text{if } 11 \leq n \leq 15, \\ RH(S_n^4) & \text{if } n \geq 16. \end{cases}$$

Proof. (i) *For $n \geq 16$.*

Case 1. Let H_1 be the common subgraph of S_n^3 and G_1. Thus, we can view graphs S_n^3 and G_1 as the graphs depicted in Figure 4.

Then, we have

$$RH(S_n^3) = RH(H_1) + \frac{1}{2} + 2 \sum_{x \in H_1} \frac{1}{1 + r(x, v_1)}$$
$$= RH(H_1) + \frac{1}{2} + 2\left[1 + \frac{n-5}{2} + \frac{6}{5}\right],$$
$$RH(G_3) = RH(H_1) + 1 + \sum_{x \in H_2} \frac{1}{1 + r(x, v_1)} + \sum_{x \in H_2} \frac{1}{2 + r(x, v_1)}$$
$$= RH(H_1) + 1 + \left(1 + \frac{6}{5} + \frac{n-5}{2} + \frac{1}{2} + \frac{n-5}{3} + \frac{3}{4}\right).$$

Therefore, we can get the difference

$$RH(S_n^3) - RH(G_1) = \frac{n}{6} - \frac{23}{60}.$$

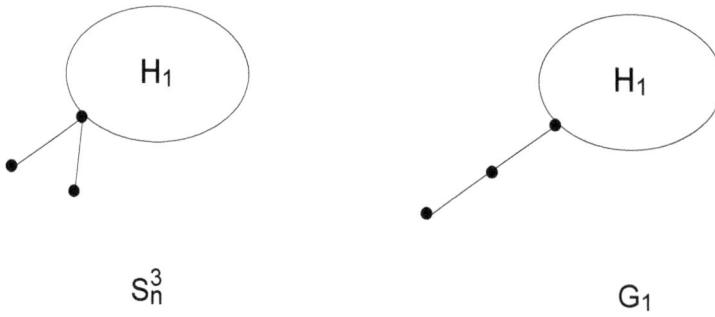

Figure 4. The graphs S_n^3 and G_1.

Case 2. Let H_2 be the common subgraph of S_n^3 and G_2. Thus, we can view graphs S_n^3 and G_2 as the graphs depicted in Figure 5.

Then, we have

$$RH(S_n^3) = RH(S_n^3) + \sum_{x \in H_2} \frac{1}{1 + r(x, v_1)}$$
$$= RH(H_2) + \left[1 + \frac{n-4}{2} + \frac{6}{5}\right],$$
$$RH(G_2) = RH(H_2) + \sum_{x \in H_2} \frac{1}{1 + r(x, v_2)}$$
$$= RH(H_2) + \left[1 + \frac{3(n-4)}{8} + \frac{6}{5}\right].$$

Therefore, we can get the difference

$$RH(S_n^3) - RH(G_2) = \frac{n}{8} - \frac{1}{2}.$$

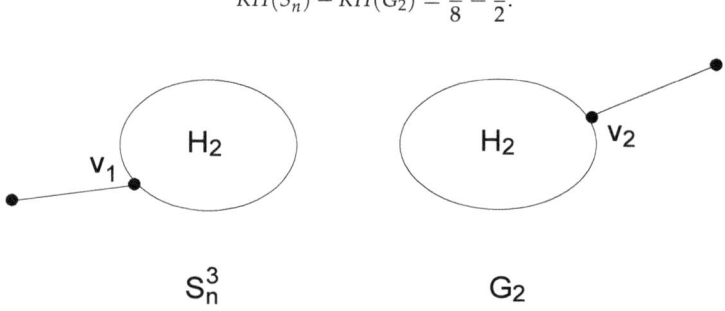

Figure 5. The graphs S_n^3 and G_2.

Case 3. Let H_3 be the common subgraph of S_n^3 and G_3. Thus, we can view graphs S_n^3 and G_3 as the graphs depicted in Figure 6.

Then, we have

$$RH(S_n^3) = RH(H_3) + RH(S_4^3) + \sum_{x \in H_3, y \in S_4^3} \frac{1}{r(x,y)}$$

$$= RH(H_3) + \frac{67}{10} + \frac{27(n-4)}{10},$$

$$RH(G_3) = RH(H_3) + RH(C_4) + \sum_{x \in H_3, y \in C_4} \frac{1}{r(x,y)}$$

$$= RH(H_3) + \frac{22}{3} + \frac{37(n-4)}{14}.$$

Therefore, we can get the difference

$$RH(S_n^3) - RH(G_3) = \frac{2n}{35} - \frac{181}{210}.$$

By the above expressions for the Resistance-Harary index of G_1, G_2 and G_3, we immediately have the desired result.

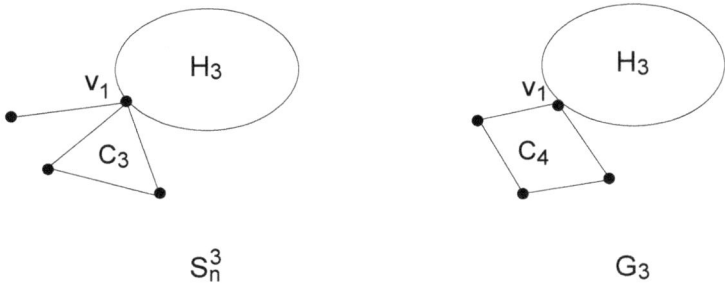

Figure 6. The graphs S_n^3 and G_3.

(ii) *For $9 \leq n \leq 15$.*

By the same arguments as used in (i), we conclude that the possible candidates having the second-largest Resistance-Harary index must be one of the graphs G_4, G_5, G_6, $G_7(S_n^5)$ (as shown in Figure 7) and S_n^3.

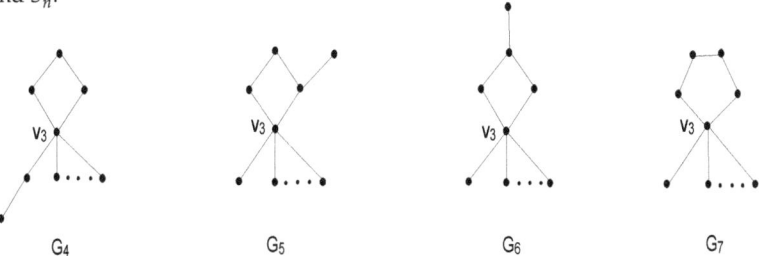

Figure 7. The graphs $G_4 - G_7$.

Let H_4, H_5, H_6 denote the common subgraphs of S_n^4 and $G_4 - G_7$, respectively. Thus, we can view graphs $G_4 - G_7$ as the graphs depicted in Figure 8.

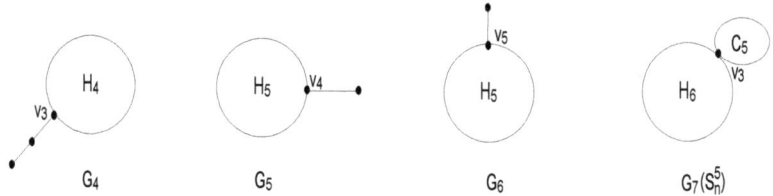

Figure 8. The graphs $G_4 - G_7$.

Then, in a similar way, we have

$$\begin{cases} RH(S_n^4) - RH(G_4) = \frac{n}{6} - \frac{193}{462}, \\ RH(S_n^4) - RH(G_5) = \frac{3n}{22} - \frac{15}{22}, \\ RH(S_n^4) - RH(G_6) = \frac{n}{6} - \frac{5}{6}, \\ RH(S_n^4) - RH(G_7) = \frac{85n}{693} - \frac{2921}{2772}. \end{cases}$$

Therefore, we have $HR(G_4) < HR(G_6) < HR(G_5) < HR(G_7)$. In connection with Equation (2), we have $G_7(S_n^5) < S_n^3$ if $11 \le n \le 15$, so for $11 \le n \le 15$, S_n^3 is the second largest. For $n = 9, 10$, in connection with Equation (2), we have S_n^5 is the second largest.

(iii) For $n \le 7$ and $n = 8$.

In connection with Equation (2), we have S_n^{n-1}, S_n^4 is the second largest, respectively.

The result follows. □

4. Application

Now, we give a specific application of formation mentioned in the Section 3. Fully loaded graphs as a special class of unicyclic graphs also have some special properties about Resistance-Harary index. In this section, we determine the largest Resistance-Harary index among all fully loaded unicyclic graphs.

By a sequence of α and β transformations to a fully loaded graph G, we can obtain a new graph, denoted by Q_n^l, which is obtained by attaching a pendent edge to each vertex of the unique cycle C_l and attaching $n - 2l + 1$ pendent edges to a vertex of C_l. Then, by Lemma 2 and Corollary 1, we arrive at,

Theorem 4. $G \in \mathfrak{U}(n; g)$, then $RH(G) \le RH(Q_n^g)$.

Next, we determine the graph in $\mathfrak{U}(n)$ with the largest Resistance-Harary index.

Theorem 5. If $G \in \mathfrak{U}(n)$, then

$$\max_{G \in \mathfrak{U}(n)} \{RH(G)\} = \begin{cases} RH(Q_n^3) & \text{if } n \le 7, \\ RH(Q_n^4) & \text{if } n = 8, 9, \\ RH(Q_n^3) & \text{if } n \ge 10. \end{cases}$$

Proof. Using a similar way as in Section 3.2, we can conclude that the unicyclic graphs with $n \ge 16$ in Figure 9 have the second largest or third largest Resistance-Harary index.

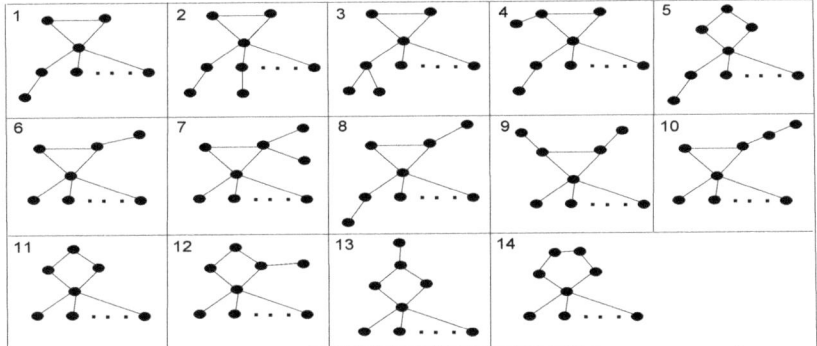

Figure 9. The graphs with second maximal or third maximal Resistance-Harary index.

Only one graph Q_n^3 is fully loaded (Graph 9 in Figure 9). Thus, Q_n^3 has the largest Resistance-Harary index among all fully loaded graphs with $n \geq 16$. For $n \leq 15$, from Lemmas 2 and 3 we can conclude that the fully loaded graph with largest Resistance-Harary index must be one of the five situations $Q_n^3, Q_n^4, Q_n^5, Q_n^6, Q_n^7$.

For completeness of the proof, we list all possible values as follows. For $n \leq 7$, there is only one situation Q_7^3 with $n = 7$ and Q_6^3 with $n = 6$, so we begin at $n = 8$.

Case 1. $n = 8$.

$$RH(Q_8^3) = 19.625, RH(Q_8^4) = 20.026.$$

Then, $\max\limits_{G \in \mathfrak{U}(n)} \{RH(G)\} = RH(Q_8^4)$.

Case 2. $n = 9$.

$$RH(Q_9^3) = 24.075, RH(Q_9^4) = 24.229.$$

Then, $\max\limits_{G \in \mathfrak{U}(n)} \{RH(G)\} = RH(Q_9^4)$.

Case 3. $n = 10$.

$$RH(Q_{10}^3) = 29.025, RH(Q_{10}^4) = 28.933, RH(Q_{10}^5) = 28.866.$$

Then, $\max\limits_{G \in \mathfrak{U}(n)} \{RH(G)\} = RH(Q_{10}^3)$.

Case 4. $n = 11$.

$$RH(Q_{11}^3) = 34.475, RH(Q_{11}^4) = 34.136, RH(Q_{11}^5) = 33.725.$$

Then, $\max\limits_{G \in \mathfrak{U}(n)} \{RH(G)\} = RH(Q_{11}^3)$.

Case 5. $n = 12$.

$$RH(Q_{12}^3) = 40.425, RH(Q_{12}^4) = 39.840, RH(Q_{12}^5) = 39.085, RH(Q_{12}^6) = 38.563.$$

Then, $\max\limits_{G \in \mathfrak{U}(n)} \{RH(G)\} = RH(Q_{12}^3)$.

Case 6. $n = 13$.

$$RH(Q_{13}^3) = 46.875, RH(Q_{13}^4) = 46.043, RH(Q_{13}^5) = 44.944, RH(Q_{13}^6) = 44.003.$$

Then, $\max_{G\in\mathfrak{U}(n)}\{RH(G)\} = RH(Q_{13}^3)$.

Case 7. $n = 14$.

$$RH(Q_{14}^3) = 53.825, RH(Q_{14}^4) = 52.747, RH(Q_{14}^5) = 51.303,$$
$$RH(Q_{14}^6) = 49.942, RH(Q_{14}^7) = 49.987.$$

Then, $\max_{G\in\mathfrak{U}(n)}\{RH(G)\} = RH(Q_{14}^3)$.

Case 8. $n = 15$.

$$RH(Q_{15}^3) = 61.275, RH(Q_{15}^4) = 59.950, RH(Q_{15}^5) = 58.163,$$
$$RH(Q_{15}^6) = 56.382, RH(Q_{15}^7) = 54.946.$$

Then, $\max_{G\in\mathfrak{U}(n)}\{RH(G)\} = RH(Q_{15}^3)$.

The proof is completed. □

5. Conclusions

This paper focuses on Resistance-Harary index in unicyclic graphs. Let $\mathcal{U}(n)$ and $\mathfrak{U}(n)$ be the set of unicyclic graphs and fully loaded unicyclic graphs, respectively. Here, we first give a more precise proof about the largest Resistance-Harary index among all unicyclic graphs, then determine the graph of $\mathcal{U}(n)$ with second-largest Resistance-Harary index and apply this way to fully loaded unicyclic graphs determine the graph of $\mathfrak{U}(n)$ with largest Resistance-Harary index.

Author Contributions: Funding Acquisition, J.L. and J.-B.L.; Methodology, J.-B.L. and J.L.; Supervision, X.-F.P.; and Writing—Original Draft, J.L. and S.-B.C. All authors read and approved the final manuscript.

Funding: This work was supported by the National Natural Science Foundation of China (11601006), the China Postdoctoral Science Foundation (2017M621579), the Postdoctoral Science Foundation of Jiangsu Province (1701081B), the Project of Anhui Jianzhu University (2016QD116 and 2017dc03) and the Anhui Province Key Laboratory of Intelligent Building and Building Energy Saving.

Conflicts of Interest: The authors declare no conflict of interest.

References

1. Klein, D.J.; Randić, M. Resistance distance. *J. Math. Chem.* **1993**, *12*, 81–95. [CrossRef]
2. Du, J.; Su, G.; Tu, J.; Gutman, I. The degree resistance distance of cacti. *Discrete Appl. Math.* **2015**, *188*, 16–24. [CrossRef]
3. Bu, C.; Yan, B.; Zhou, X.; Zhou, J. Resistance distance in subdivision-vertex join and subdivision-edge join of graphs. *Linear Algebra Appl.* **2014**, *458*, 454–462. [CrossRef]
4. Feng, L.H.; Yu, G.; Liu, W. Futher results regarding the degree Kirchhoff index of a graph. *Miskolc Math. Notes* **2014**, *15*, 97–108. [CrossRef]
5. Feng, L.H.; Yu, G.; Xu, K.; Jiang, Z. A note on the Kirchhoff index of bicyclic graphs. *ARS Combin.* **2014**, *114*, 33–40.
6. Gao, X.; Luo, Y.; Liu, W. Resistance distance and the Kirchhoff index in Cayley graphs. *Discrete Appl. Math.* **2011**, *159*, 2050–2057. [CrossRef]
7. Gao, X.; Luo, Y.; Liu, W. Kirchhoff index in line, subdivision and total graphs of a regular graph. *Discrete Appl. Math.* **2012**, *160*, 560–565. [CrossRef]
8. Gutman, I.; Feng, L.; Yu, G. On the degree resistance distance of unicyclic graphs. *Trans. Comb.* **2012**, *1*, 27–40.
9. Liu, J.; Pan, X.; Yu, L.; Li, D. Complete characterization of bicyclic graphs with minimal Kirchhoff index. *Discrete Appl. Math.* **2016**, *200*, 95–107. [CrossRef]
10. Liu, J.; Wang, W.; Zhang, Y.; Pan, X. On degree resistance distance of cacti. *Discrete Appl. Math.* **2016**, *203*, 217–225. [CrossRef]
11. Liu, J.; Pan, X. Minimizing Kirchhoff index among graphs with a given vertex bipartiteness. *Appl. Math. Comput.* **2016**, *291*, 84–88. [CrossRef]

12. Pirzada, S.; Ganie, H.A.; Gutman, I. On Laplacian-Energy-Like Invariant and Kirchhoff Index. *MATCH Commun. Math. Comput. Chem.* **2015**, *73*, 41–59.
13. Plavšić, D.; Nikolić, S.; Mihalić, Z. On the Harary index for the characterization of chemical graphs. *J. Math. Chem.* **1993**, *12*, 235–250.
14. Ivanciuc, O.; Balaban, T.S.; Balaban, A.T. Reciprocal distance matrix, related local vertex invariants and topological indices. *J. Math. Chem.* **1993**, *12*, 309–318. [CrossRef]
15. Furtula, B.; Gutman, I.; Katanić, V. Three-center Harary index and its applications. *Iranian J. Math. Chem.* **2016**, *7*, 61–68.
16. Feng, L.H.; Lan, Y.; Liu, W.; Wang, X. Minimal Harary index of graphs with samll parameters. *MATCH Commun. Math. Comput. Chem.* **2016**, *76*, 23–42.
17. Li, X.; Fan, Y. The connectivity and the Harary index of a graph. *Discrete Appl. Math.* **2015**, *181*, 167–173. [CrossRef]
18. Xu, K.; Das, K.C. On Harary index of graphs. *Discrete Appl. Math.* **2011**, *159*, 1631–1640. [CrossRef]
19. Xu, K. Trees with the seven smallest and eight greatest Harary indices. *Discrete Appl. Math.* **2012**, *160*, 321–331. [CrossRef]
20. Xu, K.; Das, K.C. Extremal unicyclic and bicyclic graphs with respect to Harary index. *Bull. Malays. Math. Sci. Soc.* **2013**, *36*, 373–383.
21. Xu, K.; Wang, J.; Das, K.C.; Klavžar, S. Weighted Harary indices of apex trees and k-apex trees. *Discrete Appl. Math.* **2015**, *189*, 30–40. [CrossRef]
22. Yu, G.; Feng, L. On the maximal Harary index of a class of bicyclic graphs. *Util. Math.* **2010**, *82*, 285–292.
23. Chen, S.B.; Guo, Z.J.; Zeng, T.; Yang, L. On the Resistance-Harary index of unicyclic graphs. *MATCH Commun. Math. Comput. Chem.* **2017**, *78*, 189–119.
24. Wang, H.; Hua, H.; Zhang, L.; Wen, S. On the Resistance-Harary Index of Graphs Given Cut Edges. *J. Chem.* **2017**, *2017*, 3531746.

© 2019 by the authors. Licensee MDPI, Basel, Switzerland. This article is an open access article distributed under the terms and conditions of the Creative Commons Attribution (CC BY) license (http://creativecommons.org/licenses/by/4.0/).

Article

Fractional Metric Dimension of Generalized Jahangir Graph

Jia-Bao Liu [1], Agha Kashif [2], Tabasam Rashid [2] and Muhammad Javaid [2,*]

1. School of Mathematics and Physics, Anhui Jianzhu University, Hefei 230601, China; liujiabaoad@163.com
2. Department of Mathematics, School of Science, University of Management and Technology, Lahore 54770, Pakistan; kashif.khan@umt.edu.pk or aghakashifkhan@hotmail.com (A.K.); tabasam.rashid@umt.edu.pk (T.R.)
* Correspondence: javaidmath@gmail.com

Received: 30 November 2018; Accepted: 9 January 2019; Published: 18 January 2019

Abstract: Arumugam and Mathew [*Discret. Math.* **2012**, *312*, 1584–1590] introduced the notion of fractional metric dimension of a connected graph. In this paper, a combinatorial technique is devised to compute it. In addition, using this technique the fractional metric dimension of the generalized Jahangir graph $J_{m,k}$ is computed for $k \geq 0$ and $m = 5$.

Keywords: resolving neighbourhood; Fractional metric dimension; generalized Jahangir graph

---

1. Introduction and Preliminaries

In this paper, $G = (V(G), E(G))$ is a finite, undirected, connected and simple graph of order $|V(G)|$ and size $|E(G)|$. For any two vertices $u, v \in V(G)$, the distance $d(u, v)$ is the length of a shortest path $u \sim v$ in G. For graph theoretic terminology, we refer to [1–3].

An ordered set of vertices, we mean a set $W = \{w_1, w_2, \ldots, w_k\}$ on which the ordering $(w_1, w_2, \ldots, w_k)$ has been imposed. For an ordered subset $W = \{w_1, w_2, \ldots, w_k\}$ of $V(G)$, we refer to the k-vector (ordered k-tuple) $r(v|W) = (d(v, w_1), d(v, w_2), \ldots, d(v, w_k))$ as the (metric) representation of v with respect to W. The set W is called a resolving set for G if $r(u|W) = r(v|W)$ implies that $u = v$ for all $u, v \in V(G)$. Hence, if W is a resolving set of cardinality k for a graph G of order n, then the set $\{r(v|W) : v \in V(G)\}$ consists of n distinct k-vectors. A vertex $x \in V(G)$ is said to resolve $\{u, v\} \subseteq V(G)$ in G if $d(u, x) \neq d(v, x)$. The collection of all such x in $V(G)$ is called resolving neighbourhood of the pair $\{u, v\}$, denoted by $R\{u, v\}$. Explicitly, $R\{u, v\} = \{x \in V(G) : d(u, x) \neq d(v, x)\}$. Let V_p denote the collection of all $\binom{|V(G)|}{2}$ pairs of vertices of G. Then for each $x \in V(G)$ the set $R\{x\} = \{\{u, v\} \in V_p : d(u, x) \neq d(v, x)\}$ is called resolvent neighbourhood of x.

Definition 1 ([4]). *Let $G = (V(G), E(G))$ be a connected graph of order n. A function $f : V(G) \to [0, 1]$ is called a resolving function (RF) of G if $f(R\{u, v\}) \geq 1$ for any two distinct vertices $u, v \in V(G)$, where $f(R\{u, v\}) = \sum_{x \in R\{u,v\}} f(x)$. A resolving function g of a graph G is minimal (MRF) if any function $f : V(G) \to [0, 1]$ such that $f \leq g$ and $f(v) \neq g(v)$ for at least one $v \in V(G)$ is not a resolving function of G. Then, the fractional metric dimension of the graph G is $\dim_f(G) = \min\{|g| : g \text{ is a minimal resolving function of } G\}$, where $|g| = \sum_{v \in V(G)} g(v)$.*

In [5,6], Slatter introduced the notion of resolving set of a connected graph under the term locating set. Harary and Melter in [7], independently discovered these concepts and termed them as the metric dimension of graph. Resolving sets enjoy their several applications in various areas of computer sciences such as network discovery and verification [8], robot navigation [9], mastermind game [10], coin weighing problem [11], integer programming [12] and drug discovery [13]. The problem of finding metric dimension of a graph as an integer programming problem (IPP) has been introduced by Chartrand et al. [13], and independently by Currie and Oellermann [12]. As a further refinement, Currie and Oellermann [8] devised the notion of fractional metric dimension as the optimal solution of the linear relaxation of the IPP. An equivalent formulation for the fractional metric dimension of a graph has been proposed by Fehr et al. [14] as follows:

Suppose $V = \{v_1, v_2, \ldots, v_n\}$ and $V_p = \{s_1, s_2, \ldots, s_{\binom{n}{2}}\}$. Let $A = (a_{ij})$ be the $\binom{n}{2} \times n$ matrix with $a_{ij} = 1$ if $s_i v_j \in E(R(G))$ and 0 otherwise, where $1 \leq i \leq \binom{n}{2}$ and $1 \leq j \leq n$. The IPP of the metric dimension is given by;

Minimize $f(x_1, x_2, \ldots, x_n) = x_1 + x_2 +, \ldots, + x_n$ subject to $A\bar{x} \geq \bar{1}$, where $\bar{x} = (x_1, x_2, \ldots, x_n)^T$, $x_i \in \{0, 1\}$ and $\bar{1}$ is the $\binom{n}{2} \times 1$ column vector with all entries as 1.

The optimal solution of the aforementioned linear programming relaxation, with replacement $x_i \in \{0, 1\}$ by $0 \leq x_i \leq 1$ gives the fractional metric dimension of G, represented by $\dim_f(G)$. The optimal solution of the dual of this LPP is referred to as the metric independence number of G ($mi_f(G)$). Therefore, the duality and weak duality theorem in linear programming implies that $mi(G) \leq mif(G) = \dim_f(G) \leq \dim(G)$, as discussed by Arumugam and Mathew in [4]. For further details of the duality and weak duality theorem, we refer to [15].

In [16], Ali et al. introduced the generalized Jahangir graph as follows:

Definition 2. *The generalized Jahangir graph $J_{m,k}$, for $m \geq 3, k \geq 1$, is a graph on $m(k+1) + 1$ vertices i.e., a graph consisting of a cycle $C_{m(k+1)}$ with one additional vertex which is adjacent to m vertices of $C_{m(k+1)}$ at distance $k+1$ to each other on $C_{m(k+1)}$. The vertex set of $J_{m,k}$ is $V(J_{m,k}) = \{u, u_0, u_1, \ldots, u_{m-1}\} \cup \{v_i^1, v_i^2, \ldots, v_i^k | i = 0, 1, \ldots, m-1\}$ with $|V(J_{m,k})| = n = m(k+1) + 1$.*

The vertices of the generalized Jahangir graph $J_{m,k}$ can be classified into three different types. The vertices of degree 2, 3 and m are respectively named as minors, major and center. The generalized Jahangir graph $J_{m,k}$ have km minor vertices, m major vertices and one center vertex. In this article, we have discussed results for $m = 5$, shown in Figure 1. For $k = 1$, the generalized Jahangir graph $J_{m,k}$ is the Jahangir graph J_{2m}, for $m \geq 4$, discussed by Tomescu et al. in [17].

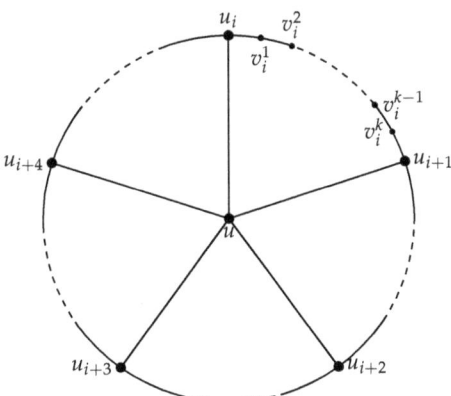

Figure 1. Generalized Jahangir graph $J_{5,k}$.

Arumugam and Mathew [4] formally introduced the notion of fractional metric dimension and discussed some fundamental results. The fractional metric dimension of the cartesian product, hierarchical product, corona product, lexicographic product and comb product of connected graphs, see [18–21]. YI [22] computed the fractional metric dimension of permutation graphs. Mainly, Arumugama et al. [4] studied the graphs whose fractional metric dimension graphs equals half of their orders and Feng et al. [23] investigated the fractional metric dimension of vertex transitive and distance regular graphs. This motivated us to devise a criterion to compute fractional metric dimension of those graphs which are neither vertex transitive and distance regular graphs nor their fractional metric dimension is half of their orders. In particular, the criterion is applied to compute fractional metric dimension of the generalized Jahangir graph $J_{m,k}$ for $k \geq 0$ and $m = 5$.

The paper is organized as follows: Section 1 is for introduction and preliminaries and in Section 2, the resolving neighbourhood of each possible pair of the vertices of the generalized Jahangir graph $J_{m,k}$ for $k \geq 0$ and $m = 5$ are obtained. The main results are included in Section 3. Finally, the paper is concluded with some future prospects in Section 4.

2. Resolving Neighbourhoods of the Generalized Jahangir Graph $J_{m,k}$ for $k \geq 0$ and $m = 5$

The possible pairs of vertices of the generalized Jahangir graph $J_{m,k}$ for $k \geq 1$ and $m = 5$ are majors with majors, major with minors, center with majors, center with minors, and minors with minors. In this section, the resolving neighbourhoods for each pair of vertices of $J_{m,k}$ $k \geq 0$ and $m = 5$ are classified.

Lemma 1. *Let $J_{m,k}$ be the generalized Jahangir graph for $k \geq 4$ and $m = 5$. Then*

$$|R_i| = |R\{v_{i-1}^k, v_i^1\}| = \begin{cases} k+4 & \text{if } k \equiv 0 \pmod{2} \\ k+3 & \text{if } k \equiv 1 \pmod{2}. \end{cases}$$

Moreover, $\cup_{i=0}^{4} R_i = \{v_i^1, v_i^2, ..., v_i^k | i = 0, 1, ..., m-1\}$ and $\hat{\beta} = |\cup_{i=0}^{4} R_i| = 5k$.

Proof. The resolving neighborhood of $\{v_{i-1}^k, v_i^1\}$ for $k \equiv 0 \pmod{2}$ is $R\{v_{i-1}^k, v_i^1\} = \{v_{i-1}^j | \frac{k}{2} - 1 \leq j \leq k\} \cup \{v_i^j | 1 \leq j \leq \frac{k}{2} + 2\}$ with $|R_i| = k+4$. Similarly, the resolving neighborhood of $\{v_{i-1}^k, v_i^1\}$ for $k \equiv 1 \pmod{2}$ is $R\{v_{i-1}^k, v_i^1\} = \{v_{i-1}^j | \frac{k-1}{2} \leq j \leq k\} \cup \{v_i^j | 1 \leq j \leq \frac{k-1}{2} + 2\}$ with $|R_i| = k+3$.

Also in both cases, $\cup_{i=0}^{4} R_i = \{v_i^1, v_i^2, ..., v_i^k | i = 0, 1, ..., m-1\}$ and hence $\hat{\beta} = |\cup_{i=0}^{4} R_i| = 5k$. □

In the following lemma resolving neighbourhoods of the center vertex with major vertices in $J_{5,k}$ are computed.

Lemma 2. *Let $J_{m,k}$ be the generalized Jahangir graph for $k \geq 4$ and $m = 5$. Then $|R_i| < |R\{u, u_i\}|$ and $|R\{u, u_i\} \cap (\cup_{i=0}^{4} R_i)| \geq |R_i|$.*

Proof. For $k \equiv 0 \pmod{2}$, the resolving neighbourhood $R\{u, u_i\}$ is $V(J_{5,k}) - \{v_{i-1}^{\frac{k}{2}}, v_i^{\frac{k}{2}+1}\}$ with $|R\{u, u_i\}| = 5k+4 > k+4 = |R_i|$ and $R\{u, u_i\} \cap (\cup_{i=0}^{4} R_i) = \cup_{i=0}^{4} R_i) - \{v_{i-1}^{\frac{k}{2}}, v_i^{\frac{k}{2}+1}\}$. Therefore, $|R\{u, u_i\} \cap (\cup_{i=0}^{4} R_i)| = 5k - 2 > |R_i|$. Similarly, for $k \equiv 1 \pmod{2}$, $R\{u, u_i\} = V(J_{5,k})$ with $|R\{u, u_i\}| = n > k+3 = |R_i|$ and $R\{u, u_i\} \cap (\cup_{i=0}^{4} R_i) = \cup_{i=0}^{4} R_i)$. Therefore, $|R\{u, u_i\} \cap (\cup_{i=0}^{4} R_i)| = 5k = |R_i|$. This completes the proof. □

In the following lemma resolving neighbourhoods of center vertex with minor vertices in $J_{5,k}$ are computed.

Lemma 3. *Let $J_{m,k}$ be the generalized Jahangir graph for $k \geq 4$ and $m = 5$. Then $|R_i| < |R\{u, v_i^j\}|$ and $|R\{u, v_i^j\} \cap (\cup_{i=0}^{4} R_i)| \geq |R_i|$.*

Proof.

Case 1: (When $k \equiv 0 \pmod 2$)

Since, $R\{u, v_i^1\} = V(J_{5,k}) - \{v_{i-1}^{k-t} | 0 \leq t \leq \frac{k}{2} - 1\} \cup \{u_i\}$ with $|R\{u, v_i^1\}| = 4k + \frac{k}{2} + 5 > k + 4 = |R_i|$ and $R\{u, v_i^1\} \cap (\cup_{i=0}^4 R_i) = \cup_{i=0}^4 R_i - \{v_{i-1}^{k-t} | 0 \leq t \leq \frac{k}{2} - 1\}$. Therefore, $|R\{u, v_i^1\} \cap (\cup_{i=0}^4 R_i)| = 4k + \frac{k}{2}$. Now for $1 \leq j \leq \frac{k}{2}$, the resolving neighbourhood $R(u, v_i^j) = V(J_{5,k}) - \{v_i^{\frac{k-4}{2}}\}$ with $|R\{u, v_i^j\}| = 5k + 5 > k + 4 = |R_i|$. Also, $R\{u, v_i^j\} \cap (\cup_{i=0}^4 R_i) = \cup_{i=0}^4 R_i - \{v_i^{\frac{k-4}{2}}\}$ and therefore, $|R\{u, v_i^j\} \cap (\cup_{i=0}^4 R_i)| = 5k + 5 > |R_i|$.

Case 2: (When $k \equiv 1 \pmod 2$)

Since, $R\{u, v_i^1\} = V(J_{5,k}) - \{v_{i-1}^t | \frac{k+1}{2} \leq t \leq k\} \cup \{u_i, v_i^{\frac{k+3}{2}}\}$ with $|R\{u, v_i^1\}| = 3k + \frac{3k+1}{2} + 3 > k + 3 = |R_i|$ and $R\{u, v_i^1\} \cap (\cup_{i=0}^4 R_i) = \cup_{i=0}^4 R_i - \{v_{i-1}^t | \frac{k+1}{2} \leq t \leq k\} \cup \{v_i^{\frac{k+3}{2}}\}$. Therefore, $|R\{u, v_i^1\} \cap (\cup_{i=0}^4 R_i)| = 4k + \frac{k-1}{2} - 1 > |R_i|$. Now for $3 \leq j \leq \lceil \frac{k}{2} \rceil$ & j is odd, the resolving neighbourhood $R(u, v_i^j) = V(J_{5,k}) - \{v_i^{\frac{k+1}{2}}, v_i^{\frac{k+5}{2}}\}$ with $|R\{u, v_i^j\}| = 5k + 4 > k + 3 = |R_i|$. Also, $R\{u, v_i^j\} \cap (\cup_{i=0}^4 R_i) = \cup_{i=0}^4 R_i - \{v_i^{\frac{k+1}{2}}, v_i^{\frac{k+5}{2}}\}$ and therefore, $|R\{u, v_i^j\} \cap (\cup_{i=0}^4 R_i)| = 5k - 2 > |R_i|$. Finally, for $2 \leq j \leq \lceil \frac{k}{2} \rceil$ & j is even, $R\{u, v_i^j\} = V(J_{5,k})$, and the case is easy to see. This completes the proof. □

In the following lemma resolving neighbourhoods of the pair of major vertices in $J_{5,k}$ are computed.

Lemma 4. *Let $J_{m,k}$ be the generalized Jahangir graph for $k \geq 4$ and $m = 5$. Then $|R_i| < |R\{u_i, u_{i+p}\}|$ and $|R\{u_i, u_{i+p}\} \cap (\cup_{i=0}^4 R_i)| \geq |R_i|$ for $p = 1, 2$.*

Proof. The symmetry of the generalized Jahangir graph $J_{5,k}$ allows us to discuss only the following case:

Case 1: (When $k \equiv 0 \pmod 2$ and $p = 1$)

Since, $R\{u_i, u_{i+1}\} = V(J_{5,k}) - \{u, u_{i+2}, u_{i+3}, u_{i+4}\} \cup \{v_{i+1}^r, v_{i+2}^s, v_{i+3}^s, v_{i+4}^t | \frac{k+4}{2} \leq r \leq k, 1 \leq s \leq k, 1 \leq t \leq \frac{k-2}{2}\}$ with $|R\{u_i, u_{i+1}\}| = 2(k+2) > k + 4 = |R_i|$ and $R\{u_i, u_{i+1}\} \cap (\cup_{i=0}^4 R_i) = \cup_{i=0}^4 R_i - \{v_{i+1}^r, v_{i+2}^s, v_{i+3}^s, v_{i+4}^t | \frac{k+4}{2} \leq r \leq k, 1 \leq s \leq k, 1 \leq t \leq \frac{k-2}{2}\}$. Therefore, $|R\{u_i, u_{i+1}\} \cap (\cup_{i=0}^4 R_i)| = 2k + 2 > |R_i|$.

Case 2: (When $k \equiv 1 \pmod 2$ and $p = 1$)

Since, $R\{u_i, u_{i+1}\} = V(J_{5,k}) - \{u, u_{i+2}, u_{i+3}, u_{i+4}\} \cup \{v_i^{\frac{k+1}{2}}, v_{i+1}^r, v_{i+2}^s, v_{i+3}^s, v_{i+4}^t | \frac{k+3}{2} \leq r \leq k, 1 \leq s \leq k, 1 \leq t \leq \frac{k-1}{2}\}$ with $|R\{u_i, u_{i+1}\}| = 2(k+1) > k + 4 = |R_i|$ and $R\{u_i, u_{i+1}\} \cap (\cup_{i=0}^4 R_i) = \cup_{i=0}^4 R_i - \{v_i^{\frac{k+1}{2}}, v_{i+1}^r, v_{i+2}^s, v_{i+3}^s, v_{i+4}^t | \frac{k+3}{2} \leq r \leq k, 1 \leq s \leq k, 1 \leq t \leq \frac{k-1}{2}\}$. Therefore, $|R\{u_i, u_{i+1}\} \cap (\cup_{i=0}^4 R_i)| = 2k > |R_i|$.

Case 3: (When $k \equiv 0 \pmod 2$ and $p = 2$)

Since, $R\{u_i, u_{i+2}\} = V(J_{5,k}) - \{u, u_{i+1}, u_{i+3}, u_{i+4}\} \cup \{v_i^r, v_{i+1}^s, v_{i+2}^r, v_{i+3}^t, v_{i+4}^s | \frac{k+4}{2} \leq r \leq k, 1 \leq s \leq \frac{k-2}{2}, 1 \leq t \leq k\}$ with $|R\{u_i, u_{i+2}\}| = 2(k+3) > k + 4 = |R_i|$ and $R\{u_i, u_{i+2}\} \cap (\cup_{i=0}^4 R_i) = \cup_{i=0}^4 R_i - \{v_i^r, v_{i+1}^s, v_{i+2}^r, v_{i+3}^t, v_{i+4}^s | \frac{k+4}{2} \leq r \leq k, 1 \leq s \leq \frac{k-2}{2}, 1 \leq t \leq k\}$. Therefore, $|R\{u_i, u_{i+2}\} \cap (\cup_{i=0}^4 R_i)| = 2(k+2) > |R_i|$.

Case 4: (When $k \equiv 1 \pmod 2$ and $p = 0$)

Since, $R\{u_i, u_{i+2}\} = V(J_{5,k}) - \{u, u_{i+1}, u_{i+3}, u_{i+4}\} \cup \{v_i^r, v_{i+1}^s, v_{i+2}^r, v_{i+3}^t, v_{i+4}^s | \frac{k+3}{2} \leq r \leq k, 1 \leq s \leq \frac{k-1}{2}, 1 \leq t \leq k\}$ with $|R\{u_i, u_{i+2}\}| = 2(k+2) > k + 4 = |R_i|$ and $R\{u_i, u_{i+2}\} \cap (\cup_{i=0}^4 R_i) = \cup_{i=0}^4 R_i - \{v_i^r, v_{i+1}^s, v_{i+2}^r, v_{i+3}^t, v_{i+4}^s | \frac{k+3}{2} \leq r \leq k, 1 \leq s \leq \frac{k-1}{2}, 1 \leq t \leq k\}$. Therefore, $|R\{u_i, u_{i+2}\} \cap (\cup_{i=0}^4 R_i)| = 2(k+1) > |R_i|$. □

In the following lemma resolving neighbourhoods of major vertices with minor vertices in $J_{5,k}$ are computed.

Lemma 5. *Let $J_{m,k}$ be the generalized Jahangir graph for $k \geq 4$ and $m = 5$. Then $|R_i| < |R\{u_i, v_{i+p}^j\}|$ and $|R\{u_i, v_{i+p}^j\} \cap (\cup_{i=0}^4 R_i)| \geq |R_i|$ for $p = 0, 1, 2$.*

Proof.

Case 1: (When $k \equiv 0 \pmod 2$ and $p = 0$)

For $1 \leq j \leq k-2$, the resolving neighbourhood $R\{u_i, v_i^j\} = V(J_{5,k}) - \{v_i^{\frac{j}{2}}\}$ and $R\{u_i, v_i^j\} = V(J_{5,k}) - \{v_i^{\frac{k+j+3}{2}}\}$ for j is even and odd respectively. Also, $|R\{u_i, v_i^j\}| = 5k + 5 > k + 4 > |R_i|$ and $|R\{u_i, v_i^j\} \cap (\cup_{i=0}^4 R_i)| = 5k - 1 > |R_i|$. Now $R\{u_i, v_i^{k-1}\} = V(J_{5,k}) - \{u_{i+1}, v_{i+1}^j | 1 \leq j \leq \frac{k}{2}\}$ and $R\{u_i, v_i^k\} = V(J_{5,k}) - \{v_i^{\frac{k}{2}-1}, v_{i+1}^{\frac{k}{2}+1}\}$, therefore, $|R\{u_i, v_i^{k-1}\}| = \frac{9k+10}{2} > |R_i|$, $|R\{u_i, v_i^k\}| = 5k + 4 > |R_i|$, $|R\{u_i, v_i^{k-1}\} \cap (\cup_{i=0}^4 R_i)| = 5k - \frac{k}{2} > |R_i|$ and $|R\{u_i, v_i^k\} \cap (\cup_{i=0}^4 R_i)| = 5k - 2 > |R_i|$.

Case 2: (When $k \equiv 0 \pmod 2$ and $p = 1$)

In this case, the resolving neighbourhoods are $R\{u_i, v_{i+1}^1\} = V(J_{5,k}) - \{v_i^{\frac{k}{2}+1}, v_{i+1}^{\frac{k+4}{2}}\}$, $R\{u_i, v_{i+1}^2\} = V(J_{5,k}) - \{u_i, v_i^j | \frac{k+4}{2} \leq j \leq k\}$, $R\{u_i, v_{i+1}^j\}_{j=3}^{k-2} = V(J_{5,k}) - \{v_{i+1}^{\frac{j-2}{2}}\}$ for even j, $R\{u_i, v_{i+1}^j\}_{j=3}^{k-2} = V(J_{5,k}) - \{v_{i+1}^{\frac{k+j+3}{2}}\}$ for odd j, $R\{u_i, v_i^{k-1}\} = V(J_{5,k}) - \{u_{i+2}, v_{i+2}^j | 1 \leq j \leq \frac{k}{2}\}$ and $R\{u_i, v_i^k\} = V(J_{5,k}) - \{v_{i+1}^{\frac{k}{2}-1}, v_{i+2}^{\frac{k}{2}+1}\}$. Therefore, $|R\{u_i, v_{i+1}^j\}_{j=3}^{k-2}| = 5k + 5 > 5k + 4 = |R\{u_i, v_{i+1}^1\}| = |R\{u_i, v_i^k\}| > 4k + \frac{k}{2} + 6 = |R\{u_i, v_{i+1}^2\}| > 4k + \frac{k}{2} + 5 = |R\{u_i, v_i^{k-1}\}| > k + 4 = |R_i|$. Also, $|R\{u_i, v_{i+1}^j\}_{j=3}^{k-2} \cap (\cup_{i=0}^4 R_i)| = 5k - 1 > 5k - 2 = |R\{u_i, v_{i+1}^1\} \cap (\cup_{i=0}^4 R_i)| = |R\{u_i, v_i^k\} \cap (\cup_{i=0}^4 R_i)| > 4k + \frac{k}{2} + 1 = |R\{u_i, v_{i+1}^2\} \cap (\cup_{i=0}^4 R_i)| > 4k + \frac{k}{2} = |R\{u_i, v_{i+1}^{k-1}\} \cap (\cup_{i=0}^4 R_i)| > |R_i|$.

Case 3: (When $k \equiv 0 \pmod 2$ and $p = 2$)

In this case, the resolving neighbourhoods are $R\{u_i, v_{i+2}^1\} = V(J_{5,k}) - \{v_{i+2}^{\frac{k}{2}}, v_{i+2}^{\frac{k}{2}+2}\}$, $R\{u_i, v_{i+2}^2\} = V(J_{5,k}) - \{u_{i+2}, v_{i+1}^j | \frac{k}{2} + 1 \leq j \leq k\}$, $R\{u_i, v_{i+2}^j\}_{j=3}^{\frac{k}{2}} = V(J_{5,k}) - \{v_{i+2}^{\frac{k+j+3}{2}}\}$ for odd j and $R\{u_i, v_{i+2}^j\}_{j=3}^{k-2} = V(J_{5,k}) - \{v_{i+2}^{\frac{j-2}{2}}\}$ for even j. Therefore, $|R\{u_i, v_{i+2}^j\}_{j=3}^{\frac{k}{2}}| = 5k + 5 > 5k + 4 = |R\{u_i, v_{i+2}^1\}| > 4k + \frac{k}{2} + 5 = |R\{u_i, v_{i+2}^2\}| > k + 4 = |R_i|$. Also, $|R\{u_i, v_{i+2}^j\}_{j=3}^{\frac{k}{2}} \cap (\cup_{i=0}^4 R_i)| = 5k - 1 > 5k - 2 = |R\{u_i, v_{i+2}^1\} \cap (\cup_{i=0}^4 R_i)| > 4k + \frac{k}{2} = |R\{u_i, v_{i+2}^2\} \cap (\cup_{i=0}^4 R_i)| > |R_i|$.

Case 4: (When $k \equiv 1 \pmod 2$ and $p = 0$)

In this case, $R\{u_i, v_i^j\} = V(J_{5,k}) - \{v_i^{\frac{j}{2}}, v_i^{\frac{k+j+3}{2}}\}$ for even $j \in \{2, \ldots, k-3\}$, $R\{u_i, v_i^j\} = V(J_{5,k})$ for odd $j \in \{3, \ldots, k-2\}$ and $R\{u_i, v_i^{k-1}\} = V(J_{5,k}) - \{u_{i+1}, v_i^{\frac{k-1}{2}}, v_{i+1}^j | 1 \leq j \leq \frac{k+1}{2}\}$. Therefore, in each of the above cases $|R\{u_i, v_i^j\}| = 5k + 4, 5k + 6, 4k + \frac{k+7}{2}$ respectively, is greater than $|R_i|$. Also each of $|R\{u_i, v_i^j\}_{j=2}^{k-3} \cap (\cup_{i=0}^4 R_i)| = 5k - 2$, for even j, $|R\{u_i, v_i^j\}_{j=3}^{k-2} \cap (\cup_{i=0}^4 R_i)| = 5k$ for odd j and $|R\{u_i, v_i^{k-1}\} \cap (\cup_{i=0}^4 R_i)| = 5k - 2$ are greater than $|R_i| = k + 3$.

Case 5: (When $k \equiv 1 \pmod 2$ and $p = 1$)

In this case, $R\{u_i, v_{i+1}^j\} = V(J_{5,k})$ for odd $j \in \{1, \ldots, k\}$, $R\{u_i, v_{i+1}^2\} = V(J_{5,k}) - \{u_{i+1}, v_i^{\frac{k+5}{2}}, v_{i+1}^{\frac{k+3}{2}} | \frac{k+3}{2} \leq j \leq k\}$, $R\{u_i, v_{i+1}^j\} = V(J_{5,k}) - \{v_{i+1}^{\frac{j-2}{2}}, v_{i+1}^{\frac{k+j+3}{2}}\}$ for even $j \in \{4, \ldots, k-3\}$ and $R\{u_i, v_{i+1}^{k-1}\} = V(J_{5,k}) - \{u_{i+2}, v_{i+1}^{\frac{k-3}{2}}, v_{i+2}^j | 1 \leq j \leq \frac{k+1}{2}\}$. Therefore, in each of the above cases $|R\{u_i, v_{i+1}^j\}| = 5k + 6, 4k + \frac{k+9}{2}, 5k + 4, 4k + \frac{k+7}{2}$ respectively, is greater than $|R_i| = k + 3$.

Also each of $|R\{u_i, v_{i+1}^j\}_{j=1}^2 \cap (\cup_{i=0}^4 R_i)| = 5k$, for odd j, $|R\{u_i, v_{i+1}^k\} \cap (\cup_{i=0}^4 R_i)| = 4k + \frac{k-1}{2}$, $|R\{u_i, v_{i+1}^j\}_{j=4}^{k-2} \cap (\cup_{i=0}^4 R_i)| = 5k - 2$ for even j and $|R\{u_i, v_{i+1}^{k-1}\} \cap (\cup_{i=0}^4 R_i)| = 5k + \frac{k-3}{2}$ are greater than $|R_i| = k + 3$.

Case 6: (When $k \equiv 1 \pmod{2}$ and $p = 2$)

In this case, $R\{u_i, v_{i+2}^j\} = V(J_{5,k})$ for odd $j \in \{1, \ldots, \frac{k-1}{2}\}$, $R\{u_i, v_{i+2}^2\} = V(J_{5,k}) - \{u_{i+2}, v_{i+1}^{\frac{k+5}{2}}, v_{i+2}^{\frac{k+1}{2}} | \frac{k+1}{2} \leq j \leq k\}$ and $R\{u_i, v_{i+2}^j\} = V(J_{5,k}) - \{v_{i+2}^{\frac{j-2}{2}}, v_{i+2}^{\frac{k+j+3}{2}}\}$ for even $j \in \{4, \ldots, \frac{k-1}{2}\}$. Therefore, in each of the above cases $|R\{u_i, v_{i+2}^j\}| = 5k + 6, 4k + \frac{k+7}{2}$ and $5k + 4$ respectively, is greater than $|R_i| = k + 3$. Also each of $|R\{u_i, v_{i+2}^j\}_{j=1}^k \cap (\cup_{i=0}^4 R_i)| = 5k$, for odd j, $|R\{u_i, v_{i+2}^2\} \cap (\cup_{i=0}^4 R_i)| = 4k + \frac{k+3}{2}$ and $|R\{u_i, v_{i+1}^j\}_{j=4}^{k-2} \cap (\cup_{i=0}^4 R_i)| = 5k - 2$ for even j are greater than $|R_i| = k + 3$. □

In the following lemma resolving neighbourhoods of each pair of minor vertices in $\tilde{J}_{5,k}$ are computed.

Lemma 6. *Let $J_{m,k}$ be the generalized Jahangir graph for $k \geq 4$ and $m = 5$. Then $|R_i| < |R\{v_i^r, v_{i+1}^j\}|$ and $|R\{v_i^r, v_{i+l}^j\} \cap (\cup_{i=0}^4 R_i)| \geq |R_i|$ for $l = 0, 1, 2$.*

Proof.

Case 1: When $k \equiv 0 \pmod{2}$:

Case 1.1: For $r = 1$ and $0 \leq l \leq 1$

Here, $R\{v_i^1, v_i^{k-2}\} = V(J_{5,k}) - \{u_{i+1}, v_{i+1}^s | 1 \leq s \leq \frac{k}{2}\}$, $R\{v_i^1, v_i^{k-1}\} = V(J_{5,k}) - \{v_i^{\frac{k}{2}}, v_{i+1}^{\frac{k+2}{2}}\}$ and $R\{v_i^1, v_i^k\} = V(J_{5,k}) - \{u, u_{i+2}, u_{i+3}, u_{i+4}, v_{i+1}^s, v_{i+2}^t, v_{i+3}^t, v_{i+4}^p | \frac{k+4}{2} \leq s \leq k, 1 \leq t \leq k, 1 \leq p \leq \frac{k-2}{2}\}$. Also, $|R\{v_i^1, v_i^{k-2}\}| = \frac{9k}{2} + 5 > k + 4 = |R_i|$, $|R\{v_i^1, v_i^{k-1}\}| = 5k + 4 > |R_i|$ and $|R\{v_i^1, v_i^k\}| = 2k + 4 > |R_i|$. Now $|R\{v_i^1, v_i^{k-1}\} \cap (\cup_{i=0}^4 R_i)| = 5k - 2 \geq |R\{v_i^1, v_i^{k-2}\} \cap (\cup_{i=0}^4 R_i)| = \frac{9k}{2} > |R\{v_i^1, v_i^k\} \cap (\cup_{i=0}^4 R_i)| = 2k - 6 > |R_i|$.

Case 1.2: For $r = 1$, $0 \leq l \leq 2$ and $2 + 2\lceil \frac{l}{2} \rceil \leq j \leq k - 3$

$R\{v_i^1, v_{i+l}^j\} = V(J_{5,k}) - \{v_{i+l}^{\frac{k+j+4}{2}}\}$ for even j and $0 \leq l \leq 2$, $R\{v_i^1, v_i^j\} = V(J_{5,k}) - \{v_i^{\frac{j+1}{2}}\}$ for odd j and $R\{v_i^1, v_{i+l}^j\} = V(J_{5,k}) - \{v_{i+l}^{\frac{j-3}{2}}\}$ for odd j and $1 \leq l \leq 2$. Also, $|R\{v_i^1, v_{i+l}^j\}| = 5k + 5 > k + 4 = |R_i|$. Now $|R\{v_i^1, v_{i+l}^j\} \cap (\cup_{i=0}^4 R_i)| = 5k - 1 > |R_i|$.

Case 1.3: For $r = 1$ and $1 \leq l \leq 2$

Here, $R\{v_i^1, v_{i+1}^1\} = V(J_{5,k}) - \{u, u_{i+1}, u_{i+2}, u_{i+3}, u_{i+4}, v_{i+1}^s, v_{i+2}^t, v_{i+3}^t, v_{i+4}^p | \frac{k+6}{2} \leq s \leq k, 1 \leq t \leq k, 1 \leq p \leq \frac{k-2}{2}\}$, $R\{v_i^1, v_{i+2}^1\} = V(J_{5,k}) - \{u, u_{i+1}, u_{i+3}, u_{i+4}, v_{i+1}^s, v_{i+1}^t, v_{i+2}^s, v_{i+3}^p, v_{i+4}^t| \frac{k+4}{2} \leq s \leq k, 1 \leq t \leq \frac{k-2}{2}, 1 \leq p \leq k\}$, $R\{v_i^1, v_{i+1}^2\} = V(J_{5,k}) - \{v_i^{\frac{k+4}{2}}, v_{i+1}^{\frac{k+6}{2}} | k > 4\}$, $R\{v_i^1, v_{i+2}^2\} = V(J_{5,k}) - \{v_{i+1}^{\frac{k}{2}}, v_{i+2}^{\frac{k+6}{2}} | k > 4\}$, $R\{v_i^1, v_{i+1}^2\} = V(J_{5,k}) - \{u_{i+2}, v_i^k, v_{i+2}^1, v_{i+2}^2 | k = 4\}$, $R\{v_i^1, v_{i+2}^2\} = V(J_{5,k}) - \{u_{i+3}, v_{i+1}^2, v_{i+3}^1, v_{i+3}^2 | k = 4\}$, $R\{v_i^1, v_{i+1}^3\} = V(J_{5,k}) - \{u_{i+1}, v_i^r | \frac{k+6}{2} \leq r \leq k, k > 4\}$, $R\{v_i^1, v_{i+2}^3\} = V(J_{5,k}) - \{u_{i+2}, v_{i+1}^r | \frac{k+6}{2} \leq r \leq k, k > 4\}$, $R\{v_i^1, v_{i+1}^3\} = V(J_{5,k}) - \{u_{i+1}, v_{i+2}^2 | k = 4\}$, $R\{v_i^1, v_{i+2}^3\} = V(J_{5,k}) - \{u_{i+2}, v_{i+1}^2, v_{i+1}^2, v_{i+3}^3 | k = 4\}$. Also, $|R\{v_i^1, v_{i+1}^1 | k > 4\}| = |R\{v_i^1, v_{i+1}^1 | k = 4\}| = 5k + 4 > |R\{v_i^1, v_{i+l}^2\}_{k=4}| = |R\{v_i^1, v_{i+2}^2 | k = 4\}| = 5k + 2 > |R\{v_i^1, v_{i+l}^3| k > 4\}| = 4k + \frac{k}{2} + 7 > |R\{v_i^1, v_{i+l}^2\}| = 2k + 8 > |R\{v_i^1, v_{i+l}^1\}| = 2k + 5 > |R_i| = k + 4$.

Now $|R\{v_i^1, v_{i+1}^3 | k = 4\} \cap (\cup_{i=0}^4 R_i)| = 5k - 1 > |R\{v_i^1, v_{i+1}^2 | k > 4\} \cap (\cup_{i=0}^4 R_i)| = |R\{v_i^1, v_{i+2}^2 | k > 4\} \cap (\cup_{i=0}^4 R_i)| = 5k - 2 > |R\{v_i^1, v_{i+1}^2 | k = 4\} \cap (\cup_{i=0}^4 R_i)| = |R\{v_i^1, v_{i+2}^2 | k = 4\} \cap (\cup_{i=0}^4 R_i)| = |R\{v_i^1, v_{i+2}^3 | k = 4\} \cap (\cup_{i=0}^4 R_i)| = 5k - 3 > |R\{v_i^1, v_{i+l}^3 | k > 4\} \cap (\cup_{i=0}^4 R_i)| = \frac{9k}{2} + 2 > |R\{v_i^1, v_{i+2}^1\} \cap (\cup_{i=0}^4 R_i)| = 2k + 6 > |R\{v_i^1, v_{i+1}^1\} \cap (\cup_{i=0}^4 R_i)| = 2k + 3 > |R_i| = k + 4$. Similarly, it can be done for $2 \leq r \leq k$.

Case 2: When $k \equiv 1 \pmod{2}$:

The proof is same as of case 1. □

3. Fractional Metric Dimension of the Generalized Jahangir Graph $J_{m,k}$ for $k \geq 0$ and $m = 5$

In this section, the fractional metric dimension of the generalized Jahangir graph $J_{m,k}$ for $k \geq 0$ and $m = 5$ is computed. Before achieving the main result a combinatorial criterion to compute fractional metric dimension of a graph is devised in Lemma 7. The criteria is then used in main theorems of this section.

Lemma 7. Let $R = \{R_i, \bar{R}_j | i \in I \ \& j \in J\}$ be the collection of all pair wise resolving sets of $G = (V, E)$ such that $|R_i| = \alpha < |\bar{R}_j|$ and $|\bar{R}_j \cap (\cup R_i)| \geq \alpha$. Then

$$\dim_f(G) = \sum_{t=1}^{\beta} \frac{1}{\alpha},$$

where, $\beta(G) = |\cup_{i \in I} R_i|$.

Proof. Define a function $g : V \to [0,1]$ defined by

$$g(v) = \begin{cases} \frac{1}{\alpha} & \text{if } v \in \cup R_i \\ 0 & \text{if } v \in V - \cup R_i. \end{cases}$$

Then g is indeed a minimal resolving function for G. Since $|R_i| = \alpha < |\bar{R}_j|$ and $|\bar{R}_j \cap (\cup R_i)| \geq \alpha$, therefore, assigning zero to all $v \in \bar{R}_j - \cup R_i$ is required to attain minimum possible weight of $|g|$. Consequently, zero is assigned to all $v \in V - \cup R_i$. Therefore, computing summation of $\frac{1}{\alpha}$ over all $v \in \cup R_i$ gives $\dim_f(G) = \sum_{t=1}^{\beta} \frac{1}{\alpha}$ □

Theorem 1. The fractional metric dimension of the generalized Jahangir graph $J_{m,k}$ for $0 \leq k \leq 3$ and $m = 5$ is

$$\dim_f(J_{m,k}) = \begin{cases} \frac{3}{2} & \text{if } k = 0 \\ \frac{5}{2} & \text{if } k = 1 \\ \frac{15}{8} & \text{if } k = 2 \\ \frac{5}{2} & \text{if } k = 3. \end{cases}$$

Proof.

Case 1: When $k = 0$;

The resolving neighbourhood of all possible pairs of vertices in $V(J_{5,0})$ are $R\{u_i, u_{i+1}\} = \{u_i, u_{i+1}, u_{i+2}, u_{i+4}\}$, $R\{u_i, u_{i+2}\} = \{u_i, u_{i+2}, u_{i+3}, u_{i+4}\}$ and $R\{u, u_i\} = \{u, u_i, u_{i+2}, u_{i+3}\}$. Hence, $\alpha = |R\{u,v\}| = 4$ for all $u, v \in V(J_{5,0})$. Also, $\bigcup_{i=0}^{4} R\{u_i, u_{i+1}\} \cup \bigcup_{i=0}^{4} R\{u_i, u_{i+2}\} \cup \bigcup_{i=0}^{4} R\{u, u_i\} = V(J_{5,0})$. Therefore, from Lemma 7 $\dim_f(J_{5,0}) = \sum_{i=1}^{6} \frac{1}{4} = \frac{3}{2}$.

Case 2: When $k = 1$;

The resolving neighbourhood of any pair of consecutive major vertices u_i, u_{i+1} in $V(J_{5,1})$ is $R\{u_i, u_{i+1}\} = \{u_i, u_{i+1}, v_{i-1}^1, v_{i+1}^1\}$ and $\bigcup_{i=0}^{4} R\{u_i, u_{i+1}\} = V(J_{5,1}) - \{u_0\}$. It is indeed easy to see that $|R\{u_i, u_{i+1}\}| = 4 \leq |R\{u,v\}|$ and $|R\{u_i, u_{i+1}\}| = 4 \leq |R\{u,v\} \cap (\bigcup_{i=0}^{4} R\{u_i, u_{i+1}\})|$ for any pair of vertices u, v in $V(J_{5,1})$ such that $u \neq u_i$ and $v \neq u_{i+1}$. Therefore, from Lemma 7 $\dim_f(J_{5,1}) = \sum_{i=1}^{10} \frac{1}{4} = \frac{5}{2}$.

Case 3: When $k = 2$;

The resolving neighbourhood of any pair of consecutive major vertices u_i, u_{i+1} in $V(J_{5,2})$ is $R\{u_i, u_{i+1}\} = \{u_i, u_{i+1}, v_{i-1}^1, v_{i-1}^2, v_i^1, v_i^2, v_{i+1}^1, v_{i+1}^2\}$ and the resolving neighbourhood of the pair of minors v_{i-1}^2, v_i^1 in $V(J_{5,2})$ is $R\{v_{i-1}^2, v_i^1\} = \{u_{i-1}, u_{i+1}, v_{i-2}^2, v_{i-1}^1, v_{i-1}^2, v_i^1, v_i^2, v_{i+1}^1\}$. Also, $\bigcup\{\bigcup_{i=0}^4 R\{u_i, u_{i+1}\}, \bigcup_{i=0}^4 R\{v_{i-1}^2, v_i^1\}\} = V(J_{5,1}) - \{u_0\}$. It is indeed easy to see that $|R\{u_i, u_{i+1}\}| = |R\{v_{i-1}^2, v_i^1\}| = 8 \leq |R\{u, v\}|$ and $|R\{u_i, u_{i+1}\}| = |R\{v_{i-1}^2, v_i^1\}| = 4 \leq |R\{u, v\} \cap (\bigcup\{\bigcup_{i=0}^4 R\{u_i, u_{i+1}\}, \bigcup_{i=0}^4 R\{v_{i-1}^2, v_i^1\}\})|$ for any pair of vertices u, v in $V(J_{5,2})$ such that either $u \neq u_i$ and $v \neq u_{i+1}$ or $u \neq v_{i-1}^2$ and $v \neq v_i^1$. Therefore, from Lemma 7 $\dim_f(J_{5,2}) = \sum_{i=1}^{15} \frac{1}{8} = \frac{15}{8}$.

Case 4: When $k = 3$;

The resolving neighbourhood of the pair of minors v_{i-1}^2, v_i^1 in $V(J_{5,3})$ is $R\{v_{i-1}^2, v_i^1\} = \{v_{i-1}^1, v_{i-1}^2, v_{i-1}^3, v_i^1, v_i^2, v_i^3\}$. Also, $\bigcup_{i=0}^4 R\{v_{i-1}^3, v_i^1\} = V(J_{5,3}) - \{u, u_0, u_1, u_2, u_3, u_4\}$. It is indeed easy to see that $|R\{v_{i-1}^3, v_i^1\}| = 6 \leq |R\{u, v\}|$ and $|R\{v_{i-1}^3, v_i^1\}| = 6 \leq |R\{u, v\} \cap (\bigcup_{i=0}^4 R\{v_{i-1}^3, v_i^1\})|$ for any pair of vertices u, v in $V(J_{5,3})$ such that $u \neq v_{i-1}^3$ and $v \neq v_i^1$. Therefore, from Lemma 7 $\dim_f(J_{5,3}) = \sum_{i=1}^{15} \frac{1}{6} = \frac{5}{2}$. □

Remark 1. *In [4], Arumugam and Mathew computed fractional metric dimension of the wheel graph W_n as $\frac{3}{2}$ for $n = 6$. It is to be noted that the graph W_6 is a special case of the generalized Jahangir graph $J_{m,k}$ for $m = 5, k = 0$. Also, the fractional dimension $\dim_f(J_{m,k}) = \frac{3}{2}$ for $m = 5, k = 0$ computed above is in consensus with [4].*

Theorem 2. *The fractional metric dimension of the generalized Jahangir graph $J_{m,k}$ for $k \geq 4$ and $m = 5$ is*

$$\dim_f(J_{m,k}) = \begin{cases} \frac{5k}{k+4} & \text{if } k \equiv 0 \pmod{2} \\ \frac{5k}{k+3} & \text{if } k \equiv 1 \pmod{2}. \end{cases}$$

Proof. In view of Lemma 1,

$$|R_i| = |R\{v_{i-1}^k, v_i^1\}| = \begin{cases} k+4 & \text{if } k \equiv 0 \pmod{2} \\ k+3 & \text{if } k \equiv 1 \pmod{2}. \end{cases}$$

and $\acute{\beta} = |\bigcup_{i=0}^4 R_i| = 5k$. Also from Lemma 2 to Lemma 6, $|R\{v_{i-1}^k, v_i^1\}| \leq |R\{x, y\}|$ for all $x, y \in V(J_{5,k})$ such that $x \neq v_{i-1}^k$ and $y \neq v_i^1$. Therefore, from the criteria given in Lemma 7, the fractional metric of $J_{5,k}$ is given as follows:

$$\dim_f(J_{5,k}) = \sum_{t=1}^{\beta} \frac{1}{|R_i|}.$$

Here, $\beta = \acute{\beta} = 5k$. This implies

$$\dim_f(J_{5,k}) = \sum_{t=1}^{5k} \frac{1}{|R\{v_{i-1}^k, v_i^1\}|}.$$

Hence,

$$\dim_f(J_{5,k}) = \begin{cases} \frac{5k}{k+4} & \text{if } k \equiv 0 \pmod{2} \\ \frac{5k}{k+3} & \text{if } k \equiv 1 \pmod{2}. \end{cases}$$

This completes the proof. □

Theorem 3. *The fractional metric dimension of the generalized Jahangir graph $J_{m,k}$ is $\frac{5}{2}$ for $m = 5, k = 4$ and $\frac{25}{8}$ for $m = 5, k = 5$.*

Proof. Clear from Theorem 2. □

4. Conclusions

In this paper, a combinatorial criteria is developed to compute fractional metric dimension of a connected graph. The criteria is applied to compute fractional metric dimension of the generalized Jahangir graph $J_{m,k}$ for $k \geq 0$ and $m = 5$. The problem to investigate the fractional metric dimension of the generalized Jahangir graph $J_{m,k}$ for $k \geq 0$ and $m > 5$ is still open.

Author Contributions: J.-B.L. contributed the discussion on problem, validation of results, funding and final reading, A.K. and M.J. contributed the source of problem, collection of material, analyze and compute the results, and wrote the paper, and T.R. contributed for discussion on problem, methodology, and prepared the final draft.

Funding: The work was partially supported by the China Postdoctoral Science Foundation under Grant No. 2017M621579 and the Postdoctoral Science Foundation of Jiangsu Province under Grant No. 1701081B. Project of Anhui Jianzhu University under Grant No. 2016QD116 and 2017dc03. Anhui Province Key Laboratory of Intelligent Building & Building Energy Saving.

Acknowledgments: The authors are indebted to all the anonymous referees for their careful reading and valuable comments to improve the original version of this paper.

Conflicts of Interest: The authors declare that there are no conflicts of interest regarding the publication of this paper.

References

1. Chartrand, G.; Lesniak, L. *Graphs & Digraphs*, 4th ed.; Chapman & Hall, CRC: London, UK, 2005.
2. Gross, J.L.; Yellen, J. *Graph Theory and Its Applications*, 2nd ed.; Chapman and Hall/CRC: London, UK, 2005.
3. West, D.B. *Introduction to Graph Theory*; Prentice Hall: Upper Saddle River, NJ, USA, 2001.
4. Arumugam, S.; Mathew, V. The fractional metric dimension of graphs. *Discret. Math.* **2012**, *312*, 1584–1590. [CrossRef]
5. Slater, P.J. Leaves of trees. *Congr. Numer.* **1975**, *14*, 549–559.
6. Slater, P.J. Domination and location in acyclic graphs. *Networks* **1987**, *17*, 55–64. [CrossRef]
7. Harary, F.; Melter, R.A. On the metric dimension of a graph. *ARS Combin.* **1976**, *2*, 191–195.
8. Beerliova, Z.; Eberhard, F.; Erlebach, T.; Hall, A.; Hoffman, M.; Mihalak, M.; Ram, L. Network discovery and verification. *IEEE J. Sel. Areas Commun.* **2006**, *24*, 2168–2181. [CrossRef]
9. Khuller, S.; Raghavachari, B.; Rosenfield, A. Landmarks in graphs. *Discret. Appl. Math.* **1996**, *70*, 217–229. [CrossRef]
10. Chvátal, V. Mastermind. *Combinatorica* **1983**, *3*, 325–329. [CrossRef]
11. Shapiro, H.; Soderberg, S. A combinatory detection problem. *Am. Math. Mon.* **1963**, *70*, 1066–1070.
12. Currie, J.; Oellermann, O.R. The metric dimension and metric independence of a graph. *J. Combin. Math. Combin. Comput.* **2001**, *39*, 157–167.
13. Chartrand, G.; Eroh, L.; Johnson, M.; Oellermann, O.R. Resolvability in graphs and the metric dimension of a graph. *Discret. Appl. Math.* **2000**, *105*, 99–113. [CrossRef]
14. Fehr, M.; Gosselin, S.; Oellermann, O.R. The metric dimension of Cayley digraphs. *Discret. Math.* **2006**, *306*, 31–41. [CrossRef]
15. Bot, R.I.; Grad, S.M.; Wanka, G. *Duality in Vector Optimization*; Springer: Berlin, Germany, 2009; ISBN 978-3-642-02885-4.
16. Ali, K.; Baskoro, E.T.; Tomescu, I. On the Ramsey numbers for paths and generalized Jahangir graphs $J_{s,m}$. *Bull. Math. Soc. Sci. Math.* **2008**, *51*, 177–182.
17. Tomescu, I.; Javaid, I. On the metric dimension of the Jahangir graph. *Bull. Math. Soc. Sci. Math.* **2007**, *50*, 371–376.
18. Arumugam, S.; Mathew, V.; Shen, J. On fractional metric dimension of graphs Discrete Mathematics. *Algorithms Appl.* **2013**, *5*, 1–8.
19. Feng, M.; Wang, K. On the metric dimension and fractional metric dimension of the hierarchical product of graphs. *Appl. Anal. Discret. Math.* **2013**, *7*, 302–313. [CrossRef]
20. Feng, M.; Wang, K. On the fractional metric dimension of corona product graphs and lexicographic product graphs. *arXiv* **2012**, arXiv:1206.1906v1.

21. Saputro, S.W.; Fenovcikova, A.S.; Baca, M.; Lascsakova, M. On fractional metric dimension of comb product graphs. *Stat. Optim. Inf. Comput.* **2018**, *6*, 150–158. [CrossRef]
22. Yi, E. The fractional metric dimension of permutation graphs. *Acta Math. Sin.* **2015**, *31*, 367–382. [CrossRef]
23. Feng, M.; Lv, B.; Wang, K. On the fractional metric dimension of graphs. *Discret. Appl. Math.* **2014**, *170*, 55–63. [CrossRef]

© 2019 by the authors. Licensee MDPI, Basel, Switzerland. This article is an open access article distributed under the terms and conditions of the Creative Commons Attribution (CC BY) license (http://creativecommons.org/licenses/by/4.0/).

Article

Fault-Tolerant Resolvability and Extremal Structures of Graphs

Hassan Raza [1], Sakander Hayat [2,*], Muhammad Imran [3,4] and Xiang-Feng Pan [1]

1. School of Mathematical Sciences, Anhui University, Hefei 230601, China; hassan_raza783@yahoo.com (H.R.); xfpan@ahu.edu.cn (X.-F.P.)
2. Faculty of Engineering Sciences, GIK Institute of Engineering Sciences and Technology, Topi, Swabi 23460, Pakistan
3. Department of Mathematical Sciences, United Arab Emirates University, Al Ain 15551, UAE; imrandhab@gmail.com
4. School of Natural Sciences, National University of Sciences and Technology, H-12, Islamabad 44000, Pakistan
* Correspondence: sakander1566@gmail.com; Tel.: +92-342-4431402

Received: 25 November 2018; Accepted: 10 January 2019; Published: 14 January 2019

Abstract: In this paper, we consider fault-tolerant resolving sets in graphs. We characterize n-vertex graphs with fault-tolerant metric dimension n, $n-1$, and 2, which are the lower and upper extremal cases. Furthermore, in the first part of the paper, a method is presented to locate fault-tolerant resolving sets by using classical resolving sets in graphs. The second part of the paper applies the proposed method to three infinite families of regular graphs and locates certain fault-tolerant resolving sets. By accumulating the obtained results with some known results in the literature, we present certain lower and upper bounds on the fault-tolerant metric dimension of these families of graphs. As a byproduct, it is shown that these families of graphs preserve a constant fault-tolerant resolvability structure.

Keywords: resolving set; fault-tolerant resolving set; extended Petersen graphs; anti-prism graphs; squared cycle graphs

MSC: 05C12; 05C90

---

1. Introduction

In 1975, Slater [1] introduced the concept of a resolving set and its minimality within the graph, known as the metric dimension. Independently, Harary and Melter [2] proposed the same concept by explaining its diverse applicability. The research on this graph-theoretic parameter is excelling, and hundreds of manuscripts have been published from both theoretic and applicability perspectives. By considering its applicability perspective, the metric dimension significantly possesses many potentially diverse applications in different areas of science, social science, and technology. Next, we discuss applications of the metric dimension in other scientific disciplines.

The emergence and diversity of metric dimension applications prevail in many scientific areas, such as the navigation of robots in robotics [3], determining routing protocols geographically [4], and telecommunication [5]. The vertex–edge relation in graphs and its equivalence to the atom–bond relation derive many applications in chemistry [6]. Network discovery and its verification [5] is another area in which interesting applications of the metric dimension emerge. Based on its importance in other scientific areas, it is natural to study the mathematical properties of this parameter. Next, we review some literature on the mathematical significance of this graph-theoretic parameter.

Various families of graphs of mathematical interest have been studied from the metric dimension perspective. Here, we mention some of the important work: the metric dimension of certain families of distance-regular graphs, such as Grassmann graphs [7] and Johnson graphs [8], which have been studied by Bailey and others. The metric dimension of Kneser graphs was also studied by Bailey at al. [8]. Graphs of group-theoretic interest, such as Cayely digraphs [9] and Cayley graphs generated by certain finite groups [10], have also been studied from the metric dimension viewpoint. The metric dimension and resolving sets of product graphs, such as the Cartesian product of graphs [11] and categorical product of graphs [12], have also been investigated. Certain infinite families generated from wheel graphs have been studied by Siddiqui et al. [13]. The metric dimension of rotationally symmetric convex polytopes (resp. convex polytopes produced by wheel-related graphs) has been studied by Kratica et al. [14] (resp. Imran et al. [15]). The question of whether or not the metric dimension is a finite number was answered in [16]. They showed this result by constructing some infinite families of graphs possessing infinite metric dimension. Similar to many other graph-theoretic parameters, the computational complexity of the metric dimension problem was investigated in [17].

Metric dimension has also been generalized and extended by providing more mathematical rigorous general concepts, such as the k-metric dimension. Hernando et al. [18] introduced another concept: fault tolerance in resolvability, which tolerates the removal of any arbitrary vertex and preserves the resolvability status of the underlying set. By considering the vertices in a resolving set as the location for loran/sonar stations, we can say that the location of any such vertex is distinctly measured by its vertex distances from the site of the stations. From this perspective, a fault-tolerant (unique) resolving set is the one which still preserves the property of a resolving set when neglecting any station at a uniquely determined location of a vertex in the resolving set. Consequently, fault-tolerant resolving sets enhance the applicability of classical resolving sets in graphs. In addition, this shows that the fault-tolerant metric dimension possesses applicative superiority over the metric dimension.

Chartrand [19] investigated certain applications by referring to components of a metric basis as sensors. From the fault-tolerant resolvability point of view, if some sensor is lacking in performance and does not convey information efficiently, the system will not have enough information process in order to tackle the thief/intruder/fire, etc. A fault-tolerant resolving set from this perspective deals with this problem by conveying the information efficiently when one of the sensors does not catch the intruder. It turns out that fault tolerance in resolvability has applicative superiority over classical resolvability in graphs. In other words, the fault-tolerant metric dimension has application wherever the metric dimension is applicable. Nevertheless, fault-tolerant resolving sets have not received much attention from researchers. The fault-tolerant metric dimension of certain interesting graphs possessing chemical importance was studied in [20]. Recently, Raza et al. [21,22] considered certain rotationally symmetric convex polytopes and studied their fault-tolerant metric dimension and binary-locating dominating sets. The reader is referred to [23] for consideration of fault-tolerant resolvability as an optimization problem and its applicative perspective. We also refer the reader to [24–28] for a study of other interesting graph-theoretic parameters having potential applications in chemistry.

Based on the importance of fault-tolerant resolvability from both mathematical and applicative perspectives as discussed above, it is natural to study the mathematical properties of fault-tolerant resolving sets in graphs. In this paper, we study the fault-tolerant resolvability in graphs. We characterize the graphs with fault-tolerant metric dimension n, $n-1$, and 2, which are the non-trivial extremal values of the fault-tolerant metric dimension. We utilize a lemma to trace a fault-tolerant resolving set from a given resolving set. This results in proving a non-trivial upper bound on the fault-tolerant metric dimension of a graph with a given resolving set. We study the fault-tolerant resolvability for three infinite families of regular graphs and show some upper and lower bounds on their fault-tolerant metric dimension.

2. Preliminaries

This section defines the terminologies and explains the undefined terms from the previous section. We also provide an overview of basic results in the literature which are used in subsequent sections. Notations and graph-theoretic concepts were taken from Bondy and Murty [29].

A graph is an ordered pair $\Gamma = (V, E)$, where V is considered to be the vertex set and E is called the edge set. Γ is called finite if V is finite; it is said to be simple if it does not contain any loop and parallel edges; it is called undirected if its edges do not possess direction; and it is called connected if any two vertices in it are connected by a path. The length of the shortest path between two given vertices is called the distance between them. For $u, v \in V$, the distance between u and v is usually denoted as $d_{u,v}$.

For two arbitrary vertices x and y, a vertex u is said to resolve the pair x, y if it satisfies $d_{u,x} \neq d_{u,y}$. If this resolvability condition is satisfied by a number of vertices composing a subset $R \subseteq V$, i.e., any pair of vertices in the graph is resolved by at least one vertex in R, then L is said to be a resolving set. The idea behind this definition goes back to Harary and Melter [2], who showed that this concept naturally arises from communication networks. The minimum cardinality of a resolving set in a given graph is said to be the metric dimension. It is usually denoted by $\beta(G)$. A resolving set in which the number of elements is β is called the metric basis. For an ordered subset $R = (x_1, x_2, \ldots, x_r)$, the R-coordinate/code/representation of vertex u in V is $C_R(u) = (d_{u,x_1}, d_{u,x_2}, \ldots, d_{u,x_r})$. In these terms, L is said to be a resolving set of Γ if any two vertices in Γ have distinct codes or distance vectors.

Chartrand et al. [6] determined all the connected graphs with metric dimension 1. Let P_ν be the ν-vertex path graph.

Theorem 1. [6] *A connected graph has metric dimension 1 if and only if it is the path graph.*

They also showed that a graph having metric dimension 2 cannot possess $K_{3,3}$ and K_5 as its subgraphs. Let K_ν be the complete graph on ν vertices. They also classified the connected graphs possessing metric dimension $\nu - 1$.

Theorem 2. [6] *A connected ν-vertex graph has metric dimension $\nu - 1$ if and only if it is the complete graph.*

Let $\Gamma \cup \Omega$ denote the disjoint union of two graphs Γ and Ω. The join of two graphs Γ and Ω, symbolized as $\Gamma + \Omega$, is obtained by joining any vertex of Γ to all the vertices of Ω and vice versa. Graphs having ν vertices sharing the metric dimension $\nu - 2$ are classified in the following result.

Theorem 3. [6] *A connected ν-vertex graph Γ with $\nu \geq 4$ shares the metric dimension $\nu - 2$ if and only if $\Gamma \in \{K_s + \overline{K_t} \, (s \geq 1, t \geq 2), K_{s,t} \, (s, t \geq 1), K_s + (K_1 \cup K_t) \, (s, t \geq 1)\}$.*

A fault-tolerant resolving set is a resolving set in which the removal of an arbitrary vertex maintains the resolvability. The idea of a fault-tolerant resolving set (also known as resilient) has been widely investigated in networked systems; see, for example, [30,31]. The fault-tolerant metric dimension and fault-tolerant metric basis are defined similarly as metric dimension. We denote the fault-tolerant metric dimension of graph Γ by $\beta'(\Gamma)$.

A family of graphs on ν vertices is said to possess a constant (resp. bounded) resolvability/fault-tolerant resolvability structure if the metric dimension/fault-tolerant metric dimension does not depend on the parameter ν (resp. is a function of ν). Note that our definition of a constant/bounded metric/fault-tolerant metric dimension could be different from the one in the literature. In view of Theorem 1, path graphs are a family of graphs with a constant metric dimension. On the other hand, in view of Theorem 2, complete graphs provide a family of graphs possessing a bounded resolvability structure.

In a path graph, there exists a unique fault-tolerant metric basis comprising the initial and terminal vertices. Thus, we obtain $\beta'(P_n) = 2$. Hernando et al. [18] showed that the tree T in Figure 1 has $\beta(T) = 10$ and $\beta'(T) = 14$. The set $P = (1, 2, 3, 4, \ldots, 10)$ (resp. $Q = P \cup \{y, v, r, s\}$) forms the metric basis (resp. fault-tolerant metric basis) of T.

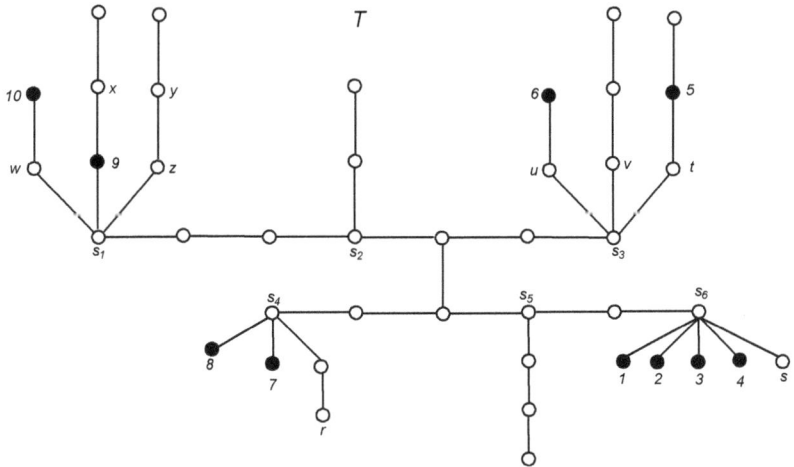

Figure 1. The tree example from Hernando et al. [18].

Javaid et al. proved the following lemma, which shows an alternative way to trace a fault-tolerant resolving set in a graph.

Lemma 1. [32] *A resolving set R of graph Γ is fault-tolerant if and only if any arbitrary pair of vertices of Γ is resolved by at least two vertices of R.*

Proof. Let R be a fault-tolerant resolving set of G. Assume contrarily that two vertices x and y of G are resolved by a single vertex $r \in R$. Then, $R \setminus \{r\}$ is not a resolving set since both x and y have the same codes with respect to $r \in R$. This raises a contradiction to the assumption that R is a fault-tolerant resolving set of G.

Now, we assume that every pair of vertices of G is resolved by at least two vertices of R. Then, $R \setminus \{r\}$ for any $r \in R$ is a resolving set by definition. This shows the lemma. □

Hernando et al. [18] showed the following upper bound on β' in terms of β.

Theorem 4. [18] *The upper bound $\beta'(\Gamma) \leq \beta(\Gamma)(1 + 2 \times 5^{\beta(\Gamma)-1})$ holds for any arbitrary graph.*

The following result demonstrates that the difference between the two parameters β and β' can be increasingly large enough.

Theorem 5. [32] *There always exists a graph Γ for which $\beta'(\Gamma) \geq \beta(\Gamma) + p$ holds for any integer p.*

From this, we can also note that, with the defining structures of β and β', we can have $\beta'(\Gamma) \geq \beta(\Gamma) + 1$. In the next section, we discuss graphs which hold equality in this lower bound.

3. Main Results

This section contains the main result presented in this paper.

3.1. Some Characterizations

In this subsection, we prove some characterization results on extreme values of the fault-tolerant metric dimension of graphs. These results are the fault-tolerant metric dimension analogs of Theorems 1–3, where similar results on the metric dimension of graphs are obtained. Note that from the interpretation of the fault-tolerant metric dimension of a graph Γ with n vertices, we have $2 \leq \beta'(\Gamma) \leq n$.

In the following result, graphs with fault-tolerant metric dimension 2 are characterized.

Theorem 6. *A graph has $\beta'(\Gamma) = 2$ if and only if it is the path graph.*

Proof. First, we assume that $\Gamma \cong P_n$. By Theorem 1, we obtain $\beta(\Gamma) = 1$. By the definition of the fault-tolerant metric dimension, it is noted that

$$\beta'(\Gamma) \geq \beta(\Gamma) + 1. \tag{1}$$

By inserting $\beta(\Gamma) = 1$ in Equation (1), we get $\beta'(\Gamma) \geq 2$. Let $R' = \{a, b\} \subseteq V(\Gamma)$, where a and b are the vertices with degree one in Γ. Clearly, R' is a resolving set in Γ. Note that both $R' \setminus \{a\}$ and $R' \setminus \{b\}$ are also resolving sets in Γ, because any vertex of degree one resolves the path graph. This implies that R' is a fault-tolerant resolving set of Γ, and thus, $\beta'(\Gamma) \leq 2$. By combining two inequalities, we obtain $\beta'(\Gamma = P_n) = 2$.

Conversely, suppose that Γ is a graph with fault-tolerant metric dimension 2. Since both $\beta(\Gamma)$ and $\beta'(\Gamma)$ are positive integers, by Equation (1), we get $\beta(\Gamma) < \beta'(\Gamma)$. By implying $\beta'(\Gamma) = 2$, we obtain $\beta(\Gamma) < 2$, which indicates that $\beta(\Gamma) = 1$. By Theorem 1, we find that the only graphs with metric dimension 1 are the path graphs. This implies that $\Gamma \cong P_n$. □

In the next theorem, we characterize the equality in $\beta'(\Gamma) \leq n$, where Γ is an n-ordered graph.

Theorem 7. *An n-vertex connected graph has $\beta'(\Gamma) = n$ if and only if it is the complete graph K_n.*

Proof. Let Γ be an n-ordered complete graph. Then, by Theorem 2, we have $\beta(\Gamma) = n - 1$. By putting this in Equation (1), we get $\beta'(\Gamma) \geq n$. Let $R' = V(\Gamma)$; for some $c \in V(\Gamma)$, the set $R' \setminus \{c\}$ is a resolving set, because any collection of $n - 1$ vertices of Γ resolve Γ completely. Thus, R' is a fault-tolerant resolving set of Γ, and thus, $\beta'(\Gamma) \leq n$. By combining these two cases, we obtain $\beta'(\Gamma) = n$.

Conversely, suppose that Γ is a graph with fault-tolerant metric dimension n. From Equation (1), we have $\beta(\Gamma) < \beta'(\Gamma)$, which shows that $\beta(\Gamma) \leq n - 1$. In Theorem 2, it is shown that equality holds in $\beta(\Gamma) \leq n - 1$ if and only if $\Gamma = K_n$. This shows that equality holds in $\beta(\Gamma) \leq \beta'(\Gamma) - 1 = n - 1$. This implies that Γ is a complete graph on n vertices. □

In the next theorem, graphs with fault-tolerant metric dimension $n - 1$ are characterized.

Theorem 8. *Let Γ be a graph with order $n \geq 4$. Then, $\beta'(\Gamma) = n - 1$ if and only if $\Gamma = K_{s,t}$ ($s, t \geq 1$), $\Gamma = K_s + \overline{K_t}$ ($s \geq 1, t \geq 2$) and $\Gamma = K_s + (K_1 \cup K_t)$ ($s, t \geq 1$).*

Proof. Let $\Gamma_1 = K_{s,t}$ ($s, t \geq 1$), $\Gamma_2 = K_s + \overline{K_t}$ ($s \geq 1, t \geq 2$), and $\Gamma_3 = K_s + (K_1 \cup K_t)$ ($s, t \geq 1$). Assume that Γ belongs to one of the three infinite families Γ_i, $i = 1, 2, 3$. Then, by Theorem 3, $\beta(\Gamma) = n - 2$. By using this in Inequality (1), we get $\beta'(\Gamma) \geq n - 1$. Since Γ is not a complete graph, by Theorem 7, we obtain $\beta'(\Gamma) < n$. This implies that $\beta'(\Gamma) \leq n - 1$. Now, we combine the two inequalities to achieve $\beta'(\Gamma) = n - 1$.

Conversely, when we let Γ be a graph with fault-tolerant metric dimension $n - 1$, by using Equation (1), $\beta'(\Gamma) \geq \beta(G) + 1$ implies

$$\beta(\Gamma) \leq n - 2. \tag{2}$$

By Theorem 3, equality holds in Equation (2) if $\Gamma \in \{\Gamma_1, \Gamma_2, \Gamma_3\}$, if $n \geq 4$. This implies that the equality holds in $\beta(\Gamma) \leq \beta'(\Gamma) - 1$, and thus, for $n \geq 4$, $\Gamma \in \Gamma_i$ for $i = 1, 2, 3$. This completes the proof. □

By Theorems 6–8, if Γ is a graph with $\Gamma \notin \{P_n, K_n, \Gamma_1, \Gamma_2, \Gamma_3\}$, then $3 \leq \beta'(\Gamma) \leq n - 2$. Next, we focus on the graphs for which $3 \leq \beta'(\Gamma) \leq n - 2$.

3.2. Relation between Resolving Sets and Fault-Tolerant Resolving Sets of Graphs

In Theorem 4, Hernando et al. [18] showed that the fault-tolerant metric dimension is bounded by a function of metric dimension. They also showed a relation between a resolving set and a fault-tolerant resolving set for an arbitrary graph. Now, let $N(w)$ (resp. $N[w]$) represent the open and close neighborhood of a vertex $w \in V(\Gamma)$, where $N(w) := \{u \in V(\Gamma) \mid uw \in E(\Gamma)\}$ and $N[w] := \{w\} \cup N(w)$.

Lemma 2. [18] *Let R be a resolving set of graph Γ. For all $w \in R$, let $T(w) := \{x \in V(\Gamma) : N(w) \subseteq N(x)\}$. Then, $R' := \cup_{w \in R}(N[w] \cup T(w))$ is a fault-tolerant resolving set of Γ.*

Now, the following lemma will help us to obtain upper bounds on the fault-tolerant metric dimension of a given graph. It uses R in a graph to produce a fault-tolerant resolving set within it. In view of Lemma 2, for a given resolving set R of a graph Γ, finding the set R' to evaluate the corresponding fault-tolerant resolving set seems tedious due to the calculation of the set $T(w)$ for a vertex $w \in R$. Raza et al. [21] further simplify this lemma so that one does not have to check every vertex x of Γ to verify whether or not it belongs to $T(w)$ for some $w \in R$. Now, for vertices x and y in Γ, we let $\lambda(x, y)$ be a set of common neighbors of these vertices and, for some $Q \subset V(\Gamma)$, let $\lambda(Q)$ be the set of common neighbors of each vertex in Q. The following lemma is a key result for finding upper bounds on the fault-tolerant metric dimension of a given graph.

Lemma 3. [21] *For a graph Γ, let R be a distinguishing or resolving set, and $R' := \cup_{w \in R}(N[w] \cup \lambda(N(w)))$. Then, $\beta'(G) \leq |R'|$.*

Proof. Let R be a resolving set of graph Γ. For $v \in R$, let $T(v) := \{x \in V(\Gamma) : N(v) \subseteq N(x)\}$. Then, for any $x \in T(v)$, we notice that $d(x, v) = 2$ (see Figure 2).

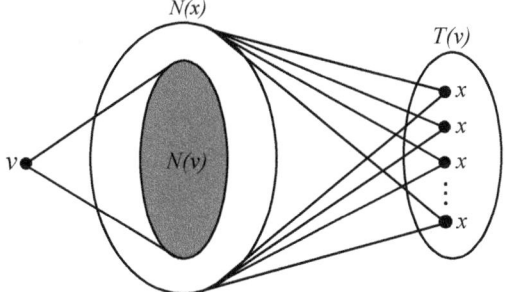

Figure 2. A depiction of the proof of Lemma 3.

Moreover, for $y, z \in N(v)$, we obtain $\lambda(y, z) = x$ for some $x \in T(v)$. This implies that $T(v) = \lambda(N(v)) \setminus \{v\}$ for any $v \in R$. Now, by Lemma 2, $R' := \cup_{v \in R}(N[v] \cup T(v))$ is a fault-tolerant resolving set of Γ. Since v is contained in $N[v]$, then, for any $v \in R$,

$$N[v] \cup T(v) = N[v] \cup \lambda(N(v)).$$

This shows the lemma. □

We use Lemma 3 in later subsections to calculate upper bounds on the fault-tolerant metric dimension for certain families of regular graphs.

3.3. Extended Petersen Graphs

The extended Petersen graph $P(n)$, $n \geq 3$, has a vertex set

$$V = \{z_1, z_2, \ldots z_n, y_1, y_2, \ldots y_n\}$$

and an edge set

$$E = \{z_i z_{i+1}, z_i y_i, y_i y_{i+2} | \text{with indices taken as modulo } n\}.$$

The extended Petersen graph $P(n)$ is a special case of the generalized Petersen graphs which were first studied by Watkins [33].

We studied the problem of the fault-tolerant metric dimension of the extended Petersen graph. The set $\{z_1, z_2, \ldots, z_n\}$ prompts a cycle in $P(n)$, with $z_k z_{k+1}$ ($1 \leq k \leq n$) and $y_k y_{k+2}$ ($1 \leq k \leq n$), with indices taken modulo n, as edges. For even n, $\{y_1, y_2, \ldots, y_n\}$ induces two cycles, again with edges $y_k y_{k+2}$ ($1 \leq k \leq n$), with indices taken modulo n. For example, $P(5)$ is the standard Petersen graph. For the sake of simplicity, we denote the cycle induced by $\{z_1, z_2, \ldots, z_n\}$ as the outer cycle and the cycle induced by $\{y_1, y_2, \ldots, y_n\}$ as the inner cycle or cycles.

The following result was shown by Javaid et al. [34].

Proposition 1. [34] *Let Γ be the extended Petersen graph $P(n)$ with $n \geq 5$; then, $\beta(\Gamma) = 3$.*

They also showed the following:

Proposition 2. [34] *$P(n)$, the extended Petersen graph, can be classified as a family of graphs with a constant metric dimension.*

In this section, we present our main results. We derive the upper as well as lower bounds on the fault-tolerant metric dimension of the extended Petersen graph $P(n)$. Note that Claim 1 in the following result was essentially shown in Proposition 1.

Theorem 9. *Let Γ be the extended Petersen graph $P(n)$; then,*

$$4 \leq \beta'(\Gamma) \leq \begin{cases} 10, & \text{if } n \equiv 0 (\mod 2) \text{ with } n \geq 8; \\ 12, & \text{if } n \equiv 1 (\mod 2) \text{ with } n \geq 11. \end{cases}$$

Proof. Let Γ be the extended Petersen graph $P(n)$, with $n \geq 4$.

Case 1: When $n \equiv 0 (\mod 2)$ with $n \geq 8$.

Claim 1: Resolving set R of order 3 exists in Γ.

Based on the location of basis elements in Γ, we further divide this case into two subcases.

Subcase 1.1: When $n \equiv 0 (\mod 4)$.

It can be written as $n = 4\ell$, $2 \leq \ell \in \mathbb{Z}^+$. We prove that $R = \{y_1, y_2, y_3\}$ resolves $V(\Gamma)$. In order to show that R resolves vertices of $V(\Gamma)$, we first represent the vertices in Γ with respect to $R \setminus \{y_3\}$.

Indeed, the vertices y_1 and y_2 distinguish the inner cycle vertices and a few of the outer cycle vertices. The vertices in the outer cycle are represented by $C_{R\setminus\{y_3\}}(z_1) = (1,2)$, $C_{R\setminus\{y_3\}}(z_2) = (2,1)$,

$$C_{R\setminus\{y_3\}}(z_{2k}) = \begin{cases} (k+1,k), & 2 \leq k \leq \ell; \\ (2\ell-k+2, 2\ell-k+2), & \ell+1 \leq k \leq 2\ell. \end{cases}$$

$$C_{R\setminus\{y_3\}}(z_{2k+1}) = \begin{cases} (k+1,k+1), & 1 \leq k \leq \ell; \\ (2\ell-k+1, 2\ell-k+2), & \ell+1 \leq k \leq 2\ell-1. \end{cases}$$

In the inner cycle,

$$C_{R\setminus\{y_3\}}(y_{2k}) = \begin{cases} (k+2,k-1), & 2 \leq k \leq \ell; \\ (2\ell-k+3, 2\ell-k+1), & \ell+1 \leq k \leq 2\ell. \end{cases}$$

and

$$C_{R\setminus\{z_3\}}(y_{2k+1}) = \begin{cases} (k,k+2), & 1 \leq k \leq \ell; \\ (2\ell-k, 2\ell-k+3), & \ell+1 \leq k \leq 2\ell-1. \end{cases}$$

From the above discussion, it is clear that there are no two vertices with the same representation in the inner cycle. However, in the outer cycle, $C_{R\setminus\{y_3\}}(z_{3+k}) = C_{R\setminus\{y_3\}}(z_{n-k})$ for $k = 0, 2, \ldots, 2\ell-2$. Vertex y_3 distinguishes these pairs with the same representation as $d(y_3, z_{3+k}) = \lfloor\frac{3+k}{2}\rfloor \neq d(y_3, z_{n-k}) = \lfloor\frac{3+k}{2}\rfloor + 2$ for $k = 0, 2, \ldots, 2\ell-4$ and $d(y_3, z_{2\ell+2}) = d(y_3, z_{2\ell+1}) + 1$. This shows that R resolves vertices of Γ, which means $\beta(\Gamma) \leq 3$ when $n \equiv 0 \pmod{4}$.

Subcase 1.2: When $n \equiv 2 \pmod{4}$.

It can be written as $n = 4\ell+2, 2 \leq \ell \in \mathbb{Z}^+$. In this case, again, $R = \{y_1, y_2, y_3\}$ resolves $V(\Gamma)$. In order to show that R resolves the vertices of $V(P(n))$, we first represent the vertices in Γ with respect to $R \setminus \{y_3\}$. Again, it is clear that the vertices y_1 and y_2 distinguish the inner and outer cycle vertices. Note that for the outer cycle, we have $C_{R\setminus\{y_3\}}(z_1) = (1,2)$, $C_{R\setminus\{y_3\}}(z_2) = (2,1)$,

$$C_{R\setminus\{y_3\}}(z_{2k}) = \begin{cases} (k+1,k), & 2 \leq k \leq \ell+1; \\ (2\ell-k+3, 2\ell-k+3), & \ell+2 \leq k \leq 2\ell+1. \end{cases}$$

and

$$C_{R\setminus\{y_3\}}(z_{2k+1}) = \begin{cases} (k+1,k+1), & 1 \leq k \leq \ell; \\ (2\ell-k+2, 2\ell-k+3), & \ell+1 \leq k \leq 2\ell. \end{cases}$$

In the inner cycle,

$$C_{R\setminus\{y_3\}}(y_{2k}) = \begin{cases} (k+2,k-1), & 2 \leq k \leq \ell+1; \\ (2\ell-k+4, 2\ell-k+2), & \ell+2 \leq k \leq 2\ell+1. \end{cases}$$

and

$$C_{R\setminus\{y_3\}}(y_{2k+1}) = \begin{cases} (k,k+2), & 1 \leq k \leq \ell; \\ (2\ell-k+1, 2\ell-k+4), & \ell+1 \leq k \leq 2\ell. \end{cases}$$

Again, in this case, it is clear for the inner cycle that there are no two vertices with the same representation. However, for the outer cycle, $C_{R\setminus\{y_3\}}(z_{3+k}) = C_{R\setminus\{y_3\}}(z_{n-k})$ for $k = 0, 2, \ldots, 2\ell-2$. Note that the pairs with the same representations are distinguished by y_3 since $d(y_3, z_{3+k}) = \lfloor\frac{3+k}{2}\rfloor \neq d(y_3, z_{n-k}) = \lfloor\frac{3+k}{2}\rfloor + 2$ for $k = 0, 2, \ldots, 2\ell-2$. This shows that R resolves the vertices of Γ, which means $\beta(\Gamma) \leq 3$, when $n \equiv 2 \pmod{4}$.

Claim 2: When $n \geq 8$, the cardinality of the fault-tolerant resolving set in Γ is 10.

We can write $n = 4\ell$, $\ell \geq 2$, $\ell \in \mathbb{Z}^+$. Note that, for this, $R = \{y_1, y_2, y_3\}$ is a resolving set of Γ. We show that Γ has a fault-tolerant resolving set of cardinality 10.

As seen from Figure 3, it can be observed that $N[y_1] = \{y_1, y_3, y_{n-1}, z_1\}$, $N[y_2] = \{y_2, y_4, y_n, z_2\}$, and $N[y_3] = \{y_1, y_3, y_5, z_3\}$. Moreover, we find that $\lambda(N_\Gamma(y_1)) = \lambda(N_\Gamma(y_2)) = \lambda(N_\Gamma(y_3)) = \emptyset$. Thus, by using Lemma 3, we find that $R' = \{y_1, y_2, y_3, y_4, y_5, y_{n-1}, y_n, z_1, z_2, z_3\}$ is a fault-tolerant resolving set of Γ. Thus, a fault-tolerant resolving set of Γ with cardinality 10 exists when $n \geq 8$.

Case 2: When $n \equiv 1 \pmod{2}$ with $n \geq 11$.

Based on the location of basis elements in Γ, we further divide this case into two subcases.

Subcase 2.1: When $n \equiv 1 \pmod{4}$.

Claim 1: Γ has a resolving set R of order 3.

In this case, we can write $n = 4\ell + 1$, $1 \leq \ell \in \mathbb{Z}^+$. It can be seen that $\{y_1, y_2, z_3\}$ is a resolving set for the standard Petersen graph $P(5)$. For $P(9)$, we see that $W = \{y_1, y_2, z_4\}$ is a resolving set. Now, we show that, for $n \geq 9$, $R = \{y_1, y_2, z_{2\ell-1}\}$ resolves the vertices of Γ, where $n \equiv 1 \pmod{4}$. In order to show this, first we present representations of the vertices with respect to $R \setminus \{z_{2\ell-1}\}$. The representations of the vertices in the outer cycle are $C_{R \setminus \{z_{2\ell-1}\}}(z_1) = (1,2)$, $C_{R \setminus \{z_{2\ell-1}\}}(z_2) = (2,1)$,

$$C_{R \setminus \{z_{2\ell-1}\}}(z_{2k}) = \begin{cases} (k+1, k), & 2 \leq k \leq \ell; \\ (k, k), & k = \ell + 1; \\ (2\ell - k + 2, 2\ell - k - 3), & \ell + 2 \leq k \leq 2\ell. \end{cases}$$

and

$$C_{R \setminus \{z_{2\ell-1}\}}(z_{2k+1}) = \begin{cases} (k+1, k+1), & 1 \leq k \leq \ell; \\ (2\ell - k + 2, 2\ell - k + 2), & \ell + 1 \leq k \leq 2\ell. \end{cases}$$

Now, the representations of the vertices in the inner cycle are

$$C_{R \setminus \{y_{z_{2\ell-1}}\}}(y_{2k}) = \begin{cases} (k+2, k-1), & 2 \leq k \leq \ell - 1; \\ (k+1, k-1), & k = \ell; \\ (k-1, k-1), & k = \ell + 1; \\ (k-3, k-1), & k = \ell + 2; \\ (2\ell - k + 1, 2\ell - k + 4), & \ell + 3 \leq k \leq 2\ell. \end{cases}$$

and

$$C_{R \setminus \{z_{2\ell-1}\}}(y_{2k+1}) = \begin{cases} (k, k+2), & 1 \leq k \leq \ell - 1; \\ (k, k+1), & k = \ell; \\ (k, k-1), & k = \ell + 1; \\ (2\ell - k + 3, 2\ell - k + 1), & \ell + 2 \leq k \leq 2\ell. \end{cases}$$

From the above discussion, it is clear that $R \setminus \{z_{2\ell-1}\}$ distinguishes all but the following vertices. (i) z_{3+k} and z_{n-k} for $i = 0, 2, \ldots, 2\ell - 6$. (ii) $z_{2\ell-1}$ and $z_{2\ell+5}$ and $y_{2\ell+2}$. (iii) $z_{2\ell+1}$, $z_{2\ell+2}$, and $z_{2\ell+3}$. (iv) $y_{2\ell-1}$ and $y_{2\ell+4}$. (v) $y_{2\ell}$ and $y_{2\ell+5}$. (vi) $z_{2\ell}$ and $y_{2\ell+3}$. (vii) $y_{2\ell+1}$ and $z_{2\ell+4}$. It is easy to see that vertices with the same representation in the outer cycle are at different distances from $z_{2\ell-1}$. $d(z_{2\ell-1}, z_{2\ell+5}) = 5$ and $d(z_{2\ell-1}, y_{2\ell+2}) = 3$, $d(z_{2\ell-1}, y_{2\ell-1}) = 1$ and $d(z_{2\ell-1}, y_{2\ell+4}) = 4$, $d(z_{2\ell-1}, y_{2\ell}) = 2$ and $d(z_{2\ell-1}, y_{2\ell+5}) = 4$, $d(z_{2\ell-1}, z_{2\ell}) = 1$ and $d(z_{2\ell-1}, y_{2\ell+3}) = 3$, $d(z_{2\ell-1}, y_{2\ell+1}) = 2$ and $d(z_{2\ell-1}, z_{2\ell+4}) = 5$. The above discussion shows that R is a resolving set for $V(\Gamma)$ when $n \equiv 1 \pmod{4}$. Hence, $\beta(\Gamma) \leq 3$ for $n \equiv 1 \pmod{4}$.

Claim 2: Γ has a fault-tolerant resolving set of cardinality 12 when $n \geq 11$.

We can write $n = 4\ell + 1$, $\ell \geq 3$ and $\ell \in \mathbb{Z}^+$. Note that, in this case, $R = \{y_1, y_2, z_{2\ell-1}\}$ is a resolving set of Γ. We prove here that Γ has a fault-tolerant resolving set of cardinality 12. From Figure 3, it can be observed that $N[y_1] = \{y_1, y_{n-1}, y_n, z_1\}$, $N[y_2] = \{y_2, y_4, y_n, z_2\}$ and $N[z_{2\ell-1}] =$

$\{z_{2\ell-2}, z_{2\ell-1}, z_{2\ell}, y_{2\ell-1}\}$. Moreover, we find that $\lambda(N_\Gamma(y_1)) = \lambda(N_\Gamma(y_2)) = \lambda(N_\Gamma(z_{2\ell-1})) = \emptyset$. Thus, by using Lemma 3, we find that $R' = \{y_1, y_2, y_3, y_4, y_{2\ell-1}, y_{n-1}, y_n, z_1, z_2, z_{2\ell-2}, z_{2\ell-1}, z_{2\ell}\}$ is a fault-tolerant resolving set of Γ. Thus, there exists a fault-tolerant resolving set of Γ with cardinality 12.

Subcase 2.2: When $n \equiv 3 \pmod 4$.
Claim 1: Resolving set R of order 3 in Γ exists.

We can write $n = 4\ell + 3$, $1 \leq \ell \in \mathbb{Z}^+$. It is not difficult to see that $U = \{y_1, y_2, z_3\}$ resolves $V(P(7))$. For $n \equiv 3 \pmod 4$ and $n \geq 11$, we show that $R = \{y_1, y_2, z_{2\ell+1}\}$ resolves $V(\Gamma = P(n))$. Representations of the vertices in the outer cycle are $C_{R \setminus \{z_{2\ell+1}\}}(z_1) = (1,2)$, $C_{R \setminus \{z_{2\ell+1}\}}(z_2) = (2,1)$,

$$C_{R \setminus \{z_{2\ell+1}\}}(z_{2k}) = \begin{cases} (k+1, k), & 2 \leq k \leq \ell+1; \\ (2\ell-k+3, 2\ell-k+4), & \ell+2 \leq k \leq 2\ell+1. \end{cases}$$

and

$$C_{R \setminus \{z_{2\ell+1}\}}(z_{2k+1}) = \begin{cases} (k+1, k+1), & 1 \leq k \leq \ell+1; \\ (2\ell-k+3, 2\ell-k+3), & \ell+2 \leq k \leq 2\ell+1. \end{cases}$$

Now, in the inner cycle,

$$C_{R \setminus \{z_{2\ell+1}\}}(y_{2k}) = \begin{cases} (k+2, k-1), & 2 \leq k \leq \ell; \\ (k, k-1), & k = \ell+1; \\ (k-2, k-1), & k = \ell+2; \\ (2\ell-k+2, 2\ell-k+5), & \ell+3 \leq k \leq 2\ell+1. \end{cases}$$

and

$$C_{R \setminus \{z_{2\ell+1}\}}(2k+1) = \begin{cases} (k, k+2), & 1 \leq k \leq \ell; \\ (k, k), & k = \ell+1; \\ (2\ell-k+4, 2\ell-k+2), & \ell+2 \leq k \leq 2\ell+1. \end{cases}$$

Again, in this case, $R \setminus \{z_{2\ell+1}\}$ distinguishes all the vertices in Γ except the following vertices: (i) z_{3+i} and z_{n-i} for $i = 0, 2, \ldots, 2\ell - 4$. (ii) $z_{2\ell}, y_{2\ell+2}$. (iii) $z_{2\ell+1}, z_{2\ell+5}$, and $y_{2\ell+3}$. (iv) $y_{2\ell+4}$ and $z_{2\ell+6}$. It is easy to see that vertices with same representation in the outer cycle are at different distances from $z_{2\ell+1}$. $d(z_{2\ell+1}, z_{2\ell}) = 1$, $d(z_{2\ell+1}, y_{2\ell+2}) = 2$ and $d(z_{2\ell+1}, y_{2\ell+5}) = 4$, $d(z_{2\ell+1}, y_{2\ell+3}) = 2$ and $d(z_{2\ell+1}, y_{2\ell+4}) = 3$, $d(z_{2\ell+1}, y_{2\ell+6}) = 5$. The above discussion shows that R is a resolving set for $V(\Gamma)$ when $n \equiv 3 \pmod 4$ and $n \geq 11$. Hence, $\beta(\Gamma) \leq 3$ for $n \equiv 3 \pmod 4$.

Claim 2: Γ has a fault-tolerant resolving set of cardinality 12 with $n \geq 11$.

We can write $n = 4\ell + 3$, $\ell \geq 2$, $\ell \in \mathbb{Z}^+$. Note that, in this case, $R = \{y_1, y_2, z_{2\ell+1}\}$ is a resolving set of Γ.

We show that Γ has a fault-tolerant resolving set of cardinality 12.
From Figure 3, it can be observed that $N[y_1] = \{y_1, y_3, y_{n-1}, z_1\}$, $N[y_2] = \{y_2, y_4, y_n, z_2\}$, and $N[z_{2\ell+1}] = \{z_{2\ell}, z_{2\ell+1}, z_{2\ell+2}, y_{2\ell+1}\}$. Moreover, we find that $\lambda(N_\Gamma(y_1)) = \lambda(N_\Gamma(y_2)) = \lambda(N_\Gamma(z_{2\ell+1})) = \emptyset$. Thus, by using Lemma 3, we find that $R' = \{y_1, y_2, y_3, y_4, y_{n-1}, y_n, y_{2\ell+1}, z_1, z_2, z_{2\ell}, z_{2\ell+1}, z_{2\ell+2}\}$ is a fault-tolerant resolving set of $P_{n,2}$. Thus, a fault-tolerant resolving set of $P_{n,2}$ with cardinality 12 exists.

By using Proposition 1, the above discussion, and Inequality (1), we find that $\beta'(\Gamma) \geq 4$. □

As a consequence of Theorem 9, we have the following corollary. It provides a fault-tolerant metric dimension analog of Proposition 2.

Corollary 1. *The extended Petersen graph $P(n)$ is a family of graphs with a constant fault-tolerant metric dimension.*

Proof. By Theorem 9, we have

$$4 \leq \beta'(P(n)) \leq \begin{cases} 10, & \text{if } n \equiv 0 (\mod 2) \text{ with } n \geq 8; \\ 12, & \text{if } n \equiv 1 (\mod 2) \text{ with } n \geq 11. \end{cases}$$

This implies that the fault-tolerant metric dimension of $P(n)$ does not depend on the defining parameter n. Thus, by definition, $P(n)$ is a family of graphs with a constant fault-tolerant metric dimension. □

In view of Lemma 3 and Proposition 1, we find enough reasoning to propose the following conjecture on the greatest lower bound of the fault-tolerant metric dimension for the extended Petersen graph $P(n)$.

Conjecture 1. *Let Γ be the extended Petersen graph $P(n)$; then,*

$$\beta'(\Gamma) \geq \begin{cases} 10, & \text{if } n \equiv 0 (\mod 2) \text{ with } n \geq 8; \\ 12, & \text{if } n \equiv 1 (\mod 2) \text{ with } n \geq 11, \end{cases}$$

and thus, we have

$$\beta'(\Gamma) = \begin{cases} 10, & \text{if } n \equiv 0 (\mod 2) \text{ with } n \geq 8; \\ 12, & \text{if } n \equiv 1 (\mod 2) \text{ with } n \geq 11. \end{cases}$$

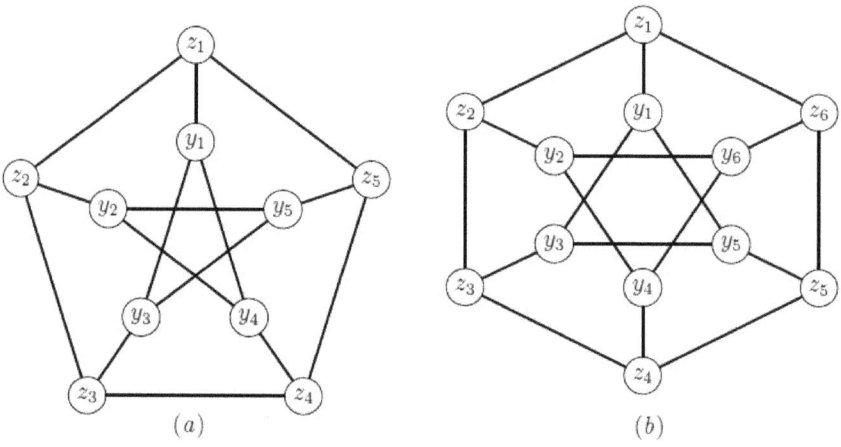

Figure 3. (**a**) The extended Petersen graph $P(5)$, (**b**) The extended Petersen graph $P(6)$.

3.4. Anti-Prism Graphs

The cross product of a cycle C_n and P_2 is actually called a prism, usually denoted by $D(n)$. In [11], it was shown that

$$\beta(P_m \square C_n) = \begin{cases} 2, & \text{if } n \text{ is odd}; \\ 3, & \text{if } n \text{ is even}. \end{cases}$$

This implies that

$$\beta(D(n)) = \begin{cases} 2, & \text{if } n \text{ is odd}; \\ 3, & \text{if } n \text{ is even}. \end{cases}$$

By applying Equation (1) and Theorem 4 to the prism graph $D(n)$, we find the following result.

Proposition 3. *The prism graph $D(n)$ has a constant fault-tolerant metric dimension.*

We investigate fault-tolerant resolvability in the anti-prism graphs. The anti-prism $A(n)$ [35] is a 4-regular graph. It is the octahedron for $n \geq 3$. For $n \geq 3$, the anti-prism $A(n)$ consists of an inner cycle $y_1, y_2, \ldots, y_n$, an outer cycle $z_1, z_2, \ldots, z_n$, and a set of n spokes $y_k z_k$ and $y_{k+1} z_k$, $k = 1, 2, \ldots, n$, with indices taken as modulo n. Thus, $|V(A(n))| = 2n$ and $|E(A(n))| = 4n$.

Javaid et al. [34] showed the following result.

Proposition 4. [34] *Let Γ be the anti-prism graph $A(n)$ with $n \geq 3$; then, $\beta(\Gamma) = 3$.*

They also showed the following:

Proposition 5. [34] *The anti-prism graph $A(n)$ has a constant metric dimension.*

In this section, we present the main results, and, for the anti-prism graph $A(n)$, the upper and lower bounds on the fault-tolerant metric dimension are proved. Note that Claim 1 in the following result was essentially shown in Proposition 4.

Theorem 10. *Let Γ be the anti-prism graph $A(n)$, with $n \geq 10$; then, $4 \leq \beta'(\Gamma) \leq 14$.*

Proof. Let $n = 2\ell$ or $n = 2\ell + 1$ for even or odd n, respectively.

Claim 1: A resolving set R of order 3 exists in Γ.

Based on the location of basis elements in G, we divide this in two cases.

Case 1: When n is even, $n = 2\ell$, with $\ell \geq 3$.

For $n \geq 6$, there exists a resolving set R of cardinality 3. $R = \{z_1, z_3, z_{\ell+1}\}$ is a resolving set. Representation of the vertices in the outer cycle with respect to $\{z_1, z_3\}$ is as follows. As we can see, $C_{R\setminus\{z_{\ell+1}\}}(z_2) = (1,1)$; in general, the representations of the vertices in the outer cycle are

$$C_{R\setminus\{z_{\ell+1}\}}(z_k) = \begin{cases} (k-1, k-3), & 4 \leq k \leq \ell+1; \\ (n-k+1, k-3), & k = \ell+2, k = \ell+3; \\ (n-k+1, n-k+3), & \ell+4 \leq k \leq n. \end{cases}$$

Representations of the vertices in the inner cycle are $C_{R\setminus\{z_{\ell+1}\}}(y_1) = (1,3)$, $C_{R\setminus\{z_{\ell+1}\}}(y_2) = (1,2)$, $C_{R\setminus\{z_{\ell+1}\}}(y_3) = (2,1)$. In general,

$$C_{R\setminus\{z_{\ell+1}\}}(y_k) = \begin{cases} (k-1, k-3), & 4 \leq k \leq \ell+1; \\ (\ell, \ell-1), & k = \ell+2; \\ (\ell-1, \ell), & k = \ell+3; \\ (n-k+2, n-k+4), & \ell+4 \leq k \leq n. \end{cases}$$

Case 2: For odd n, $n = 2\ell + 1$ with $\ell \geq 3$. Then,

$$C_{R\setminus\{z_{\ell+1}\}}(y_k) = \begin{cases} (k-1, k-3), & 4 \leq k \leq \ell+2; \\ (\ell, \ell), & k = \ell+3; \\ (n-k+2, n-k+4), & \ell+4 \leq k \leq n. \end{cases}$$

From the above discussion, we can see there are few vertices with the same representation y_k, z_k, with $4 \leq k \leq \ell+1$; for even and odd n, y_1, z_n and y_{s+1}, z_s with $\ell+3 \leq s \leq n-1$ and $\ell+4 \leq s \leq n-1$, respectively. In order to distinguish the pairs with the same vertices, we take $y_{\ell+1}$ in the outer and inner cycle. Representation in the outer cycle is

$$d(y_{\ell+1}, z_s) = \begin{cases} \ell - s + 1, & 1 \leq s \leq \ell; \\ s - \ell - 1, & \ell + 2 \leq s \leq n. \end{cases}$$

Now, representation in the inner cycle is

$$d(y_{\ell+1}, y_k) = \begin{cases} \ell - k + 2, & 1 \leq k \leq \ell; \\ 1, & s = \ell + 1; \\ k - \ell - 1, & \ell + 2 \leq k \leq n. \end{cases}$$

Also, $d(z_{\ell+1}, y_1) = n - \ell$. So, from the above discussion, we see that $z_{\ell+1}$ distinguishes the vertices of Γ. Hence, $R = \{z_1, z_3, z_{\ell+1}\}$ is a resolving set of Γ. This shows that $\beta(\Gamma) \leq 3$.

Claim 2: There exists a fault-tolerant resolving set of cardinality 14 in Γ.

Γ contains a resolving set R of order 3. We show that Γ has a fault-tolerant resolving set of 14. Now, we can see from Figure 4 that $N[z_1] = \{z_1, z_2, z_n, y_1, y_2\}$, $N[z_3] = \{z_2, z_3, z_4, y_3, y_4\}$, and $N[z_{\ell+1}] = \{z_\ell, z_{\ell+1}, z_{\ell+2}, y_{\ell+1}, y_{\ell+2}\}$. Moreover, we find that $\lambda(N_\Gamma(z_1)) = \lambda(N_\Gamma(z_2)) = \lambda(N_\Gamma(z_{\ell+1})) = \emptyset$. Thus, by using Lemma 3, we find that $R' = \{y_1, y_2, y_3, y_4, z_1, z_2, z_3, z_4, y_{\ell+1}, y_{\ell+2}, z_\ell, z_{\ell+1}, z_{\ell+2}, z_n\}$. Thus, there exists a fault-tolerant resolving set of Γ with cardinality 14 when $n \geq 10$.

By using Proposition 4, the above discussion, and Inequality (1), we find that $\beta'(\Gamma) \geq 4$. □

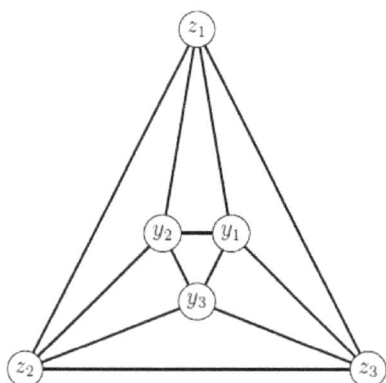

Figure 4. The anti-prism graph A_3.

As a result of Theorem 10, we present the following corollary. It provides a fault-tolerant metric dimension analog of Proposition 5.

Corollary 2. *The anti-prism graph $A(n)$ has a constant fault-tolerant metric dimension.*

Proof. By Theorem 10, we have $4 \leq \beta'(A(n)) \leq 14$. This implies that the fault-tolerant metric dimension of $A(n)$ does not depend on the defining parameter n. Thus, by definition, $A(n)$ is a family of graphs with a constant fault-tolerant metric dimension. □

In view of Lemma 3 and Proposition 4, we propose the following conjecture on the greatest lower bound on the fault-tolerant metric dimension for the anti-prism graph $A(n)$.

Conjecture 2. *Let Γ be an anti-prism graph $A(n)$ and $n \geq 10$; then, $\beta'(\Gamma) \geq 14$, and thus, $\beta'(\Gamma) = 14$.*

3.5. Squared Cycle Graphs

Javaid et al. [32] proved that the fault-tolerant metric dimension of cycle graphs is 3.

Lemma 4. *Let Γ be the cycle graph C_n, where $n \geq 3$. Then, $\beta'(\Gamma) = 3$.*

In the subsequent section, we study fault-tolerant resolvability of squared cycle graphs, which are somewhat of an extension of cycle graphs. The squared cycle graph $S(n)$ is a 4-regular graph of order n, with $V(S(n)) = \{y_1, y_2, \ldots, y_n\}$. For each k ($1 \leq k \leq n$), we join y_k to y_{k+1}, y_{k+2} and to y_{k-1}, y_{k-2}. If we cyclically arrange the vertices $y_1, y_2, \ldots, y_n$, then each vertex y_k is adjacent to the 2 vertices that immediately follow y_k and 2 vertices that immediately precede y_k. Thus, $S(n)$ is a *four*-regular graph. In Figure 5, we depict the squared cycle graph $S(n)$ for $n = 8$ and $n = 9$. Note that the squared cycle graph is a special case of the Harary graph $H(m, n)$, with $m = 4$.

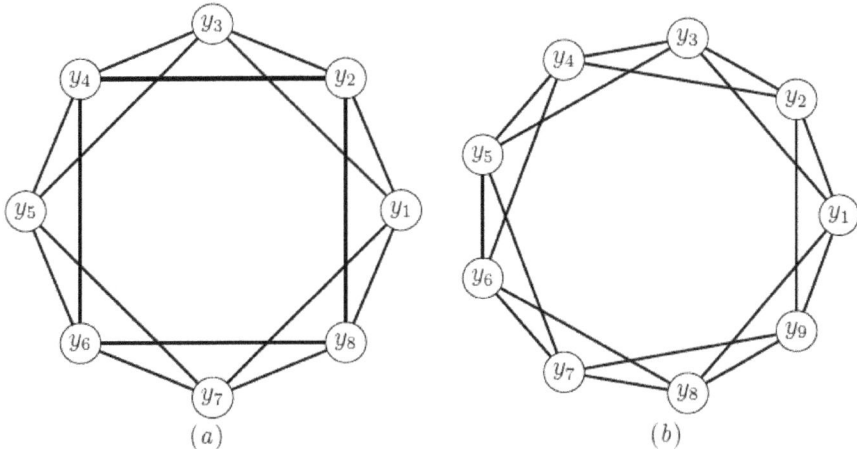

Figure 5. (a) The squared cycle graph $S(8)$, (b) the squared cycle graph $S(9)$.

Javaid et al. [34] showed the following result.

Proposition 6. [34] *For $n \equiv 0, 2, 3 \pmod 4$, let Γ be the squared cycle graph $S(n)$ with $n \geq 5$. Then, $\beta(\Gamma) = 3$.*

They also showed the following:

Proposition 7. [34] *For a positive integer n, the squared cycle graph $S(n)$ is a family of graphs with a constant metric dimension.*

The following is the main result of this section. Note that Claim 1 in the following result was essentially shown in Proposition 6.

Theorem 11. *Let Γ be the squared cycle graph $S(n)$; then,*

$$\beta'(\Gamma) \leq \begin{cases} 7, & \text{if } n \equiv 0, 2, 3 \pmod 4 \text{ with } n \geq 7; \\ 12, & \text{if } n \equiv 1 \pmod 4 \text{ with } n \geq 13, \end{cases}$$

and
$$\beta'(\Gamma) \geq \begin{cases} 4, & \text{if } n \equiv 0,2,3(\mod 4) \text{ with } n \geq 5; \\ \delta, & \text{if } n \equiv 1(\mod 4) \text{ with } n \geq 5. \end{cases}$$

where
$$\delta = \begin{cases} 4, & \text{if } \beta(\Gamma) > 2; \\ 5, & \text{if } \beta(\Gamma) > 3. \end{cases}$$

Proof. Let Γ be the squared cycle graph $S(n)$. We show the following claims to complete the proof.

Claim 1: There exists a resolving set R of order 3 in Γ.

Case 1: When $n \equiv 0,2,3(\mod 4)$ with $n \geq 7$.

Based on the location of basis elements in Γ, we further divide this case into three subcases.

Subcase 1.1: When $n \equiv 0(\mod 4)$.

We can write $n = 4\ell$, $\ell \in \mathbb{Z}^+$. We prove that $R = \{y_1, y_2, y_3\}$ resolves $V(\Gamma)$. In order to show that R resolves vertices of $V(\Gamma)$, the representation of the vertices of $V(\Gamma)$ with respect to the resolving set is given.

$$C_R(y_{2k}) = \begin{cases} (k, k-1, k-1), & 2 \leq k \leq \ell; \\ (\ell, \ell, \ell), & k = \ell+1; \\ (2\ell-k+1, 2\ell-k+1, 2\ell-k+2), & \ell+2 \leq k \leq 2\ell. \end{cases}$$

and

$$C_R(y_{2k+1}) = \begin{cases} (k, k, k-1), & 2 \leq k \leq \ell; \\ (2\ell-k, 2\ell-k+1, 2\ell-k+1), & \ell+1 \leq k \leq 2\ell-1. \end{cases}$$

From the above discussion, it is shown that all vertices have a distinct representation for $n \equiv 0(\mod 4)$, so $\beta(G) \leq 3$.

Subcase 1.2: When $n \equiv 2(\mod 4)$.

It can be written as $n = 4\ell + 2$, $\ell \in \mathbb{Z}^+$.

$$C_R(y_{2k}) = \begin{cases} (k, k-1, k-1), & 2 \leq k \leq \ell+1; \\ (2\ell-k+2, 2\ell-k+2, 2\ell-k+3), & \ell+2 \leq k \leq 2\ell+1. \end{cases}$$

and

$$C_R(y_{2k+1}) = \begin{cases} (k, k, k-1), & 2 \leq k \leq \ell; \\ (\ell, \ell+1, \ell), & k = \ell+1; \\ (2\ell-k+1, 2\ell-k+2, 2\ell-k+2), & \ell+2 \leq k \leq 2\ell. \end{cases}$$

Again, all vertices in Γ have a distinct representation, which shows that $\beta(\Gamma) \leq 3$ when $n \equiv 2(\mod 4)$.

Subcase 1.3: When $n \equiv 3(\mod 4)$.

We can write $n = 4\ell + 3$, $\ell \in \mathbb{Z}^+$.

$$C_R(y_{2k}) = \begin{cases} (k, k-1, k-1), & 2 \leq k \leq \ell+1; \\ (2\ell-k+2, 2\ell-k+3, 2\ell-k+3), & \ell+2 \leq k \leq 2\ell+1. \end{cases}$$

and

$$C_R(y_{2k+1}) = \begin{cases} (k, k, k-1), & 2 \leq k \leq \ell+1; \\ (2\ell-k+2, 2\ell-k+2, 2\ell-k+3), & \ell+2 \leq k \leq 2\ell+1. \end{cases}$$

Once again, we can see that all vertices in Γ have a distinct representation, which shows that $\beta(\Gamma) \leq 3$ when $n \equiv 3(\mod 4)$.

Claim 2: Γ has a fault-tolerant resolving set of cardinality 7 when $n \geq 7$.

We can write $n = 4\ell$, $\ell \geq 2$, $\ell \in \mathbb{Z}^+$. Note that, in this case, $R = \{y_1, y_2, y_3\}$ is a resolving set of Γ. We show that Γ is the graph in which there exists a fault-tolerant resolving set of cardinality 7. From Figure 5, it can be observed that $N[y_1] = \{y_1, y_2, y_3, y_{n-1}, y_n\}$, $N[y_2] = \{y_1, y_2, y_3, y_4, y_n\}$, and $N[y_3] = \{y_1, y_2, y_3, y_4, y_5\}$. Moreover, we find that $\lambda(N_\Gamma(y_1)) = \lambda(N_\Gamma(y_2)) = \lambda(N_\Gamma(y_3)) = \emptyset$. Thus, by using Lemma 3, we find that $R' = \{y_1, y_2, y_3, y_4, y_5, y_{n-1}, y_n\}$ is a fault-tolerant resolving set of Γ. Thus, it is shown that a fault-tolerant resolving set of Γ with cardinality 7 exists when $n \geq 7$.

Claim 1: There exists a resolving set R of order 4 in Γ.
Case 1: When $n \equiv 1(\mod 4)$.

Now, we can write $n = 4\ell + 1$, $\ell \in \mathbb{Z}^+$.

$$C_R(y_{2k}) = \begin{cases} (k, k-1, k-1), & 2 \leq k \leq \ell; \\ (\ell, \ell, \ell), & k = \ell + 1; \\ (2\ell - k + 1, 2\ell - k + 2, 2\ell - k + 2), & \ell + 2 \leq k \leq 2\ell. \end{cases}$$

and

$$C_R(y_{2k+1}) = \begin{cases} (k, k, k-1), & 2 \leq k \leq \ell; \\ (\ell, \ell, \ell), & k = \ell + 1; \\ (2\ell - k + 1, 2\ell - k + 1, 2\ell - k + 2), & \ell + 2 \leq k \leq 2\ell. \end{cases}$$

For $n \equiv 1(\mod 4)$, the vertices $y_{2\ell+2}$ and $y_{2\ell+3}$ have the same representation. In order to have distinct representations, we add $y_{2\ell+2}$ to the resolving set R. Now, $R' = \{y_1, y_2, y_3, y_{2\ell+2}\}$ resolves $V(\Gamma)$. So, it is shown that $\beta(\Gamma) \leq 4$ for $n \equiv 1(\mod 4)$.

Claim 2: When $n \geq 13$, Γ has a fault-tolerant resolving set of cardinality 12. It can be written $n = 4\ell + 1$, $\ell \geq 3$, $\ell \in \mathbb{Z}^+$. Now, for this, $R = \{y_1, y_2, y_3, y_{2\ell+2}\}$ is a resolving set of Γ. We show that Γ has a fault-tolerant resolving set of cardinality 12. From Figure 5, it can be observed that $N[y_1] = \{y_1, y_2, y_3, y_{n-1}, y_n\}$, $N[y_2] = \{y_1, y_2, y_3, y_4, y_n\}$, $N[y_3] = \{y_1, y_2, y_3, y_4, y_5\}$, and $N[y_{2\ell+2}] = \{y_{2\ell}, y_{2\ell+1}, y_{2\ell+2}, y_{2\ell+3}, y_{2\ell+4}\}$. Moreover, we find that $\lambda(N_\Gamma(y_1)) = \lambda(N_\Gamma(y_2)) = \lambda(N_\Gamma(y_3)) = \lambda(N_\Gamma(y_{2\ell+2})) = \emptyset$. Thus, by using Lemma 3, we find that $R' = \{y_1, y_2, y_3, y_4, y_5, y_{n-1}, y_n, y_{2\ell}, y_{2\ell+1}, y_{2\ell+2}, y_{2\ell+3}, y_{2\ell+4}\}$ is a fault-tolerant resolving set of Γ. Thus, Γ is the graph in which there exists a fault-tolerant resolving set of cardinality 12 when $n \geq 13$. In view of Lemma 3 and Proposition 1, we find enough reasoning to propose the following conjecture on the lower bound of the fault-tolerant metric dimension for the squared cycle graph $S(n)$.

From the above discussion, Inequality, and Proposition 6, we find that

$$\beta'(\Gamma) \geq \begin{cases} 4, & \text{if } n \equiv 0, 2, 3(\mod 4) \text{ with } n \geq 5; \\ \delta, & \text{if } n \equiv 1(\mod 4) \text{ with } n \geq 5. \end{cases}$$

where

$$\delta = \begin{cases} 4, & \text{if } \beta(\Gamma) > 2; \\ 5, & \text{if } \beta(\Gamma) > 3. \end{cases}$$

□

Because of Theorem 11, the following corollary is presented. It provides a fault-tolerant metric dimension analogous to Proposition 7.

Corollary 3. *The squared cycle graph $S(n)$ is a family of graphs with a constant fault-tolerant metric dimension.*

Proof. By Theorem 11, we have

$$\beta'(S(n)) \leq \begin{cases} 7, & \text{if } n \equiv 0,2,3(\mod 4) \text{ with } n \geq 7; \\ 12, & \text{if } n \equiv 1(\mod 4) \text{ with } n \geq 13, \end{cases}$$

and

$$\beta'(\Gamma) \geq \begin{cases} 4, & \text{if } n \equiv 0,2,3(\mod 4) \text{ with } n \geq 5; \\ \delta, & \text{if } n \equiv 1(\mod 4) \text{ with } n \geq 5. \end{cases}$$

where

$$\delta = \begin{cases} 4, & \text{if } \beta(\Gamma) > 2; \\ 5, & \text{if } \beta(\Gamma) > 3. \end{cases}$$

This implies that the fault-tolerant metric dimension of $S(n)$ does not depend on the defining parameter n. Thus, by definition, $S(n)$ is a family of graphs with a constant fault-tolerant metric dimension. □

In view of Lemma 3 and Proposition 6, the following conjecture is proposed.

Conjecture 3. *Let Γ be the squared cycle graph $S(n)$ such that $n \equiv 0,2,3(\mod 4)$, with $n \geq 7$. Then, $\beta'(\Gamma) \geq 7$; thus, we have $\beta'(\Gamma) = 7$.*

4. Concluding Remarks

This paper investigates the fault-tolerant metric dimension of graphs. We present certain characterizations of graphs with some extreme values of the fault-tolerant metric dimension. A method is presented to calculate the upper bounds on the fault-tolerant metric dimension of graphs. We study fault-tolerant resolvability in three non-finite families of regular graphs and show that they are the families of graphs with a constant fault-tolerant metric dimension. The following remark shows a comparison between the upper bound produced by our method and the upper bound by Hernando et al.

Remark 1. *Note that the upper bound on the fault-tolerant metric dimension provided by Theorem 4 is always crude. For example, if $\Gamma \in \{P(n), A(n)\}$ or $S(n)$, with $n \equiv 0,2,3(\mod 4)$, then by using $\beta(\Gamma) = 3$ in Theorem 4, we obtain $\beta'(\Gamma) \leq 153$, which is not interesting. In view of this fact, Lemma 3 always gives a much better bound on $\beta'(\Gamma)$.*

Recently, Raza et al. [36] studied the fault-tolerant metric dimension of hexagonal, honeycomb, and hex-derived networks. See [37] for a study of hexagonal and honeycomb networks. We conclude the paper with some open problems.

Problem 1. *In view of the characterizations of graphs with fault-tolerant metric dimension 2 and $n - 1$, the following open problems are proposed.*

(i) *Characterize n-ordered graphs with fault-tolerant metric dimension 3.*
(ii) *Characterize n-ordered graphs with fault-tolerant metric dimension $n - 2$.*

We also propose the following open problems:

(i) *Study the fault-tolerant metric dimension of other interesting families of the regular graph, such as the prism graphs, and the generalized Petersen graphs $P(n,m)$, $m > 2$.*
(ii) *Investigate the fault-tolerant metric dimension of strongly regular graphs, such as the square grid graphs and the triangular graphs.*
(iii) *In view of Raza et al. [36], study the fault-tolerant resolvability in other direct and multiplex interconnection networks, such as the butterfly and Benes networks.*

(iv) Study the applicability of fault-tolerant resolvability in the optimal flow control of multiplex interconnection networks; see, for example, [38–40] for a through study on multiplex networks.

Author Contributions: The idea to study the fault-tolerant resolvability was proposed by S.H. After several discussion with X.-F.P. and M.I., they approved the idea to work on these problems. H.R. worked on the problem with assistance from S.H. The Results section was written by H.R. and S.H. The Introduction was written by M.I., and the Preliminaries section was arranged and written by X.-F.P. The final version was carefully read by M.I. and X.-F.P. H.R. finalized the write-up of the paper by following suggestions from other authors.

Funding: This research was supported by the Startup Research Grant Program of Higher Education Commission (HEC) Pakistan under Project# 2285 and grant No. 21-2285/SRGP/R&D/HEC/2018 received by Sakander Hayat. Muhammad Imran was supported by the Start-up Research Grant 2016 of United Arab Emirates University, Al Ain, United Arab Emirates via Grant No. G00002233 and UPAR Grant of United Arab Emirates University via Grant No. G00002590. APC was covered by Hassan Raza who was funded by a Chinese Government Scholarship.

Acknowledgments: The authors are grateful to the anonymous reviewers for a careful reading of this paper and for all their comments, which lead to a number of improvements of the paper.

Conflicts of Interest: The authors declare no conflict of interest.

References

1. Slater, P.J. Leaves of trees. Proceedings of the 6th Southeastern Conference on Combinatorics, Graph Theory, and Computing. *Congr. Numer.* **1975**, *14*, 549–559.
2. Harary, F.; Melter, R.A. On the metric dimension of a graph. *Ars Comb.* **1976**, *2*, 191–195.
3. Khuller, S.; Raghavachari, B.; Rosenfeld, A. Landmarks in graphs. *Discret. Appl. Math.* **1996**, *70*, 217–229. [CrossRef]
4. Liu, K.; Abu-Ghazaleh, N. Virtual coordinate back tracking for void travarsal in geographic routing. *Lect. Notes Comput. Sci.* **2006**, *4104*, 46–59.
5. Beerloiva, Z.; Eberhard, F.; Erlebach, T.; Hall, A.; Hoffmann, M.; Mihalák, M.; Ram, L. Network discovery and verification. *IEEEE J. Sel. Area Commun.* **2006**, *24*, 2168–2181. [CrossRef]
6. Chartrand, G.; Eroh, L.; Johnson, M.A.; Oellermann, O.R. Resolvability in graphs and the metric dimension of a graph. *Discret. Appl. Math.* **2000**, *150*, 99–113. [CrossRef]
7. Bailey, R.F.; Meagher, K. On the metric dimension of Grassmann graphs. *Discret. Math. Theor. Comput. Sci.* **2011**, *13*, 97–104.
8. Bailey, R.F.; Cameron, P.J. Basie size, metric dimension and other invariants of groups and graphs. *Bull. Lond. Math. Soc.* **2011**, *43*, 209–242. [CrossRef]
9. Fehr, M.; Gosselin, S. Oellermann, O. The metric dimension of Cayley digraphs. *Discret. Math.* **2006**, *306*, 31–41. [CrossRef]
10. Ahmad, A.; Imran, M.; Al-Mushayt, O.; Bokhary, S.A.U.H. On the metric dimension of barycentric subdividion of Cayley graph $Cay(Z_n \oplus Z_m)$. *Miskolc Math. Notes* **2015**, *16*, 637–646.
11. Cáceres, J.; Hernando, C.; Mora, M.; Pelayoe, I.M.; Puertas, M.L.; Seara, C.; Wood, D.R. On the metric dimension of cartesian products of graphs. *SIAM J. Discret. Math.* **2007**, *21*, 423–441. [CrossRef]
12. Vetrík, T.; Ahmad, A. Computing the metric dimension of the categorial product of some graphs. *Int. J. Comput. Math.* **2015**, *94*, 363–371. [CrossRef]
13. Siddiqui, H.M.A.; Imran, M. Computing the metric dimension of wheel related graphs. *Appl. Math. Comput.* **2014**, *242*, 624–632.
14. Kratica, J.; Kovačević-Vujčić, V.; Čangalović, M.; Stojanović, M. Minimal doubly resolving sets and the strong metric dimension of some convex polytopes. *Appl. Math. Comput.* **2012**, *218*, 9790–9801. [CrossRef]
15. Imran, M.; Siddiqui, H.M.A. Computing the metric dimension of conves polytopes generated by the wheel related graphs. *Acta Math. Hung.* **2016**, *149*, 10–30. [CrossRef]
16. Cáceres, J.; Hernando, C.; Mora, M.; Pelayoe, I.M.; Puertas, M.L. On the metric dimension of infinite graphs. *Electron. Notes Discret. Math.* **2009**, *35*, 15–20. [CrossRef]
17. Garey, M.R.; Johnson, D.S. *Computers and Intractability: A Guide to the Theory of NP–Completeness*; W.H. Freeman and Company: New York, NY, USA, 1979.

18. Hernando, C.; Mora, M.; Slater, P.J.; Wood, D.R. Fault-tolerant metric dimension of graphs. In *Proceedings International Conference on Convexity in Discrete Structures*; Ramanujan Mathematical Society Lecture Notes; Ramanujan Mathematical Society: Tiruchirappalli, India, 2008; pp. 81–85.
19. Chartrand, G.; Zhang, P. The theory and applications of resolvability in graphs: A survey. *Congr. Numer.* **2003**, *160*, 47–68.
20. Krishnan, S.; Rajan, B. Fault-tolerant resolvability of certain crystal structures. *Appl. Math.* **2016**, *7*, 599–604. [CrossRef]
21. Raza, H.; Hayat, S.; Pan, X.-F. On the fault-tolerant metric dimension of convex polytopes. *Appl. Math. Comput.* **2018**, *339*, 172–185. [CrossRef]
22. Raza, H.; Hayat, S.; Pan, X.-F. Binary locating-dominating sets in rotationally-symmetric convex polytopes. *Symmetry* **2018**, *10*, 727. [CrossRef]
23. Salman, M.; Javaid, I.; Chaudhry, M.A. Minimum fault-tolerant, local and strong metric dimension of graphs. *arXiv* **2014**, arxiv:1409.2695. [CrossRef]
24. Hayat, S. Computing distance-based topological descriptors of complex chemical networks: New theoretical techniques. *Chem. Phys. Lett.* **2017**, *688*, 51–58. [CrossRef]
25. Hayat, S.; Imran, M. Computation of topological indices of certain networks. *Appl. Math. Comput.* **2014**, *240*, 213–228. [CrossRef]
26. Hayat, S.; Malik, M.A.; Imran, M. Computing topological indices of honeycomb derived networks. *Rom. J. Inf. Sci. Technol.* **2015**, *18*, 144–165.
27. Hayat, S.; Wang, S.; Liu, J.-B. Valency-based topological descriptors of chemical networks and their applications. *Appl. Math. Model.* **2018**, *60*, 164–178. [CrossRef]
28. Imran, M.; Hayat, S.; Malik, M.Y.H. On topological indices of certain interconnection networks. *Appl. Math. Comput.* **2014**, *244*, 936–951. [CrossRef]
29. Bondy, J.A.; Murty, U.S.R. *Graph Theory*; Springer: New York, NY, USA, 2008.
30. Shang, Y. Resilient consensus of switched multi-agent systems. *Syst. Control Lett.* **2018**, *122*, 12–18. [CrossRef]
31. Shang, Y. Resilient multiscale coordination control against adversarial nodes. *Energies* **2018**, *11*, 1844. [CrossRef]
32. Javaid, I.; Salman, M.; Chaudhry, M.A.; Shokat, S. Fault-tolerance in resolvibility. *Util. Math.* **2009**, *80*, 263–275.
33. Watkins, M.E. A theorem on Tait colorings with an application to the generalized Petersen graphs. *J. Comb. Theory* **1969**, *6*, 152–164. [CrossRef]
34. Javaid, I.; Rahim, T.; Ali, K. Families of regular graphs with constant metric dimension. *Util. Math.* **2008**, *65*, 21–33.
35. Gallian, J.A. A dynamic survey of graph labeling. *Electron. J. Comb.* **2018**, #DS6, 1–219. [PubMed]
36. Raza, H.; Hayat, S.; Pan, X.-F. On the fault-tolerant metric dimension of certain interconnection networks. *J. Appl. Math. Comput.* **2018**. [CrossRef]
37. Chen, M.S.; Shin, K.G.; Kandlur, D.D. Addressing, routing and broadcasting in hexagonal mesh multiprocessors. *IEEE Trans. Comput.* **1990**, *39*, 10–18. [CrossRef]
38. Wang, W.-H.; Palaniswami, M.; Low, H.L. Optimal flow control and routing in multi-path networks. *Perform. Eval.* **2003**, *52*, 119–132. [CrossRef]
39. Shang, Y. Deffuant model of opinion formation in one-dimensional multiplex networks. *J. Phys. A Math. Theor.* **2015**, *48*, 395101. [CrossRef]
40. Antonopoulos, C.G.; Shang, Y. Opinion formation in multiplex networks with general initial distributions. *Sci. Rep.* **2018**, *8*, 2852. [CrossRef]

© 2019 by the authors. Licensee MDPI, Basel, Switzerland. This article is an open access article distributed under the terms and conditions of the Creative Commons Attribution (CC BY) license (http://creativecommons.org/licenses/by/4.0/).

Article

Distance and Adjacency Energies of Multi-Level Wheel Networks

Jia-Bao Liu [1], Mobeen Munir [2,*], Amina Yousaf [2], Asim Naseem [3] and Khudaija Ayub [4]

[1] School of Mathematics and Physics, Anhui Jianzhu University, Hefei 230601, China; liujiabaoad@163.com
[2] Department of Mathematics, Division of Science and Technology, University of Education, Lahore 54000, Pakistan; aminakhan1056@gmail.com
[3] Department of Mathematics, Government College University Lahore, Lahore 54000, Pakistan; asimroz@gmail.com
[4] Department of Mathematical Sciences, Federal Urdu University of Science and Technology, Karachi 75270, Pakistan; khudaijaayub@yahoo.com
* Correspondence: mmunir@ue.edu.pk

Received: 11 December 2018; Accepted: 27 December 2018; Published: 4 January 2019

Abstract: Energies of molecular graphs have various applications in chemistry, polymerization, computer networking and pharmacy. In this paper, we give general closed forms of distance and adjacency energies of generalized wheel networks $W_{n,m}$. Consequently, we give these results for classical wheel graphs. We also give pictorial dependencies of energies on the involved parameters $m \geq 3$ and n.

Keywords: distance matrix; adjacency matrix; distance energy; adjacency energy; wheel graphs

1. Introduction

Energy is referred to as the sum of absolute values of any operator. In quantum chemistry, the solutions of the Schrodinger equation is approximately reduced to the evaluation of eigenvalues and corresponding eigenvectors of the Hamiltonian operator. Often, Hamiltonian operators are approximately expressed as

$$H = \alpha I + \beta A(G), \qquad (1)$$

where α and β are the empirical constants of Huckel molecular orbital theory and $A(G)$ is the adjacency matrix of the Huckel graph constructed for the π-electron network of conjugated hydro-carbons [1]. In this way, characteristic polynomials entered the arena of chemical graph theory. It has also attracted keen interest even from pure mathematicians due to the interesting problems that originate from the mathematical structures and their symmetries involved. The ordinary energy of the graph is defined as the sum of the absolute values of the eigenvalues of its adjacency matrix. This graph invariant is very closely connected to a chemical quantity known as the total π-electron energy of conjugated hydro-carbon molecules. In recent times, analogous energies are being considered, based on eigenvalues of a variety of other graph matrices associated to the graph [1–4]. In [5], authors computed incidence energy of a graph. In [6], authors computed general forms of energies of non-regular graphs.

Gutman introduced this idea of the energy of a graph in 1978 in the context of Mathematics [4]; however, inspiration for his definition seems to emerge from the popular Huckel molecular orbital theory. Huckel's technique enabled scientific experts to predict energies related to p-electron orbitals for a unique class of particles. The basic idea behind this is the Hamiltonian operator, which is a basic linear combination of certain orbitals [7,8]. It is somewhat less known than the one Heilbronner et al. developed, a model resulting in a fact that the roots of the characteristic polynomial of the line graph of the molecular graph are in a linear manner related to the s-electron energy levels of the corresponding saturated hydrocarbon [7,8], where these molecular graphs have vertices of both carbon and hydrogen atoms. Its popularity among mathematical chemists came from the fact that the Hamiltonian matrix of the Huckel molecular orbital theory is a simple linear function of the adjacency matrix of the corresponding molecular graph G. Thus, each π-electron energy level is a linear function of the corresponding zero of the characteristic polynomial of G [9]. In addition, under certain sensible presumptions about the particle, its "aggregate π electron energy" can be composed as the sum of the total eigenvalues of this graph.

Since the definition of energy for a graph in [4] is rather strange, not many mathematicians appear to be pulled by the definition. However, with the passage of time, the idea became powerful and in the previous decade enthusiasm for graph energy has expanded resulting in numerous different forms [3]. In 2006, Gutman and Zhou defined the Laplacian energy of a graph [10]. The authors of [11,12] discussed distance energy of a graph based on the idea of distance matrix associated with the graph. Nikiforov et al. computed some energies of non-regular graphs [13]. In [14], the authors discussed signless Laplacian energies of some finite graphs. In [15], the author discussed graph theoretical analyses in analyzing the changes in interactions between solvent and solute. In [16,17], the authors computed some asymptotic Laplacian and incidence energies of lattice.

Let G be a graph having vertex set $V(G)$ and edge set $E(G)$ denoted by $G = (V, E)$. A Graph $G = (V, E)$ is said to be connected if there is a connection between any pair of vertices in G. The number of vertices in a graph represents its order, the number of edges represents its size, and the number of edges connected to a single vertex represents the degree of that vertex denoted as d_u. The distance matrix associated to a graph is defined as the square matrix $D = [d_{ab}]$ where d_{ab} consists of all graph distances from vertex v_a to vertex v_b. An $n \times n$ matrix M for a graph having order n, called an adjacency matrix, can be associated to the graph as,

$$[M_{ab}] = \begin{cases} 1 & p_1 \mapsto p_2 \\ 0 & \text{otherwise} \end{cases}$$

The roots of a characteristics polynomial are the eigenvalues of a matrix associated to a graph. In most cases, the associated matrices are real and symmetric so eigenvalues are necessarily real-valued numbers. The collection of all eigenvalues of graph G forms the spectrum of G. Spectral properties of graphs have been widely studied. If G is not connected, then the energy of a graph is the sum of energies of its connected components. If a graph is connected, then its distance and adjacency energies are defined as the sum of the absolute values of associated eigenvalues. Energy of some non-regular graphs and Laplacian energy of a simple graph are discussed in [14,18].

In the current article, we want to find closed expressions for distance and adjacency energies of generalized wheel graphs, also known as m-level wheel, $W_{n,m}$. An m-wheel graph $W_{n,m}$ is a graph obtained from m copies of cycles C_n and one copy of vertex v, such that all vertices of every copy of C_n are adjacent to v. Thus, $W_{n,m}$ has $nm + 1$ vertices, i.e., the center and n-rim vertices, and has diameter 2. Figure 1 is an example of m-wheel graph $W_{12,m}$.

Vertices that lay on the same cycle C_n and adjacent to central vertex are termed as rim vertices. This graph can be considered as generalization of classical wheel graph W_n. Figure 2 is another instance of m-wheel graph, $W_{3,4}$.

This m-wheel network is an extension of the classical wheel graph $W_{1,n}$. Figure 3 is an example of wheel graph W_6.

The wheel graph has been used in different areas such as the wireless sensor networks and the vulnerability of networks [19]. The wheel graph has many good properties. From the standpoint of the hub vertex, all elements, including vertices and edges, are in its one-hop neighborhood, which indicates that the wheel structure is fully included in the neighborhood graph of the hub vertex. Wheel and related graphs are extensively studied recently. In [20], the authors computed partition dimension and connected partition dimension of wheel graphs and showed that, for $n \geq 4$, $[(2n)]^{\frac{1}{3}} \leq pd(G) \leq$

$2[n^{\frac{1}{2}}] + 1$. In [21], the authors gave an algorithm to compute average lower two-domination number and also computed this number for some wheel related graphs. In [22], authors computed the metric dimension of generalised wheel. In [23], Zafar et al. generalized the above results to multi-level wheel and obtained that for every $n \geq 4$, $[(2nm)]^{\frac{1}{3}} \leq pd(W_{n,m}) \leq 2[nm^{\frac{1}{2}}] + 1$.

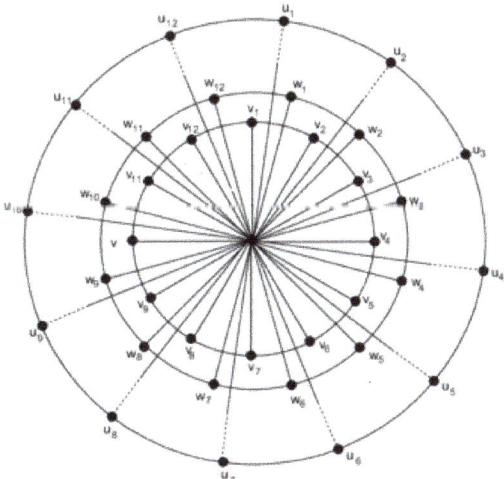

Figure 1. An m-level wheel, $W_{12,m}$.

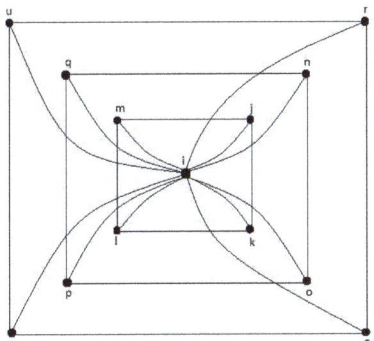

Figure 2. $W_{3,4}$.

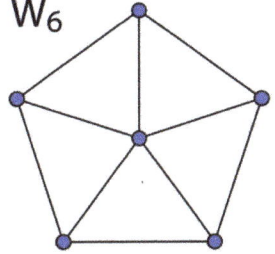

Figure 3. W_6.

2. Main Results

In this section, we give some results on distance and adjacency energies of wheel related graphs $W_{n,m}$.

Theorem 1. *The distance energy of the wheel graph $W_{n,m}$ is given by*

$$E_D(W_{n,m}) = 2(mn - 2 + \sqrt{m^2n^2 - 3mn + 4}), \qquad (2)$$

where $m \geq 3$ and $n \geq 1$.

Proof. Let A be adjacency matrix of cycle graph C_m given by

$$A = \begin{pmatrix} 0 & 1 & 0 & 0 & . & . & . & 0 & 1 \\ 1 & 0 & 1 & 0 & . & . & . & 0 & 0 \\ 0 & 1 & 0 & 1 & . & . & . & 0 & 0 \\ 0 & 0 & 1 & 0 & . & . & . & 0 & 0 \\ . & . & . & . & . & . & . & . & . \\ . & . & . & . & . & . & . & . & . \\ . & . & . & . & . & . & . & . & . \\ 0 & 0 & 0 & 0 & . & . & . & 0 & 1 \\ 1 & 0 & 0 & 0 & . & . & . & 1 & 0 \end{pmatrix}$$

where $a_{ij} = 1$ for $|i - j| = 1$ or $m - 1$ and $a_{ij} = 0$ otherwise.
Generally, the m-cycle has adjacency spectrum

$$Spec(C_m) = 2\cos(\frac{2\pi j}{m}) \text{ where } j = 0, 1, 2, ... n - 1.$$

The distance matrix of wheel graph $W_{n,m}$ obtained by joining of m-vertex cycle C_m and K_n can be given as,

$$C_{m \times m} = \begin{pmatrix} 0 & J_{1 \times m} & J_{1 \times m} & . & . & . & J_{1 \times m} \\ J_{m \times 1} & [A + 2\bar{A}]_{m \times m} & T_{m \times m} & . & . & . & T_{m \times m} \\ J_{m \times 1} & T_{m \times m} & [A + 2\bar{A}]_{m \times m} & . & . & . & T_{m \times m} \\ . & . & . & . & . & . & . \\ . & . & . & . & . & . & . \\ . & . & . & . & . & . & . \\ J_{m \times 1} & T_{m \times m} & T_{m \times m} & . & . & . & T_{m \times m} \\ J_{m \times 1} & T_{m \times m} & T_{m \times m} & . & . & . & [A + 2\bar{A}]_{m \times m} \end{pmatrix}$$

where

$$J_{1 \times m} = \begin{pmatrix} 1 & 1 & . & . & . & 1 \end{pmatrix},$$

$$T_{m \times m} = \begin{pmatrix} 2 & 2 & . & . & . & 2 \\ 2 & 2 & . & . & . & 2 \\ . & . & . & . & . & . \\ . & . & . & . & . & . \\ . & . & . & . & . & . \\ 2 & 2 & . & . & . & 2 \end{pmatrix},$$

and
$$A + 2\overline{A} = \begin{pmatrix} 0 & 1 & 2 & 2 & . & . & . & 1 & 1 \\ 1 & 0 & 1 & 2 & . & . & . & 2 & 1 \\ 2 & 1 & 0 & 1 & . & . & . & 2 & 1 \\ . & . & . & . & . & . & . & . & . \\ . & . & . & . & . & . & . & . & . \\ . & . & . & . & . & . & . & . & . \\ 1 & 2 & 2 & 2 & . & . & . & 0 & 1 \\ 1 & 1 & 1 & 1 & . & . & . & 1 & 0 \end{pmatrix}.$$

We get the distance spectrum of $W_{n,m}$ by using binomial series and adjacency spectrum of cycle graph. Thus, we get,

$$spec_D(W_{n,m}) = \begin{pmatrix} mn - 2 \pm \sqrt{m^2n^2 - 3mn + 4} & -4 & -(\lambda_i + 2) \\ 1 & n-1 & n \end{pmatrix} \text{ for } i = 2, 3, ..., m,$$

where λ_i are the eigenvalues of the adjacency matrix of cycle graph.

Since $\lambda_i > 0$ for all $i = 2, 3, ..., p$, by using the definition and summing up the eigenvalues, we arrive at the desired result of distance energy, which is $E_D(W_{n,m}) = 2(mn - 2 + \sqrt{m^2n^2 - 3mn + 4})$. □

Theorem 2. *The adjacency energy of the wheel graph $W_{n,m}$ is given by*

$$E_A(W_{n,m}) = 4n - 2 + 2\sqrt{nm + 1} \tag{3}$$

where m is even.

Proof. Let A be adjacency matrix of cycle graph C_m.

$$A = \begin{pmatrix} 0 & 1 & 0 & 0 & . & . & . & 0 & 1 \\ 1 & 0 & 1 & 0 & . & . & . & 0 & 0 \\ 0 & 1 & 0 & 1 & . & . & . & 0 & 0 \\ 0 & 0 & 1 & 0 & . & . & . & 0 & 0 \\ . & . & . & . & . & . & . & . & . \\ . & . & . & . & . & . & . & . & . \\ . & . & . & . & . & . & . & . & . \\ 0 & 0 & 0 & 0 & . & . & . & 0 & 1 \\ 1 & 0 & 0 & 0 & . & . & . & 1 & 0 \end{pmatrix}$$

where $a_{ij} = 1$ if $|i - j| = 1$ or $m - 1$ and $a_{ij} = 0$ otherwise.
Generally, the m cycles has adjacency spectrum.

$$Spec(C_m) = 2\cos(\frac{2\pi j}{m}) \text{ where } j = 0, 1, 2, ...n - 1.$$

Then, the adjacency matrix of wheel graph $W_{n,m}$ obtained by joining of m-vertex cycle C_m and K_n can be given as,

$$T_{m \times m} = \begin{pmatrix} 0 & J_{1 \times m} & J_{1 \times m} & \cdots & J_{1 \times m} \\ J_{m \times 1} & [B]_{m \times m} & [0]_{m \times m} & \cdots & [0]_{m \times m} \\ J_{m \times 1} & [0]_{m \times m} & [B]_{m \times m} & \cdots & [0]_{m \times m} \\ \cdot & \cdot & \cdot & \cdot & \cdot \\ \cdot & \cdot & \cdot & \cdot & \cdot \\ \cdot & \cdot & \cdot & \cdot & \cdot \\ J_{m \times 1} & [0]_{m \times m} & [0]_{m \times m} & \cdots & [0]_{m \times m} \\ J_{m \times 1} & [0]_{m \times m} & [0]_{m \times m} & \cdots & [B]_{m \times m} \end{pmatrix},$$

where

$$J_{1 \times m} = \begin{pmatrix} 1 & 1 & \cdots & 1 \end{pmatrix},$$

and

$$B_{m \times m} = \begin{pmatrix} 0 & 1 & 0 & 0 & \cdots & 0 & 1 \\ 1 & 0 & 1 & 0 & \cdots & 0 & 0 \\ 0 & 1 & 0 & 1 & \cdots & 0 & 0 \\ \cdot & \cdot & \cdot & \cdot & \cdot & \cdot & \cdot \\ \cdot & \cdot & \cdot & \cdot & \cdot & \cdot & \cdot \\ \cdot & \cdot & \cdot & \cdot & \cdot & \cdot & \cdot \\ 0 & 0 & 0 & 0 & \cdots & 0 & 1 \\ 1 & 0 & 0 & 0 & \cdots & 1 & 0 \end{pmatrix}.$$

We get the following adjacency spectrum of $W_{n,m}$ by using binomial series and adjacency spectrum of a cycle graph.

$$spec_A(W_{n,m}) = \begin{pmatrix} -2 & 2 & 1 \pm \sqrt{mn+1} & \lambda_i \\ n & n-1 & 1 & n \end{pmatrix}, for\ i = 3, 4, \ldots, m,$$

where λ_i are the eigenvalues of the adjacency matrix of cycle graph.

As $\lambda_i > 0$ for all $i = 2, 3, \ldots, p$, by using the definition and summing up the eigenvalues, we arrive at the desired result of adjacency energy, $E_A(W_{n,m}) = 4n - 2 + 2\sqrt{nm+1}$. □

Theorem 3. *Distance energy of wheel graph $W_{3,m}$ is*

$$E_D(W_{3,m}) = 2(3m - 2 + \sqrt{9m^2 - 9m + 4}) \tag{4}$$

Proof. As a classical wheel is a special case of generalized wheels for $n = 3$, the proof follows immediately from the first result. □

Theorem 4. *Adjacency energy of wheel graph $W_{3,m}$ is*

$$E_A(W_{3,m}) = 10 + 2\sqrt{3m+1} \tag{5}$$

Proof. As a classical wheel is a special case of generalized wheels for $n = 3$, the proof follows immediately from the second result. □

Conclusion and Analysis

In the current article, we compute general forms of distance and adjacency energies of multi-level wheels, which are the extension of classical wheel graph. In the attached figure, dependencies of distance energies on the parameters m and n are given. Figure 4 represents the trends of distance energies with change in m and n. The first part is a 3D plot showing the trends of distance energies with change in m and n.

Figure 5 represents increasing behaviour of distance energy with respect to n while keeping m constant. The three different colored lines correspond to three different values of m.

Figure 6 shows that, with the rise in m and n, the values of adjacency energies rise. It is the 3D plot showing trends with changes in both m and n.

Figure 7 represents behaviour of adjacency energy with respect to n while keeping m constant. The three different colored lines correspond to three different values of m.

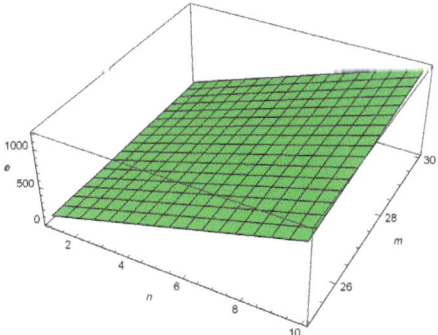

Figure 4. View of distance energy of $W_{n,m}$.

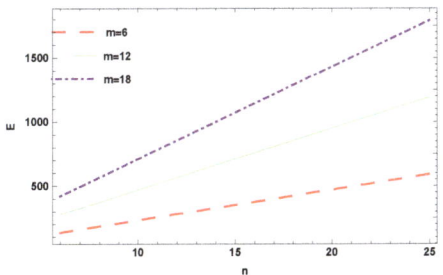

Figure 5. Distance energy of $W_{n,m}$ while keeping m constant.

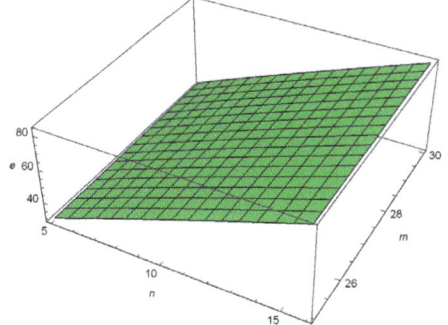

Figure 6. View of adjacency energy of $W_{n,m}$.

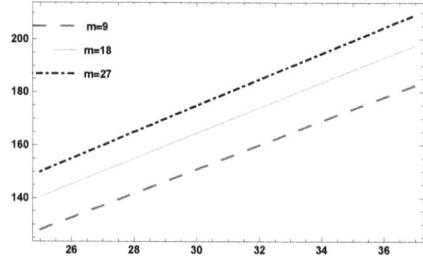

Figure 7. Adjacency energy of $W_{n,m}$ while keeping m constant.

In this paper, we compute closed forms of distance and adjacency energies of generalized wheels and particularize these for classical wheels. These results are helpful for mathematicians and chemists working in industry as generalized wheels can be considered as particular cyclic structures having a common hub.

Author Contributions: Conceptualization has been done by J.-B.L. and A.N. Main article has been drafted by M.M., A.Y. and K.A.

Funding: The work was partially supported by the China Postdoctoral Science Foundation under grant No. 2017M621579 and the Postdoctoral Science Foundation of Jiangsu Province under grant No. 1701081B, Project of Anhui Jianzhu University under Grant no. 2016QD116 and 2017dc03, Anhui Province Key Laboratory of Intelligent Building and Building Energy Saving.

Conflicts of Interest: The authors declare no conflict of interest.

References

1. Diudea, M.V.; Gutman, I.; Lorentz, J. *Molecular Topology*; Babes-Bolyai University: Cluj-Napoca, Romania, 1999; ISBN 1-56072-957-0.
2. Gutman, I.; Kiobucar, A.; Majstrovic, S. *Selected Topics from the Theory of Graph Energy: Hypoenergetic Graphs*; Applications of Graph Spectra Mathematical Institution: Belgrade, Serbia, 2009; pp. 65–105.
3. Meenakshi, S.; Lavanya, S. A Survey on Energy of Graphs. *Ann. Pure Appl. Math.* **2014**, *8*, 183–191.
4. Gutman, I. The energy of a graph. *Steiermark. Math. Symp.* **1978**, *103*, 1–22.
5. Jooyandeh, M.; Kiani, D.; Mirzakhah, M. Incidence energy of a graph. *MATCH. Commun. Math. Comput. Chem.* **2009**, *62*, 561–572.
6. Indulal, G.; Vijaykumar, A. Energies of some non-regular graphs. *J. Math. Chem.* **2007**, *42*, 377–386. [CrossRef]
7. Bieri, G.; Dill, J.; Heilbronner, E.; Schmelzer, A. Application of the Equivalent Bond Orbital Model to the C2s-Ionization Energies of Saturated Hydrocarbons. *Helv. Chim. Acta* **1977**, *60*, 2234–2247. [CrossRef]
8. Heilbronner, E. A Simple Equivalent Bond Orbital Model for the Rationalization of the C2s-Photoelectron Spectra of the Higher n-Alkanes, in Particular of Polyethylene. *Helv. Chim. Acta* **1977**, *60*, 2248–2257. [CrossRef]
9. Gunthard, H.; Primas, H. Zusammenhang von Graphentheorie und MO-Theorie von Molekeln mit Systemen konjugierter Bindungen. *Helv. Chim. Acta* **1956**, *39*, 1645–1653. [CrossRef]
10. Gutman, I.; Zhou, B. Laplacian energy of a graph. *Lin. Algebra Appl.* **2006**, *414*, 29–37. [CrossRef]
11. Gutman, I.; Indulal, G.; Vijaykumar, A. On distance energy of graphs. *MATCH Commun. Math. Compul. Chen.* **2008**, *60*, 461–472.
12. Gutman, I.; Li, X.; Shi, Y. *Graph Energy*; Springer: New York, NY, USA, 2012.
13. Nikiforov, V. The energy of graphs and matrices. *J. Math. Anal. Appl.* **2007**, *326*, 1472–1475. [CrossRef]
14. Rowlinson, D.C.P.; Simic, K. Signless Laplacians of finite graphs. *MATCH Commun. Math. Comput. Chem.* **2007**, *57*, 211–220.
15. Sandberg, T.O.; Weinberger, C.; Smatt, J.H. Molecular Dynamics on Wood-Derived Lignans Analyzed by Intermolecular Network Theory. *Molecules* **2018**, *23*, 1990. [CrossRef] [PubMed]
16. Liu, J.B.; Pan, X.F.; Hu, F.T. Asymptotic Laplacian-energy-like invariant of lattices. *Appl. Math. Comput.* **2015**, *253*, 205–214. [CrossRef]

17. Liu, J.B.; Pan, X.F. Asymptotic incidence energy of lattices. *Physica A* **2015**, *422*, 193–202. [CrossRef]
18. Zhou, B.; Gutman, I. On Laplacian energy of graphs. *MATCH Commun. Math. Comput. Chem.* **2007**, *57*, 211–220.
19. Aytac, A.; Turaci, T. Vertex vulnerablility parameter of Gear Graphs. *Int. J. Found. Comput. Sci.* **2011**, *22*, 1187–1195. [CrossRef]
20. Tomescu, I.; Javaid, I. Slamin On the partition dimension and connected partition dimension of wheels. *Ars Comb.* **2007**, *84*, 311–317.
21. Turaci, T. The Average Lower 2-domination Number of Wheels Related Graphs and an Algorithm. *Math. Comput. Appl.* **2016**, *21*, 29. [CrossRef]
22. Siddique, H.M.A.; Imran, H. Computing the metric dimension of wheel related graphs. *Appl. Math. Comput.* **2014**, *242*, 624–632.
23. Hussain, Z.; Muqaddas, M.; Munir, M.; Ali, U.; Zahid, A.; Saleem, S. Bounds for partition dimension of *m*-Wheels. *Open Phys.* **2018**, in press.

© 2019 by the authors. Licensee MDPI, Basel, Switzerland. This article is an open access article distributed under the terms and conditions of the Creative Commons Attribution (CC BY) license (http://creativecommons.org/licenses/by/4.0/).

Article

Construction Algorithm for Zero Divisor Graphs of Finite Commutative Rings and Their Vertex-Based Eccentric Topological Indices

Kashif Elahi [1,2,]*, Ali Ahmad [3,]* and Roslan Hasni [2,]*

1. Deanship of E-learning and Information Technology, Jazan University, Jazan 45142, Saudi Arabia
2. Department of Mathematics, University Malaysia Terengganu, Kuala Terengganu 21030, Terengganu, Malaysia
3. College of Computer Science and Information Technology, Jazan University, Jazan 45142, Saudi Arabia
* Correspondence: kashif_elahi@hotmail.com (K.E.); ahmadsms@gmail.com (A.A.); hroslan@umt.edu.my (R.H.)

Received: 26 October 2018; Accepted: 2 December 2018; Published: 4 December 2018

Abstract: Chemical graph theory is a branch of mathematical chemistry which deals with the non-trivial applications of graph theory to solve molecular problems. Graphs containing finite commutative rings also have wide applications in robotics, information and communication theory, elliptic curve cryptography, physics, and statistics. In this paper we discuss eccentric topological indices of zero divisor graphs of commutative rings $\mathbb{Z}_{p_1 p_2} \times \mathbb{Z}_q$, where p_1, p_2, and q are primes. To enhance the importance of these indices a construction algorithm is also devised for zero divisor graphs of commutative rings $\mathbb{Z}_{p_1 p_2} \times \mathbb{Z}_q$.

Keywords: topological index; zero divisor graphs; commutative ring

MSC: 05C12; 05CO5; 05C90

---

1. Introduction

A single number that can be utilized to depict properties of the graph of a molecule is known as a topological descriptor for that graph. There are different topological descriptors that have found a number of applications in theoretical science. Topological descriptors are numerical parameters of a graph that characterize its topology and are usually graph-invariant. Topological descriptors are utilized within the improvement of quantitative structure-activity connections (QSARs) and quantitative structure-property connections (QSPR) in which the organic movement or other properties of atoms are connected with their chemical structure. Topological descriptors are utilized in QSPR/QSAR. These days, there exists a variety of topological descriptors that have some applications in chemistry, physics, robotics, statistics, and computer networks. The topological descriptors deal with the distance among the vertices in a graph are "distance-based topological indices". Other topological descriptors that deal with the degree of vertices in graph are "degree-based topological indices". The Wiener index is the first distance based topological index and it has eminent applications in chemistry. Wiener index is based on topological distance of vertices within the individual graph, the Hosoya index is calculated by checking of non-incident edges in a graph, the energy and the Estrada index are based on the range of the graph, the Randic connectivity index is calculated utilizing the degrees of vertices. For further detail about other indices [1–9] can be explored.

2. Definitions and Notations

Let G be a connected graph with vertex and edge sets $V(G)$ and $E(G)$, respectively. A numerical quantity related to a graph that is invariant under graph automorphisms is topological index or topological descriptor. For a graph G, the degree of a vertex v is the number of edges incident with v and denoted by $d(v)$. The maximum degree of a graph G, denoted by $\Delta(G)$, and the minimum degree of a graph, denoted by $\delta(G)$, are the maximum and minimum degree of its vertices. The sum of degree of all vertices u which are adjacent to vertex v is denoted by $S(v)$. The distance between the vertices u and v of G is denoted by $d(u,v)$ and it is defined as the number of edges in a minimal path connecting them.

Connectivity descriptors are important among topological descriptors and used in various fields like chemistry, physics, and statistics. Let $x_1, x_2 \in V(G)$, the distance $d(x_1, x_2)$ between x_1 and x_2, be defined as the length of any shortest path in G connecting x_1 and x_2. In mathematical, eccentricity is defined as:

$$e(u) = max\{d(u,v) : \forall \ v \in V(G)\} \qquad (1)$$

In 1997 eccentric connectivity index was introduced by Sharma [10]. By using eccentric connectivity index, the mathematical modeling of biological activities of diverse nature is done. The general formula of eccentric connectivity index is defined as:

$$\xi(G) = \sum_{v \in V} d_v\, e(v) \qquad (2)$$

where $e(v)$ is the eccentricity of vertex v in G. Some applications and mathematical properties of eccentric connectivity index can be found in [11–14]. The total eccentricity index is the sum of eccentricity of the all the vertex v in G. Total eccentricity index is introduced by Farooq and Malik [15], which is defined as:

$$\zeta(G) = \sum_{v \in V} e(v) \qquad (3)$$

The first Zagreb index of a graph G is studied in [16] based on degree and the new version of the first Zagreb index based on eccentricity was introduced by Ghorbani and Hosseinzadeh [17], as follows:

The eccentric connectivity polynomial is the polynomial version of the eccentric-connectivity index which was proposed by Alaeiyan, Mojarad, and Asadpour [18] and some graph operations can be found in [19]. The eccentric connectivity polynomial of a graph G is defined as:

$$ECP(G, x) = \sum_{v \in V} d(v) x^{e(v)} \qquad (4)$$

Gupta, Singh and Madan [20] defined the augmented eccentric connectivity index of a graph G as follows:

$$\xi^{ac}(G) = \sum_{v \in V} \frac{M(v)}{e(v)} \qquad (5)$$

where $M(v)$ denotes the product of degrees of all vertices u which are adjacent to vertex v. Some interesting results on augmented eccentric connectivity index are discussed in [21,22]. Another very relevant and special eccentricity based topological index is connective eccentric index. The connective eccentric index was defined by Gupta, Singh, and Madan [20] defined as follows:

$$\xi^{C}(G) = \sum_{v \in V} \frac{d(v)}{e(v)} \qquad (6)$$

Ediz [23,24] introduced the Ediz eccentric connectivity index and reverse eccentric connectivity index of graph G, which is used in various branches of sciences, molecular science, and chemistry etc. The Ediz eccentric connectivity index and reverse eccentric connectivity index are defined as:

$$E\zeta(G) = \sum_{v \in V(G)} \frac{S(v)}{e(v)} \tag{7}$$

$$^{Re}\zeta(G) = \sum_{v \in V(G)} \frac{e(v)}{S(v)} \tag{8}$$

where $S(v)$ is the sum of degrees of all vertices, u, adjacent to vertex v, $e(v)$ is the eccentricity of v.

Let R be a commutative ring with identity and $Z(R)$ is the set of all zero divisors of R. $G(R)$ is said to be a zero divisor graph if $x, y \in V(G(R)) = Z(R)$ and $(x, y) \in E(G(R))$ if and only if $x.y = 0$. Beck [25] introduced the notion of zero divisor graph. Anderson and Livingston [26] proved that $G(R)$ is always connected if R is commutative. Anderson and Badawi [27] introduced the total graph of R as: There is an edge between any two distinct vertices $u, v \in R$ if and only if $u + v \in Z(R)$. For a graph G, the concept of graph parameters have always a high interest. Numerous authors briefly studied the zero-divisor and total graphs from commutative rings [28–32]. Similar problems were investigated in [33,34].

Let p_1, p_2, and q be prime numbers, with $p_2 > p_1$ and $\Gamma(\mathbb{Z}_{p_1 p_2} \times \mathbb{Z}_q)$ being zero divisor graph of the commutative rings $\mathbb{Z}_{p_1 p_2} \times \mathbb{Z}_q$. In this paper, we investigate the eccentric topological descriptors namely, eccentric connectivity index, total eccentric index, first Zagreb eccentricity index, connective eccentric index, Ediz eccentric index, eccentric connectivity polynomial, and augmented eccentric connectivity index of zero divisor graphs $\Gamma(\mathbb{Z}_{p_1 p_2} \times \mathbb{Z}_q)$. Now onward, we use G as a zero divisor graph of the commutative rings $\mathbb{Z}_{p_1 p_2} \times \mathbb{Z}_q$.

3. Methods

In this paper, we adopted interdisciplinary methods by combining algorithmic approach for graph construction and outcome of algorithm are aligned with eccentric topological indices. For prime numbers p_1, p_2, q with $p_2 > p_1$, we consider the commutative ring $R = \mathbb{Z}_{p_1 p_2} \times \mathbb{Z}_q$ with usual addition and multiplication. The zero divisor graph $G = \Gamma(\mathbb{Z}_{p_1 p_2} \times \mathbb{Z}_q)$ associated with ring R is defined as: For $a \in \mathbb{Z}_{p_1 p_2}$, $b \in \mathbb{Z}_q$, $(a, b) \notin V(G)$ if and only if $a \neq kp_1, a \neq sp_2$ for $k = 1, 2, \cdots, p_2 - 1, s = 1, 2, \cdots, p_1 - 1$ and $y \neq 0$. Let $J = \{(a, b) \notin V(G) : a \neq kp_1, a \neq sp_2, k = 1, 2, \cdots, p_2 - 1, s = 1, 2, \cdots, p_1 - 1 \ \& \ y \neq 0\}$, then $|J| = (p_1 p_2 - p_1 - p_2 + 1)(q - 1)$. The elements of the set J are the non zero divisors of R. Also $(0, 0) \in \mathbb{Z}_{p_1 p_2} \times \mathbb{Z}_q$ is a non zero divisor. Therefore, $|J| + 1 = (p_1 p_2 - p_1 - p_2 + 1)(q - 1) + 1$ are the total number of non zero divisors of R and the total number of elements of R are $p_1 p_2 q$. Hence, $p_1 p_2 q - (p_1 p_2 - p_1 - p_2 + 1)(q - 1) + 1 = (p_1 + p_2 - 1)(q - 1) + p_1 p_2 - 1$ are the total number of zero divisors. This implies that $|V(G)| = (p_1 + p_2 - 1)(q - 1) + p_1 p_2 - 1$. We can construct the zero divisor graph of commutative ring $R = \mathbb{Z}_{p_1 p_2} \times \mathbb{Z}_q$ by the following algorithm:

Input: p_1, p_2 and q are three prime numbers.
Output: ordered pairs for zero divisor.

Algorithm 1 ZeroDivisorGraph(p_1, p_2, q)

1: **if** ($p1 < p2$)
2:
3:     **for** $x1 \leftarrow 0$ **to** $p1 \times p2$
4:
5:         **for** $y1 \leftarrow 0$ **to** q
6:
7:             **if** ($x1 \neq 0$ **OR** $y1 \neq 0$)
8:
9:                 createGraph(x_1, y_1, p_1, p_2, q)

Algorithm 2 createGraph (x_1, y_1, p_1, p_2, q)

1: **for** $x2 \leftarrow x1$ **to** $p1 \times p2$
2:
3:     **for** $y2 \leftarrow y1$ **to** q
4:
5:         **if** ($x1 \neq x2$ **AND** $y1 \neq y2$)
6:
7:             **if** ($x1 \neq 0$ **OR** $y1 \neq 0$)
8:
9:                 $k1 = 0$
10:
11:             **else**
12:
13:                 $k1 = x1 \times x2$
14:
15:             **if** ($y1 \neq 0$ **OR** $y2 \neq 0$)
16:
17:                 $k2 = 0$
18:
19:             **else**
20:
21:                 $k2 = y1 \times y2$
22:
23:             **if** ($k1$ **mod** $p1 = 0$ **AND** $k1$ **mod** $p2 = 0$ **AND** $k2 = 0$)
24:
25:                 **return** x_1, y_1, x_1, y_2

Outcomes of above algorithm, the degree of each vertex $(a,b) \in V(G)$ can be depicted mathematically in the following cases:

Case 1: If $a = 0$ and any $b \in \mathbb{Z}_q \setminus \{0\}$, then each such type of vertex $(0,b)$ is adjacent to the vertices $(a',0)$ for every $a' \in \mathbb{Z}_{p_1p_2} \setminus \{0\}$. Hence the degree of each vertex $(0,b)$ is $p_1p_2 - 1$.

Case 2: If $a = kp_1, k = 1, 2, \cdots, p_2 - 1$ and $b = 0$, then each such type of vertex $(a,0)$ is adjacent to the vertices $(0,b), (a',0)$ & (a',b') for every $b' = \{1, 2, \cdots, q-1\}$, and $a' = sp_2, s = 1, 2, \cdots, p_1 - 1$. Hence the degree of each vertex $(a,0)$ is $q - 1 + p_1 - 1 + (p_1 - 1)(q - 1) = p_1q - 1$. Similarly, if $a = sp_2, s = 1, 2, \cdots, p_1 - 1$ and $b = 0$, then the degree of each such type of vertices $(a,0)$ is $p_2q - 1$.

Case 3: If $a \in \mathbb{Z}_{p_1p_2} \setminus \{0, kp_1, sp_2$ with $k = 1, 2, \cdots, p_2 - 1, s = 1, 2, \cdots, p_1 - 1\}$ and $b = 0$, then each such type of vertex $(a,0)$ is adjacent with only $(0,b')$ for every $b' \in \mathbb{Z}_q \setminus \{0\}$. Hence the degree of each vertex $(a,0)$ is $q - 1$.

Case 4: If $a = kp_1, k = 1, 2, \cdots, p_2 - 1$ and $b \in \mathbb{Z}_q \setminus \{0\}$, then each such type of vertex (a,b) is adjacent with only $(a',0)$ for every $a' = sp_2, s = 1, 2, \cdots, p_1 - 1$. Therefore, the degree of each vertex (a,b) is $p_1 - 1$. Similarly, if $a = sp_2, s = 1, 2, \cdots, p_1 - 1$ and $b \in \mathbb{Z}_q \setminus \{0\}$, then degree of each such type of vertices (a,b) is $p_2 - 1$.

From the above discussion and our convenance, let us partitioned the vertex set of G based one their degrees as follows:

$$V_1 = \{(0,x) : x \in \mathbb{Z}_q, x \neq 0\}$$
$$V_2 = \{(x,0) : x = kp_1, k = 1, 2, \ldots, p_2 - 1\}$$
$$V_3 = \{(x,0) : x = sp_2, s = 1, 2, \ldots, p_1 - 1\}$$
$$V_4 = \{(x,0) : x \in \mathbb{Z}_{p_1p_2} \setminus \{0\}, x \neq kp_1, x \neq sp_2, k = 1, 2, \ldots, p_2 - 1, s = 1, 2, \ldots, p_1 - 1\}$$
$$V_5 = \{(x,y) : x = kp_1, k = 1, 2, \ldots, p_2 - 1, y \in \mathbb{Z}_q \setminus \{0\}\}$$
$$V_6 = \{(x,y) : x = sp_2, s = 1, 2, \ldots, p_1 - 1, y \in \mathbb{Z}_q \setminus \{0\}\}$$

This shows that $V(G) = V_1 \cup V_2 \cup V_3 \cup V_4 \cup V_5 \cup V_6$. It is easy to see that $|V_1| = q-1$, $|V_2| = p_2 - 1$, $|V_3| = p_1 - 1$, $|V_4| = (p_1-1)(p_2-1)$, $|V_5| = (p_2-1)(q-1)$, and $|V_1| = (p_1-1)(q-1)$.

4. Main Results

Let $d_U(u)$ denote the degree of a vertex u in U and $d(U, V)$ denotes the distance between the vertices of two sets U and V. In the following theorem, we determined the eccentricity of the vertices of G.

Theorem 1. *Let G be the zero divisor graph of the commutative ring R, then the eccentricity of the vertices of G is 2 or 3.*

Proof. From case 1, the vertices of the set V_1 are at distance 1 with the vertices of the sets V_2, V_3, & V_4 i.e., $d(V_1, V_2) = d(V_1, V_3) = d(V_1, V_4) = 1$. From Case 4, the vertices of the sets V_2 and V_3 are adjacent with the vertices of the sets V_6 and V_5, respectively. This implies that $d(V_1, V_5) = d(V_1, V_6) = 2$. The distance between any two different vertices of the set V_1 is also 2. Therefore the eccentricity of the vertices of set V_1 is 2, i.e., $e(V_1) = 2$. Similarly, it is easy to see that $e(V_2) = e(V_3) = 2$.

As $d(V_1, V_2) = d(V_1, V_3) = d(V_1, V_4) = 1$ and $d(V_1, V_5) = d(V_1, V_6) = 2$. This implies that $d(V_4, V_5) = d(V_4, V_1) + d(V_1, V_5) = 3$. This shows that $e(V_4) = 3$. Similarly, it is easy to calculate that $e(V_5) = e(V_6) = 3$. This completes the proof. □

Summarizing the above cases, partition of vertices and their cardinality and Theorem 1 in Table 1.

Table 1. The representation of vertices, their degree, eccentricity, and frequency of the vertices in G.

Representatives of Vertices	Degree	Eccentricity	Frequency
V_1	$p_1 p_2 - 1$	2	$q - 1$
V_2	$p_1 q - 1$	2	$p_2 - 1$
V_3	$p_2 q - 1$	2	$p_1 - 1$
V_4	$q - 1$	3	$(p_1 - 1)(p_2 - 1)$
V_5	$p_1 - 1$	3	$(p_2 - 1)(q - 1)$
V_6	$p_2 - 1$	3	$(p_1 - 1)(q - 1)$

In the following theorem, we determined the eccentric connectivity index of the graph G.

Theorem 2. *Let $p_1 < p_2$, q be prime numbers, then eccentric connectivity index of graph G is $\xi(G) = p_1 p_2 (15q - 11) - (p_1 + p_2)(11q - 7) + 7q - 3$.*

Proof. By using the degree of each vertex partition and corresponding their eccentricity from Table 1 in the Equation (2), we obtain:

$$\xi(G) = \sum_{v \in V} d_v \, e(v)$$
$$= 2(p_1 p_2 - 1)(q - 1) + 2(p_1 q - 1)(p_2 - 1) + 2(p_2 q - 1)(p_1 - 1)$$
$$+ 3(p_1 - 1)(p_2 - 1)(q - 1) + 3(p_1 - 1)(p_2 - 1)(q - 1) + 3(p_1 - 1)(p_2 - 1)(q - 1)$$

After simplification, we get:
$\xi(G) = p_1 p_2 (15q - 11) - (p_1 + p_2)(11q - 7) + 7q - 3$.
This completes the proof. □

The eccentricity of the vertices and their frequency is given in the Table 1 of the graph G, by putting these values and after simplification we obtain the following two corollaries.

Corollary 1. *Let $p_1 < p_2$, q be prime numbers, then the total-eccentricity index of G is given by $\zeta(G) = 3(p_1 p_2 + p_1 q + p_2 q + 1) - 4(p_1 + p_2 + q)$.*

Corollary 2. Let $p_1 < p_2$, q be prime numbers, then the first Zagreb eccentricity index of G is given by $M_1^*(G) = 9(p_1p_2 + p_1q + p_2q) - 14(p_1 + p_2 + q) + 15$.

Theorem 3. Let $p_1 < p_2$, q be prime numbers, then the connective eccentric index of graph G is $\xi^C(G) = (p_1 - 1)(p_2 - 1)(q - 1) + 2 + \frac{p_1p_2(3q-1)-(p_1+p_2+1)(q+1)}{2}$.

Proof. By using the values of degrees and their eccentricity in the Equation (6), we obtain the following:

$$\xi^C(G) = \sum_{v \in V} \frac{d(v)}{e(v)}$$
$$= \frac{(p_1p_2 - 1)(q - 1)}{2} + \frac{(p_1q - 1)(p_2 - 1)}{2} + \frac{(p_2q - 1)(p_1 - 1)}{2}$$
$$+ \frac{(p_1 - 1)(p_2 - 1)(q - 1)}{3} + \frac{(p_1 - 1)(p_2 - 1)(q - 1)}{3}$$
$$+ \frac{(p_1 - 1)(p_2 - 1)(q - 1)}{3}$$
$$= (p_1 - 1)(p_2 - 1)(q - 1) + 2 + \frac{p_1p_2(3q - 1) - (p_1 + p_2 + 1)(q + 1)}{2}.$$

After simplification, we get
$\xi^C(G) = (p_1 - 1)(p_2 - 1)(q - 1) + 2 + \frac{p_1p_2(3q-1)-(p_1+p_2+1)(q+1)}{2}$.
This completes the proof. □

Theorem 4. Let $p_1 < p_2$, q be prime numbers, then the Ediz eccentric connectivity index of graph G is $E\zeta(G) = \frac{9(p_1-1)(p_2-1)(q-1)+8[(p_1-1)(p_2q-1)+(p_2-1)(p_1q-1)+(p_1p_2-1)(q-1)]}{6}$.

Proof. $S(v)$ is the sum of degrees of all vertices u which are adjacent to vertex v. Calculate the values of $S(v)$ with the help of Table 1. The eccentricity of each vertex is also given in Table 1. Putting these vales in Equation (7), we obtain the following:

$$E\zeta(G) = \sum_{v \in V(G)} \frac{S(v)}{e(v)}$$
$$= \frac{(p_1 - 1)(p_2 - 1)(q - 1) + (p_1 - 1)(p_2q - 1) + (p_2 - 1)(p_1q - 1)}{2}$$
$$+ \frac{(p_1 - 1)(p_2 - 1)(q - 1) + (p_1 - 1)(p_2q - 1) + (q - 1)(p_1p_2 - 1)}{2}$$
$$+ \frac{(p_1 - 1)(p_2 - 1)(q - 1) + (p_2 - 1)(p_1q - 1) + (q - 1)(p_1p_2 - 1)}{2}$$
$$+ \frac{(q - 1)(p_1p_2 - 1)}{3} + \frac{(p_1 - 1)(p_2q - 1)}{3} + \frac{(p_2 - 1)(p_1q - 1)}{3}$$

After simplification, we get
$E\zeta(G) = \frac{9(p_1-1)(p_2-1)(q-1)+8[(p_1-1)(p_2q-1)+(p_2-1)(p_1q-1)+(p_1p_2-1)(q-1)]}{6}$.
This completes the proof. □

Theorem 5. Let $p_1 < p_2$, q be prime numbers, then the eccentric connectivity polynomial of graph G is $ECP(G, x) = (3p_1p_2q - p_1p_2 - p_1q - p_1 - p_2q - p_2 - q + 3)x^2 + 3(p_1 - 1)(p_2 - 1)(q - 1)x^3$.

Proof. By using the degree of each vertex partition and their corresponding eccentricities from Table 1 Equation (4), we obtain:

$$ECP(G,x) = \sum_{v\in V} d(v)x^{e(v)}$$
$$=(p_1p_2-1)(q-1)x^2 + (p_1q-1)(p_2-1)x^2$$
$$+(p_2q-1)(p_1-1)x^2 + (p_1-1)(p_2-1)(q-1)x^3$$
$$+(p_1-1)(p_2-1)(q-1)x^3 + (p_1-1)(p_2-1)(q-1)x^3$$
$$=(3p_1p_2q - p_1p_2 - p_1q - p_1 - p_2q - p_2 - q + 3)x^2$$
$$+3(p_1-1)(p_2-1)(q-1)x^3.$$

After simplification, we get
$$ECP(G,x) = (3p_1p_2q - p_1p_2 - p_1q - p_1 - p_2q - p_2 - q + 3)x^2 + 3(p_1-1)(p_2-1)(q-1)x^3.$$
This completes the proof. □

Theorem 6. *Let* $p_1 < p_2$, q *be prime numbers, then augmented eccentric connectivity index of graph* G *is* $\zeta^{ac}(G) = \frac{(p_1-1)(p_2-1)(p_1p_2-1)^{q-1} + (p_1-1)(q-1)(p_1q-1)^{p_2-1} + (p_2-1)(q-1)(p_2q-1)^{p_1-1}}{3} + \frac{(p_1-1)^{p_2q-q-p_2+2}(p_1q-1)^{p_2-1}(p_1p_2-1)^{q-1} + (p_2-1)^{p_1q-p_1-q+2}(p_1p_2-1)^{q-1}(p_2q-1)^{p_1-1}}{2} + \frac{(q-1)^{p_1p_2-p_1-p_2+2}(p_1q-1)^{p_2-1}(p_2q-1)^{p_1-1}}{2}.$

Proof. $M(v)$ is the product of degrees of all vertices u which are adjacent to vertex v. Calculate the values of $M(v)$ with the help of Table 1. The eccentricity of each vertex is also given in the Table 1. Putting these vales in Equation (5), we obtain the following:

$$\zeta^{ac}(G) = \sum_{v\in V} \frac{M(v)}{e(v)}$$
$$= \frac{(p_1-1)(p_2-1)(p_1p_2-1)^{q-1}}{3} + \frac{(p_1-1)(q-1)(p_1q-1)^{p_2-1}}{3}$$
$$++ \frac{(p_2-1)(q-1)(p_2q-1)^{p_1-1}}{3}$$
$$+ \frac{(p_1-1)(p_1-1)^{(p_1-1)(q-1)}(p_1q-1)^{p_2-1}(p_1p_2-1)^{q-1}}{2}$$
$$+ \frac{(p_2-1)(p_2-1)^{(p_2-1)(q-1)}(p_1p_2-1)^{q-1}(p_2q-1)^{p_1-1}}{2}$$
$$+ \frac{(q-1)(q-1)^{(p_1-1)(p_2-1)}(p_1q-1)^{p_2-1}(p_2q-1)^{p_1-1}}{2}$$

After simplification, we get
$\zeta^{ac}(G) = \frac{(p_1-1)(p_2-1)(p_1p_2-1)^{q-1} + (p_1-1)(q-1)(p_1q-1)^{p_2-1} + (p_2-1)(q-1)(p_2q-1)^{p_1-1}}{3} + \frac{(p_1-1)^{p_2q-q-p_2+2}(p_1q-1)^{p_2-1}(p_1p_2-1)^{q-1} + (p_2-1)^{p_1q-p_1-q+2}(p_1p_2-1)^{q-1}(p_2q-1)^{p_1-1}}{2} + \frac{(q-1)^{p_1p_2-p_1-p_2+2}(p_1q-1)^{p_2-1}(p_2q-1)^{p_1-1}}{2}.$
This completes the proof. □

If p_1, p_2 and q are prime numbers with $p_1 = p_2 = p$, then Ahmad et al. [35] determined the vertex-based eccentric topological indices of zero divisor graph of the commutative ring $\mathbb{Z}_{p^2} \times \mathbb{Z}_q$ as follows:

Theorem 7 ([35]). *Let* p, q *be prime numbers. If* $G(R)$ *is the zero divisor graph of the commutative ring* $R = \mathbb{Z}_{p^2} \times \mathbb{Z}_q$, *then*

- $\zeta(G(R)) = 10p^2q - 8p^2 - 11pq + 5p + q + 3.$

- $\zeta(G(R)) = 3p^2 + 3pq - 4p - q - 1$
- $M_1^*(G(R)) = 9p^2 + 9pq - 14p - 5q + 1$.
- $\zeta^C(G) = \frac{(p-1)(10pq - 7p + q - 7)}{6}$
- $\zeta^{ac}(G(R)) = (\frac{p-1}{3} + \frac{(q-1)^{p^2-p}}{2})(pq-2)^{p-1}(q-1) + (\frac{p}{3} + \frac{p^{(p-1)(q-1)}(pq-2)^{p-2}}{2})(p^2-1)^{q-1}(p-1)$.

5. Conclusions

In this paper, we discussed the vertex-based eccentric topological indices, namely eccentric connectivity index, total-eccentricity index, first Zabreb eccentricity index, connective eccentric index, Ediz eccentric connectivity index, eccentric connectivity polynomial, and augmented eccentric index for zero divisor graphs of commutative rings $\mathbb{Z}_{p_1 p_2} \times \mathbb{Z}_q$ where p_1, p_2 and q are primes. These indices are helpful in understanding the characteristics of different physical structures like carbon nanostructures, hexagonal belts and chains, Fullerence and Nanocone, structure-boiling point, and the relationships of various alkanes. They can be used in estimating and trouble shooting computer network problems regarding distance, speed, and time. They can also be helpful in developing efficient physical structure in robotics.

Author Contributions: R.H. contribute for supervision and analyzed the data curation. A.A. contribute for Investigation, visualization, validation, computation and Methodology. K.E. contribute for conceptualization, validation, designing the experiments, resources, software and wrote the initial draft of the paper. All authors read and approved the final version of the paper.

Funding: This research received no external funding.

Acknowledgments: The authors are grateful to the reviewers for suggestions to improve the presentation of the manuscript.

Conflicts of Interest: The authors declare no conflict of interest.

References

1. Ahmad, A. On the degree based topological indices of benzene ring embedded in P-type-surface in 2D network. *Hacet. J. Math. Stat.* **2018**, *47*, 9–18. [CrossRef]
2. Bača, M.; Horvràthovà, J.; Mokrišovà, M.; Suhànyiovà, A. On topological indices of fullerenes. *Appl. Math. Comput.* **2015**, *251*, 154–161.
3. Baig, A.Q.; Imran, M.; Ali, H.; Rehman, S.U. Computing topological polynomial of certain nanostructures. *J. Optoelectron. Adv. Mater.* **2015**, *17*, 877–883.
4. Estrada, E. Atom-Bond Connectivity and the Energetic of Branched Alkanes. *Chem. Phys. Lett.* **2008**, *463*, 422–425. [CrossRef]
5. Estrada, E.; Torres, L.; Rodriguez, L.; Gutman, I. An atom-bond connectivity index: Modelling the enthalpy of formation of alkanes. *Indian J. Chem.* **1998**, *37A*, 849–855.
6. Gravovac, A.; Ghorbani, M.; Hosseinzadeh, M.A. Computing fifth geometric-arithmatic index ABC_4 index of nanostar dendrimers. *Optoelectron. Adv. Mater. Rapid Commun.* **2010**, *4*, 1419–1422.
7. Hayat, S.; Imran, M. Computation of topological indices of certain networks. *Appl. Math. Comput.* **2014**, *240*, 213–228. [CrossRef]
8. Nadeem, M.F.; Zafar, S.; Zahid, Z. On certain topological indices of the line graph of subdivision graphs. *Appl. Math. Comput.* **2015**, *271*, 790–794. [CrossRef]
9. Nadeem, M.F.; Zafar, S.; Zahid, Z. On topological properties of the line graphs of subdivision graphs of certain nanostructures. *Appl. Math. Comput.* **2016**, *273*, 125–130. [CrossRef]
10. Sharma, V.; Goswami, R.; Madan, A.K. Eccentric connectivity index: A novel highly discriminating topological descriptor for structure property and structure activity studies. *J. Chem. Inf. Comput. Sci.* **1997**, *37*, 273–282. [CrossRef]
11. Dureja, H.; Madan, A.K. Topochemical models for prediction of cyclin-dependent kinase 2 inhibitory activity of indole-2-ones. *J. Mol. Model.* **2005**, *11*, 525–531. [CrossRef] [PubMed]
12. Ilic, A.; Gutman, I. Eccentric-connectivity index of chemical trees. *MATCH Commun. Math. Comput. Chem.* **2011**, *65*, 731–744.

13. Kumar, N.; Madan, A.K. Application of graph theory: Prediction of cytosolic phospholipase A(2) inhibitory activity of propan-2-ones. *J. Math. Chem.* **2006**, *39*, 511–521. [CrossRef]
14. Zhou, B. On eccentric-connectivity index. *MATCH Commun. Math. Comput. Chem.* **2010**, *63*, 181–198.
15. Farooq, R.; Malik, M.A. On some eccentricity based topological indices of nanostar dendrimers. *Optoelectron. Adv. Mater. Rapid Commun.* **2015**, *9*, 842–849.
16. Li, X.; Zhao, H. Trees with the first three smallest and largest generalized topological indices. *MATCH Commun. Math. Comput. Chem.* **2004**, *50*, 57–62.
17. Ghorbani, M.; Hosseinzadeh, M.A. A new version of Zagreb indices. *Filomat* **2012**, *26*, 93–100. [CrossRef]
18. Alaeiyan, M.; Asadpour, J.; Mojarad, R. A numerical method for MEC polynomial and MEC index of one pentagonal carbon nanocones. *Fuller. Nanotub. Carbon Nanostruct.* **2013**, *21*, 825–835. [CrossRef]
19. Ashrafi, A.R.; Ghorbani, M.; Hossein-Zadeh, M.A. The eccentric-connectivity polynomial of some graph operations. *Serdica J. Comput.* **2011**, *5*, 101–116.
20. Gupta, S.; Singh, M.; Madan, A.K. Connective eccentricity index: A novel topological descriptor for predicting biological activity. *J. Mol. Graph. Model.* **2000**, *18*, 18–25. [CrossRef]
21. De, N. Relationship between augmented eccentric-connectivity index and some other graph invariants. *Int. J. Adv. Math.* **2013**, *1*, 26–32. [CrossRef]
22. Došlić, T.; Saheli, M. Augmented eccentric-connectivity index. *Miskolc Math. Notes* **2011**, *12*, 149–157. [CrossRef]
23. Ediz, S. On the Ediz eccentric connectivity index of a graph. *Optoelectron. Adv. Mater. Rapid Commun.* **2011**, *5*, 1263–1264.
24. Ediz, S. Reverse eccentric connectivity index. *Optoelectron. Adv. Mater. Rapid Commun.* **2012**, *6*, 664–667.
25. Beck, I. Coloring of a commutative ring. *J. Algebra* **1988**, *116*, 208–226. [CrossRef]
26. Anderson, D.F.; Livingston, P.S. The Zero-divisor Graph of Commutative Ring. *J. Algebra* **1999**, *217*, 434–447. [CrossRef]
27. Anderson, D.F.; Badawi, A. On the Zero-Divisor Graph of a Ring. *Commun. Algebra* **2008**, *36*, 3073–3092. [CrossRef]
28. Akbari, S.; Mohammadian, A. On the zero-divisor graph of a commutative ring. *J. Algebra* **2004**, *274*, 847–855. [CrossRef]
29. Anderson, D.F.; Mulay, S.B. On the diameter and girth of a zero-divisor graph. *J. Pure Appl. Algebra* **2008**, *210*, 543–550. [CrossRef]
30. Asir, T.; Tamizh Chelvam, T. On the total graph and its complement of a commutative ring. *Commun. Algebra* **2013**, *41*, 3820–3835. [CrossRef]
31. Samei, K. The zero-divisor graph of a reduced ring. *J. Pure Appl. Algebra* **2007**, *209*, 813–821. [CrossRef]
32. Tamizh Chelvam, T.; Asir, T. A note on total graph of $\mathbb{Z}_n$. *J. Discret. Math. Sci. Cryptogr.* **2011**, *14*, 1–7. [CrossRef]
33. Belov, A.Y. Linear Recurrence Equations on a Tree. *Math. Notes* **2005**, *78*, 603–609. [CrossRef]
34. Belov, A.Y.; Borisenko, V.V.; Latyshev, V.N. Monomial algebras. *J. Math. Sci.* **1997**, *87*, 3463–3575. [CrossRef]
35. Ahmad, A.; Bača, M.; Semaničová–Feňovčíková, A. Computation of vertex based eccentric topological indices of zero divisor graph of $\mathbb{Z}_{p^2} \times \mathbb{Z}_q$. **2018**, submitted.

© 2018 by the authors. Licensee MDPI, Basel, Switzerland. This article is an open access article distributed under the terms and conditions of the Creative Commons Attribution (CC BY) license (http://creativecommons.org/licenses/by/4.0/).

Article
Resistance Distance in H-Join of Graphs $G_1, G_2, \ldots, G_k$

Li Zhang [1], Jing Zhao [1], Jia-Bao Liu [1,*] and Micheal Arockiaraj [2]

1. School of Mathematics and Physics, Anhui Jianzhu University, Hefei 230601, China; zhang12@mail.ustc.edu.cn (L.Z.); zhaojing94823@163.com (J.Z.)
2. Department of Mathematics, Loyola College, Chennai 600034, India; marockiaraj@gmail.com
* Correspondence: liujiabaoad@163.com

Received: 11 October 2018; Accepted: 21 November 2018; Published: 26 November 2018

Abstract: In view of the wide application of resistance distance, the computation of resistance distance in various graphs becomes one of the main topics. In this paper, we aim to compute resistance distance in H-join of graphs $G_1, G_2, \ldots, G_k$. Recall that H is an arbitrary graph with $V(H) = \{1, 2, \ldots, k\}$, and $G_1, G_2, \ldots, G_k$ are disjoint graphs. Then, the H-join of graphs $G_1, G_2, \ldots, G_k$, denoted by $\bigvee_H \{G_1, G_2, \ldots, G_k\}$, is a graph formed by taking $G_1, G_2, \ldots, G_k$ and joining every vertex of G_i to every vertex of G_j whenever i is adjacent to j in H. Here, we first give the Laplacian matrix of $\bigvee_H \{G_1, G_2, \ldots, G_k\}$, and then give a $\{1\}$-inverse $L(\bigvee_H \{G_1, G_2, \ldots, G_k\})^{\{1\}}$ or group inverse $L(\bigvee_H \{G_1, G_2, \ldots, G_k\})^{\#}$ of $L(\bigvee_H \{G_1, G_2, \ldots, G_k\})$. It is well know that, there exists a relationship between resistance distance and entries of $\{1\}$-inverse or group inverse. Therefore, we can easily obtain resistance distance in $\bigvee_H \{G_1, G_2, \ldots, G_k\}$. In addition, some applications are presented in this paper.

Keywords: graph; Laplacian matrix; resistance distance; group inverse

1. Introduction

Throughout this paper, "G is a graph" always means that "G is a simple and undirected graph". Moreover, we denote a graph G by $G = (V(G), E(G))$, where $V(G) = \{v_1, v_2, \ldots, v_n\}$ is the vertex set and $E(G) = \{e_1, e_2, \ldots, e_m\}$ is the edge set of G. Associated with a graph G, some matrices characterize the structure of G, such as the adjacency matrix $A(G)$, which is an $n \times n$ matrix with entry $a_{ij} = 1$ if v_i and v_j are adjacent in G, and $a_{ij} = 0$ otherwise, the diagonal matrix $D(G)$ with diagonal entries $d_G(v_1), d_G(v_2), \ldots, d_G(v_n)$ and the Laplacian matrix $L(G)$, which is $D(G) - A(G)$. Let I_n denote the unit matrix of order n, $\mathbf{1}_n$ be the all-one column vector of dimension n and $J_{n \times m}$ be the all-one $n \times m$-matrix. For more detail, one can refer to [1,2] for the definitions and notions in the paper.

It is rather clear that, from some given graphs, a big graph arises by the help of graph operations, such as the Cartesian product, the Kronecker product, the corona graph, the neighborhood corona graph and subdivision-vertex join and subdivision-edge join of graphs (see [3–7]). Furthermore, following [8], from an arbitrary graph H of order k and graphs $G_1, G_2, \ldots, G_k$, we obtain a new graph called H-join of graphs $G_1, G_2, \ldots, G_k$, which is denoted by $\bigvee_H \{G_1, G_2, \ldots, G_k\}$, for detail:

Definition 1. *Let H be an arbitrary graph with $V(H) = \{1, 2, \ldots, k\}$, and $G_1, G_2, \ldots, G_k$ be disjoint graphs of orders $n_1, n_2, \ldots, n_k$. The H-join of graphs $G_1, G_2, \ldots, G_k$, which is denoted by $\bigvee_H \{G_1, G_2, \ldots, G_k\}$, is a graph formed by taking $G_1, G_2, \ldots, G_k$ and joining every vertex of G_i to every vertex of G_j whenever i is adjacent to j in H. Particularly, $\bigvee_H \{G_1, G_1, \ldots, G_1\}$ is denoted by $H \odot G_1$.*

Example 1. *Let P_n and C_n be a path and a cycle with n vertices. Then, $\bigvee_{P_3} \{P_3, P_1, P_2\}$, $P_3 \odot P_2$ and $C_3 \odot P_3$ are as follows (Figures 1 and 2).*

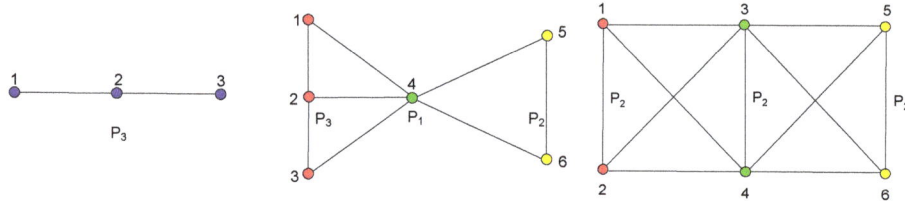

Figure 1. $\vee_{P_3}\{P_3, P_1, P_2\}$ and $P_3 \odot P_2$.

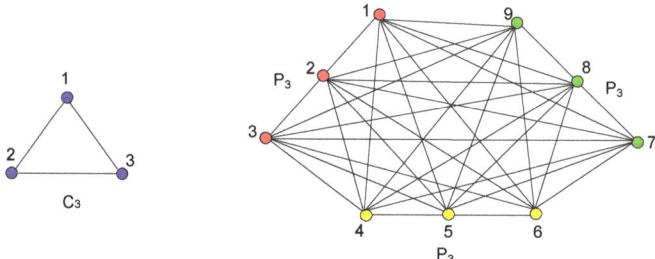

Figure 2. $C_3 \odot P_3$.

As we know, the length of a shortest path between vertices v_i and v_j, which is denoted by d_{ij}, is the conventional distance. However, it does not apply to some practical situations, such as electrical network. Thus, based on electrical network theory, Klein and Randić introduced a new distance called resistance distance ([9]). The resistance distance between vertices v_i and v_j is denoted by r_{ij}, and, in fact, r_{ij} is the effective electrical resistance between v_i and v_j if every edge of G is replaced by a unit resistor. In view of its practical application, resistance distance was widely explored by many authors. One of the main topics in the study of resistance distance is to determine it in various graphs. For example, from [10], one would know that how r_{ij} can be computed from the Laplacian matrix of the graph; in [11], authors gave the resistance distance between any two vertices of a wheel and a fan; in [3], authors obtained formulae for resistance distance in subdivision-vertex join and subdivision-edge join of graphs; recently, in [12], authors gave the resistance distance in corona and the neighborhood corona graphs of two disjoint graphs. Except for the above, one can refer to [13–20] for more information.

Motivated by the study of resistance distance and graph operations, a natural question arises: *what is the resistance distance in* $\vee_H\{G_1, G_2, \ldots, G_k\}$? In fact, this paper focuses on this question, gives resistance distance in H-join of graphs $G_1, G_2, \ldots, G_k$ and finally presents some applications.

2. Preliminaries

Recall that, for a matrix M, a $\{1\}$-inverse of M, which is always denoted by $M^{\{1\}}$, is a matrix X such that $MXM = M$. For a square matrix M, the group inverse of M, which is denoted by $M^{\#}$, is the unique matrix X such that the following hold: $(1) MXM = M; (2) XMX = X; (3) MX = XM$. It is well-known that $M^{\#}$ exists if and only if rank(M)=rank(M^2). Therefore, $A^{\#}$ exists and it is a

{1}-inverse of A, whenever A is a real symmetric. In fact, assume that A is a real symmetric matrix and U is an orthogonal matrix (i.e., $UU^T = U^T U = I$), such that $A = U^T diag\{\lambda_1, \lambda_2, \cdots, \lambda_n\} U$, where $\lambda_1, \lambda_2, \cdots, \lambda_n$ are eigenvalues of A. Then, $A^\# = U^T diag\{f(\lambda_1), f(\lambda_2), \cdots, f(\lambda_n)\} U$, where

$$f(\lambda_i) = \begin{cases} 1/\lambda_i, & \text{if } \lambda_i \neq 0, \\ 0, & \text{if } \lambda_i = 0. \end{cases}$$

Note that the Laplacian matrix $L(G)$ of a graph G is real symmetric. Thus, $L(G)^\#$ exists. For more detail about the group inverse of the Laplacian matrix of a graph, see [21].

Lemma 1 ([3,22]). *Let* $L = \begin{pmatrix} L_1 & L_2 \\ L_2^T & L_3 \end{pmatrix}$ *be the Laplacian matrix of a connected graph. Assume that L_1 is nonsingular. Denote $S = L_3 - L_2^T L_1^{-1} L_2$. Then,*

(1) $\begin{pmatrix} L_1^{-1} + L_1^{-1} L_2 S^\# L_2^T L_1^{-1} & -L_1^{-1} L_2 S^\# \\ -S^\# L_2^T L_1^{-1} & S^\# \end{pmatrix}$ *is a symmetric {1}-inverse of L.*

(2) *If each column vector of L_2 is $\mathbf{1}$ or a zero vector, then* $\begin{pmatrix} L_1^{-1} & 0 \\ 0 & S^\# \end{pmatrix}$ *is a symmetric {1}-inverse of L.*

In order to compute the inverse of a matrix, the next lemma is useful.

Lemma 2 ([3]). *Let* $M = \begin{pmatrix} A & B \\ C & D \end{pmatrix}$ *be a nonsingular matrix. If A and D are nonsingular, then*

$$M^{-1} = \begin{pmatrix} A^{-1} + A^{-1} B S^{-1} C A^{-1} & -A^{-1} B S^{-1} \\ -S^{-1} C A^{-1} & S^{-1} \end{pmatrix},$$

where $S = D - CA^{-1}B$ is the Schur complement of A in M.

One of the important applications of group inverse $L(G)^\#$ or {1}-inverse $L(G)^{\{1\}}$ is based on the following fact, which gives the formulae for resistance distance.

Lemma 3 ([3]). *Let G be a connected graph and $(L(G))_{ij}$ be the (i,j)-entry of the Laplacian matrix $L(G)$. Then,*

$$r_{ij}(G) = (L(G)^{\{1\}})_{ii} + (L(G)^{\{1\}})_{jj} - (L(G)^{\{1\}})_{ij} - (L(G)^{\{1\}})_{ji}$$
$$= (L(G)^\#)_{ii} + (L(G)^\#)_{jj} - 2(L(G)^\#)_{ij}.$$

3. Main Results

Now, we turn to compute resistance distance in H-join of graphs $G_1, G_2, \ldots, G_k$. Denote $G = \bigvee_H \{G_1, G_2, \ldots, G_k\}$. Keeping Lemma 3 in mind, we only need to compute the group inverse $L(G)^\#$ or a {1}-inverse $L(G)^{\{1\}}$.

First, we give the Laplacian matrix $L(G)$ of G.

Theorem 1. *Let H be an arbitrary graph with $V(H) = \{1, 2, \ldots, k\}$, and G_i be the disjoint graph of order n_i ($i = 1, 2, \ldots, k$). Assume that the adjacency matrix of H is $A(H) = (a_{ij})_k$ and*

$$A(H)(n_1, n_2, \ldots, n_k)^T = (m_1, m_2, \ldots, m_k)^T.$$

Denote $G = \bigvee_H \{G_1, G_2, \ldots, G_k\}$, and label the n_i vertices of G_i with

$$V(G_i) = \{v_i^{n_1 + \cdots + n_{i-1} + 1}, v_i^{n_1 + \cdots + n_{i-1} + 2}, \ldots, v_i^{n_1 + \cdots + n_{i-1} + n_i}\}.$$

Then, $V(G) = \{v_1^1, \ldots, v_1^{n_1}, \ldots, v_i^{n_1+\cdots+n_{i-1}+1}, \ldots, v_i^{n_1+\cdots+n_{i-1}+n_i}, \ldots, v_k^{n_1+\cdots+n_{k-1}+1}, \ldots, v_k^{n_1+\cdots+n_{k-1}+n_k}\}$,
and the Laplacian matrix $L(G)$ of G is

$$\begin{pmatrix} L(G_1)+m_1I_{n_1} & 0 & \cdots & 0 \\ 0 & L(G_2)+m_2I_{n_2} & \cdots & 0 \\ \vdots & \vdots & \ddots & \vdots \\ 0 & 0 & \cdots & L(G_k)+m_kI_{n_k} \end{pmatrix} - \begin{pmatrix} a_{11}J_{n_1\times n_1} & a_{12}J_{n_1\times n_2} & \cdots & a_{1k}J_{n_1\times n_k} \\ a_{21}J_{n_2\times n_1} & a_{22}J_{n_2\times n_2} & \cdots & a_{2k}J_{n_2\times n_k} \\ \vdots & \vdots & \ddots & \vdots \\ a_{k1}J_{n_k\times n_1} & a_{k2}J_{n_k\times n_2} & \cdots & a_{kk}J_{n_k\times n_k} \end{pmatrix}.$$

Proof. Clearly, all of the diagonal matrix $D(G)$, the adjacency matrix $A(G)$ and the Laplacian matrix $L(G)$ are partitioned $k \times k$-matrixes, whose (ij)-entry is a $n_i \times n_j$-matrix. We proceed via the following steps:

(1) *The diagonal matrix $D(G)$ of G.*

Obviously, the degree increment of $V(G_i)$ depends on the i-th line $(a_{i1}\ a_{i2}\cdots a_{ik})$ of $A(H)$. For detail, if $a_{ij} = 1, j = 1, 2, \cdots, k$, then every vertex of G_j is joined to every vertex of G_i, that is, the increment of each vertex in $V(G_i)$ is $a_{ij}n_j$. Otherwise, that is $a_{ij} = 0$, the increment is zero, which can also be written by $a_{ij}n_j$. In general, the degree increment of each vertex of $V(G_i)$ is

$$a_{i1}n_1 + a_{i2}n_2 + \cdots + a_{ik}n_k = m_i.$$

Consequently, the diagonal matrix of G is

$$D(G) = \begin{pmatrix} D(G_1)+m_1I_{n_1} & 0 & \cdots & 0 \\ 0 & D(G_2)+m_2I_{n_2} & \cdots & 0 \\ \vdots & \vdots & \ddots & \vdots \\ 0 & 0 & \cdots & D(G_k)+m_kI_{n_k} \end{pmatrix}.$$

(2) *The adjacency matrix $A(G)$ of G.*

Similarly, the i-th line of the partitioned matrixes $A(G)$ also relies on $(a_{i1}\ a_{i2}\cdots a_{ik})$. Assume that $a_{ij} = 1$. Then, every vertex of G_j is joined to every vertex of G_i. Thus, the (ij)-entry of $A(G)$ is $J_{n_i\times n_j}$, which is $a_{ij}J_{n_i\times n_j}$. If $a_{ij} = 0$, then there is no edge between $V(G_i)$ and $V(G_j)$, that is, the (ij)-entry of $A(G)$ is zero. However, in this case, we can also denote it by $a_{ij}J_{n_i\times n_j}$. Note that the above holds for $i = j$. Therefore, the adjacency matrix of G is

$$A(G) = \begin{pmatrix} A(G_1) & 0 & \cdots & 0 \\ 0 & A(G_2) & \cdots & 0 \\ \vdots & \vdots & \ddots & \vdots \\ 0 & 0 & \cdots & A(G_k) \end{pmatrix} + \begin{pmatrix} a_{11}J_{n_1\times n_1} & a_{12}J_{n_1\times n_2} & \cdots & a_{1k}J_{n_1\times n_k} \\ a_{21}J_{n_2\times n_1} & a_{22}J_{n_1\times n_2} & \cdots & a_{2k}J_{n_2\times n_k} \\ \vdots & \vdots & \ddots & \vdots \\ a_{k1}J_{n_k\times n_1} & a_{k2}J_{n_k\times n_2} & \cdots & a_{2k}J_{n_k\times n_k} \end{pmatrix}.$$

(3) *The Laplacian matrix $L(G)$ of G.*

With respect to the above results, the Laplacian matrix $L(G)$ of G is the Theorem 1. □

According to Theorem 1 and Lemma 1, we finally obtain a symmetric $\{1\}$-inverse of $L(G)$.

Theorem 2. *Let H be an arbitrary connected graph with $V(H) = \{1, 2, \ldots, k\}$, and G_i be disjoint connected graph of order n_i $(i = 1, 2, \ldots, k)$. Assume that $A(H) = (a_{ij})_k$ and $A(H)(n_1, n_2, \ldots, n_k)^T = (m_1, m_2, \ldots, m_k)^T$. Denote $G = \bigvee_H\{G_1, G_2, \ldots, G_k\}$. Then, the following matrix*

$$\begin{pmatrix} L_1^{-1} + L_1^{-1}L_2 S^{\#} L_2^T L_1^{-1} & -L_1^{-1}L_2 S^{\#} \\ -S^{\#} L_2^T L_1^{-1} & S^{\#} \end{pmatrix}$$

is a symmetric $\{1\}$-inverse of $L(G)$, where

$$L_1 = L(G_1) + m_1 I_{n_1};$$
$$L_2 = -(a_{12} J_{n_1 \times n_2}\ a_{13} J_{n_1 \times n_3} \cdots a_{1k} J_{n_1 \times n_k});$$
$$L_3 = diag\{L(G_2) + m_2 I_{n_2}, \ldots, L(G_k) + m_k I_{n_k}\} - (a_{ij} J_{n_i \times n_j})_{i,j=2,3,\ldots,k};$$
$$S = L_3 - L_2^T L_1^{-1} L_2$$
$$= diag\{L(G_2) + m_2 I_{n_2}, \ldots, L(G_k) + m_k I_{n_k}\} - ((a_{ij} + a_{i1} a_{1j} s) J_{n_i \times n_j})_{i,j=2,3,\ldots,k}$$
$$= L_3 - ((a_{i1} a_{1j} s) J_{n_i \times n_j})_{i,j=2,3,\ldots,k}$$
$$= L_3 - sBB^T.$$

Here, $s = \mathbf{1}_{n_1}^T L_1^{-1} \mathbf{1}_{n_1}$ and $B^T = \left(a_{12} \mathbf{1}_{n_2}^T\ a_{13} \mathbf{1}_{n_3}^T\ \cdots\ a_{1k} \mathbf{1}_{n_k}^T\right)$.

Proof. Note that all of H and $G_1, G_2, \ldots, G_k$ are connected. Thus, it is easy to show that G is connected. By Theorem 1, we have the Laplacian matrix $L(G)$ of G. In order to give a $\{1\}$-inverse of $L(G)$ with the help of Lemma 1, we further divide $L(G)$ into blocks $L(G) = \begin{pmatrix} L_1 & L_2 \\ L_2^T & L_3 \end{pmatrix}$, where

$$L_1 = L(G_1) + m_1 I_{n_1} - a_{11} J_{n_1 \times n_1} = L(G_1) + m_1 I_{n_1};$$
$$L_2 = -(a_{12} J_{n_1 \times n_2}\ a_{13} J_{n_1 \times n_3} \cdots a_{1k} J_{n_1 \times n_k});$$
$$L_3 = \begin{pmatrix} L(G_2) + m_2 I_{n_2} & \cdots & 0 \\ \vdots & \ddots & \vdots \\ 0 & \cdots & L(G_k) + m_k I_{n_k} \end{pmatrix} - \begin{pmatrix} a_{22} J_{n_2 \times n_2} & \cdots & a_{2k} J_{n_2 \times n_k} \\ \vdots & & \vdots \\ a_{k2} J_{n_k \times n_2} & \cdots & a_{kk} J_{n_k \times n_k} \end{pmatrix}.$$

Note that $L_2^T = \begin{pmatrix} -a_{12} J_{n_2 \times n_1} \\ -a_{13} J_{n_3 \times n_1} \\ \vdots \\ -a_{1k} J_{n_k \times n_1} \end{pmatrix}$. Thus, we have

$$L_2^T L_1^{-1} L_2 = \begin{pmatrix} a_{12} J_{n_2 \times n_1} \\ a_{13} J_{n_3 \times n_1} \\ \vdots \\ a_{1k} J_{n_k \times n_1} \end{pmatrix} L_1^{-1} (a_{12} J_{n_1 \times n_2}\ a_{13} J_{n_1 \times n_3} \cdots a_{1k} J_{n_1 \times n_k})$$

$$= \begin{pmatrix} a_{12} a_{12} J_{n_2 \times n_1} L_1^{-1} J_{n_1 \times n_2} & \cdots & a_{12} a_{1k} J_{n_2 \times n_1} L_1^{-1} J_{n_1 \times n_k} \\ a_{13} a_{12} J_{n_3 \times n_1} L_1^{-1} J_{n_1 \times n_2} & \cdots & a_{13} a_{1k} J_{n_3 \times n_1} L_1^{-1} J_{n_1 \times n_k} \\ \vdots & & \vdots \\ a_{1k} a_{12} J_{n_k \times n_1} L_1^{-1} J_{n_1 \times n_2} & \cdots & a_{1k} a_{1k} J_{n_k \times n_1} L_1^{-1} J_{n_1 \times n_k} \end{pmatrix}.$$

Since $J_{n_i\times n_1}L_1^{-1}J_{n_1\times n_j} = sJ_{n_i\times n_j}$, where $s = \mathbf{1}_{n_1}^T L_1^{-1}\mathbf{1}_{n_1} \in \mathbb{R}$, we have

$$L_2^T L_1^{-1} L_2 = s\begin{pmatrix} a_{12}a_{12}J_{n_2\times n_2} & \cdots & a_{12}a_{1k}J_{n_2\times n_k} \\ a_{13}a_{12}J_{n_3\times n_2} & \cdots & a_{13}a_{1k}J_{n_3\times n_k} \\ \vdots & & \vdots \\ a_{1k}a_{12}J_{n_k\times n_2} & \cdots & a_{1k}a_{1k}J_{n_k\times n_k} \end{pmatrix}$$

$$= s\begin{pmatrix} a_{12}\mathbf{1}_{n_2} \\ a_{13}\mathbf{1}_{n_3} \\ \vdots \\ a_{1k}\mathbf{1}_{n_k} \end{pmatrix} \begin{pmatrix} a_{12}\mathbf{1}_{n_2}^T & a_{13}\mathbf{1}_{n_3}^T & \cdots a_{1k}\mathbf{1}_{n_k}^T \end{pmatrix}.$$

Assume that B is a column vector of dimension $n_2 + n_3 + \cdots + n_k$ satisfying

$$B^T = \begin{pmatrix} a_{12}\mathbf{1}_{n_2}^T & a_{13}\mathbf{1}_{n_3}^T & \cdots a_{1k}\mathbf{1}_{n_k}^T \end{pmatrix}.$$

Therefore, $S = L_3 - L_2^T L_1^{-1} L_2$ has three forms:

$$S = \text{diag}\{L(G_2) + m_2 I_{n_2}, \ldots, L(G_k) + m_k I_{n_k}\} - ((a_{ij} + a_{i1}a_{1j}s)J_{n_i\times n_j})_{i,j=2,3,\ldots,k}$$
$$= L_3 - s(a_{i1}a_{1j}J_{n_i\times n_j})_{i,j=2,3,\ldots,k}$$
$$= L_3 - sBB^T.$$

By Lemma 1, we know that Theorem 2 holds. □

Recall that the Kronecker product $A \otimes B$ ([23]) of two matrices $A = (a_{ij})_{m\times n}$ and $B = (b_{ij})_{p\times q}$ is an $mp \times nq$-matrix obtained from A by replacing every element a_{ij} by $a_{ij}B$. As an application of Theorem 2, we easily obtain a symmetric $\{1\}$-inverse of $L(H \odot G)$.

Corollary 1. *Let H be an arbitrary connected graph with k vertices and G be a connected graph with n vertices. Assume that $A(H) = \begin{pmatrix} 0_{1\times 1} & H_2 \\ H_2^T & H_3 \end{pmatrix}$ and $nA(H)\mathbf{1}_n = nD(H)\mathbf{1}_n = (m_1, m_2, \ldots, m_k)^T$. Then, the following matrix*

$$\begin{pmatrix} L_1^{-1} + L_1^{-1}L_2 S^\# L_2^T L_1^{-1} & -L_1^{-1}L_2 S^\# \\ -S^\# L_2^T L_1^{-1} & S^\# \end{pmatrix}$$

is a symmetric $\{1\}$-inverse of $L(H \odot G)$, where

$$L_1 = L(G) + m_1 I_n;$$
$$L_2 = -H_2 \otimes J_{n\times n};$$
$$L_3 = I_{k-1} \otimes L(G) + \text{diag}\{m_2, \ldots, m_k\} \otimes I_n - H_3 \otimes J_{n\times n};$$
$$S = L_3 - L_2^T L_1^{-1} L_2$$
$$= L_3 - s(H_2^T \otimes \mathbf{1}_n)(H_2 \otimes \mathbf{1}_n^T)$$
$$= L_3 - s(H_2^T H_2) \otimes J_{n\times n}.$$

Here, $s = \mathbf{1}_n^T L_1^{-1} \mathbf{1}_n$.

4. Some Applications

Now, we give a specific application of formation mentioned in the Section 2. Let A be a real symmetric such that $\lambda_1, \lambda_2, \cdots, \lambda_{n-1}, 0$ are eigenvalues of A and 0 is a simple eigenvalue. Assume that

A is a real symmetric and U is an orthogonal matrix such that $A = U^T diag\{\lambda_1, \lambda_2, \cdots, \lambda_{n-1}, 0\} U$. Then, $A^{\#} = U^T diag\{\frac{1}{\lambda_1}, \frac{1}{\lambda_2}, \cdots, \frac{1}{\lambda_{n-1}}, 0\} U$.

Example 2. *Compute resistance distance in $G = \vee_{P_3}\{P_3, P_1, P_2\}$ (see Figure 1).*

Step 1. We label the vertices $P_3 = \{v_1^1, v_1^2, v_1^3\}$, $P_1 = \{v_2^4\}$, $P_2 = \{v_3^5, v_3^6\}$. Then,

$$V(G) = \{v_1^1, v_1^2, v_1^3, v_2^4, v_3^5, v_3^6\}.$$

Note that $A(P_3)\begin{pmatrix} 3 \\ 1 \\ 2 \end{pmatrix} = \begin{pmatrix} 0 & 1 & 0 \\ 1 & 0 & 1 \\ 0 & 1 & 0 \end{pmatrix}\begin{pmatrix} 3 \\ 1 \\ 2 \end{pmatrix} = \begin{pmatrix} 1 \\ 5 \\ 1 \end{pmatrix}$. Thus, the Laplacian matrix of G is

$$L(G) = \begin{pmatrix} L(P_3) + I_3 & 0 & 0 \\ 0 & L(P_1) + 5I_1 & 0 \\ 0 & 0 & L(P_2) + I_2 \end{pmatrix} - \begin{pmatrix} 0_{3\times3} & J_{3\times1} & 0_{3\times2} \\ J_{1\times3} & 0_{1\times1} & J_{1\times2} \\ 0_{2\times3} & J_{2\times1} & 0_{2\times2} \end{pmatrix} = \begin{pmatrix} L_1 & L_2 \\ L_2^T & L_3 \end{pmatrix},$$

where $L_1 = L(P_3) + I_3 = \begin{pmatrix} 2 & -1 & 0 \\ -1 & 3 & -1 \\ 0 & -1 & 2 \end{pmatrix}$, $L_2 = -(J_{3\times1} \; 0_{3\times2}) = \begin{pmatrix} -1 & 0 & 0 \\ -1 & 0 & 0 \\ -1 & 0 & 0 \end{pmatrix}$ and

$$L_3 = \begin{pmatrix} L(P_1) + 5I_1 & -J_{1\times2} \\ -J_{2\times1} & L(P_2) + I_2 \end{pmatrix} = \begin{pmatrix} 5 & -1 & -1 \\ -1 & 2 & -1 \\ -1 & -1 & 2 \end{pmatrix}.$$

Step 2. $L_1^{-1} = \frac{1}{8}\begin{pmatrix} 5 & 2 & 1 \\ 2 & 4 & 2 \\ 1 & 2 & 5 \end{pmatrix}$ and so $s = 1_3^T L_1^{-1} 1_3 = 3$. By Theorem 2, $B = \begin{pmatrix} 1 \\ 0 \\ 0 \end{pmatrix}$ and

$S = \begin{pmatrix} 2 & -1 & -1 \\ -1 & 2 & -1 \\ -1 & -1 & 2 \end{pmatrix}$. By the formula at the beginning of this section, $S^{\#} = \frac{1}{9}\begin{pmatrix} 2 & -1 & -1 \\ -1 & 2 & -1 \\ -1 & -1 & 2 \end{pmatrix}$.

Furthermore, $-L_1^{-1} L_2 S^{\#} = \frac{1}{9}\begin{pmatrix} 2 & -1 & -1 \\ 2 & -1 & -1 \\ 2 & -1 & -1 \end{pmatrix}$ and $L_1^{-1} L_2 S^{\#} L_2^T L_1^{-1} = \frac{2}{9} J_{3\times3}$.

Step 3. By Lemma 1 or Theorem 2, $\begin{pmatrix} \frac{1}{8}\begin{pmatrix} 5 & 2 & 1 \\ 2 & 4 & 2 \\ 1 & 2 & 5 \end{pmatrix} + \frac{2}{9} J_{3\times3} & \frac{1}{9}\begin{pmatrix} 2 & -1 & -1 \\ 2 & -1 & -1 \\ 2 & -1 & -1 \end{pmatrix} \\ \frac{1}{9}\begin{pmatrix} 2 & 2 & 2 \\ -1 & -1 & -1 \\ -1 & -1 & -1 \end{pmatrix} & \frac{1}{9}\begin{pmatrix} 2 & -1 & -1 \\ -1 & 2 & -1 \\ -1 & -1 & 2 \end{pmatrix} \end{pmatrix}$ is a

$\{1\}$-inverse of $L(G)$.

Step 4. In view of Lemma 3, the matrix whose (i,j)-entry is the resistance distance r_{ij} between vertices v^i and v^j is

$$\begin{pmatrix} 0 & \frac{5}{8} & 1 & \frac{5}{8} & \frac{31}{24} & \frac{31}{24} \\ \frac{5}{8} & 0 & \frac{5}{8} & \frac{1}{2} & \frac{7}{6} & \frac{7}{6} \\ 1 & \frac{5}{8} & 0 & \frac{5}{8} & \frac{31}{24} & \frac{31}{24} \\ \frac{5}{8} & \frac{1}{2} & \frac{5}{8} & 0 & \frac{2}{3} & \frac{2}{3} \\ \frac{31}{24} & \frac{7}{6} & \frac{31}{24} & \frac{2}{3} & 0 & \frac{2}{3} \\ \frac{31}{24} & \frac{7}{6} & \frac{31}{24} & \frac{2}{3} & \frac{2}{3} & 0 \end{pmatrix}.$$

Example 3. Assume that $G = P_3 \odot P_2$ (see Figure 1). Then, the Laplacian matrix of G is

$$L(G) = \begin{pmatrix} L(P_2) + 2I_2 & 0 & 0 \\ 0 & L(P_2) + 4I_2 & 0 \\ 0 & 0 & L(P_2) + 2I_2 \end{pmatrix} - \begin{pmatrix} 0_{2\times 2} & J_{2\times 2} & 0_{2\times 2} \\ J_{2\times 2} & 0_{2\times 2} & J_{2\times 2} \\ 0_{2\times 2} & J_{2\times 2} & 0_{2\times 2} \end{pmatrix}.$$

From Theorem 2, we have that the matrix

$$\begin{pmatrix} \frac{1}{16}\begin{pmatrix} 7 & 3 \\ 3 & 7 \end{pmatrix} & \frac{1}{16}\begin{pmatrix} 1 & 1 \\ 1 & 1 \end{pmatrix} & \frac{1}{16}\begin{pmatrix} 1 & 1 & -1 & -1 \\ 1 & 1 & -1 & -1 \end{pmatrix} \\ \frac{1}{16}\begin{pmatrix} 1 & 1 \\ 1 & 1 \\ -1 & -1 \\ -1 & -1 \end{pmatrix} & & \frac{1}{48}\begin{pmatrix} 7 & -1 & -3 & -3 \\ -1 & 7 & -3 & -3 \\ -3 & -3 & 9 & -3 \\ -3 & -3 & -3 & 9 \end{pmatrix} \end{pmatrix}$$ is

a $\{1\}$-inverse of $L(G)$.

Thus, the matrix whose (i,j)-entry is r_{ij} is

$$\begin{pmatrix} 0 & \frac{1}{2} & \frac{11}{24} & \frac{11}{24} & \frac{3}{4} & \frac{3}{4} \\ \frac{1}{2} & 0 & \frac{11}{24} & \frac{11}{24} & \frac{3}{4} & \frac{3}{4} \\ \frac{11}{24} & \frac{11}{24} & 0 & \frac{1}{3} & \frac{11}{24} & \frac{11}{24} \\ \frac{11}{24} & \frac{11}{24} & \frac{1}{3} & 0 & \frac{11}{24} & \frac{11}{24} \\ \frac{3}{4} & \frac{3}{4} & \frac{11}{24} & \frac{11}{24} & 0 & \frac{1}{2} \\ \frac{3}{4} & \frac{3}{4} & \frac{11}{24} & \frac{11}{24} & \frac{1}{2} & 0 \end{pmatrix}.$$

Example 4. Assume that $G = C_3 \odot P_3$ (see Figure 2). Then, the Laplacian matrix of G is

$$L(G) = \begin{pmatrix} L(P_3) + 6I_3 & 0 & 0 \\ 0 & L(P_3) + 6I_3 & 0 \\ 0 & 0 & L(P_3) + 6I_3 \end{pmatrix} - \begin{pmatrix} 0_{3\times 3} & J_{3\times 3} & J_{3\times 3} \\ J_{3\times 3} & 0_{3\times 3} & J_{3\times 3} \\ J_{3\times 3} & J_{3\times 3} & 0_{3\times 3} \end{pmatrix}.$$

Based on Theorem 2, the matrix $\begin{pmatrix} A & \frac{1}{27}J_{3\times 3} & 0_{3\times 3} \\ \frac{1}{27}J_{3\times 3} & B & 0_{3\times 3} \\ 0_{3\times 3} & 0_{3\times 3} & S^{\#} \end{pmatrix}$ is a $\{1\}$-inverse of $L(G)$, where

$$A = B = \begin{pmatrix} \frac{31}{189} & \frac{1}{27} & \frac{4}{189} \\ \frac{1}{27} & \frac{4}{27} & \frac{1}{27} \\ \frac{4}{189} & \frac{1}{27} & \frac{31}{189} \end{pmatrix}, S^{\#} = \begin{pmatrix} \frac{17}{189} & \frac{-1}{27} & \frac{-10}{189} \\ \frac{-1}{27} & \frac{2}{27} & \frac{-1}{27} \\ \frac{-10}{189} & \frac{-1}{27} & \frac{17}{189} \end{pmatrix}.$$

Thus, the matrix whose (i,j)-entry is r_{ij} is

$$\begin{pmatrix} 0 & \frac{5}{21} & \frac{2}{7} & \frac{16}{63} & \frac{5}{21} & \frac{16}{63} & \frac{16}{63} & \frac{5}{21} & \frac{16}{63} \\ \frac{5}{21} & 0 & \frac{5}{21} & \frac{5}{21} & \frac{2}{9} & \frac{5}{21} & \frac{5}{21} & \frac{2}{9} & \frac{5}{21} \\ \frac{2}{7} & \frac{5}{21} & 0 & \frac{16}{63} & \frac{5}{21} & \frac{16}{63} & \frac{16}{63} & \frac{5}{21} & \frac{16}{63} \\ \frac{16}{63} & \frac{5}{21} & \frac{16}{63} & 0 & \frac{5}{21} & \frac{2}{7} & \frac{16}{63} & \frac{5}{21} & \frac{16}{63} \\ \frac{5}{21} & \frac{2}{9} & \frac{5}{21} & \frac{5}{21} & 0 & \frac{5}{21} & \frac{5}{21} & \frac{2}{9} & \frac{5}{21} \\ \frac{16}{63} & \frac{5}{21} & \frac{16}{63} & \frac{2}{7} & \frac{5}{21} & 0 & \frac{16}{63} & \frac{5}{21} & \frac{16}{63} \\ \frac{16}{63} & \frac{5}{21} & \frac{16}{63} & \frac{16}{63} & \frac{5}{21} & \frac{16}{63} & 0 & \frac{5}{21} & \frac{2}{7} \\ \frac{5}{21} & \frac{2}{9} & \frac{5}{21} & \frac{5}{21} & \frac{2}{9} & \frac{5}{21} & \frac{5}{21} & 0 & \frac{5}{21} \\ \frac{16}{63} & \frac{5}{21} & \frac{16}{63} & \frac{16}{63} & \frac{5}{21} & \frac{16}{63} & \frac{2}{7} & \frac{5}{21} & 0 \end{pmatrix}.$$

5. Conclusions

This paper focuses on resistance distance in H-join of graphs $G_1, G_2, \ldots, G_k$. Let G be H-join of graphs $G_1, G_2, \ldots, G_k$. Here we first give the Laplacian matrix $L(G)$ of G. Then we compute a symmetric $\{1\}$-inverse of $L(G)$. Note that there exists a relationship between resistance distance and entries of $\{1\}$-inverse. So we can easily obtain resistance distance in G.

Author Contributions: Funding Acquisition, L.Z. and J.-B.L.; Methodology, J.-B.L. and L.Z.; Supervision, M.A.; Writing—Original Draft, L.Z. and J.Z.; All authors read and approved the final manuscript.

Funding: This work was supported by the Start-Up Scientific Research Foundation of Anhui Jianzhu University (2017QD20), the National Natural Science Foundation of China (11601006), the China Postdoctoral Science

Foundation (2017M621579), the Postdoctoral Science Foundation of Jiangsu Province (1701081B), the Project of Anhui Jianzhu University (2016QD116 and 2017dc03) and the Anhui Province Key Laboratory of Intelligent Building and Building Energy Saving.

Acknowledgments: The authors are grateful to the anonymous reviewers and the editor for the valuable comments and suggestions.

Conflicts of Interest: The authors declare no conflict of interest.

References

1. Bapat, R.B. *Graphs and Matrices*; Universitext; Springer-Hindustan Book Agency: London, UK; New Delhi, India, 2010.
2. Bondy, J.A.; Murty, U.S.R. *Graph Theory with Applications*; Macmillan Press: New York, NY, USA, 1976.
3. Bu, C.J.; Yan, B.; Zhang, X.Q.; Zhou, J. Resistance distance in subdivision-vertex join and subdivision-edge of graphs. *Linear Algebra Appl.* **2014**, *458*, 454–462. [CrossRef]
4. Gopalapillai, I. The spectrum of neghborhood corona of graphs. *Kragujevac J. Math.* **2011**, *35*, 493–500.
5. Liu, X.G.; Lu, P.L. Spectra of the subdivision-vertex and subdivision neighborhood coronae. *Linear Algebra Appl.* **2013**, *438*, 3547–3559. [CrossRef]
6. McLeman, C.; McNicholas, E. Spectra of coronae. *Linear Algebra Appl.* **2011**, *435*, 998–1007. [CrossRef]
7. Wang, S.L.; Zhou, B. The signless Laplacian spectra of the corona and edge corona of two graphs. *Linear Multilinear Algebra* **2013**, *61*, 197–204. [CrossRef]
8. Cardoso, D. M.; De Freitas, M. A. A.; Martins, E. A.; Robbiano, María. Spectra of graphs obtained by a generalization of the join graph operation. *Discrete Math.* **2013**, *313*, 733–741. [CrossRef]
9. Klein, D.J.; Randić, M. Resistance distance. *J. Math. Chem.* **1993**, *12*, 81–95. [CrossRef]
10. Bapat, R.B.; Gutman, I.; Xiao, W. A simple method for computing resistance distance. *Z. Naturforschung A* **2003**, *58*, 494–498. [CrossRef]
11. Bapat, R.B.; Gupta, S. Resistance distance in wheels and fans. *Indian J. Pure Appl. Math.* **2010**, *41*, 1–13. [CrossRef]
12. Cao, J.; Liu, J.B.; Wang, S. Resistance distance in corona and neighborhood corona networks based on Laplacian generalized inverse approach. *J. Algebra Appl.* **2018**. [CrossRef]
13. Liu, J.B.; Pan, X.F. Minimizing Kirchhoffindex among graphs with a given vertex bipartiteness. *Appl. Math. Comput.* **2016**, *291*, 84–88.
14. Feng, L.; Yu, G.; Xu, K.; Jiang, Z. A note on the Kirchhoff index of bicyclic graphs. *Ars Comb.* **2014**, *114*, 33–40.
15. Sun, L.Z.; Wang, W.Z.; Zhou, J.; Bu, C.J. Some results on resistance distance and resistance matrices. *Linear Multilinear Algebra* **2015**, *63*, 523–533. [CrossRef]
16. Wang, C.; Liu, J.B.; Wang, S. Sharp upper bounds for mulitiplicative Zagreb indices of bipartite graphs with given diameter. *Discret. Appl. Math.* **2017**, *227*, 156–165. [CrossRef]
17. Liu, J.B.; Pan, X.F.; Yu, L.; Li, D. Complete characterization of bicyclic graphs with minimal Kirchhoff index. *Discret. Appl. Math.* **2016**, *200*, 95–107. [CrossRef]
18. Liu, J.B.; Wang, W.R.; Zhang, Y.M.; Pan, X.F. On degree resistance distance of cacti. *Discret. Appl. Math.* **2016**, *203*, 217–225. [CrossRef]
19. Liu, J.B.; Cao, J. The resistance distance of electrical networks based on Laplacian generalized inverse. *Neurocomputing* **2015**, *167*, 306–313. [CrossRef]
20. Liu, J.B.; Pan, X.F.; Hu, F.T. The {1}-inverse of the Laplacian of subdivision-vertex and subdivision-edge coronae with applications. *Linar Multilinear Algebra* **2017**, *65*, 178–191. [CrossRef]
21. Kirkland, S. The Group Inverse of the Laplacian Matrix of a Graph. In *Combinatorial Matrix Theory*; Advanced Courses in Mathematics-CRM Barcelona; Birkhäuser: Cham, Switzerland, 2018. [CrossRef]
22. Zhou, J.; Sun, L.Z.; Wang, W.Z.; Bu, C.J. Line star sets for Laplacian eigenvalues. *Linear Algebra Appl.* **2014**, *440*, 164–176. [CrossRef]
23. Horn, R.A.; Johnson, C.R. *Topics in Matrix Analysis*; Cambridge University Press: Cambridge, UK, 1991.

© 2018 by the authors. Licensee MDPI, Basel, Switzerland. This article is an open access article distributed under the terms and conditions of the Creative Commons Attribution (CC BY) license (http://creativecommons.org/licenses/by/4.0/).

Article

The Extremal Graphs of Some Topological Indices with Given Vertex k-Partiteness

Fang Gao [1], Xiaoxin Li [1], Kai Zhou [1] and Jia-Bao Liu [2,*]

[1] School of Mathematics and Computer Science, Chizhou University, Chizhou 247000, China; gaofang@czu.edu.cn (F.G.); lxx@czu.edu.cn (X.L.); zk1984@163.com (K.Z.)
[2] School of Mathematics and Physics, Anhui Jianzhu University, Hefei 230601, China
* Correspondence: liujiabaoad@163.com

Received: 12 October 2018; Accepted: 16 November 2018; Published: 21 November 2018

Abstract: The vertex k-partiteness of graph G is defined as the fewest number of vertices whose deletion from G yields a k-partite graph. In this paper, we characterize the extremal value of the reformulated first Zagreb index, the multiplicative-sum Zagreb index, the general Laplacian-energy-like invariant, the general zeroth-order Randić index, and the modified-Wiener index among graphs of order n with vertex k-partiteness not more than m.

Keywords: topological index; vertex k-partiteness; extremal graph

1. Introduction

All graphs considered in this paper are simple, undirected, and connected. Let G be a graph with vertex set $V(G) = \{v_1, \cdots, v_n\}$ and edge set $E(G) = \{e_1, \cdots, e_m\}$. The degree of a vertex $u \in V(G)$ is the number of edges incident to u, denoted by $d_G(u)$. The distance between two vertices u and v is the length of the shortest path connecting u and v, denoted by $d_G(u,v)$. The complement of G, denoted by $\overline{G}$, is the graph with vertex set $V(\overline{G}) = V(G)$ and edge set $E(\overline{G}) = \{uv : uv \notin E(G)\}$. A subgraph of G induced by H, denoted by $\langle H \rangle$, is the subgraph of G that has the vertex set H, and for any two vertices $u, v \in V(H)$, they are adjacent in H iff they are adjacent in G. The adjacency matrix of G is a square $n \times n$ matrix such that its element a_{ij} is one when there is an edge from vertex u_i to vertex u_j, and zero when there is no edge, denoted by $A(G)$. Let $D(G) = diag(d_1, d_2, \cdots, d_n)$ be the diagonal matrix of vertex degrees of G. The Laplacian matrix of G is defined as $L(G) = D(G) - A(G)$, and the eigenvalues of $L(G)$ are called Laplacian eigenvalues of G, denoted by $\mu_1, \cdots, \mu_n$ with $\mu_1 \geq \cdots \geq \mu_n$. It is well known that $\mu_n = 0$, and the multiplicity of zero corresponds to the number of connected components of G.

A bipartite graph is a graph whose vertex set can be partitioned into two disjoint sets U_1 and U_2, such that each edge has an end vertex in U_1 and the other one in U_2. A complete bipartite graph, denoted by $K_{s,t}$, is a bipartite graph with $|U_1| = s$ and $|U_2| = t$, where any two vertices $u \in U_1$ and $v \in U_2$ are adjacent. If every pair of distinct vertices in G is connected by a unique edge, we call G a complete graph. The complete graph with n vertices is denoted by K_n. An independent set of G is a set of vertices, no two of which are adjacent. A graph G is called k-partite if its vertex-set can be partitioned into k different independent sets $U_1, \cdots, U_k$. When $k = 2$, they are the bipartite graphs, and $k = 3$ the tripartite graphs. The vertex k-partiteness of graph G, denoted by $v_k(G)$, is the fewest number of vertices whose deletion from G yields a k-partite graph. A complete k-partite graph, denoted by $K_{s_1,\cdots,s_k}$, is a k-partite graph with k different independent sets $|U_1| = s_1, \cdots, |U_k| = s_k$, where there is an edge between every pair of vertices from different independent sets.

A topological index is a numerical value that can be used to characterize some properties of molecule graphs in chemical graph theory. Recently, many researchers have paid much attention to studying different topological indices. Dimitrov [1] studied the structural properties of trees with minimal atom-bond connectivity index. Li and Fan [2] obtained the extremal graphs of the Harary index. Xu et al. [3] determined the eccentricity-based topological indices of graphs. Hayat et al. [4] studied the valency-based topological descriptors of chemical networks and their applications. Let $G + uv$ be the graph obtained from G by adding an edge $uv \in E(\overline{G})$. Let $I(G)$ be a graph invariant, if $I(G + uv) > I(G)$ (or $I(G + uv) < I(G)$, respectively) for any edge $uv \in E(\overline{G})$, then we call $I(G)$ a monotonic increasing (or decreasing, respectively) graph invariant with the addition of edges [5]. Let $\mathscr{G}_{n,m,k}$ be the set of graphs with order n and vertex k-partiteness $v_k(G) \leq m$, where $1 \leq m \leq n - k$. In [5–7], the authors have researched several monotonic topological indices in $\mathscr{G}_{n,m,2}$, such as the Kirchhoff index, the spectral radius, the signless Laplacian spectral radius, the modified-Wiener index, the connective eccentricity index, and so on. Inspired by these results, we extend the parameter of graph partition from two-partiteness to arbitrary k-partiteness. Moreover, we study some monotonic topological indices and characterize the graphs with extremal monotonic topological indices in $\mathscr{G}_{n,m,k}$.

2. Preliminaries

The join of two-vertex-disjoint graphs G_1, G_2, denoted by $G = G_1 \vee G_2$, is the graph obtained from the disjoint union $G_1 \cup G_2$ by adding edges between each vertex of G_1 and each of G_2. It is to say that $V(G) = V(G_1) \cup V(G_2)$ and $E(G) = E(G_1) \cup E(G_2) \cup \{uv : u \in V(G_1), v \in V(G_2)\}$.

The join operation can be generalized as follows. Let $F = \{G_1, \cdots, G_k\}$ be a set of vertex-disjoint graphs and H be an arbitrary graph with vertex set $V(H) = \{1, \cdots, k\}$. Each vertex $i \in V(H)$ is assigned to the graph $G_i \in F$.

The H-join of the graphs $G_1, \cdots, G_k$ is the graph $G = H[G_1, \cdots, G_k]$, such that $V(G) = \bigcup_{j=1}^{k} V(G_j)$ and:

$$E(G) = \bigcup_{j=1}^{k} E(G_j) \bigcup \left(\bigcup_{ij \in E(H)} \{uv : u \in V(G_i), v \in V(G_j)\} \right).$$

If $H = K_2$, the H-join is the usual join operation of graphs, and the complete k-partite graph $K_{s_1, \cdots, s_k}$ can be seen as the K_k-join graph $K_k[O_{s_1}, \cdots, O_{s_k}]$, where O_{s_i} is an empty graph of order s_i, $1 \leq i \leq k$.

For $U \subseteq V(G)$, let $G - U$ be the graph obtained from G by deleting the vertices in U and the edges incident with them.

Lemma 1. *Let G be an arbitrary graph in $\mathscr{G}_{n,m,k}$ and $I(G)$ be a monotonic increasing graph invariant. Then, there exists k positive integers $s_1, \cdots, s_k$ satisfying $\sum_{i=1}^{k} s_i = n - m$, such that $I(G) \leq I(\widehat{G})$ holds for all graphs $G \in \mathscr{G}_{n,m,k}$, where $\widehat{G} = K_m \vee (K_k[O_{s_1}, \cdots, O_{s_k}]) \in \mathscr{G}_{n,m,k}$, with equality holds if and only if $G \cong \widehat{G}$.*

Proof. Choose $\widehat{G} \in \mathscr{G}_{n,m,k}$ with the maximum value of a monotonic increasing graph invariant such that $I(G) \leq I(\widehat{G})$ for all $G \in \mathscr{G}_{n,m,k}$. Assume that the k-partiteness of graph $\widehat{G}$ is m', then there exists a vertex set U of graph $\widehat{G}$ with order m' such that $\widehat{G} - U$ is a k-partite graph with k-partition $\{U_1, \cdots, U_k\}$. For $1 \leq i \leq k$, let s_i be the order of U_i; hence, $n = \sum_{i=1}^{k} s_i + m'$.

Firstly, we claim that $\widehat{G} - U = K_k[O_{s_1}, \cdots, O_{s_k}]$. Otherwise, there exists at least two vertices $u \in U_{s_i}$ and $v \in U_{s_j}$ for some $i \neq j$, which are not adjacent in $\widehat{G}$. By joining the vertices u and v, we get a new graph $\widehat{G} + uv$, obviously, $\widehat{G} + uv \in \mathscr{G}_{n,m,k}$. Then, $I(\widehat{G}) < I(\widehat{G} + uv)$, which is a contradiction.

Secondly, we claim that U is the complete graph $K_{m'}$. Otherwise, there exists at least two vertices $u, v \in U$, which are not adjacent. By connecting the vertices u and v, we arrive at a new graph $\widehat{G} + uv$, obviously, $\widehat{G} + uv \in \mathscr{G}_{n,m,k}$. Then, we have $I(\widehat{G}) < I(\widehat{G} + uv)$, a contradiction again.

Using a similar method, we can get $\widehat{G} = K_{m'} \vee (K_k[O_{s_1}, \cdots, O_{s_k}])$.

Finally, we prove that $m' = m$. If $m' \leq m - 1$, then $\sum_{i=1}^{k} s_i = n - m' \geq n - m + 1 > n - m \geq k$; thus, $\sum_{i=1}^{k} s_i > k$. Without loss of generality, we assume that $s_1 \geq 2$. By moving a vertex $u \in O_{s_1}$ to the set of U and adding edges between u and all the other vertices in O_{s_1}, we get a new graph $\widetilde{G} = K_{m'+1} \vee (K_k[O_{s_1-1}, O_{s_2}, \cdots, O_{s_k}])$. It is easy to check that $\widetilde{G} \in \mathscr{G}_{n,m,k}$ has $s_1 - 1$ edges more than the graph $\widehat{G}$. By the definition of the monotonic increasing graph invariant, we get $I(\widehat{G}) < I(\widetilde{G})$, which is obviously another contradiction.

Therefore, $\widehat{G}$ is the join of a complete graph with order m and a complete k-partite graph with order $n - m$. That is to say $\widehat{G} = K_m \vee (K_k[O_{s_1}, \cdots, O_{s_k}])$.

The proof of the lemma is completed. □

Lemma 2. *Let G be an arbitrary graph in $\mathscr{G}_{n,m,k}$ and $I(G)$ be a monotonic decreasing graph invariant. Then, there exists k positive integers $s_1, \cdots, s_k$ satisfying $\sum_{i=1}^{k} s_i = n - m$, such that $I(G) \geq I(\widehat{G})$ holds for all graphs $G \in \mathscr{G}_{n,m,k}$, where $\widehat{G} = K_m \vee (K_k[O_{s_1}, \cdots, O_{s_k}]) \in \mathscr{G}_{n,m,k}$, with equality holds if and only if $G \cong \widehat{G}$.*

3. Main Results

In this section, we will characterize the graphs with an extremal monotonic increasing (or decreasing, respectively) graph invariant in $\mathscr{G}_{n,m,k}$. Assume that $n - m = sk + t$, where s is a positive integer and t is a non-negative integer with $0 \leq t < k$.

3.1. The Reformulated First Zagreb Index, Multiplicative-Sum Zagreb Index, and k-Partiteness

The first Zagreb index is used to analyze the structure-dependency of total π-electron energy on the molecular orbitals, introduced by Gutman and Trinajsté [8]. It is denoted by:

$$M_1(G) = \sum_{uv \in E(G)} (d_G(u) + d_G(v)),$$

which can be also calculated as:

$$M_1(G) = \sum_{u \in V(G)} d_G(u)^2.$$

Todeschini and Consonni [9] considered the multiplicative version of the first Zagreb index in 2010, defined as:

$$\Pi_1(G) = \prod_{u \in V(G)} d_G(u)^2.$$

For an edge $e = uv \in E(G)$, we define the degree of e as $d_G(e) = d_G(u) + d_G(v) - 2$. Milličević et al. [10] introduced the reformulated first Zagreb index, defined as:

$$\widetilde{M}_1(G) = \sum_{e \in E(G)} d_G(e)^2 = \sum_{uv \in E(G)} (d_G(u) + d_G(v) - 2)^2.$$

Eliasi et al. [11] introduced another multiplicative version of the first Zagreb index, which is called the multiplicative-sum Zagreb index and defined as:

$$\Pi_1^*(G) = \prod_{uv \in E(G)} (d_G(u) + d_G(v)).$$

They are widely used in chemistry to study the heat information of heptanes and octanes. For some recent results on the fourth Zagreb indices, one can see [12–17].

Lemma 3. *Let G be a graph with $u, v \in V(G)$. If $uv \in E(\overline{G})$, then $\widetilde{M}_1(G) < \widetilde{M}_1(G + uv)$.*

Lemma 4. *Let G be a graph with $u, v \in V(G)$. If $uv \in E(\overline{G})$, then $\Pi_1^*(G) < \Pi_1^*(G + uv)$.*

Note that $s_1, \cdots, s_k$ are k positive integers with $\sum\limits_{i=1}^{k} s_i = n - m$.

Theorem 1. *Let $\widehat{G}$ be a graph of order $n > 2$, and the join of a complete graph with order m and a complete k-partite graph with order $n - m$ in $\mathscr{G}_{n,m,k}$, i.e., $\widehat{G} = K_m \vee (K_k[O_{s_1}, \cdots, O_{s_k}])$. By moving one vertex from the part of O_{s_1} to the part of O_{s_2}, we get a new graph $\widetilde{G} = K_m \vee (K_k[O_{s_1-1}, O_{s_2+1}, \cdots, O_{s_k}])$. If $s_1 - 1 \geq s_2 + 1$, then $\widetilde{M}_1(\widetilde{G}) > \widetilde{M}_1(\widehat{G})$.*

Proof. By the definition of the reformulated first Zagreb index $\widetilde{M}_1(G)$, we can calculate as follows:

$$\widetilde{M}_1(\widehat{G}) = \frac{m(m-1)}{2}(2n-4)^2 + \sum_{i=1}^{k} ms_i(2n - s_i - 3)^2 + \sum_{1 \leq i < j \leq k} s_i s_j (2n - s_i - s_j - 2)^2.$$

Therefore,

$$\begin{aligned}\widetilde{M}_1(\widetilde{G}) - \widetilde{M}_1(\widehat{G}) &= m(s_1 - 1)(2n - s_1 - 2)^2 + m(s_2 + 1)(2n - s_2 - 4)^2 \\&+ (s_1 - 1)(s_2 + 1)(2n - s_1 - s_2 - 2)^2 - ms_1(2n - s_1 - 3)^2 \\&- ms_2(2n - s_2 - 3)^2 - s_1 s_2 (2n - s_1 - s_2 - 2)^2 \\&+ \sum_{i=3}^{k}(s_1 - 1)s_i(2n - s_1 - s_i - 1)^2 + \sum_{i=3}^{k}(s_2 + 1)s_i(2n - s_2 - s_i - 3)^2 \\&- \sum_{i=3}^{k} s_1 s_i (2n - s_1 - s_i - 2)^2 - \sum_{i=3}^{k} s_2 s_i (2n - s_2 - s_i - 2)^2 \\&= (s_1 - s_2 - 1)[(5n + 3p - 12)p + (n + p - 2)^2 \\&+ (7n + 8m - 12)\sum_{i=3}^{k} s_i + (\sum_{i=3}^{k} s_i)^2 + \sum_{i=3}^{k} s_i(3\sum_{i=3}^{k} s_i - 4s_i) \\&= (s_1 - s_2 - 1)[(n - 2)^2 + (7n - 16)m + 4m^2 \\&+ (7n + 8m - 12)\sum_{i=3}^{k} s_i + 4(\sum_{i=3}^{k} s_i)^2 - 4\sum_{i=3}^{k} s_i^2] \\&> (s_1 - s_2 - 1)[(n - 2)^2 + (4n - 8)m + 4m^2] \\&= (s_1 - s_2 - 1)(n - 2 + 2m)^2 > 0. \quad \square\end{aligned}$$

Note that we have $n - m = sk + t = (k - t)s + t(s + 1)$, where s is a positive integer and t is a non-negative integer with $0 \leq t < k$. For simplicity, we write $K_m \vee (K_k[\{k - t\}O_s, \{s\}O_{s+1}]) = K_m \vee (K_k[\underbrace{O_s, \cdots, O_s}_{k-t}, \underbrace{O_{s+1}, \cdots, O_{s+1}}_{t}])$. Then, the extremal value and the corresponding graph of the reformulated first Zagreb index $\widetilde{M}_1(G)$ can be shown as follows.

Theorem 2. *Let G be an arbitrary graph in $\mathscr{G}_{n,m,k}$. Then:*

$$\begin{aligned}\widetilde{M}_1(G) &\leq \frac{m(m-1)}{2}(2n - 4)^2 + m(n - m)(6n - 3s - 11) \\&+ 2(n - m)(n - m - s)(n - s - 1)^2 \\&+ t(s + 1)[-6(n - s - 1)^2 + n + 2m(5 - 2n + s) + (t - 2)(s + 1)],\end{aligned}$$

with the equality holding if and only if $G \cong K_m \vee (K_k[\{k-t\}O_s, \{s\}O_{s+1}])$.

Proof. By Lemmas 1, 3, and Theorem 1, the extremal graph having the maximum reformulated first Zagreb index in $\mathscr{G}_{n,m,k}$ is the graph $K_m \vee (K_k[\{k-t\}O_s, \{s\}O_{s+1}])$.

Let $\hat{G} = K_m \vee (K_k[\{k-t\}O_s, \{s\}O_{s+1}])$.

Then, we obtain that:

$$\widetilde{M}_1(\hat{G}) = \frac{m(m-1)}{2}(2n-4)^2 + (k-t)ms(2n-s-3)^2$$
$$+ tm(s+1)(2n-s-4)^2 + \frac{t(t-1)}{2}(s+1)^2(2n-2s-4)^2$$
$$+ \frac{(k-t)(k-t-1)}{2}s^2(2n-2s-2)^2 + t(k-t)s(s+1)(2n-2s-3)^2$$
$$= \frac{m(m-1)}{2}(2n-4)^2 + m(n-m)(6n-3s-11)$$
$$+ 2(n-m)(n-m-s)(n-s-1)^2$$
$$+ t(s+1)[-6(n-s-1)^2 + n + 2m(5-2n+s) + (t-2)(s+1)]. \quad \square$$

Theorem 3. *Let $\hat{G}$ be a graph of order $n > 2$, and the join of a complete graph with order m and a complete k-partite graph with order $n - m$ in $\mathscr{G}_{n,m,k}$, i.e., $\hat{G} = K_m \vee (K_k[O_{s_1}, \cdots, O_{s_k}])$. If $s_1 - 1 \geq s_2 + 1$, by moving one vertex from the part of O_{s_1} to the part of O_{s_2}, we get a new graph $\widetilde{G} = K_m \vee (K_k[O_{s_1-1}, O_{s_2+1}, \cdots, O_{s_k}])$. Then, $\Pi_1^*(\widetilde{G}) > \Pi_1^*(\hat{G})$.*

Proof. By the definition of the multiplicative-sum Zagreb index $\Pi_1^*(G)$, it is easy to see that:

$$\Pi_1^*(\hat{G}) = (2n-2)^{\frac{m(m-1)}{2}} \Pi_{i=1}^k (2n-s_i-1)^{ms_i} \Pi_{1 \leq i < j \leq k}(2n-s_i-s_j)^{s_i s_j}.$$

Hence,

$$\frac{\Pi_1^*(\widetilde{G})}{\Pi_1^*(\hat{G})} = (2n-s_1-s_2)^{(s_1-s_2-1)} \frac{2n-s_2-2}{2n-s_1-1} a^{m(s_1-1)} b^{ms_2}$$
$$\Pi_{i=3}^k c^{(s_1-1)s_i} \Pi_{i=3}^k d^{s_2 s_i} \Pi_{i=3}^k \left(\frac{2n-s_2-s_i-1}{2n-s_1-s_i}\right)^{s_i}$$
$$> (ab)^{ms_2} \Pi_{i=3}^k (cd)^{s_2 s_i},$$

where $a = \frac{2n-s_1}{2n-s_1-1}, b = \frac{2n-s_2-2}{2n-s_2-1}, c = \frac{2n-s_1-s_i+1}{2n-s_1-s_i}, d = \frac{2n-s_2-s_i-1}{2n-s_2-s_i}$.

By a simple calculation, we have:

$$(2n-s_1)(2n-s_2-2) - (2n-s_1-1)(2n-s_2-1) = s_1 - s_2 - 1 > 0,$$

$$(2n-s_1-s_i+1)(2n-s_2-s_i-1) - (2n-s_1-s_i)(2n-s_2-s_i) = s_1 - s_2 - 1 > 0.$$

Therefore, $\frac{\Pi_1^*(\widetilde{G})}{\Pi_1^*(\hat{G})} > 1$. $\quad \square$

Theorem 4. *Let G be an arbitrary graph in $\mathscr{G}_{n,m,k}$. Then:*

$$\Pi_1^*(G) \leq (2n-2)^{\frac{m(m-1)}{2}} (2n-s-1)^{ms(k-t)} (2n-s-2)^{m(s+1)t}$$
$$(2n-2s)^{\frac{s^2(k-t)(k-t-1)}{2}} (2n-2s-2)^{\frac{(s+1)^2 t(t-1)}{2}} (2n-2s-1)^{s(s+1)t(k-t)},$$

with the equality holding if and only if $G \cong K_m \vee (K_k[\{k-t\}O_s, \{s\}O_{s+1}])$.

Proof. By Lemmas 1, 4, and Theorem 3, the extremal graph having the maximum multiplicative-sum Zagreb index in $\mathscr{G}_{n,m,k}$ should be the graph $K_m \vee (K_k[\{k-t\}O_s, \{s\}O_{s+1}])$.

Let $\widehat{G} = K_m \vee (K_k[\{k-t\}O_s, \{s\}O_{s+1}])$. We get that,

$$\Pi_1^*(\widehat{G}) = (2n-2)^{\frac{m(m-1)}{2}} (2n-s-1)^{ms(k-t)} (2n-s-2)^{m(s+1)t}$$
$$(2n-2s)^{\frac{s^2(k-t)(k-t-1)}{2}} (2n-2s-2)^{\frac{(s+1)^2 t(t-1)}{2}} (2n-2s-1)^{s(s+1)t(k-t)}. \quad \square$$

3.2. The General Laplacian-Energy-Like Invariant and k-Partiteness

The general Laplacian-energy-like invariant (also called the sum of powers of the Laplacian eigenvalues) of a graph G is defined by Zhou [18] as:

$$S_\alpha(G) = \sum_{i=1}^{n-1} \mu_i^\alpha,$$

where α is an arbitrary real number.

$S_\alpha(G)$ is the Laplacian-energy-like invariant [19], and the Laplacian energy [20] when $\alpha = \frac{1}{2}$ and $\alpha = 2$, respectively. For $\alpha = -1$, $nS_{-1}(G)$ is equal to the Kirchhoff index [21], and $\alpha = 1$, $\frac{1}{2}S_1(G)$ is equal to the number of edges in G. For some recent results on the general Laplacian-energy-like invariant, one can see [22–25].

Lemma 5. *[18] Let G be a graph with $u, v \in V(G)$. If $uv \in E(\overline{G})$, then $S_\alpha(G) > S_\alpha(G + uv)$ for $\alpha < 0$, and $S_\alpha(G) < S_\alpha(G + uv)$ for $\alpha > 0$.*

Lemma 6. *[26] If $\mu_1 \geq \cdots \geq \mu_{i-1} \geq \mu_i = 0$ are the Laplacian eigenvalues of graph G and $\mu_1' \geq \cdots \geq \mu_{j-1}' \geq \mu_j' = 0$ are the Laplacian eigenvalues of graph G', then the Laplacian eigenvalues of $G \vee G'$ are:*

$$i+j, \mu_1+j, \mu_2+j, \cdots, \mu_{i-1}+j, \mu_1'+i, \mu_2'+i, \cdots, \mu_{j-1}'+i, 0.$$

It is well known that Laplacian eigenvalues of the complete graph K_p are $0, p, \cdots, p$, and Laplacian eigenvalues of O_p are $0, 0, \cdots, 0$. Then, the Laplacian eigenvalues of $K_{s_1, s_2} = O_{s_1} \vee O_{s_2}$ are $s_1 + s_2, s_2, \cdots, s_2, s_1, \cdots, s_1, 0$, where the multiplicity of s_2 is $s_1 - 1$ and the multiplicity of s_1 is $s_2 - 1$. The Laplacian eigenvalues of $K_{s_1, s_2, s_3} = K_{s_1, s_2} \vee O_{s_3}$ are $s_1 + s_2 + s_3, s_1 + s_2 + s_3, s_2 + s_3, \cdots, s_2 + s_3, s_1 + s_3, \cdots, s_1 + s_3, 0$, where the multiplicity of $s_2 + s_3$ is $s_1 - 1$ and the multiplicity of $s_1 + s_3$ is $s_2 - 1$.

By induction, we have that the Laplacian eigenvalues of $K_{s_1, \cdots, s_k}$ are $\sum_{i=1}^{k} s_i, \cdots, \sum_{i=1}^{k} s_i, \sum_{i=1}^{k} s_i - s_1, \cdots, \sum_{i=1}^{k} s_i - s_1, \cdots, \sum_{i=1}^{k} s_i - s_k, \cdots, \sum_{i=1}^{k} s_i - s_k, 0$, where the multiplicity of $\sum_{i=1}^{k} s_i$ is $k - 1$ and the multiplicity of $\sum_{i=1}^{k} s_i - s_j$ is $s_j - 1$, for $1 \leq j \leq k$.

From Lemma 6 and the above analysis, we obtain the following lemma.

Lemma 7. *Let $\widehat{G}$ be a graph of order n, and the join of a complete graph with order m and a complete k-partite graph with order $n - m$ i.e., $\widehat{G} = K_m \vee (K_k[O_{s_1}, \cdots, O_{s_k}])$. Then, the Laplacian eigenvalues of $\widehat{G}$ are $n, \cdots, n, n - s_1, \cdots, n - s_1, \cdots, n - s_k, \cdots, n - s_k, 0$, where the multiplicity of n is $m + k - 1$ and the multiplicity of $n - s_j$ is $s_j - 1$, for $1 \leq j \leq k$.*

Theorem 5. *Let $\widehat{G}$ be a graph of order $n > 2$, and the join of a complete graph with order m and a complete k-partite graph with order $n - m$ in $\mathscr{G}_{n,m,k}$, i.e., $\widehat{G} = K_m \vee (K_k[O_{s_1}, \cdots, O_{s_k}])$. If $s_1 - 1 \geq s_2 + 1$, by moving* one vertex from the part of O_{s_1} to the part of O_{s_2}, we get a new graph $\widetilde{G} = K_m \vee (K_k[O_{s_1-1}, O_{s_2+1}, \cdots, O_{s_k}])$. Then, $S_\alpha(\widetilde{G}) < S_\alpha(\widehat{G})$ for $\alpha < 0$, and $S_\alpha(\widetilde{G}) > S_\alpha(\widehat{G})$ for $0 < \alpha < 1$.

Proof. By the definition of the general Laplacian-energy-like invariant $S_\alpha(G)$ and Lemma 7, we conclude that:

$$S_\alpha(\widehat{G}) = (m+k-1)n^\alpha + \sum_{i=1}^{k}(s_i-1)(n-s_i)^\alpha.$$

Therefore:

$$\begin{aligned} S_\alpha(\widetilde{G}) - S_\alpha(\widehat{G}) &= (s_1-2)(n-s_1+1)^\alpha + s_2(n-s_2-1)^\alpha \\ &\quad - (s_1-1)(n-s_1)^\alpha - (s_2-1)(n-s_2)^\alpha \\ &= (s_1-2)[(n-s_1+1)^\alpha - (n-s_1)^\alpha] \\ &\quad + (s_2-1)[(n-s_2-1)^\alpha - (n-s_2)^\alpha] + (n-s_2-1)^\alpha - (n-s_1)^\alpha. \end{aligned}$$

For $\alpha < 0$, we have:

$$\begin{aligned} S_\alpha(\widetilde{G}) - S_\alpha(\widehat{G}) &< (s_1-2)[(n-s_1+1)^\alpha - (n-s_1)^\alpha] + (s_2-1)[(n-s_2-1)^\alpha - (n-s_2)^\alpha] \\ &< (s_1-2)[(n-s_1+1)^\alpha - (n-s_1)^\alpha + (n-s_2-1)^\alpha - (n-s_2)^\alpha] \\ &= (s_1-2)[f(n-s_1) - f(n-s_2-1)], \end{aligned}$$

where $f(x) = (x+1)^\alpha - x^\alpha$, $f'(x) = \alpha(x+1)^{\alpha-1} - \alpha x^{\alpha-1} > 0$.
Then, $f(n-s_1) < f(n-s_2-1)$, and $S_\alpha(\widetilde{G}) < S_\alpha(\widehat{G})$.
For $0 < \alpha < 1$, we have:

$$\begin{aligned} S_\alpha(\widetilde{G}) - S_\alpha(\widehat{G}) &> (s_1-2)[(n-s_1+1)^\alpha - (n-s_1)^\alpha] + (s_2-1)[(n-s_2-1)^\alpha - (n-s_2)^\alpha] \\ &> (s_2-1)[(n-s_1+1)^\alpha - (n-s_1)^\alpha + (n-s_2-1)^\alpha - (n-s_2)^\alpha] \\ &= (s_2-1)[f(n-s_1) - f(n-s_2-1)], \end{aligned}$$

where $f(x) = (x+1)^\alpha - x^\alpha$, $f'(x) = \alpha(x+1)^{\alpha-1} - \alpha x^{\alpha-1} < 0$.
Then, $f(n-s_1) > f(n-s_2-1)$, and $S_\alpha(\widetilde{G}) > S_\alpha(\widehat{G})$. □

Theorem 6. Let G be an arbitrary graph in $\mathscr{G}_{n,m,k}$. Then,
for $\alpha < 0$, $S_\alpha(G) \geq (m+k-1)n^\alpha + (k-t)(s-1)(n-s)^\alpha + ts(n-s-1)^\alpha$,
for $0 < \alpha < 1$, $S_\alpha(G) \leq (m+k-1)n^\alpha + (k-t)(s-1)(n-s)^\alpha + ts(n-s-1)^\alpha$,
with the equality holding if and only if $G \cong K_m \vee (K_k[\{k-t\}O_s, \{s\}O_{s+1}])$.

Proof. By Lemmas 1, 2, and Theorem 5, the extremal graph having the extremal value of the general Laplacian-energy-like invariant in $\mathscr{G}_{n,m,k}$ should be the graph $K_m \vee (K_k[\{k-t\}O_s, \{s\}O_{s+1}])$.
Let $\widehat{G} = K_m \vee (K_k[\{k-t\}O_s, \{s\}O_{s+1}])$, then we can verify that
$S_\alpha(\widehat{G}) = (m+k-1)n^\alpha + (k-t)(s-1)(n-s)^\alpha + ts(n-s-1)^\alpha$. □

3.3. The General Zeroth-Order Randić Index and k-Partiteness

The general zeroth-order Randić index is introduced by Li [27] as:

$$^0R_\alpha(G) = \sum_{u \in V(G)} (d_G(u))^\alpha,$$

where α is a non-zero real number.

$^0R_\alpha(G)$ is the inverse degree [28], the zeroth-Randić index [29], the first Zagreb index [30], and the forgotten index [31] when $\alpha = -1, \alpha = -\frac{1}{2}, \alpha = 2$, and $\alpha = 3$, respectively. For some recent results on the general zeroth-order Randić index, one can see [32–34].

Lemma 8. *Let G be a graph with $u, v \in V(G)$. If $uv \in E(\overline{G})$, then $^0R_\alpha(G) > {}^0R_\alpha(G + uv)$ for $\alpha < 0$, and $^0R_\alpha(G) < {}^0R_\alpha(G + uv)$ for $\alpha > 0$.*

Theorem 7. *Let $\widehat{G}$ be a graph of order $n > 2$, and the join of a complete graph with order m and a complete k-partite graph with order $n - m$ in $\mathscr{G}_{n,m,k}$, i.e., $\widehat{G} = K_m \vee (K_k[O_{s_1}, \cdots, O_{s_k}])$. If $s_1 - 1 \geq s_2 + 1$, by moving one vertex from the part of O_{s_1} to the part of O_{s_2}, we get a new graph $\widetilde{G} = K_m \vee (K_k[O_{s_1-1}, O_{s_2+1}, \cdots, O_{s_k}])$. Then, $^0R_\alpha(\widetilde{G}) < {}^0R_\alpha(\widehat{G})$ for $\alpha < 0$, and $^0R_\alpha(\widetilde{G}) > {}^0R_\alpha(\widehat{G})$ for $0 < \alpha < 1$.*

Proof. By the definition of the general zeroth-order Randić index $^0R_\alpha(G)$, we have:

$$^0R_\alpha(\widehat{G}) = m(n-1)^\alpha + \sum_{i=1}^k s_i(n-s_i)^\alpha$$

Then,

$$\begin{aligned}^0R_\alpha(\widetilde{G}) - {}^0R_\alpha(\widehat{G}) &= (s_1 - 1)(n - s_1 + 1)^\alpha - s_1(n - s_1)^\alpha \\ &\quad + (s_2 + 1)(n - s_2 - 1)^\alpha - s_2(n - s_2)^\alpha \\ &= (n - s_2 - 1)^\alpha - (n - s_1)^\alpha \\ &\quad + (s_1 - 1)[(n - s_1 + 1)^\alpha - (n - s_1)^\alpha] + s_2[(n - s_2 - 1)^\alpha - (n - s_2)^\alpha].\end{aligned}$$

For $\alpha < 0$, we have:

$$\begin{aligned}^0R_\alpha(\widetilde{G}) - {}^0R_\alpha(\widehat{G}) &< (s_1 - 1)[(n - s_1 + 1)^\alpha - (n - s_1)^\alpha + (n - s_2 - 1)^\alpha - (n - s_2)^\alpha] \\ &= (s_1 - 1)[f(n - s_1) - f(n - s_2 - 1)],\end{aligned}$$

where $f(x) = (x+1)^\alpha - x^\alpha$, $f'(x) = \alpha(x+1)^{\alpha-1} - \alpha x^{\alpha-1} > 0$. Then, $f(n - s_1) < f(n - s_2 - 1)$, $^0R_\alpha(\widetilde{G}) < {}^0R_\alpha(\widehat{G})$.

For $0 < \alpha < 1$, we have:

$$\begin{aligned}^0R_\alpha(\widetilde{G}) - {}^0R_\alpha(\widehat{G}) &> s_2[(n - s_1 + 1)^\alpha - (n - s_1)^\alpha + (n - s_2 - 1)^\alpha - (n - s_2)^\alpha] \\ &= s_2[f(n - s_1) - f(n - s_2 - 1)],\end{aligned}$$

where $f(x) = (x+1)^\alpha - x^\alpha$, $f'(x) = \alpha(x+1)^{\alpha-1} - \alpha x^{\alpha-1} < 0$.
Then, $f(n - s_1) > f(n - s_2 - 1)$, $R_\alpha(\widetilde{G}) > R_\alpha(\widehat{G})$. □

Theorem 8. *Let G be an arbitrary graph in $\mathscr{G}_{n,m,k}$. Then,
for $\alpha < 0$, $^0R_\alpha(G) \geq m(n-1)^\alpha + (k-t)s(n-s)^\alpha + t(s+1)(n-s-1)^\alpha$,
for $0 < \alpha < 1$, $^0R_\alpha(G) \leq m(n-1)^\alpha + (k-t)s(n-s)^\alpha + t(s+1)(n-s-1)^\alpha$,
with the equality holding if and only if $G \cong K_m \vee (K_k[\{k-t\}O_s, \{s\}O_{s+1}])$.*

Proof. By Lemma 8 and Theorem 7, in view of Lemmas 1 and 2, the extremal graph having the extremal value of the general zeroth-order Randić index in $\mathscr{G}_{n,m,k}$ should be the graph $K_m \vee (K_k[\{k-t\}O_s, \{s\}O_{s+1}])$.

Let $\widehat{G} = K_m \vee (K_k[\{k-t\}O_s, \{s\}O_{s+1}])$. By a simple calculation, we have
$^0R_\alpha(\widehat{G}) = m(n-1)^\alpha + (k-t)s(n-s)^\alpha + t(s+1)(n-s-1)^\alpha$. □

3.4. The Modified-Wiener Index and k-Partiteness

The modified-Wiener index is defined by Gutman [35] as:

$$W_\lambda(G) = \sum_{u,v \in V(G)} d_G^\lambda(u,v),$$

where λ is a non-zero real number.

Lemma 9. *Let G be a graph with $u, v \in V(G)$. If $uv \in E(\overline{G})$, then $W_\lambda(G) < W_\lambda(G + uv)$ for $\lambda < 0$, and $W_\lambda(G) > W_\lambda(G + uv)$ for $\lambda > 0$.*

Theorem 9. *Let $\widehat{G}$ be a graph of order $n > 2$, and the join of a complete graph with order m and a complete k-partite graph with order $n - m$ in $\mathscr{G}_{n,m,k}$, i.e., $\widehat{G} = K_m \vee (K_k[O_{s_1}, \cdots, O_{s_k}])$. If $s_1 - 1 \geq s_2 + 1$, by moving one vertex from the part of O_{s_1} to the part of O_{s_2}, we get a new graph $\widetilde{G} = K_m \vee (K_k[O_{s_1-1}, O_{s_2+1}, \cdots, O_{s_k}])$. Then, $W_\lambda(\widetilde{G}) > W_\lambda(\widehat{G})$ for $\lambda < 0$, and $W_\lambda(\widetilde{G}) < W_\lambda(\widehat{G})$ for $\lambda > 0$.*

Proof. By the definition of the modified-Wiener index $W_\lambda(G)$, we have the following result.

$$W_\lambda(\widehat{G}) = \frac{m(m-1)}{2} + \sum_{i=1}^{k} \frac{s_i(s_i-1)}{2} 2^\lambda + \sum_{i=1}^{k} m s_i + \sum_{1 \leq i < j \leq k} s_i s_j$$

Then,

$$W_\lambda(\widetilde{G}) - W_\lambda(\widehat{G}) = \frac{(s_1-1)(s_1-2)}{2} 2^\lambda + \frac{(s_2+1)s_2}{2} 2^\lambda + m(s_1 - 1)$$

$$+ m(s_2 + 1) + (s_1 - 1)(s_2 + 1) + \sum_{i=3}^{k}(s_1 - 1)s_i + \sum_{i=3}^{k}(s_2 + 1)s_i$$

$$- \frac{s_1(s_1-1)}{2} 2^\lambda - \frac{s_2(s_2-1)}{2} 2^\lambda - m s_1 - m s_2 - s_1 s_2 - \sum_{i=3}^{k} s_1 s_i - \sum_{i=3}^{k} s_2 s_i$$

$$= (s_1 - s_2 - 1)(1 - 2^\lambda).$$

For $\lambda > 0$, we have $W_\lambda(\widetilde{G}) < W_\lambda(\widehat{G})$. For $\lambda < 0$, we have $W_\lambda(\widetilde{G}) > W_\lambda(\widehat{G})$. □

Theorem 10. *Let G be an arbitrary graph in $\mathscr{G}_{n,m,k}$. Then,
for $\alpha < 0$, $W_\lambda(G) \leq \frac{1}{2}[m(m-1) + (n-m)(n+m-s) - (s+1)t + s(n-m+t-k)2^\lambda]$,
for $\alpha > 0$, $W_\lambda(G) \geq \frac{1}{2}[m(m-1) + (n-m)(n+m-s) - (s+1)t + s(n-m+t-k)2^\lambda]$,
with the equality holding if and only if $G \cong K_m \vee (K_k[\{k-t\}O_s, \{s\}O_{s+1}])$.*

Proof. By Lemma 9 and Theorem 9, in view of Lemmas 1 and 2, the extremal graph having the extremal value of the modified-Wiener index in $\mathscr{G}_{n,m,k}$ should be the graph $K_m \vee (K_k[\{k-t\}O_s, \{s\}O_{s+1}])$.
Let $\widehat{G} = K_m \vee (K_k[\{k-t\}O_s, \{s\}O_{s+1}])$. Consequently, we have that:

$$W_\lambda(\widehat{G}) = \frac{m(m-1)}{2} + (k-t)\frac{s(s-1)}{2}2^\lambda + t\frac{s(s+1)}{2}2^\lambda + tm(s+1) + (k-t)ms$$

$$= \frac{1}{2}[m(m-1) + (n-m)(n+m-s) - (s+1)t + s(n-m+t-k)2^\lambda]. \quad \square$$

4. Conclusions

In this paper, we consider connected graphs of order n with vertex k-partiteness not more than m and characterize some extremal monotonic graph invariants such as the reformulated first Zagreb index, the multiplicative-sum Zagreb index, the general Laplacian-energy-like invariant, the general zeroth-order Randić index, and the modified-Wiener index among these graphs, and we investigate the corresponding extremal graphs of these invariants.

Author Contributions: The authors made equal contributions in the article. All authors read and approved the final manuscript.

Funding: This research was funded by the National Science Foundation of China under Grant 11601006; the China Postdoctoral Science Foundation under Grant 2017M621579; the Postdoctoral Science Foundation of Jiangsu Province under Grant 1701081B; Anhui Provincial Natural Science Foundation under Grant 1708085QA13; the Natural Science Foundation of the Anhui Provincial Education Department under Grant KJ2016A517; and the Project of Chizhou University under Grants 2017ZRZ009, 2016XJXTD02.

Acknowledgments: The authors are grateful to the anonymous reviewers and the editor for the valuable comments and suggestions.

Conflicts of Interest: The authors declare no conflict of interest.

References

1. Dimitrov, D. On structural properties of trees with minimal atom-bond connectivity index. *Discret. Appl. Math.* **2014**, *172*, 28–44. [CrossRef]
2. Li, X.; Fan, Y. The connectivity and the Harary index of a graph. *Discret. Appl. Math.* **2015**, *181*, 167–173. [CrossRef]
3. Xu, K.; Alizadeh, Y.; Das, K.C. On two eccentricity-based topological indices of graphs. *Discret. Appl. Math.* **2017**, *233*, 240–251. [CrossRef]
4. Hayat, S.; Wang, S.; Liu, J. Valency-based topological descriptors of chemical networks and their applications. *Appl. Math. Model.* **2018**, *60*, 164–178. [CrossRef]
5. Chen, H.; Wu, R.; Deng, H. The extremal values of some monotonic topological indices in graphs with given vertex bipartiteness. *MATCH Commun. Math. Comput. Chem.* **2017**, *78*, 103–120.
6. Liu, J.; Pan, X. Minimizing Kirchhoff index among graphs with a given vertex bipartiteness. *Appl. Math. Comput.* **2016**, *291*, 84–88. [CrossRef]
7. Robbiano, M.; Morales, K.T.; Martin, B.S. Extremal graphs with bounded vertex bipartiteness number. *Linear Algebra Appl.* **2016**, *493*, 28–36. [CrossRef]
8. Gutman, I.; Trinajstić, N. Graph theory and molecular orbitals.Total π-electron energy of alternant hydrocarbons. *Chem. Phys. Lett.* **1972**, *17*, 535–538. [CrossRef]
9. Todeschini, R.; Consonni, V. New local vertex invariants and molecular descriptors based on functions of the vertex degrees. *Match Commun. Math. Comput. Chem.* **2010**, *64*, 359–372.
10. Milićević, A.; Nikolić, S.; Trinajstić, N. On reformulated Zagreb indices. *Mol. Divers.* **2004**, *8*, 393–399. [CrossRef] [PubMed]
11. Eliasi, M.; Iranmanesh, A.; Gutman, I. Multiplicative versions of first Zagreb index. *Match Commun. Math. Comput. Chem.* **2012**, *68*, 217–230.
12. Borovićanin, B.; Furtula, B. On extremal Zagreb indices of trees with given domination number. *Appl. Math. Comput.* **2016**, *279*, 208–218. [CrossRef]
13. Gao, W.; Jamil, M.K.; Farahani, M.R. The hyper-Zagreb index and some graph operations. *J. Math. Anal. Appl.* **2017**, *54*, 263–275. [CrossRef]
14. Gutman, I.; Furtula, B.; Vukićević, Ḱ.; Popivoda, G. On Zagreb indices and coindices. *Match Commun. Math. Comput. Chem.* **2015**, *74*, 5–16.
15. Milovanović, E.I.; Milovanović, I.; Dolićanin, E.; Glogić, E. A note on the first reformulated Zagreb index. *Appl. Math. Comput.* **2016**, *273*, 16–20. [CrossRef]
16. Wang, C.; Liu, J.; Wang, S. Sharp upper bounds for multiplicative Zagreb indices of bipartite graphs with given diameter. *Discret. Appl. Math.* **2017**, *227*, 156–165. [CrossRef]
17. Wang, S.; Wang, C.; Liu, J. On extremal multiplicative Zagreb indices of trees with given domination number. *Appl. Math. Comput.* **2018**, *332*, 338–350. [CrossRef]
18. Zhou, B. On sum of powers of the Laplacian eigenvalues of graphs. *Linear Algebra Appl.* **2008**, *429*, 2239–2246. [CrossRef]
19. Liu, J.; Liu, B. A Laplacian-energy-like invariant of a graph. *Match Commun. Math. Comput. Chem.* **2011**, *66*, 713–730.

20. Lazić, M. On the Laplacian energy of a graph. *Czechoslovak Math. J.* **2006**, *56*, 1207–1213. [CrossRef]
21. Klein, D.J.; Randić, M. Resistance distance. *J. Math. Chem.* **1993**, *12*, 81–95. [CrossRef]
22. Das, K.C.; Xu, K.; Liu, M. On sum of powers of the Laplacian eigenvalues of graphs. *Linear Algebra Appl.* **2013**, *439*, 3561–3575. [CrossRef]
23. Liu, M.; Liu, B. A note on sum of powers of the Laplacian eigenvalues of graphs. *Appl. Math. Lett.* **2011**, *24*, 249–252. [CrossRef]
24. Qiao, L.; Zhang, S.; Jing, B.; Li, J. Coulson-type integral formulas for the general Laplacian-energy-like invariant of graphs I. *J. Math. Anal. Appl.* **2016**, *435*, 1246–1261. [CrossRef]
25. Tian, G.; Huang, T.; Zhou, B. A note on sum of powers of the Laplacian eigenvalues of bipartite graphs. *Linear Algebra Appl.* **2009**, *430*, 2503–2510. [CrossRef]
26. Merris, R. Laplacian graph eigenvectors. *Linear Algebra Appl.* **1998**, *278*, 221–236. [CrossRef]
27. Li, X.; Zheng, J. A unified approach to the extremal trees for different indices. *Match Commun. Math. Comput. Chem.* **2005**, *54*, 195–208.
28. Fajtlowicz, S. On conjectures of graffiti II. *Congr. Numer.* **1987**, *60*, 189–197.
29. Klein, L.B.; Hall, L.H. The meaning of molecular connectivity: A bimolecular accessibility model. *Croat. Chem. Acta* **2002**, *75*, 371–382.
30. Nikolić, S.; Kovačenić, G.; Milićević, A.; Trinajstić, N. The Zagreb indices 30 years after. *Croat. Chem. Acta* **2003**, *76*, 113–124.
31. Furtula, B.; Gutman, I. On forgotten topological index. *J. Math. Chem.* **2015**, *53*, 1184–1190. [CrossRef]
32. Chen, Z.; Su, G.; Volkmann, L. Sufficient conditions on the zeroth-order general Randić index for maximally edge-connected graphs. *Discret. Appl. Math.* **2017**, *218*, 64–70. [CrossRef]
33. Su, G.; Tu, J.; Das, K.C. Graphs with fixed number of pendent vertices and minimal Zeroth-order general Randić index. *Appl. Math. Comput.* **2015**, *270*, 705–710. [CrossRef]
34. Zhang, B.; Zhou, B. On zeroth-order general Randić indices of trees and unicyclic graphs. *Match Commun. Math. Comput. Chem.* **2007**, *58*, 139–146.
35. Gutman, I. A property of the Wiener number and its modifications. *Indian J. Chem.* **1997**, *36*, 128–132.

© 2018 by the authors. Licensee MDPI, Basel, Switzerland. This article is an open access article distributed under the terms and conditions of the Creative Commons Attribution (CC BY) license (http://creativecommons.org/licenses/by/4.0/).

Article

Scheduling and Planning in Service Systems with Goal Programming: Literature Review

Şeyda Gür and Tamer Eren *

Department of Industrial Engineering, Faculty of Engineering, Kirikkale University, 71450 Kirikkale, Turkey; seydaaa.gur@gmail.com
* Correspondence: tamereren@gmail.com; Tel.: +90-318-3574242

Received: 1 November 2018; Accepted: 14 November 2018; Published: 19 November 2018

Abstract: Background: People want to be able to evaluate different kinds of information in a good way. There are various methods that they develop in such situations. Among the optimization methods, the goal programming method is often used when there are multiple objectives that decision makers want to accomplish. Because scheduling and planning problems have multiple objectives that are desired to be achieved, the goal programming method helps the researcher in contradictory situations between these goals. Methods: This study includes, examines, and analyzes recent research on service scheduling and planning. In the literature, service scheduling and planning studies have been examined using goal programming method from past to today. Results: The studies are detailed according to the type of goal programming, according to scheduling types, the purpose used in the studies, and the methods integrated with the goal programming. There are 142 studies in Emerald, Science Direct, Jstor, Springer, Taylor and Francis, Google Scholar, etc. databases that are examined in detail. For readers, diversification has been made to facilitate the identification of these studies and a detailed overview has been presented. Conclusion: As a result of the study, studies with the goal programming in the literature have been seen. The readers' perspectives for planning and scheduling are discussed.

Keywords: goal programming; scheduling and planning; service system

1. Introduction

Even at any time in everyday life, people may be faced with situations that need to be decided. Deciding is to choose the most appropriate option among many. Optimal results may not always be obtained when a comparison is made between options. Some of the aims may conflict with each other, while others may be proportional to each other. However, too many factors may need to be ignored in order to achieve an optimal solution. Multi-criteria decision making is the decision-making tool to choose the best option among multiple criteria. One of the multi-criteria decision-making methods, the goal programming method, is a method that helps decision-makers when more than one criterion is concerned. By trying to reduce complexity problems, it is tried to reach the determined aims as much as possible. The goal programming method, which is an extension of linear programming, is a commonly used method in the literature. The difference of the goal programming method from the linear programming is to consider many objectives at the same time [1].

There are many purposes in production and service systems that are required to be realized, and there are many factors that affect these goals. In production systems, it is planned in what order and when to do jobs on machines. In service systems, this definition of planning differs and varies for each sector. Each task defined in production systems represents activities that transform a piece and add value to it. In service systems, this activity generally involves people. So, the resources needed can take many different forms and basically all serve humanity. In the service systems, these resources are varied in the health environment such as operating rooms, polyclinics, surgeons and else in the transportation such as airline, ship, train, passenger, pilot, or general reservation, course-exam programs. In this system, where there are so many varieties, scheduling and planning are very important. There are many factors that affect scheduling and planning activities. Taking these factors into account, synchronizing the use of different resource types is very difficult in real life. For decision makers, multi-criteria decision-making methods that can take into account multiple objectives that are influenced by various factors are at the forefront. Among these methods, the goal programming method, which is frequently used in the literature and has a high efficiency in order to reach the desired results, is an effective tool. As an extension of linear programming, the goal programming method allows flexibility in performing many purposes in planning and scheduling studies. Therefore, it is mostly preferred by the researchers in the literature. The researchers provide solutions for each scheduling and planning activities in the service sector by using the goal programming method using different performance criteria [2].

When literature studies related to goal programming method are examined; Tamiz et al. [3] examined the literature on two types of goal programming methods. They analyzed the application areas of these 70 studies. Tamiz et al. [4] presented a detailed analysis of the literature on the goal programming method. They emphasized to application areas in order to guide future work by looking from a general point of view. Jones et al. [5] presented a review of 280 studies on goal programming over a period of ten years. By determining the goal programming method as a keyword, they analyzed the application areas of the studies within the ten-year period. Azmi et al. [6] focused on portfolio selection and examined the work done with goal programming in this respect. They talked about the factors that affect portfolio selection in their studies and they included applications that can be worked on for readers. Colapinto et al. [7] focused on a topic rather than examining the goal programming method from a general point of view like other studies. In financial portfolio management, they have examined applications related to goal programming. They have categorized countries, years and so on, and talked about the importance of the subject and its relation to goal programming.

This study intends to examine in detail the studies related to scheduling and planning with goal programming method in service systems. This is the first study to analyze the scheduling and planning studies of the goal programming method which is frequently preferred by the researchers in the literature according to our studies. In addition, unlike other studies in the literature, we have classified the studies according to scheduling and planning types. We have believed that the contributions obtained as a result of the examinations made may be useful for readers who wish to conduct research in these areas. By putting together, the extensive literature covered in detail, the studies have been reflected the extent that readers can understand. Goal programming, scheduling, and planning keywords in Emerald, Science Direct, Jstor, Springer, Taylor and Francis, and Google Scholar databases are scanned while the literature is being searched. The results of the review of 142 studies are compiled.

All of the studies include all the studies that can be achieved as much as the day-to-day study of the first year of the goal programming method being used in the literature. Although the number of studies in the years that the first definition of the goal programming method was made is very small, the number of studies done in recent years has increased [5]. The majority of the studies examined is varied after 2000. With the development of technology and the changing needs of people, planning, and scheduling activities in service systems have also been shaped and differentiated according to needs. Especially in the last decade, these activities have increased and are expected to become even more diverse.

The review structure of this study is basically based on the combination of scheduling and planning activities of the goal programs. This work, which is more specifically structured to allow readers to easily access the information they seek, is divided into 5 sections. Section 2 provides information on which scheduling and planning activities the goal programming method is used for. In Section 3, the types of goal programming that are frequently used in the literature are given. The mathematical formulations of these methods are given to give technical information to the reader. In Section 4, it is mentioned what methods are integrated with the goal programming method in the literature. In Section 5 the information obtained in the investigation is interpreted.

2. Goal Programming According to Types of Scheduling and Planning Activities

Planning and scheduling is an effective tool for decision making in production and service systems. The mechanism to control the sequence of tasks to be performed manually or automatically can be defined as scheduling [2]. Scheduling and planning studies are carried out according to the determined goals and constraints in order to balance the load in a system and ensure that the existing resources are distributed evenly. Mathematical or heuristic methods are used to allocate these jobs to limited resources. This balanced distribution of resources enables businesses to optimize their objectives and reach their goals. Scheduling and planning activities differ in terms of process and service processes, although they are defined as an alignment of tasks and balance of resources. Scheduling and scheduling activities in manufacturing systems are specified as machining or hand-machining in a specific sequence of orders that will be driven to the market in a business environment. Works can be delayed when machines are busy, when machine breakdowns occur, when processing times are longer than planned, when capacities are inadequate. In such cases, detailed scheduling of the tasks or tasks planned to be done helps to increase the efficiency of the processes and ensure continuous control. In manufacturing systems, it is aimed to optimize the allocation of resources based on stock levels, demands, and resource requirements [8].

In scheduling and planning activities in service systems, there are many different problems. Though basically the same as the planning and scheduling function in the manufacturing environment, detailed information systems and decision-making functions are included in service systems. Differences between manufacturing systems and service systems also affect scheduling and planning activities. While the number of resources is kept constant in the production process of a job in manufacturing systems, the number of resources in service systems can change with time. Such variability affects the objective function. For this reason, planning and scheduling activities in service systems are related to capacity management and productivity management [2]. Scheduling and planning activities in service systems have many field applications. It is applied in many different subjects such as manpower scheduling, reservation scheduling, nurse scheduling, personnel scheduling, shift scheduling, transportation systems scheduling, and course scheduling. The goal programming method in the literature has been used in a wide variety of fields in service systems. Table 1 shows the applications in the service sector where researchers use the goal programming method.

Table 1. Studies by scheduling and planning types.

Course scheduling	[9–11]
Financial planning	[12,13]
Tour scheduling	[14–16]
Shift scheduling	[17–22]
Menu planning	[23,24]
Manpower planning	[25–30]
Maintenance scheduling	[31,32]
Urban planning	[33–38]
Other	[39–55]
Personnel	
Nurse scheduling	[56–74]
Staff scheduling	[75–87]
Examiner scheduling	[88,89]
Advertisement	
Media planning	[90–92]
Advertisement planning	[93]

Table 1. Cont.

Agriculture		
	Agriculture planning	[94–96]
	Harvest planning	[97–101]
	Land planning	[102–105]
	Forest planning	[106–108]
Transportation		
	Transportation planning	[109–112]
	Passenger scheduling	[113]
Waste		
	Waste planning	[114]
	Solid waste management planning	[115]
Healthcare		
	Master Surgical Scheduling	[116–120]
	Health planning	[121]
	Polyclinic schedules	[122]
Energy		[123–130]

As shown in Table 1, scheduling and planning activities in service systems vary widely in the literature. With this diversity being too much, the work that a particular inland destination programming method is used to is limited. Nurse scheduling and staff scheduling studies under the heading of personnel appear to be frequently addressed in the literature. Increasing the quality of service provided to customers in service systems is a priority goal. It is also important to increase staff satisfaction in order to provide this service quality at the top level. Taking into consideration the preferences of the staff in working conditions and creating the schedules according to this, causes performance increases. Louly et al. [76], who draw attention to this point and improves productivity with the program they have created, has developed a mathematical model with goal programming. They aimed to create an optimized cyclic program by combining the staff preferences and operating constraints. The flexibility of the goal programming method is an alternative tool for many constraint and objective problems. In a set of work models, soft constraints provide the convenience of developing solutions to these goals and boundaries. At the same time, the excess of the work load on the staff, the staff can tire and reduce the motivation to work. Therefore, the retirement of the staff must be distributed equally. The equal division of staff effort means that the work load of all the staff is balanced. Todovic et al. [79] have developed a methodology to be able to allocate this workload in a balanced way.

In the nurse scheduling problem, which is another type of personnel scheduling, basically, the same goals are sought. Providing patient satisfaction at the top level in health care units is linked to ensuring a high level of employee satisfaction. Careful and productive work by healthcare professionals has vital preventive measures. However, it is seen that there is motivation and loss of performance on the staff through wrong and unfair schedules. Azaiez et al. [56–58] developed a mathematical model for fairness of these schedules and plans by addressing the nurse scheduling problem.

In Table 1, very different application areas are covered by the researchers. While some areas have become the focus of researchers' interest, some studies have remained limited in the literature. In the studies under the other title; the authors of [40] in the planning of information resources for strategic planning in health systems, the authors of [43] in strategic planning for human resources in health systems, the authors of [44] in a basketball league game schedule, the authors of [47] for pre-scheduling in wind power, and the authors of [55] in mine planning used goal programming. When we look at the studies, it is pointed out that real life problems contain too many limitations. It seems that it is very difficult to transfer all of these constraints to mathematical models. At this point, the goal programming method that will soften most constraints, which will help most situations, is at the forefront. Many objectives can be achieved by allowing deviations from these constraints with the goal programming method. In the future, researchers should focus on the work in the areas that need to use the goal programming method. They should develop alternative approaches to real-life problems by replicating the limited applications of existing studies.

3. Goal Programming Types

There are many purposes to be realized in the problems encountered in everyday life. These aims can be contradictory to each other as well as in the same direction. In such cases, researchers resort to multi-criteria programming methods in order to achieve the objectives simultaneously. One of these methods, Goal Programming, was first described by Charnes et al. [131] in 1961. Decision makers have a hard time developing complex mathematical approaches when there are conflicts of interest or lack of knowledge in complex situations. To reach the desired values for each goal, it is necessary to extend the mathematical approaches to include multiple objectives. In such decision problems, decision makers want to achieve their goals as much as possible. All these concerns place the goal programming method within the multi-criteria programming paradigm [132,133]. There are three different goal programming methods used by researchers in the literature. Although Lexicographic Goal Programming and Weighted Goal Programming are frequently used, Chevyshev Goal Programming, also known as Minmax Goal Programming, is another less commonly used method.

Extensions of the goal programming method include extended goal programming, interval goal programming, lexicographic extended goal programming, and lexicographic Minmax goal programming methods (minimize the maximum deviation between goals). The extended goal programming method is used when decision makers wish to consider the number of goals reached. Researchers benefit from the flexibility of the expanded goal programming method to bring together the philosophies underlying the problems. They talk about the ability to produce solutions that fully reflect the basic criteria of the problems [134]. Another variant of this method is the lexicographic extended goal programming method [135]. Interval goal programming method minimizes the weighted sum of unwanted deviation variables within a given set of ranges [136]. The lexicographic Minmax goal programming method (minimize the maximum deviation between goals) represents the preferences of researchers more accurately in certain situations [137].

Researchers use these methods when the classical goal programming approach is not sufficient. In the multi-choice goal programming method developed in cases where the current goal formulation is not solved, multi-choice aspiration situations are taken into consideration. These multi-choice aspiration levels may be present in decision-making. It allows decision makers to determine multi aspiration levels for yield "higher/better" and "less/better" problems at aspiration levels [138]. While expressing these levels, there are difficulties in understanding the multiplicative terms of binary variables. To overcome these challenges, Chang et al. [139] proposed a revised multi-choice goal programming method. In this method, the multiplicative values of binary variables are not included. This leads to more efficient use and understanding of this method. In the proposed new method, it is also possible to direct the relations between the goals in problems involving multiple goals. At the same time, the goal programming method has been diversified according to in the case of fuzzy and uncertainty. Table 2 lists the studies in which the goal programming method is used in the fuzzy state. Table 3 also shows the use of the goal programming method in uncertain situations.

Table 2. Studies by fuzzy conditions.

Fuzzy	[11,27,29,36,38,42,48,49,67,88,104,111,112,115]
Non-fuzzy	[9,10,12–26,28,30–35,39–41,43–47,50–66,68–87,89–103,105–110,113,114,116–122]

Table 3. Studies by Uncertainty Status.

Stochastic	
Chance-Constraint	[47,93]
Stochastic	[37,84,107]
Deterministic	[9–36,38–46,48–83,85–92,94–116,118–122]

Tables 2 and 3 show that there is a limited number of fuzzy and stochastic studies. Uncertainty situations vary according to the problems researchers address. Most researchers are doing solutions under hypotheses in their work. However, even if the number is small, it seems that they are taken into account in their uncertainties.

3.1. Lexicographic Goal Programming

In some cases, decision-makers may be faced with prioritizing the solution options to achieve their goals. In other words, in order to optimize mathematical approaches in the problems encountered, it is the status of ranking among the objectives in the model. According to this approach, priority structure is mentioned among the preferences. Each component in the objective function represents the deviation variables of the goals placed at the priority level to which it corresponds. Then, according to these priorities, the model is solved, and the result obtained from each priority is added to run the next priority on the model. This resolution continues until the last priority is executed. This is defined as sequential reduction of each priority. The mathematical formulation of priority goal programming is as follows [137,140]:

$$LEXMIN_a = \left[\sum_{i \in h_1}(\alpha_i.d_i^- + \beta_i.d_i^+), \ldots, \sum_{i \in h_r}(\alpha_i.d_i^- + \beta_i.d_i^+), \ldots, \sum_{i \in h_Q}(\alpha_i.d_i^- + \beta_i.d_i^+)\right] \quad (1)$$

subject to

$$f_i(x) + d_i^- - d_i^+ = b_i \; i \in \{1, \ldots, q\}, i \in h_r, r \in \{1, \ldots, Q\} \quad (2)$$

$$d_i^-, d_i^+ \geq 0. \quad (3)$$

The expressions in the given mathematical model, h_r represents the cluster index with the goals at the r. priority level, α_q and β_q represents the weight factors for the d_q^+ and d_q^- deviation values, $f_s(x)$ represents the goal constraint. $\alpha_i = w_i/k_i$ if d_i^- is unwanted, otherwise $\alpha_i = 0$ and $\beta_i = w_i/k_i$ if d_i^+ is unwanted, otherwise $\beta_i = 0$. The parameters w_i and k_i are the weights reflecting preferential and normalizing purposes attached to the achievement of the ith goal. Each component in the objective function minimizes unwanted deviation variables in the goals placed at the level of priority it corresponds to.

The basic logic in priority goal programming starts with giving priorities to the identified goals. Then the model continues with resolving the goals with each priority one by one. The deviation variables d_q^+ and d_q^- in the goal constraints are defined as the difference between the achievement level in reaching the goals set by the decision makers and the actual level. If a goal value is below a desired level, a negative deviation is reached, and a positive deviation occurs if a desired value is reached. Deviation variables cannot have a value less than zero. Any variance that is undesirable to be minimized is given a zero value. In Table 4, there are scheduling, and planning studies made using the lexicographic goal programming method in the literature.

Table 4. Studies in the literature according to lexicographic goal programming and weighted goal programming method.

Lexicographic goal programming	[9,17,21,24,36,42,43,52,60,64,69,93,94,116–118,122]
Weighted goal programming	[10,19,22,35,38,40,56,57,75,77,86,100,108]

In some problems, the results of the solution are affected by the decisions of the decision makers. When there is an importance level among the objectives, it is necessary to prioritize the objectives. Sungur et al. [17,24,36] have identified priority levels among goals using the lexicographic goal programming method in their work. In lexicographic goal programming, decision-makers may not achieve the desired level of satisfaction at the specified goals. In this point, priority is given to the most important goals and the solution process is going on. Lexicographic goal programming is used when decision-makers cannot achieve relative importance of their goals by weight.

3.2. Weighted Goal Programming

When decision-makers' demands are determined precisely, a certain weight is given to the objectives. In the objective function, this weighted sum of deviations is minimized. The deviation variables of the goals have different relative weight in the objective function. Weighted goal programming also makes an effort to achieve multiple goals at the same time. Weighted goal programming is used for problems that cannot be prioritized among goals and can be measured by weighting goals where all goals are same important. The mathematical formulation of weighted goal programming is as follows [137,141]:

$$Min_z = \sum_i^k (\alpha_i d_i^- + \beta_i d_i^+) \quad (4)$$

subject to

$$f_i(x) + d_i^- - d_i^+ = b_i, \quad i = 1\ldots Q, \quad x \in C_s. \quad (5)$$

In the weighted goal programming, the basic logic is to minimize the sum of the deviations of each goal weighted relative importance weights. Expressions in the given mathematical model; $f_i(x)$ represents a linear function of x, the attainment of b_i represents the desired goal value, d_i^-, d_i^+ represents the deviation values in the negative and positive directions from the goal values, C_s represents a set of constraints in linear programming. $\alpha_i = w_i/k_i$ if d_i^- is unwanted, otherwise $\alpha_i = 0$ and $\beta_i = w_i/k_i$ if d_i^+ is unwanted, otherwise $\beta_i = 0$. The parameters w_i and k_i are the weights reflecting preferential and normalizing purposes attached to the achievement of the ith goal. For decision makers, the weight of each goal may be different. If a goal value is below a desired level, a negative deviation is reached, and a positive deviation occurs if a desired value is reached. Deviation variables cannot have a value less than zero. Any variance that is undesirable to be minimized is given a zero value. Table 4 contains the scheduling and planning studies using the weighted goal programming method in the literature.

Looking at the studies in Table 4, it appears that decision makers have weighted on the goals in the decision-making process. Since these weights are factors that affect the goals in some studies, various methods are integrated. [10,19,56–77] used weighted goal programming method in their studies. Weighted goal programming, which minimizes the weighted sum of the deviations in the goals, can balance the opposites between goals.

3.3. Chebyshev Goal Programming

Weighted goal programming and lexicographic goal programming methods are often preferred by the researchers in the literature. However, Chebyshev Goal Programming method, known as Minmax goal programming, is less common in the literature. Although it is not used very often, it has a theoretically important structure. In the Chebyshev goal programming method, there is a tendency to minimize the maximum deviation between goals, rather than the minimization of the priority of deviations or weighted summation of the deviations. In the model, the goals are shown separately and there is no prioritization among the goals.

In this method, first proposed by the authors of [142] in 1976, the objective function consists only of the distance parameter giving the minimization of the maximum deviation [143]. The mathematical formulation of the Chebyshev goal programming method is as follows [137]:

$$Min\ D \quad (6)$$

subject to

$$(\alpha_i n_i + \beta_i p_i) - D \leq 0 \quad (7)$$

$$f_i(x) + d_i^- - d_i^+ = t_i, \quad i \in \{1,\ldots,q\} \quad (8)$$

$$d_i^+, d_i^- \geq 0 \quad x \in F. \quad (9)$$

In the given mathematical model expressions, d_i^+ and d_i^- represents deviations in the positive and negative direction from the i goal. If the positive direction deviation is d_i^+ for any value greater than zero and the negative direction deviation takes the value "0" for d_i^-, the value of the objective function is greater than the goal value. Similarly, for any value greater than zero in the negative direction deviation is d_i^-, if the deviation variable d_i^+ in the positive direction has a value of "0", the objective function value is smaller than the goal value. t_i is the target level for the ith goal, x is vector of decision variables, F is feasible set of constraints, D is a maximum deviation. In this goal programming approach, the maximum deviation D is minimized. Therefore, is called Minmax goal programming.

In this method, normalization process is performed because there are different units among the goals. Methods such as percent normalization, Euclidean normalization, total normalization, and Zero-one normalization are recommended for normalization. The first and important difference between the other goal programming methods is the phasing of the maximum discovery. The general effect of this punishment is to provide a balance between the levels of the goals, rather than reducing the sum to the minimum if possible. When considering real-life problems, decision-makers can use it to define needs as balancing in many applications.

4. Goal Programming According to Integrated Method

In the goal programming method which allows flexibility in the solution process, the goals are transferred with the model goal constraints. In the model of decision makers, the optimal value of the objective function is sought in the solution allowed by the system and goal constraints. In other words, the desired solution is determined according to the area of the desired goals. In the literature, goal programming method is mostly used alone in scheduling and planning studies. However, in recent years it has been integrated with various methods and started to be used. Traditional goal programming methods use simplex-based optimization techniques in the solution process. As the number of factors to consider in the problem structure increases, the difficulty and complexity of the problem also increase. The work integrated with the heuristic methods in the literature facilitates the solution process of the difficult models that cannot be solved by traditional methods. Table 5 shows the studies integrated with the goal programming in the scheduling and planning studies in the literature.

Table 5. The studies integrated with goal programming.

Multi-Criteria Decision Making	
Analytic Hierarchy Process	[10,40,75,77,86,130]
Analytic Network Process	[22,57]
Heuristic Methods	
Particle Swarm Optimization	[29]
Annealing Simulation	[111]
Other Methods	
Data Envelopment Analysis	[50,130]
Benchmarking	[51]
Not Integrated	
Only Goal Programming	[9,11–21,23–28,30–39,41–49,52–56,58–74,76–85,87–110,112–122]

As can be seen from Table 5, the number of studies related to the methods in which the goal programming method is integrated is very limited. The factors that make the solution process difficult can cause the inclusion of the stochastic functions in the studies. For such complicated situations, researchers can increase the effectiveness of the goal programming method by increasing the variety and application area of the models.

In the literature, the goal programming method is often integrated with multi-criteria decision-making methods so that decision makers can weight their goals. The analytical hierarchy process method seems to be preferred. Decision makers first identify the factors that influence goals.

Then, comparisons are made according to the hierarchical structure or interactions among these factors. According to these comparisons, factors are weighted. Kırış [10] in the course scheduling, [40] in planning information sources in health systems, Güler et al. [75] in planning anesthesia patients, used the analytic hierarchy process method. Hamurcu et al. [22] in staff scheduling, Bağ et al. [57] nurse scheduling used the analytical network process method.

Shahnazari-Shahrezaei et al. [29] have integrated particle swarm optimization with the goal programming method. They have considered the preferences of the employees of the problem type they deal with, and they have developed an algorithm for the complexity of the problem. The performance of the schedules created with this algorithm has been verified. The performance of the schedule created with this algorithm has been verified. During the studies, the effectiveness of the approaches developed by integrating the goal programming method with different methods is being increased. By evaluating the performance of these integrations and approaches, researchers can create more effective schedules in future work.

The goal programming method integrated with methods such as AHP is the solution to the problems experienced in the ongoing weighting situations. In this section, researchers can be interpreted that the researchers have recently turned towards these integrations. According to this evaluation, it is predicted that such integrations will increase. These integrations are composed of potential study topics for future researchers.

5. Conclusions

There are many factors and constraints that decision-makers consider in planning and scheduling study in production and service systems. In line with these constraints and limits, there are many objectives that need to be realized at the same time. Since it is impossible to transfer such real-life problems entirely to modeling, researchers are developing solutions algorithms under various assumptions. Optimization of scheduling and planning studies in these systems is tried to be achieved by multi-criteria programming models that simultaneously satisfy conflicting objectives. Today, service systems that operate with the idea of developing technology and meeting the growing desire of consumers face many limitations. Many approaches are being developed to cope with these limitations. Various studies are being carried out in order to be able to cope with these limiting conditions as well as to achieve the determined aims. The goal programming method, which is a multi-criteria programming model, is an effective tool for solving these complex situations. It offers an optimal solution for problems with two or more aims. At the same time, contradictory goals are also included in the modeling. Due to the complicated structure of the problem, sometimes it is faced to there is no solution in the processes with linear programming methods. The goal programming method is used by decision makers as a tool to help with such problems.

In this study, studies about planning and scheduling studies in service systems are examined. We have been researched studies from the first definition of the goal programming method to the today. Goal programming, scheduling, and planning keywords in Emerald, Science Direct, Jstor, Springer, Taylor and Francis, and Google Scholar databases are scanned while the literature is being searched. The studies examined are listed under various headings according to scheduling types, goal programming types, goal programming with integrated methods. The contributions of these studies to the literature and readers are mentioned. The theoretical structure of the goal programming method is discussed, and technical information is provided to the readers. For researchers, a systematic structure of these studies has been established. This structure makes it easier for readers to focus on the topics they are researching. In addition, the studies listed according to scheduling and planning types help the readers to navigate to which areas. Comprehensible lists have been created with the tables presented in this study and accessibility has been facilitated.

It can be seen from the planning and scheduling studies made by the goal programming method that the researchers have applied in a wide range of fields. However, there are a limited number of applications in these areas. Researchers are trying to achieve many goals at the same time by taking advantage of the flexibility of the goal programming method. But as with every method, there is a lack of this method. All limitations and restrictions on real life problems are not reflected in the model. Even though it is an indirect way, there are contradictions between goals and these limitations make solution difficult. For this reason, there are various assumptions in studies. In applications performed with the goal programming method, researchers can be satisfied with the results of the solution as much as possible. However, this satisfaction is not always fully realized. For this reason, researchers can make different researches in order to get desired results by going to different approaches. At the same time, in spite of this diversity in scheduling types, it is possible to make an interpretation that developing technology and application fields may have changed if there are so few studies. So, as technology develops, demands and needs change. For this reason, while some areas of service systems are at the foreground, some areas remain behind. The areas shaped according to these desires and needs, the researchers also directed the same direction.

The goal programming method is a method that can allow flexibility on the objectives in decision problems. At this point, researchers can take a look at the different areas of application taking into account other studies in this study. Researchers can build models that offer solutions to different problems. The basis of these models can be taken from other studies presented as a reference in this study. Based on changing technology, it can adapt these studies to today's problems and extend the performance criteria mentioned here. Thus, it can become a source of research for different studies. In addition, the goal programming method helps researchers to achieve the closest successful outcome as possible to various goals and constraints. It makes it possible for researchers to reach multiple goals that conflict with their preferences.

The goal programming method is presented as an effective method to researchers by prioritizing or weighting among the objectives. However, it is foreseen that there may be some points where this advantageous situation becomes a disadvantage. Researchers may find it difficult to prioritize or weight their intended objectives. At this point, they should establish a decision support system for these purposes. This method, which is one of the most suitable tools for researchers for real life problems, may not provide a solution for some problems in polynomial time. In these challenging situations faced by the researchers, it is recommended to continue by making assumptions. In some cases, the problem sufficiently stretched by deviations can be supported by assumptions. Another difficult situation faced by researchers is that sometimes not all goals are accessible. In this case, the researchers can accept the most satisfactory result. Another alternative for difficult-to-solve problems is the integration of goal programming and meta-heuristic algorithms. Utilizing such advances in the solution phase is a good opportunity to achieve goals of the problem.

The subjects surrounding the determination and sensitivity of the solutions in the goal programming method are one of the other areas that can be developed for researchers. Furthermore, unlike the classical formulation, which is insufficient in the solution processes, researchers have developed various extensions of the goal programming method. It is necessary to test the robustness of the solutions offered by the new formulations developed and to determine how the model result will react in variable and parameter variability.

In the study, theoretical information about the frequently used types of the goal programming method in the literature is given and the basic steps of the modeling structure are mentioned. In the studies examined, decision makers use different types according to their importance levels in the goals they set. Some goals are at a more important level in the problem, while others can stay in the background more than others. In this case, the decision makers either prioritize or weight the objectives. Researchers can use different methods integrated with the goal programming method in their work when they are weighing. When weighting is done, it has generally been seen that multi-criteria decision-making methods are utilized. The factors that are effective on the goals weighted and integrated to the solution with multi-criteria decision-making methods. With the other methods used in the integration, the productivity of the planning and scheduling is improved, and their performance is evaluated.

Often, in manual planning and schedules, the incentive to use the goal programming method needs to be increased. It is thought that these planning and schedules should be made more systematic. The flexibility and effectiveness of the goal programming method needs to be exploited. In changing areas of application, researchers can use this method to transfer many objectives to the objective function. Thus, they can carry out contradictory purposes together with misconceptions. At the same time, by integrating the goal programming method with different methods, the efficiency can be increased, and the performance of the solution results can be improved. With the quality of the programs made, decision-makers can achieve satisfactory results.

Author Contributions: Ş.G. conceptualized the study, conducted analyses, and contributed to writing the manuscript. T.E. provided overall guidance and expertise in conducting the analysis and was a contributor to writing the manuscript. All authors read and approved the final manuscript.

Funding: This research received no external funding.

Conflicts of Interest: The authors declare that there is no conflict of interest regarding the publication of this paper.

References

1. Uçakcıoğlu, B. Selection of Investment Projects with Multi-Criteria Decision Making and Goal Programming in the Air Defense Industry. Ph.D. Thesis, Kırıkkale University, Kırıkkale, Turkey, 2017.
2. Pinedo, M. *Planning and Scheduling in Manufacturing and Services*; Springer: New York, NY, USA, 2005.
3. Tamiz, M.; Jones, D.; El-Darzi, E. A review of goal programming and its applications. *Ann. Oper. Res.* **1995**, *58*, 39–53. [CrossRef]
4. Tamiz, M.; Jones, D.; Romero, C. Goal programming for decision making: An overview of the current state-of-the-art. *Eur. J. Oper. Res.* **1998**, *111*, 569–581. [CrossRef]
5. Jones, D.F.; Tamiz, M. *Goal Programming in the Period 1990–2000, Multiple Criteria Optimization: State of the Art Annotated Bibliographic Surveys*; Springer: Berlin, Germany, 2003; pp. 129–170.
6. Azmi, R.; Tamiz, M. *A Review of Goal Programming for Portfolio Selection, New Developments in Multiple Objective and Goal Programming*; Springer: Berlin, Germany, 2010; pp. 15–33.
7. Colapinto, C.; la Torre, D.; Aouni, B. Goal programming for financial portfolio management: A state-of-the-art review. *Oper. Res.* **2017**, 1–20. [CrossRef]
8. Baker, K.R.; Trietsch, D. *Principles of Sequencing and Scheduling*; John Wiley & Sons: Hoboken, NJ, USA, 2013.
9. Badri, M.A.; Davis, D.L.; Davis, D.F.; Hollingsworth, J. A multi-objective course scheduling model: Combining faculty preferences for courses and times. *Comput. Oper. Res.* **1998**, *25*, 303–316. [CrossRef]
10. Kırış, Ş. AHP and multichoice goal programming integration for course planning. *Int. Trans. Oper. Res.* **2014**, *21*, 819–833. [CrossRef]
11. Ertuğrul, İ.; Öztaş, G.Z. Ders Programı Oluşturulmasında 0-1 Tam Sayılı Bulanık Hedef Programlama Yaklaşımı. *Ömer Halisdemir Üniversitesi İktisadi ve İdari Bilimler Fakültesi Dergisi* **2016**, *9*, 159–177.
12. Spronk, J. *Interactive Multiple Goal Programming as an Aid for Capital Budgeting and Financial Planning with Multiple Goals, Capital Budgeting under Conditions of Uncertainty*; Springer: Berlin, Germany, 1981; pp. 188–212.
13. Cook, W.D. Goal programming and financial planning models for highway rehabilitation. *J. Oper. Res. Soc.* **1984**, *35*, 217–223. [CrossRef]
14. Topaloglu, S.; Ozkarahan, I. An implicit goal programming model for the tour scheduling problem considering the employee work preferences. *Ann. Oper. Res.* **2004**, *128*, 135–158. [CrossRef]
15. Mathirajan, M.; Ramanathan, R. A (0–1) goal programming model for scheduling the tour of a marketing executive. *Eur. J. Oper. Res.* **2007**, *179*, 554–566. [CrossRef]
16. Sungur, B. Development of a mixed integer goal programming model for the tour scheduling problem of a beauty salon. *Istanb. Univ. J. Sch. Bus.* **2008**, *37*, 49–64.
17. Sungur, B.; Özgüven, C.; Kariper, Y. Shift scheduling with break windows, ideal break periods, and ideal waiting times. *Flex. Serv. Manuf. J.* **2017**, *29*, 203–222. [CrossRef]
18. Özcan, E.C.; Varlı, E.; Eren, T. Goal programming approach for shift scheduling problems in hydroelectric power plants. *Int. J. Inf. Technol.* **2017**, *10*, 363–370.
19. Eren, T.; Varlı, E. Shift Scheduling Problems and A Case Study. *Int. J. Inf. Technol.* **2017**, *10*, 185.

20. Ciritcioğlu, C.; Akgün, S.; Varlı, E.; Eren, T. Shift Scheduling Problem a Solution Suggestion for Safety Officers in University of Kırıkkale. *Int. J. Eng. Res. Dev.* **2017**, *9*, 1–23. [CrossRef]
21. Eren, T.; Ünal, F.M. The Solution of Shift Scheduling Problem by Using Goal Programming. *Acad. Platf. J. Eng. Sci.* **2016**, *4*, 28–37.
22. Hamurcu, M.; Ünal, F.; Eren, T. The Solution of Shift Scheduling Problem by Using Analytic Network Process and Goal Programming Method. In Proceedings of the International Conference on Multiple Objective Programming, Tlemcen, Algeria, 13–15 December 2015; pp. 17–19.
23. Anderson, A.; Earle, M. Diet planning in the third world by linear and goal programming. *J. Oper. Res. Soc.* **1983**, *34*, 9–16. [CrossRef]
24. Körpeli, S.; Şahin, B.; Eren, T. Menu planning with goal programming: A case study. *Kırıkkale Üniv. J. Soc. Sci.* **2012**, *2*, 121–142.
25. Charnes, A.; Cooper, W.W.; Niehaus, R.J. *A Goal Programming Model for Manpower Planning*; Carnegie-Mellon Univ Pittsburgh Pa Management Sciences Research Group: Pittsburgh, PA, USA, 1967.
26. Charnes, A.; Cooper, W.; Niehaus, R.; Sholtz, D. *An Extended Goal Programming Model for Manpower Planning*; Carnegie-Mellon Univ Pittsburgh Pa Management Sciences Research Group: Pittsburgh, PA, USA, 1968.
27. Shahnazari-Shahrezaei, P.; Tavakkoli-Moghaddam, R.; Kazemipoor, H. Solving a multi-objective multi-skilled manpower scheduling model by a fuzzy goal programming approach. *Appl. Math. Model.* **2013**, *37*, 5424–5443. [CrossRef]
28. Bektur, G.; Hasgül, S. Workforce scheduling problem according to seniority levels: An application for a service system. *J. Econ. Adm. Sci.* **2013**, *15*, 385–402.
29. Shahnazari-Shahrezaei, P.; Tavakkoli-Moghaddam, R.; Kazemipoor, H. Solving a new fuzzy multi-objective model for a multi-skilled manpower scheduling problem by particle swarm optimization and elite tabu search. *Int. J. Adv. Manuf. Technol.* **2013**, *64*, 1517–1540. [CrossRef]
30. Goodman, D.A. A goal programming approach to aggregate planning of production and work force. *Manag. Sci.* **1974**, *20*, 1569–1575. [CrossRef]
31. Moro, L.M.; Ramos, A. Goal programming approach to maintenance scheduling of generating units in large scale power systems. *IEEE Trans. Power Syst.* **1999**, *14*, 1021–1028. [CrossRef]
32. Orhan, İ.; Kapanoğlu, M.; Karakoç, T.H. Concurrent aircraft routing and maintenance scheduling using goal programming. *J. Fac. Eng. Archit. Gazi Univ.* **2012**, *27*, 11–16.
33. Stern, H.I. A goal-programming approach to planning for population balance in a multiregional system. *Environ. Plan. A* **1974**, *6*, 431–437. [CrossRef]
34. Taylor, B.W., III; Keown, A.J. Planning urban recreational facilities with integer goal programming. *J. Oper. Res. Soc.* **1978**, *29*, 751–758. [CrossRef]
35. Levary, R.R.; Choi, T.S. A linear goal programming model for planning the exports of emerging countries. *J. Oper. Res. Soc.* **1983**, *34*, 1057–1067. [CrossRef]
36. Bravo, M.; Gonzalez, I. Applying stochastic goal programming: A case study on water use planning. *Eur. J. Oper. Res.* **2009**, *196*, 1123–1129. [CrossRef]
37. Sharma, D.K.; Ghosh, D.; Alade, J.A. A fuzzy goal programming approach for regional rural development planning. *Appl. Math. Comput.* **2006**, *176*, 141–149. [CrossRef]
38. Subulan, K.; Taşan, A.S.; Baykasoğlu, A. A fuzzy goal programming model to strategic planning problem of a lead/acid battery closed-loop supply chain. *J. Manuf. Syst.* **2015**, *37*, 243–264. [CrossRef]
39. Schroeder, R.G. Resource planning in university management by goal programming. *Oper. Res.* **1974**, *22*, 700–710. [CrossRef]
40. Lee, C.; Kwak, N. Information resource planning for a health-care system using an AHP-based goal programming method. *J. Oper. Res. Soc.* **1999**, *50*, 1191–1198. [CrossRef]
41. Kim, G.C.; Emery, J. An application of zero–one goal programming in project selection and resource planning—A case study from the Woodward Governor Company. *Comput. Oper. Res.* **2000**, *27*, 1389–1408. [CrossRef]
42. Oruç, K.O. Menu planning with fuzzy goal programming. *J. Manag. Econ. Res.* **2014**, *23*, 33–51.
43. Kwak, N.; Lee, C. A linear goal programming model for human resource allocation in a health-care organization. *J. Med. Syst.* **1997**, *21*, 129–140. [CrossRef] [PubMed]
44. Yang, T.-H.; Wang, R.-T.; Tseng, C.-H. The application of goal programming to the Scheduling problem of the professional baseball league. *J. Chin. Inst. Ind. Eng.* **2009**, *26*, 135–146. [CrossRef]

45. Steuer, R.E. Multiple criterion function goal programming applied to managerial compensation planning. *Comput. Oper. Res.* **1983**, *10*, 299–309. [CrossRef]
46. De Wit, C.; van Keulen, H.; Seligman, N.; Spharim, I. Application of interactive multiple goal programming techniques for analysis and planning of regional agricultural development. *Agric. Syst.* **1988**, *26*, 211–230. [CrossRef]
47. Wang, Y.; Zhou, Z.; Zhao, S.; Xu, Y.; Chen, R.; Yin, J.; Botterud, A. Chance-Constrained Goal-Programming Based Day ahead Scheduling in Wind Power Integrated System. In Proceedings of the Power and Energy Society General Meeting (PESGM), Boston, MA, USA, 17–21 July 2016; pp. 1–5.
48. Peng, J.; Song, K. Expected Value Goal Programming Model for Fuzzy Scheduling Problem. In Proceedings of the 10th IEEE International Conference on Fuzzy Systems, Melbourne, Australia, 2–5 December 2001; pp. 292–295.
49. Ravi, V.; Reddy, P. Fuzzy linear fractional goal programming applied to refinery operations planning. *Fuzzy Sets Syst.* **1998**, *96*, 173–182. [CrossRef]
50. Athanassopoulos, A.D. Goal programming & data envelopment analysis (GoDEA) for target-based multi-level planning: Allocating central grants to the Greek local authorities. *Eur. J. Oper. Res.* **1995**, *87*, 535–550.
51. Cherif, M.S.; Chabchoub, H.; Aouni, B. Integrating customer's preferences in the QFD planning process using a combined benchmarking and imprecise goal programming model. *Int. Trans. Oper. Res.* **2010**, *17*, 85–102. [CrossRef]
52. Abdallah, M.; Kapelan, Z. Iterative Extended Lexicographic Goal Programming Method for Fast and Optimal Pump Scheduling in Water Distribution Networks. *J. Water Resour. Plan. Manag.* **2017**, *143*, 04017066. [CrossRef]
53. Pang, Q.; Wu, X. Optimization scheduling model of double line Shiplock based on nonlinear goal programming. *J. Appl. Res. Technol.* **2014**, *12*, 192–200. [CrossRef]
54. Taylor, B.W., III; Anderson, P.F. Goal programming approach to marketing/production planning. *Ind. Mark. Manag.* **1979**, *8*, 136–144. [CrossRef]
55. Ben-Awuah, E.; Askari-Nasab, H.; Awuah-Offei, K. Production Scheduling and Waste Disposal Planning for Oil Sands Mining Using Goal Programming. *J. Environ. Inform.* **2012**, *20*, 20–33. [CrossRef]
56. Azaiez, M.N.; al Sharif, S.S. A 0–1 goal programming model for nurse scheduling. *Comput. Oper. Res.* **2005**, *32*, 491–507. [CrossRef]
57. Bağ, N.; Özdemir, N.M.; Eren, T. Solving A 0–1 Goal Programming and ANP Methods with Nurse Scheduling Problem. *Int. J. Eng. Res. Dev.* **2012**, *4*, 2–6.
58. Jenal, R.; Ismail, W.R.; Yeun, L.C.; Oughalime, A. A cyclical nurse schedule using goal programming. *J. Math. Fundam. Sci.* **2011**, *43*, 151–164. [CrossRef]
59. Wang, S.-P.; Hsieh, Y.-K.; Zhuang, Z.-Y.; Ou, N.-C. Solving an outpatient nurse scheduling problem by binary goal programming. *J. Ind. Prod. Eng.* **2014**, *31*, 41–50. [CrossRef]
60. Sundari, V.; Mardiyati, S. Solving Cyclical Nurse Scheduling Problem Using Preemptive Goal Programming. In *AIP Conference Proceedings*; AIP Publishing: Melville, NY, USA, 2017; p. 030132.
61. Hakim, L.; Bakhtiar, T. The Nurse Scheduling Problem: A Goal Programming and Nonlinear Optimization Approaches. In *IOP Conference Series: Materials Science and Engineering*; IOP Publishing: Bristol, UK, 2017; p. 012024.
62. Musa, A.; Saxena, U. Scheduling nurses using goal-programming techniques. *IIE Trans.* **1984**, *16*, 216–221. [CrossRef]
63. Huarng, F. A primary shift rotation nurse scheduling using zero-one linear goal programming. *Comput. Nurs.* **1999**, *17*, 135–144. [PubMed]
64. Varlı, E.; Ergişi, B.; Eren, T. Nurse scheduling problem with special constraints: Goal programming approach. *Erciyes Univ. Fac. Econ. Adm. Sci. J.* **2017**, *0*, 189–206.
65. Ferland, J.A.; Berrada, I.; Nabli, I.; Ahiod, B.; Michelon, P.; Gascon, V.; Gagné, É. Generalized assignment type goal programming problem: Application to nurse scheduling. *J. Heuristics* **2001**, *7*, 391–413. [CrossRef]
66. Agyei, W.; Obeng-Denteh, W.; Andaam, E.A. Modeling nurse scheduling problem using 0–1 goal programming: A case study of Tafo Government Hospital, Kumasi-Ghana. *Int. J. Sci. Technol. Res.* **2015**, *4*, 5–10.
67. Tamiz, M.; Yaghoobi, M.A. *Nurse Scheduling by Fuzzy Goal Programming, New Developments in Multiple Objective and Goal Programming*; Springer: Berlin, Germany, 2010; pp. 151–163.

68. Atmaca, E.; Pehlivan, C.; Aydoğdu, C.B.; Yakıcı, M. Nurse scheduling problem and application. *Erciyes Univ. Sci. Inst. J.* **2012**, *28*, 351–358.
69. Eren, T.; Varlı, E.; Aktürk, M.S. The Solutions of Nurse Scheduling Problem of Full-Time Shift and Special Days Off with Goal Programming. *Kırıkkale Univ. J. Soc. Sci.* **2017**, *7*, 1–16.
70. Eren, T.; Şahiner, M.; Aktürk, M.S.; Bedir, N.; Ünlüsoy, S. A nursing scheduling for model suggestion: A case study. *Trakya Univ. Fac. Econ. Adm. Sci. J.* **2017**, *6*, 62–77.
71. Varlı, E.; Eren, T. Nurse scheduling problems and an application in hospital. *APJES* **2017**, *5*, 34–40.
72. Aktunc, E.A.; Tekin, E. Nurse Scheduling with Shift Preferences in a Surgical Suite Using Goal Programming. In *Industrial Engineering in the Industry 4.0 Era*; Springer: Berlin, Germany, 2018; pp. 23–36.
73. Ismail, W.R.; Jenal, R.; Hamdan, N.A. Goal programming based master plan for cyclical nurse scheduling. *J. Theor. Appl. Inf. Technol.* **2012**, *46*, 499–504.
74. Ozkarahan, I.; Bailey, J.E. Goal programming model subsystem of a flexible nurse scheduling support system. *IIE Trans.* **1988**, *20*, 306–316. [CrossRef]
75. Güler, M.G.; İdi, K.; Güler, E.Y. A goal programming model for scheduling residents in an anesthesia and reanimation department. *Expert Syst. Appl.* **2013**, *40*, 2117–2126. [CrossRef]
76. Louly, M.A.O. A goal programming model for staff scheduling at a telecommunications center. *J. Math. Model. Algorithms Oper. Res.* **2013**, *12*, 167–178. [CrossRef]
77. Topaloglu, S. A multi-objective programming model for scheduling emergency medicine residents. *Comput. Ind. Eng.* **2006**, *51*, 375–388. [CrossRef]
78. Yaacob, W.F.W.; Jauhari, N.E.; Yaacob, W.F.W. Development of 0–1 goal programming model for bus driver scheduling. *AIP Conf. Proc.* **2012**, *1482*, 376–381.
79. Todovic, D.; Makajic-Nikolic, D.; Kostic-Stankovic, M.; Martic, M. Police officer scheduling using goal programming. *Polic. Int. J. Police Strateg. Manag.* **2015**, *38*, 295–313. [CrossRef]
80. Özcan, E.; Varlı, E.; Eren, T. Shift Personnel Scheduling in Hydroelectric Power Plants with Goal Programming Approach. *J. Inf. Technol.* **2017**, *10*, 363–370.
81. Lin, H.-T.; Chen, Y.-T.; Chou, T.-Y.; Liao, Y.-C. Crew rostering with multiple goals: An empirical study. *Comput. Ind. Eng.* **2012**, *63*, 483–493. [CrossRef]
82. Chu, S.C. Generating, scheduling and rostering of shift crew-duties: Applications at the Hong Kong International Airport. *Eur. J. Oper. Res.* **2007**, *177*, 1764–1778. [CrossRef]
83. Gordon, L.; Erkut, E. Improving volunteer scheduling for the Edmonton Folk Festival. *Interfaces* **2004**, *34*, 367–376. [CrossRef]
84. Easton, F.F.; Rossin, D.F. A stochastic goal program for employee scheduling. *Decis. Sci.* **1996**, *27*, 541–568. [CrossRef]
85. Min, H. A disaggregate zero-one goal programming model for the flexible staff scheduling problem. *Soc. Econ. Plan. Sci.* **1987**, *21*, 271–282. [CrossRef]
86. Bedir, N.; Eren, T.; Dizdar, E.N. Ergonomic staff scheduling and an application in the retail sector. *Eng. Sci. Des. J.* **2017**, *5*, 657–674.
87. Eren, T.; Özder, E.H.; Varlı, E. A Model Suggestion for Cleaning Staff Scheduling Problem with Goal Programming Approach. *Black Sea J. Sci.* **2017**, *7*, 114–127.
88. Kağnıcıoğlu, C.H.; Yıldız, A. Solution to job assignment problem by a 0–1 integer fuzzy goal programming approach. *Anadolu Univ. Sci. Technol. J.* **2006**, *7*, 413–429.
89. Varlı, E.; Alagaş, H.; Eren, T.; Özder, E.H. Goal Programming Solution of the Examiner Assignment Problem. *Bilge Int. J. Sci. Technol. Res.* **2017**, *1*, 105–118.
90. Charnes, A.; Cooper, W.W.; Learner, D.B.; Snow, E.F. Note on an application of a goal programming model for media planning. *Manag. Sci.* **1986**, *14*, B-431–B-436. [CrossRef]
91. Kluyver, C.A. An exploration of various goal programming formulations—With application to advertising media scheduling. *J. Oper. Res. Soc.* **1979**, *30*, 167–171.
92. Charnes, A.; Cooper, W.W.; DeVoe, J.; Learner, D.B.; Reinecke, W. A goal programming model for media planning. *Manag. Sci.* **1968**, *14*, B-423–B-430. [CrossRef]
93. Bhattacharya, U. A chance constraints goal programming model for the advertising planning problem. *Eur. J. Oper. Res.* **2009**, *192*, 382–395. [CrossRef]
94. Ortuño, M.T.; Vitoriano, B. A goal programming approach for farm planning with resources dimensionality. *Ann. Oper. Res.* **2011**, *190*, 181–199. [CrossRef]

95. Wheeler, B.; Russell, J. Goal programming and agricultural planning. *J. Oper. Res. Soc.* **1977**, *28*, 21–32. [CrossRef]
96. Romero, C.; Rehman, T. Goal programming and multiple criteria decision-making in farm planning: Some extensions. *J. Agric. Econ.* **1985**, *36*, 171–185. [CrossRef]
97. Da Silva, A.F.; Marins, F.A.S.; Dias, E.X. Addressing uncertainty in sugarcane harvest planning through a revised multi-choice goal programming model. *Appl. Math. Model.* **2015**, *39*, 5540–5558. [CrossRef]
98. Zengin, H.; Asan, Ü.; Destan, S.; Engin Ünal, M.U.; Yeşil, A.; Bettinger, P.; Değermenci, A.S. Modeling harvest scheduling in multifunctional planning of forests for longterm water yield optimization. *Nat. Resour. Model.* **2015**, *28*, 59–85. [CrossRef]
99. Field, R.C.; Dress, P.E.; Fortson, J.C. Complementary linear and goal programming procedures for timber harvest scheduling. *For. Sci.* **1980**, *26*, 121–133.
100. Kao, C.; Brodie, J.D. Goal programming for reconciling economic, even-flow, and regulation objectives in forest harvest scheduling. *Can. J. For. Res.* **1979**, *9*, 525–531. [CrossRef]
101. Hof, J.G.; Pickens, J.B.; Bartlett, E. A MAXMIN approach to nondeclining yield timber harvest scheduling problems. *For. Sci.* **1986**, *32*, 653–666.
102. Cornett, D.; Williams, W.A. Goal programming for multiple land use planning at Mineral King, California. *J. Soil Water Conserv.* **1991**, *46*, 373–376.
103. El-Shishiny, H. A goal programming model for planning the development of newly reclaimed lands. *Agric. Syst.* **1988**, *26*, 245–261. [CrossRef]
104. Biswas, A.; Pal, B.B. Application of fuzzy goal programming technique to land use planning in agricultural system. *Omega* **2005**, *33*, 391–398. [CrossRef]
105. Arp, P.A.; Lavigne, D.R. Planning with goal programming: A case study for multiple-use of forested land. *For. Chron.* **1982**, *58*, 225–232. [CrossRef]
106. Gómez, T.; Hernández, M.; León, M.; Caballero, R. A forest planning problem solved via a linear fractional goal programming model. *For. Ecol. Manag.* **2006**, *227*, 79–88. [CrossRef]
107. Eyvindson, K.; Kangas, A. Stochastic goal programming in forest planning. *Can. J. For. Res.* **2014**, *44*, 1274–1280. [CrossRef]
108. Hotvedt, J.E. Application of linear goal programming to forest harvest scheduling. *J. Agric. Appl. Econ.* **1983**, *15*, 103–108. [CrossRef]
109. Prakash, J.; Sinha, S.; Sahay, S. Bus transportation crews planning by goal programming. *Soc. Econ. Plan. Sci.* **1984**, *18*, 207–210. [CrossRef]
110. Strang, K.D. Logistic planning with nonlinear goal programming models in spreadsheets. *Int. J. Appl. Logist. (IJAL)* **2012**, *3*, 1–14. [CrossRef]
111. Mokhtari, H.; Hasani, A. A multi-objective model for cleaner production-transportation planning in manufacturing plants via fuzzy goal programming. *J. Manuf. Syst.* **2017**, *44*, 230–242. [CrossRef]
112. Liang, T.-F. Applying fuzzy goal programming to production/transportation planning decisions in a supply chain. *Int. J. Syst. Sci.* **2007**, *38*, 293–304. [CrossRef]
113. Yaghini, M.; Alimohammadian, A.; Sharifi, S. A goal programming technique for railroad passenger scheduling. *Manag. Sci. Lett.* **2002**, *2*, 535–542. [CrossRef]
114. Ben-Awuah, E.; Askari-Nasab, H. Oil sands mine planning and waste management using mixed integer goal programming. *Int. J. Min. Reclam. Environ.* **2011**, *25*, 226–247. [CrossRef]
115. Chang, N.-B.; Wang, S. A fuzzy goal programming approach for the optimal planning of metropolitan solid waste management systems. *Eur. J. Oper. Res.* **1997**, *99*, 303–321. [CrossRef]
116. Cappanera, P.; Visintin, F.; Banditori, C. A Goal-Programming Approach to the Master Surgical Scheduling Problem. In *Health Care Systems Engineering for Scientists and Practitioners*; Springer: Berlin, Germany 2016; pp. 155–166.
117. Cappanera, P.; Visintin, F.; Banditori, C. Addressing conflicting stakeholders' priorities in surgical scheduling by goal programming. *Flex. Serv. Manuf. J.* **2018**, *30*, 252–271. [CrossRef]
118. Ozkarahan, I. Allocation of surgeries to operating rooms by goal programing. *J. Med. Syst.* **2000**, *24*, 339–378. [CrossRef] [PubMed]
119. Ogulata, S.N.; Erol, R. A hierarchical multiple criteria mathematical programming approach for scheduling general surgery operations in large hospitals. *J. Med. Syst.* **2003**, *27*, 259–270. [CrossRef] [PubMed]

120. Arenas, M.; Bilbao, A.; Caballero, R.; Gómez, T.; Rodriguez, M.; Ruiz, F. Analysis via goal programming of the minimum achievable stay in surgical waiting lists. *J. Oper. Res. Soc.* **2002**, *53*, 387–396. [CrossRef]
121. Rifai, A.K.; Pecenka, J.O. An application of goal programming in healthcare planning. *Int. J. Oper. Prod. Manag.* **1990**, *10*, 28–37. [CrossRef]
122. Güler, M.G. A hierarchical goal programming model for scheduling the outpatient clinics. *Expert Syst. Appl.* **2013**, *40*, 4906–4914. [CrossRef]
123. Amiri, S.; Honarvar, M.; Sadegheih, A. Providing an integrated Model for Planning and Scheduling Energy Hubs and preventive maintenance. *Energy* **2018**, *163*, 1093–1114. [CrossRef]
124. Hemmati, R.; Saboori, H.; Jirdehi, M.A. Stochastic planning and scheduling of energy storage systems for congestion management in electric power systems including renewable energy resources. *Energy* **2017**, *133*, 380–387. [CrossRef]
125. Koltsaklis, N.E.; Giannakakis, M.; Georgiadis, M.C. Optimal energy planning and scheduling of microgrids. *Chem. Eng. Res. Des.* **2018**, *131*, 318–332. [CrossRef]
126. Liu, Y.; Yu, S.; Zhu, Y.; Wang, D.; Liu, J. Modeling, planning, application and management of energy systems for isolated areas: A review. *Renew. Sustain. Energy Rev.* **2018**, *82*, 460–470. [CrossRef]
127. Ma, T.; Wu, J.; Hao, L.; Lee, W.-J.; Yan, H.; Li, D. The optimal structure planning and energy management strategies of smart multi energy systems. *Energy* **2018**, *160*, 122–141. [CrossRef]
128. Deshmukh, S.S.; Deshmukh, M.K. A new approach to micro-level energy planning—A case of northern parts of Rajasthan, India. *Renew. Sustain. Energy Rev.* **2009**, *13*, 634–642. [CrossRef]
129. Jinturkar, A.M.; Deshmukh, S.S. A fuzzy mixed integer goal programming approach for cooking and heating energy planning in rural India. *Expert Syst. Appl.* **2011**, *38*, 11377–11381. [CrossRef]
130. Özcan, E.C.; Ünlüsoy, S.; Eren, T. A combined goal programming–AHP approach supported with TOPSIS for maintenance strategy selection in hydroelectric power plants. *Renew. Sustain. Energy Rev.* **2017**, *78*, 1410–1423. [CrossRef]
131. Charnes, A.; Cooper, W.W.; Ferguson, R.O. Optimal estimation of executive compensation by linear programming. *Manag. Sci.* **1955**, *1*, 138–151. [CrossRef]
132. Charnes, A.; Cooper, W. *Management Models and Industrial Applications of Linear Programming*; John Wiley and Sons: New York, NY, USA, 1961.
133. Türkoğlu, S.P. Goal programming method and applications in decision making. *Osmaniye Korkut Ata Univ. J. Econ. Adm. Sci.* **2017**, *1*, 29–46.
134. Jones, D.F.; Wall, G. An extended goal programming model for site selection in the offshore wind farm sector. *Ann. Oper. Res.* **2016**, *245*, 121–135. [CrossRef]
135. Romero, C. Extended lexicographic goal programming: A unifying approach. *Omega* **2001**, *29*, 63–71. [CrossRef]
136. Vitoriano, B.; Romero, C. Extended interval goal programming. *J. Oper. Res. Soc.* **1999**, *50*, 1280–1283. [CrossRef]
137. Romero, C. A general structure of achievement function for a goal programming model. *Eur. J. Oper. Res.* **2004**, *153*, 675–686. [CrossRef]
138. Chang, C.T. Multi-choice goal programming. *Omega* **2007**, *35*, 389–396. [CrossRef]
139. Chang, C.T. Revised multi-choice goal programming. *Appl. Math. Model.* **2008**, *32*, 2587–2595. [CrossRef]
140. Lee, S.M. *Goal Programming for Decision Analysis*; Auerbach Publishers: Philadelphia, PA, USA, 1972.
141. Romero, C. *Handbook of Critical Issues in Goal Programming*; Elsevier: Amsterdam, Netherlands, 2014.
142. Flavell, R. A new goal programming formulation. *Omega* **1976**, *4*, 731–732. [CrossRef]
143. Güngör, M.; Umarusman, N.; Güneş, M. Use of goal programming and fuzzy goal programming under capital constraints in best price determination processes and an application. In Proceedings of the 31st National Operations Research and Industrial Engineering Congress, Sakarya, Turkey, 8–9 January 2011; pp. 1–9.

© 2018 by the authors. Licensee MDPI, Basel, Switzerland. This article is an open access article distributed under the terms and conditions of the Creative Commons Attribution (CC BY) license (http://creativecommons.org/licenses/by/4.0/).

Article

Edge Version of Metric Dimension and Doubly Resolving Sets of the Necklace Graph

Jia-Bao Liu [1], Zohaib Zahid [2], Ruby Nasir [2] and Waqas Nazeer [3,*]

[1] School of Mathematics and Physics, Anhui Jianzhu University, Hefei 230601, China; liujiabaoad@163.com
[2] Department of Mathematics, University of Management and Technology, Lahore 54000, Pakistan; zohaib_zahid@hotmail.com (Z.Z.); rubynasir76@gmail.com (R.N.)
[3] Division of Science and Technology, University of Education, Lahore 54000, Pakistan
* Correspondence: nazeer.waqas@ue.edu.pk; Tel.: +9-232-1470-7379

Received: 23 September 2018; Accepted: 29 October 2018; Published: 7 November 2018

Abstract: Consider an undirected and connected graph $G = (V_G, E_G)$, where V_G and E_G represent the set of vertices and the set of edges respectively. The concept of edge version of metric dimension and doubly resolving sets is based on the distances of edges in a graph. In this paper, we find the edge version of metric dimension and doubly resolving sets for the necklace graph.

Keywords: necklace graph; resolving sets; edge version of metric dimension; edge version of doubly resolving sets

1. Introduction and Preliminaries

Let G be a connected, simple and undirected graph consisting of nonempty finite sets V_G of vertices and E_G of edges. The order of a graph G is $|V_G|$ and $|E_G|$ is the size of G. The number of vertices joining to v, where $v \in V_G$ is called a degree of that vertex and written as d_v. $\Delta(G)$ is the maximum degree in a graph G.

For any two vertices $x, y \in V_G$, the distance $d(x,y)$ is the length of a shortest path between x and y. Let $R = \{r_1, r_2, \ldots, r_l\} \subset V_G$ be an ordered set and let $x \in V_G$, then $r(x, R)$ representation of x with respect to R is the l-tuple $\big(d(x, r_1), d(x, r_2), \ldots, d(x, r_l)\big)$. R is said to be a resolving set if different vertices of G have different representations with respect to R. The minimum number of vertices in a resolving set is called a basis for G and the cardinality of the basis is known as the metric dimension of G, represented by $dim(G)$. For $R = \{r_1, r_2, \ldots, r_l\} \subset V_G$, the ith component of $r(x, R)$ is 0 if and only if $x = r_i$. Hence, to prove that R is a resolving set it is enough to show that $r(x, R) \neq r(y, R)$ for each pair $x \neq y \in V_G \setminus R$.

The following lemma is very helpful for determining resolving set for $dim(G)$:

Lemma 1. *Let R be a resolving set for a simple connected graph G and $x, y \in V_G$. If $d(x, r) = d(y, r)$ for all vertices $r \in V_G \setminus \{x, y\}$, then $\{x, y\} \cap R \neq \emptyset$.*

The idea of resolving sets and metric dimension was presented by Slater in [1] and also by Hararay and Melter in [2]. Metric dimension is applied in different branches of navigation [3], robotics [3], chemistry [4], and network discovery and verification. It is well-known in [5] that computing the metric dimension of a graph is an NP-hard problem. Metric dimension has been deeply elaborated in surveys [6,7]. The line graph $L(G)$ of a graph G is defined as, the graph whose vertices are the edges of G, with two adjacent vertices if the corresponding edges share the common vertex in G. Also, metric properties of line graphs were studied to a great extent in [8–18]. The line graph of a graph G is helpful to find edge distances using the same technique of finding vertex distances of the graph G.

The concept of edge metric dimension was set up by Kelenc, Tratnik and Yero in [19] in 2016. They computed the edge metric dimension of different families of graphs and showed edge metric dimension i.e., $edim(G)$ can be less, equal to or more than $dim(G)$. They also showed computing $edim(G)$ is NP-hard in general. Since in literature edge metric dimension exists and that is entirely different from edge metric dimension defined in [20], so we renamed edge metric dimension proposed in [20] as an edge version of metric dimension. The edge version of metric dimension is defined as:

Definition 1.

1. The edge distance $d_E(f,g)$ between two edges $f,g \in E_G$ is the length of a shortest path between vertices f and g in the line graph $L(G)$.
2. If $d_E(e,f) \neq d_E(e,g)$, then the edge $e \in E_G$ is said to resolve two edges f and g of E_G.
3. Suppose that $R_E = \{f_1, f_2, \ldots, f_k\} \subset E_G$ is an ordered set and e is an edge of F_G, then $r_E(e, R_E)$ the edge version of representation of e with respect to R_E is the k-tuple $(d_E(e,f_1), d_E(e,f_2), \ldots, d_E(e,f_k))$.
4. If different edges of G have different edge version of representations with respect to R_E, then the set R_E is said to be a an edge version of resolving set of G.
5. The edge version of the metric basis of G is basically an edge version of the resolving set having minimum cardinality. The cardinality of the edge version of metric basis is represented by $dim_E(G)$, and is called the edge version of metric dimension of G.

In literature the edge version of metric dimension is known for few classes of graphs. Bounds of an edge version of metric dimension are also known and these bounds are given in the next theorem:

Theorem 1 ([21]). *If G is a connected graph with $|V_G| \geq 5$, then*

$$\lceil log_2 \Delta(G) \rceil \leq dim_E(G) \leq |V_G| - 2.$$

Table 1, represents all those graphs for which the edge version of metric dimension is known. In the table P_n, C_n and K_n represent the path graph, the cycle graph and the complete graph on n vertices respectively. $W_{1,n} = K_1 + C_n$ is a wheel graph on $n+1$ vertices, $K_{s,t}$ is a complete bipartite graph on $s+t$ vertices and for $n \geq 2$, $B_n = (k_1, k_2, \ldots, k_n)$ is a bouquet of circles $C^1, C^2, \ldots, C^n$ with a cut-vertex where k_i is the number of vertices of C^i ($1 \leq i \leq n$). Also S_n represents the n-sunlet graph and D_n is the prism graph on $2n$ vertices.

Table 1. Edge version of the metric dimension of graphs.

G	dim_E G
P_n	1 [4]
C_n	2
K_n	$n-1$ [6]
$K_{s,t}$	$\begin{cases} \lfloor \frac{2(s+t-1)}{3} \rfloor & \text{if } s \leq t \leq 2s; \\ t-1 & \text{if } t \geq 2s. \end{cases}$ [22]
$W_{1,n}$	$\begin{cases} 3 & \text{if } n = 3,4; \\ 4 & \text{if } n = 5; \\ n - \lceil \frac{n}{3} \rceil & \text{if } n \geq 6. \end{cases}$ [23]
B_n	$2n - 1$ [23]
S_n	$\begin{cases} 2 & \text{if } n \text{ is even}; \\ 3 & \text{if } n \text{ is odd}. \end{cases}$ [20]
D_n	3 [20]

Caceres et al. define the notion of a doubly resolving set in [22]. The doubly resolving sets present a valuable source for finding upper bounds of the metric dimension of graphs. Let the vertices a and b of the graph G with order $|V_G| \geq 2$ doubly resolve vertices c and d of the graph G if $d(c,a) - d(c,b) \neq d(d,a) - d(d,b)$. A subset D of vertices doubly resolves G if every two vertices in G are doubly resolved by some two vertices of D. Moreover, in G there do not exist any two different vertices having the same difference between their corresponding metric coordinates with respect to D. A doubly resolving set with minimum cardinality is called the minimal doubly resolving set. The minimum cardinality of a doubly resolving set for G is represented by $\psi(G)$. In case of some convex prism, hamming and polytopes graphs, the minimal doubly resolving sets have been obtained in [24–26] respectively.

Clearly, every doubly resolving set is a resolving set, which implies $dim(G) \leq \psi(G)$ for all graphs G. Also, if a and b doubly resolve c and d, then $d(c,a) - d(a,a) \neq 0$ or $d(f,b) - d(g,b) \neq 0$, and thus a or b resolve c and d, this shows that a doubly resolving set is also a resolving set.

Ahmed et al. in [27] proposed the idea of minimal edge version of doubly resolving sets of graph G, based on the distances of the edges of graph G which is defined as follows:

Definition 2.

1. The edges f and g of the graph G with size $|E_G| \geq 2$ are supposed to edge doubly resolve edges f_1 and f_2 of the graph G if $d_E(f_1, f) - d_E(f_1, g) \neq d_E(f_2, f) - d_E(f_2, g)$ in G.
2. Let $D_E = \{e_1, e_2, \ldots, e_k\}$ be an ordered set of the edges of G. If any two edges $e \neq f \in E_G$ are doubly resolved by any two edges of set D_E in G, then the set $D_E \subset E_G$ is said to be an edge version of doubly resolving set of G. The minimum cardinality of an edge version of doubly resolving set of G is represented by $\psi_E(G)$.

Note that every edge version of a doubly resolving set is an edge version of a resolving set, which implies $dim_E(G) \leq \psi_E(G)$ for all graphs G.

In this paper we compute the edge version of metric dimension and doubly resolving set for the necklace graph. At the end, we conclude that edge version of metric dimension and doubly resolving set are independent of choice of n.

2. The Edge Version of Metric Dimension for N_{e_n}

The necklace graph (see Figure 1) denoted by N_{e_n} [28] is a cubic Halin graph [29] obtained by joining a cycle with all vertices of degree 1 of a caterpillar (also called a comb) having n vertices of degree 3 and $n+2$ vertices of degree 1, denoted by $x_0, x_1, \ldots, x_{n+1}$ and $y_1, y_2, \ldots, y_n$, respectively. We have $V_{N_{e_n}} = \{x_0, \ldots, x_{n+1}, y_1, \ldots, y_n\}$ and $E_{N_{e_n}} = F \cup H \cup K$, where $F = \{f_1, f_2, \ldots, f_{n+1}\}$, $H = \{h_1, h_2, \ldots, h_{n+1}\}$ and $K = \{g_1, g_2, \ldots, g_{n+1}\}$. The necklace graph is 3-regular graph with constant metric dimension, which is computed in [30] given below:

$$dim(N_{e_n}) = \begin{cases} 2 & \text{if } n \text{ is even}; \\ 3 & \text{if } n \text{ is odd}. \end{cases}$$

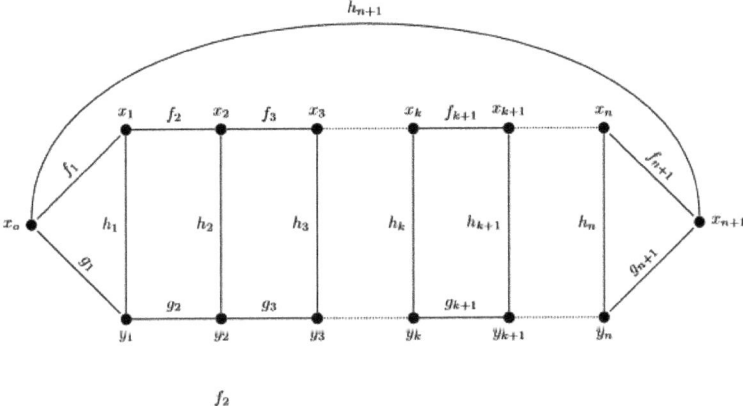

Figure 1. The necklace graph N_{e_n}.

For the edge version of metric dimension of the necklace graph, we have to construct a line graph $L(N_{e_n})$ of N_{e_n} with $n \geq 2$. (see Figure 2).

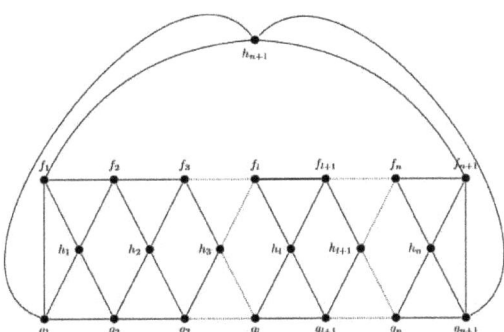

Figure 2. The line graph of a necklace graph: $L(N_{e_n})$.

Theorem 2. *The edge version of metric dimension of N_{e_n} is 3 for $n \geq 2$.*

Proof. Let $l = \lfloor \frac{n}{2} \rfloor$. For $n = 2$ and 3, consider the set $R_E = \{f_1, f_n, f_{n+1}\} \subset E_{N_{e_n}}$, then the edge version of representation of each edge of N_{e_n} with respect to R_E is given below:

The edge version of representation of the edges $f_p \in F$ with respect to R_E is:

$$r_E(f_p, R_E) = \begin{cases} (0, n-1, 2) & \text{if } p = 1; \\ (p-1, |n-p|, n-p+1) & \text{if } 2 \leq p \leq n; \\ (2, l, 0) & \text{if } p = n+1. \end{cases}$$

The edge version of representation of the inner edges $h_p \in H$ with respect to R_E is:

$$r_E(h_p, R_E) = \begin{cases} (p, n-p, n-p+1), & \text{if } 1 \leq p \leq n-1; \\ (n, 1, 1), & \text{if } p = n; \\ (1, l+1, 1), & \text{if } p = n+1. \end{cases}$$

The edge version of representation of the edges $g_p \in K$ with respect respect to R_E is:

$$r_E(g_p, R_E) = \begin{cases} (1, n, 2), & \text{if } p = 1; \\ (p, 2, n-p+2), & \text{if } 2 \leq p \leq n; \\ (2, l+1, 1), & \text{if } p = n+1. \end{cases}$$

For $n \geq 4$, take a set $R_E = \{f_1, f_l, f_n\} \subset E_{N_{e_n}}$, we will show that R_E is an edge version of resolving set for N_{e_n}.

The edge version of representation of the edges $f_p \in F$ with respect to R_E is:

$$r_E(f_p, R_E) = \begin{cases} (p-1, l-p, p+2) & \text{if } 1 \leq p \leq l-1; \\ (p-1, |l-p|, n-p) & \text{if } l \leq p \leq l+2; \\ (n-p+3, |l-p|, |n-p|) & \text{if } l+3 \leq p \leq n; \\ (2, l+1, 1), & \text{if } p = n+1. \end{cases}$$

The edge version of representation of the inner edges $h_p \in H$ with respect to R_E is:

$$r_E(h_p, R_E) = \begin{cases} (p, l-p, p+3), & \text{if } 1 \leq p \leq l-2; \\ (p, |l-p|+1, n-p), & \text{if } l-1 \leq p \leq l+1; \\ (n-p+3, |l-p|+1, n-p), & \text{if } l+2 \leq p \leq n-1; \\ (3, |l-n|+1, 1), & \text{if } p = n; \\ (1, l, 2), & \text{if } p = n+1. \end{cases}$$

The edge version of representation of the edges $g_p \in K$ with respect respect to R_E is:

$$r_E(g_p, R_E) = \begin{cases} (p, l-p+1, p+2), & \text{if } 1 \leq p \leq l-1; \\ (p, 2, n-p+1), & \text{if } l \leq p \leq l+1; \\ (n-p+3, p-l+1, n-p+1), & \text{if } l+2 \leq p \leq n-1; \\ (3, n-l+1, 2), & \text{if } p = n; \\ (2, l+1, 2), & \text{if } p = n+1. \end{cases}$$

From the above representations it is clear that no two edges of N_{e_n} have the same edge version of representations, which implies R_E is the edge version of resolving set and hence $dim_E(N_{e_n}) \leq 3$. Next, we have to show that $dim_E(N_{e_n}) \geq 3$. Suppose on the contrary that $dim_E(N_{e_n}) = 2$, then we have the following possibilities:

1. Let two edges h_1 and h_p from the edge set H with $2 \leq p \leq l+1$. For $R_E = \{h_1, h_p\} \subset E_{N_{e_n}}$, we have $r_E(f_1, R_E) = r_E(g_1, R_E) = (1, p)$, a contradiction.

2. Now suppose that both edges are from the edge set F. Suppose without loss of generality that $R_E = \{f_1, f_p\} \subset E_{N_{e_n}}$, where $2 \leq p \leq l+1$. Then, $r_E(g_1, R_E) = r_E(h_{n+1}, R_E) = (1, p)$, a contradiction.
3. Now suppose that both edges are from the edge set K. Suppose without loss of generality that $R_E = \{g_1, g_p\} \subset E_{N_{e_n}}$, where $2 \leq p \leq l+1$. Since $r_E(f_1, R_E) = r_E(h_{n+1}, R_E) = (1, p)$, so we have a contradiction.
4. If one edge belongs to the set F and the second edge is from H, without loss of generality we can take $R_E = \{f_1, h_p\} \subset E_{N_{e_n}}$ with $1 \leq p \leq l$. For $2 \leq n \leq 5$, we have $r_E(g_{n+1}, R_E) = r_E(f_{n+1}, R_E) = (2, 3)$ for $p = 1$ and $r_E(g_{n+1}, R_E) = r_E(f_{n+1}, R_E) = (2, n-1)$ for $p = 2$. For $n \geq 6$, we have $r_E(f_n, R_E) = r_E(g_n, R_E) = (3, p+3)$, a contradiction.
5. If one edge belongs to the set G and the second edge is from H. i.e. $R_E = \{g_1, h_p\} \subset E_{N_{e_n}}$. This case is similar to (4).
6. If one edge belongs to the set F and the second edge is from K, then we have the following five subcases:
   (a) Let $R_E = \{f_1, g_1\} \subset E_{N_{e_n}}$. For $2 \leq n \leq 5$, we have $r_E(h_1, R_E) = r_E(h_{n+1}, R_E) = (1, 1)$. For $n \geq 6$ and $l+4 \leq p \leq n+1$, we have $r_E(g_p, R_E) = r_E(f_p, R_E) = (n-p+3, n-p+3)$, a contradiction.
   (b) If $R_E = \{f_1, g_p\} \subset E_{N_{e_n}}$ and $2 \leq p \leq l+1$, then we have $r_E(g_1, R_E) = r_E(h_1, R_E) = (1, p-1)$, a contradiction.
   (c) Let $R_E = \{g_1, f_p\} \subset E_{N_{e_n}}$ with $2 \leq p \leq l+1$. This case is similar to 6 (b).
   (d) Let $R_E = \{f_2, g_p\} \subset E_{N_{e_n}}$ with $1 \leq p \leq l$. For $2 \leq n \leq 5$ and $p = 1$, we have $r(f_1, R_E) = r_E(h_1, R_E) = (1, 1)$ and when $p = 2$, then $r_E(h_1, R_E) = r_E(h_2, R_E) = (1, 1)$. For $n \geq 6$, we have $r_E(f_n, R_E) = r_E(h_n, R_E) = (4, p+2)$, a contradiction.
   (e) Let $R_E = \{g_2, f_p\} \subset E_{N_{e_n}}$. This case is similar to 6 (e).

All the above possibilities lead to a contradiction. Hence, there is no edge version of resolving set of cardinality 2 for edges $E_{N_{e_n}}$, which implies that $dim_E(N_{e_n}) = 3$. □

3. The Minimal Edge Version of Doubly Resolving Sets for N_{e_n}

The minimum doubly resolving set for the necklace graph N_{e_n} has been discussed in [31]. In this section, we determine minimal edge version of doubly resolving sets for the necklace graph. Define $S_j(h_{n+1}) = \{g \in E_{N_{e_n}} : d_E(h_{n+1}, g) = j\}$ be the set of edges in N_{e_n} at edge distance j from edge h_{n+1}. The Table 2 can be easily formulated for $S_j(h_{n+1})$ and it will be used to get the edge distances between two arbitrary edges in $E_{N_{e_n}}$.

Table 2. $S_j(h_{n+1})$ for N_{e_n}.

n	j	$S_j(h_{n+1})$
	1	$\{g_1, f_1, g_{n+1}, f_{n+1}\}$
	$2 \leq j \leq t$	$\{g_j, f_j, g_{n+2-j}, f_{n+2-j}, h_{j-1}, h_{n+2-j}\}$
$2t(t \geq 2)$	$t+1$	$\{h_t, f_{t+1}, g_{t+1}\}$
$2t+1(t \geq 2)$	$t+1$	$\{h_t, f_{t+1}, g_{t+1}\}$

By the symmetry of the necklace graph N_{e_n}, it is clear that $d_E(f_j, f_s) = d_E(g_j, g_s) = d_E(h_{n+1}, f_{s-j}) = d_E(h_{n+1}, g_{s-j})$ for $s > j$

For $n = 2t$

$$d_E(g_j, f_s) = \begin{cases} d_E(h_{n+1}, g_{|s-j|}) + 1 & \text{if } |j-s| \leq t, 1 \leq j, s \leq n; \\ d_E(h_{n+1}, g_{|s-j|}) & \text{if } |j-s| > t, 1 \leq j, s \leq n; \\ d_E(h_{n+1}, g_s) & \text{if } j = s = 1, \text{ or } n+1; \\ d_E(h_j, g_{j+2}) & \text{if } 1 < j = s < n; \\ d_E(h_{n+1}, f_n) & \text{if } j = s = n. \end{cases}$$

For $n = 2t + 1$

$$d_E(g_j, f_s) = \begin{cases} d_E(h_{n+1}, g_{|s-j|}) & \text{if } s > j; \\ d_E(h_{n+1}, g_s) & \text{if } j = s = 1, \text{ or } n + 1; \\ d_E(h_j, g_{j+2}) & \text{if } 1 < j = s < n; \\ d_E(h_{n+1}, f_n) & \text{if } j = s = n. \end{cases}$$

Lemma 2. $\psi_E(N_{e_n}) = 3$, whenever $n = 2t, t \geq 2$.

Proof. The Table 3 represents the vectors of edge version of representations of N_{e_n} with respect to $D_E = \{f_1, f_{t+1}, f_{n+1}\}$

Table 3. Vectors of edge version of representations of $N_{e_n}, n = 2t$.

j	$S_j(h_{n+1})$	$D_E = \{f_1, f_{t+1}, f_{n+1}\}$
0	h_{n+1}	$(1, t+1, 1)$
1	g_1	$(1, t+2, 2)$
	f_1	$\{0, t, 2\}$
	g_{n+1}	$\{2, t+1, 1\}$
	f_{n+1}	$\{2, t, 0\}$
$2 \leq j \leq k$	g_j	$\{j, t+2-j, j+1\}$
	f_j	$\{j, t+1-j, j+1\}$
	g_{n+2-j}	$\{n-j+3, j-t, n-j+2\}$
	f_{n+2-j}	$\{n-j+3, |t+1-j|, n-j+1\}$
	h_{j-1}	$\{j, t+1-j, j+2\}$
	h_{n+2-j}	$\{n-j+3, t-j, n-j+1\}$
	h_t	$\{t, 1, t\}$
	h_{t+1}	$\{t+1, 1, t+1\}$
	f_{k+1}	$\{t, 0, t\}$
	g_{t+1}	$\{t+1, 2, t+1\}$

It can be verified that for each $j \in \{1, 2, 3, \ldots, t+1\}$, no two edges $f, g \in S_j(h_{n+1})$ exist such that $r_E(f, D_E) - r_E(g, D_E) = 0$ holds. Also for any $j, s \in \{1, 2, 3, \ldots, t+1\}$, there do not exist any two edges $f \in S_i(w_{n+1})$ and $g \in S_j(h_{n+1})$ such that $r_E(f, D_E) - r_E(g, D_E) = i - j$. So, $D_E = \{f_1, f_{t+1}, f_{n+1}\}$ becomes the minimal edge version of doubly resolving set for $n = 2t, t \geq 2$ and therefore the Lemma 2 holds. □

Lemma 3. $\psi_E(N_{e_n}) = 3$ whenever, $n = 2t + 1, t \geq 2$.

Proof. As we know that $dim_E(N_{e_n}) \leq \psi_E(N_{e_n})$ holds. Now the Table 4 represents the vectors of edge version of representations of N_{e_n} with respect to $D_E = \{f_1, f_n, h_{t+1}\}$.

Table 4 shows that for $j \in \{1, 2, 3, \ldots, t+1\}$ there do not exist two edges $f, g \in S_j(h_{n+1})$ such that the following condition $r_E(f, D_E) - r_E(g, D_E) = 0$ holds. Also, for any $i, j \in \{1, 2, 3, \ldots, t+1\}$, there do not exist any two edges $f \in S_i(h_{n+1})$ and $g \in S_j(h_{n+1})$ such that $r_E(f, D_E) - r_E(g, D_E) = i - j$. So, $D_E = \{f_1, f_n, h_{t+1}\}$ becomes the minimal edge version of doubly resolving set for $n = 2t + 1, t \geq 2$ and therefore the Lemma 3 holds. □

Table 4. Vectors of edge version of representations of N_{e_n}, for $n = 2t+1$.

j	$S_j(h_{n+1})$	$D_E = \{f_1, f_n, h_{t+1}\}$
0	h_{n+1}	$(1, 2, t+2)$
1	g_1	$(1, 3, t+1)$
	f_1	$\{0, 3, t+1\}$
	g_{n+1}	$\{2, 2, t+1\}$
	f_{n+1}	$\{2, 1, t+1\}$
2	g_n	$\{j+1, 2, t+2-j\}$
	h_n	$\{j+1, 1, t+3-j\}$
$2 \leq j \leq t$	g_j	$\{j, j+2, t+2-j\}$
	f_j	$\{j, j+2, j\}$
	g_{n+1-j}	$\{j+1, j-1, t-j+2\}$
	f_{n+2-j}	$\{j+1, j-2, t-j+2\}$
	h_{j-1}	$\{j-1, j+2, j\}$
	h_{n+1-j}	$\{j+1, j-2, t-j+3\}$
$t+1$	f_{t+1}	$\{t, t, 1\}$
	g_{t+1}	$\{t+1, t+1, 1\}$
	f_{t+2}	$\{t+1, t-2, 1\}$
	g_{t+2}	$\{t+2, t+1, 1\}$
	h_{t+2}	$\{t+2, t-1, 2\}$

Note: A counting technique determines that $\psi_E(N_{e_n}) = 3$ for $n = 2$ and 3. The sets $\{f_1, f_2, f_3\}$ and $\{f_1, f_3, h_2\}$ are the minimal edge version of doubly resolving sets for N_{e_2} and N_{e_3} respectively. When Lemma 2 and Lemma 3 is combined, then the following main theorem is formulated.

Theorem 3. Let N_{e_n} be the necklace graph. Then $\psi_E(N_{e_n}) = 3$ for $n \geq 2$.

4. Conclusions

In this paper, we have extended the notion of metric dimension to the edge version of metric dimension for the necklace graph N_{e_n} which is the least cardinality over all edge versions of resolving sets. We also calculated the minimal edge version of doubly resolving sets for N_{e_n}. It is interesting to consider the necklace graph because its edge version of metric dimension and the minimal edge version of doubly resolving set are independent of parity of n. In previous work on necklace graphs, (see [30,31]) resolving sets were based on vertices and distances were calculated between vertices only. While, in this paper edges have been considered for getting resolving sets and distances have been calculated between edges. Finally, we get $dim_E(N_{e_n}) = \psi_E(N_{e_n}) = 3$ for every n.

Author Contributions: J.-B.L. designed the problem. Z.Z. investigate the problem. R.N. wrote the paper and W.N. validate the results.

Funding: This research was funded by China Postdoctoral Science Foundation under grant No. 2017M621579 and Postdoctoral Science Foundation of Jiangsu Province under grant No. 1701081B. Project of Anhui Jianzhu University under Grant no. 2016QD116 and 2017dc03. Anhui Province Key Laboratory of Intelligent Building & Building Energy Saving.

Acknowledgments: The authors are grateful to the reviewers for suggestions to improve the presentation of the manuscript.

Conflicts of Interest: The authors declare no conflict of interest.

Open Problem: Characterize all classes of graphs in which metric dimension/doubly resolving sets coincides with edge version of metric dimension/doubly resolving sets.

References

1. Slater, P.J. Leaves of trees. *Congr. Numer.* **1975**, *14*, 549–559.
2. Harary, F.; Melter, R.A. On the metric dimension of a graph. *Ars Combin.* **1976**, *2*, 191–195.
3. Khuller, S.; Raghavachari, B.; Rosenfeld, A. Landmarks in Graphs. *Discret. Appl. Math.* **1996**, *70*, 217–229. [CrossRef]
4. Chartrand, G.; Eroh, L.; Johnson, M.A.; Oellermann, O.R. Resolvability in graphs and the metric dimension of a graph. *Discret. Appl. Math.* **2000**, *105*, 99–113. [CrossRef]
5. Garey, M.R.; Johnson, D.S. *Computers and Intractability: A Guide to the Theory of NP-Completeness*; Freeman: New York, NY, USA, 1979.
6. Bailey, R.F.; Cameron, P.J. Base size, metric dimension and other invariants of groups and graphs. *Bull. Lond. Math. Soc.* **2011**, *43*, 209–242. [CrossRef]
7. Chartrand, G.; Zhang, P. The theory and applications of resolvability in graphs. A Survey. *Congr. Numer.* **2003**, *160*, 47–68.
8. Buckley, F. Mean distance in line graphs. *Congr. Numer.* **1981**, *32*, 153–162.
9. Cohen, N.; Dimitrov, D.; Krakovski, R.; Skrekovski, R.; Vukasinovic, V. On Wiener index of graphs and their line graphs. *MATCH Commun. Math. Comput. Chem.* **2010**, *64*, 683–698.
10. Gutman, I. Distance of line graphs. *Graph. Theory Notes N. Y.* **1996**, *31*, 49–52.
11. Gutman, I.; Pavlovic, L. More on distance of line graphs. *Graph. Theory Notes N. Y.* **1997**, *33*, 14–18.
12. Imran, M.; Bokhary, S.A. On resolvability in double-step circulant graphs. *UPB Sci. Bull. Ser. A* **2014**, *76*, 31–42.
13. Iranmanesh, A.; Gutman, I.; Khormali, O.; Mahmiani, A. The edge versions of the Wiener index. *MATCH Commun. Math. Comput. Chem.* **2009**, *61*, 663–672.
14. Ramane, H.S.; Ganagi, A.B.; Gutman, I. On a conjecture of the diameter of line graphs of graphs of diameter two. *Kragujev. J. Math.* **2012**, *36*, 59–62.
15. Ramane, H.S.; Gutman, I. Counterexamples for properties of line graphs of graphs of diameter two. *Kragujev. J. Math.* **2010**, *34*, 147–150.
16. Ramane, H.S.; Revankar, D.S.; Gutman, I.; Walikar, H.B. Distance spectra and distance energies of iterated line graphs of regular graphs. *Publ. Inst. Math.* **2009**, *85*, 39–46. [CrossRef]
17. Su, G.; Xu, L. Topological indices of the line graph of subdivision graphs and their Schur-bounds. *Appl. Math. Comput.* **2015**, *253*, 395–401. [CrossRef]
18. Wu, B. Wiener index of line graphs. *MATCH Commun. Math. Comput. Chem.* **2010**, *64*, 699–706.
19. Kelenc, A.; Tratnik, N.; Yero, I.G. Uniquely identifying the edges of a graph: The edge metric dimension. *Discret. Appl. Math.* **2018**. [CrossRef]
20. Nasir, R.; Zafar, S.; Zahid, Z. Edge metric dimension of graphs. *Ars Combin.* **2018**, in press.
21. Feng, M.; Xu, M.; Wang, K. On the metric dimension of line graphs. *Discret. Appl. Math.* **2013**, *161*, 802–805. [CrossRef]
22. Cáceres, J.; Hernado, C.; Mora, M.; Pelayo, I.M.; Puertas, M.L.; Seara, C.; Wood, D.R. On the Metric Dimension of Cartesian Products of Graphs. *SIAM J. Discret. Math.* **2007**, *21*, 423–441. [CrossRef]
23. Eroh, L.; Kang, C.X.; Yi, E. Metric Dimension and Zero Forcing Number of Two Families of Line Graphs. *Math. Biochem.* **2014**, *139*, 467–483.
24. Cangalovic, M.; Kratica, J.; Kovacevic-Vujcic, V.; Stojanovic, M. Minimal doubly resolving sets of prism graphs. *Optimization* **2013**, *62*, 1037–1043. [CrossRef]
25. Kratica, J.; Kovacevic, V.; Cangalovic, M.; Stojanovic, M. Minimal doubly resolving sets and the strong metric dimension of Hamming graphs. *Appl. Anal. Discret. Math.* **2012**, *6*, 63–71. [CrossRef]
26. Kratica, J.; Kovacevic, V.; Cangalovic, M.; Stojanovic, M. Minimal doubly resolving sets and the strong metric dimension of some convex polytope. *Appl. Math. Comput.* **2012**, *218*, 9790–9801. [CrossRef]
27. Ahmad, M.; Zahid, Z.; Zafar, S. On minimal edge version of doubly resolving sets of a graph. *arXiv* **2018**, arXiv:1807.02365.
28. Syslo, M.M.; Proskurowski, A. On Halin graphs. In *Graph Theory*; Lecture Notes in Mathematics; Springer: New York, NY, USA, 1983; Volume 1018, pp. 248–256.
29. Lovasz, L.; Plummer, M.D. On a family of planar bicritical graphs. *Proc. Lond. Math. Soc.* **1975**, *30*, 160–176. [CrossRef]

30. Tomescu, I.; Imran, M. R-Sets and Metric Dimension of Necklace Graphs. *Appl. Math. Inf. Sci.* **2015**, *9*, 63–67. [CrossRef]
31. Ahmad, A.; Baca, M.; Sultan, S. Minimal Doubly Resolving Sets of Necklace Graph. *Math. Rep.* **2018**, *20*, 123–129.

© 2018 by the authors. Licensee MDPI, Basel, Switzerland. This article is an open access article distributed under the terms and conditions of the Creative Commons Attribution (CC BY) license (http://creativecommons.org/licenses/by/4.0/).

Article

Maximizing and Minimizing Multiplicative Zagreb Indices of Graphs Subject to Given Number of Cut Edges

Shaohui Wang [1,*,†], Chunxiang Wang [2,†], Lin Chen [2,†], Jia-Bao Liu [3,†] and Zehui Shao [4,†]

1. Department of Mathematics, Savannah State University, Savannah, GA 31419, USA
2. School of Mathematics and Statistics and Hubei key Laboratory Mathematics Sciences, Central China Normal University, Wuhan 430079, China; wcxiang@mail.ccnu.edu.cn (C.W.); clcycl@mails.ccnu.edu.cn (L.C.)
3. School of Mathematics and Physics, Anhui Jianzhu University, Hefei 230601, China; liujiabaoad@163.com
4. Institute of Computing Science and Technology, Guangzhou University, Guangzhou 510006, China; zshao@gzhu.edu.cn
* Correspondence: shaohuiwang@yahoo.com; Tel.: +1-352-665-3381
† These authors contributed equally to this work.

Received: 21 September 2018; Accepted: 22 October 2018; Published: 29 October 2018

Abstract: Given a (molecular) graph, the first multiplicative Zagreb index Π_1 is considered to be the product of squares of the degree of its vertices, while the second multiplicative Zagreb index Π_2 is expressed as the product of endvertex degree of each edge over all edges. We consider a set of graphs $\mathbb{G}_{n,k}$ having n vertices and k cut edges, and explore the graphs subject to a number of cut edges. In addition, the maximum and minimum multiplicative Zagreb indices of graphs in $\mathbb{G}_{n,k}$ are provided. We also provide these graphs with the largest and smallest $\Pi_1(G)$ and $\Pi_2(G)$ in $\mathbb{G}_{n,k}$.

Keywords: cut edge; graph transformation; multiplicative zagreb indices; extremal values

1. Introduction

Within the areas of theoretical chemistry and mathematics, the structure invariant is an important tool to study the quantitative molecular properties [1]. One type of the most classical topological molecular expression is called as Zagreb indices M_1 and M_2 [2]. This information can be used as qualitative levels for integral π-electron energy of the conjugated molecules. In the view of successful considerations on the applications on Zagreb indices [3], Todeschini et al., (2010) [4–6] introduced the multiplicative Zagreb indices of molecular graphs, denoted by Π_1 and Π_2 the multiplicative Zagreb indices. (Multiplicative) Zagreb indices are employed as molecular expressions in quantitative structure–property relationships and quantitative structure–activity relationships [7,8].

Mathematicians have been interested in the information of Zagreb indices about the upper and lower bounds for special (chemical) graphs, as well as corresponding areas of determining their extremal graphs [9–23]. In addition to a plenty of applications for the usage of Zagreb indices in theoretical chemistry, there are many studies for multiplicative Zagreb indices, which attracted one of the focus of interests in physics and graph theory. Borovićanin et al. [24] investigated upper bounds on Zagreb indices of noncyclic graphs with given domination number. Wang and Wei [6] determined the maximal and minimal values of multiplicative Zagreb indices in the extended noncyclic graph, k-trees. In some graph classes, Liu and Zhang provided some upper bounds for Π_1-index and Π_2-index of graphs subject to structure parameters [25]. Xu and Hua [26] explored a common method to characterize the bounds of 0, 1, 2-cyclic graphs. Iranmanesh et al. [27] gave these indices for a type of chemical molecules, specific dendrimers. Kazemi [28] found interesting extremal values for related moments and probability generating functions in random trees. The graphs subject to a given number of cut edges (or vertices) are intriguing in extremal mathematics [29–33]. It is a natural observation that trees having largest and smallest multiplicative Zagreb indices have been considered as interesting topics [27,34,35].

In view of mentioned outcomes, we continue this way and study multiplicative Zagreb indices of graphs subject to a given number of cut edges. In addition, the maximum and minimum of $\Pi_1(G)$ and $\Pi_2(G)$ of graphs in $\mathbb{G}_{n,k}$ subject to fixed number of cut edges are provided. Lastly, the corresponding graphs with the largest and smallest multiplicative Zagreb indices in $\mathbb{G}_{n,k}$ are determined.

2. Preliminaries

Denote by $G = (V(G), E(G))$ a simple undirected connected graph of vertex number n and edge number m with vertex set $V = V(G)$ and edge set $E = E(G)$. For $w \in V(G)$, $N(w)$ denotes the neighbors of w, that is, $N(w) = \{v| \ wv \in E(G)\}$, and $d(w) = |N(w)|$ is the degree of w. The Zagreb indices [3] of a connected graph are given by

$$M_1(G) = \sum_{u \in V(G)} d(u)^2 \text{ and } M_2(G) = \sum_{uv \in E(G)} d(u)d(v).$$

The first multiplicative Zagreb index $\Pi_1 = \Pi_1(G)$ and the second multiplicative Zagreb index $\Pi_2 = \Pi_2(G)$ [4,5] of any graph G are considered as

$$\Pi_1(G) = \prod_{u \in V(G)} d(u)^2 \text{ and } \Pi_2(G) = \prod_{uv \in E(G)} d(u)d(v) = \prod_{u \in V(G)} d(u)^{d(u)}.$$

A vertex of degree one is called pendent vertex. The supporting vertex is a vertex in a graph which is incident to at least one pendent vertex. A pendent edge is an edge connecting a pendent vertex and a supporting vertex. If $G_1, G_2, \cdots, G_l$ with $l \geq 2$ share a common vertex v, then $G_1vG_2v\cdots vG_l$ denote the graph with edge set $E(G_1) \cup E(G_2) \cup \cdots \cup E(G_l)$ and $V(G_1) \cap V(G_2) \cap \cdots \cap V(G_l) = \{v\}$. For $u_1 \in V(G_1)$ and $u_s \in V(G_2)$, if $P = u_1u_2\cdots u_s$ is a path, then denote this graph by G_1PG_2 or $G_1u_1u_2\cdots u_sG_2$ in which P is called an internal path. By deleting a vertex or an edge, the resulting graph has at least two components, and this vertex or edge is called a cut. If G has no cut vertex, then G is 2-connected. A block is 2-connected, and an endblock has not more than two cut vertices. $G_1 \cong G_2$ means that G_1 is isomorphic to G_2. As usual, P_n, K_n, S_n and C_n are a path, a clique, a star and a cycle on n vertices, respectively. The cyclomatic number $c(G)$ of a graph G is defined as $m - n + 1$. In particular, if $c(G) = 0$, 1 and 2, then G will be trees, unicyclic graphs and bicyclic graphs, respectively. If $c(G) \geq 1$, then G has at most $n - 3$ cut edges. Thus, we suppose that G contains $1 \leq k \leq n - 3$ cut edges in our following discussion.

Let $\mathbb{G}_{n,k}$ be the set of the connected graphs with $k \in [1, n-3]$ cut edges, and $E_c = \{e_1, e_2, \cdots, e_k\}$ be a set of cut edges of the graph $G \in \mathbb{G}_{n,k}$. Then E_c can be considered as two categories, which are the pendent edges and nonpendent edges (or internal paths of length 1). $G - E_c$ contains some 2-connected graphs and isolated vertices. Denote by K_n^S (or K_n^P, respectively) a graph obtained by identifying (connecting to, respectively) the nonpendent vertex of a star S_{k+1} (or a pendent vertex of a path P_k, respectively) to a vertex of K_{n-k} (see Figure 1). In addition, let C_n^S (or C_n^P, respectively) be a graph obtained by identifying (connecting to, respectively) the nonpendent vertex of a star S_k (or a pendent vertex of a path P_k, respectively) to a vertex of C_{n-k}.

In our work, we may use some terminologies and notations of these textbooks of graph theory (see [36,37]). By elementary processes, the following results are not hard.

Proposition 1. *If $s(l) = \frac{l}{l+t}$ is a function for $t > 0$, then $s(l)$ is an increasing function in $\mathbb{R}$.*

Proposition 2. *If $k(l) = \frac{l^l}{(l+t)^{l+t}}$ is a function for $t > 0$, then $k(l)$ is a decreasing function in $\mathbb{R}$.*

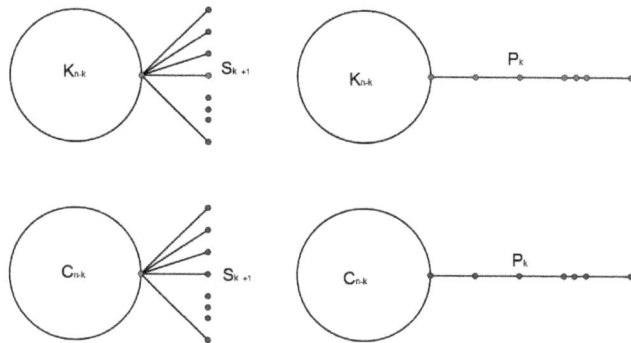

Figure 1. K_n^S, K_n^P, C_n^S and C_n^P.

Based on the concepts of $\Pi_1(G)$ and $\Pi_2(G)$ and the fact that adding edges increases the degrees, we have

Lemma 1. *Suppose that $G = (V, E)$ is a connected graph and $i = 1, 2$.*

(i) *If u, v are not adjacent in G, then $\Pi_i(G + uv) > \Pi_i(G)$.*

(ii) *If $uv \in E(G)$, we have $\Pi_i(G - e) < \Pi_i(G)$.*

Lemma 2 yields the following result.

Lemma 2. *Suppose that $G = (V, E)$ is a 2-connected graph with $i = 1, 2$.*

(i) *If $\Pi_i(G)$ is maximal, then $G \cong K_n$.*

(ii) *If $\Pi_i(G)$ is minimal, then $G \cong C_n$.*

Lemma 3. *Let C^1, C^2 be cycles, and $P_s = u_1 u_2 \cdots u_s$ be an internal path of $G = C^1 P_s C^2$ such that $u_1 \in V(C^1)$ and $u_s \in V(C^2)$. Assume that $u_1 v_1, u_1 v_2 \in E(C^1)$ and $u_s w_1, u_s w_2 \in E(C^2)$ such that $v_1 \neq v_2$ and $w_1 \neq w_2$. Let $G' = G - \{u_1 v_2, u_s w_1, u_s w_2\} + \{v_2 w_2, u_1 w_1\}$. Then $\Pi_i(G) > \Pi_i(G')$ with $i = 1, 2$.*

Proof. By the graph operations from G to G', we have $d_{G'}(u_s) = 1 < d_G(u_s) = 3$. For $v \in V(G) - \{u_s\}$, $d_G(v) = d_{G'}(v)$. Then $\Pi_i(G) > \Pi_i(G')$ with $i = 1, 2$, and we complete the proof. □

Lemma 4. *Let $G_1 P_m G_2$ and $G_1 G_2 P_m$ be graphs (see Figure 2), in which P_m is a path, and G_1, G_2 are connected. Then $\Pi_1(G_1 P_m G_2) \geq \Pi_1(G_1 G_2 P_m)$ and $\Pi_2(G_1 P_m G_2) \leq \Pi_2(G_1 G_2 P_m)$.*

Proof. Let $d_{G_1 P_m G_2}(u) = x$ and $d_{G_1 P_m G_2}(v) = y$. Then $d_{G_1 G_2 P_m}(u) = x + y - 1$. From the formulas of multiplicative Zagreb indices, we obtain

$$\frac{\Pi_1(G_1 P_m G_2)}{\Pi_1(G_1 G_2 P_m)} = \frac{x^2 y^2}{(x+y-1)^2 1^2} = \left(\frac{\frac{x}{x+y-1}}{\frac{1}{1+(y-1)}}\right)^2.$$

Since $x \geq 1, y \geq 1$, and by Proposition 1, we have $\Pi_1(G_1 P_m G_2) \geq \Pi_1(G_1 G_2 P_m)$. Note that

$$\frac{\Pi_2(G_1 P_m G_2)}{\Pi_2(G_1 G_2 P_m)} = \frac{x^x y^y}{(x+y-1)^{(x+y-1)} 1^1} = \frac{\frac{x^x}{(x+y-1)^{(x+y-1)}}}{\frac{1^1}{(1+y-1)^{(1+y-1)}}}.$$

By $x \geq 1$ and Proposition 2, we have $\frac{\Pi_2(G_1 P_m G_2)}{\Pi_2(G_1 G_2 P_m)} \leq 1$, that is, $\Pi_2(G_1 P_m G_2) \leq \Pi_2(G_1 G_2 P_m)$. Thus, this completes the proof. □

From Lemma 4, if we have an internal path, then we can move out it. By keeping this process, we have the useful lemma below.

Lemma 5. *Let GT be a graph by identifying a vertex of a tree T (not S_n) to a vertex u of G, and GS be a graph by attaching $|E(T)|$ pendent edges to u (see Figure 3). Then $\Pi_1(GT) > \Pi_1(GS)$ and $\Pi_2(GT) < \Pi_2(GS)$.*

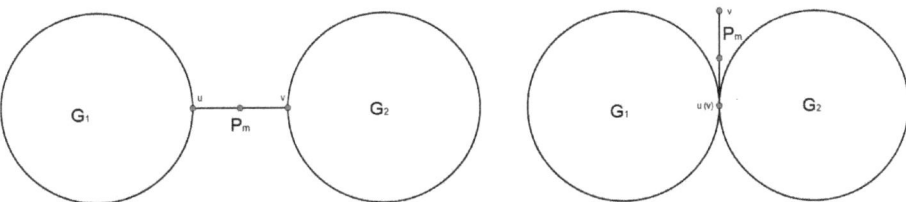

Figure 2. $G_1 P_m G_2$ and $G_1 G_2 P_m$.

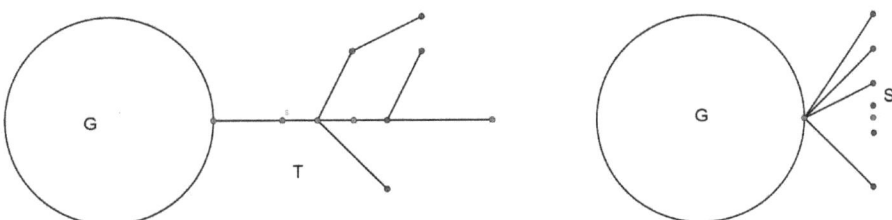

Figure 3. GT and GS.

Lemma 6. *Let u (v, respectively) be a vertex in G, and $u_1, u_2, \ldots, u_s$ be the endvertices of pendent path $P_1, P_2, \cdots, P_s$ ($v_1, v_2, \ldots, v_t$ be the endvertices of $P_1', P_2', \cdots, P_t'$, respectively). Set $uu_i' \in E(P_i)$ with $1 \leq i \leq s$, and $vv_j' \in E(P_j')$ with $1 \leq j \leq t$. Let $G' = G - \{uu_i'\} + \{vu_i'\}$ with $1 \leq i \leq s$, $G'' = G - \{vv_j'\} + \{uv_j'\}$ with $1 \leq j \leq t$ and $|V(G_0)| \geq 3$ (see Figure 4). Then either $\Pi_1(G) \geq \Pi_1(G')$ and $\Pi_2(G) \leq \Pi_2(G')$, or $\Pi_1(G) > \Pi_1(G'')$ and $\Pi_2(G) < \Pi_2(G'')$.*

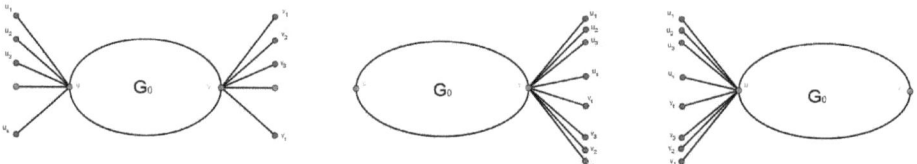

Figure 4. G, G' and G''.

Proof. Let $d_G(u) = x$, $d_G(v) = y$. By the constructions of G' and G'', we have $d_{G'}(u) = d_G(u) - s = x - s$, $d_{G'}(v) = d_G(v) + s = y + s$, $d_{G''}(u) = d_G(u) + t = x + t$ and $d_{G''}(v) = d_G(v) - t = y - t$. Combining with the concepts of multiplicative Zagreb indices, we have

$$\frac{\Pi_1(G)}{\Pi_1(G')} = \frac{x^2 y^2}{(x-s)^2(y+s)^2} = \frac{(\frac{y}{y+s})^2}{(\frac{x-s}{(x-s)+s})^2},$$

$$\frac{\Pi_2(G)}{\Pi_2(G')} = \frac{x^x y^y}{(x-s)^{x-s}(y+s)^{y+s}} = \frac{\frac{y^y}{(y+s)^{y+s}}}{\frac{(x-s)^{x-s}}{x^x}} = \frac{\frac{y^y}{(y+s)^{y+s}}}{\frac{(x-s)^{x-s}}{[(x-s)+s]^{(x-s)+s}}},$$

$$\frac{\Pi_1(G)}{\Pi_1(G'')} = \frac{x^2 y^2}{(x+t)^2(y-t)^2} = \frac{(\frac{x}{x+t})^2}{(\frac{y-t}{(y-t)+t})^2},$$

$$\frac{\Pi_2(G)}{\Pi_2(G'')} = \frac{x^x y^y}{(x+t)^{x+t}(y-t)^{y-t}} = \frac{\frac{x^x}{(x+t)^{x+t}}}{\frac{(y-t)^{y-t}}{y^y}} = \frac{\frac{x^x}{(x+t)^{x+t}}}{\frac{(y-t)^{y-t}}{[(y-t)+t]^{(y-t)+t}}}.$$

If $x - s \leq y$, by Propositions 1 and 2, we can obtain that $\Pi_1(G) \geq \Pi_1(G')$ and $\Pi_2(G) \leq \Pi_2(G')$. If $x - s - 1 \geq y$, then $x \geq y + s + 1 > y - t$. Propositions 1 and 2 yield that $\Pi_1(G) > \Pi_1(G'')$ and $\Pi_2(G) < \Pi_2(G'')$. Thus, the lemma is proved. □

Lemma 7. *Let $P_1 = u_1 u_2 \cdots u_s$ and $P_2 = v_1 v_2 \cdots v_t$ be two pendent paths of G with $s, t \geq 2$ and $d(u_s) = d(v_t) = 1$ (see Figure 5). Let $G' = G - v_1 v_2 + u_s v_2$. Then $\Pi_1(G) < \Pi_1(G')$ and $\Pi_2(G) > \Pi_2(G')$.*

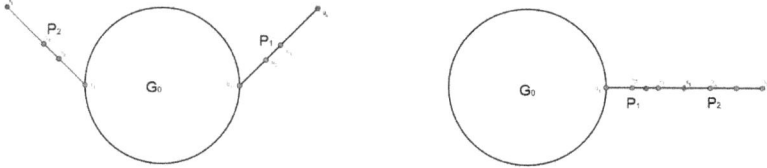

Figure 5. G and G'.

Proof. Note that $d(u_1) \geq 3$, $d(v_1) \geq 3$. From the expressions of multiplicative Zagreb indices, we have

$$\frac{\Pi_1(G)}{\Pi_1(G')} = \frac{d(u_s)^2 d(v_1)^2}{d_{G'}(u_s)^2 d_{G'}(v_1)^2} = \left(\frac{\frac{1}{2}}{\frac{d(v_1)-1}{d(v_1)}}\right)^2.$$

By Proposition 1, we have $\frac{\Pi_1(G)}{\Pi_1(G')} < 1$, that is, $\Pi_1(G) < \Pi_1(G')$.

$$\frac{\Pi_2(G)}{\Pi_2(G')} = \frac{d(u_s)^{d(u_s)} d(v_1)^{d(v_1)}}{d_{G'}(u_s)^{d_{G'}(u_s)} d_{G'}(v_1)^{d_{G'}(v_1)}} = \left(\frac{\frac{1^1}{2^2}}{\frac{(d(v_1)-1)^{d(v_1)-1}}{d(v_1)^{d(v_1)}}} \right)^2.$$

By Proposition 2, we have $\frac{\Pi_2(G)}{\Pi_2(G')} > 1$, that is, $\Pi_2(G) > \Pi_2(G')$.
Thus, this completes the proof. □

3. Graphs with Smallest Multiplicative Zagreb Indices in $\mathbb{G}_{n,k}$

We begin to determine the graphs having the smallest $\Pi_1(G)$ and $\Pi_2(G)$ in $\mathbb{G}_{n,k}$.

Theorem 1. *Let G be a graph in $\mathbb{G}_{n,k}$ with $1 \leq k \leq n-3$. Then*

$$\Pi_1(G) \geq 4^{n-k-1}(k+2)^2,$$

where the equality holds if and only $G \cong C_n^S$, respectively.

Proof. Choose a graph $G \in \mathbb{G}_{n,k}$ such that the value of $\Pi_1(G)$ is as small as possible. Let E_c be a cut edge set of G and $B_1, B_2, \cdots, B_{k+1}$ be the components of $G - E_c$. We first do some graph operations by previous lemmas. By Lemma 2, we have B_i is a cycle or an isolated vertex. Lemma 3 implies that G has a unique cycle. By Lemma 5, all cut edges in G are pendent edge. By Lemma 6, all pendent edges share a common supporting vertex, that is, $G \cong C_n^S$. Thus, this completes the proof. □

Theorem 2. *Assume that G is a graph in $\mathbb{G}_{n,k}$ for $1 \leq k \leq n-3$. We have*

$$\Pi_2(G) \geq 27 * 4^{n-2},$$

where the equality holds if and only $G \cong C_n^P$.

Proof. Let $G \in \mathbb{G}_{n,k}$ be a graph such that $\Pi_2(G)$ is minimal. Let E_c be a cut edge set of G and $B_1, B_2, \cdots, B_{k+1}$ be the components of $G - E_c$. By Lemma 2, we have B_i is a cycle or an isolated vertex. Lemma 3 implies that G has a unique cycle. By Lemma 7, there is only one pendent path in G. Thus $G \cong C_n^P$, and we prove this theorem. □

4. Graphs with Largest Multiplicative Zagreb Indices in $\mathbb{G}_{n,k}$

We proceed to consider graphs with the largest $\Pi_1(G)$ and $\Pi_2(G)$ in $\mathbb{G}_{n,k}$ in this section.

Theorem 3. *If G is a graph in $\mathbb{G}_{n,k}$ for $1 \leq k \leq n-3$, we have*

$$\Pi_1(G) \leq 4^{k-1}(n-k-1)^{2(n-k-1)}(n-k)^2,$$

where the equality holds if and only $G \cong K_n^P$.

Proof. Denote by a graph $G \in \mathbb{G}_{n,k}$ such that $\Pi_1(G)$ is maximal. Set E_c to be a cut edge set of G and $B_1, B_2, \cdots, B_{k+1}$ the components of $G - E_c$. By Lemma 2, we have B_i is a clique of size at least 3 or an isolated vertex. Next we start with the following claims.

Claim 1. *Every two cliques of size at least 3 do not share a common vertex.*

Proof of Claim 1. We prove it by a contradiction. Assume there are at least two blocks B_1, B_2 sharing a common vertex v_0 in G such that $|B_1|, |B_2| \geq 3$. Choose $v_1 \in V(B_1)$, $v_2 \in V(B_2)$ and $v_1, v_2 \neq v_0$.

Let $G' = G + v_1v_2$. By Lemma 1, $\Pi_2(G') > \Pi_2(G)$, that is a contradiction to the assumption of G. The claim is proved. □

We introduce a graph transformation that is used in the rest of our proof.

Claim 2. *Let K_{n_1} and K_{n_2} be two farthest endblocks of $K_{n_1}G_0K_{n_2}$ such that $v_{11} \in V(K_{n1}) \cap V(G_0)$ and $v_{l1} \in V(K_{n2}) \cap V(G_0)$ (see Figure 6). If $d(v_{11}) = n_1 \geq 3$ and $d(v_{l1}) = n_2 \geq 3$, then $\Pi_1(K_{n_1}G_0K_{n_2}) < \Pi_1(K_{n_1+n_2-1}G_0)$.*

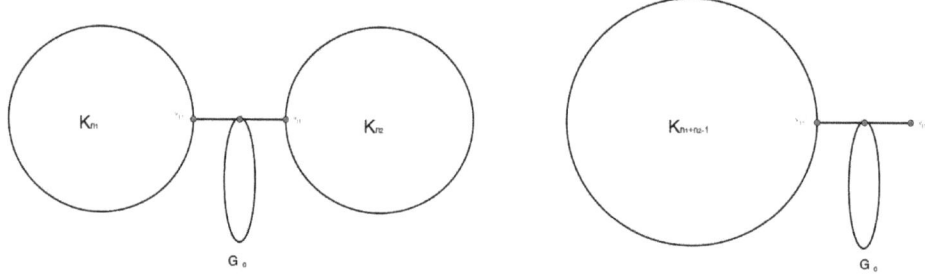

Figure 6. G and G'.

Proof of Claim 2. Let $V(K_{n_1}) = \{v_{11}, v_{12}, \cdots, v_{1n_1}\}$ and $V(K_{n_2}) = \{v_{l1}, v_{l2}, \cdots, v_{ln_2}\}$. Denote by $G = K_{n_1}G_0K_{n_2}$ and $G' = G - \{v_{l1}v_{li}, i \geq 2\} + \{v_{li}v_{1j}, i \geq 2, j \geq 1\} = K_{n_1+n_2-1}G_0$. From concepts of multiplicative Zagreb indices, one may obtain that

$$\frac{\Pi_1(G)}{\Pi_1(G')} = \left(\frac{d(v_{11})d(v_{12})d(v_{13})\cdots d(v_{1n_1})d(v_{l1})d(v_{l2})d(v_{l3})\cdots d(v_{ln_2})}{d'(v_{11})d'(v_{12})d'(v_{13})\cdots d'(v_{1n_1})d'(v_{l1})d'(v_{l2})d'(v_{l3})\cdots d'(v_{ln_2})}\right)^2$$

$$= \left(\frac{n_1n_2(n_1-1)^{n_1-1}(n_2-1)^{n_2-1}}{(n_1+n_2-1)(n_1+n_2-2)^{n_1+n_2-2}}\right)^2$$

$$\leq \left(\frac{n_1n_2(n_1-1)^{n_1-1}(n_2-1)^{n_2-1}}{(n_1+n_2-2)^{n_1+n_2-1}}\right)^2.$$

Let $f(x) = \frac{xn_2(x-1)^{x-1}(n_2-1)^{n_2-1}}{(x+n_2-2)^{x+n_2-1}}$. Then we take a derivative of $\ln(f(x))$ as $\frac{1}{x} + \ln(x-1) + 1 - \ln(x+n_2-2) - \frac{x+n_2-1}{x+n_2-2} < \frac{1}{x} + \ln(x-1) - \ln(x+n_2-2) \leq \frac{1}{x} + \ln(x-1) - \ln(x+1)$, by $n_2 \geq 3$. Set $g(x) = \frac{1}{x} + \ln(x-1) - \ln(x+1)$. Note that $g'(x) = \frac{x^2+1}{x^2(x^2-1)} > 0$ and $\lim_{x\to\infty} g(x) = \lim_{x\to\infty} \ln(\frac{(x-1)e^{\frac{1}{x}}}{x+1}) = 0$, by L' Hospital's Rule. Thus, $g(x) < 0$, that is, the function $f(x)$ is decreasing. We have

$$\frac{\Pi_1(G_1)}{\Pi_1(G_2)} \leq \frac{3n_2(3-1)^{3-1}(n_2-1)^{n_2-1}}{(3+n_2-2)^{3+n_2-1}} = \frac{12*n_2*(n_2-1)^{n_2-1}}{(n_2+1)^2(n_2+1)(n_2+1)^{n_2-1}}.$$

Since $12 \leq (n_2+1)^2$ and $n_2 < n_2+1$, then $\frac{\Pi_1(G_1)}{\Pi_1(G_2)} < 1$. This completes the proof of Claim 2. □

Claim 3. *If $\Pi_1(G)$ is maximal, then there exists exactly one path in G.*

Proof of Claim 3. We prove it by contradictions. Assume that there are at least two paths $P_1 = u_1u_2\cdots u_s$, $P_2 = v_1v_2\cdots v_l$ with $d(u_1), d(v_1) \geq 3$. We consider three cases that P_i is either a pendent path or an internal path with $i = 1, 2$. □

Case 1. $d(u_s) = d(v_l) = 1$.

Proof of Case 1. By Lemma 7, there is another graph $G' \in \mathbb{G}_n^k$ such that $\Pi_1(G) < \Pi_1(G')$, which is a contradiction to the choice of G. □

Case 2. $d(u_s) = 1, d(v_l) \geq 3$.

Proof of Case 2. Let $G'' = G - \{v_1v_2, u_1u_2\} + \{v_1u_2, v_2u_s\}$. Note that

$$\frac{\Pi_1(G)}{\Pi_1(G'')} = \frac{d(u_1)^2 d(u_s)^2}{d_{G''}(u_1)^2 d_{G''}(u_s)^2} = \left(\frac{\frac{1}{2}}{\frac{d(u_1)-1}{d(u_1)}}\right)^2.$$

Since $d(u_1) \geq 3$, by Proposition 1, we have $\Pi_1(G) < \Pi_1(G'')$, that is a contradiction to the choice of G. □

Case 3. $d(u_s) \geq 3, d(v_l) \geq 3$.

Proof of Case 3. By Case 2, there does not exist any pendent paths in G. Then every cut edge is in an internal path. By choosing two farthest endblocks and Claim 2, there is another graph G''' such that $\Pi_1(G''') > \Pi_1(G)$, which contradicts that $\Pi_1(G)$ is maximal. This completes the proof of Case 3. □

Therefore, G contains a unique clique of size at least 3 and the unique path is a pendent path. Thus $G \cong K_n^P$, and this completes the proof. □

Theorem 4. *Let G be a graph in $\mathbb{G}_{n,k}$ with $1 \leq k \leq n-3$. Then*

$$\Pi_2(G) \leq (n-1)^{n-1}(n-k-1)^{(n-k-1)^2},$$

where the equality holds if and only $G \cong K_n^S$.

Proof. Pick a graph $G \in \mathbb{G}_{n,k}$ such that $\Pi_2(G)$ is as large as possible. Denote by E_c a cut edge set of G and $B_1, B_2, \cdots, B_{k+1}$ be the components of $G - E_c$. By Lemma 2, we have B_i is a clique of size at least 3 or an isolated vertex. By Lemma 4, if two blocks are connected by a path, then they share a common vertex.

Claim 4. *There is a unique block B such that $|B| \geq 3$.*

Proof of Claim 4. We prove it by a contradiction. Assume that there are at least two blocks B_1, B_2 sharing a common vertex v_0 in G such that $|B_1|, |B_2| \geq 3$. Choose $v_1 \in V(B_1)$ and $v_2 \in V(B_2)$ and $v_1, v_2 \neq v_0$. Let $G' = G + v_1v_2$. By Lemma 1, $\Pi_2(G') > \Pi_2(G)$ and this claim is proved. □

By Lemmas 5 and 6, we have $G \cong K_n^S$, and this completes the proof. □

Author Contributions: All authors contributed equally to this work. Investigation: C.W. and Z.S.; Methodology: S.W. and J.-B.L.; Validation: L.C.

Funding: The work was partially supported by the National Natural Science Foundation of China under Grants 11771172 and 11571134, and Anhui Province Key Laboratory of Intelligent Building & Building Energy Saving.

Acknowledgments: The authors would like to express their sincere gratitude to the anonymous referees and the editor for many friendly and helpful suggestions, which led to great deal of improvement of the original manuscript.

Conflicts of Interest: The authors declare no conflict of interest.

References

1. Klavžar, S.; Gutman, I. The Szeged and the Wiener index of graphs. *Appl. Math. Lett.* **1996**, *9*, 45–49. [CrossRef]
2. Gutman, I.; Trinajstić, N. Graph theory and molecular orbitals. Total π-electron energy of alternant hydrocarbons. *Chem. Phys. Lett.* **1972**, *17*, 535–538. [CrossRef]
3. Gutman, I. On the origin of two degree-based topological indices. *Bull. Acad. Serbe Sci. Arts* **2014**, *146*, 39–52.
4. Todeschini, R.; Ballabio, D.; Consonni, V. Novel molecular descriptors based on functions of new vertex degrees. In *Novel Molecular Structure Descriptors Theory and Applications I*; Gutman, I., Furtula, B., Eds.; University Kragujevac: Kragujevac, Serbia, 2010; pp. 72–100.
5. Todeschini, R.; Consonni, V. New local vertex invariants and molecular descriptors based on functions of the vertex degrees. *MATCH Commun. Math. Comput. Chem.* **2010**, *64*, 359–372.
6. Wang, S.; Wei, B. Multiplicative Zagreb indices of k-trees. *Discret. Appl. Math.* **2015**, *180*, 168–175. [CrossRef]
7. Wang, C.; Liu J.; Wang S. Sharp upper bounds for multiplicative Zagreb indices of bipartite graphs with given diameter. *Discret. Appl. Math.* **2017**, *227*, 156–165. [CrossRef]
8. Basak, S.C.; Grunwald, G.D.; Niemi, G.J. Use of graph-theoretic geometric molecular descriptors in structure-activity relationships. In *From Chemical Topology to Three-Dimensional Geometry*; Balaban, A.T., Ed.; Plenum Press: New York, NY, USA, 1997; pp. 73–116.
9. Hu, Y.; Li, X.; Shi, Y.; Xu, T.; Gutman, I. On molecular graphs with smallest and greatest zeroth order general randić index. *MATCH Commun. Math. Comput. Chem.* **2005**, *54*, 425–434.
10. Li, X.; Shi, Y. A survey on the randić index. *MATCH Commun. Math. Comput. Chem.* **2008**, *59*, 127–156.
11. Shi, Y. Note on two generalizations of the randić index. *Appl. Math. Comput.* **2015**, *265*, 1019–1025. [CrossRef]
12. Furtula, B.; Gutman, I.; Ediz, S. On difference of Zagreb indices. *Discret. Appl. Math.* **2014**, *178*, 83–88. [CrossRef]
13. Hosamani, S.M.; Gutman, I. Zagreb indices of transformation graphs and total transformation graphs. *Appl. Math. Comput.* **2014**, *247*, 1156–1160. [CrossRef]
14. Xu, K.; Das, K.C.; Balachandran, S. Maximizing the Zagreb indices of (n, m)-graphs. *MATCH Commun. Math. Comput. Chem.* **2014**, *72*, 641–654.
15. Wang, J.F.; Belardo, F. A lower bound for the first Zagreb index and its application. *MATCH Commun. Math. Comput. Chem.* **2015**, *74*, 35–56.
16. Gao, W.; Farahani, M.; Husin, M.; Wang, S. On the edge-version atom-bond connectivity and geometric arithmetic indices of certain graph operations. *Appl. Math. Comput.* **2017**, *308*, 11–17. [CrossRef]
17. Liu, J.; Pan, X.; Hu, F.; Hu, F. Asymptotic Laplacian-energy-like invariant of lattices. *Appl. Math. Comput.* **2015**, *253*, 205–214. [CrossRef]
18. Ji, S.; Wang, S. On the sharp lower bounds of Zagreb indices of graphs with given number of cut vertices. *J. Math. Anal. Appl.* **2018**, *458*, 21–29. [CrossRef]
19. Matejić, M.; Milovanović, I.; Milovanović, E. On Bounds for Harmonic Topological Index. *Filomat* **2018**, *32*, 311–317. [CrossRef]
20. Upadhyay, A.K.; Maity, D. On the enumeration of a class of toroidal graphs. *Contrib. Discret. Math.* **2018**, *13*, 79–119.
21. Zhang, X. Equitable vertex arboricity of planar graphs. *Taiwan J. Math.* **2015**, *19*, 123–131. [CrossRef]
22. Tan, L.; Zhu, Z. The extremal graphs with respect to Hosoya index and Merrifield-Simmons index. *MATCH Commun. Math. Comput. Chem.* **2010**, *63*, 789–798.
23. Chen, G.; Zhu, Z. The number of independent sets in unicyclic graph with given size of maximum matchings. *Discret. Appl. Math.* **2012**, *160*, 108–115. [CrossRef]
24. Borovićanin, B.; Furtula, B. On extremal Zagreb indices of trees with given domination number. *Appl. Math. Comput.* **2016**, *279*, 208–218. [CrossRef]
25. Liu, J.; Zhang, Q. Sharp upper bounds for multiplicative Zagreb indices. *MATCH Commun. Math. Comput. Chem.* **2012**, *68*, 231–240.
26. Xu, K; Hua, H. A unified approach to extremal multiplicative Zagreb indices for trees, unicyclic and bicyclic graphs. *MATCH Commun. Math. Comput. Chem.* **2012**, *68*, 241–256.
27. Iranmanesh, A.; Hosseinzadeh, M.A.; Gutman, I. On multiplicative Zagreb indices of graphs. *Iran. J. Math. Chem.* **2012**, *3*, 145–154.

28. Kazemi, R. Note on the multiplicative Zagreb indices. *Discret. Appl. Math.* **2016**, *198*, 147–154. [CrossRef]
29. Liu, H.; Lu, M.; Tian, F. On the spectral radius of graphs with cut edges. *Linear Algebra Appl.* **2004**, *389*, 139–145. [CrossRef]
30. Wu, Y.R.; He, S.; Shu, J.L. Largest spectral radius among graphs with cut edges. *J. East China Norm. Univ. Nat. Sci. Ed.* **2007**, *3*, 67–74.
31. Zhao, Q.; Li, S.C. On the maximum Zagreb indices of graphs with k cut edges. *Acta Appl. Math.* **2010**, *111*, 93–106. [CrossRef]
32. Deng, H. On the minimum Kirchhoff index of graphs with a given cut edges. *MATCH Commun. Math. Comput. Chem.* **2010**, *63*, 171–180.
33. Borovićanin, B.; Lampert, T.A. On the maximum and minimum Zagreb indices of trees with a given number of vertices of maximum degree. *MATCH Commun. Math. Comput. Chem.* **2015**, *74*, 81–96.
34. Wang, S.; Wang, C.; Liu, J. On extremal multiplicative Zagreb indices of trees with given domination number. *Appl. Math. Comput.* **2018**, *332*, 338–350. [CrossRef]
35. Wang, S.; Wang, C.; Chen, L.; Liu, J. On extremal multiplicative Zagreb indices of trees with given number of vertices of maximum degree. *Discret. Appl. Math.* **2017**, *227*, 166–173. [CrossRef]
36. Bollobás, B. *Modern Graph Theory*; Springer: Berlin, Germany, 1998.
37. Trinajstić, N. *Chemical Graph Theory*; CRC Press: Boca Raton, FL, USA, 1992.

© 2018 by the authors. Licensee MDPI, Basel, Switzerland. This article is an open access article distributed under the terms and conditions of the Creative Commons Attribution (CC BY) license (http://creativecommons.org/licenses/by/4.0/).

Article

The Double Roman Domination Numbers of Generalized Petersen Graphs $P(n, 2)$

Huiqin Jiang [1], Pu Wu [2], Zehui Shao [2], Yongsheng Rao [2] and Jia-Bao Liu [3,*]

[1] Key Laboratory of Pattern Recognition and Intelligent Information Processing, Institutions of Higher Education of Sichuan Province, Chengdu University, Chengdu 610106, China; hq.jiang@hotmail.com
[2] Institute of Computing Science and Technology, Guangzhou University, Guangzhou 510006, China; puwu1997@126.com (P.W.); zshao@gzhu.edu.cn (Z.S.); rysheng@gzhu.edu.cn (Y.R.)
[3] School of Mathematics and Physics, Anhui Jianzhu University, Hefei 230601, China
* Correspondence: liujiabao@ahjzu.edu.cn or liujiabaoad@163.com

Received: 11 September 2018; Accepted: 10 October 2018; Published: 16 October 2018

Abstract: A double Roman dominating function (DRDF) f on a given graph G is a mapping from $V(G)$ to $\{0, 1, 2, 3\}$ in such a way that a vertex u for which $f(u) = 0$ has at least a neighbor labeled 3 or two neighbors both labeled 2 and a vertex u for which $f(u) = 1$ has at least a neighbor labeled 2 or 3. The weight of a DRDF f is the value $w(f) = \sum_{u \in V(G)} f(u)$. The minimum weight of a DRDF on a graph G is called the double Roman domination number $\gamma_{dR}(G)$ of G. In this paper, we determine the exact value of the double Roman domination number of the generalized Petersen graphs $P(n, 2)$ by using a discharging approach.

Keywords: double Roman domination; discharging approach; generalized Petersen graphs

1. Introduction

In this paper, only graphs without multiple edges or loops are considered. For two vertices u and v of a graph G, we say $u \sim v$ in G if $uv \in E(G)$. For positive integer k and $u, v \in V(G)$, let $d(u, v)$ be the distance between u and v and $N_k(v) = \{u | d(u, v) = k\}$. The neighborhood of v in G is defined to be $N_1(v)$ (or simply $N(v)$). The closed neighborhood $N[v]$ of v in G is defined to be $N[v] = \{v\} \cup N(v)$. For a vertex subset $S \subseteq V(G)$, we denote by $G[S]$ the subgraph induced by S. For a positive integer n, we denote $[n] = \{1, 2, \cdots, n\}$. For a set $S = \{x_1, x_2, \cdots, x_n\}$, if $x_i = x_j$ for some i and j, then S is considered as a multiset. Otherwise, S is an ordinary set.

For positive integer numbers n and k with n at least $2k + 1$, the generalized Petersen graph $P(n, k)$ is a graph with its vertex set $\{u_i | i = 1, 2, \cdots, n\} \cup \{v_i | i = 1, 2, \cdots, n\}$ and its edge set the union of $\{u_i u_{i+1}, u_i v_i, v_i v_{i+k}\}$ for $1 \leq i \leq n$, where subscripts are reduced modulo n (see [1]).

A subset D of the vertex set of a graph G is a dominating set if every vertex in $V(G) \setminus D$ has at least one neighbor in D. The domination number, denoted by $\gamma(G)$, is the minimum number of vertices over all dominating sets of G.

There have been more than 200 papers studying various domination on graphs in the literature [2–6]. Among them, Roman domination and double Roman domination appear to be a new variety of interest [3,7–15].

A double Roman dominating function (DRDF) f on a given graph G is a mapping from $V(G)$ to $\{0, 1, 2, 3\}$ in such a way that a vertex u for which $f(u) = 0$ has at least a neighbor labeled 3 or two neighbors both labeled 2 and a vertex u for which $f(u) = 1$ has at least a neighbor labeled 2 or 3. The weight of a DRDF f is the value $w(f) = \sum_{u \in V(G)} f(u)$. The minimum weight of a DRDF on a graph G is called the double Roman domination number $\gamma_{dR}(G)$ of G. A DRDF f of G with $w(f) = \gamma_{dR}(G)$ is called a $\gamma_{dR}(G)$-function. Given a DRDF f of G, we denote $E^f_{\{x_1, x_2\}} = \{uv \in E(G) | \{f(u), f(v)\} = \{x_1, x_2\}\}$. A graph G is a double Roman Graph if $\gamma_{dR}(G) = 3\gamma(G)$.

Mathematics **2018**, *6*, 206; doi:10.3390/math6100206 www.mdpi.com/journal/mathematics

In [7], Beeler et al. obtained the following results:

Proposition 1 ([7]). *In a double Roman dominating function of weight $\gamma_{dR}(G)$, no vertex needs to be assigned the value one.*

By Proposition 1, we now consider the DRDF of a graph G in which there exists no vertex assigned with one in the following.

Given a DRDF f of a graph G, suppose (V_0^f, V_2^f, V_3^f) is the ordered partition of the vertex set of G induced by f in such a way that $V_i^f = \{v : f(v) = i\}$ for $i = 0, 2, 3$. It can be seen that there is a 1-1 mapping between f and (V_0^f, V_2^f, V_3^f), and we write $f = (V_0^f, V_2^f, V_3^f)$, or simply (V_0, V_2, V_3). Given a DRDF f of $P(n,2)$ and letting $w_i \in \{0,2,3\}$ for $i = 1,2,3$ with $w_1 \geq w_2 \geq w_3$, we write $V_j^{w_1 w_2 w_3} = \{x \in V(P(n,2)) | f(x) = j, \{w_1, w_2, w_3\} = \{f(x_1), f(x_2), f(x_3)\}\}$, where $N(x) = \{x_1, x_2, x_3\}$.

Now, we will use $f(\cdot) = q^+$ to represent the value scope $f(\cdot) \geq q$ for an integer q. We say a path $t_1 t_2 \cdots t_k$ is a path of type $c_1 - c_2 - \cdots - c_k$ if $f(t_i) = c_i$ for $i \in [k]$. Let H be a subgraph induced by five vertices s_1, s_2, s_3, s_4, s_5 with $s_1 \sim s_2, s_2 \sim s_3, s_3 \sim s_4, s_3 \sim s_5$ satisfying $f(s_3) = 0$ and $f(s_1) = a$, $f(s_2) = b$, $f(s_4) = c$, $f(s_5) = d$ for some $a, b, c, d \in \{0, 2, 3\}$, then we say H is a subgraph of type $a - b - 0_{-d}^{-c}$.

Let W be a subgraph induced by four vertices s_1, s_2, s_3, s_4 with $s_1 \sim s_2, s_2 \sim s_3, s_2 \sim s_4$, satisfying $f(s_1) = a, f(s_2) = 0, f(s_3) = b$ and $f(s_4) = c$ for some $a, b, c \in \{0, 2, 3\}$, then we say W is a subgraph of type $a - 0_{-c}^{-b}$.

In the graph $P(n,2)$, we will denote the set of vertices of $\{u_i, v_i\}$ with $L^{(i)}$. For a given DRDF f of $P(n,2)$, let $w_f(L^{(i)})$ denote the weight of $L^{(i)}$, that is $w_f(L^{(i)}) = \sum_{u \in V(L^{(i)})} f(u)$. Let $\mathcal{B}_i = \{L^{(i-2)}, L^{(i-1)}, L^{(i)}, L^{(i+1)}, L^{(i+2)}\}$, where the subscripts are taken modulo n. We define $w_f(\mathcal{B}_i) = \sum_{j=-2}^{2} w_f(L^{(i+j)})$, and:

$$f(\mathcal{B}_i) = f \begin{pmatrix} u_{i-2} & u_{i-1} & u_i & u_{i+1} & u_{i+2} \\ v_{i-2} & v_{i-1} & v_i & v_{i+1} & v_{i+2} \end{pmatrix}.$$

Motivation: Beeler et al. [7] put forward an open problem about characterizing the double Roman graphs. As an interesting family of graphs, the domination and its variations of generalized Petersen graphs have attracted considerable attention [1,16]. Therefore, it is interesting to characterize the double Roman graphs in generalized Petersen graphs. In this paper, we focus on finding the double Roman graphs in $P(n,2)$.

2. Double Roman Domination Number of $P(n,2)$

2.1. Upper Bound for the Double Roman Domination Number of $P(n,2)$

Lemma 1. *If $n \geq 5$, then:*

$$\gamma_{dR}(P(n,2)) \leq \begin{cases} \lceil \frac{8n}{5} \rceil, & n \equiv 0 \pmod{5}, \\ \lceil \frac{8n}{5} \rceil + 1, & n \equiv 1, 2, 3, 4 \pmod{5}. \end{cases}$$

Proof. We consider the following five cases.

Case 1: $n \equiv 0 \pmod{5}$.

Let:
$$P_5 = \begin{bmatrix} 2 & 0 & 2 & 0 & 0 \\ 0 & 0 & 0 & 2 & 2 \end{bmatrix}.$$

Then, by repeating the pattern of P_5, we obtain a DRDF of weight $8k$ of $P(5k,2)$, and the upper bound is obtained.

Case 2: $n \equiv 1 \pmod 5$.

If $n = 6$, let:
$$P_6 = \begin{bmatrix} 0 & 2 & 0 & 2 & 0 & 0 \\ 2 & 0 & 0 & 0 & 2 & 3 \end{bmatrix}.$$

Then, the pattern P_6 induces a DRDF of weight 11 of $P(6,2)$, and the desired upper bound is obtained.

If $n \geq 11$, let:
$$P_{11} = \begin{bmatrix} 2 & 0 & 2 & 0 & 0 & 2 & 2 & 0 & 2 & 0 & 0 \\ 0 & 0 & 0 & 2 & 2 & 0 & 0 & 0 & 0 & 3 & 2 \end{bmatrix}.$$

Then, by repeating the leftmost five columns of the pattern of P_{11}, we obtain a DRDF of weight $8k+3$ of $P(5k+1,2)$, and the desired upper bound is obtained.

Case 3: $n \equiv 2 \pmod 5$.

If $n = 7$, let:
$$P_7 = \begin{bmatrix} 2 & 0 & 2 & 0 & 0 & 3 & 0 \\ 0 & 0 & 2 & 2 & 0 & 0 & 2 \end{bmatrix}.$$

Then, the pattern P_7 induces a DRDF of weight 13 of $P(7,2)$, and the desired upper bound is obtained.

If $n \geq 12$, let:
$$P_{12} = \begin{bmatrix} 2 & 0 & 2 & 0 & 0 & 2 & 0 & 3 & 0 & 2 & 0 & 0 \\ 0 & 0 & 0 & 2 & 2 & 0 & 2 & 0 & 0 & 0 & 2 & 2 \end{bmatrix}.$$

Then, by repeating the leftmost five columns of the pattern of P_{12}, we obtain a DRDF of weight $8k+6$ of $P(5k+2,2)$, and the desired upper bound is obtained.

Case 4: $n \equiv 3 \pmod 5$.

If $n \geq 8$, let:
$$P_8 = \begin{bmatrix} 2 & 0 & 2 & 0 & 0 & 2 & 0 & 0 \\ 0 & 0 & 0 & 2 & 2 & 0 & 2 & 2 \end{bmatrix}.$$

Then, by repeating the leftmost five columns of the pattern of P_8, we obtain a DRDF of weight $8k+6$ of $P(5k+3,2)$, and the desired upper bound is obtained.

Case 5: $n \equiv 4 \pmod 5$.

If $n \geq 9$, let:
$$P_9 = \begin{bmatrix} 2 & 0 & 2 & 0 & 0 & 3 & 0 & 0 & 0 \\ 0 & 0 & 0 & 2 & 2 & 0 & 0 & 3 & 2 \end{bmatrix}.$$

Then, by repeating the leftmost five columns of the pattern of P_9, we obtain a DRDF of weight $8k+8$ of $P(5k+4,2)$, and the desired upper bound is obtained. □

2.2. Lower Bound for Double Roman Domination Number of $P(n,2)$

Lemma 2. *Let f be a γ_{dR}-function of $P(n,2)$ with $n \geq 5$. Then, $w_f(\mathcal{B}_i) \geq 4$.*

Proof. Since u_i, v_i, u_{i+1} and u_{i-1} need to be double Roman dominated by vertices in $\mathcal{B}_i$, we have $w_f(\mathcal{B}_i) \geq 3$. Now, we will show that $w_f(\mathcal{B}_i) \neq 3$. Otherwise, it is clear that $f(u_i) = 3$, and $f(x) = 0$ for any $x \in \mathcal{B}_i \setminus \{u_i\}$. Since $v_{i\pm 1}, u_{i\pm 2}$ and $v_{i\pm 2}$ need to be double Roman dominated, we have $f(u_{i\pm 3}) = f(v_{i\pm 3}) = f(v_{i\pm 4}) = 3$. Now, we can obtain a DRDF f' from f by letting $f'(u_{i-2}) = 2$, $f'(u_{i-3}) = 0$ and $f'(v) = f(v)$ for $v \in V(P(n,2)) \setminus \{u_{i-2}, u_{i-3}\}$. Then, we have $w(f') < w(f)$, a contradiction (see Figure 1). Therefore, $w_f(\mathcal{B}_i) \geq 4$. □

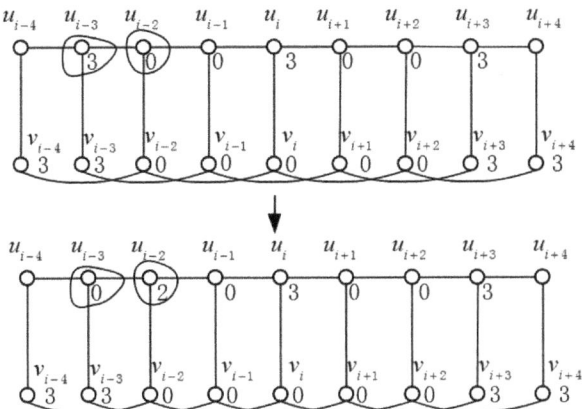

Figure 1. Construct a function f' from f used in Lemma 2.

Lemma 3. *Let f be a γ_{dR}-function of $P(n,2)$ with $n \geq 5$. Then, for any $i \in [n]$, it is impossible that $f(v_{i-1}) = f(v_i) = f(v_{i+1}) = 3$ and $f(x) = 0$ for any $x \in \mathcal{B}_i \setminus \{v_{i-1}, v_i, v_{i+1}\}$.*

Proof. Suppose to the contrary that $f(v_{i-1}) = f(v_i) = f(v_{i+1}) = 3$ and $f(x) = 0$ for $x \in \mathcal{B}_i \setminus \{v_{i-1}, v_i, v_{i+1}\}$. Then, we have $f(u_{i\pm 3}) = 3$. Now, we can obtain a DRDF f' from f by letting $f'(u_{i-1}) = 2$, $f'(v_{i-1}) = 0$ and $f'(v) = f(v)$ for $v \in V(P(n,2)) \setminus \{v_{i-1}, u_{i-1}\}$. Then, we have $w(f') < w(f)$, a contradiction (see Figure 2). □

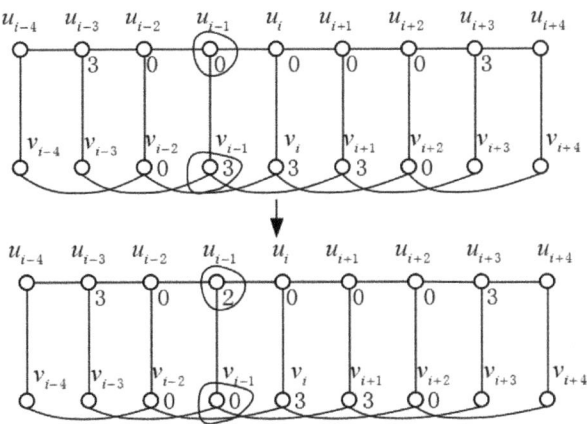

Figure 2. Construct a function f' from f in Lemma 3.

Lemma 4. *Let f be a γ_{dR}-function of $P(n,2)$ with $n \geq 5$. Then, for each $x \in V_3^{000}$, there exists a neighbor y of x such that $y \in V_0^{320} \cup V_0^{330} \cup V_0^{322} \cup V_0^{332} \cup V_0^{333}$, or equivalently, it is impossible that for any $x \in V_3^{000}$, $f(z) = 0$ for any $z \in N_2(x)$.*

Proof. Suppose to the contrary that there is a vertex $x \in V_3^{000}$ such that $y \in V_0^{300}$ for every neighbor y of x. Now, it is sufficient to consider the following two cases.

Case 1: $x = u_i$ for some i.

In this case, we have $f(u_i) = 3$ and $f(x) = 0$ for $x \in \mathcal{B}_i \setminus \{u_i\}$. Then, we have $w_f(\mathcal{B}_i) = 3 < 4$, contradicting Lemma 2.

Case 2: $x = v_i$ for some i.

In this case, since $u_{i\pm 1}$ and $u_{i\pm 2}$ need to be double Roman dominated, we have $f(v_{i\pm 1}) = 3$ and $f(u_{i\pm 3}) = 3$. By Lemma 3, such a case is impossible. □

Discharging procedure: Let f be a DRDF of $P(n,2)$. We set the initial charge of every vertex x be $s(x) = f(x)$. We use the discharging procedure, leading to a final charge s', defined by applying the following rules:

R1: Each $s(x)$ for which $s(x) = 3$ transmits 0.8 charge to each neighbor y with $y \in V_0^{300}$ transmits 0.6 charge to each neighbor y with $y \in V_0^{320} \cup V_0^{330} \cup V_0^{322} \cup V_0^{332} \cup V_0^{333}$.

R2: Each $s(x)$ for which $s(x) = 2$ transmits 0.4 charge to each neighbor y with $y \in V_0$.

Proposition 2. *If $n \geq 5$, then $\gamma_{dR}(P(n,2)) \geq \lceil \frac{8n}{5} \rceil$.*

Proof. Assume f is a γ_{dR}-function of $P(n,2)$. We use the above discharging procedure. Now, it is sufficient to consider the following three cases.

Case 1: By Lemma 4, there exists a vertex z with $f(z) \geq 2$ for some $z \in N_2(x)$, for any $x \in V_3^{000}$. Therefore, by rule R1, for each $v \in V_3^{000}$, the final charge $s'(v)$ is at least $3 - 0.6 - 0.8 - 0.8 = 0.8$. For each $v \in V_3 \setminus V_3^{000}$, then the final charge $s'(v)$ is at least $3 - 0.8 - 0.8 = 1.4$.

Case 2: By rule R2, for each $v \in V_2$, the final charge $s'(v)$ is at least $2 - 0.4 - 0.4 - 0.4 = 0.8$.

Case 3: For each $v \in V_0^{300}$, the final charge $s'(v)$ is 0.8 by rule R1. For each $v \in V_0 \setminus V_0^{300}$, the final charge $s'(v)$ is at least 0.8 by rules R1 and R2.

From the above, we have:

$$s'(v) \geq 0.8 \text{ for any } v \in P(n,2). \tag{1}$$

Hence, $w(f) = \sum_{v \in V(P(n,2))} s(v) = \sum_{v \in V(P(n,2))} s'(v) \geq 0.8 \times 2n = \frac{8n}{5}$. Since $w(f)$ is an integer, we have $w(f) \geq \lceil \frac{8n}{5} \rceil$. □

By using the above discharging rules, we have the following lemma immediately, and the proof is omitted.

Lemma 5. *Let f be a γ_{dR}-function of $P(n,2)$ with $n \geq 5$. If we use the above discharging procedure for f on $P(n,2)$, then:*

(a) *if there exists a path P of type $2-2-2$, or type 2^+-3, or type $2-2-0-3$, or type $3-0-2^+-0-3-0-2^+-0-3$, or type $3-0-2^+-0-3-0-3$, or type $3-0-3-0-3$, or type $2^+-0-3-0-3-0-2^+$ or a subgraph P of type $3-0^{-3}_{-3}$, then $\sum_{v \in V(P)}(s'(v) - 0.8) \geq 1$.*

(b) *if there exist a path P_1 of type $2-2$ and a path P_2 of type 2^+-0-3, then $\sum_{v \in V(P_1) \cup V(P_2)}(s'(v) - 0.8) \geq 1$.*

(c) *if there exists a subgraph H of type $2-2-0^{-2}_{-2}$, then $\sum_{v \in V(H)}(s'(v) - 0.8) \geq 1.2$.*

(d) *if there exist a path P of type $3-0-3$, together with a subgraph H of type $2^+-0-3-0-2^+$ or type $3-0^{-2^+}_{-2^+}$, then $\sum_{v \in V(P) \cup V(H)}(s'(v) - 0.8) \geq 1$.*

(e) *if there exist three paths P_1, P_2, P_3 of type $3-0-3$, then $\sum_{v \in V(P_1) \cup V(P_2) \cup V(P_3)}(s'(v) - 0.8) \geq 1.2$.*

Lemma 6. *Let f be a γ_{dR}-function of $P(n,2)$ with weight $\lceil \frac{8n}{5} \rceil$, then there exists no edge $uv \in E(P(n,2))$ for which $uv \in E^f_{\{2,2\}} \cup E^f_{\{2,3\}} \cup E^f_{\{3,3\}}$.*

Proof. First, we have:

$$\gamma_{dR}(P(n,2)) = w(f) = \lceil \frac{8n}{5} \rceil \leq \frac{8n+4}{5} = \frac{8n}{5} + 0.8,$$

and so:

$$w(f) - \frac{8n}{5} \leq 0.8.$$

We use the above discharging procedure for f on $P(n,2)$, and similar to the proof of Proposition 2, we have:

$$w(f) = \sum_{v \in V(P(n,2))} s'(v),$$

and oor

$$\sum_{v \in V(P(n,2))} (s'(v) - \frac{4}{5}) \leq 0.8 \qquad (2)$$

By Lemma 5a and Equation (2), we have that there exists no edge $uv \in E^f_{\{2,3\}} \cup E^f_{\{3,3\}}$.

Now, suppose to the contrary that there exists an edge $uv \in E^f_{\{2,2\}}$, and it is sufficient to consider the following three cases.

Case 1: $f(u_i) = f(u_{i+1}) = 2$.

We have $f(u_{i-1}) = f(u_{i+2}) = f(v_{i+1}) = f(v_i) = 0$. Otherwise, there exists a path P of type $2-2-2$ or type 2^+-3. By Lemma 5a, we have $\sum_{v \in V(P)} (s'(v) - 0.8) \geq 1$, contradicting Equation (2).

Since u_{i+2} needs to be double Roman dominated, we have $\{f(u_{i+3}), f(v_{i+2})\} = \{0, 2\}$. Otherwise, $f(x) = 3$ for some $x \in \{u_{i+3}, v_{i+2}\}$ or $f(u_{i+3}) = f(v_{i+2}) = 2$.

If $f(x) = 3$ for some $x \in \{u_{i+3}, v_{i+2}\}$, there exists a path P of type $2-2-0-3$. By Lemma 5a, we have $\sum_{v \in V(P)} (s'(v) - 0.8) \geq 1$, contradicting Equation (2).

If $f(u_{i+3}) = f(v_{i+2}) = 2$, there exists a subgraph H of type $2-2-0^{-2}_{-2}$. By Lemma 5c, we have $\sum_{v \in V(H)} (s'(v) - 0.8) \geq 1.2$, contradicting Equation (2).

Now, it is sufficient to consider the following two cases.

Case 1.1: $f(v_{i+2}) = 2, f(u_{i+3}) = 0$.

To double Roman dominate v_{i+1}, we have $f(v_{i+3}) \geq 2$ or $f(v_{i-1}) \geq 2$. First, we have $f(v_{i+3}) \neq 3$ and $f(v_{i-1}) \neq 3$. Otherwise, $u_i u_{i+1} v_{i+1} v_{i+3}$ or $u_i u_{i+1} v_{i+1} v_{i-1}$ is a path P of type $2-2-0-3$. By Lemma 5a, we have $\sum_{v \in V(P)} (s'(v) - 0.8) \geq 1$, contradicting Equation (2).

Now, we have that it is impossible $f(v_{i+3}) = f(v_{i-1}) = 2$. Otherwise, the set $\{u_i, u_{i+1}, v_{i+1}, v_{i+3}, v_{i-1}\}$ induces a subgraph H of type $2-2-0^{-2}_{-2}$. By Lemma 5c, we have $\sum_{v \in V(H)} (s'(v) - 0.8) \geq 1.2$, contradicting Equation (2).

Therefore, we have $\{f(v_{i+3}), f(v_{i-1})\} = \{0, 2\}$. Now, it is sufficient to consider the following two cases.

Case 1.1.1: $f(v_{i+3}) = 2, f(v_{i-1}) = 0$.

Since v_{i-1} and u_{i-1} need to be double Roman dominated, we have $f(v_{i-3}) = 3, f(u_{i-2}) = 2^+$. Then, there exists a path P_1 of type $2-2$ and a path P_2 of type $2^+ - 0 - 3$. By Lemma 5b, we have $\sum_{v \in V(P_1) \cup V(P_2)} (s'(v) - 0.8) \geq 1$, contradicting Equation (2).

Case 1.1.2: $f(v_{i+3}) = 0, f(v_{i-1}) = 2$.

Since u_{i+3} and v_{i+3} need to be double Roman dominated, we have $f(u_{i+4}) = f(v_{i+5}) = 3$. Then, there exist a path P_1 of type $2-2$ and a path P_2 of type $3-0-3$. By Lemma 5b, $\sum_{v \in V(P_1) \cup V(P_2)} (s'(v) - 0.8) \geq 1$, contradicting Equation (2).

Case 1.2: $f(v_{i+2}) = 0, f(u_{i+3}) = 2$.

Since v_{i+2} needs to be double Roman dominated, we have $f(v_{i+4}) = 3$. Then, there exist a path P_1 of type $2-2$ and a path P_2 of type $2-0-3$. By Lemma 5b, $\sum_{v \in V(P_1) \cup V(P_2)}(s'(v) - 0.8) \geq 1$, contradicting Equation (2).

Case 2: $f(v_i) = f(u_i) = 2$.

We have $f(u_{i\pm 1}) = f(v_{i\pm 2}) = 0$. Otherwise, there exists a path P of type $2-2-2$ or type $2^+ - 3$. By Lemma 5a, we have $\sum_{v \in V(P)}(s'(v) - 0.8) \geq 1$, contradicting Equation (2).

Since u_{i+1} needs to be double Roman dominated, we have $\{f(u_{i+2}), f(v_{i+1})\} = \{0, 2\}$. Otherwise, by Lemma 5a or Lemma 5c, we obtain a contradiction with Equation (2).

Now, we consider the following two subcases.

Case 2.1: $f(v_{i+1}) = 2, f(u_{i+2}) = 0$.

Since u_{i+2} needs to be double Roman dominated, we have $f(u_{i+3}) = 3$. Then, there exist a path P_1 of type $2-2$ and a path P_2 of type $2-0-3$. By Lemma 5b, $\sum_{v \in V(P_1) \cup V(P_2)}(s'(v) - 0.8) \geq 1$, contradicting Equation (2).

Case 2.2: $f(v_{i+1}) = 0, f(u_{i+2}) = 2$.

Since v_{i+1} needs to be double Roman dominated, we have $f(x) = 3$ for some $x \in \{v_{i+3}, v_{i-1}\}$ or $f(v_{i+3}) = f(v_{i-1}) = 2$. If $f(x) = 3$ for some $x \in \{v_{i+3}, v_{i-1}\}$, there exist a path P_1 of type $2-2$ and a path P_2 of type $2-0-3$. By Lemma 5b, $\sum_{v \in V(P_1) \cup V(P_2)}(s'(v) - 0.8) \geq 1$, contradicting Equation (2).

If $f(v_{i+3}) = f(v_{i-1}) = 2$, then by Lemma 5b,c, we have $u_{i-2} = 0$. Since u_{i-2} needs to be double Roman dominated, we have $f(u_{i-3}) = 3$. Then, there exist a path P_1 of type $2-2$ and a path P_2 of type $2-0-3$. By Lemma 5b, $\sum_{v \in V(P_1) \cup V(P_2)}(s'(v) - 0.8) \geq 1$, contradicting Equation (2).

Case 3: $f(v_{i+1}) = f(v_{i-1}) = 2$.

We have $f(u_{i\pm 1}) = f(v_{i\pm 3}) = 0$. Otherwise, there exists a path P of type $2-2-2$ or type $2^+ - 3$. By Lemma 5a, we have $\sum_{v \in V(P)}(s'(v) - 0.8) \geq 1$, contradicting Equation (2).

Since u_i needs to be double Roman dominated, we have $f(u_i) = 2$ or $f(v_i) = 3$.

Case 3.1: $f(u_i) = 2, f(v_i) = 0$.

By Lemma 5b,c and Equation (2), we have $f(u_{i\pm 2}) = 0$. Since v_i needs to be double Roman dominated, we have $\{f(v_{i-2}), f(v_{i+2})\} = \{0, 2\}$. Considering isomorphism, we without loss of generality assume $f(v_{i+2}) = 2$ and $f(v_{i-2}) = 0$. Since u_{i-2} needs to be double Roman dominated, $f(u_{i-3}) = 3$. Then, there exist a path P_1 of type $2-2$ and a path P_2 of type $2-0-3$. By Lemma 5b, $\sum_{v \in V(P_1) \cup V(P_2)}(s'(v) - 0.8) \geq 1$, contradicting Equation (2).

Case 3.2: $f(u_i) = 0, f(v_i) = 3$.

By Lemma 5a and Equation (2), we have $f(v_{i\pm 2}) = 0$. Since u_{i+1} needs to be double Roman dominated, we have $f(u_{i+2}) = 2$. Then, there exist a path P_1 of type $2-2$ and a path P_2 of type $2-0-3$. By Lemma 5b, $\sum_{v \in V(P_1) \cup V(P_2)}(s'(v) - 0.8) \geq 1$, contradicting Equation (2).

Therefore, the proof is complete. □

Lemma 7. *Let f be a γ_{dR}-function of $P(n, 2)$ with weight $\lceil \frac{8n}{5} \rceil$, $v \in V_3^{000}$ and $S = \{x | x \in N_2(v), f(x) \geq 2\}$, then $1 \leq |S| \leq 2$.*

Proof. We use the above discharging procedure for f on $P(n, 2)$. By Lemma 4, we have $|S| \geq 1$. Now, suppose to the contrary that $|S| \geq 3$. By rules R1 and R2 and Equation (1), we have:

$$\sum_{v \in V(P(n,2))} (s'(v) - \frac{4}{5}) \geq \sum_{x \in N[v] \cup N_2(v)} (s'(x) - \frac{4}{5}) \geq 1,$$

contradicting Equation (2). □

Lemma 8. *If $n \geq 5$ and f is a γ_{dR}-function of $P(n,2)$ with $f(u_i) = 3$ for some $i \in [n]$, then $w(f) \geq \lceil \frac{8n}{5} \rceil + 1$.*

Proof. Suppose to the contrary that there exists a γ_{dR}-function f with $w(f) = \lceil \frac{8n}{5} \rceil$ such that $f(u_i) = 3$ for some $i \in [n]$. By Lemma 6, we have $f(v_i) = f(u_{i\pm 1}) = 0$. Let $S = \{x | x \in N_2(v), f(x) \geq 2\}$. By Lemma 7, we have $|S| \in \{1,2\}$. Therefore, we just need to consider the following two cases.

Case 1: $|S| = 1$.

We may w.l.o.g assume that $\{f(u_{i-2}), f(v_{i-1}), f(v_{i-2})\} = \{0,0,2\}$ or $\{0,0,3\}$ and $f(v_{i+1}) = f(v_{i+2}) = f(u_{i+2}) = 0$. Since u_{i+2}, v_{i+2} need to be double Roman dominated, we have $f(u_{i+3}) = f(v_{i+4}) = 3$, and thus, $f(v_{i+3}) = 0$. Since v_{i+1} needs to be double Roman dominated, we have $f(v_{i-1}) = 3$. Thus, $f(u_{i-2}) = f(v_{i-2}) = 0$. Since u_{i-2}, v_{i-2} need to be double Roman dominated, we have $f(u_{i-3}) = f(v_{i-4}) = 3$. Then, there exist three paths P_1, P_2, P_3 of type $3-0-3$. By Lemma 5e, we have $\sum_{v \in V(P_1) \cup V(P_2) \cup V(P_3)}(s'(v) - 0.8) \geq 1.2$, contradicting Equation (2).

Case 2: $|S| = 2$.

It is sufficient to consider the following cases.

Case 2.1: $S \subseteq \{v_{i-1}, v_{i-2}, u_{i-2}\}$ and $f(v_{i+1}) = f(v_{i+2}) = f(u_{i+2}) = 0$.

Since u_{i+2}, v_{i+2} need to be double Roman dominated, we have $f(u_{i+3}) = f(v_{i+4}) = 3$. Then, there exist a path P of type $3-0-3$, and a subgraph H of type $2^+ - 0 - 3 - 0 - 2^+$ or type $3 - 0_{-2^+}^{-2^+}$. By Lemma 5d, we have $\sum_{v \in V(P) \cup V(H)}(s'(v) - 0.8) \geq 1$, contradicting Equation (2).

Case 2.2: $S = \{s_1, s_2\}, s_1 \in \{v_{i-1}, v_{i-2}, u_{i-2}\}$ and $s_2 \in \{v_{i+1}, v_{i+2}, u_{i+2}\}$.

First, we have $f(v_{i\pm 1}) = 0$. Otherwise, we may without loss of generality assume that $f(v_{i+1}) \geq 2$. Since u_{i+2}, v_{i+2} need to be double Roman dominated, we have $f(u_{i+3}) = f(v_{i+4}) = 3$. Then, there exist a path P of type $3-0-3$, and a path H of type $2^+ - 0 - 3 - 0 - 2^+$. By Lemma 5d, we have $\sum_{v \in V(P) \cup V(H)}(s'(v) - 0.8) \geq 1$, contradicting Equation (2).

Then, since v_{i+1}, v_{i-1} need to be double Roman dominated, we have $f(v_{i+3}) = f(v_{i-3}) = 3$. By Lemma 6, we have $f(u_{i+3}) = f(u_{i-3}) = 0$. Since $u_{i\pm 2}$ need to be double Roman dominated, we have $(f(u_{i-2}), f(v_{i-2})) \in \{(0,3), (2,0), (3,0)\}$ and $(f(u_{i+2}), f(v_{i+2})) \in \{(0,3), (2,0), (3,0)\}$.

It is impossible that $f(v_{i+2}) + f(u_{i+2}) = 3$ and $f(v_{i-2}) + f(u_{i-2}) = 3$. Otherwise, there exists a path P of type $3-0-3-0-3$ or a subgraph P of type $3-0_{-3}^{-3}$. By Lemma 5a, we have $\sum_{v \in V(P)}(s'(v) - 0.8) \geq 1$, contradicting Equation (2).

It is impossible $f(u_{i\pm 2}) \geq 2$. Otherwise, there exists a path P of type $3 - 0 - 2^+ - 0 - 3 - 0 - 2^+ - 0 - 3$. By Lemma 5a, we have $\sum_{v \in V(P)}(s'(v) - 0.8) \geq 1$, contradicting Equation (2).

Then, we may without loss of generality assume that $f(u_{i+2}) = 2$ and $f(v_{i-2}) = 3$. Then, there exists a path P of type $3 - 0 - 2 - 0 - 3 - 0 - 3$. By Lemma 5a, we have $\sum_{v \in V(P)}(s'(v) - 0.8) \geq 1$, contradicting Equation (2). □

Lemma 9. *If $n \geq 5$ and f is a γ_{dR}-function of $P(n,2)$ with $f(v_i) = 3$ for some $i \in [n]$, then $w(f) \geq \lceil \frac{8n}{5} \rceil + 1$.*

Proof. Suppose to the contrary that there exists a γ_{dR}-function f with $w(f) = \lceil \frac{8n}{5} \rceil$ such that $f(v_i) = 3$ for some $i \in [n]$. By Lemma 6, we have $f(u_i) = f(v_{i\pm 2}) = 0$. Let $S = \{x | x \in N_2(v), f(x) \geq 2\}$. By Lemma 7, we have $1 \leq |S| \leq 2$, and we just need to consider the following two cases.

Case 1: $|S| = 1$.

We may without loss of generality assume that $\{f(u_{i-1}), f(u_{i-2}), f(v_{i-4})\} = \{0,0,2\}$ or $\{0,0,3\}$ and $f(u_{i+1}) = f(u_{i+2}) = f(v_{i+4}) = 0$. Since u_{i+1} and u_{i+2} need to be double Roman dominated, we have $f(v_{i+1}) = f(u_{i+3}) = 3$, contradicting Lemma 8.

Case 2: $|S| = 2$.

Now, it is sufficient to consider the following two cases.

Case 2.1: $S \subseteq \{u_{i-1}, u_{i-2}, v_{i-4}\}$ and $f(u_{i+1}) = f(u_{i+2}) = f(v_{i+4}) = 0$.

Since u_{i+1}, u_{i+2} need to be double roman dominated, we have $f(v_{i+1}) = f(u_{i+3}) = 3$, contradicting Lemma 8.

Case 2.2: $S = \{s_1, s_2\}$, where $s_1 \in \{u_{i-1}, u_{i-2}, v_{i-4}\}$ and $s_2 \in \{u_{i+1}, u_{i+2}, v_{i+4}\}$.

By Lemma 8, $f(u_k) \neq 3$ for each $k \in \{1, 2, \cdots, n\}$, and thus, $\{f(u_{i+1}), f(u_{i+2}), f(u_{i-2}), f(u_{i-1})\} = \{0, 2\}$.

Then, we have $f(v_{i+4}) = f(v_{i-4}) = 0$. Otherwise, $f(v_{i+4}) \neq 0$ or $f(v_{i-4}) \neq 0$. By symmetry, we may assume without loss of generality that $f(v_{i+4}) \neq 0$. Thus, we have $f(u_{i+1}) = f(u_{i+2}) = 0$. Since u_{i+1}, u_{i+2} need to be double Roman dominated, we have $f(v_{i+1}) = f(u_{i+3}) = 3$, contradicting Lemma 8.

Now, it is sufficient to consider the following three cases.

Case 2.2.1: $f(u_{i+1}) = f(u_{i-1}) = 2$.

By Lemma 6, we have $f(u_{i \pm 2}) = f(v_{i \pm 1}) = 0$.

Since u_{i+2} needs to be double Roman dominated and by Lemma 8, we have $f(u_{i+3}) = 2$. Since v_{i+1} needs to be double Roman dominated, we have $f(v_{i+3}) \geq 2$. Thus, there exists an edge $e \in E^f_{\{2,2^+\}}$, a contradiction with Lemma 6.

Case 2.2.2: $f(u_{i+2}) = f(u_{i-2}) = 2$.

By Lemma 6, we have $f(u_{i \pm 3}) = f(u_{i \pm 1}) = 0$.

Since u_{i+1}, u_{i-1} need to be double Roman dominated, we have $f(v_{i \pm 1}) = 2$. Thus, there exists an edge $e \in E^f_{\{2,2\}}$, a contradiction with Lemma 6.

Case 2.2.3: $f(u_{i+1}) = f(u_{i-2}) = 2$.

By Lemma 6, we have $f(u_{i-3}) = f(v_{i+1}) = f(u_{i+2}) = 0$.

Since u_{i+2} needs to be double Roman dominated, we have $f(u_{i+3}) = 2$. By Lemma 6, we have $f(v_{i+3}) = f(u_{i+4}) = 0$. Since u_{i+4} needs to be double Roman dominated and by Lemma 8, we have $f(u_{i+5}) = 2$. Since v_{i+3} needs to be double Roman dominated, we have $f(v_{i+5}) \geq 2$. Thus, there exists an edge $e \in E^f_{\{2,2^+\}}$, a contradiction with Lemma 6. □

Lemma 10. *Let $n \geq 5$ and $n \not\equiv 0$ (mod 5). If f is a γ_{dR}-function of $P(n, 2)$, then $w(f) \geq \lceil \frac{8n}{5} \rceil + 1$.*

Proof. Suppose to the contrary that $w(f) = \lceil \frac{8n}{5} \rceil$. By Lemmas 8 and 9, we have $|V_3| = 0$. Now, we have:

Claim 1. $|V_2 \cap N(v)| = 2$ *for any $v \in V(P(n, 2))$ with $f(v) = 0$.*

Proof. Suppose to the contrary that there exists a vertex $v \in V(P(n, 2))$ with $f(v) = 0$ and $|V_2 \cap N(v)| = 3$. We consider the following two cases.

Case 1: $v = u_i$ for some $i \in [n]$.

Since $|V_2 \cap N(v)| = 3$, we have $f(u_{i-1}) = f(u_{i+1}) = f(v_i) = 2$. By Lemma 6, we have $f(u_{i \pm 2}) = 0$, $f(v_{i \pm 1}) = 0$ and $f(v_{i \pm 2}) = 0$. Since v_{i+1} needs to be double Roman dominated, we have $f(v_{i+3}) = 2$. Since u_{i+2} needs to be double Roman dominated, we have $f(u_{i+3}) = 2$. Since $v_{i+3}u_{i+3} \in E^f_{\{2,2\}}$, contradicting Lemma 6.

Case 2: $v = v_i$ for some $i \in [n]$.

Since $|V_2 \cap N(v)| = 3$, we have $f(v_{i-2}) = f(v_{i+2}) = f(u_i) = 2$. By Lemma 6, we have $f(u_{i\pm 1}) = f(u_{i\pm 2}) = f(v_{i\pm 4}) = 0$. Since u_{i+1} needs to be double Roman dominated, we have $f(v_{i+1}) = 2$. Since u_{i-1} needs to be double Roman dominated, we have $f(v_{i-1}) = 2$. Since $v_{i+1}v_{i-1} \in E^f_{\{2,2\}}$, contradicting Lemma 6. □

We assume without loss of generality that $f(u_i) = 2$. By Lemma 6, we have $f(u_{i-1}) = 0, f(v_i) = 0$ and $f(u_{i+1}) = 0$. Since v_i needs to be double Roman dominated, we assume without loss of generality that $f(v_{i-2}) = 2$. By Claim 1, we have $f(v_{i+2}) = 0$. Since $f(v_{i-2}) = 2$, together with Lemma 6, we have $f(u_{i-2}) = 0$. Since u_{i-1} needs to be double Roman dominated, we have $f(v_{i-1}) = 2$. Then, by Lemma 6, we have $f(v_{i+1}) = 0$. Since v_{i+2} needs to be double Roman dominated, we have $f(u_{i+2}) = 2$. That is to say, we have:

$$f(\mathcal{B}_i) = f\begin{pmatrix} u_{i-2} & u_{i-1} & u_i & u_{i+1} & u_{i+2} \\ v_{i-2} & v_{i-1} & v_i & v_{i+1} & v_{i+2} \end{pmatrix} = \begin{pmatrix} 0 & 0 & 2 & 0 & 2 \\ 2 & 2 & 0 & 0 & 0 \end{pmatrix}.$$

By repeatedly applying Claim 1 and Lemma 6, $f(x)$ can be determined for each $x \in \mathcal{B}_{i+5}$, and we have $f(\mathcal{B}_i) = f(\mathcal{B}_{i+5})$. It is straightforward to see that $w(f) = \lceil \frac{8n}{5} \rceil$ only if $n \equiv 0 \pmod 5$, a contradiction. □

3. Conclusions

By Lemma 1, Proposition 2 and Lemma 10, we have

Theorem 1. *If $n \geq 5$, then:*

$$\gamma_{dR}(P(n,2)) = \begin{cases} \lceil \frac{8n}{5} \rceil, & n \equiv 0 \pmod 5, \\ \lceil \frac{8n}{5} \rceil + 1, & n \equiv 1,2,3,4 \pmod 5. \end{cases}$$

Remark 1. *Beeler et al. [7] proposed the concept of the double Roman domination. They showed that $2\gamma(G) \leq \gamma_{dR}(G) \leq 3\gamma(G)$. Moreover, they suggested to find double Roman graphs.*

In [17], it was proven that:

Theorem 2. *If $n \geq 5$, then $\gamma(P(n,2)) = \lceil \frac{3n}{5} \rceil$.*

Therefore, we have that $P(n,2)$ is not double Roman for all $n \geq 5$.

In fact, there exist many double Roman graphs among Petersen graph $P(n,k)$. For example, in [12], it was shown that $P(n,1)$ is a double Roman graph for any $n \not\equiv 2 \pmod 4$. Therefore, it is interesting to find other Petersen graphs that are double Roman.

Author Contributions: Z.S. contributes for supervision, methodology, validation, project administration and formal analysing. H.J., P.W., Y.R., J.-B.L. contribute for resources, some computations and wrote the initial draft of the paper which were investigated and approved by Z.S. and J.-B.L. wrote the final draft.

Funding: This research work is supported by Key Supported Disciplines of Guizhou Province Computer Application Technology (No. QianXueWeiHeZi ZDXX[2016]20); Anhui Province Key Laboratory of Intelligent Building & Building Energy Saving.

Conflicts of Interest: The authors declare no conflict of interest.

References

1. Xu, G. 2-rainbow domination in generalized Petersen graphs $P(n,3)$. *Discret. Appl. Math.* **2009**, *157*, 2570–2573. [CrossRef]
2. Garey, M.R.; Johnson, D.S. *Computers and Intractability: A Guide to the Theory of NP-Completeness*; W. H. Freeman and Co.: San Francisco, CA, USA, 1979.

3. Henning, M.A. A Characterization of Roman trees. *Discuss. Math. Graph Theory* **2002**, *22*, 325–334. [CrossRef]
4. Ahangar, H.A.; Amjadi, J.; Sheikholeslami, S.M.; Volkmann, L.; Zhao, Y. Signed Roman edge domination numbers in graphs. *J. Comb. Optim.* **2016**, *31*, 333–346. [CrossRef]
5. Ore, O. *Theory of Graphs*; American Mathematical Society: Providence, RI, USA, 1967.
6. Shao, Z.; Xu, J.; Sheikholeslami, S.M.; Wang, S. The domination complexity and related extremal values of large 3D torus. *Complexity* **2018**, 3041426. [CrossRef]
7. Beeler, R.A.; Haynes, T.W.; Hedetniemi, S.T. Double Roman domination. *Discret. Appl. Math.* **2016**, *211*, 23–29. [CrossRef]
8. Liu, C.H.; Chang, G.J. Roman domination on 2-connected graphs. *SIAM J. Discret. Math.* **2012**, *26*, 193–205. [CrossRef]
9. Liu, C.H.; Chang, G.J. Upper bounds on Roman domination numbers of graphs. *Discret. Math.* **2012**, *312*, 1386–1391. [CrossRef]
10. Liu, C.H.; Chen, S.H.; Chang, G.J. Edge Roman domination on graphs. *Graphs Comb.* **2016**, *32*, 1731–1747.
11. Pushpam, P.R.; Mai, T.N. Roman domination in unicyclic graphs. *J. Discret. Math. Sci. Cryptogr.* **2012**, *15*, 237–257. [CrossRef]
12. Shao, Z.; Jiang, H.; Li, Z.; Wu, P.; Zerovnik, J.; Zhang, X. Discharging approach for double Roman domination in graphs. *IEEE Access* **2018**, accepted for publication.
13. Shao, Z.; Klavžar, S.; Li, Z.; Wu, P.; Xu, J. On the signed Roman k-domination: Complexity and thin torus graphs. *Discret. Appl. Math.* **2017**, *233*, 175–186. [CrossRef]
14. Zhang, X.; Li, Z.; Jiang, H.; Shao, Z. Double Roman domination in trees. *Inf. Process. Lett.* **2018**, *134*, 31–34. [CrossRef]
15. Li, Z.; Shao, Z.; Lang, F.; Zhang, X.; Liu, J.B. Computational complexity of outer-Independent total and total Roman domination numbers in trees. *IEEE Access* **2018**, *6*, 35544–35550. [CrossRef]
16. Tong, C.; Lin, X.; Yang, Y.; Luo, M. 2-rainbow domination of generalized Petersen graphs $P(n,2)$. *Discret. Appl. Math.* **2009**, *157*, 1932–1937. [CrossRef]
17. Ebrahimi, B.J.; Jahanbakht, N.; Mahmoodian, E.S. Vertex domination of generalized Petersen graphs. *Discret. Math.* **2009**, *309*, 4355–4361. [CrossRef]

© 2018 by the authors. Licensee MDPI, Basel, Switzerland. This article is an open access article distributed under the terms and conditions of the Creative Commons Attribution (CC BY) license (http://creativecommons.org/licenses/by/4.0/).

Article

On Metric Dimensions of Symmetric Graphs Obtained by Rooted Product

Shahid Imran [1,*], Muhammad Kamran Siddiqui [2,3], Muhammad Imran [3,4] and Muhammad Hussain [5]

1. Govt Khawaja Rafique Shaheed College Walton Road Lahore, Lahore 54000, Pakistan
2. Department of Mathematics, COMSATS University Islamabad, Sahiwal Campus, Punjab 57000, Pakistan; kamransiddiqui75@gmail.com
3. Department of Mathematical Sciences, United Arab Emirates University, Al Ain, P.O. Box 15551, UAE; imrandhab@gmail.com
4. Department of Mathematics, School of Natural Sciences (SNS), National University of Sciences and Technology (NUST), Sector H-12, Islamabad 44000, Pakistan
5. Department of Mathematics, COMSATS University Islamabad, Lahore Campus 54000, Pakistan; mhmaths@gmail.com
* Correspondence: imran_gon@yahoo.com

Received: 25 July 2018; Accepted: 26 September 2018; Published: 8 October 2018

Abstract: Let $G = (V, E)$ be a connected graph and $d(x, y)$ be the distance between the vertices x and y in G. A set of vertices W resolves a graph G if every vertex is uniquely determined by its vector of distances to the vertices in W. A metric dimension of G is the minimum cardinality of a resolving set of G and is denoted by $dim(G)$. In this paper, Cycle, Path, Harary graphs and their rooted product as well as their connectivity are studied and their metric dimension is calculated. It is proven that metric dimension of some graphs is unbounded while the other graphs are constant, having three or four dimensions in certain cases.

Keywords: metric dimension; basis; resolving set; cycle; path; Harary graphs; rooted product

MSC: 05C15; 05C62; 05C12; 05C07; 05C10; 05C90

1. Introduction

In a connected graph $G(V, E)$, where V is the set of vertices and E is the set of edges, the distance $d(u, v)$ between two vertices $u, v \in V$ is the length of shortest path between them. Let $W = \{w_1, w_2, ..., w_k\}$ be an order set of vertices of G and let v be a vertex of G. The representation $r(v|W)$ of v with respect to W is the k-tuple $(d(v, w_1), d(v, w_2), d(v, w_3), ..., d(v, w_k))$, where W is called a resolving set [1] or locating set [2] if every vertex of G is uniquely identified by its distances from the vertices of W, or equivalently, if distinct vertices of G have distinct representations with respect to W. A resolving set of minimum cardinality is called a basis for G and cardinality is the metric dimension of G, denoted by $dim(G)$ [3]. The concept of resolving set and metric basis have previously appeared in the literature [4–6].

For a given ordered set of vertices $W = \{w_1, w_2, ..., w_k\}$ of a graph G, the ith component of $r(v|W)$ is 0 if and only if $v = w_i$. Thus, to show that W is a resolving set it suffices to verify that $r(x|W) \neq r(y|W)$ for each pair of distinct vertices $x, y \in V(G) \setminus W$.

Motivated by the problem of uniquely determining the location of an intruder in a network, the concept of metric dimension was introduced by Slater in [2,7] and studied independently by Harary and Melter in [5]. Application of this invariant to the navigation of robots in networks are discussed in [8] and application to chemistry is discussed in [1], while application to the problem of pattern recognition and image processing, some of which involve the use of hierarchical data structures, are given in [6].

Let F be a family of connected graphs. If all graphs in F have the same metric dimension, then F is called a family with constant metric dimension [9]. A connected graph G has $dim(G) = 1$ if and only if G is a path [1], cycle C_n have metric dimension 2 for every $n \geq 3$, also honeycomb networks [10] have metric dimension 3.

Metric dimension is a parameter that has appeared in various applications of graph theory, as diverse as pharmaceutical chemistry [1,11], robot navigation [8,12] and combinatorial optimization [13], to name a few. A chemical compound can be represented by more than one suggested structure but only one of them, which expresses the physical and chemical properties of compound, is acceptable. The chemists require mathematical representation for a set of chemical compounds in a way that gives distinct representations to distinct compounds. As described in [1,11], the structure of chemical compounds can be represented by a labeled graph whose vertex and edge labels specify the atom and bond types, respectively. Thus, a graph theoretic interpretation of this problem is to provide representations for the vertices of a graph in such a way that distinct vertices have distinct representations. This is the subject of the papers [1,6,14–17].

Other families of graphs with unbounded metric dimension are regular bipartite graphs [4], wheel graph and jahangir graph [18].

Our main aim of this paper is to compute the metric dimension of graphs obtained from the rooted product graphs. For this purpose, we need the following definitions.

Definition 1 ([19]). *A rooted graph is a graph in which one vertex has been distinguished as the root. Both directed and undirected versions of rooted graphs have been studied, and there are also variant definitions that allow multiple roots.*

Definition 2 ([20]). *Let H be a labelled graph on n vertices. Let G be a sequence of n rooted graphs $G_1, G_2, ...G_n$. The graph $H(G)$ obtained by identifying the root of G_i with the ith vertex of H. The graph $H(G)$ is called the rooted product of H by G.*

Definition 3 ([19]). *The Harary graph $H_{m,n}$ is defined as follows and depicted in Figure 1:*

Case 1. *m is even. Let $m = 2r$, then $H_{2r,n}$ is constructed as follows: It has vertices $0, 1, \ldots, n-1$ and two vertices i and j are joined if $i - r \leq j \leq i + r$ (where addition is taken modulo n).*

Case 2. *m is odd and n is even. Let $m = 2r + 1$, then the $H_{2r+1,n}$ is constructed by first drawing $H_{2r,n}$ and then adding edges joining vertex i to vertex $i + (n/2)$ for $1 \leq i \leq n/2$.*

Case 3. *m, n are odd. Let $m = 2r + 1$, then $H_{2r+1,n}$ is constructed by first drawing $H_{2r,n}$ and then adding edges joining vertex 0 to vertices $(n-1)/2$ and $(n+1)/2$ and vertex i to vertex $i + (n+1)/2$ for $1 \leq i \leq (n-1)/2$.*

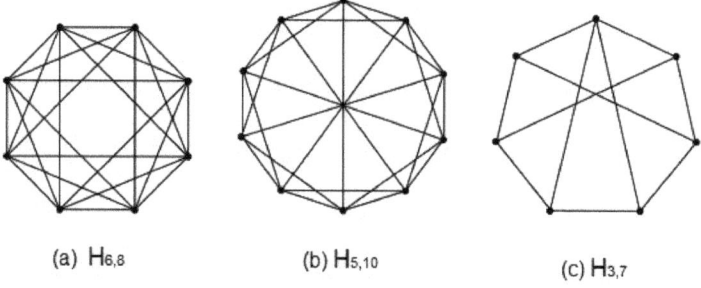

(a) $H_{6,8}$ (b) $H_{5,10}$ (c) $H_{3,7}$

Figure 1. (a) The Harary graph $H_{6,8}$; (b) The Harary graph $H_{5,10}$; (c) The Harary graph $H_{3,7}$.

2. The Rooted Product of Harary Graphs with Cycle Graph

Suppose $C_3^i, 1 \leq i \leq n$, $C_4^i, 1 \leq i \leq n$ and $C_5^i, 1 \leq i \leq n$ be n copies of C_3, C_4 and C_5 having vertices $\{v_i^j, 1 \leq i \leq n, 1 \leq j \leq 3\}$, $\{v_i^j, 1 \leq i \leq n, 1 \leq j \leq 4\}$ and $\{v_i^j, 1 \leq i \leq n, 1 \leq j \leq 5\}$ respectively and $\{v_1, v_2, v_3, ..., v_n\}$ be the set of vertices of $H_{m,n}$. By definition of rooted product $\{v_i^j, 1 \leq i \leq n, 1 \leq j \leq 3\}$, $\{v_i^j, 1 \leq i \leq n, 1 \leq j \leq 4\}$ and $\{v_i^j, 1 \leq i \leq n, 1 \leq j \leq 5\}$ will be sets of vertices of $H_{m,n}(C_3), H_{m,n}(C_4)$ and $H_{m,n}(C_5)$ respectively with indices taken modulo n. After rooted product, it is considered that all the cycles share $\{v_i^1, 1 \leq i \leq n\}$ with $H_{m,n}$.

More preciously, the graphs $H_{m,n}(C_3)$, $H_{m,n}(C_4)$ and $H_{m,n}(C_5)$ are the rooted product of Harary graphs $H_{m,n}$ by cycles C_3, C_4 and C_5 respectively.

Now we present our main results on metric dimension of $H_{m,n}(C_3)$, $H_{m,n}(C_4)$ and $H_{m,n}(C_5)$.

Theorem 1. *If $G_1 \cong H_{m,n}(C_3)$, then there exists a resolving set W of G_1 such that*

$$\{v_i^2; 1 \leq i \leq n\} \subseteq W(G_1), \quad \{v_i^3; 1 \leq i \leq n\} \nsubseteq W(G_1),$$

$$|W(G_1)| \geq n.$$

Proof. As $d(v_i^2, v_i^1) = d(v_i^3, v_i^1), \forall, 1 \leq i \leq n$

and $d(v_i^2, v_k^j) = d(v_i^3, v_k^j), \forall, 1 \leq i, k \leq n, k \neq i$ and $j = 1, 2, 3$.

$\Rightarrow$ either $v_i^2 \in W(G_1)$ or $v_i^3 \in W(G_1)$.

To minimize the cardinality of $W(G_1)$, we can say without loss of any generality:

$\{v_i^2; 1 \leq i \leq n\} \subseteq W(G_1)$ and $\{v_i^3; 1 \leq i \leq n\} \nsubseteq W(G_1)$.

$\Rightarrow |W(G_1)| \geq n$.
This conclude the proof. □

Theorem 2. *If $G_1 \cong H_{m,n}(C_3)$ and W be a minimum resolving set of G_1 then $|W(G_1)| = n$.*

Proof. From Theorem 1, we have $|W(G_1)| \geq n$. Now to prove the reverse inequality, i.e., $|W(G_1)| \leq n$, we proceed as follows:

If we take $\{v_i^1, v_i^3; 1 \leq i \leq n\} \cap W = \phi$, then W is also resolving set.

By Theorem 1, $v_i^2 \in W$ for all $1 \leq i \leq n$ and $d(v_i^2, v_i^1) \neq d(v_i^2, v_k^1), \forall 1 \leq i, k \leq n, i \neq k$.

$\Rightarrow r(v_i^1|W) \neq r(v_k^1|W), \forall 1 \leq i, k \leq n, i \neq k$.

As $v_i^2 \in W \Rightarrow v_{i+1}^2 \in W$ and $d(v_{i+1}^2, v_i^1) \neq d(v_{i+1}^2, v_i^3), \forall 1 \leq i \leq n$

$\Rightarrow r(v_i^1|W) \neq r(v_i^3|W), \forall, 1 \leq i \leq n,$

$r(v_i^1|W) \neq r(v_i^2|W)$ as $\{v_i^2; 1 \leq i \leq n\} \subseteq W$

also $r(v_i^3|W) \neq r(v_i^2|W)$ as $\{v_i^2; 1 \leq i \leq n\} \subseteq W$

$d(v_i^3, v_i^2) \neq d(v_k^3, v_i^2), \forall, 1 \leq i, k \leq n, i \neq k.$

$\Rightarrow r(v_i^3|W) \neq r(v_k^3|W), \forall, 1 \leq i, k \leq n, i \neq k.$

So we conclude that $W \setminus \{v_i^1; 1 \leq i \leq n\}$ is also the resolving set. This shows that $|W(G_1)| \leq n$. Hence, the required result is proved. □

Theorem 3. *If $G_2 \cong H_{m,n}(C_4)$, then there exists a resolving set W of G_2 such that*

$$\{v_i^2; 1 \leq i \leq n\} \subseteq W(G_2), \quad \{v_i^4; 1 \leq i \leq n\} \nsubseteq W(G_2), \quad |W(G_2)| \geq n$$

Proof. As $d(v_i^2, v_i^1) = d(v_i^4, v_i^1), \forall, 1 \leq i \leq n$

and $d(v_i^2, v_k^j) = d(v_i^4, v_k^j), \forall, 1 \leq i, k \leq n, k \neq i$ and $j = 1, 2, 3$.

$\Rightarrow$ either $v_i^2 \in W(G_2)$ or $v_i^4 \in W(G_2)$.

To minimize the cardinality of $W(G_2)$, we can say without loss of any generality:

$\{v_i^2; 1 \leq i \leq n\} \subseteq W(G_2)$ and $\{v_i^4; 1 \leq i \leq n\} \nsubseteq W(G_2)$.

$\Rightarrow |W(G_2)| \geq n$.
This conclude the proof. □

Theorem 4. *If $G_2 \cong H_{m,n}(C_4)$ and W be a minimum resolving set of G_2 then $|W(G_2)| = n$.*

Proof. From Theorem 3, $|W(G_2)| \geq n$. Now to prove the reverse inequality, i.e., $|W(G_2)| \leq n$, we proceed as follows:

If we take $\{v_i^1, v_i^3, v_i^4; 1 \leq i \leq n\} \cap W = \phi$ then W is also resolving set.

By theorem 3, $v_i^2 \in W$ for all $1 \leq i \leq n$

and $d(v_i^2, v_i^1) \neq d(v_i^2, v_k^1), \forall, 1 \leq i, k \leq n, i \neq k.$

$\Rightarrow r(v_i^1|W) \neq r(v_k^1|W), \forall, 1 \leq i, k \leq n, i \neq k.$

and $r(v_i^1|W) \neq r(v_i^2|W) \forall 1 \leq i \leq n$, by definition of resolving set.

$d(v_i^2, v_i^1) \neq d(v_i^2, v_i^4), \forall, 1 \leq i \leq n.$

$\Rightarrow r(v_i^1|W) \neq r(v_i^4|W), \forall, 1 \leq i \leq n.$

As $v_i^2 \in W$ for all $1 \leq i \leq n \Rightarrow v_{i+1}^2 \in W.$

$d(v_{i+1}^2, v_i^3) \neq d(v_{i+1}^2, v_i^1), \forall 1 \leq i \leq n.$

$\Rightarrow r(v_i^1|W) \neq r(v_i^3|W), \forall, 1 \leq i \leq n.$

$r(v_i^2|W) \neq r(v_k^2|W), \forall, 1 \leq i, k \leq n, i \neq k$, by definition of resolving set.

$r(v_i^2|W) \neq r(v_k^3|W), \forall, 1 \leq i,k \leq n, i \neq k$, by definition of resolving set.

$r(v_i^2|W) \neq r(v_k^4|W), \forall, 1 \leq i,k \leq n, i \neq k$, by definition of resolving set.

As $d(v_i^2, v_i^3) \neq d(v_i^2, v_k^3), \forall\, 1 \leq i,k \leq n, i \neq k$.

$\Rightarrow r(v_i^3|W) \neq r(v_k^3|W), \forall, 1 \leq i,k \leq n, i \neq k$.

$d(v_i^2, v_i^3) \neq d(v_i^2, v_i^4), \forall, 1 \leq i \leq n$.

$\Rightarrow r(v_i^4|W) \neq r(v_i^3|W), \forall, 1 \leq i \leq n$.

$d(v_i^2, v_i^4) \neq d(v_i^2, v_k^4), \forall, 1 \leq i,k \leq n, i \neq k$.

$\Rightarrow r(v_i^4|W) \neq r(v_k^4|W), \forall, 1 \leq i,k \leq n, i \neq k$.

$\Rightarrow$ representation of all the vertices is unique if $\{v_i^1, v_i^3; 1 \leq i \leq n\} \nsubseteq W(G_2)$

In addition, from theorem 3, $\{v_i^4; 1 \leq i \leq n\} \nsubseteq W(G_2)$ and $\{v_i^2; 1 \leq i \leq n\} \subseteq W(G_2)$.

Hence $W = \{v_i^2; 1 \leq i \leq n\}$ is the minimum resolving set of G_2. This shows that $|W(G_2)| = n$. □

Theorem 5. *If $G_3 \cong H_{m,n}(C_5)$, then there exists a resolving set W of G_3 such that*

$$\{v_i^2; 1 \leq i \leq n\} \subseteq W(G_3) \text{ and } |W(G_3)| \geq n.$$

Proof. As $d(v_i^2, v_k^j) = d(v_i^5, v_k^j), \forall, 1 \leq i,k \leq n, i \neq k$ and $1 \leq j \leq 5$.

and $d(v_i^2, v_i^1) = d(v_i^5, v_i^1), \forall, 1 \leq i \leq n$.

$d(v_i^2, v_i^3) \neq d(v_i^5, v_i^3), \forall, 1 \leq i \leq n$,

$d(v_i^2, v_i^4) \neq d(v_i^5, v_i^4) \,\forall\, 1 \leq i \leq n$.

$\Rightarrow$ For all $1 \leq i \leq n$, $r(v_i^2|W) = r(v_i^5|W), \forall$, resolving sets W in which

$\{v_i^2, v_i^3, v_i^4, v_i^5\} \cap W = \phi$.

and For all $1 \leq i \leq n$, $r(v_i^3|W) = r(v_i^4|W), \forall$, resolving sets W in which

$\{v_i^2, v_i^3, v_i^4, v_i^5\} \cap W = \phi$.

To make the representation unique, we can say $\{v_i^2, v_i^3, v_i^4, v_i^5\} \cap W \neq \phi$. Without loss of any generality we can assume that $\{v_i^2; 1 \leq i \leq n\} \subseteq W(G_3) \Rightarrow |W(G_3)| \geq n$. This concludes the proof. □

Theorem 6. *If $G_3 \cong H_{m,n}(C_5)$ and W be a minimum resolving set of G_3 then $|W(G_3)| = n$.*

Proof. From Theorem 5, $|W(G_3)| \geq n$. Now to prove the reverse inequality, i.e., $|W(G_3)| \leq n$, we proceed as follows:

If we take $\{v_i^1, v_i^3, v_i^4, v_i^5; 1 \leq i \leq n\} \cap W = \phi$, then W is also resolving set.

By Theorem 5, $v_i^2 \in W$ for all $1 \leq i \leq n$

and $d(v_i^2, v_i^1) \neq d(v_i^2, v_k^1), \forall, 1 \leq i, k \leq n, i \neq k$.

$\Rightarrow r(v_i^1|W) \neq r(v_k^1|W), \forall, 1 \leq i, k \leq n, i \neq k$.

and $r(v_k^1|W) \neq r(v_i^2|W) \forall, 1 \leq i, k \leq n$ by definition of resolving set.

$d(v_i^1, v_{i+1}^2) \neq d(v_i^3, v_{i+1}^2), \forall, 1 \leq i \leq n$.

and $d(v_i^1, v_i^2) \neq d(v_k^3, v_i^2), \forall, 1 \leq i, k \leq n$ and $i \neq k$.

$r(v_i^1|W) \neq r(v_k^3|W) \forall 1 \leq i, k \leq n$.

As $d(v_i^1, v_i^2) \neq d(v_k^4, v_i^2), \forall, 1 \leq i, k \leq n$.

$\Rightarrow r(v_i^1|W) \neq r(v_k^4|W), \forall, 1 \leq i, k \leq n$.

As $d(v_i^1, v_i^2) \neq d(v_k^5, v_i^2), \forall, 1 \leq i, k \leq n$.

$\Rightarrow r(v_i^1|W) \neq r(v_k^5|W), \forall 1 \leq i, k \leq n$.

$r(v_i^2|W) \neq r(v_k^j|W) \forall 1 \leq i, k \leq n, 1 \leq j \leq 5$, by definition of resolving set.

As $d(v_i^3, v_i^2) \neq d(v_k^3, v_i^2), \forall, 1 \leq i, k \leq n \; i \neq k$.

$\Rightarrow r(v_i^3|W) \neq r(v_k^3|W), \forall, 1 \leq i, k \leq n \; i \neq k$.

$d(v_i^3, v_i^2) \neq d(v_k^4, v_i^2), \forall, 1 \leq i, k \leq n$.

$\Rightarrow r(v_i^3|W) \neq r(v_k^4|W), \forall, 1 \leq i, k \leq n$.

$d(v_i^3, v_i^2) \neq d(v_k^5, v_i^2), \forall, 1 \leq i, k \leq n$.

$\Rightarrow r(v_i^3|W) \neq r(v_k^5|W), \forall, 1 \leq i, k \leq n$.

As $d(v_i^4, v_i^2) \neq d(v_k^4, v_i^2), \forall, 1 \leq i, k \leq n \; i \neq k$.

$\Rightarrow r(v_i^4|W) \neq r(v_k^4|W), \forall, 1 \leq i, k \leq n \; i \neq k$.

$d(v_i^4, v_{i+1}^2) \neq d(v_i^5, v_{i+1}^2), \forall, 1 \leq i \leq n$.

and $d(v_i^4, v_i^2) \neq d(v_k^5, v_i^2), \forall, 1 \leq i, k \leq n$ and $i \neq k$.

$r(v_i^4|W) \neq r(v_k^5|W) \, \forall, 1 \leq i, k \leq n$.

$d(v_i^5, v_i^2) \neq d(v_k^5, v_i^2), \forall, 1 \leq i, k \leq n \, i \neq k$.

$\Rightarrow r(v_i^5|W) \neq r(v_k^5|W), \forall, 1 \leq i, k \leq n \, i \neq k$.

Hence $W \setminus \{v_i^1, v_i^3, v_i^4, v_i^5; 1 \leq i \leq n\}$ is the resolving set.
This shows that $|W(G_3)| = n$. □

3. The Rooted Product of Harary Graphs with Path Graph

The graph $H_{4,n}(P_m)$ is the rooted product of Harary graph $H_{4,n}$ by path P_m, see Figure 2. To construct the graph $H_{4,n}(C_3)^c$ we first construct rooted product of Harary graph $H_{4,n}$ by cycle C_3 as shown in Figure 3a and then connect the remaining two vertices of each rooted C_3 with both neighboring C_3 as shown in Figure 3b.

The graphs $H_{4,n}(P_m)$ and $H_{4,n}(C_3)^c$ are an important class of graphs, which can be used in the design of local area networks [18].

Now we present our main results on metric dimension of $H_{4,n}(P_m)$ and $H_{4,n}(C_3)^c$. To calculate metric dimension of $H_{4,n}(C_3)^c$, $H_{4,n}(P_m)$ and $(P_2 \times P_k)(C_4)^c$ we need the following result of khuller et al. [8].

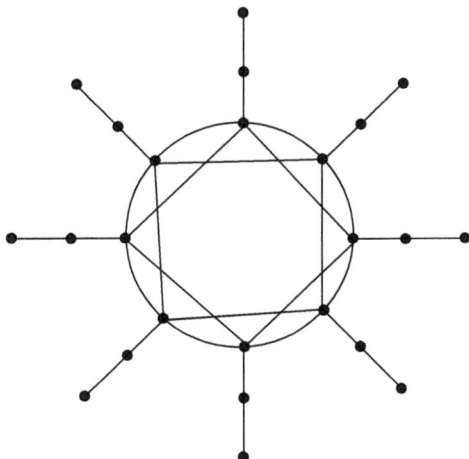

Figure 2. The graph $H_{4,8}(P_3)$.

Theorem 7. *Let G be a graph with minimum metric dimension 2 and let $\{u, v\} \subset V$ be the metric basis in G. Then the following statements are true:*

(a) *There is a unique shortest path between u and v.*
(b) *The degree of each u and v is at most 3.*

Theorem 8. *For $G \cong H_{4,n}(C_3)^c$, where $H_{4,n}$ be a 4-regular Harary graph with $n \geq 5$ and C_3 is the cycle of length 3; then we have $dim(G) = 3$ when $n \equiv 0, 1, 3 \pmod{4}$ and $dim(G) \leq 4$ otherwise.*

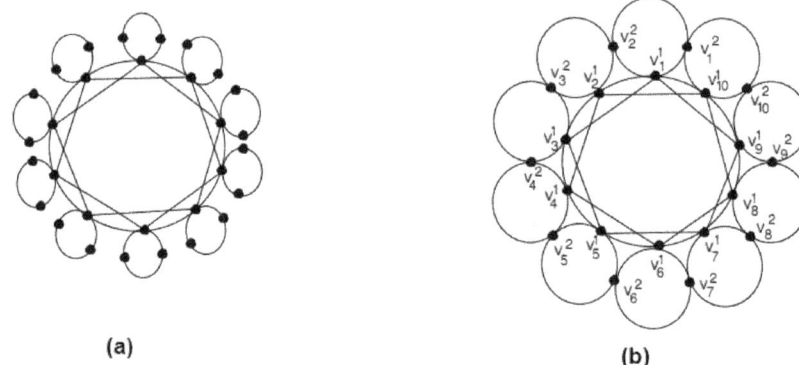

Figure 3. (a) The graph of $H_{4,10}(C_3)$; (b) The graph of $H_{4,10}(C_3)^c$.

Proof. Case-I when $n \equiv 0 \pmod 4$ i.e., $n = 4k, k \geq 2$ and $k \in N$.

be the resolving set of G then $r(v_2^1|W) = (1,2,1)$,

$r(v_3^1|W) = (1,1,1), r(v_4^1|W) = (2,1,2), r(v_6^1|W) = (2,1,3), r(v_7^1|W) = (1,1,3)$,

$r(v_8^1|W) = (1,2,2), r(v_1^2|W) = (1,3,2), r(v_2^2|W) = (1,3,1), r(v_4^2|W) = (2,2,1)$,

$r(v_5^2|W) = (3,1,2), r(v_6^2|W) = (3,1,3), r(v_7^2|W) = (2,2,4), r(v_8^2|W) = (2,2,3)$,

For $n = 12$ let $W = \{v_1^1, v_4^1, v_7^1\}$ be the resolving set of G then

$r(v_2^1|W) = (1,3,1), r(v_3^1|W) = (1,2,1), r(v_5^1|W) = (2,1,1), r(v_6^1|W) = (3,1,1)$,

$r(v_8^1|W) = (3,1,2), r(v_9^1|W) = (2,1,3), r(v_{10}^1|W) = (2,2,3), r(v_{11}^1|W) = (1,2,3)$,

$r(v_{12}^1|W) = (1,3,2), r(v_1^2|W) = (1,4,3), r(v_2^2|W) = (1,4,2), r(v_3^2|W) = (2,3,2)$,

$r(v_4^2|W) = (2,3,1), r(v_5^2|W) = (3,2,1), r(v_6^2|W) = (3,2,2), r(v_7^2|W) = (4,1,2)$,

$r(v_8^2|W) = (4,1,3), r(v_9^2|W) = (3,2,3), r(v_{10}^2|W) = (3,2,4), r(v_{11}^2|W) = (2,3,4)$,

$r(v_{12}^2|W) = (2,3,3)$.

For $n \geq 16$ let $W = \{v_1^2, v_4^2, v_{2k+2}^2\}$ be the resolving set of G then

$$r(v_{2i}^1|W) = \begin{cases} (i+1, i-1, k+2-i) & 1 \leq i \leq k \\ (i-1, i-1, 1) & i = k+1 \\ (2k+1-i, 2k+3-i, i-k) & k+2 \leq i \leq 2k \end{cases}$$

$$r(v_{2i+1}^1|W) = \begin{cases} (i+1, i, k+1-i) & 2 \leq i \leq k \\ (2k+1-i, 2k+2-i, i-k+1) & k+1 \leq i \leq 2k-1 \end{cases}$$

$$r(v_{2i}^2|W) = \begin{cases} (i+1, i, k+3-i) & 4 \leq i \leq k-1 \\ (2k+2-i, 2k+4-i, i+1-k) & k+3 \leq i \leq 2k-1 \end{cases}$$

$$r(v_{2i+1}^2|W) = \begin{cases} (i+2, i, k+2-i) & 3 \leq i \leq k-1 \\ (2k+2-i, 2k+3-i, i+1-k) & k+2 \leq i \leq 2k-2 \end{cases}$$

$r(v_1^1|W) = (1, 2, k+1), r(v_2^1|W) = (2, 2, k+1), r(v_3^1|W) = (2, 1, k)$,

$r(v_{2k}^2|W) = (k+1, k, 2), r(v_{2k+1}^2|W) = (k+2, k, 1), r(v_{2k+3}^2|W) = (k+1, k+1, 1)$,

$r(v_{2k+4}^2|W) = (k, k+2, 2), r(v_{4k}^2|W) = (1, 4, k+1), r(v_{4k-1}^2|W) = (2, 4, k)$,

$r(v_2^2|W) = (1, 2, k+2), r(v_3^2|W) = (2, 1, k+1), r(v_5^2|W) = (4, 1, k)$.

Since distinct vertices have distinct representation, $dim(G) \leq 3$ in this case. However, by Theorem 1 no two vertices can resolve G into distinct representation so $dim(G) > 2$. Hence $dim(G) = 3$.

Case-II when $n \equiv 1 \pmod 4$ i.e., $n = 4k+1, k \in N$.

For $n = 5$ let $W = \{v_1^2, v_4^2, v_4^1\}$ be the resolving set of G then $r(v_1^1|W) = (1, 3, 1)$,

$r(v_2^1|W) = (2, 2, 1), r(v_3^1|W) = (3, 1, 1), r(v_5^1|W) = (1, 2, 1), r(v_2^2|W) = (1, 2, 2)$,

$r(v_3^2|W) = (2, 1, 2), r(v_5^2|W) = (1, 1, 1)$.

For $n \geq 9$ let $W = \{v_1^2, v_4^2, v_{2k+1}^1\}$ be the resolving set of G then

$$r(v_{2i}^1|W) = \begin{cases} (i+1, i-1, k+1-i) & 2 \leq i \leq k \\ (2k+2-i, 2k+3-i, i-k) & k+2 \leq i \leq 2k \end{cases}$$

$$r(v_{2i+1}^1|W) = \begin{cases} (i+1, i, k-i) & 1 \leq i \leq k-1 \\ (2k+1-i, 2k+3-i, i-k) & k+2 \leq i \leq 2k \end{cases}$$

$$r(v_{2i}^2|W) = \begin{cases} (i+1, i, k+2-i) & 4 \leq i \leq k \\ (2k+3-i, 2k+4-i, i-k) & k+2 \leq i \leq 2k-1 \end{cases}$$

$$r(v_{2i+1}^2|W) = \begin{cases} (i+2, i, k+1-i) & 3 \leq i \leq k \\ (2k+2-i, 2k+4-i, i-k+1) & k+2 \leq i \leq 2k-1 \end{cases}$$

$r(v_{2k+2}^1|W) = (k+1, k, 1), r(v_{2k+3}^1|W) = (k, k+1, 1), r(v_2^1|W) = (2, 2, k)$,

$r(v_1^1|W) = (1, 2, k), r(v_{2k+2}^2|W) = (k+2, k+1, 1), r(v_{2k+3}^2|W) = (k+1, k+1, 2)$,

$r(v_{4k}^2|W) = (2, 3, k), r(v_{4k+1}^2|W) = (1, 3, k), r(v_2^2|W) = (1, 2, k+1)$,

$r(v_3^2|W) = (2, 1, k), r(v_5^2|W) = (4, 1, k-1), r(v_6^2|W) = (4, 2, k-1)$.

Since distinct vertices have distinct representation, $dim(G) \leq 3$ in this case. However, by Theorem 1 no two vertices can resolve G into distinct representation so $dim(G) > 2$. Hence $dim(G) = 3$.

Case-III when $n \equiv 3 \pmod 4$ i.e., $n = 4k+3, k \in N$.

For $n = 7$ let $W = \{v_1^2, v_6^2, v_7^2\}$ be the resolving set of G then $r(v_1^1|W) = (1,2,2)$,

$r(v_2^1|W) = (2,3,2), r(v_3^1|W) = (2,2,3), r(v_4^1|W) = (3,2,2), r(v_5^1|W) = (2,1,2)$,

$r(v_6^1|W) = (2,1,1), r(v_7^1|W) = (1,2,1), r(v_2^2|W) = (1,3,2), r(v_3^2|W) = (2,3,3)$,

$r(v_4^2|W) = (3,2,3), r(v_5^2|W) = (3,1,2)$.

For $n = 11$ let $W = \{v_1^2, v_4^2, v_7^1\}$ be the resolving set of G then

$r(v_1^1|W) = (1,2,3), r(v_2^1|W) = (2,2,3), r(v_3^1|W) = (2,1,2), r(v_4^1|W) = (3,1,2)$,

$r(v_5^1|W) = (3,2,1), r(v_6^1|W) = (4,2,1), r(v_8^1|W) = (3,3,1), r(v_9^1|W) = (2,4,1)$,

$r(v_{10}^1|W) = (2,3,2), r(v_{11}^1|W) = (1,3,2), r(v_2^2|W) = (1,2,4), r(v_3^2|W) = (2,1,3)$,

$r(v_5^2|W) = (4,1,2), r(v_6^2|W) = (4,2,2), r(v_7^2|W) = (4,3,1), r(v_8^2|W) = (4,4,1)$,

$r(v_9^2|W) = (3,4,2), r(v_{10}^2|W) = (2,4,2), r(v_{11}^2|W) = (1,4,3)$.

For $n \geq 15$ let $W = \{v_1^2, v_6^2, v_{2k+5}^2\}$ be the resolving set of G then

$$r(v_{2i}^1|W) = \begin{cases} (i+1, i-2, k+3-i) & 3 \leq i \leq k+1 \\ (2k+3-i, 2k+5-i, i-k-1) & k+4 \leq i \leq 2k+1 \end{cases}$$

$$r(v_{2i+1}^1|W) = \begin{cases} (i+1, i-1, k+3-i) & 2 \leq i \leq k \\ (2k+2-i, 2k+5-i, i-k-1) & k+3 \leq i \leq 2k+1 \end{cases}$$

$$r(v_{2i}^2|W) = \begin{cases} (i+1, i-1, k+4-i) & 5 \leq i \leq k+1 \\ (2k+4-i, 2k+6-i, i-k-1) & k+4 \leq i \leq 2k \end{cases}$$

$$r(v_{2i+1}^2|W) = \begin{cases} (i+2, i-1, k+4-i) & 4 \leq i \leq k \\ (2k+3-i, 2k+6-i, i-k) & k+4 \leq i \leq 2k \end{cases}$$

$r(v_{2k+3}^1|W) = (k+1, k, 2), r(v_{2k+4}^1|W) = (k+1, k, 1), r(v_{2k+5}^1|W) = (k, k+1, 1)$,

$r(v_{2k+6}^1|W) = (k, k+1, 2), r(v_1^1|W) = (1, 3, k+1), r(v_2^1|W) = (2, 3, k+1)$,

$r(v_3^1|W) = (2, 2, k+2), r(v_4^1|W) = (3, 2, k+1), r(v_{2k+3}^2|W) = (k+2, k, 2)$,

$r(v_{2k+4}^2|W) = (k+2, k+1, 1), r(v_{2k+6}^2|W) = (k+1, k+2, 1)$,

$r(v_{2k+7}^2|W) = (k, k+2, 2), r(v_{4k+2}^2|W) = (2, 5, k), r(v_{4k+3}^2|W) = (1, 5, k+1)$,

$r(v_2^2|W) = (1, 4, k+2), r(v_3^2|W) = (2, 3, k+2), r(v_4^2|W) = (3, 2, k+2)$,

$r(v_5^2|W) = (4, 1, k+2), r(v_7^2|W) = (5, 1, k+1), r(v_8^2|W) = (5, 2, k)$.

Since distinct vertices have distinct representation, $dim(G) \leq 3$ in this case. However, by theorem 1 no two vertices can resolve G into distinct representation so $dim(G) > 2$.

Hence $dim(G) = 3$.

Case-IV when $n \equiv 2(mod 4)$ i.e., $n = 4k+2, k \in N$.

For $n = 6$ let $W_1 = \{v_1^1, v_1^2, v_5^1\}$ be the subset of $V(G)$ and $r(v_2^1|W_1) = (2,1,2)$,

$r(v_3^1|W_1) = (2,1,1), r(v_4^1|W_1) = (2,2,1), r(v_6^1|W_1) = (1,1,1), r(v_2^2|W_1) = (1,1,2)$,

$r(v_3^2|W_1) = (2,2,2), r(v_4^2|W_1) = (3,2,2), r(v_5^2|W_1) = (2,2,1), r(v_6^2|W_1) = (1,2,1)$,

since $r(v_5^2|W_1) = r(v_4^1|W_1) \Rightarrow W = W_1 \cup \{v_4^1\}$ is the resolving set of G.

$\Rightarrow dim(G) \leq 4$

For $n = 10$ let $W_1 = \{v_1^2, v_4^2, v_8^2\}$ be the subset of $V(G)$ and $r(v_1^1|W_1) = (1,2,3)$,

$r(v_2^1|W_1) = (2,2,3), r(v_3^1|W_1) = (2,1,3), r(v_4^1|W_1) = (3,1,3), r(v_5^1|W_1) = (3,2,2)$,

$r(v_6^1|W_1) = (3,2,2), r(v_7^1|W_1) = (3,3,1), r(v_8^1|W_1) = (2,3,1), r(v_9^1|W_1) = (2,3,2)$,

$r(v_{10}^1|W_1) = (1,3,2), r(v_2^2|W_1) = (1,2,4), r(v_3^2|W_1) = (2,1,4), r(v_5^2|W_1) = (4,1,3)$,

$r(v_6^2|W_1) = (4,2,2), r(v_7^2|W_1) = (4,3,1), r(v_9^2|W_1) = (2,4,1)$,

$r(v_{10}^2|W_1) = (1,4,2)$.

since $r(v_5^1|W_1) = r(v_6^1|W_1) \Rightarrow W = W_1 \cup \{v_5^1\}$ is the resolving set of G.

$\Rightarrow dim(G) \leq 4$

For $n \geq 14$ let $W = \{v_1^2, v_4^2, v_{2k+4}^2\}$ be the subset of $V(G)$ then

$$r(v_{2i}^1|W) = \begin{cases} (i+1, i-1, k+3-i) & 2 \leq i \leq k \\ (2k+2-i, 2k+4-i, i-k-1) & k+3 \leq i \leq 2k+1 \end{cases}$$

$$r(v_{2i+1}^1|W) = \begin{cases} (i+1, i, k+2-i) & 1 \leq i \leq k \\ (2k+2-i, 2k+3-i, i-k) & k+2 \leq i \leq 2k \end{cases}$$

$$r(v_{2i}^2|W) = \begin{cases} (i+1, i, k+4-i) & 4 \leq i \leq k \\ (2k+3-i, 2k+5-i, i-k) & k+4 \leq i \leq 2k \end{cases}$$

$$r(v_{2i+1}^2|W) = \begin{cases} (i+2, i, k+3-i) & 3 \leq i \leq k \\ (2k+3-i, 2k+4-i, i-k) & k+3 \leq i \leq 2k-1 \end{cases}$$

$r(v_{2k+2}^1|W) = (k+1, k, 2), r(v_{2k+3}^1|W) = (k+1, k+1, 1)$,

$r(v^1_{2k+4}|W_1) = (k, k+1, 1), r(v^1_1|W_1) = (1, 2, k+1), r(v^1_2|W_1) = (2, 2, k+1),$

$r(v^2_{2k+2}|W_1) = (k+2, k+1, 2), r(v^2_{2k+3}|W_1) = (k+2, k+1, 1),$

$r(v^2_{2k+5}|W_1) = (k+1, k+2, 1), r(v^2_{2k+6}|W_1) = (k, k+2, 2), r(v^2_{4k+1}|W_1) = (2, 4, k),$

$r(v^2_{4k+2}|W_1) = (1, 4, k+1), r(v^2_2|W_1) = (1, 2, k+2), r(v^2_3|W_1) = (2, 1, k+2),$

$r(v^2_5|W_1) = (4, 1, k+1), r(v^2_6|W_1) = (4, 2, k+1).$ since $r(v^1_{2k+1}|W_1) = r(v^1_{2k+2}|W_1) \Rightarrow W = W_1 \cup \{v^1_{2k+1}\}$ is the resolving set of G.

$\Rightarrow dim(G) \leq 4$. This complete the proof. □

Theorem 9. *For $G \cong H_{4,n}(P_m)$ where $H_{4,n}$ be a 4-regular Harary graph with $n \geq 5$ and P_m is the path of length $m-1$; then we have $dim(G) = 3$ when $n \equiv 0, 2, 3 \pmod 4$ and $dim(G) \leq 4$ otherwise.*

Proof. Case-I when $n \equiv 0 \pmod 4$ i.e., $n = 4k, k \geq 2$ and $k \in N$.
Let $W = \{v^1_1, v^1_2, v^1_{2k+1}\}$ be the resolving set of G then

$$r(v^j_{2i}|W) = \begin{cases} (i+j-1, i+j-2, k-i+j) & 2 \leq i \leq k, 1 \leq j \leq m \\ (2k-i+j, 2k-i+j, i-k+j-1) & k+1 \leq i \leq 2k, 1 \leq j \leq m \end{cases}$$

$$r(v^j_{2i+1}|W) = \begin{cases} (i+j-1, i+j-1, k-i+j-1) & 1 \leq i \leq k-1, 1 \leq j \leq m \\ (2k-i+j-1, 2k-i+j, i-k+j-1) & k+1 \leq i \leq 2k-1, 1 \leq j \leq m \end{cases}$$

For $2 \leq j \leq m, r(v^j_1|W) = (j-1, j, k+j-1),$

$r(v^j_2|W) = (j, j-1, k+j-1), r(v^j_{2k+1}|W) = (k+j-1, k+j-1, j-1).$

Since distinct vertices have distinct representation, $dim(G) \leq 3$ in this case. Now we prove that $dim(G) \neq 2$ when $n \equiv 0 \pmod 4$. Since every vertex that lies on cycle has degree 5, by Theorem 1 we shall take the vertices on pendents uncommon to the cycle when $|W| = 2$. Without loss of generality we can say
$W = \{v^2_1, v^3_1\}$ and $W = \{v^2_1, v^2_i\}, 2 \leq i \leq 2k+1$ represent all possible cases in which $|W| = 2$ and in each case the following contradictions arise.
Take $W = \{v^2_1, v^3_1\}$ then $r(v^1_2/W) = r(v^1_{4k}|W) = (2, 3)$ a contradiction.

Take $W = \{v^2_1, v^2_{2i}\}, 1 \leq i \leq k$ then $r(v^1_{2k+1}|W) = r(v^1_{2k+2}|W) = (k+1, k+2-i)$ a contradiction.

Take $W = \{v^2_1, v^2_{2i+1}\}, 1 \leq i \leq k-1$ then $r(v^1_{2i+2}|W) = r(v^1_{2i+3}|W) = (i+2, 2)$ a contradiction.

Take $W = \{v^2_1, v^2_{2k+1}\}$, then $r(v^1_{2k}|W) = r(v^1_{2k+2}|W) = (k+1, 2)$ a contradiction.

hence $dim(G) = 3$.

Case-II when $n \equiv 2 \pmod 4$ i.e., $n = 4k+2, k \in N$.
Let $W = \{v^1_1, v^1_3, v^1_{2k+3}\}$ be the resolving set of G then

$$r(v^j_{2i}|W) = \begin{cases} (i+j-1, i+j-2, k-i+j+1) & 2 \leq i \leq k+1, 1 \leq j \leq m \\ (2k-i+j+1, 2k-i+j+2, i-k+j-2) & k+2 \leq i \leq 2k+1, 1 \leq j \leq m \end{cases}$$

$$r(v^j_{2i+1}|W) = \begin{cases} (i+j-1, i+j-2, k-i+j) & 2 \leq i \leq k, 1 \leq j \leq m \\ (2k-i+j, 2k-i+j+1, i-k+j-2) & k+2 \leq i \leq 2k, 1 \leq j \leq m \end{cases}$$

For $2 \leq j \leq m$, $r(v^j_1|W) = (j-1, j, k+j-1)$, $r(v^j_2|W) = (j, j, k+j)$,

$r(v^j_3|W) = (j, j-1, k+j-1)$, $r(v^j_{2k+3}|W) = (k+j-1, k+j-1, j-1)$.

Since distinct vertices have distinct representation, $dim(G) \leq 3$ in this case. Now we prove that $dim(G) \neq 2$ when $n \equiv 2(mod 4)$. Since every vertex lies that on cycle has degree 5, by theorem 1 we shall take the vertices on pendents uncommon to the cycle when $|W| = 2$. Without loss of generality we can say:
$W = \{v^2_1, v^3_1\}$ and $W = \{v^2_1, v^2_i\}$, $2 \leq i \leq 2k+1$ represent all possible cases in which $|W| = 2$ and in each case the following contradictions arise. Take $W = \{v^2_1, v^3_1\}$ then $r(v^1_2|W) = r(v^1_{4k+2}|W) = (2,3)$ a contradiction.

Take $W = \{v^2_1, v^2_2\}$, then $r(v^1_3|W) = r(v^1_{4k+2}|W) = (2,2)$ a contradiction.

Take $W = \{v^2_1, v^2_{2i}\}$, $2 \leq i \leq k+1$ then $r(v^1_{2k+3}|W) = r(v^1_{2k+4}|W) = (k+1, k+3-i)$ a contradiction.

Take $W = \{v^2_1, v^2_{2i+1}\}$, $2 \leq i \leq k-1$ then $r(v^1_{2i+2}|W) = r(v^1_{2i+3}|W) = (i+2, 2)$ a contradiction.

Take $W = \{v^2_1, v^2_{2k+1}\}$ then $r(v^1_{2k}|W) = r(v^1_{2k+3}|W) = (k+1, 2)$ a contradiction.

hence $dim(G) = 3$.

Case-III when $n \equiv 3(mod 4)$ i.e., $n = 4k+3, k \in N$.

Let $W = \{v^1_1, v^1_2, v^1_{2k+2}\}$ be the resolving set of G then

$$r(v^j_{2i}|W) = \begin{cases} (i+j-1, i+j-2, k-i+j) & 2 \leq i \leq k, 1 \leq j \leq m \\ (2k-i+j+1, 2k-i+j+2, i-k+j-2) & k+2 \leq i \leq 2k+1, 1 \leq j \leq m \end{cases}$$

$$r(v^j_{2i+1}|W) = \begin{cases} (i+j-1, i+j-1, k-i+j) & 1 \leq i \leq k, 1 \leq j \leq m \\ (2k-i+j+1, 2k-i+j+1, i-k+j-1) & k+1 \leq i \leq 2k+1, 1 \leq j \leq m \end{cases}$$

For $2 \leq j \leq m$, $r(v^j_1|W) = (j-1, j, k+j)$, $r(v^j_2|W) = (j, j-1, k+j-1)$, $r(v^j_{2k+2}|W) = (k+j, k+j-1, j-1)$.

Since distinct vertices have distinct representation, $dim(G) \leq 3$ in this case. Now we prove that $dim(G) \neq 2$ when $n \equiv 2 \pmod 4$. Since every vertex that lies on cycle has degree 5, by Theorem 1 we shall take the vertices on pendents uncommon to the cycle when $|W| = 2$. Without loss of generality we can say:
$W = \{v^2_1, v^3_1\}$ and $W = \{v^2_1, v^2_i\}$, $2 \leq i \leq 2k+2$ represent all possible cases in which $|W| = 2$ and in each case the following contradictions arise. Take $W = \{v^2_1, v^3_1\}$ then $r(v^1_2|W) = r(v^1_{4k+3}|W) = (2,3)$ a contradiction.

Take $W = \{v^2_1, v^2_2\}$, then $r(v^1_3|W) = r(v^1_{4k+3}|W) = (2,2)$ a contradiction.

Take $W = \{v_1^2, v_{2i}^2\}$, $2 \leq i \leq k+1$ then $r(v_{2i-1}^1|W) = r(v_{2i-2}^1|W) = (i,2)$ a contradiction.

Take $W = \{v_1^2, v_{2i+1}^2\}$, $1 \leq i \leq k$ then $r(v_{2i+2}^1|W) = r(v_{2i+3}^1|W) = (i+2,2)$ a contradiction.

hence $dim(G) = 3$.

Case-IV when $n \equiv 1 \pmod 4$ i.e., $n = 4k+1, k \in N$.
Let $W = \{v_1^1, v_2^1, v_{2k+2}^1, v_{2k+3}^1\}$ be the resolving set of G then

$$r(v_{2i}^j|W) = \begin{cases} (i+j-1, i+j-2, k-i+j, k-i+j+1) & 2 \leq i \leq k, 1 \leq j \leq m \\ (2k-i+j, 2k-i+j+1, k-i+j+2, k-ij+2) & k+2 \leq i \leq 2k, 1 \leq j \leq m \end{cases}$$

$$r(v_{2i+1}^j|W) = \begin{cases} (i+j-1, i+j-1, k-i+j, k-i+j) & 1 \leq i \leq k, 1 \leq j \leq m \\ (2k-i+j, 2k-i+j, k-i+j+3, k-i+j+2) & k+2 \leq i \leq 2k, 1 \leq j \leq m \end{cases}$$

For $2 \leq j \leq m$, $r(v_1^j|W) = (j-1, j, k+j-1, k+j-1)$,
$r(v_2^j|W) = (j, j-1, k+j-1, k+j-1)$, $r(v_{2k+2}^j|W) = (k+j-1, k+j-1, j-1, j)$,

$r(v_{2k+3}^j|W) = (k+j-1, k+j-1, j, j-1)$. Since distinct vertices have distinct representation so $dim(G) \leq 4$ in this case. This complete the proof. □

4. The Rooted Product of Ladder Graph with Cycle Graph

To construct the graph $G \cong (P_2 \times P_k)(C_4)^c$ we first construct rooted product of ladder graph $(P_2 \times P_k)$ by cycle C_4 as shown in Figure 4a and then connect each rooted C_4 with both neighboring C_4 as shown in Figure 4b.

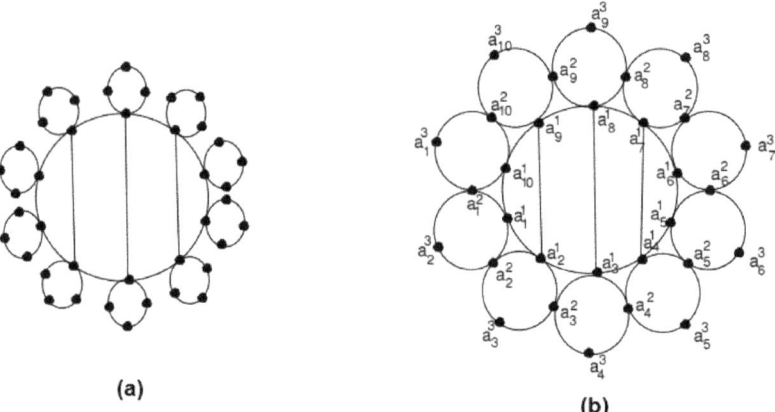

(a) (b)

Figure 4. (a) The graph of $(P_2 \times P_5)(C_4)$; (b) The graph of $(P_2 \times P_5)(C_4)^c$.

Theorem 10. *For $G \cong (P_2 \times P_k)(C_4)^c$ where C_4 be a cycle of length 4 and P_k is the path of length $k-1$; then we have $dim(G) = 3$.*

Proof. When $n = 2k, k \in N$ let $W = \{a_1^1, a_k^1, a_n^1\}$ be the resolving set of G then

$$r(a_i^1|W) = \begin{cases} (i-1, i, k-i) & 2 \leq i \leq k-1 \\ (2k-i+1, 2k-i, i-k) & k+1 \leq i \leq 2k-1 \end{cases}$$

$$r(a_i^2|W) = \begin{cases} (i-1, i, k-i+1) & 2 \leq i \leq k \\ (2k-i+2, 2k-i+1, i-k) & k+2 \leq i \leq 2k \end{cases}$$

$$r(a_i^3|W) = \begin{cases} (i-1, i, k-i+2) & 3 \leq i \leq k \\ (2k-i+3, 2k-i+2, i-k) & k+2 \leq i \leq n \end{cases}$$

$r(a_1^2|W) = (1,1,k), r(a_{k+1}^2|W) = (k,k,1), r(a_1^3|W) = (2,2,k+1), r(a_2^3|W) = (2,2,k), r(a_{k+1}^3|W) = (k, k+1, 2)$.

Since distinct vertices have distinct representation, $dim(G) \leq 3$. Now we prove that $dim(G) \neq 2$. Since all vertices have degree either 4 or 5 except a_i^3, by theorem 1 we can say $W = \{a_1^3, a_i^3\}, 2 \leq i \leq n$ and $W = \{a_n^3, a_i^3\}, 1 \leq i \leq n-1$ represent all possible cases in which $|W| = 2$ and in each case the following contradictions arise.

take $W = \{a_1^3, a_2^3\}$ then $r(a_n^1|W) = r(a_1^1|W) = (2,2)$, a contradiction.

take $W = \{a_1^3, a_3^3\}$ then $r(a_{n-1}^1|W) = r(a_n^1|W) = (2,3)$, a contradiction.

take $W = \{a_1^3, a_i^3\}, 4 \leq i \leq k+1$ then $r(a_n^1|W) = r(a_1^1|W) = (2,2)$, a contradiction.

take $W = \{a_1^3, a_{k+2}^3\}$ then $r(a_{k+1}^1|W) = r(a_{k+3}^3|W) = (k,2)$, a contradiction.

take $W = \{a_1^3, a_i^3\}, k+3 \leq i \leq n$ then $r(a_k^1|W) = r(a_{k+1}^2|W) = (k+1, i-k)$ a contradiction.

take $W = \{a_n^3, a_i^3\}, 1 \leq i \leq k-1$ then $r(a_{k+1}^1|W) = r(a_{k+2}^2|W) = (k-1, k+3-i)$, a contradiction.

take $W = \{a_n^3, a_k^3\}$ then $r(a_{k-1}^1|W) = r(a_{k-1}^3|W) = (k-1, 2)$, a contradiction.

take $W = \{a_n^3, a_{k+1}^3\}$ then $r(a_{k+1}^1|W) = r(a_k^3|W) = (k, 2)$, a contradiction.

take $W = \{a_n^3, a_{k+2}^3\}$ then $r(a_{k+1}^1|W) = r(a_{k+3}^3|W) = (k-1, 2)$, a contradiction.

take $W = \{a_n^3, a_i^3\}, k+3 \leq i \leq n-1$ then $r(a_k^1|W) = r(a_{k+1}^2|W) = (k, i-k)$, a contradiction.

So $dim(G) \geq 3$. Combining both inequalities, we get $dim(G) = 3$. This conclude the proof. □

5. Conclusions

In the foregoing section, graphs $H_{4,n}(C_3)^c$, $(P_2 \times P_k)(C_4)^c$ and $H_{m,n}(C_i)$ for $i = 3, 4, 5$ are constructed. It is proven that metric dimension of $H_{4,n}(C_3)^c$ and $(P_2 \times P_k)(C_4)^c$ is either three or four in certain cases but the family of graphs $H_{m,n}(C_3)$ for $i = 3, 4, 5$ have unbounded metric dimension. This section is closed by raising the following open problems.

Open Problem 1. Determine the metric dimension of $H_{4,n}(C_3)$ and $(P_2 \times P_k)(C_4)$.

Open Problem 2. Determine the metric dimension of $H_{m,n}(C_n)$.

Author Contributions: S.I. contribute for conceptualization, resources, computations, funding, and analyzed the data. M.K.S. and M.I. contribute for supervision, methodology, software, funding, validation, designing the experiments and formal analysing. M.H. contribute for performed experiments, resources, funding and wrote the initial draft of the paper. M.K.S. contribute for analyzed the data, investigated this draft and wrote the final draft. All authors read and approved the final version of the paper.

Funding: This research is supported by the Start-Up Research Grant 2016 of United Arab Emirates University (UAEU), Al Ain, United Arab Emirates via Grant No. G00002233 and UPAR Grant of UAEU via Grant No. G00002590 for (M.Imran and M.K.Siddiqu). This research is also supported by The Higher Education

Commission of Pakistan Under Research and Development Division, National Research Program for Universities via Grant No.: 5348/Federal/NRPU/R&D/HEC/2016 for (M.Hussain).

Acknowledgments: We are thankful to the referees for their valuable remarks and suggestions that improved the current version of the paper.

Conflicts of Interest: The authors declare no conflict of interest.

References

1. Chartrand, G.; Eroh, L.; Johnson, M.A.; Oellermann, O.R. Resolvability in graphs and metric dimension of a graph. *Discret. Appl. Math.* **2000**, *105*, 99–113. [CrossRef]
2. Slater, P.J. Leaves of trees. *Congress. Number* **1975**, *14*, 549–559.
3. Imran, M.; Baig, A.Q.; Bokhary, S.A.U.H.; Javaid, I. On the metric dimension of circulant graphs. *Appl. Math. Lett.* **2012**, *5*, 320–325. [CrossRef]
4. Bača, M.; Baskoro, E.T.; Salman, A.N.M.; Saputro, S.W.; Suprijanto, D. On metric dimension of regular bipartite graphs. *Bull. Math. Soc. Sci. Math. Roum.* **2011**, *54*, 15–28.
5. Harary, F.; Melter, R.A. On the metric dimension of a graph. *Ars Comb.* **1976**, *2*, 191–195.
6. Melter, R.A.; Tomescu, I. Metric bases in digital geometry, Computer vision. *Gr. Image Process.* **1984**, *25*, 113–121. [CrossRef]
7. Slater, P.J. Dominating and references sets in graphs. *J. Math. Phys. Sci.* **1988**, *22*, 445–455.
8. Khuller, S.; Raghavachari, B.; Rosenfeld, A. *Localization in Graphs*; Technical Report CS-TR-3326; University of Maryland at College Park: College Park, MD, USA, 1994.
9. Tomescu, I.; Imran, M. Metric dimension and R-Sets of connected graph. *Gr. Comb.* **2011**, *27*, 585–591. [CrossRef]
10. Manuel, P.; Rajan, B.; Rajasingh, I.; Monica, C. On minimum metric dimension of honeycom networks. *J. Discret. Algorithms* **2008**, *6*, 20–27. [CrossRef]
11. Cameron, P.J.; VanLint, J.H. *Designs, Graphs, Codes and Their Links, in London Mathematical Society Student Texts*; Cambridge University Press: Cambridge, UK, 1991; Volume 22.
12. Bermound, J.C.; Comellas, F.; Hsu, D.F. Distributed loop computer networks: Survey. *J. Parallel Distrib. Comput.* **1995**, *24*, 2–10. [CrossRef]
13. Sebö, A.; Tannier, E. On metric generators of graphs. *Math. Oper. Res.* **2004**, *29*, 383–393. [CrossRef]
14. Wu, C.; Feng, T.Y. On a class of multistage interconnection networks. *IEEE Trans. Comput.* **1980**, *29*, 694–702.
15. Hoffmann, S.; Elterman, A.; Wanke, E. A linear time algorithm for metric dimension of cactus block graphs. *Theor. Comput. Sci.* **2016**, *630*, 43–62. [CrossRef]
16. Buczkowski, P.S.; Chartrand, G.; Poisson, C.; Zhang, P. On k-dimensional graphs and their bases. *Perioddica Math. HUNG* **2003**, *46*, 9–15. [CrossRef]
17. Imran, S.; Siddiqui, M.K.; Imran, M.; Hussain, M.; Bilal, H.M.; Cheema, I.Z.; Tabraiz, I.; Saleem, Z. Computing the metric dimension of gear graphs. *Symmetry* **2018**, *10*, 209. [CrossRef]
18. Tomescu, I.; Javaid, I. On the metric dimension of the jahangir graph. *Bull. Math. Soc. Sci. Math. Roum.* **2007**, *50*, 371–376.
19. West, B. *Introduction to Graph Theory*; Prentice Hall of India: Delhi, India, 2003.
20. Godsil, C.D.; Mckay, B.D. A new product and its spectrum. *Bull. Aust. Math. Soc.* **1978**, *18*, 21–28. [CrossRef]

© 2018 by the authors. Licensee MDPI, Basel, Switzerland. This article is an open access article distributed under the terms and conditions of the Creative Commons Attribution (CC BY) license (http://creativecommons.org/licenses/by/4.0/).

Article

Optimizing Three-Dimensional Constrained Ordered Weighted Averaging Aggregation Problem with Bounded Variables

Hui-Chin Tang * and Shen-Tai Yang *

Department of Industrial Engineering and Management, National Kaohsiung University of Science and Technology, Kaohsiung 80778, Taiwan
* Correspondence: tang@nkust.edu.tw (H.-C.T.); 1105407103@nkust.edu.tw (S.-T.Y.)

Received: 3 September 2018; Accepted: 14 September 2018; Published: 19 September 2018

Abstract: A single constrained ordered weighted averaging aggregation (COWA) problem is of considerable importance in many disciplines. Two models are considered: the maximization COWA problem with lower bounded variables and the minimization COWA problem with upper bounded variables. For a three-dimensional case of these models, we present the explicitly optimal solutions theoretically and empirically. The bounds and weights can affect the optimal solution of the three-dimensional COWA problem with bounded variables.

Keywords: constrained ordered weighted averaging aggregation problem; mixed integer linear programming; bounded variables

1. Introduction

An ordered weighted averaging (OWA) operator [1] is a general class of parametric aggregation operators that appears in many research fields such as decision making [2–6], fuzzy system [7,8], statistics [9–11], risk analysis [12] and others [13,14]. For more details, see Carlsson and Fullér [15], Emrouznejad and Marra [16] and Yager et al. [17]. A constrained OWA aggregation problem (COWA) attempts to optimize the OWA aggregation problem with multiple constraints. Yager [18] developed a mixed integer linear programming problem to solve a single COWA problem. Later, Carlsson et al. [19] proposed an algorithm to solve the single constrained OWA optimization problem for any dimensions. Furthermore, Coroianu and Fullér [20] presented an explicitly optimal solution for the single COWA problem with any constraint coefficients. In addition, there are other important references [21–27] dedicated to constrained OWA optimization problem with multiple constraints. However, the decision variables are usually bounded for the most practical problems. Recently, Chen and Tang [28] proposed a three-dimensional COWA problem with lower bounded variables. This paper presents the explicitly optimal solutions for the three-dimensional COWA problem with bounded variables. Two models are considered. One is a maximizing three-dimensional constrained OWA aggregation problem with lower bounded variables (3COWAL). The other is a minimizing three-dimensional constrained OWA aggregation problem with upper bounded variables (3COWAU).

The organization of this paper is as follows. Section 2 briefly reviews the COWA problem. For maximizing 3COWAL, there are two parameters (w_1, w_2, w_3) and (l_1, l_2, l_3) that affect the optimal solution types. We discuss the optimal solution behaviors in Section 3 for $w_1 \geq w_2 \geq w_3$ and Section 4 for $l_1 \geq l_2 \geq l_3$. Section 5 analyzes the optimal solution behaviors of minimizing 3COWAU. Finally, some concluding remarks are presented.

2. Constrained OWA Aggregation Problem

An OWA operator of dimension n is a mapping $F : \mathcal{R}^n \to \mathcal{R}$ that has an associated weighting vector $W = (w_1, w_2, \ldots, w_n)$ satisfying

$$w_1 + w_2 + \ldots + w_n = 1, \ 0 \leq w_i \leq 1, \ i = 1, 2, \ldots, n$$

and such that

$$G(x_1, x_2, \ldots, x_n) = \sum_{i=1}^{n} w_i y_i \tag{1}$$

with y_i being the ith largest of $\{x_1, x_2, \ldots, x_n\}$. For simplicity, we will denote this expression as $F(y_1, y_2, \ldots, y_n)$.

Consider the following single COWA problem:

$$\text{Max } W^T Y, \text{ s.t. } \mathcal{I}^T X \leq 1, \ X \geq 0, \tag{2}$$

where the column vectors X, Y, W and $\mathcal{I}$ are

$$X = \begin{bmatrix} x_1 \\ x_2 \\ \vdots \\ x_n \end{bmatrix}, \ Y = \begin{bmatrix} y_1 \\ y_2 \\ \vdots \\ y_n \end{bmatrix}, \ W = \begin{bmatrix} w_1 \\ w_2 \\ \vdots \\ w_n \end{bmatrix}, \ \mathcal{I} = \begin{bmatrix} 1 \\ 1 \\ \vdots \\ 1 \end{bmatrix}.$$

By introducing the $(n-1) \times n$ matrix

$$G = \begin{bmatrix} -1 & 1 & 0 & 0 & \cdots & 0 & 0 \\ 0 & -1 & 1 & 0 & & 0 & 0 \\ & & \vdots & & \ddots & & \vdots \\ 0 & 0 & 0 & 0 & \cdots & -1 & 1 \end{bmatrix}$$

and the column binary vectors $Z_i \in \{0,1\}^n$, $i = 1, 2, \ldots, n$, Yager [18] transformed the nonlinear programming single COWA problem (2) to the following mixed integer linear programming problem (MILP):

$$\text{Max } W^T Y, \text{ s.t. } \mathcal{I}^T X \leq 1, \ GY \leq 0, \ y_i \mathcal{I} - X - M Z_i \leq 0, \ i = 1, 2, \ldots, n-1,$$
$$y_n \mathcal{I} - X \leq 0, \ \mathcal{I}^T Z_i \leq n - i, \ i = 1, 2, \ldots, n-1, \ Z_i \in \{0,1\}^n, \ i = 1, 2, \ldots, n-1, \ X \geq 0, \tag{3}$$

where M is a very large positive number. To reduce the multiple solutions of the MILP (3), Chen and Tang [28] introduced the following constraints:

$$Z_{i+1} \leq Z_i, \ i = 1, 2, \ldots, n-2.$$

Then, the more efficient MILP of a single COWA problem is as follows:

$$\text{Max } W^T Y, \text{ s.t. } \mathcal{I}^T X \leq 1, \ GY \leq 0, \ y_i \mathcal{I} - X - M Z_i \leq 0, \ i = 1, 2, \ldots, n-1, \ y_n \mathcal{I} - X \leq 0,$$
$$\mathcal{I}^T Z_i \leq n - i, \ i = 1, 2, \ldots, n-1, \ Z_{i+1} \leq Z_i, \ i = 1, 2, \ldots, n-2, \ Z_i \in \{0,1\}^n, \tag{4}$$
$$i = 1, 2, \ldots, n-1, \ X \geq 0.$$

3. Maximizing a Three-Dimensional Constrained OWA Aggregation Problem with Lower Bounded Variables for $w_1 \geq w_2 \geq w_3$

It is fairly common in practical optimization problems that the decision variables are usually bounded. A typical decision variable x_i is bounded from below by l_i and from above by u_i, where $l_i \leq u_i$. Sections 3 and 4 analyze the maximization COWA problem with the lower bound constraints. Section 5 analyzes the minimization COWA problem with the upper bound constraints. Chen and Tang [28] proposed the following COWAL:

$$\text{Max } W^T Y, \text{ s.t. } \mathcal{I}^T X \leq 1, GY \leq 0, \, , y_i \mathcal{I} - X - MZ_i \leq 0, \, i = 1, 2, \ldots, n-1,$$
$$y_n \mathcal{I} - X \leq 0, \mathcal{I}^T Z_i \leq n - i, \, i = 1, 2, \ldots, n-1, Z_{i+1} \leq Z_i, \, i = 1, 2, \ldots, n-2, Z_i \in \{0,1\}^n, \quad (5)$$
$$i = 1, 2, \ldots, n-1, X \geq L,$$

where the lower bounded vector

$$L = \begin{bmatrix} l_1 \\ l_2 \\ \vdots \\ l_n \end{bmatrix}.$$

The lower bounded vector can be transformed into the zero vector by using the standard transformations $X' = X - L$. The COWAL is as follows:

$$\text{Max } W^T Y, \text{ s.t. } \mathcal{I}^T X' \leq 1 - \mathcal{I}^T L, GY \leq 0, y_i \mathcal{I} - X' - MZ_i \leq L, \, i = 1, 2, \ldots, n-1,$$
$$y_n \mathcal{I} - X' \leq L, \mathcal{I}^T Z_i \leq n - i, \, i = 1, 2, \ldots, n-1, Z_{i+1} \leq Z_i, \, i = 1, 2, \ldots, n-2, Z_i \in \{0,1\}^n, \quad (6)$$
$$i = 1, 2, \ldots, n-1, X' \geq \mathbf{0}.$$

If $1 - \mathcal{I}^T L < 0$, then the COWAL has no feasible solution. If $1 - \mathcal{I}^T L = 0$, then $X' = \mathbf{0}$ is the unique optimal solution, so $X = L$. The following will discuss the case that $1 - \mathcal{I}^T L > 0$.

Consider the 3COWAL for the case of

$$l_1 + l_2 + l_3 \leq 1. \quad (7)$$

Two parameters (w_1, w_2, w_3) and (l_1, l_2, l_3) are considered in 3COWAL. This section discusses 3COWAL with

$$w_1 \geq w_2 \geq w_3. \quad (8)$$

There are six permutations of (l_1, l_2, l_3). First, consider the case of

$$l_1 \geq l_2 \geq l_3. \quad (9)$$

At optimality, the first constraint of model (6) becomes

$$x_1' + x_2' + x_3' = 1 - l_1 - l_2 - l_3. \quad (10)$$

There are three types (A, B, C) of (x_1', x_2', x_3') according to the number of zero components. The number of zero components of first type A is two. The possible values of (x_1', x_2', x_3') are

$$(1 - l_1 - l_2 - l_3, 0, 0), \, (0, 1 - l_1 - l_2 - l_3, 0) \text{ and } (0, 0, 1 - l_1 - l_2 - l_3).$$

For the case of $(x_1', x_2', x_3') = (1 - l_1 - l_2 - l_3, 0, 0)$, we have

$$(x_1, x_2, x_3) = (1 - l_2 - l_3, l_2, l_3)$$

and

$$(y_1, y_2, y_3) = (1 - l_2 - l_3, l_2, l_3), \, (l_2, 1 - l_2 - l_3, l_3), \, (l_2, l_3, 1 - l_2 - l_3),$$
$$(1 - l_2 - l_3, l_3, l_2), \, (l_3, 1 - l_2 - l_3, l_2) \text{ or } (l_3, l_2, 1 - l_2 - l_3).$$

Consider $(y_1, y_2, y_3) = (l_2, 1 - l_2 - l_3, l_3)$, so $l_2 \geq 1 - l_2 - l_3 \geq l_3$, implying $2l_2 + l_3 \geq 1$. From Label (7), it follows that $l_2 \geq l_1$, in contradiction to assumption (9). The same contradiction is also for $(y_1, y_2, y_3) = (l_2, l_3, 1 - l_2 - l_3)$, $(1 - l_2 - l_3, l_3, l_2)$, $(l_3, 1 - l_2 - l_3, l_2)$ and $(l_3, l_2, 1 - l_2 - l_3)$. Therefore, for $(x'_1, x'_2, x'_3) = (1 - l_1 - l_2 - l_3, 0, 0)$, the reasonable candidate for the optimal solution is $(y_1, y_2, y_3) = (1 - l_2 - l_3, l_2, l_3)$. For cases of $(0, 1 - l_1 - l_2 - l_3, 0)$ and $(0, 0, 1 - l_1 - l_2 - l_3)$, the reasonable candidates of (y_1, y_2, y_3) are shown in Table 1.

Table 1. The possible values of (x'_1, x'_2, x'_3), (x_1, x_2, x_3) and (y_1, y_2, y_3) for 3COWAL with $l_1 \geq l_2 \geq l_3$.

	(x'_1, x'_2, x'_3)	(x_1, x_2, x_3)	(y_1, y_2, y_3)
A-1	$(1 - l_1 - l_2 - l_3, 0, 0)$	$(1 - l_2 - l_3, l_2, l_3)$	$(1 - l_2 - l_3, l_2, l_3)$
A-2	$(0, 1 - l_1 - l_2 - l_3, 0)$	$(l_1, 1 - l_1 - l_3, l_3)$	$(1 - l_1 - l_3, l_1, l_3), (l_1, 1 - l_1 - l_3, l_3)$
A-3	$(0, 0, 1 - l_1 - l_2 - l_3)$	$(l_1, l_2, 1 - l_1 - l_2)$	$(1 - l_1 - l_2, l_1, l_2), (l_1, 1 - l_1 - l_2, l_2), (l_1, l_2, 1 - l_1 - l_2)$
B1-1	$(\frac{1-2l_1-l_3}{2}, \frac{1-2l_2-l_3}{2}, 0)$	$(\frac{1-l_3}{2}, \frac{1-l_3}{2}, l_3)$	$(\frac{1-l_3}{2}, \frac{1-l_3}{2}, l_3)$
B1-2	$(\frac{1-2l_1-l_2}{2}, 0, \frac{1-l_2-2l_3}{2})$	$(\frac{1-l_2}{2}, l_2, \frac{1-l_2}{2})$	$(\frac{1-l_2}{2}, \frac{1-l_2}{2}, l_2)$
B1-3	$(0, \frac{1-l_1-2l_2}{2}, \frac{1-l_1-2l_3}{2})$	$(l_1, \frac{1-l_1}{2}, \frac{1-l_1}{2})$	$(l_1, \frac{1-l_1}{2}, \frac{1-l_1}{2})$
B2-1	$(l_3 - l_1, 1 - l_2 - 2l_3, 0)$	$(l_3, 1 - 2l_3, l_3)$	
B2-2	$(1 - l_1 - 2l_3, l_3 - l_2, 0)$	$(1 - 2l_3, l_3, l_3)$	
B2-3	$(l_2 - l_1, 0, 1 - 2l_2 - l_3)$	$(l_2, l_2, 1 - 2l_2)$	
B2-4	$(1 - l_1 - 2l_2, 0, l_2 - l_3)$	$(1 - 2l_2, l_2, l_2)$	$(1 - 2l_2, l_2, l_2)$
B2-5	$(0, l_1 - l_2, 1 - 2l_1 - l_3)$	$(l_1, l_1, 1 - 2l_1)$	$(l_1, l_1, 1 - 2l_1)$
B2-6	$(0, 1 - 2l_1 - l_2, l_1 - l_3)$	$(l_1, 1 - 2l_1, l_1)$	$(l_1, l_1, 1 - 2l_1)$
C	$(1/3 - l_1, 1/3 - l_2, 1/3 - l_3)$	$(1/3, 1/3, 1/3)$	$(1/3, 1/3, 1/3)$

In Table 1, there are six candidates for optimal solution (y_1, y_2, y_3) for type A. Among these six candidates, we will show that the largest objective function $F(Y) = w_1 y_1 + w_2 y_2 + w_3 y_3$ is that of $(y_1, y_2, y_3) = (1 - l_2 - l_3, l_2, l_3)$. Before we prove this result in detail, we present a well-known fact.

Theorem 1. *For* $(x_1, x_2 \ldots, x_n)$, $(x'_1, x'_2 \ldots, x'_n)$, $s_k = \sum_{i=1}^{k} x_i$ *and* $s'_k = \sum_{i=1}^{k} x'_i$, $k = 1, 2, \ldots, n$, *if* $s_k \geq s'_k$, $k = 1, 2, \ldots, n$, *then for all* $(w_1, w_2, \ldots, w_n)$ *with* $w_k \geq w_{k+1}$, $k = 1, 2, \ldots, n - 1$, *we have*

$$\sum_{i=1}^{n} w_i x_i \geq \sum_{i=1}^{n} w_i x'_i.$$

Comparing the objective function value of $(y_1, y_2, y_3) = (1 - l_2 - l_3, l_2, l_3)$ with that of $(1 - l_1 - l_3, l_1, l_3)$, we get that

$$s_1 = 1 - l_2 - l_3 \geq s'_1 = 1 - l_1 - l_3,$$

$$s_2 = 1 - l_3 \geq s'_2 = 1 - l_3,$$

$$s_3 = 1 \geq s'_3 = 1.$$

It implies that the most favorable value of the objective function is that with $(1 - l_2 - l_3, l_2, l_3)$. A similar argument shows that $F(1 - l_2 - l_3, l_2, l_3)$ is larger than those of $(l_1, 1 - l_1 - l_3, l_3)$, $(1 - l_1 - l_2, l_1, l_2)$, $(l_1, 1 - l_1 - l_2, l_2)$ and $(l_1, l_2, 1 - l_1 - l_2)$. Therefore, the optimal solution for type A is $(1 - l_2 - l_3, l_2, l_3)$.

For the one zero component of (x'_1, x'_2, x'_3), the possible values are

$$(x'_1, x'_2, 0), \; (x'_1, 0, x'_3) \text{ and } (0, x'_2, x'_3).$$

At optimal, the possible values of x'_1, x'_2 and x'_3 with at least one $x'_i = 0$, $i = 1, 2, 3$ satisfy

$$x'_1 + l_1 = x'_2 + l_2, \; x'_1 + l_1 = x'_3 + l_3 \text{ or } x'_2 + l_2 = x'_3 + l_3.$$

We choose $x'_i + l_i = x'_j + l_j$ for type B1, and $x'_i + l_i = l_k$ or $x'_j + l_j = l_k$, $i \neq j \neq k$, $i, j, k = 1, 2, 3$, for type B2. A similar argument shows that all possible candidates for optimal solutions (y_1, y_2, y_3) are

$$\left(\frac{1-l_3}{2}, \frac{1-l_3}{2}, l_3\right), \left(\frac{1-l_2}{2}, \frac{1-l_2}{2}, l_2\right), \left(l_1, \frac{1-l_1}{2}, \frac{1-l_1}{2}\right)$$

for type B1, and

$$(1-2l_2, l_2, l_2), (l_1, l_1, 1-2l_1)$$

for type B2. The largest objective function value is that with $(\frac{1-l_3}{2}, \frac{1-l_3}{2}, l_3)$ for type B1 and $(l_1, l_1, 1-2l_1)$ for type B2. Furthermore, $F(\frac{1-l_3}{2}, \frac{1-l_3}{2}, l_3) \geq F(l_1, l_1, 1-2l_1)$. Therefore, the optimal solution for type B is $(\frac{1-l_3}{2}, \frac{1-l_3}{2}, l_3)$.

Type C is the nonzero components. From Label (10), it follows that

$$(x'_1, x'_2, x'_3) = (1/3 - l_1, 1/3 - l_2, 1/3 - l_3), (x_1, x_2, x_3) = (1/3, 1/3, 1/3) \text{ and}$$
$$(y_1, y_2, y_3) = (1/3, 1/3, 1/3).$$

Therefore, there are six candidate optimal solutions for type A, five candidate optimal solutions for type B and one candidate optimal solution for type C. Detailed results of (x'_1, x'_2, x'_3), (x_1, x_2, x_3), (y_1, y_2, y_3), $F(y_1, y_2, y_3)$ and condition for 3COWAL with $l_1 \geq l_2 \geq l_3$ are presented in Table 2.

Table 2. The candidate optimal solutions of (x'_1, x'_2, x'_3), (x_1, x_2, x_3) and (y_1, y_2, y_3), $F(y_1, y_2, y_3)$ and condition for 3COWAL with $l_1 \geq l_2 \geq l_3$.

	(x'_1, x'_2, x'_3)	(x_1, x_2, x_3)	(y_1, y_2, y_3)	$F(y_1, y_2, y_3)$	Condition
A1	$(1-l_1-l_2-l_3, 0, 0)$	$(1-l_2-l_3, l_2, l_3)$	$(1-l_2-l_3, l_2, l_3)$	$w_1 + l_2(-w_1+w_2) + l_3(-w_1+w_3)$	$2l_1 + l_3 \leq 1$
A2	$(0, 1-l_1-l_2-l_3, 0)$	$(l_1, 1-l_1-l_3, l_3)$	$(1-l_1-l_3, l_1, l_3)$	$w_1 + l_1(-w_1+w_2) + l_3(-w_1+w_3)$	$2l_1 + l_3 \geq 1$
A3	$(0, 1-l_1-l_2-l_3, 0)$	$(l_1, 1-l_1-l_3, l_3)$	$(l_1, 1-l_1-l_3, l_3)$	$w_2 + l_1(w_1-w_2) + l_3(-w_2+w_3)$	$2l_1 + l_2 \leq 1$
A4	$(0, 0, 1-l_1-l_2-l_3)$	$(l_1, 1-l_1-l_2, l_2)$	$(1-l_1-l_2, l_1, l_2)$	$w_1 + l_1(-w_1+w_2) + l_2(-w_1+w_3)$	$2l_1 + l_2 \leq 1$
A5	$(0, 0, 1-l_1-l_2-l_3)$	$(l_1, 1-l_1-l_2, l_2)$	$(l_1, 1-l_1-l_2, l_2)$	$w_2 + l_1(w_1-w_2) + l_2(-w_1+w_3)$	$2l_1 + l_2 \geq 1, l_1 + 2l_2 \leq 1$
A6	$(0, 0, 1-l_1-l_2-l_3)$	$(l_1, l_2, 1-l_1-l_2)$	$(l_1, l_2, 1-l_1-l_2)$	$w_3 + l_1(w_1-w_3) + l_2(w_2-w_3)$	$l_1 + 2l_2 \geq 1$
B1	$(\frac{1-2l_1-l_3}{2}, \frac{1-2l_2-l_3}{2}, 0)$	$(\frac{1-l_3}{2}, \frac{1-l_3}{2}, l_3)$	$(\frac{1-l_3}{2}, \frac{1-l_3}{2}, l_3)$	$\frac{1-w_3-l_3+3l_3w_3}{2}$	$l_3 \leq 1/3, 2l_1 + l_3 \leq 1$
B2	$(\frac{1-2l_1-l_2}{2}, 0, \frac{1-l_1-2l_3}{2})$	$(\frac{1-l_2}{2}, l_2, \frac{1-l_2}{2})$	$(\frac{1-l_2}{2}, \frac{1-l_2}{2}, l_2)$	$\frac{1-w_3-l_2+3l_2w_3}{2}$	$l_2 \leq 1/3, 2l_1 + l_2 \leq 1$
B3	$(0, \frac{1-l_1-2l_2}{2}, \frac{1-l_1-2l_3}{2})$	$(l_1, \frac{1-l_1}{2}, \frac{1-l_1}{2})$	$(l_1, \frac{1-l_1}{2}, \frac{1-l_1}{2})$	$\frac{1-w_1-l_1+3l_1w_1}{2}$	$l_1 \geq 1/3, l_1 + 2l_2 \leq 1$
B4	$(1-l_1-2l_2, 0, l_2-l_3)$	$(1-2l_2, l_2, l_2)$	$(1-2l_2, l_2, l_2)$	$w_1 + l_2 - 3l_2 w_1$	$l_2 \leq 1/3, l_1 + 2l_2 \leq 1$
B5	$(0, l_1-l_2, 1-2l_1-l_3)$	$(l_1, l_1, 1-2l_1)$	$(l_1, l_1, 1-2l_1)$	$w_3 + l_1 - 3l_1 w_3$	$l_1 \geq 1/3, 2l_1 + l_3 \leq 1$
C	$(1/3-l_1, 1/3-l_2, 1/3-l_3)$	$(1/3, 1/3, 1/3)$	$(1/3, 1/3, 1/3)$	$1/3$	$l_1 \leq 1/3, l_2 \leq 1/3, l_3 \leq 1/3$

The largest objective function value is that of $A1(1 - l_2 - l_3, l_2, l_3)$ for type A, $B1(\frac{1-l_3}{2}, \frac{1-l_3}{2}, l_3)$ for type B and $C(1/3, 1/3, 1/3)$ for type C. A similar argument shows that

$$F(A1) \geq F(B1) \text{ and } F(A1) \geq F(C).$$

Therefore, for the case of $w_1 \geq w_2 \geq w_3$, the optimal solution for $l_1 \geq l_2 \geq l_3$ is A1. Similarly, the optimal solutions of the remaining five permutations $l_1 \geq l_3 \geq l_2$, $l_2 \geq l_1 \geq l_3$, $l_2 \geq l_3 \geq l_1$, $l_3 \geq l_1 \geq l_2$ and $l_3 \geq l_2 \geq l_1$ can be derived. Detailed optimal solutions are described as follows.

Theorem 2. *For $w_1 \geq w_2 \geq w_3$ and $l_1 + l_2 + l_3 \leq 1$, the optimal solution of 3COWAL is as follows:*

$$(y_1^*, y_2^*, y_3^*) = \begin{cases} (1 - l_2 - l_3, l_2, l_3), & \text{if } l_1 \geq l_2 \geq l_3 \\ (1 - l_2 - l_3, l_3, l_2), & \text{if } l_1 \geq l_3 \geq l_2 \\ (1 - l_1 - l_3, l_1, l_3), & \text{if } l_2 \geq l_1 \geq l_3 \\ (1 - l_1 - l_3, l_3, l_1), & \text{if } l_2 \geq l_3 \geq l_1 \\ (1 - l_1 - l_2, l_1, l_2), & \text{if } l_3 \geq l_1 \geq l_2 \\ (1 - l_1 - l_2, l_2, l_1), & \text{if } l_3 \geq l_2 \geq l_1. \end{cases} \tag{11}$$

4. Maximizing Three-Dimensional Constrained OWA Aggregation Problem with Lower Bounded Variables for $l_1 \geq l_2 \geq l_3$

This section considers the optimal solution behaviors for 3COWAL with $l_1 \geq l_2 \geq l_3$. The main result is described as follows.

Theorem 3. *For $l_1 \geq l_2 \geq l_3$ and $l_1 + l_2 + l_3 \leq 1$, the optimal solution Y^* of 3COWAL is as follows.*

(1) For $w_1 \geq w_2 \geq w_3$ or $w_1 \geq w_3 \geq w_2$, the optimal solution is $A1(1 - l_2 - l_3, l_2, l_3)$.
(2) For $w_2 \geq w_1 \geq w_3$, the optimal solution Y^* is

$$\text{if } 2l_1 + l_3 \geq 1, \text{ then } Y^* = A3(l_1, 1 - l_1 - l_3, l_3) \text{ else } Y^* = B1\left(\frac{1-l_3}{2}, \frac{1-l_3}{2}, l_3\right).$$

(3) For $w_2 \geq w_3 \geq w_1$, the optimal solution Y^* is

$$\text{if } 2l_1 + l_3 \geq 1, \text{ then } Y^* = A3(l_1, 1 - l_1 - l_3, l_3).$$

$$\text{else if } w_3 \leq 1/3 \text{ then } Y^* = B1\left(\frac{1-l_3}{2}, \frac{1-l_3}{2}, l_3\right);$$

$$\text{else if } l_1 \geq 1/3, \text{ then } Y^* = B5(l_1, l_1, 1 - 2l_1) \text{ else } Y^* = C(1/3, 1/3, 1/3).$$

(4) For $w_3 \geq w_1 \geq w_2$, the optimal solution Y^* is

$$\text{if } l_1 + 2l_2 \geq 1, \text{ then } Y^* = A6(l_1, l_2, 1 - l_1 - l_2).$$

$$\text{else if } w_1 \geq 1/3 \text{ then } Y^* = B4\,(1 - 2l_2, l_2, l_2);$$

$$\text{else if } l_1 \geq 1/3 \text{ then } Y^* = B3\left(l_1, \frac{1-l_1}{2}, \frac{1-l_1}{2}\right) \text{ else } Y^* = C(1/3, 1/3, 1/3).$$

(5) For $w_3 \geq w_2 \geq w_1$, the optimal solution Y^* is

$$\text{if } l_1 + 2l_2 \geq 1, \text{ then } Y^* = A6(l_1, l_2, 1 - l_1 - l_2).$$

$$\text{else if } l_1 \geq 1/3, \text{ then } Y^* = B3\left(l_1, \frac{1-l_1}{2}, \frac{1-l_1}{2}\right) \text{ else } Y^* = C(1/3, 1/3, 1/3).$$

Proof. There are six permutations of (w_1, w_2, w_3). From Theorem 2, for $w_1 \geq w_2 \geq w_3$, the optimal solution is A1$(1 - l_2 - l_3, l_2, l_3)$. Similarly, the optimal solution also is A1 for $w_1 \geq w_3 \geq w_2$.

We now consider the case that $w_2 \geq w_1 \geq w_3$. From Table 2, all of the twelve candidates are divided into two categories to obtain optimal solution: (I) A1, A3, A4, A5, A6 and C; (II) A2, B1, B2, B3, B4 and B5. We will show that the largest objective function value is that of A3 $(l_1, 1 - l_1 - l_3, l_3)$ for category I.

Comparing the objective function value of A3 with that of A1, from Theorem 1, since $w_2 \geq w_1 \geq w_3$, we have to compare $s_1 = y_2$, $s_2 = y_1 + y_2$ and $s_3 = y_1 + y_2 + y_3$ with those of $s_1' = y_2'$, $s_2' = y_1' + y_2'$ and $s_3' = y_1' + y_2' + y_3'$. From

$$s_1 = 1 - l_1 - l_3 \geq s_1' = l_2,$$

$$s_2 = 1 - l_3 \geq s_2' = 1 - l_3,$$

$$s_3 = 1 \geq s_3' = 1,$$

the comparison results imply that A3 is superior to A1. Similarly, $F(A3)$ is larger than those of A2, A5, A6 and C. Therefore, the optimal solution for category I is A3. A similar argument shows that the optimal solution for category II is B1 $(\frac{1-l_3}{2}, \frac{1-l_3}{2}, l_3)$. From the conditions of A3 and B1 displayed in Table 2, the optimal solution for $w_2 \geq w_1 \geq w_3$ is A3 for $2l_1 + l_3 \geq 1$, and B1 for $2l_1 + l_3 \leq 1$.

Similarly, for $w_2 \geq w_3 \geq w_1$, $w_3 \geq w_1 \geq w_2$ and $w_3 \geq w_2 \geq w_1$, the optimal solutions can be derived. □

We next present two numerical experiments to evaluate the optimal solutions of 3COWAL with $l_1 \geq l_2 \geq l_3$.

Tables 3 and 4 entries correspond to a pair (S, W) and give the number of different instances of $(l_1, l_2, l_3, w_1, w_2, w_3)$ satisfying type of candidate solution (S) and weight (W). The adopted measure is the number of instances. From Table 2, we adopt twelve types of candidate solutions and six permutations of weight. More precisely, $S \in \{A1, A2, A3, A4, A5, A6, B1, B2, B3, B4, B5, C\}$, $W \in \{w_1 > w_2 > w_3, w_1 > w_3 > w_2, w_2 > w_1 > w_3, w_2 > w_3 > w_1, w_3 > w_1 > w_2, w_3 > w_2 > w_1\}$, $l_i \in \{-lb, -0.9, -0.8, \ldots, lb\}$ and $w_i \in \{0, 0.1, 0.2, \ldots, 1\}$, $i = 1, 2, 3$.

The value of bound lb is $lb = 1$ for Table 3 and $lb = 2$ Table 4. For each weight, the instances $(l_1, l_2, l_3, w_1, w_2, w_3)$ of 3COWAL are 8744 for $lb = 1$ and 57,464 for $lb = 2$. The total instances of 3COWAL are 397,248. An examination of Tables 3 and 4 reveals that the largest number of instances is A1 for $w_1 > w_2 > w_3$ and $w_1 > w_3 > w_2$, B1 for $w_2 > w_1 > w_3$ and $w_2 > w_3 > w_1$, and B3 for $w_3 > w_1 > w_2$ and $w_3 > w_2 > w_1$. Among all the instances of 3COWAL, the zero number is A2, A4, A5 and B2. Therefore, A1, B1 and B3 are superior in the number of the instances, while A2, A4, A5 and B2 are inferior ones for 3COWAL with $l_1 \geq l_2 \geq l_3$.

Table 3. The number of instances satisfying solution type and weight for 3COWAL with $-1 \leq l_3 < l_2 < l_1 \leq 1$.

	(y_1, y_2, y_3)	$w_1 > w_2 > w_3$	$w_1 > w_3 > w_2$	$w_2 > w_1 > w_3$	$w_2 > w_3 > w_1$	$w_3 > w_1 > w_2$	$w_3 > w_2 > w_1$	Total
A1	$(1 - l_2 - l_3, l_2, l_3)$	8744	8744	0	0	0	0	17,488
A2	$(1 - l_1 - l_3, l_1, l_3)$	0	0	0	0	0	0	0
A3	$(l_1, 1 - l_1 - l_3, l_3)$	0	0	1632	1632	0	0	3264
A4	$(1 - l_1 - l_2, l_1, l_2)$	0	0	0	0	0	0	0
A5	$(l_1, 1 - l_1 - l_2, l_2)$	0	0	0	0	0	0	0
A6	$(l_1, l_2, 1 - l_1 - l_2)$	0	0	0	0	1920	1920	3840
B1	$(\frac{1-l_3}{2}, \frac{1-l_3}{2}, l_3)$	0	0	7112	5474	0	0	12,586
B2	$(\frac{1-l_2}{2}, \frac{1-l_2}{2}, l_2)$	0	0	0	0	0	0	0
B3	$(l_1, \frac{1-l_1}{2}, \frac{1-l_1}{2})$	0	0	0	0	3026	3912	6938
B4	$(1 - 2l_2, l_2, l_2)$	0	0	0	0	1614	0	1614
B5	$(l_1, l_1, 1 - 2l_1)$	0	0	0	910	0	0	910
C	$(1/3, 1/3, 1/3)$	0	0	0	728	2184	2912	5824

Table 4. The number of instances satisfying solution type and weight for 3COWAL with $-2 \leq l_3 < l_2 < l_1 \leq 2$.

	(y_1, y_2, y_3)	$w_1 > w_2 > w_3$	$w_1 > w_3 > w_2$	$w_2 > w_1 > w_3$	$w_2 > w_3 > w_1$	$w_3 > w_1 > w_2$	$w_3 > w_2 > w_1$	Total
A1	$(1 - l_2 - l_3, l_2, l_3)$	57,464	57,464	0	0	0	0	114,928
A2	$(1 - l_1 - l_3, l_1, l_3)$	0	0	0	0	0	0	0
A3	$(l_1, 1 - l_1 - l_3, l_3)$	0	0	19,352	19,352	0	0	38,704
A4	$(1 - l_1 - l_2, l_1, l_2)$	0	0	0	0	0	0	0
A5	$(l_1, 1 - l_1 - l_2, l_2)$	0	0	0	0	0	0	0
A6	$(l_1, l_2, 1 - l_1 - l_2)$	0	0	0	0	15,640	17,008	32,648
B1	$(\frac{1-l_3}{2}, \frac{1-l_3}{2}, l_3)$	0	0	38,112	29,004	0	0	67,116
B2	$(\frac{1-l_2}{2}, \frac{1-l_2}{2}, l_2)$	0	0	0	0	0	0	0
B3	$(l_1, \frac{1-l_1}{2}, \frac{1-l_1}{2})$	0	0	0	0	19,566	28,312	47,878
B4	$(1 - 2l_2, l_2, l_2)$	0	0	0	0	10,114	0	10,114
B5	$(l_1, l_1, 1 - 2l_1)$	0	0	0	5060	0	0	5060
C	$(1/3, 1/3, 1/3)$	0	0	0	4048	12,144	12,144	28,336

5. Minimizing Three-Dimensional Constrained OWA Aggregation Problem with Upper Bounded Variables

Consider the minimizing COWAU problem described as follows:

$$\text{Min } W^T Y, \text{ s.t. } \mathcal{I}^T X \geq 1, GY \leq 0, y_i \mathcal{I} - X - MZ_i \leq 0, i = 1, 2, \ldots, n-1, y_n \mathcal{I} - X \leq 0,$$
$$\mathcal{I}^T Z_i \leq n - i, i = 1, 2, \ldots, n-1, Z_{i+1} \leq Z_i, i = 1, 2, \ldots, n-2, Z_i \in \{0, 1\}^n, \quad (12)$$
$$i = 1, 2, \ldots, n-1, X \leq U$$

where the column vector

$$U = \begin{bmatrix} u_1 \\ u_2 \\ \vdots \\ u_n \end{bmatrix}.$$

Using the standard transformations $X' = U - X$, these lead to the following model

$$\text{Min } W^T Y, \text{ s.t. } \mathcal{I}^T X' \leq \mathcal{I}^T U - 1, GY \leq 0, y_i \mathcal{I} + X' - MZ_i \leq U, i = 1, 2, \ldots, n-1,$$
$$y_n \mathcal{I} + X' \leq U, \mathcal{I}^T Z_i \leq n - i, i = 1, 2, \ldots, n-1, Z_{i+1} \leq Z_i, i = 1, 2, \ldots, n-2, \quad (13)$$
$$Z_i \in \{0, 1\}^n, i = 1, 2, \ldots, n-1, X' \geq 0.$$

If $\mathcal{I}^T U - 1 < 0$, we conclude that the COWAU has no feasible solutions. If $\mathcal{I}^T U - 1 = 0$, then $X' = 0$ is the unique optimal solution, so $X = U$.

This section considers 3COWAU for

$$\mathcal{I}^T U - 1 = u_1 + u_2 + u_3 \geq 1. \quad (14)$$

Similar analyses to Sections 3 and 4 can be derived. The results are described as follows.

At optimality, the first constraint of the model (13) becomes

$$x'_1 + x'_2 + x'_3 = u_1 + u_2 + u_3 - 1. \quad (15)$$

There are three types (A', B', C') of (x'_1, x'_2, x'_3) according to the number of zero components.

For 3COWAU with

$$u_1 \geq u_2 \geq u_3, \quad (16)$$

there are six candidate optimal solutions for type A', seven candidate optimal solutions for type B' and one candidate optimal solution for type C'. Detailed results of (x'_1, x'_2, x'_3), (x_1, x_2, x_3), (y_1, y_2, y_3), $F(y_1, y_2, y_3)$ and condition are presented in Table 5.

Table 5. The candidate optimal solutions of (x'_1, x'_2, x'_3), (x_1, x_2, x_3) and (y_1, y_2, y_3), $F(y_1, y_2, y_3)$ and condition for 3COWAU with $u_1 \geq u_2 \geq u_3$.

	(x'_1, x'_2, x'_3)	(x_1, x_2, x_3)	(y_1, y_2, y_3)	$F(y_1, y_2, y_3)$	Condition
A'1	$(u_1 + u_2 + u_3 - 1, 0, 0)$	$(1 - u_2 - u_3, u_2, u_3)$	$(1 - u_2 - u_3, u_2, u_3)$	$w_1 + u_2(-w_1 + w_2) + u_3(-w_1 + w_3)$	$2u_2 + u_3 \leq 1$
A'2	$(u_1 + u_2 + u_3 - 1, 0, 0)$	$(1 - u_2 - u_3, u_2, u_3)$	$(u_2, 1 - u_2 - u_3, u_3)$	$w_2 + u_2(w_1 - w_2) + u_3(-w_2 + w_3)$	$2u_2 + u_3 \geq 1,$ $u_2 + 2u_3 \leq 1$
A'3	$(u_1 + u_2 + u_3 - 1, 0, 0)$	$(1 - u_2 - u_3, u_2, u_3)$	$(u_2, u_3, 1 - u_2 - u_3)$	$w_3 + u_2(w_1 - w_3) + u_3(w_2 - w_3)$	$u_2 + 2u_3 \geq 1, u_2 \geq 1/3$
A'4	$(0, u_1 + u_2 + u_3 - 1, 0)$	$(u_1, 1 - u_1 - u_3, u_3)$	$(u_1, 1 - u_1 - u_3, u_3)$	$w_2 + u_1(w_1 - w_2) + u_3(-w_2 + w_3)$	$u_1 + 2u_3 \leq 1, u_3 \leq 1/3$
A'5	$(0, u_1 + u_2 + u_3 - 1, 0)$	$(u_1, u_3, 1 - u_1 - u_3)$	$(u_1, u_3, 1 - u_1 - u_3)$	$w_3 + u_1(w_1 - w_3) + u_3(w_2 - w_3)$	$u_1 + 2u_3 \geq 1$
A'6	$(0, 0, u_1 + u_2 + u_3 - 1)$	$(u_1, u_2, 1 - u_1 - u_2)$	$(u_1, u_2, 1 - u_1 - u_2)$	$w_3 + u_1(w_1 - w_3) + u_2(w_2 - w_3)$	
B'1	$\left(\frac{2u_1+u_3-1}{2}, \frac{2u_2+u_3-1}{2}, 0\right)$	$\left(\frac{1-u_3}{2}, \frac{1-u_3}{2}, u_3\right)$	$\left(\frac{1-u_3}{2}, \frac{1-u_3}{2}, u_3\right)$	$\frac{1-w_3-u_3+3u_3w_3}{2}$	$u_3 \leq 1/3, 2u_2 + u_3 \geq 1$
B'2	$\left(\frac{2u_1+u_3-1}{2}, \frac{2u_2+u_3-1}{2}, 0\right)$	$\left(\frac{1-u_3}{2}, \frac{1-u_3}{2}, u_3\right)$	$\left(u_3, \frac{1-u_3}{2}, \frac{1-u_3}{2}\right)$	$\frac{1-w_1-u_3+3u_3w_1}{2}$	$u_3 \geq 1/3$
B'3	$\left(\frac{2u_1+u_2-1}{2}, 0, \frac{2u_3+u_2-1}{2}\right)$	$\left(\frac{1-u_2}{2}, u_2, \frac{1-u_2}{2}\right)$	$\left(\frac{1-u_2}{2}, u_2, \frac{1-u_2}{2}\right)$	$\frac{1-w_1-u_2+3u_2w_1}{2}$	$u_2 \geq 1/3, u_2 + 2u_3 \geq 1$
B'4	$\left(0, \frac{2u_2+u_1-1}{2}, \frac{2u_3+u_1-1}{2}\right)$	$\left(u_1, \frac{1-u_1}{2}, \frac{1-u_1}{2}\right)$	$\left(u_1, \frac{1-u_1}{2}, \frac{1-u_1}{2}\right)$	$\frac{1-w_1-u_1+3u_1w_1}{2}$	$u_1 + 2u_3 \geq 1$
B'5	$(u_1 - u_3, u_2 + 2u_3 - 1, 0)$	$(u_3, 1 - 2u_3, u_3)$	$(u_3, u_3, 1 - 2u_3)$	$w_3 + u_3 - 3u_3 w_3$	$u_3 \geq 1/3$
B'6	$(u_1 - u_3, u_2 + 2u_3 - 1, 0)$	$(u_3, 1 - 2u_3, u_3)$	$(1 - 2u_3, u_3, u_3)$	$w_1 + u_3 - 3u_3 w_1$	$u_3 \leq 1/3,$ $u_2 + 2u_3 \geq 1$
B'7	$(u_1 - u_2, 0, 2u_2 + u_3 - 1)$	$(u_2, u_2, 1 - 2u_2)$	$(u_2, u_2, 1 - 2u_2)$	$w_3 + u_2 - 3u_2 w_3$	$u_2 \geq 1/3, 2u_2 + u_3 \geq 1$
C'	$(u_1 - 1/3, u_2 - 1/3, u_3 - 1/3)$	$(1/3, 1/3, 1/3)$	$(1/3, 1/3, 1/3)$	$1/3$	$u_1 \geq 1/3, u_2 \geq 1/3, u_3 \geq 1/3$

Theorem 4. For 3COWAU with $u_1 \geq u_2 \geq u_3$ and $w_1 \geq w_2 \geq w_3$, the smallest objective function value is that of $(y_1, y_2, y_3) = A'1(1 - u_2 - u_3, u_2, u_3)$ for type A', $B'1(\frac{1-u_3}{2}, \frac{1-u_3}{2}, u_3)$ for type B' and $C'(1/3, 1/3, 1/3)$ for type C'.

For 3COWAU with $u_1 \geq u_2 \geq u_3$, the optimal solutions of different permutations of weight are described as follows.

Theorem 5. For 3COWAU with $u_1 \geq u_2 \geq u_3$ and $u_1 + u_2 + u_3 \geq 1$, the optimal solution Y^* is described as follows.

(1) For $w_1 \geq w_2 \geq w_3$, the optimal solution Y^* is

if $u_3 \geq 1/3$, then $Y^* = C'(\frac{1}{3}, \frac{1}{3}, \frac{1}{3})$ else if $2u_2 + u_3 \leq 1$
then $Y^* = A'1(1 - u_2 - u_3, u_2, u_3)$ else $Y^* = B'1(\frac{1-u_3}{2}, \frac{1-u_3}{2}, u_3)$.

(2) For $w_1 \geq w_3 \geq w_2$, the optimal solution Y^* is

if $2u_2 + u_3 \leq 1$, then $Y^* = A'1(1 - u_2 - u_3, u_2, u_3)$.

else if $w_3 \geq 1/3$, then $Y^* = B'7(u_2, u_2, 1 - 2u_2)$;

else if $u_3 \leq 1/3$, then $Y^* = B'1(\frac{1-u_3}{2}, \frac{1-u_3}{2}, u_3)$ else $Y^* = C'(\frac{1}{3}, \frac{1}{3}, \frac{1}{3})$.

(3) For $w_2 \geq w_1 \geq w_3$, the optimal solution Y^* is

if $u_1 + 2u_3 \leq 1$, then $Y^* = A'4(u_1, 1 - u_1 - u_3, u_3)$.

else if $w_1 \leq 1/3$, then $Y^* = B'4(u_1, \frac{1-u_1}{2}, \frac{1-u_1}{2})$;

else if $u_3 \leq 1/3$, then $Y^* = B'6(1 - 2u_3, u_3, u_3)$ else $Y^* = C'(\frac{1}{3}, \frac{1}{3}, \frac{1}{3})$.

(4) For $w_2 \geq w_3 \geq w_1$, the optimal solution Y^* is

if $u_1 + 2u_3 \leq 1$, then $Y^* = A'4(u_1, 1 - u_1 - u_3, u_3)$ else $Y^* = B'4(u_1, \frac{1-u_1}{2}, \frac{1-u_1}{2})$.

(5) For $w_3 \geq w_1 \geq w_2$ and $w_3 \geq w_2 \geq w_1$, the optimal solution is $A'6(u_1, u_2, 1 - u_1 - u_2)$.

To compare the optimal solution behaviors of maximizing 3COWAL with those of minimizing 3COWAU, the performance is shown in Figure 1. The first bar corresponds to the number of optimal solutions of maximizing 3COWAL and second to the minimizing 3COWAU, where the weight type $W[i]$ denotes the ith component of $W = \{w_1 > w_2 > w_3, w_1 > w_3 > w_2, w_2 > w_1 > w_3, w_2 > w_3 > w_1, w_3 > w_1 > w_2, w_3 > w_2 > w_1\}$. The number of optimal solutions of $W[i]$, $i = 1, 2, \ldots, 6$, for maximizing 3COWAL is the same as that of $W[6 - i]$ for minimizing 3COWAU. Therefore, the numbers of optimal solutions for maximizing 3COWAL are same as those of minimizing 3COWAU but in reverse order. The correspondence between the optimal solution of these two mathematical models is worthy of future research.

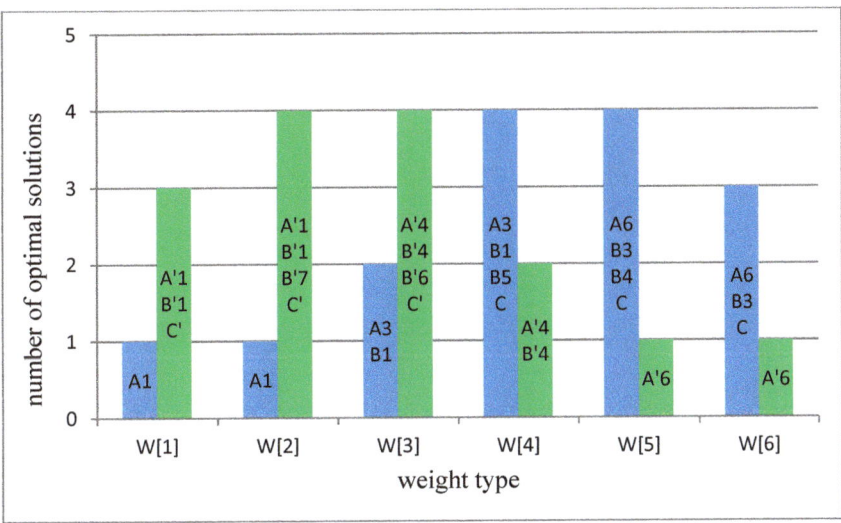

Figure 1. The number of optimal solutions for maximizing 3COWAL and minimizing 3COWAU.

We perform two numerical experiments to evaluate the optimal solution behaviors of 3COWAU with $u_1 \geq u_2 \geq u_3$.

Tables 6 and 7 give the number of different instances $(u_1, u_2, u_3, w_1, w_2, w_3)$ satisfying type of candidate solution (S) and weight (W). More precisely,

$$S \in \{A'1, A'2, \ldots, A'6, B'1, B'2, \ldots, B'7, C'\},$$
$$W \in \{w_1 > w_2 > w_3, w_1 > w_3 > w_2, w_2 > w_1 > w_3, w_2 > w_3 > w_1, w_3 > w_1 > w_2, w_3 > w_2 > w_1\},$$
$$u_i \in \{-ub, -0.9, -0.8, \ldots, ub\} \text{ and } w_i \in \{0, 0.1, 0.2, \ldots, 1\} i = 1, 2, 3.$$

The value of bound ub is $ub = 1$ for Table 6 and $ub = 2$ Table 7. For each weight, the number of the instances of 3COWAU is 8744 for $ub = 1$ and 57,464 for $ub = 2$. The total instances of 3COWAU are 397,248. From Tables 6 and 7, the largest number of instances is $B'1(\frac{1-u_3}{2}, \frac{1-u_3}{2}, u_3)$ for $w_1 > w_2 > w_3$, $A'1 (1 - u_2 - u_3, u_2, u_3)$ for $w_1 > w_3 > w_2$, $A'4 (u_1, 1 - u_1 - u_3, u_3)$ for $w_2 > w_1 > w_3$ and $w_2 > w_3 > w_1$, and $A'6(u_1, u_2, 1 - u_1 - u_2)$ for $w_3 > w_1 > w_2$ and $w_3 > w_2 > w_1$. We also notice that the number of instances is zero for $A'2, A'3, A'5, B'2, B'3$ and $B'5$. Therefore, $A'1, A'4, A'6$ and $B'1$ are the best candidates, while $A'2, A'3, A'5, B'2, B'3$ and $B'5$ are inferior ones for 3COWAU with $u_1 \geq u_2 \geq u_3$.

Table 6. The number of instances satisfying solution type and weight for 3COWAU with $-1 \leq u_3 \leq u_2 \leq u_1 \leq 1$.

	(y_1, y_2, y_3)	$w_1 > w_2 > w_3$	$w_1 > w_3 > w_2$	$w_2 > w_1 > w_3$	$w_2 > w_3 > w_1$	$w_3 > w_1 > w_2$	$w_3 > w_2 > w_1$	Total
A'1	$(1 - u_2 - u_3, u_2, u_3)$	624	624	0	0	0	0	1248
A'2	$(u_2, 1 - u_2 - u_3, u_3)$	0	0	0	0	0	0	0
A'3	$(u_2, u_3, 1 - u_2 - u_3)$	0	0	0	0	0	0	0
A'4	$(u_1, 1 - u_1 - u_3, u_3)$	0	0	912	888	0	0	1800
A'5	$(u_1, u_3, 1 - u_1 - u_3)$	0	0	0	0	0	0	0
A'6	$(u_1, u_2, 1 - u_1 - u_2)$	0	0	0	0	1632	1632	3264
B'1	$(\frac{1-u_3}{2}, \frac{1-u_3}{2}, u_3)$	728	546	0	0	0	0	1274
B'2	$(u_3, \frac{1-u_3}{2}, \frac{1-u_3}{2})$	0	0	0	0	0	0	0
B'3	$(u_2, \frac{1-u_2}{2}, \frac{1-u_2}{2})$	0	0	0	0	0	0	0
B'4	$(u_1, \frac{1-u_1}{2}, \frac{1-u_1}{2})$	0	0	558	744	0	0	1302
B'5	$(u_3, u_3, 1 - 2u_3)$	0	0	0	0	0	0	0
B'6	$(1 - 2u_3, u_3, u_3)$	0	0	92	0	0	0	92
B'7	$(u_2, u_2, 1 - 2u_2)$	0	252	0	0	0	0	252
C'	$(1/3, 1/3, 1/3)$	280	210	70	0	0	0	560

Table 7. The number of instances satisfying solution type and weight for 3COWAU with $-2 \leq u_3 \leq u_2 \leq u_1 \leq 2$.

	(y_1, y_2, y_3)	$w_1 > w_2 > w_3$	$w_1 > w_3 > w_2$	$w_2 > w_1 > w_3$	$w_2 > w_3 > w_1$	$w_3 > w_1 > w_2$	$w_3 > w_2 > w_1$	Total
A'1	$(1 - u_2 - u_3, u_2, u_3)$	9184	9184	0	0	0	0	18,368
A'2	$(u_2, 1 - u_2 - u_3, u_3)$	0	0	0	0	0	0	0
A'3	$(u_2, u_3, 1 - u_2 - u_3)$	0	0	0	0	0	0	0
A'4	$(u_1, 1 - u_1 - u_3, u_3)$	0	0	13,472	13,328	0	0	26,800
A'5	$(u_1, u_3, 1 - u_1 - u_3)$	0	0	0	0	0	0	0
A'6	$(u_1, u_2, 1 - u_1 - u_2)$	0	0	0	0	26,352	26,352	52,704
B'1	$(\frac{1-u_3}{2}, \frac{1-u_3}{2}, u_3)$	11,728	8796	0	0	0	0	20,524
B'2	$(u_3, \frac{1-u_3}{2}, \frac{1-u_3}{2})$	0	0	0	0	0	0	0
B'3	$(u_2, \frac{1-u_2}{2}, \frac{1-u_2}{2})$	0	0	0	0	0	0	0
B'4	$(u_1, \frac{1-u_1}{2}, \frac{1-u_1}{2})$	0	0	9768	13,024	0	0	22,792
B'5	$(u_3, u_3, 1 - 2u_3)$	0	0	0	0	0	0	0
B'6	$(1 - 2u_3, u_3, u_3)$	0	0	1752	0	0	0	1752
B'7	$(u_2, u_2, 1 - 2u_2)$	0	4292	0	0	0	0	4292
C'	$(1/3, 1/3, 1/3)$	5440	4080	1360	0	0	0	10,880

6. Conclusions

This paper presents the optimal solutions for both maximizing 3COWAL and minimizing 3COWAU. For maximizing 3COWAL with $l_1 \geq l_2 \geq l_3$, there are six candidate optimal solutions for type A, five candidate optimal solutions for type B and one candidate optimal solution for type C. Theoretically and empirically, the largest number of instances is A1 $(1 - l_2 - l_3, l_2, l_3)$ for $w_1 > w_2 > w_3$ and $w_1 > w_3 > w_2$, B1 $(\frac{1-l_3}{2}, \frac{1-l_3}{2}, l_3)$ for $w_2 > w_1 > w_3$ and $w_2 > w_3 > w_1$, and B3 $(l_1, \frac{1-l_1}{2}, \frac{1-l_1}{2})$ for $w_3 > w_1 > w_2$ and $w_3 > w_2 > w_1$. For minimizing 3COWAU with $u_1 \geq u_2 \geq u_3$, there are six candidate optimal solutions for type A$'$, seven candidate optimal solutions for type B$'$ and one candidate optimal solution for type C$'$. The largest number of instances is B$'$1 $(\frac{1-u_3}{2}, \frac{1-u_3}{2}, u_3)$ for $w_1 > w_2 > w_3$, A$'$1 $(1 - u_2 - u_3, u_2, u_3)$ for $w_1 > w_3 > w_2$, A$'$4 $(u_1, 1 - u_1 - u_3, u_3)$ for $w_2 > w_1 > w_3$ and $w_2 > w_3 > w_1$, and A$'$6 $(u_1, u_2, 1 - u_1 - u_2)$ for $w_3 > w_1 > w_2$ and $w_3 > w_2 > w_1$. Therefore, the best candidate optimal solutions are A1, B1 and B3 for maximizing 3COWAL with $l_1 \geq l_2 \geq l_3$, and A$'$1, A$'$4, A$'$6 and B$'$1 for minimizing 3COWAU with $u_1 \geq u_2 \geq u_3$.

Extending the analysis to high dimensions is worthy of future research in addition to analysis of the correspondence between the optimal solution of maximizing 3COWAL and minimizing 3COWAU. Thus, the analysis of maximizing COWAL and minimizing COWAU is a subject of considerable ongoing research.

Author Contributions: H.T. analyzed the method and wrote the paper. S.Y. performed the experiments.

Funding: This research received no external funding.

Conflicts of Interest: The authors declare that they have no competing interests.

References

1. Yager, R.R. On ordered weighted averaging aggregation operators in multicriteria decision making. *IEEE Trans. Syst. Man Cybern.* **1988**, *18*, 183–190. [CrossRef]
2. Chaji, A.; Fukuyama, H.; Shiraz, R.K. Selecting a model for generating OWA operator weights in MAGDM problems by maximum entropy membership function. *Comp. Ind. Eng.* **2018**, *124*, 370–378. [CrossRef]
3. De Miguel, L.; Sesma-Sara, M.; Elkano, M.; Asiain, M.; Bustince, H. An algorithm for group decision making using n-dimensional fuzzy sets, admissible orders and OWA operators. *Inf. Fusion* **2017**, *37*, 126–131. [CrossRef]
4. Liu, P.; Wang, Y. Interval neutrosophic prioritized OWA operator and its application to multiple attribute decision making. *J. Syst. Sci. Complex.* **2016**, *29*, 681–697. [CrossRef]
5. Merigó, J.M.; Gil-Lafuente, A.M.; Zhou, L.G.; Chen, H.Y. Induced and linguistic generalized aggregation operators and their application in linguistic group decision making. *Group Decis. Negot.* **2012**, *21*, 531–549. [CrossRef]
6. Zhou, L.; Chen, H.; Liu, J. Generalized multiple averaging operators and their applications to group decision making. *Group Decis. Negot.* **2013**, *22*, 331–358. [CrossRef]
7. Vigier, H.P.; Scherger, V.; Terceño, A. An application of OWA operators in fuzzy business diagnosis. *Appl. Soft Comput.* **2017**, *54*, 440–448. [CrossRef]
8. Yager, R.R. On the analytic representation of the Leximin ordering and its application to flexible constraint propagation. *Eur. J. Oper. Res.* **1997**, *102*, 176–192. [CrossRef]
9. Garg, B.; Garg, R. Enhanced accuracy of fuzzy time series model using ordered weighted aggregation. *Appl. Soft Comput.* **2016**, *48*, 265–280. [CrossRef]
10. Mohammed, E.A.; Naugler, C.T.; Far, B.H. Breast tumor classification using a new OWA operator. *Exp. Syst. Appl.* **2016**, *61*, 302–313. [CrossRef]
11. Yager, R.R.; Beliakov, G. OWA operators in regression problems. *IEEE Trans. Fuzzy Syst.* **2010**, *18*, 106–113. [CrossRef]
12. Ogryczak, W.; Śliwiński, T. On solving linear programs with the ordered weighted averaging objective. *Eur. J. Oper. Res.* **2003**, *148*, 80–91. [CrossRef]
13. Ameri, F.; Zoej, M.J.V.; Mokhtarzade, M. Multi-Criteria, Graph-Based Road Centerline Vectorization Using Ordered Weighted Averaging Operators. *Photogramm. Eng. Remote Sens.* **2016**, *82*, 107–120. [CrossRef]

14. Chen, S.M.; Kuo, L.W. Autocratic decision making using group recommendations based on interval type-2 fuzzy sets, enhanced Karnik–Mendel algorithms, and the ordered weighted aggregation operator. *Inf. Sci.* **2017**, *412*, 174–193. [CrossRef]
15. Carlsson, C.; Fullér, R. Maximal Entropy and Minimal Variability OWA Operator Weights: A Short Survey of Recent Developments. In *Soft Computing Applications for Group Decision-Making and Consensus Modeling*; Mikael, C., Janusz, K., Eds.; Springer: Cham, Switzerland, 2018; pp. 187–199.
16. Emrouznejad, A.; Marra, M. Ordered weighted averaging operators 1988–2014: A citation-based literature survey. *Int. J. Intell. Syst.* **2014**, *29*, 994–1014. [CrossRef]
17. Yager, R.R.; Kacprzyk, J.; Beliakov, G. *Recent Developments in the Ordered Weighted Averaging Operators: Theory and Practice*; Springer: Berlin, Germany, 2011.
18. Yager, R.R. Constrained OWA aggregation. *Fuzzy Sets Syst.* **1996**, *81*, 89–101. [CrossRef]
19. Carlsson, C.; Fullér, R.; Majlender, P. A note on constrained OWA aggregation. *Fuzzy Sets Syst.* **2003**, *139*, 543–546. [CrossRef]
20. Coroianu, L.; Fullér, R. On the constrained OWA aggregation problem with single constraint. *Fuzzy Sets Syst.* **2018**, *332*, 37–43. [CrossRef]
21. Ahn, B.S. Parameterized OWA operator weights: An extreme point approach. *Int. J. Approx. Reason.* **2010**, *51*, 820–831. [CrossRef]
22. Ahn, B.S. A New Approach to Solve the Constrained OWA Aggregation Problem. *IEEE Trans. Fuzzy Syst.* **2017**, *25*, 1231–1238. [CrossRef]
23. Fernández, E.; Pozo, M.A.; Puerto, J.; Scozzari, A. Ordered Weighted Average optimization in Multiobjective Spanning Tree Problem. *Eur. J. Oper. Res.* **2017**, *260*, 886–903. [CrossRef]
24. Fullér, R.; Majlender, P. On obtaining minimal variability OWA operator weights. *Fuzzy Sets Syst.* **2003**, *136*, 203–215. [CrossRef]
25. Kasperski, A.; Zieliński, P. Using the WOWA operator in robust discrete optimization problems. *Int. J. Approx. Reason.* **2016**, *68*, 54–67. [CrossRef]
26. Ogryczak, W.; Olender, P. Ordered median problem with demand distribution weights. *Optim. Lett.* **2016**, *10*, 1071–1086. [CrossRef]
27. Ogryczak, W.; Śliwiński, T. On efficient WOWA optimization for decision support under risk. *Int. J. Approx. Reason.* **2009**, *50*, 915–928. [CrossRef]
28. Chen, Y.F.; Tang, H.C. A Three Dimensional Constrained OWA Aggregation Problem with Lower Bounded Variables. *Symmetry* **2018**, *10*, 339. [CrossRef]

© 2018 by the authors. Licensee MDPI, Basel, Switzerland. This article is an open access article distributed under the terms and conditions of the Creative Commons Attribution (CC BY) license (http://creativecommons.org/licenses/by/4.0/).

Article

Computing The Irregularity Strength of Planar Graphs

Hong Yang [1], Muhammad Kamran Siddiqui [2,*], Muhammad Ibrahim [3] and Sarfraz Ahmad [4] and Ali Ahmad [5]

1. School of Information Science and Engineering, Chengdu University, Chengdu 610106, China; yanghong01@cdu.edu.cn
2. Department of Mathematics, COMSATS University Islamabad, Sahiwal Campus, Sahiwal 57000, Pakistan
3. Center for Advanced Studies in Pure and Applied Mathematics, Bahauddin Zakariya University Multan, Multan 60800, Pakistan; mibtufail@gmail.com
4. Department of Mathematics, COMSATS University Islamabad, Lahore Campus, Lahore 54000, Pakistan; sarfrazahmad@cuilahore.edu.pk
5. College of Computer Science & Information Systems, Jazan University, Jazan 45142, Saudi Arabia; ahmadsms@gmail.com
* Correspondence: kamransiddiqui75@gmail.com

Received: 23 July 2018; Accepted: 27 August 2018; Published: 30 August 2018

Abstract: The field of graph theory plays a vital role in various fields. One of the important areas in graph theory is graph labeling used in many applications such as coding theory, X-ray crystallography, radar, astronomy, circuit design, communication network addressing, and data base management. In this paper, we discuss the totally irregular total k labeling of three planar graphs. If such labeling exists for minimum value of a positive integer k, then this labeling is called totally irregular total k labeling and k is known as the total irregularity strength of a graph G. More preciously, we determine the exact value of the total irregularity strength of three planar graphs.

Keywords: total edge irregularity strength; total vertex irregularity strength; total irregularity strength; planar graph

MSC: 05C12; 05C78; 05C90

1. Introduction

All graphs considered here are finite, undirected, without loops or multiple edges. Denote by $V(G)$ and $E(G)$ the set of vertices and the set of edges of a graph G, respectively. Let $|V(G)| = n$ and $|E(G)| = m$.

A labeling of a graph is any mapping that sends some set of graph elements to a set of numbers or colors. Graph labeling provides valuable information used in several application areas (see [1]). It is interesting to consider labeling the elements of the graph by the elements of a finite field.

For a graph G, we characterize a labeling $\zeta : V \cup E \to \{1, 2, \ldots, k\}$ to be total k-labeling. A total k-labeling is characterized to be an edge irregular total k-labeling of the graph G if for each two distinct edges rs and $r's'$ their weights $\phi(r) + \phi(rs) + \phi(s)$ and $\phi(r') + \phi(r's') + \phi(s')$ are distinct. In addition, total k-labeling is characterized to be a vertex irregular total k-labeling of the graph G if for each two distinctive vertices r and s their weights $wt(r)$ and $wt(s)$ are distinct. Here, the weight of a vertex r in G is the sum of the label of r and the labels of all edges incident with the vertex r. The least k for which the graph G has an edge irregular total k-labeling is called the total irregularity strength of G, represented by $tes(G)$. Analogously, the minimum k for which the graph G has a vertex irregular total k-labeling is called the total vertex irregularity strength of G, denoted by $tvs(G)$.

Chartrand et al. [2] introduced two graph invariants namely irregular assignments and the irregularity strength. Baca et al. [3] modified these graph invariants and introduced the concept of total edge irregularity strength and total vertex irregularity strength for a graph G. A simple lower bound for $tes(G)$ and $tvs(G)$ of a (p,q)—graph G in terms of maximum degree $\Delta(G)$ and the minimum degree $\delta(G)$, determine in the following theorems.

Theorem 1. [3] *Let G be a finite graph with p vertices, q edges and having maximum degree $\Delta = \Delta(G)$, the upper square brackets represent the ceiling function, and then*

$$tes(G) \geq \max\left\{ \left\lceil \frac{q+2}{3} \right\rceil, \left\lceil \frac{\Delta+1}{2} \right\rceil \right\}$$

Theorem 2. [3] *Let G be a finite graph with p vertices, q edges, minimum degree $\delta = \delta(G)$ and maximum degree $\Delta = \Delta(G)$, the upper square brackets represent the ceiling function, and then*

$$\left\lceil \frac{p+\delta}{\Delta+1} \right\rceil \leq tvs(G) \leq p + \Delta - 2\delta + 1$$

In [4], Ivančo and Jendroľ posed the following conjecture:

Conjecture 1. [4] *Let G be a finite graph with p vertices, q edges, different from K_5 with minimum degree $\delta = \delta(G)$, maximum degree $\Delta = \Delta(G)$, the upper square brackets represent the ceiling function, and then*

$$tes(G) = \max\left\{ \left\lceil \frac{q+2}{3} \right\rceil, \left\lceil \frac{\Delta+1}{2} \right\rceil \right\}$$

In [5], Nurdin et al. posed the following conjecture:

Conjecture 2. [5] *Let G be a connected graph having n_i vertices of degree $i (i = \delta, \delta+1, \delta+2, \ldots, \Delta)$, where δ and Δ are the minimum and the maximum degree of G, respectively. Moreover, the upper square brackets represent the ceiling function, and then*

$$tvs(G) = \max\left\{ \left\lceil \frac{\delta + n_\delta}{\delta+1} \right\rceil, \left\lceil \frac{\delta + n_\delta + n_{\delta+1}}{\delta+2} \right\rceil, \ldots, \left\lceil \frac{\delta + \sum_{i=\delta}^{\Delta} n_i}{\Delta+1} \right\rceil \right\}.$$

Conjecture 1 has been shown for complete graphs and complete bipartite graphs [6,7], for hexagonal grid graphs [8], for toroidal grid [9], for generalized prism [10], for strong product of cycles and paths [11], for categorical product of two cycles [12], for zigzag graphs [13] and for strong product of two paths [14].

Conjecture 2 has been verified for for circulant graphs [15].

Combining both total edge irregularity strength and total vertex irregularity strength notions, Marzuki et al. [16] introduced a new irregular total k-labeling of a graph G, which is required to be at the same time both vertex and edge irregular as follows:

Definition 1. *A total labeling $\phi : V \cup E \to \{1, 2, \ldots, k\}$ is called totally irregular total k-labeling of G if every two distinct vertices u and v in $V(G)$ satisfy $wt(u) \neq wt(v)$, and every two distinct edges u_1u_2 and v_1v_2 in $E(G)$ satisfy $wt(u_1u_2) \neq wt(v_1v_2)$, where $wt(u) = \phi(u) + \sum_{uv \in E(G)} \phi(uv)$ and $wt(u_1u_2) = \phi(u_1) + \phi(u_1u_2) + \phi(u_2)$. The minimum k for which a graph G has a totally irregular total k-labeling is called the total irregularity strength of G, denoted by $ts(G)$.*

Marzuki, et al. [16] gave a lower bond of $ts(G)$ as follows:

$$\text{For every graph G,} \quad ts(G) \geq \max\{tes(G), tvs(G)\} \tag{1}$$

Ramdani and Salman [17] showed that the lower bound in Equation (1) for some cartesian product graphs is tight. Besides that, they determined the total irregularity strength of cycles and paths. For more details, see [18–20]. In [21], Ahmad et al. found the exact value of total irregularity strength of generalized Petersen graph.

Example 1. *For illustration, the concept of the* totally irregular total k-labeling, *we give an example from our recent paper [21] in which we show the totally irregular total 10-labeling for generalized Petersen graph $P(9,2)$ (see Figure 1).*

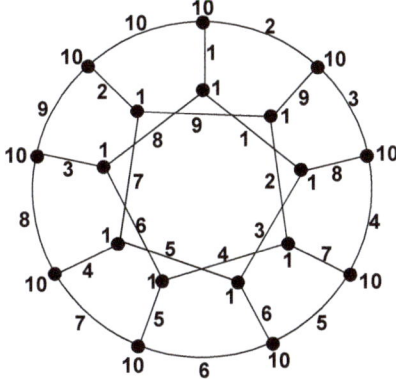

Figure 1. A totally irregular total 10—labeling for $P(9,2)$.

The weights for all vertices and the weights for all edges under the totally irregular total 10-labeling are given in Figure 2.

Now, from Figure 2, it is easy to check that edge weights are different and represented by blue. On the other hand, the vertex weights are different and represented by black.

In this paper, we investigate the total irregularity strength of planar graphs.

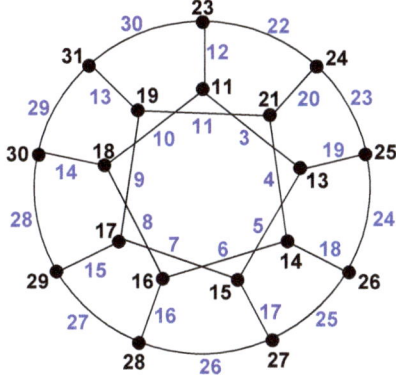

Figure 2. The weights of vertices and edges for $P(9,2)$.

2. The Planar Graph T_n

Siddiqui introduced the planar graph S_n in [22] and computed the $tes(S_n)$, $tvs(S_n)$. The planar graph T_n (see Figure 3) is obtained from the planar graph S_n by adding new edges $x_i y_{i+1}$ and having the same vertex set. The planar graph T_n has

$$V(T_n) = \{x_i; y_i; z_i; 1 \le i \le n\}$$

$$E(T_n) = \{z_i z_{i+1}; y_i y_{i+1} : 1 \le i \le n\} \cup \{x_i y_i; y_i z_i; x_i y_{i+1}; y_{i+1} z_i : 1 \le i \le n\}$$

Clearly, the planar graph T_n has $3n$ vertices and $6n$ edges. More preciously, we call the cycle induced by $\{z_i : 1 \le i \le n\}$ the inner cycle, cycle induced by $\{y_i : 1 \le i \le n\}$ the outer cycle, and the set vertices $\{x_i : 1 \le i \le n\}$, the outer vertices. All subscripts are taken under modulo n. In the next theorem, we determine the total irregularity strength of the planar graph T_n.

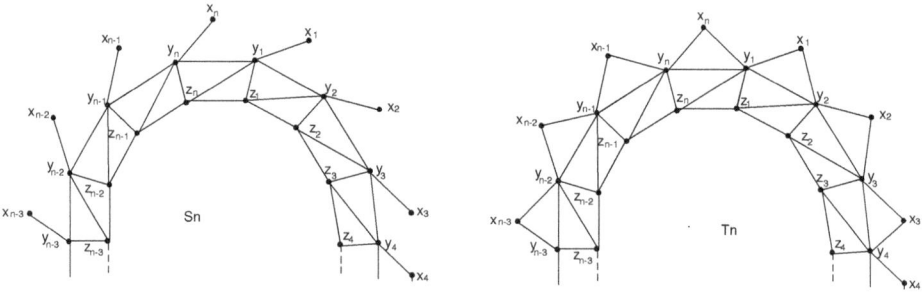

Figure 3. The planar graph S_n and T_n.

Theorem 3. *Let T_n, $n \ge 3$ be a planar graph. Then, $ts(T_n) = \left\lceil \frac{6n+2}{3} \right\rceil$.*

Proof. Since $|E(T_n)| = 6n$, from Theorem 1, $tes(T_n) \ge \left\lceil \frac{6n+2}{3} \right\rceil$. In addition, T_n has n vertices of degree 2, n vertices of degree 4, and n vertices of degree 6; thus, from Theorem 2, we get $tvs(T_n) \ge \left\lceil \frac{2n+2}{4} \right\rceil$. From Equation (1), we get $ts(T_n) \ge \left\lceil \frac{6n+2}{3} \right\rceil$. Now, we show that $ts(T_n) \le \left\lceil \frac{6n+2}{3} \right\rceil$. For this, we define a total labeling ϕ from $V(T_n) \cup E(T_n)$ into $\left\{1, 2, \ldots, \left\lceil \frac{6n+2}{3} \right\rceil\right\}$ and compute the vertex weight and edge weights in the following way. □

Let $k = \left\lceil \frac{6n+2}{3} \right\rceil$. For $1 \le i \le n$, we have

$\phi(x_i) = \phi(y_i) = i$, $\phi(z_i) = k$, $\phi(x_i y_i) = 1$, $\phi(y_i y_{i+1}) = k+1-i$, $\phi(y_i z_i) = n+1$, $\phi(y_{i+1} z_i) = k$,
$wt(x_i y_i) = 2i+1$, $wt(x_i y_{i+1}) = 2i+2$, $wt(y_i z_i) = k+n+1+i$, $wt(y_i) = k+5n+8-i$,

$$\phi(x_i y_{i+1}) = \begin{cases} 1, & \text{for } 1 \le i \le n-1 \\ n+1, & \text{for } i = n \end{cases}$$

$$wt(y_i y_{i+1}) = \begin{cases} k+2+i, & \text{for } 1 \le i \le n-1 \\ k+2, & \text{for } i = n \end{cases}$$

$$\phi(z_i z_{i+1}) = \begin{cases} k+1-i, & \text{for } 1 \leq i \leq n-3 \\ n+3, & \text{for } i = n-2 \\ n+4, & \text{for } i = n-1 \\ n+1, & \text{for } i = n, \ n \text{ is even} \\ n+2, & \text{for } i = n, \ n \text{ is odd} \end{cases}$$

$$wt(y_{i+1}z_i) = \begin{cases} 2k+1+i, & \text{for } 1 \leq i \leq n-1 \\ 2k+1, & \text{for } i = n \end{cases}$$

$$wt(z_i z_{i+1}) = \begin{cases} 3k+1-i, & \text{for } 1 \leq i \leq n-3 \\ 2k+5+i, & \text{for } n-2 \leq i \leq n-1 \\ 2k+2+i, & \text{for } i = n, \ n \text{ is odd} \\ 2k+1+i, & \text{for } i = n, \ n \text{ is even} \end{cases}$$

$$wt(x_i) = \begin{cases} 2+i, & \text{for } 1 \leq i \leq n-1 \\ 2n+2, & \text{for } i = n \end{cases}$$

$$wt(z_i) = \begin{cases} 3k+2n+2, & \text{for } i = 1, \ n \text{ is even} \\ 3k+2n+3, & \text{for } i = 1, \ n \text{ is odd} \\ 2k+5n+6-2i, & \text{for } 2 \leq i \leq n-3 \\ 2k+4n+7-i, & \text{for } n-2 \leq i \leq n \end{cases}$$

Now, the weight of the edges and vertices of T_n under the labeling ϕ are distinct. It is easy to check that there are no two edges of the same weight and there are no two vertices of the same weight. Thus, ϕ is a totally irregular total k-labeling. We conclude that $ts(T_n) = \lceil \frac{6n+2}{3} \rceil$, which complete the proof.

3. The Planar Graph R_n (Pentagonal Circular Ladder)

In [23], Bača defined the prism D_n (Circular ladder) for $n \geq 3$. It is a cubic graph which can be defined as the cartesian product $P_2 \times C_n$ on a path on two vertices with a cycle on n vertices. Prism $D_n, n \geq 3$ is considered of n-cycle $y_1, y_2, y_3, \ldots, y_n$, an inner n-cycle $x_1, x_2, x_3, \ldots, x_n$, and a set of n spokes $y_i z_i, i = 1, 2, \ldots, n$, $|V(D_n)| = 2n$, $|E(D_n)| = 3n$. The planar graph (pentagonal circular ladder) R_n (see Figure 4) is obtained from the graph of prism D_n by adding a new vertex x_i between y_i and y_{i+1}, for $i = 1, 2, 3, \ldots, n$. The planar graph (pentagonal circular ladder) R_n has

$$V(R_n) = \{x_i; y_i; z_i : 1 \leq i \leq n\}$$

$$E(R_n) = \{z_i z_{i+1}; 1 \leq i \leq n\} \cup \{x_i y_i; y_i z_i; x_i y_{i+1}; 1 \leq i \leq n\}$$

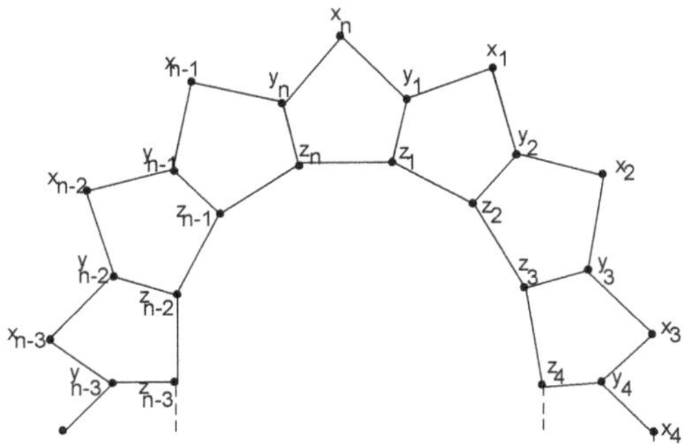

Figure 4. The planar graph R_n (Pentagonal Circular Ladder).

For our purpose, we call the cycle induced by $\{z_i : 1 \leq i \leq n\}$ the inner cycle, and the cycle induced by $\{y_i : 1 \leq i \leq n\} \cup \{x_i : 1 \leq i \leq n\}$ the outer cycle. All subscripts are taken under modulo n. In the next theorem, we determine the total irregularity strength of the planar graph R_n.

Theorem 4. *Let R_n, $n \geq 4$ be a planar graph. Then, $ts(R_n) = \left\lceil \frac{4n+2}{3} \right\rceil$.*

Proof. Since $|E(R_n)| = 4n$, from Theorem 1, $tes(R_n) \geq \left\lceil \frac{4n+2}{3} \right\rceil$. In addition, R_n has n vertices of degree 2, $2n$ vertices of degree 3; thus, from Theorem 2, we get $tvs(T_n) \geq \left\lceil \frac{3n+2}{4} \right\rceil$. From Equation (1), we get $ts(R_n) \geq \left\lceil \frac{4n+2}{3} \right\rceil$. Now, we show that $ts(R_n) \leq \left\lceil \frac{4n+2}{3} \right\rceil$. For this, we define a total labeling ϕ from $V(R_n) \cup E(R_n)$ into $\left\{1, 2, \ldots, \left\lceil \frac{4n+2}{3} \right\rceil\right\}$ and compute the vertex weight and edge weights in the following way. □

Let $k = \lceil \frac{4n+2}{3} \rceil$ and $1 \leq i \leq n$.

For $n = 4$, we have,

$\phi(x_i) = i$, $\phi(y_i) = i$, $\phi(z_i) = k$, $\phi(x_i y_i) = 1$, $\phi(x_1 y_2) = 1$, $\phi(x_2 y_3) = 1$, $\phi(x_3 y_4) = 1$, $\phi(x_4 y_1) = 6$, $\phi(y_1 z_1) = 5$, $\phi(y_2 z_2) = 2$, $\phi(y_3 z_3) = 4$, $\phi(y_4 z_4) = 4$, $\phi(z_i z_{i+1}) = 2 + i$, $wt(x_i y_i) = 1 + 2i$, $wt(x_1 y_2) = 4$, $wt(x_2 y_3) = 6$, $wt(x_3 y_4) = 8$, $wt(x_4 y_1) = 11$, $wt(x_1) = 3$, $wt(x_2) = 4$, $wt(x_3) = 5$, $wt(x_4) = 11$, $wt(y_1) = 13$, $wt(y_2) = 6$, $wt(y_3) = 9$, $wt(y_4) = 10$, $wt(z_1) = 20$, $wt(z_2) = 15$, $wt(z_3) = 19$, $wt(z_4) = 21$,

For $n = 5$, we have,

$\phi(x_i) = i$, $\phi(y_i) = i$, $\phi(z_i) = k - 1$, $\phi(x_i y_i) = 1$, $\phi(x_1 y_2) = 1$, $\phi(x_2 y_3) = 1$, $\phi(x_3 y_4) = 1$, $\phi(x_4 y_5) = 1$, $\phi(x_5 y_1) = 6$, $\phi(y_1 z_1) = 5$, $\phi(y_2 z_2) = 5$, $\phi(y_3 z_3) = 5$, $\phi(y_4 z_4) = 5$, $\phi(y_5 z_5) = 8$, $\phi(z_1 z_2) = 3$, $\phi(z_2 z_3) = 4$, $\phi(z_3 z_3) = 5$, $\phi(z_4 z_4) = 7$, $\phi(z_5 z_5) = 8$, $wt(x_i y_i) = 1 + 2i$, $wt(x_i y_{i+1}) = 2 + 2i$, $wt(x_1) = 3$, $wt(x_2) = 4$, $wt(x_3) = 5$, $wt(x_4) = 6$, $wt(x_5 z) = 12$, $wt(y_1) = 13$, $wt(y_2) = 9$, $wt(y_3) = 10$, $wt(y_4) = 11$, $wt(y_5) = 15$, $wt(z_1) = 23$, $wt(z_2) = 19$, $wt(z_3) = 21$, $wt(z_4) = 24$, $wt(z_5) = 30$,

For $n = 7$, we have,

$\phi(y_i) = i$, $\phi(z_1) = 8$, $\phi(z_2) = 9$, $\phi(z_3) = 10$, $\phi(z_4) = 11$, $\phi(z_5) = 12$, $\phi(z_6) = 13$, $\phi(z_7) = 14$, $\phi(z_8) = 14$, $\phi(z_9) = 14$, $\phi(z_{10}) = 14$, $\phi(z_1 z_2) = 7$, $\phi(z_2 z_3) = 7$, $\phi(z_3 z_4) = 7$, $\phi(z_4 z_5) = 7$, $\phi(z_5 z_6) = 7$, $\phi(z_6 z_7) = 12$, $\phi(z_7 z_8) = 13$, $\phi(z_8 z_9) = 14$, $\phi(z_9 z_{10}) = 12$, $\phi(z_{10} z_1) = 12$, $wt(z_1) = 41$, $wt(z_2) = 37$, $wt(z_3) = 38$, $wt(z_4) = 39$, $wt(z_5) = 40$, $wt(z_6) = 46$, $wt(z_7) = 53$, $wt(z_8) = 55$, $wt(z_9) = 54$, $wt(z_{10}) = 52$, $\phi(y_i z_i) = k$,

$$\phi(x_i) = \begin{cases} i, & \text{for } 1 \leq i \leq n-1 \\ 4, & \text{for } i = n \end{cases}$$

$$wt(x_i) = \begin{cases} 2+i, & \text{for } 1 \leq i \leq n-1 \\ 26, & \text{for } i = n \end{cases}$$

$$wt(y_i) = \begin{cases} 30, & \text{for } i = 1 \\ n+7+i, & \text{for } 2 \leq i \leq n-1 \\ 31, & \text{for } i = n \end{cases}$$

$$\phi(x_i y_i) = \begin{cases} 1, & \text{for } 1 \leq i \leq n-1 \\ k-n+2, & \text{for } i = n \end{cases}$$

$$\phi(x_i y_{i+1}) = \begin{cases} 1, & \text{for } 1 \leq i \leq n-1 \\ k, & \text{for } i = n \end{cases}$$

$$wt(x_iy_i) = \begin{cases} 1+2i, & \text{for } 1 \leq i \leq n-1 \\ 22, & \text{for } i = n \end{cases}$$

$$wt(x_iy_{i+1}) = \begin{cases} 2+2i, & \text{for } 1 \leq i \leq n-1 \\ 21, & \text{for } i = n \end{cases}$$

$$wt(y_iz_i) = \begin{cases} 2i + 2k - \frac{2(n-1)}{3} - 1, & \text{for } 1 \leq i \leq \frac{k}{2} \\ 2k + 1 + i, & \text{for } \frac{k+2}{2} \leq i \leq n \end{cases}$$

$$wt(z_iz_{i+1}) = \begin{cases} 2n + 2 + 2i, & \text{for } 1 \leq i \leq 5 \\ 4n - 1, & \text{for } i = 6 \\ k + 2n + i, & \text{for } i = 7, 8 \\ 4n, & \text{for } i = 9 \\ 3n + 4, & \text{for } i = 10 \end{cases}$$

For $n = 10$, we have,

$\phi(y_i) = i, \phi(z_1) = 6, \phi(z_2) = 7, \phi(z_3) = 8, \phi(z_4) = 9, \phi(z_5) = 10, \phi(z_6) = 10, \phi(z_7) = 10, \phi(z_1z_2) = 5, \phi(z_2z_3) = 5, \phi(z_3z_4) = 5, \phi(z_4z_5) = 10, \phi(z_5z_6) = 10, \phi(z_6z_7) = 8, \phi(z_7z_1) = 8, wt(x_1) = 3, wt(x_2) = 4, wt(x_3) = 5, wt(x_4) = 6, wt(x_5z) = 7, wt(x_6z) = 8, wt(x_7) = 19, wt(y_1) = 22, wt(y_2) = 14, wt(y_3) = 15, wt(y_4) = 16, wt(y_5) = 17, wt(y_6z) = 18, wt(x_7) = 23, wt(z_1) = 29, wt(z_2) = 27, wt(z_3) = 28, wt(z_4) = 34, wt(z_5) = 40, wt(z) = 38, wt(z_7) = 36, \phi(y_iz_i) = k,$

$$\phi(x_i) = \begin{cases} i, & \text{for } 1 \leq i \leq n-1 \\ 6, & \text{for } i = n \end{cases}$$

$$\phi(x_iy_i) = \begin{cases} 1, & \text{for } 1 \leq i \leq n-1 \\ k - n + 2, & \text{for } i = n \end{cases}$$

$$\phi(x_iy_{i+1}) = \begin{cases} 1, & \text{for } 1 \leq i \leq n-1 \\ k, & \text{for } i = n \end{cases}$$

$$wt(x_iy_i) = \begin{cases} 1 + 2i, & \text{for } 1 \leq i \leq n-1 \\ 16, & \text{for } i = n \end{cases}$$

$$wt(x_iy_{i+1}) = \begin{cases} 2 + 2i, & \text{for } 1 \leq i \leq n-1 \\ 15, & \text{for } i = n \end{cases}$$

$$wt(y_iz_i) = \begin{cases} 2i + 2k - \frac{2n}{3} - 1, & \text{for } 1 \leq i \leq \frac{k+2}{2} \\ 2k + i, & \text{for } \frac{k+4}{2} \leq i \leq n \end{cases}$$

$$wt(z_iz_{i+1}) = \begin{cases} 2n + 2 + 2i, & \text{for } 1 \leq i \leq \frac{k}{2} - 2 \\ 3n + 4 + i, & \text{for } \frac{k+2}{2} \leq i \leq n - 2 \\ k + 2n + 4, & \text{for } i = n - 1 \\ k + 2n, & \text{for } i = n \end{cases}$$

For $n \geq 6$ and $n \neq 7, 10$, we have $\phi(y_i) = i, \phi(y_iz_i) = k,$

$$\phi(x_iy_i) = \begin{cases} 1, & \text{for } 1 \leq i \leq n-1 \\ k - n + 2, & \text{for } i = n \end{cases}$$

$$\phi(x_iy_{i+1}) = \begin{cases} 1, & \text{for } 1 \leq i \leq n-1 \\ k, & \text{for } i = n \end{cases}$$

Case 1. *when* $n \equiv 0 \pmod{3}$

$$\phi(x_i) = \begin{cases} i, & \text{for } 1 \leq i \leq n-1 \\ \frac{k-3}{2}, & \text{for } i = n \end{cases}$$

$$\phi(z_i) = \begin{cases} k - \frac{2n}{3} - 1 + i, & \text{for } 1 \leq i \leq \frac{k+1}{2} \\ k, & \text{for } \frac{k+3}{2} \leq i \leq n \end{cases}$$

$$\phi(z_i z_{i+1}) = \begin{cases} \frac{k+1}{2}, & \text{for } 1 \leq i \leq \frac{k+1}{2} - 2 \\ n+2, & \text{for } i = \frac{k+1}{2} - 1 \\ k - n + i, & \text{for } \frac{k+1}{2} \leq i \leq n-1 \\ k-1, & \text{for } i = n \end{cases}$$

$$wt(x_i) = \begin{cases} i+2, & \text{for } 1 \leq i \leq n-1 \\ 3k - \frac{5n}{3}, & \text{for } i = n \end{cases}$$

$$wt(y_i) = \begin{cases} 2k+2, & \text{for } i = 1 \\ 4(k-n) - 1 + i, & \text{for } 2 \leq i \leq n-1 \\ 2k+3, & \text{for } i = n \end{cases}$$

$$wt(z_i) = \begin{cases} \frac{7(k+1)}{2} - \frac{2n}{3} - 4, & \text{for } i = 1 \\ 3k - \frac{2n}{3} + i, & \text{for } 2 \leq i \leq \frac{k-3}{2} \\ \frac{5(k+1)}{2} + n - 1, & \text{for } i = \frac{k-1}{2} \\ 3k + 2 + i, & \text{for } \frac{k+1}{2} \leq i \leq \frac{k+3}{2} \\ 4(k-1) - 2n + 3 + 2i, & \frac{k+5}{2} \leq i \leq n-1 \\ 4k-2, & \text{for } i = n \end{cases}$$

$$wt(x_i y_i) = \begin{cases} 2i+1, & \text{for } 1 \leq i \leq n-1 \\ 2k - \frac{2n}{3}, & \text{for } i = n \end{cases}$$

$$wt(x_i y_{i+1}) = \begin{cases} 2i+2, & \text{for } 1 \leq i \leq n-1 \\ 2k - \frac{2n}{3} - 1, & \text{for } i = n \end{cases}$$

$$wt(y_i z_i) = \begin{cases} 2i + 2k - \frac{2n}{3} - 1, & \text{for } 1 \leq i \leq \frac{k+1}{2} - 1 \\ 2k + i, & \text{for } \frac{k+1}{2} \leq i \leq n \end{cases}$$

$$wt(z_i z_{i+1}) = \begin{cases} 2n + 2 + 2i, & \text{for } 1 \leq i \leq \frac{k+1}{2} - 2 \\ 3n + 3 + i, & \text{for } \frac{k+1}{2} - 1 \leq i \leq n-1 \\ k + 2n + 1, & \text{for } i = n \end{cases}$$

Case 2. *when* $n \equiv 1 \pmod{3}$

$$\phi(x_i) = \begin{cases} i, & \text{for } 1 \leq i \leq n-1 \\ k - \frac{(2n+1)}{3} - 1, & \text{for } i = n \end{cases}$$

$$\phi(z_i) = \begin{cases} k - \frac{2n+1}{3} + i, & \text{for } 1 \leq i \leq \frac{k}{2} \\ k, & \text{for } \frac{k}{2} + 1 \leq i \leq n \end{cases}$$

$$\phi(z_i z_{i+1}) = \begin{cases} \frac{k}{2}, & \text{for } 1 \leq i \leq \frac{k}{2} - 2 \\ n+2, & \text{for } i = \frac{k}{2} - 1 \\ k - n + 1 + i, & \text{for } \frac{k}{2} \leq i \leq n-1 \\ k-2, & \text{for } i = n \end{cases}$$

$$wt(x_i) = \begin{cases} i+2, & \text{for } 1 \le i \le n-1 \\ 3k - \frac{5n+1}{3} + 1, & \text{for } i = n \end{cases}$$

$$wt(y_i) = \begin{cases} 2k+2, & \text{for } i = 1 \\ 4(k-n)+i, & \text{for } 2 \le i \le n-1 \\ 2k+3, & \text{for } i = n \end{cases}$$

$$wt(z_i) = \begin{cases} \frac{7k}{2} - \frac{2n+1}{3} - 1, & \text{for } i = 1 \\ 3k - \frac{2n+1}{3} + i, & \text{for } 2 \le i \le \frac{k}{2} - 2 \\ \frac{5k}{2} + n + 1, & \text{for } i = \frac{k}{2} - 1 \\ 3k + 3 + i, & \text{for } \frac{k}{2} \le i \le \frac{k}{2} + 1 \\ 4k - 2n + 1 + 2i, & \text{for } \frac{k}{2} + 2 \le i \le n-1 \\ 4k - 2, & \text{for } i = n \end{cases}$$

$$wt(x_i y_i) = \begin{cases} 2i+1, & \text{for } 1 \le i \le n-1 \\ 2k - \frac{2n+1}{3} + 1, & i = n. \end{cases}$$

$$wt(x_i y_{i+1}) = \begin{cases} 2i+2, & 1 \le i \le n-1 \\ 2k - \frac{2n+1}{3}, & \text{for } i = n \end{cases}$$

$$wt(y_i z_i) = \begin{cases} 2i + 2k - \frac{2n+1}{3}, & \text{for } 1 \le i \le \frac{k}{2} \\ 2k + i, & \text{for } \frac{k}{2} + 1 \le i \le n \end{cases}$$

$$wt(z_i z_{i+1}) = \begin{cases} 2n + 2 + 2i, & \text{for } 1 \le i \le \frac{k}{2} - 2 \\ 3n + 3 + i, & \text{for } \frac{k}{2} - 1 \le i \le n-1 \\ k + 2n, & \text{for } i = n \end{cases}$$

Case 3. *when* $n \equiv 2 \pmod{3}$

$$\phi(x_i) = \begin{cases} i, & \text{for } 1 \le i \le n-1 \\ \frac{k-4}{2}, & \text{for } i = n \end{cases}$$

$$\phi(z_i) = \begin{cases} k - \frac{2n+2}{3} - 1 + i, & \text{for } 1 \le i \le \frac{k+2}{2} \\ k, & \text{for } \frac{k+4}{2} \le i \le n \end{cases}$$

$$\phi(z_i z_{i+1}) = \begin{cases} \frac{k}{2} + 1, & \text{for } 1 \le i \le \frac{k}{2} - 1 \\ n + 2, & \text{for } i = \frac{k}{2} \\ k - n - 1 + i, & \text{for } \frac{k}{2} + 1 \le i \le n-1 \\ k, & \text{for } i = n \end{cases}$$

$$wt(x_i) = \begin{cases} i+2, & \text{for } 1 \le i \le n-1 \\ 3k - \frac{5n+5}{3} + 1, & \text{for } i = n \end{cases}$$

$$wt(y_i) = \begin{cases} 2k+2, & \text{for } i = 1 \\ 4(k-n) - 2 + i, & \text{for } 2 \le i \le n-1 \\ 2k+3, & \text{for } i = n \end{cases}$$

$$wt(z_i) = \begin{cases} \frac{7k}{2} - \frac{2(n+1)}{3} + 1, & \text{for } i = 1 \\ 3k - \frac{2(n+1)}{3} + 1 + i, & \text{for } 2 \le i \le \frac{k}{2} - 1 \\ \frac{5k}{2} + n + 2, & \text{for } i = \frac{k}{2} \\ 3k + 2 + i, & \text{for } \frac{k}{2} + 1 \le i \le \frac{k}{2} + 2 \\ 4k - 2n - 1 + 2i, & \text{for } \frac{k}{2} + 3 \le i \le n-1 \\ 4k - 2, & \text{for } i = n \end{cases}$$

$$wt(x_iy_i) = \begin{cases} 2i+1, & \text{for } 1 \leq i \leq n-1 \\ 2k + \frac{2n+2}{3}, & \text{for } i = n \end{cases}$$

$$wt(x_iy_{i+1}) = \begin{cases} 2i+2, & \text{for } 1 \leq i \leq n-1 \\ 2k - \frac{2n+2}{3} - 1, & \text{for } i = n \end{cases}$$

$$wt(y_iz_i) = \begin{cases} 2i + 2k - \frac{2n+2}{3} - 1, & \text{for } 1 \leq i \leq \frac{k}{2} \\ 2k + i, & \text{for } \frac{k}{2} + 1 \leq i \leq n \end{cases}$$

$$wt(z_iz_{i+1}) = \begin{cases} 2n+2+2i, & \text{for } 1 \leq i \leq \frac{k}{2} - 1 \\ 3n+3+i, & \text{for } \frac{k}{2} \leq i \leq n-1 \\ k+2n+2, & \text{for } i = n \end{cases}$$

The weight of the edges and vertices under the labeling ϕ are distinct. It is easy to check that there are no two edges of the same weight and there are no two vertices of the same weight. Thus, ϕ is a totally irregular total k-labeling. We conclude that $ts(R_n) = \lceil \frac{4n+2}{3} \rceil$, which complete the proof.

4. The Planar Graph Q_n

In [23], Bača defined the planar graph (pentagonal circular ladder) R_n. The planar graph Q_n (see Figure 5) is obtained from the planar graph (pentagonal circular ladder) R_n by adding new edges $y_iy_{i+1}, z_iw_i, w_iw_{i+1}$. The planar graph Q_n has

$$V(Q_n) = \{x_i; y_i; z_i; w_i : 1 \leq i \leq n\}$$

$$E(Q_n) = \{y_iy_{i+1}; w_iw_{i+1}; z_iz_{i+1}; x_iy_i; x_iy_{i+1}; y_iz_i; z_iw_i : 1 \leq i \leq n\}$$

The planar graph Q_n has $4n$ vertices and $7n$ edges. For our purpose, we call the cycle induced by $\{w_i : 1 \leq i \leq n\}$ the inner cycle, the cycle induced by $\{z_i : 1 \leq i \leq n\}$ the middle cycle, the cycle induced by $\{y_i : 1 \leq i \leq n\}$ the outer cycle, and the set of vertices $\{x_i : 1 \leq i \leq n\}$ the set of outer vertices. The subscript $n+1$ must be replaced by 1.

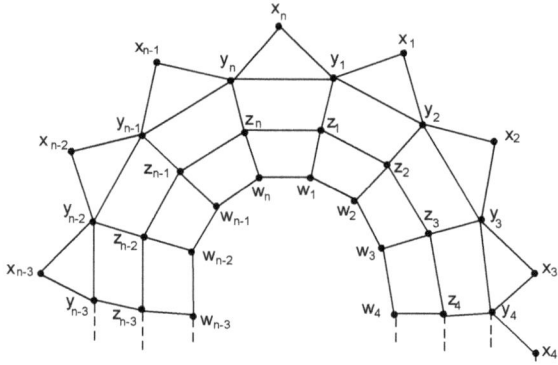

Figure 5. The planar graph Q_n.

Theorem 5. Let Q_n, $n \geq 4$ be a planar graph. Then, $ts(Q_n) = \lceil \frac{7n+2}{3} \rceil$.

Proof. Since $|E(Q_n)| = 7n$, from Theorem 1 $tes(Q_n) \geq \lceil \frac{7n+2}{3} \rceil$. In addition, Q_n has n vertices of degree 2, n vertices of degree 3, n vertices of degree 4 and n vertices of degree 5; thus, from Theorem 2, we get $tvs(Q_n) \geq \lceil \frac{4n+2}{6} \rceil$. From Equation (1), we get $ts(Q_n) \geq \lceil \frac{7n+2}{3} \rceil$. Now, we show that $ts(Q_n) \leq \lceil \frac{7n+2}{3} \rceil$.

For this, we define a total labeling ϕ from $V(Q_n) \cup E(Q_n)$ into $\left\{1, 2, \ldots, \left\lceil \frac{7n+2}{3} \right\rceil \right\}$ and compute the vertex weight and edge weights in the following way. □

Let $k = \lceil \frac{7n+2}{3} \rceil$ and $1 \leq i \leq n$,

$\phi(x_i) = i$, $\phi(y_i) = i$, $\phi(z_i) = k$, $\phi(x_i y_i) = 1$, $wt(x_i y_i) = 1 + 2i$, $wt(x_i y_{i+1}) = 2 + 2i$, $wt(y_i z_i) = 4n + 2 + i$, $wt(y_i y_{i+1}) = 2n + 2 + i$, $wt(w_i w_{i+1}) = 3n + 2 + i$,

$$\phi(x_i y_{i+1}) = \begin{cases} 1, & \text{for } 1 \leq i \leq n-1 \\ n+1, & \text{for } i = n \end{cases}$$

$$\phi(y_i y_{i+1}) = \begin{cases} 2n+1-i, & \text{for } 1 \leq i \leq n-1 \\ 2n+1, & \text{for } i = n \end{cases}$$

$$\phi(w_i w_{i+1}) = \begin{cases} i, & \text{for } 1 \leq i \leq n, \ n \text{ is even} \\ i+1, & \text{for } 1 \leq i \leq n, \ n \text{ is odd} \end{cases}$$

$$wt(x_i) = \begin{cases} 2+i, & \text{for } 1 \leq i \leq n-1 \\ 2n+2, & \text{for } i = n \end{cases}$$

Case 1. when $n \equiv 0 \pmod{6}$ and $1 \leq i \leq n$

$\phi(w_i) = \frac{3n}{2} + 1$, $\phi(y_i z_i) = \frac{5n}{3} + 1$, $\phi(z_i z_{i+1}) = \frac{4n}{3} + i$, $wt(z_i z_{i+1}) = 2k + \frac{4n}{3} + i$, $wt(z_i) = \frac{53n}{6} + 3 + i$, $wt(w_i) = \frac{11n}{3} + 2 + i$,

$$\phi(z_i w_i) = \begin{cases} \frac{7n}{6} + 1, & \text{for } i = 1 \\ \frac{13n}{6} + 2 - i, & \text{for } 2 \leq i \leq n \end{cases}$$

$$wt(z_i w_i) = \begin{cases} k + \frac{8n}{3} + 2, & \text{for } i = 1 \\ k + \frac{11n}{3} + 3 - i, & \text{for } 2 \leq i \leq n \end{cases}$$

$$wt(y_i) = \begin{cases} \frac{20n}{3} + 5, & \text{for } i = 1 \\ \frac{17n}{3} + 6 - i, & \text{for } 2 \leq i \leq n-1 \\ \frac{17n}{3} + 6, & \text{for } i = n \end{cases}$$

Case 2. when $n \equiv 1 \pmod{6}$ and $1 \leq i \leq n$

$\phi(w_i) = \frac{3(n-1)}{2} + 2$, $\phi(y_i z_i) = \frac{5(n-1)}{3} + 3$, $\phi(z_i z_{i+1}) = \frac{4(n-1)}{3} + 2 + i$, $wt(z_i z_{i+1}) = 2k + \frac{4(n-1)}{3} + 2 + i$, $wt(z_i) = \frac{53(n-1)}{6} + 14 + i$, $wt(w_i) = \frac{11(n-1)}{3} + 8 + i$,

$$\phi(z_i w_i) = \begin{cases} \frac{7(n-1)}{6} + 3, & \text{for } i = 1 \\ \frac{13(n-1)}{6} + 5 - i, & \text{for } 2 \leq i \leq n \end{cases}$$

$$wt(z_i w_i) = \begin{cases} k + \frac{8(n-1)}{3} + 5, & \text{for } i = 1 \\ k + \frac{11(n-1)}{3} + 7 - i, & \text{for } 2 \leq i \leq n \end{cases}$$

$$wt(y_i) = \begin{cases} \frac{20(n-1)}{3} + 12, & \text{for } i = 1 \\ \frac{17(n-1)}{3} + 12 - i, & \text{for } 2 \leq i \leq n-1 \\ \frac{17(n-1)}{3} + 12, & \text{for } i = n \end{cases}$$

Case 3. when $n \equiv 2 \pmod{6}$ and $1 \leq i \leq n$

$\phi(w_i) = \frac{3(n-2)}{2} + 4, \phi(y_iz_i) = \frac{5(n-2)}{3} + 4, \phi(z_iz_{i+1}) = \frac{4(n-2)}{3} + 2 + i, wt(z_iz_{i+1}) = 2k + \frac{4(n-2)}{3} + 2 + i,$
$wt(z_i) = \frac{53(n-2)}{6} + 19 + i, wt(w_i) = \frac{11(n-2)}{3} + 9 + i,$

$$\phi(z_iw_i) = \begin{cases} \frac{7(n-2)}{6} + 3, & \text{for } i = 1 \\ \frac{13(n-2)}{6} + 6 - i, & \text{for } 2 \le i \le n \end{cases}$$

$$wt(z_iw_i) = \begin{cases} k + \frac{8(n-2)}{3} + 7, & \text{for } i = 1 \\ k + \frac{11(n-2)}{3} + 10 - i, & \text{for } 2 \le i \le n \end{cases}$$

$$wt(y_i) = \begin{cases} \frac{20(n-2)}{3} + 18, & \text{for } i = 1 \\ \frac{17(n-2)}{3} + 17 - i, & \text{for } 2 \le i \le n-1 \\ \frac{17(n-2)}{3} + 17, & \text{for } i = n \end{cases}$$

Case 4. *when $n \equiv 3 \pmod{6}$ and $1 \le i \le n$*

$\phi(w_i) = \frac{3(n-3)}{2} + 5, \phi(y_iz_i) = \frac{5(n-3)}{3} + 6, \phi(z_iz_{i+1}) = \frac{4(n-2)}{3} + 4 + i, wt(z_iz_{i+1}) = 2k + \frac{4(n-3)}{3} + 4 + i,$
$wt(z_i) = \frac{53(n-3)}{6} + 30 + i, wt(w_i) = \frac{11(n-3)}{3} + 15 + i,$

$$\phi(z_iw_i) = \begin{cases} \frac{7(n-3)}{6} + 5, & \text{for } i = 1 \\ \frac{13(n-3)}{6} + 9 - i, & \text{for } 2 \le i \le n \end{cases}$$

$$wt(z_iw_i) = \begin{cases} k + \frac{8(n-3)}{3} + 10, & \text{for } i = 1 \\ k + \frac{11(n-3)}{3} + 14 - i, & \text{for } 2 \le i \le n \end{cases}$$

$$wt(y_i) = \begin{cases} \frac{20(n-3)}{3} + 25, & \text{for } i = 1 \\ \frac{17(n-3)}{3} + 23 - i, & \text{for } 2 \le i \le n-1 \\ \frac{17(n-3)}{3} + 23, & \text{for } i = n \end{cases}$$

Case 5. *when $n \equiv 4 \pmod{6}$ and $1 \le i \le n$*

$\phi(w_i) = \frac{3(n-4)}{2} + 7, \phi(y_iz_i) = \frac{5(n-4)}{3} + 8, \phi(z_iz_{i+1}) = \frac{4(n-4)}{3} + 6 + i, wt(z_iz_{i+1}) = 2k + \frac{4(n-4)}{3} + 6 + i,$
$wt(z_i) = \frac{53(n-4)}{6} + 40 + i, wt(w_i) = \frac{11(n-4)}{3} + 17 + i,$

$$\phi(z_iw_i) = \begin{cases} \frac{7(n-4)}{6} + 6, & \text{for } i = 1 \\ \frac{13(n-4)}{6} + 11 - i, & \text{for } 2 \le i \le n \end{cases}$$

$$wt(z_iw_i) = \begin{cases} k + \frac{8(n-4)}{3} + 13, & \text{for } i = 1 \\ k + \frac{11(n-4)}{3} + 18 - i, & \text{for } 2 \le i \le n \end{cases}$$

$$wt(y_i) = \begin{cases} \frac{20(n-4)}{3} + 32, & \text{for } i = 1 \\ \frac{17(n-4)}{3} + 29 - i, & \text{for } 2 \le i \le n-1 \\ \frac{17(n-4)}{3} + 29, & \text{for } i = n \end{cases}$$

Case 6. *when $n \equiv 5 \pmod{6}$ and $1 \le i \le n$*

$\phi(w_i) = \frac{3(n-5)}{2} + 8, \phi(y_iz_i) = \frac{5(n-5)}{3} + 9, \phi(z_iz_{i+1}) = \frac{4(n-5)}{3} + 6 + i, wt(z_iz_{i+1}) = 2k + \frac{4(n-5)}{3} + 6 + i,$
$wt(z_i) = \frac{53(n-5)}{6} + 46 + i, wt(w_i) = \frac{11(n-5)}{3} + 22 + i,$

$$\phi(z_iw_i) = \begin{cases} \frac{7(n-5)}{6} + 7, & \text{for } i = 1 \\ \frac{13(n-5)}{6} + 13 - i, & \text{for } 2 \le i \le n \end{cases}$$

$$wt(z_iw_i) = \begin{cases} k + \frac{8(n-5)}{3} + 15, & \text{for } i = 1 \\ k + \frac{11(n-5)}{3} + 21 - i, & \text{for } 2 \leq i \leq n \end{cases}$$

$$wt(y_i) = \begin{cases} \frac{20(n-5)}{3} + 38, & \text{for } i = 1 \\ \frac{17(n-5)}{3} + 34 - i, & \text{for } 2 \leq i \leq n-1 \\ \frac{17(n-5)}{3} + 34, & \text{for } i = n \end{cases}$$

The weight of the edges and vertices of S_n under the labeling ϕ are distinct. It is easy to check that there are no two edges of the same weight and there are no two vertices of the same weight. Thus, ϕ is a totally irregular total $k-$labeling. We conclude that $ts(Q_n) = \lceil \frac{7n+2}{3} \rceil$, which completes the proof.

5. Conclusions

In this paper, we discuss the total edge irregular k labeling, total vertex irregular k labeling and totally irregular total k labeling of planar graphs. We provide exact result of total irregularity strength ts for the planar graph T_n, the planar graph R_n (Pentagonal Circular Ladder) and the planar graph Q_n. In the future, we are interested in computing the total irregularity strength ts for the other planar graphs.

Author Contributions: H.Y. contribute for supervision, project administration, funding and analyzed the data curation. M.K.S. contribute for designing the experiments, validation, conceptualization. M.I. contribute for formal analysing experiments, resources, software and some computations. S.A and A.A. contribute for Investigation, Methodology and wrote the initial draft of the paper. M.K.S. investigated the initial draft and wrote the final draft. All authors read and approved the final version of the paper.

Funding: This work was supported by the Soft Scientific Research Foundation of Sichuan Province under grant 2018ZR0265, Project of Sichuan Military and Civilian Integration Strategy Research Center under grant JMRH-1818, and Key Project of Sichuan Provincial Department of Education under grant 18ZA0118.

Acknowledgments: The authors are grateful to the anonymous referees for their valuable comments and suggestions that improved this paper.

Conflicts of Interest: The authors declare no conflict of interest.

References

1. Gallian, J. A dynamic survey of graph labeling. *Electron. J. Comb.* **2009**, *16*, 1–442.
2. Chartrand, G.; Jacobson, M.S.; Lehel, J.; Oellermann, O.R.; Ruiz, S.; Saba, F. Irregular networks. *Congr. Numer.* **1988**, *64*, 187–192.
3. Bača, M.; Jendrol, S.; Miller, M.; Ryan, J. On irregular total labellings. *Discret. Math.* **2007**, *307*, 1378–1388. [CrossRef]
4. Ivančo, J.; Jendrol, S. Total edge irregularity strength of trees. *Discuss. Math. Graph Theory* **2006**, *26*, 449–456.
5. Nurdin; Baskoro, E.T.; Salman, A.N.M.; Gaos, N.N. On total vertex irregularity strength of trees. *Discret. Math.* **2010**, *310*, 3043–3048. [CrossRef]
6. Jendrol', S.; Miškuf, J.; Soták, R. Total edge irregularity strength of complete graphs and complete bipartite graphs. *Electron. Notes Discret. Math.* **2007**, *28*, 281–285. [CrossRef]
7. Jendrol', S.; Miškuf, J.; Soták, R. Total edge irregularity strength of complete graphs and complete bipartite graphs. *Discret. Math.* **2010**, *310*, 400–407. [CrossRef]
8. Al-Mushayt, O.; Ahmad, A.; Siddiqui, M.K. On the total edge irregularity strength of hexagonal grid graphs. *Australas. J. Comb.* **2012**, *53*, 263–271.
9. Chunling, T.; Xiaohui, L.; Yuansheng, Y.; Liping, W. Irregular total labellings of grids. *Utilitas Math.* **2010**, *81*, 3–13.
10. Bača, M.; Siddiqui, M.K. Total edge irregularity strength of generalized prism. *Appl. Math. Comput.* **2014**, *235*, 168–173. [CrossRef]
11. Ahmad, A.; Al Mushayt, O.; Siddiqui, M.K. Total edge irregularity strength of strong product of cycles and paths. *UPB Sci. Bull. Ser. A* **2014**, *76*, 147–156.
12. Ahmad, A.; Bača, M.; Siddiqui, M.K. On edge irregular total labeling of categorical product of two cycles. *Theory Comp. Syst.* **2014**, *54*, 1–12. [CrossRef]

13. Ahmad, A.; Siddiqui, M.K.; Afzal, D. On the total edge irregularity strength of zigzag graphs. *Australas. J. Comb.* **2012**, *54*, 141–149.
14. Ahmad, A.; Bača, M.; Bashir, Y.; Siddiqui, M.K. Total edge irregularity strength of strong product of two paths. *Ars Comb.* **2012**, *106*, 449–459.
15. Anholcer, M.; Palmer, C. Irregular labelings of circulant graphs. *Discret. Math.* **2012**, *312*, 3461–3466. [CrossRef]
16. Marzuki, C.C.; Salman, A.N.M.; Miller, M. On the total irregularity strength on cycles and paths. *Far East J. Math. Sci.* **2013**, *82*, 1–21.
17. Ramdani, R.; Salman, A.N.M. On the total irregularity strength of some cartesian product graphs. *AKCE Int. J. Graphs Comb.* **2013**, *10*, 199–209.
18. Bača, M.; Siddiqui, M.K. On total edge irregularity strength of strong product of two cycles. *Utilitas Math.* **2017**, *104*, 255–275.
19. Siddiqui, M.K.; Afzal, D.; Faisal, M.R. Total edge irregularity strength of accordion graphs. *J. Comb. Optim.* **2017**, *34*, 534–544. [CrossRef]
20. Siddiqui, M.K.; Miller, M.; Ryan, J. Total edge irregularity strength of octagonal grid graph. *Utilitas Math.* **2017**, *103*, 277–287.
21. Ahmad, A.; Siddiqui, M.K.; Ibrahim, M.; Asif, M. On the total irregularity strength of Generalized Petersen Graph. *Math. Rep.* **2016**, *68*, 139–147.
22. Siddiqui, M.K. On irregularity strength of convex polytope graphs with certain pendent edges added. *Ars Comb.* **2016**, *129*, 199–210.
23. Bača, M. Labeling of two classes of convex polytopes. *Utilitas Math.* **1998**, *34*, 24–31.

 © 2018 by the authors. Licensee MDPI, Basel, Switzerland. This article is an open access article distributed under the terms and conditions of the Creative Commons Attribution (CC BY) license (http://creativecommons.org/licenses/by/4.0/).

Article

Computing Topological Indices and Polynomials for Line Graphs

Shahid Imran [1], Muhammad Kamran Siddiqui [2,*], Muhammad Imran [3,4] and Muhammad Faisal Nadeem [5]

1. Govt Khawaja Rafique Shaheed College, Lahore 54000, Pakistan; imran_gon@yahoo.com
2. Department of Mathematics, COMSATS University Islamabad, Sahiwal Campus, Sahiwal 57000, Pakistan
3. Department of Mathematical Sciences, United Arab Emirates University, P. O. Box 15551, Al Ain, UAE; imrandhab@gmail.com
4. Department of Mathematics, School of Natural Sciences (SNS), National University of Sciences and Technology (NUST), Sector H-12, Islamabad 44000, Pakistan
5. Department of Mathematics, COMSATS University Islamabad, Lahore Campus, Lahore 54000, Pakistan; mfaisalnadeem@ymail.com
* Correspondence: kamransiddiqui75@gmail.com

Received: 16 July 2018; Accepted: 5 August 2018; Published: 10 August 2018

Abstract: A topological index is a number related to the atomic index that allows quantitative structure–action/property/toxicity connections. All the more vital topological indices correspond to certain physico-concoction properties like breaking point, solidness, strain vitality, and so forth, of synthetic mixes. The idea of the hyper Zagreb index, multiple Zagreb indices and Zagreb polynomials was set up in the substance diagram hypothesis in light of vertex degrees. These indices are valuable in the investigation of calming exercises of certain compound systems. In this paper, we computed the first and second Zagreb index, the hyper Zagreb index, multiple Zagreb indices and Zagreb polynomials of the line graph of wheel and ladder graphs by utilizing the idea of subdivision.

Keywords: hyper Zagreb index; first and second Zagreb index; multiple Zagreb indices; Zagreb polynomials; line graph; subdivision graph; tadpole; wheel; ladder

1. Introduction

Chemical graph theory is a branch of mathematical chemistry in which we apply apparatuses of the graph hypothesis to display the substance numerically. This hypothesis contributes noticeably to the synthetic sciences. A sub-atomic diagram is a straightforward limited graph in which vertices mean that the atoms and edges indicate concoction bonds in hidden compound structure. A topological index is actually a numerical amount related to the concoction constitution indicating the connection of the substance structure with numerous physio-synthetic properties, compound reactivity, and organic action. A decade ago, the diagram hypothesis found extensive use in research. The graph hypothesis has given physicists a variety of valuable apparatuses, such as topological files. Cheminformatics is a new subject that is a mix of science, arithmetic, and data science. It ponders quantitative structure–movement (QSAR) and structure–property (QSPR) connections that are utilized to anticipate the natural exercises and properties of synthetic mixes.

A graph G with vertex set V and edge set E are associated if there exists a connection between any combination of vertices in G. A network is just a connected diagram having no various edges and no self loops. For a graph G, the level of a vertex v is the quantity of edges occurrence to v and is indicated by $\xi(v)$.

A topological list $Top(G)$ of a graph G is a number with the property that for each chart H isomorphic to G, $Top(H) = Top(G)$. The idea of the topological file originated from the work done by Wiener [1], while at the same time, he was aiming to determine the breaking point of paraffin. He named this list as the way number. Later on, the way number was renamed as the Wiener index. The Wiener list is the first and most concentrated topological list, both from hypothetical and applications perspectives, and is characterized as the aggregate of separations between all sets of vertices in G (see [2] for details).

I. Gutman and N.Trinajstic [3] introduced the first and second Zagreb indices based on the degree of vertices as:

$$M_1(G) = \sum_{r_1 r_2 \in E(G)} [\xi(r_1) + \xi(r_2)], \tag{1}$$

$$M_2(G) = \sum_{r_1 r_2 \in E(G)} [\xi(r_1) \times \xi(r_2)]. \tag{2}$$

In 2013, Shirdel et al. [4] introduced the "hyper Zagreb index" as:

$$HM(G) = \sum_{r_1 r_2 \in E(G)} [\xi(r_1) + \xi(r_2)]^2. \tag{3}$$

M. Ghorbani and N. Azimi defined [5] multiple Zagreb indices as:

$$PM_1(G) = \prod_{r_1 r_2 \in E(G)} [\xi(r_1) + \xi(r_2)], \tag{4}$$

$$PM_2(G) = \prod_{r_1 r_2 \in E(G)} [\xi(r_1) \times \xi(r_2)]. \tag{5}$$

The properties of $PM_1(G), PM_2(G)$ indices for some chemical structures have been studied in [6]. The first Zagreb polynomial $M_1(G, x)$) and second Zagreb polynomial $M_2(G, x)$ are defined as:

$$M_1(G, x) = \sum_{r_1 r_2 \in E(G)} x^{[\xi(r_1) + \xi(r_2)]}, \tag{6}$$

$$M_2(G, x) = \sum_{r_1 r_2 \in E(G)} x^{[\xi(r_1) \times \xi(r_2)]}. \tag{7}$$

There is now extensive research activity on $HM(G)$, $PM_1(G)$, $PM_2(G)$ indices and $M_1(G, x)$, $M_2(G, x)$ polynomials. See [7–9] for details.

2. Applications of Topological Indices

A ago, graph hypothesis had found an amazing use in research. Compound graph speculation has given researchers a variety of important gadgets (e.g., topological files). The Zagreb index is a topological descriptor that is related to a considerable measure of fabricated attributes of the particles, and has been discovered parallel to setting up the limit and Kovats constants of the particles [10]. The particle bond arranged hyper Zagreb index has a superior relationship with the security of direct dendrimers, besides the expanded medication stores and for setting up the strain criticalness of cycloalkanes [11–15]. To relate with certain physico-mix properties, different Zagreb indices have particularly needed insightful control over the farsighted essentialness of the dendrimers [16,17]. The first and second Zagreb polynomials were found to aid in the calculation of the aggregate π-electron imperativeness of the particles inside particular brutal verbalizations [18,19].

3. Topological Indices for Line Graph of Subdivided Graph $L(S(G))$

The subdivision graph [20] $S(G)$ is the diagram acquired from G by supplanting every one of its edges by a way of length 2, or equivalently, by embedding an extra vertex into each edge of G. The line diagram of the chart G, composed $L(G)$, is the basic diagram whose vertices are the edges of G, with $ef \in E(L(G))$ when e and f have a typical end point in G. Likewise, the line chart of the subdivided diagram is indicated by $L(S(G))$.

The tadpole graph $T_{n,k}$ is the diagram acquired by joining a cycle diagram C_n to a way of length k. By beginning with a disjoint association of two charts G_1 and G_2 and including edges joining every vertex of G_1 to that of G_2, one gets the whole $G_1 + G_2$ of G_1 and G_2. The total $C_n + K_1$ of a cycle C_n and a solitary vertex is alluded to as a wheel chart W_{n+1} with arrange n. The Cartesian product $G_1 \times G_2$ of charts G_1 and G_2 is a diagram with vertex set $V_1 \times V_2$, and two vertices r_1, s_1 and r_2, s_2 are nearby in $G_1 \times G_2$ if and only if either $r_1 = r_2$ and $s_1 s_2 \in E_2$, or $s_1 = s_2$ and $r_1 r_2 \in E_1$. The stepping stool diagram L_n is given by $L_n = K_2 \times P_n$, where P_n is the way of length n. It is along these lines proportionate to the framework chart $G_{2,n}$. The diagram acquired by means of this definition resembles a stepping stool, having two rails and n rungs between them.

In 2011, Ranjini et al. figured the unequivocal articulations for the Schultz lists of the subdivision diagrams of the tadpole, wheel, steerage, and stepping stool charts. They additionally contemplated the Zagreb records of the line diagrams of the tadpole, haggle charts with subdivision in [21,22]. Ali et al. [23] registered the topological lists for the line diagram of the sparkler chart, and Sardar et al. [24] computed the topological files of the line diagrams of Banana tree and Firecracker diagrams. Ahmad et al. [25] discuss the m-polynomials and degree-based topological indices for the line graph of the Firecracker graph. Soleimani et al. [26] discuss the topological properties of nanostructures. In 2015, Su and Xu figured the general aggregate availability records and co-lists of the line diagrams of the tadpole and haggle charts with subdivision in [27]. Nadeem et al. [28,29] registered ABC_4 and GA_5 records of the line charts of the tadpole, wheel, stepping stool, $2D$−lattice, nanotube, and nanotorus of $TUC_4C_8[p,q]$ diagrams.

3.1. Zagreb Indices and Zagreb Polynomials of the Line Graph of the Tadpole Graph $T_{n,k}$

Theorem 1. *Let R be the line graph of the tadpole graph $T_{n,k}$. Then*

$$\begin{aligned}
M_1(R) &= 8n + 8k + 12, \\
M_2(R) &= 8n + 8k + 23, \\
HM(R) &= 32n + 32k + 96, \\
PM_1(R) &= 3 \times 4^{(2n+2k-6)} \times 5^3 \times 6^3, \\
PM_2(R) &= 2 \times 4^{(2n+2k-6)} \times 6^3 \times 9^3, \\
M_1(R, x) &= x^3 + (2n + 2k - 6)x^4 + 3x^5 + 3x^6, \\
M_2(R, x) &= x^2 + (2n + 2k - 6)x^4 + 3x^6 + 3x^9.
\end{aligned}$$

Proof. The subdivision diagram of $T_{n,k}$ and the related line chart R appear individually in Figure 1a,b. The subdivision chart $S(T_{n,k})$ contains $2n + 2k$ edges, so its line diagram contains $2n + 2k$ vertices, out of which 3 vertices are of degree 3 and one vertex is of degree 1. The rest of the $2n + 2k - 4$ vertices are all of degree 2. It is easy to see that the aggregate number of edges of R is $2n + 2k + 1$. The edge set $E(R)$ separates into our edge segments in view of degrees of end vertices:

$E_{12}(R) = \{r_1 r_2 \in E(R) \mid \xi(r_1) = 1, \xi(r_2) = 2\}$,

$E_{22}(R) = \{r_1 r_2 \in E(R) \mid \xi(r_1) = 2, \xi(r_2) = 2\}$,

$E_{23}(R) = \{r_1 r_2 \in E(R) \mid \xi(r_1) = 2, \xi(r_2) = 3\}$,

$E_{33}(R) = \{r_1 r_2 \in E(R) \mid \xi(r_1) = 3, \xi(r_2) = 3\}$.

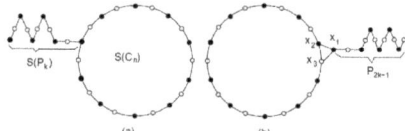

Figure 1. (a) Subdivision graph of the tadpole graph $T_{n,k}$; (b) Line graph of the subdivision graph of $(T_{n,k})$.

□

These four partitions of the edge set correspond to their degree sum of neighbors of end vertices. The number of edges in $E_{12}(R)$ is 1, in $E_{22}(R)$ there are $2n + 2k - 6$, in $E_{23}(R)$ there are 3, and in $E_{33}(R)$ there are 3. Now, using Equations (1)–(7), we have

$$M_1(G) = \sum_{r_1 r_2 \in E(G)} [\xi(r_1) + \xi(r_2)],$$

$$M_1(R) = \sum_{r_1 r_2 \in E_{12}(R)} [\xi(r_1) + \xi(r_2)] + \sum_{r_1 r_2 \in E_{22}(R)} [\xi(r_1) + \xi(r_2)] + \sum_{r_1 r_2 \in E_{23}(R)} [\xi(r_1) + \xi(r_2)]$$

$$+ \sum_{r_1 r_2 \in E_{33}(R)} [\xi(r_1) + \xi(r_2)]$$

$$= 3|E_{12}(R)| + 4|E_{22}(R)| + 5|E_{23}(R)| + 6|E_{33}(R)|$$

$$= 3(1) + 4((2n + 2k - 6)) + 5(3) + 6(3) = 8n + 8k + 12,$$

$$M_2(G) = \sum_{r_1 r_2 \in E(G)} [\xi(r_1) \times \xi(r_2)]$$

$$M_2(R) = \sum_{r_1 r_2 \in E_{12}(R)} [\xi(r_1) \times \xi(r_2)] + \sum_{r_1 r_2 \in E_{22}(R)} [\xi(r_1) \times \xi(r_2)] + \sum_{r_1 r_2 \in E_{23}(R)} [\xi(r_1) \times \xi(r_2)]$$

$$+ \sum_{r_1 r_2 \in E_{33}(R)} [\xi(r_1) \times \xi(r_2)]$$

$$= 2|E_{12}(R)| + 4|E_{22}(R)| + 6|E_{23}(R)| + 9|E_{33}(R)|$$

$$= 2(1) + 4((2n + 2k - 6)) + 6(3) + 9(3) = 8n + 8k + 23,$$

$$HM(G) = \sum_{r_1 r_2 \in E(G)} [\xi(r_1) + \xi(r_2)]^2,$$

$$HM(R) = \sum_{r_1 r_2 \in E_{12}(R)} [\xi(r_1) + \xi(r_2)]^2 + \sum_{r_1 r_2 \in E_{22}(R)} [\xi(r_1) + \xi(r_2)]^2 + \sum_{r_1 r_2 \in E_{23}(R)} [\xi(r_1) + \xi(r_2)]^2$$

$$+ \sum_{r_1 r_2 \in E_{33}(R)} [\xi(r_1) + \xi(r_2)]^2$$

$$= 9|E_{12}(R)| + 16|E_{22}(R)| + 25|E_{23}(R)| + 36|E_{33}(R)|$$

$$= 9(1) + 16(2n + 2k - 6) + 25(3) + 36(3) = 2n + 32k + 96,$$

$$PM_1(G) = \prod_{r_1 r_2 \in E(G)} [\xi(r_1) + \xi(r_2)],$$

$$PM_1(R) = \prod_{r_1 r_2 \in E_{12}(R)} [\xi(r_1) + \xi(r_2)] \times \prod_{r_1 r_2 \in E_{22}(R)} [\xi(r_1) + \xi(r_2)] \times \prod_{r_1 r_2 \in E_{23}(R)} [\xi(r_1) + \xi(r_2)]$$

$$\times \prod_{r_1 r_2 \in E_{33}(R)} [\xi(r_1) + \xi(r_2)]$$

$$= 3^{|E_{12}(R)|} \times 4^{|E_{22}(R)|} \times 5^{|E_{23}(R)|} \times 6^{|E_{33}(R)|} = 3 \times 4^{(2n+2k-6)} \times 5^3 \times 6^3,$$

$$PM_2(G) = \prod_{r_1r_2 \in E(G)} [\xi(r_1) \times \xi(r_2)],$$

$$PM_2(R) = \prod_{r_1r_2 \in E_{12}(R)} [\xi(r_1) \times \xi(r_2)] \times \prod_{r_1r_2 \in E_{22}(R)} [\xi(r_1) \times \xi(r_2)] \times \prod_{r_1r_2 \in E_{23}(R)} [\xi(r_1) \times \xi(r_2)]$$
$$\times \prod_{r_1r_2 \in E_{33}(R)} [\xi(r_1) \times \xi(r_2)]$$
$$= 2^{|E_{12}(R)|} \times 4^{|E_{22}(R)|} \times 6^{|E_{23}(R)|} \times 9^{|E_{33}(R)|} = 2 \times 4^{(2n+2k-6)} \times 6^3 \times 9^3,$$

$$M_1(G,x) = \sum_{r_1r_2 \in E(G)} x^{[\xi(r_1)+\xi(r_2)]},$$

$$M_1(R,x) = \sum_{r_1r_2 \in E_1(R)} x^{[\xi(r_1)+\xi(r_2)]} + \sum_{r_1r_2 \in E_2(R)} x^{[\xi(r_1)+\xi(r_2)]} + \sum_{r_1r_2 \in E_3(R)} x^{[\xi(r_1)+\xi(r_2)]}$$
$$+ \sum_{r_1r_2 \in E_4(R)} x^{[\xi(r_1)+\xi(r_2)]}$$
$$= \sum_{r_1r_2 \in E_1(R)} x^3 + \sum_{r_1r_2 \in E_2(R)} x^4 + \sum_{r_1r_2 \in E_3(R)} x^5 + \sum_{r_1r_2 \in E_4(R)} x^6$$
$$= |E_{12}(R)|x^3 + |E_{22}(R)|x^4 + |E_{23}(R)|x^5 + |E_{33}(R)|x^6 = x^3 + (2n+2k-6)x^4 + 3x^5 + 3x^6,$$

$$M_2(G,x) = \sum_{r_1r_2 \in E(G)} x^{[\xi(r_1) \times \xi(r_2)]},$$

$$M_2(R,x) = \sum_{r_1r_2 \in E_1(R)} x^{[\xi(r_1) \times \xi(r_2)]} + \sum_{r_1r_2 \in E_2(R)} x^{[\xi(r_1) \times \xi(r_2)]} + \sum_{r_1r_2 \in E_3(R)} x^{[\xi(r_1) \times \xi(r_2)]}$$
$$+ \sum_{r_1r_2 \in E_4(R)} x^{[\xi(r_1) \times \xi(r_2)]}$$
$$= \sum_{r_1r_2 \in E_1(R)} x^2 + \sum_{r_1r_2 \in E_2(R)} x^4 + \sum_{r_1r_2 \in E_3(R)} x^6 + \sum_{r_1r_2 \in E_4(R)} x^9$$
$$= |E_{12}(R)|x^2 + |E_{22}(R)|x^4 + |E_{23}(R)|x^6 + |E_{33}(R)|x^9 = x^2 + (2n+2k-6)x^4 + 3x^6 + 3x^9.$$

Theorem 2. *Let H be the line graph of the wheel graph W_{n+1}. Then*

$$M_1(H) = n^3 + 27n,$$
$$M_2(H) = \frac{n^4 - n^3 + 6n^2 + 72n}{2},$$
$$HM(H) = 2n^4 - n^3 + 6n^2 + 45n,$$
$$PM_1(H) = 6^{4n} \times (3+n)^n \times (2n)^{\left(\frac{n^2-n}{2}\right)},$$
$$PM_2(H) = 9^{4n} \times (3n)^n \times n^{n^2-n},$$
$$M_1(H,x) = 4nx^4 + nx^{3+n} + \left(\frac{n^2-n}{2}\right)x^{2n},$$
$$M_2(H,x) = 4nx^9 + nx^{3n} + \left(\frac{n^2-n}{2}\right)x^{n^2}.$$

Proof. The subdivision chart of wheel W_{n+1} and the relating line diagram H appear separately in Figure 2a,b. The line chart H contains $4n$ vertices, of which $3n$ vertices are of degree 3 and the others are of degree n. It is simple to determine that the aggregate number of edges in the line diagram H are $\frac{n^2+9n}{2}$. To demonstrate the above proclamation, the edge set $E(H)$ isolates into three edge segments in light of the degrees of end vertices:
$E_{33}(H) = \{r_1r_2 \in E(H) \mid \xi(r_1) = 3, \xi(r_2) = 3\},$
$E_{3n}(H) = \{r_1r_2 \in E(H) \mid \xi(r_1) = 3, \xi(r_2) = n\},$

$E_{nn}(H) = \{r_1 r_2 \in E(H) \mid \xi(r_1) = n, \xi(r_2) = n\}.$

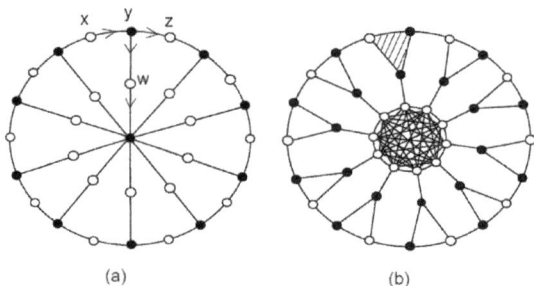

Figure 2. (**a**) Subdivision graph of wheel graph W_{n+1}; (**b**) Line graph of the subdivision graph of the wheel graph W_{n+1}.

$\square$

These three partitions of the edge set correspond to their degree sum of neighbors of end vertices. The number of edges in $E_{33}(H)$ are $4n$, in $E_{3n}(HG)$ there are n, and in $E_{nn}(H)$ there are $\dfrac{n^2 - n}{2}$. Now, using Equations (1)–(7), we have:

$$\begin{aligned}
M_1(G) &= \sum_{r_1 r_2 \in E(G)} [\xi(r_1) + \xi(r_2)], \\
M_1(H) &= \sum_{r_1 r_2 \in E_{33}(H)} [\xi(r_1) + \xi(r_2)] + \sum_{r_1 r_2 \in E_{3n}(H)} [\xi(r_1) + \xi(r_2)] + \sum_{r_1 r_2 \in E_{nn}(H)} [\xi(r_1) + \xi(r_2)] \\
&= 6|E_{33}(H)| + (3+n)|E_{3n}(H)| + 2n|E_{nn}(H)| \\
&= 6(4n) + (3+n)(n) + 2n\left(\frac{n^2-n}{2}\right) = n^3 + 27n, \\
M_2(G) &= \sum_{r_1 r_2 \in E(G)} [\xi(r_1) \times \xi(r_2)], \\
M_2(H) &= \sum_{r_1 r_2 \in E_{33}(H)} [\xi(r_1) \times \xi(r_2)] + \sum_{r_1 r_2 \in E_{3n}(H)} [\xi(r_1) \times \xi(r_2)] + \sum_{r_1 r_2 \in E_{nn}(H)} [\xi(r_1) \times \xi(r_2)] \\
&= 9|E_{33}(H)| + 3n|E_{3n}(H)| + n^2|E_{nn}(H)| \\
&= 9(4n) + 3n(n) + n^2\left(\frac{n^2-n}{2}\right) = \frac{n^4 - n^3 + 6n^2 + 72n}{2}, \\
HM(G) &= \sum_{r_1 r_2 \in E(G)} [\xi(r_1) + \xi(r_2)]^2, \\
HM(H) &= \sum_{r_1 r_2 \in E_{33}(H)} [\xi(r_1) + \xi(r_2)]^2 + \sum_{r_1 r_2 \in E_{3n}(H)} [\xi(r_1) + \xi(r_2)]^2 + \sum_{r_1 r_2 \in E_{nn}(H)} [\xi(r_1) + \xi(r_2)]^2 \\
&= 9|E_{33}(H)| + (3+n)^2|E_{3n}(H)| + 4n^2|E_{nn}(H)| \\
&= 9(4n) + n(3+n)^2 + 4n^2\left(\frac{n^2-n}{2}\right) = 2n^4 - n^3 + 6n^2 + 45n, \\
PM_1(G) &= \prod_{r_1 r_2 \in E(G)} [\xi(r_1) + \xi(r_2)], \\
PM_1(H) &= \prod_{r_1 r_2 \in E_{33}(H)} [\xi(r_1) + \xi(r_2)] \times \prod_{r_1 r_2 \in E_{3n}(H)} [\xi(r_1) + \xi(r_2)] \times \prod_{r_1 r_2 \in E_{nn}(H)} [\xi(r_1) + \xi(r_2)] \\
&= 6^{|E_{33}(H)|} \times (3+n)^{|E_{3n}(H)|} \times 2n^{|E_3(H)|} \\
&= 6^{4n} \times (3+n)^n \times (2n)^{\left(\frac{n^2-n}{2}\right)},
\end{aligned}$$

$$PM_2(G) = \prod_{r_1r_2 \in E(G)} [\xi(r_1) \times \xi(r_2)],$$

$$PM_2(H) = \prod_{r_1r_2 \in E_{33}(H)} [\xi(r_1) \times \xi(r_2)] \times \prod_{r_1r_2 \in E_{3n}(H)} [\xi(r_1) \times \xi(r_2)] \times \prod_{r_1r_2 \in E_{nn}(H)} [\xi(r_1) \times \xi(r_2)]$$

$$= 9^{|E_{33}(H)|} \times (3n)^{|E_{3n}(H)|} \times (n^2)^{|E_{nn}(H)|}$$

$$= 9^{4n} \times (3n)^n \times n^{n^2-n},$$

$$M_1(G,x) = \sum_{r_1r_2 \in E(G)} x^{[\xi(r_1)+\xi(r_2)]},$$

$$M_1(H,x) = \sum_{r_1r_2 \in E_1(H)} x^{[\xi(r_1)+\xi(r_2)]} + \sum_{r_1r_2 \in E_{3n}(H)} x^{[\xi(r_1)+\xi(r_2)]} + \sum_{r_1r_2 \in E_{nn}(H)} x^{[\xi(r_1)+\xi(r_2)]}$$

$$= \sum_{r_1r_2 \in E_1(H)} x^6 + \sum_{r_1r_2 \in E_2(H)} x^{3+n} + \sum_{r_1r_2 \in E_3(H)} x^{2n}$$

$$= |E_{33}(H)|x^6 + |E_{3n}(H)|x^{3+n} + |E_{nn}(H)|x^{2n}$$

$$= 4nx^4 + nx^{3+n} + \left(\frac{n^2-n}{2}\right)x^{2n},$$

$$M_2(G,x) = \sum_{r_1r_2 \in E(G)} x^{[\xi(r_1) \times \xi(r_2)]},$$

$$M_2(H,x) = \sum_{r_1r_2 \in E_1(H)} x^{[\xi(r_1) \times \xi(r_2)]} + \sum_{r_1r_2 \in E_{3n}(H)} x^{[\xi(r_1) \times \xi(r_2)]} + \sum_{r_1r_2 \in E_{nn}(H)} x^{[\xi(r_1) \times \xi(r_2)]}$$

$$= \sum_{r_1r_2 \in E_1(H)} x^9 + \sum_{r_1r_2 \in E_2(H)} x^{3n} + \sum_{r_1r_2 \in E_3(H)} x^{n^2}$$

$$= |E_{33}(H)|x^9 + |E_{3n}(H)|x^{3n} + +|E_{nn}(H)|x^{n^2}$$

$$= 4nx^9 + nx^{3n} + \left(\frac{n^2-n}{2}\right)x^{n^2}.$$

Theorem 3. *Let P_n be the line graph of the ladder graph L_n of order n. Then,*

$$M_1(P_n) = 154n - 76,$$
$$M_2(P_n) = 81n - 132,$$
$$HM(P_n) = 324n - 524,$$
$$PM_1(P_n) = 4^6 \times 5^4 \times 6^{(9n-20)},$$
$$PM_2(P_n) = 4^6 \times 6^4 \times 9^{(9n-20)},$$
$$M_1(P_n, x) = 6x^4 + 4x^5 + (9n-20)x^6,$$
$$M_2(P_n, x) = 6x^4 + 4x^6 + (9n-20)x^9.$$

Proof. The subdivision diagram of the stepping stool chart L_n and the comparing line chart P_n appear in Figure 3a,b, respectively. The quantity of vertices in the line chart P_n are $6n - 4$, among which 8 vertices are of degree 2 and the rest of the $6n - 12$ vertices are of degree 3. It is simple to process that the aggregate number of edges in the line chart P_n is $9n - 10$. To demonstrate the above proclamation, the edge set $E(P_n)$ isolates into three edge parcels in light of the degrees of end vertices:
$E_{22}(P_n) = \{r_1r_2 \in E(P_n) \mid \xi(r_1) = 2, \xi(r_2) = 2\}$,
$E_{23}(P_n) = \{r_1r_2 \in E(P_n) \mid \xi(r_1) = 2, \xi(r_2) = 3\}$,
$E_{33}(P_n) = \{r_1r_2 \in E(P_n) \mid \xi(r_1) = 3, \xi(r_2) = 3\}$.

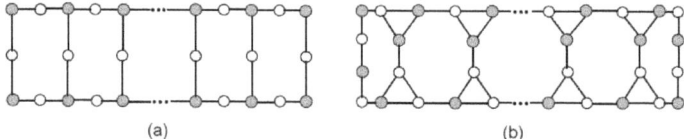

Figure 3. (a) Subdivision graph of the ladder graph L_n; (b) Line graph of the subdivision graph of the ladder graph L_n.

□

These three partitions of the edge set correspond to their degree sum of neighbors of end vertices. The number of edges in $E_{22}(P_n)$ are 6, in $E_{23}(P_n)$ there are 4, and in $E_{33}(P_n)$ there are $9n - 20$. Now, using Equations (1)–(7), we have:

$$M_1(G) = \sum_{r_1 r_2 \in E(G)} [\xi(r_1) + \xi(r_2)],$$

$$M_1(P_n) = \sum_{r_1 r_2 \in E_{22}(P_n)} [\xi(r_1) + \xi(r_2)] + \sum_{r_1 r_2 \in E_{23}(P_n)} [\xi(r_1) + \xi(r_2)] + \sum_{r_1 r_2 \in E_{33}(P_n)} [\xi(r_1) + \xi(r_2)]$$

$$= 4|E_{22}(P_n)| + 5|E_{23}(P_n)| + 6|E_{33}(P_n)|$$

$$= 4(6) + 5(4) + 6(9n - 20) = 154n - 76,$$

$$M_2(G) = \sum_{r_1 r_2 \in E(G)} [\xi(r_1) \times \xi(r_2)],$$

$$M_2(P_n) = \sum_{r_1 r_2 \in E_{22}(P_n)} [\xi(r_1) \times \xi(r_2)] + \sum_{r_1 r_2 \in E_{23}(P_n)} [\xi(r_1) \times \xi(r_2)] + \sum_{r_1 r_2 \in E_{33}(P_n)} [\xi(r_1) \times \xi(r_2)]$$

$$= 4|E_{22}(P_n)| + 6|E_{23}(P_n)| + 9|E_{33}(P_n)|$$

$$= 4(6) + 6(4) + 9(9n - 20) = 81n - 132,$$

$$HM(G) = \sum_{r_1 r_2 \in E(G)} [\xi(r_1) + \xi(r_2)]^2,$$

$$HM(P_n) = \sum_{r_1 r_2 \in E_{22}(P_n)} [\xi(r_1) + \xi(r_2)]^2 + \sum_{r_1 r_2 \in E_{23}(P_n)} [\xi(r_1) + \xi(r_2)]^2 + \sum_{r_1 r_2 \in E_{33}(P_n)} [\xi(r_1) + \xi(r_2)]^2$$

$$= 16|E_{22}(P_n)| + 25|E_{23}(P_n)| + 36|E_{33}(P_n)|$$

$$= 16(6) + 25(4) + 36(9n - 20) = 324n - 524,$$

$$PM_1(G) = \prod_{r_1 r_2 \in E(G)} [\xi(r_1) + \xi(r_2)],$$

$$PM_1(P_n) = \prod_{r_1 r_2 \in E_{22}(P_n)} [\xi(r_1) + \xi(r_2)] \times \prod_{r_1 r_2 \in E_{23}(P_n)} [\xi(r_1) + \xi(r_2)] \times \prod_{r_1 r_2 \in E_{33}(P_n)} [\xi(r_1) + \xi(r_2)]$$

$$= 4^{|E_{22}(P_n)|} \times 5^{|E_{23}(P_n)|} \times 6^{|E_{33}(P_n)|} = 4^6 \times 5^4 \times 6^{(9n-20)},$$

$$PM_2(G) = \prod_{r_1 r_2 \in E(G)} [\xi(r_1) \times \xi(r_2)],$$

$$PM_2(P_n) = \prod_{r_1 r_2 \in E_{22}(P_n)} [\xi(r_1) \times \xi(r_2)] \times \prod_{r_1 r_2 \in E_{23}(P_n)} [\xi(r_1) \times \xi(r_2)] \times \prod_{r_1 r_2 \in E_{33}(P_n)} [\xi(r_1) \times \xi(r_2)]$$

$$= 4^{|E_{22}(P_n)|} \times 6^{|E_{23}(P_n)|} \times 9^{|E_{33}(P_n)|} = 4^6 \times 6^4 \times 9^{(9n-20)},$$

$$M_1(G,x) = \sum_{r_1r_2 \in E(G)} x^{[\xi(r_1)+\xi(r_2)]},$$

$$M_1(P_n,x) = \sum_{r_1r_2 \in E_1(P_n)} x^{[\xi(r_1)+\xi(r_2)]} + \sum_{r_1r_2 \in E_2(P_n)} x^{[\xi(r_1)+\xi(r_2)]} + \sum_{r_1r_2 \in E_3(P_n)} x^{[\xi(r_1)+\xi(r_2)]}$$

$$= \sum_{r_1r_2 \in E_1(P_n)} x^4 + \sum_{r_1r_2 \in E_2(P_n)} x^5 + \sum_{r_1r_2 \in E_3(P_n)} x^6$$

$$= |E_{22}(P_n)|x^4 + |E_{23}(P_n)|x^5 + +|E_{33}(P_n)|x^6 = 6x^4 + 4x^5 + (9n-20)x^6,$$

$$M_2(G,x) = \sum_{r_1r_2 \in E(G)} x^{[\xi(r_1) \times \xi(r_2)]},$$

$$M_2(P_n,x) = \sum_{r_1r_2 \in E_1(P_n)} x^{[\xi(r_1) \times \xi(r_2)]} + \sum_{r_1r_2 \in E_2(P_n)} x^{[\xi(r_1) \times \xi(r_2)]} + \sum_{r_1r_2 \in E_3(P_n)} x^{[\xi(r_1) \times \xi(r_2)]}$$

$$= \sum_{r_1r_2 \in E_1(P_n)} x^4 + \sum_{r_1r_2 \in E_2(P_n)} x^6 + \sum_{r_1r_2 \in E_3(P_n)} x^9$$

$$= |E_{22}(P_n)|x^4 + |E_{23}(P_n)|x^6 + +|E_{33}(P_n)|x^9 = 6x^4 + 4x^6 + (9n-20)x^9.$$

4. Conclusions

In this paper we determined first and second Zagreb record, Hyper Zagreb index, first numerous Zagreb index, second different Zagreb index, and Zagreb polynomials of the line chart of tadpole and haggle diagrams by utilizing the idea of subdivision.

In the past couple of decades, investigations of the topological indices in view of end-vertex degrees of edges have seen a significant increase. The issue of determining the estimations of some outstanding degree-based topological indices is completely addressed for the line diagram of the subdivision graphs. This provides a path forward in this field of research. Also, in future we are intrigued to register these records for the line diagrams of some outstanding graphs.

Author Contributions: S.I and M.I. contributed to supervision, project administration, and funding, and analyzed the data curation. M.I. and M.K.S. contributed to designing the experiments, validation, conceptualization, formal analysis of experiments, resources, software, and some computations. M.F.N. contributed to investigation and methodology, and wrote the initial draft of the paper (which were investigated and approved by M.K.S.), and wrote the final draft. All authors read and approved the final version of the paper.

Funding: This research is supported by the Start-Up Research Grant 2016 of United Arab Emirates University (UAEU), Al Ain, United Arab Emirates via Grant No. G00002233, UPAR Grant of UAEU via Grant No. G00002590 and by the Summer Undergraduate Research Experience (SURE) plus 2017 research Grant via Grant No. G00002412.

Acknowledgments: The authors are grateful to the anonymous referees for their valuable comments and suggestions that improved this paper.

Conflicts of Interest: The authors declare no conflicts of interest.

References

1. Wiener, H. Structural determination of paraffin boiling points. *J. Am. Chem. Soc.* **1947**, *69*, 17–20. [CrossRef] [PubMed]
2. Dobrynin, A.A.; Entringer, R.; Gutman, I. Wiener index of trees: Theory and applications. *Acta Appl. Math.* **2001**, *66*, 211–249. [CrossRef]
3. Gutman, I.; Trinajstic, N. Graph theory and molecular orbitals. Total π-electron energy of alternant hydrocarbons. *Chem. Phys. Lett.* **1972**, *17*, 535–538. [CrossRef]
4. Shirdel, G.H.; Reza Pour, H.; Sayadi, A.M. The Hyper Zagreb Index of Graph Operations. *Iran. J. Math. Chem.* **2013**, *42*, 213–220.
5. Ghorbani, M.; Azimi, N. Note on multiple Zagreb indices. *Iran. J. Math. Chem.* **2012**, *32*, 137–143.
6. Eliasi, M.; Iranmanesh, A.; Gutman, I. Multiplicative version of first Zagreb index. *Match Commun. Math. Comput. Chem.* **2012**, *68*, 217–230.

7. Liu, J.B.; Siddiqui, M.K.; Zahid, M.A.; Naeem, M.; Baig, A.Q. Topological Properties of Crystallographic Structure of Molecules. *Symmetry* **2018**, *10*, 265. [CrossRef]
8. Shao, Z.; Siddiqui, M.K.; Muhammad, M.H. Computing Zagreb Indices and Zagreb Polynomials for Symmetrical Nanotubes. *Symmetry* **2018**, *10*, 244. [CrossRef]
9. Siddiqui, M.K.; Imran, M.; Ahmad, A. On Zagreb indices, Zagreb polynomials of some nanostar dendrimers. *Appl. Math. Comput.* **2016**, *280*, 132–139. [CrossRef]
10. Gao, W.; Siddiqui, M.K.; Naeem, M.; Rehman, N.A. Topological Characterization of Carbon Graphite and Crystal Cubic Carbon Structures. *Molecules* **2017**, *22*, 1496. [CrossRef] [PubMed]
11. Bača, M.; Horváthová, J.; Mokrišová, M.; Suhányiová, A. On topological indices of fullerenes. *Appl. Math. Comput.* **2015**, *251*, 154–161. [CrossRef]
12. Bača, M.; Horváthová, J.; Mokrišová, M.; Semanicová-Fenovcíková, A.; Suhányiová, A. On topological indices of carbon nanotube network. *Can. J. Chem.* **2015**, *93*, 1–4. [CrossRef]
13. Gao, W.; Farahani, M.R.; Siddiqui, M.K.; Jamil, M.K. On the First and Second Zagreb and First and Second Hyper-Zagreb Indices of Carbon Nanocones CNCk[n]. *J. Comput. Theor. Nanosci.* **2016**, *13*, 7475–7482. [CrossRef]
14. Gao, W.; Farahani, M.R.; Jamil, M.K.; Siddiqui, M.K. The Redefined First, Second and Third Zagreb Indices of Titania Nanotubes $TiO_2[m,n]$. *Open Biotechnol. J.* **2016**, *10*, 272–277. [CrossRef]
15. Gao, W.; Siddiqui, M.K.; Imran, M.; Jamil, M.K.; Farahani, M.R. Forgotten Topological Index of Chemical Structure in Drugs. *Saudi Pharm. J.* **2016**, *24*, 258–267. [CrossRef] [PubMed]
16. Imran, M.; Hayat, S.; Mailk, M.Y.H. On topological indices of certain interconnection networks. *Appl. Math. Comput.* **2014**, *244*, 936–951. [CrossRef]
17. Imran, M.; Siddiqui, M.K.; Naeem, M.; Iqbal, M.A. On Topological Properties of Symmetric Chemical Structures. *Symmetry* **2018**, *10*, 173. [CrossRef]
18. Siddiqui, M.K.; Gharibi, W. On Zagreb Indices, Zagreb Polynomials of Mesh Derived Networks. *J. Comput. Theor. Nanosci.* **2016**, *13*, 8683–8688. [CrossRef]
19. Siddiqui, M.K.; Naeem, M.; Rahman, N.A.; Imran, M. Computing topological indicesof certain networks. *J. Optoelectron. Adv. Mater.* **2016**, *18*, 884–892.
20. Rajan, M.A.; Lokesha, V.; Ranjini, P.S. A Study on Series Edge Graph Transformation. In Proceedings of the 23rd Joint Congress Iran-South Korea Jangjeon Mathematical Society, Ahvaz, Iran, 6–11 February 2010.
21. Ranjini, P.S.; Lokesha, V.; Cangül, I.N. On the Zagreb indices of the line graphs of the subdivision graphs. *Appl. Math. Comput.* **2011**, *218*, 699–702. [CrossRef]
22. Ranjini, P.S.; Lokesha, V.; Rajan, M.A. On the Shultz index of the subdivision graphs. *Adv. Stud. Contemp. Math.* **2011**, *213*, 279–290.
23. Ali, A.; Iqbal, H.; Nazeer, W.; Kang, S.M. on topological indices for the line graph of firecracker graph. *Int. J. Pure Appl. Math.* **2017**, *116*, 103–1042.
24. Sardar, M.S.; Zafar, S.; Zahid, Z. Computing topological indices of the line graphs of Banana tree graph and Firecracker graph. *Appl. Math. Nonlinear Sci.* **2017**, *2*, 83–92. [CrossRef]
25. Ahmad, M.S.; Nazeer, W.; Kang, S.M.; Jung, C.Y. M-polynomials and Degree based Topological Indices for the Line Graph of Firecracker Graph. *Global J. Pure Appl. Math.* **2017**, *13*, 2749–2776.
26. Soleimani, N.; Mohseni, E.; Rezaei, F.; Khati, F. Some Formulas for the Polynomials and Topological Indices of Nanostructures. *Acta Chem. Iasi* **2016**, *24*, 122–138. [CrossRef]
27. Su, G.; Xu, L. Topological indices of the line graph of subdivision graphs and their Schur-bounds. *Appl. Math. Comput.* **2015**, *253*, 395–401. [CrossRef]
28. Nadeem, M.F.; Zafar, S.; Zahid, Z. Certain topological indicies of the line graph of subdivsion graphs. *Appl. Math. Comput.* **2015**, *271*, 790–794.
29. Nadeem, M.F.; Zafar, S.; Zahid, Z. On topological properties of the line graphs of subdivision graphs of certain nanostructures. *Appl. Math. Comput.* **2016**, *273*, 125–130. [CrossRef]

© 2018 by the authors. Licensee MDPI, Basel, Switzerland. This article is an open access article distributed under the terms and conditions of the Creative Commons Attribution (CC BY) license (http://creativecommons.org/licenses/by/4.0/).

Article
Eccentricity Based Topological Indices of an Oxide Network

Muhammad Imran [1,2,*], Muhammad Kamran Siddiqui [1,3], Amna A. E. Abunamous [1], Dana Adi [1], Saida Hafsa Rafique [1] and Abdul Qudair Baig [4]

1. Department of Mathematical Sciences, United Arab Emirates University, Al Ain 15551, UAE; kamransiddiqui75@gmail.com (M.K.S.); 201250600@uaeu.ac.ae (A.A.E.A.); 201450261@uaeu.ac.ae (D.A.); 201350314@uaeu.ac.ae (S.H.R.)
2. Department of Mathematics, School of Natural Sciences (SNS), National University of Sciences and Technology (NUST), Sector H-12, Islamabad 44000, Pakistan
3. Department of Mathematics, COMSATS University Islamabad, Sahiwal Campus, Sahiwal 57000, Pakistan
4. Department of Mathematics, The University of Lahore, Pakpattan Campus, Pakpattan 57400, Pakistan; aqbaig1@gmail.com
* Correspondence: imrandhab@gmail.com

Received: 5 June 2018; Accepted: 11 July 2018; Published: 18 July 2018

Abstract: Graph theory has much great advances in the field of mathematical chemistry. Chemical graph theory has become very popular among researchers because of its wide applications in mathematical chemistry. The molecular topological descriptors are the numerical invariants of a molecular graph and are very useful for predicting their bioactivity. A great variety of such indices are studied and used in theoretical chemistry, pharmaceutical researchers, in drugs and in different other fields. In this article, we study the chemical graph of an oxide network and compute the total eccentricity, average eccentricity, eccentricity based Zagreb indices, atom-bond connectivity (ABC) index and geometric arithmetic index of an oxide network. Furthermore, we give analytically closed formulas of these indices which are helpful in studying the underlying topologies.

Keywords: molecular graph; total eccentricity; average eccentricity; eccentricity based Zagreb indices; atom bond connectivity index; geometric arithmetic index and oxide network

MSC: 05C12, 05C90

1. Introduction

Graph theory is a branch of mathematics that has a lot of applications in computer science, electrical systems (network), interconnected systems (network), biological networks, and in chemistry. Chemical graph theory is the rapidly developing zone among chemists and mathematicians. Chemical graph theory helps us to predict the certain physico-chemical properties of chemical compounds by just considering their pictorial representations [1,2].

Cheminformatics is a comparatively new subject, which is a combination of chemistry, mathematics and information science. There is a considerable usage of graph theory in theoretical and computational chemistry. Chemical graph theory is the topology branch of mathematical chemistry which implements graph theory to mathematically model chemical occurrences. There has been a lot of research in this area in the last few decades. A few references are given that demonstrate the significance of graph theory in Mathematical Chemistry [3,4].

Let $G = (V, E)$ be a graph, where V is a non-empty set of vertices and E is a set of edges. Chemical graph theory applies graph theory to the mathematical modeling of molecular phenomena, which is helpful for the study of molecular structures. The manipulation and examination of chemical structural information is made conceivable by using molecular descriptors. A great variety of topological indices are studied and used in theoretical chemistry by pharmaceutical researchers. In chemical graph theory, there are many topological indices for a connected graph, which are helpful in the study of chemical molecules. This theory has had a great effect in the development of chemical science.

If $p, q \in V(G)$, then the distance $d(p,q)$ between p and q is defined as the length of any shortest path in G connecting p and q. Eccentricity is the distance of vertex u from the farthest vertex in G. In mathematical form,

$$\varepsilon(u) = max\{d(u,v) | \forall\ u \in V(G)\}. \tag{1}$$

The total eccentricity index is introduced by Farooq et al. [5], which is defined as,

$$\zeta(G) = \sum_{v \in V(G)} \varepsilon(v). \tag{2}$$

where $\varepsilon(v)$ represents eccentricity of vertex v.

The average eccentricity $avec(G)$ of a graph G is the mean value of eccentricities of all vertices of a graph, that is,

$$avec(G) = \frac{1}{n} \sum_{v \in V(G)} \varepsilon(v). \tag{3}$$

The average eccentricity and standard deviation for all Sierpiński graphs S_p^n is established by [6]. The extremal properties of the average eccentricity, conjectures and Auto graphicx, about the average eccentricity are obtained by [7]. The bounds on the mean eccentricity of a graph, and also the change in mean eccentricity when a graph is replaced by a subgraph, is established by [8]. For trees with fixed diameter, fixed matching number and fixed number of pendent vertices, the lower and upper bounds of average eccentricity are found by [9].

The "eccentricity based geometric-arithmetic (GA)" index of a graph G is defined as [10],

$$GA_4(G) = \sum_{uv \in E(G)} \frac{2\sqrt{\varepsilon(u) \cdot \varepsilon(v)}}{\varepsilon(u) + \varepsilon(v)}. \tag{4}$$

Further results regarding the average eccentricity index and eccentricity-based geometric-arithmetic index can be found in [11]. A new version of the ABC index is introduced by Farahani [12] which is defined as,

$$ABC_5(G) = \sum_{uv \in E(G)} \sqrt{\frac{\varepsilon(v) + \varepsilon(u) - 2}{\varepsilon(v) \cdot \varepsilon(u)}}. \tag{5}$$

Imran et al. computed the eccentricity based ABC index and eccentricity based geometric-arithmetic index for copper oxide in [13]. Gao et al. calculated the result about the eccentric ABC index of linear polycene parallelogram benzenoid in [14].

In 2010, D. Vukičević et al. and in 2012, Ghorbani et al. proposed some new modified versions of Zagreb indices of a molecular graph G [15,16]. The first Zagreb eccentricity index is defined as:

$$M_1^*(G) = \sum_{uv \in E(G)} [\varepsilon(u) + \varepsilon(v)]. \tag{6}$$

The second Zagreb eccentricity index is defined as:

$$M_1^{**}(G) = \sum_{v \in V(G)} [\varepsilon(v)]^2. \tag{7}$$

The third Zagreb eccentricity index is defined as:

$$M_2^*(G) = \sum_{uv \in E(G)} \varepsilon(u)\varepsilon(v). \tag{8}$$

So, in this article, we extend the study of chemical graph theory to compute the total eccentricity, average eccentricity, eccentricity-based Zagreb indices, ABC index and geometric arithmetic index of oxide network. Furthermore, we give the exact result of these indices which are helpful in studying the underlying topological properties of oxide networks.

2. Applications of Topological Indices and Motivation

The ABC index provides a very good correlation for the stability of linear alkanes as well as the branched alkanes and for computing the strain energy of cyclo alkanes [17–20]. To correlate with certain physico-chemical properties, the GA index has much better predictive power than the predictive power of the Randic connectivity index [21–23]. The first and second Zagreb index were found to occur for computation of the total π-electron energy of the molecules within specific approximate expressions [24].

Since degree based topological indices are useful to analyzed the chemical properties of different molecular structures. So motivated by this idea, we focus on eccentricity based topological indices. As eccentricity based topological indices are used as an important tool to the prediction of physico-chemical, pharmacological and toxicological properties of a compound directly from its molecular structure. This analysis is known as the study of the quantitative structure–activity relationship (QSAR) [25].

3. Methods

To compute our results, we use the method of combinatorial computing, vertex partition method, edge partition method, graph theoretical tools, analytic techniques, degree counting method and sum of degrees of neighbours method [26,27]. Moreover, we use Matlab (MathWorks, Natick, MA, USA) for mathematical calculations and verifications (see https://en.wikipedia.org/wiki/MATLAB). We also use the maple software (Maplesoft, McKinney, TX, USA) for plotting these mathematical results (see https://en.wikipedia.org/wiki/Maple_(software)).

4. Oxide Network

Oxide networks play a vital role in the study of silicate networks. If we delete silicon vertices from a silicate network, we get an oxide network OX_n (see Figure 1). An n-dimensional oxide network is denoted as OX_n. The number of vertices in Oxide network are $9n^2 + 3n$ and number of edges are $18n^2$. An Oxide network OX_n with $n = 5$ is depicted in Figure 1.

4.1. Construction of Oxide Network OX_n Formulas

- To prove our main results, we make a partition of vertices of the oxide network OX_n for (n-levels) based on eccentricity of each vertex in two sets. The set V_1 contains those vertices which have the eccentricity $\varepsilon(u) = 2k + 1$, and the number of vertices in set V_1 are $6(2m - 1)$, $1 \leq m \leq n$. The set V_2 contain those vertices which have the eccentricity $\varepsilon(u) = 2k + 2$, and the number of vertices in set V_2 are $6m$, $1 \leq m \leq n$. Also, the variable k represents the distance between two vertices, which helps us to make this vertex partition. Also, k represents the range of the total number of vertices with that eccentricity. More preciously, Table 1 represents the vertex partition of Oxide network for (n-levels) based on eccentricity of each vertex.

- Now we make a partition of edges of an oxide network for (n-levels) based on eccentricity of end vertices in three sets. The set E_1 contain those edges which have the eccentricities $(\varepsilon(u), \varepsilon(v)) = (2k+1, 2k+1)$, $n \leq k \leq 2n-1$ and the number of edges in set E_1 are $6(2m-1)$, $1 \leq m \leq n$. The set E_2 contain those edges which have the eccentricities $(\varepsilon(u), \varepsilon(v)) = (2k+1, 2k+2)$, $n \leq k \leq 2n-1$, and the number of edges in set E_2 are $12m$, $1 \leq m \leq n$. The set E_3 contain those edges which have the eccentricities $(\varepsilon(u), \varepsilon(v)) = (2k+2, 2k+3)$, $n \leq k \leq 2n-1$, and the number of edges in set E_3 are $12m$, $1 \leq m \leq n$. Also k represent the range of total number of pairs with that eccentricity. More preciously Table 2 represents the edge partition of oxide network for (n-levels) based on eccentricity of end vertices.

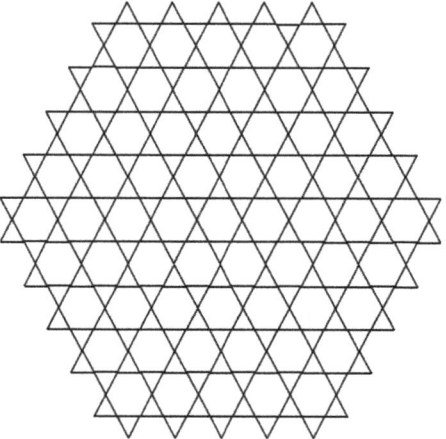

Figure 1. An oxide network OX_n with $n = 5$.

Table 1. Vertex partition of oxide network for (n-levels) based on eccentricity of each vertex.

$\varepsilon(u)$	Number of Vertices	Range of k	Range of m and n	Sets
$2k+1$	$6(2m-1)$	$n \leq k \leq 2n-1$	$1 \leq m \leq n, n \geq 1$	V_1
$2k+2$	$6m$	$n \leq k \leq 2n-1$	$1 \leq m \leq n, n \geq 1$	V_2

Table 2. Edge partition of oxide network for (n-levels) based on eccentricity of end vertices.

$(\varepsilon(u), \varepsilon(v))$	Number of Edges	Range of k	Range of m and n	Sets
$(2k+1, 2k+1)$	$6(2m-1)$	$n \leq k \leq 2n-1$	$1 \leq m \leq n, n \geq 1$	E_1
$(2k+1, 2k+2)$	$12m$	$n \leq k \leq 2n-1$	$1 \leq m \leq n, n \geq 1$	E_2
$(2k+2, 2k+3)$	$12m$	$n \leq k \leq 2n-2$	$1 \leq m \leq n-1, n > 1$	E_3

4.2. Main Results for Oxide Network

In this section, we computed the close formulae of certain topological indices for this network. Here we find the analytically closed results of total eccentricity index, average eccentricity index, eccentricity based Zagreb indices, eccentricity based geometric arithmetic and atom-bond connectivity indices for oxide networks.

Theorem 1. Let OX_n, for all $n \in \mathbb{N}$, be the oxide network, then the total eccentricity index ζ of OX_n is

$$\zeta(OX_n) = 6 \sum_{m=1}^{n} \sum_{k=n}^{2n-1} \{6mk + 4m - 2k - 1\}.$$

Proof. Let OX_n, where $n \in \mathbb{N}$, be the oxide network containing $9n^2 + 3n$ vertices and $18n^2$ edges.

Using the vertex partitioned from Table 1 and Equation (2), we have computed the total eccentricity index as:

$$\zeta(G) = \sum_{v \in V(G)} \varepsilon(v)$$

$$\zeta(OX_n) = \sum_{v \in V_1(G)} \varepsilon(v) + \sum_{v \in V_2(G)} \varepsilon(v)$$

$$= \sum_{m=1}^{n} \sum_{k=n}^{2n-1} 6(2m-1) \cdot (2k+1) + \sum_{m=1}^{n} \sum_{k=n}^{2n-1} 6m \cdot (2k+2)$$

$$= 6 \sum_{m=1}^{n} \sum_{k=n}^{2n-1} \{(2m-1) \cdot (2k+1) + m \cdot (2k+2)\}$$

After an easy simplification, we get

$$\zeta(OX_n) = 6 \sum_{m=1}^{n} \sum_{k=n}^{2n-1} \{6mk + 4m - 2k - 1\}.$$

□

Theorem 2. Let OX_n, for all $n \in \mathbb{N}$, be the oxide network, then the average eccentricity index $avec$ of OX_n is

$$avec(OX_n) = \frac{2}{3n^2 + n} \sum_{m=1}^{n} \sum_{k=n}^{2n-1} \{6mk + 4m - 2k - 1\}.$$

Proof. Let OX_n, where $n \in \mathbb{N}$, be the oxide network containing $9n^2 + 3n$ vertices and $18n^2$ edges.

Using the vertex partitioned from Table 1 and Equation (3), we have computed the average eccentricity index of oxide network $avec(OX_n)$ as:

$$avec(G) = \frac{1}{n} \sum_{v \in V(G)} \varepsilon(v)$$

$$avec(OX_n) = \frac{1}{n} \sum_{v \in V_1(G)} \varepsilon(v) + \frac{1}{n} \sum_{v \in V_2(G)} \varepsilon(v)$$

$$avec(OX_n) = \frac{1}{9n^2 + 3n} \{ \sum_{m=1}^{n} \sum_{k=n}^{2n-1} 6(2m-1) \cdot (2k+1) + \sum_{m=1}^{n} \sum_{k=n}^{2n-1} 6m \cdot (2k+2) \}$$

After an easy simplification, we get

$$avec(OX_n) = \frac{2}{3n^2 + n} \sum_{m=1}^{n} \sum_{k=n}^{2n-1} \{6mk + 4m - 2k - 1\}.$$

□

Theorem 3. Let OX_n for all $n \in \mathbb{N}$, be the oxide network, then the first Zagreb eccentricity index $M_1^*(OX_n)$ is

$$M_1^*(OX_n) = 12 \sum_{m=1}^{n} \sum_{k=n}^{2n-1} \{8mk + 5m - 2k - 1\} + 12 \sum_{m=1}^{n-1} \sum_{k=n}^{2n-2} m(4k+5).$$

Proof. Let OX_n, where $n \in \mathbb{N}$, be the oxide network containing $9n^2 + 3n$ vertices and $18n^2$ edges.

Using the vertex partitioned from Table 2 and Equation (6), we have computed first Zagreb eccentricity index $M_1^*(OX_n)$ as:

$$M_1^*(G) = \sum_{uv \in E(G)} [\varepsilon(u) + \varepsilon(v)]$$

$$M_1^*(OX_n) = \sum_{uv \in E_1(G)} [\varepsilon(u) + \varepsilon(v)] + \sum_{uv \in E_2(G)} [\varepsilon(u) + \varepsilon(v)] + \sum_{uv \in E_3(G)} [\varepsilon(u) + \varepsilon(v)]$$

$$= \sum_{m=1}^{n} \sum_{k=n}^{2n-1} 6(2m-1)(2k+1+2k+1) + \sum_{m=1}^{n} \sum_{k=n}^{2n-2} 12m(2k+1+2k+2)$$

$$+ \sum_{m=1}^{n-1} \sum_{k=n}^{2n-2} 12m(2k+2+2k+3)$$

$$= 6 \sum_{m=1}^{n} \sum_{k=n}^{2n-1} \{(2m-1)(4k+2) + 2m(4k+3)\} + 12 \sum_{m=1}^{n-1} \sum_{k=n}^{2n-2} m(4k+5).$$

After some simplification, we obtain

$$M_1^*(OX_n) = 12 \sum_{m=1}^{n} \sum_{k=n}^{2n-1} \{8mk + 5m - 2k - 1\} + 12 \sum_{m=1}^{n-1} \sum_{k=n}^{2n-2} m(4k+5).$$

□

Theorem 4. Let OX_n for all $n \in \mathbb{N}$, be the oxide network, then the second Zagreb eccentricity index $M_1^{**}(OX_n)$ is

$$M_1^{**}(OX_n) = 6 \sum_{m=1}^{n} \sum_{k=n}^{2n-1} \{2m(6k^2 + 8k + 3) - (2k+1)^2\}.$$

Proof. Let OX_n, where $n \in \mathbb{N}$, be the oxide network containing $9n^2 + 3n$ vertices and $18n^2$ edges. The general formula of second Zagreb eccentricity index is

$$M_1^{**}(G) = \sum_{v \in V(G)} [\varepsilon(v)]^2.$$

$$M_1^{**}(G) = \sum_{v \in V_1(G)} [\varepsilon(v)]^2 + \sum_{v \in V_2(G)} [\varepsilon(v)]^2.$$

By using the values from Table 1, we have

$$M_1^{**}(OX_n) = \sum_{m=1}^{n} \sum_{k=n}^{2n-1} 6(2m-1) \cdot (2k+1)^2 + \sum_{m=1}^{n} \sum_{k=n}^{2n-1} 6m \cdot (2k+2)^2.$$

$$M_1^{**}(OX_n) = 6 \sum_{m=1}^{n} \sum_{k=n}^{2n-1} \{(2m-1) \cdot (2k+1)^2 + 4m \cdot (k+1)^2\}.$$

After some simplification, we obtain

$$M_1^{**}(OX_n) = 6 \sum_{m=1}^{n} \sum_{k=n}^{2n-1} \{2m(6k^2+8k+3) - (2k+1)^2\}.$$

□

Theorem 5. *Let OX_n for all $n \in \mathbb{N}$, be the oxide network, then the third Zagreb eccentricity index $M_2^*(OX_n)$ is*

$$M_2^*(OX_n) = 12 \sum_{m=1}^{n} \sum_{k=n}^{2n-1} \{2m(8k^2+8k+3) - (4k^2+2k+1)\} + 24 \sum_{m=1}^{n-1} \sum_{k=n}^{2n-2} m(2k+3)(k+1).$$

Proof. Let OX_n, where $n \in \mathbb{N}$, be the oxide network containing $9n^2 + 3n$ vertices and $18n^2$ edges. The general formula of third Zagreb eccentricity index is

$$M_2^*(G) = \sum_{uv \in E(G)} [\varepsilon(u) \cdot \varepsilon(v)].$$

$$M_2^*(G) = \sum_{uv \in E_1(G)} [\varepsilon(u) \cdot \varepsilon(v)] + \sum_{uv \in E_2(G)} [\varepsilon(u) \cdot \varepsilon(v)] + \sum_{uv \in E_3(G)} [\varepsilon(u) \cdot \varepsilon(v)]$$

By using the values from Table 2, we have

$$M_2^*(OX_n) = \sum_{m=1}^{n} \sum_{k=n}^{2n-1} 6(2m-1)(2k+1) \cdot (2k+1) + \sum_{m=1}^{n} \sum_{k=n}^{2n-1} 12m(2k+1) \cdot (2k+2)$$

$$+ \sum_{m=1}^{n-1} \sum_{k=n}^{2n-2} 12m(2k+2) \cdot (2k+3).$$

$$M_2^*(OX_n) = 6 \sum_{m=1}^{n} \sum_{k=n}^{2n-1} \{(2m-1)(2k+1)^2 + 2m(4k^2+4k+2k+2)\} + 24 \sum_{m=1}^{n-1} \sum_{k=n}^{2n-2} m(k+1)(2k+3).$$

After some simplification, we obtain

$$M_2^*(OX_n) = 12 \sum_{m=1}^{n} \sum_{k=n}^{2n-1} \{2m(8k^2+8k+3) - (4k^2+2k+1)\} + 24 \sum_{m=1}^{n-1} \sum_{k=n}^{2n-2} m(2k+3)(k+1).$$

□

Theorem 6. *Let OX_n for all $n \in \mathbb{N}$, be the oxide network, then the geometric-arithmetic index $GA_4(OX_n)$ is*

$$GA_4(OX_n) = 12 \sum_{m=1}^{n} \sum_{k=n}^{2n-1} \left\{ \frac{2m-1}{2} + 2m \frac{\sqrt{(2k+1)(2k+2)}}{(4k+3)} \right\}$$

$$+ 24 \sum_{m=1}^{n-1} \sum_{k=n}^{2n-2} m \sqrt{\frac{(2k+2)(2k+3)}{4k+5}}.$$

Proof. Let OX_n, where $n \in \mathbb{N}$, be the oxide network containing $9n^2 + 3n$ vertices and $18n^2$ edges. The general formula of eccentricity based geometric arithmetic index is

$$GA_4(G) = \sum_{uv \in E(G)} \frac{2\sqrt{\varepsilon(u) \cdot \varepsilon(v)}}{\varepsilon(u) + \varepsilon(v)}.$$

$$GA_4(G) = \sum_{uv \in E_1(G)} \frac{2\sqrt{\varepsilon(u) \cdot \varepsilon(v)}}{\varepsilon(u) + \varepsilon(v)} + \sum_{uv \in E_2(G)} \frac{2\sqrt{\varepsilon(u) \cdot \varepsilon(v)}}{\varepsilon(u) + \varepsilon(v)} + \sum_{uv \in E_3(G)} \frac{2\sqrt{\varepsilon(u) \cdot \varepsilon(v)}}{\varepsilon(u) + \varepsilon(v)}$$

Using the edge partitioned from Table 2, we have the following computations

$$GA_4(OXn) = \sum_{m=1}^{n} \sum_{k=n}^{2n-1} 6(2m-1) \cdot 2\frac{\sqrt{(2k+1) \cdot (2k+1)}}{2k+1+2k+1} + \sum_{m=1}^{n} \sum_{k=n}^{2n-1} 12m \cdot 2\frac{\sqrt{(2k+1) \cdot (2k+2)}}{2k+1+2k+2}$$

$$+ \sum_{m=1}^{n-1} \sum_{k=n}^{2n-2} 12m \cdot 2\frac{\sqrt{(2k+2) \cdot (2k+3)}}{2k+2+2k+3}.$$

$$GA_4(OXn) = 12 \sum_{m=1}^{n} \sum_{k=n}^{2n-1} \left\{ (2m-1)\frac{\sqrt{(2k+1)^2}}{4k+2} + 2\frac{\sqrt{(2k+1) \cdot (2k+2)}}{4k+3} \right\}$$

$$+ 24 \sum_{m=1}^{n-1} \sum_{k=n}^{2n-2} m\frac{\sqrt{(2k+2) \cdot (2k+3)}}{4k+5}.$$

After some simplification, we obtain

$$GA_4(OX_n) = 12 \sum_{m=1}^{n} \sum_{k=n}^{2n-1} \left\{ \frac{2m-1}{2} + 2m\frac{\sqrt{(2k+1)(2k+2)}}{(4k+3)} \right\}$$

$$+ 24 \sum_{m=1}^{n-1} \sum_{k=n}^{2n-2} m\sqrt{\frac{(2k+2)(2k+3)}{4k+5}}.$$

□

Theorem 7. *Let OX_n for all $n \in N$, be the oxide network, then the atom-bond connectivity index $ABC_5(OX_n)$ is*

$$ABC_5(OX_n) = 12 \sum_{m=1}^{n} \sum_{k=n}^{2n-1} \left\{ \frac{(2m-1)\sqrt{k}}{2k+1} + m\sqrt{\frac{4k+1}{(2k+1)(2k+2)}} \right\}$$

$$+ 12 \sum_{m=1}^{n-1} \sum_{k=n}^{2n-2} m\sqrt{\frac{4k+3}{(2k+2)(2k+3)}}.$$

Proof. Let OX_n, where $n \in N$, be the oxide network containing $9n^2 + 3n$ vertices and $18n^2$ edges. The general formula of eccentricity based atom-bond connectivity index is

$$ABC_5(G) = \sum_{uv \in E(G)} \sqrt{\frac{\varepsilon(u) + \varepsilon(v) - 2}{\varepsilon(u) \cdot \varepsilon(v)}}.$$

$$ABC_5(G) = \sum_{uv \in E_1(G)} \sqrt{\frac{\varepsilon(u) + \varepsilon(v) - 2}{\varepsilon(u) \cdot \varepsilon(v)}} + \sum_{uv \in E_2(G)} \sqrt{\frac{\varepsilon(u) + \varepsilon(v) - 2}{\varepsilon(u) \cdot \varepsilon(v)}} + \sum_{uv \in E_3(G)} \sqrt{\frac{\varepsilon(u) + \varepsilon(v) - 2}{\varepsilon(u) \cdot \varepsilon(v)}}.$$

Using the edge partitioned from Table 2, we have the following computations

$$ABC_5(OX_n) = \sum_{m=1}^{n}\sum_{k=n}^{2n-1} 6(2m-1)\sqrt{\frac{2k+1+2k+1-2}{(2k+1)\cdot(2k+1)}} + \sum_{m=1}^{n}\sum_{k=n}^{2n-1} 12m\sqrt{\frac{2k+1+2k+2-2}{(2k+1)\cdot(2k+2)}}$$

$$+ \sum_{m=1}^{n-1}\sum_{k=n}^{2n-2} 12m\sqrt{\frac{2k+2+2k+3-2}{(2k+2)\cdot(2k+3)}}.$$

$$ABC_5(OX_n) = 6\sum_{m=1}^{n}\sum_{k=n}^{2n-1}\left\{(2m-1)\sqrt{\frac{4k}{(2k+1)^2}} + 2m\sqrt{\frac{4k+1}{(2k+1)\cdot(2k+2)}}\right\}$$

$$+ 12\sum_{m=1}^{n-1}\sum_{k=n}^{2n-2} m\sqrt{\frac{4k+3}{(2k+2)\cdot(2k+3)}}.$$

After some simplification, we obtain

$$ABC_5(OX_n) = 12\sum_{m=1}^{n}\sum_{k=n}^{2n-1}\left\{\frac{(2m-1)\sqrt{k}}{2k+1} + m\sqrt{\frac{4k+1}{(2k+1)(2k+2)}}\right\}$$

$$+ 12\sum_{m=1}^{n-1}\sum_{k=n}^{2n-2} m\sqrt{\frac{4k+3}{(2k+2)(2k+3)}}.$$

□

5. Comparisons and Discussion

For the comparison of these indices numerically for OX_n, we computed all indices for different values of m, k. Now, from Table 3, we can easily see that all indices are in increasing order as the values of m, k are increasing. The graphical representations of the all indices for OX_n are depicted in Figures 2–8 for certain values of m, k.

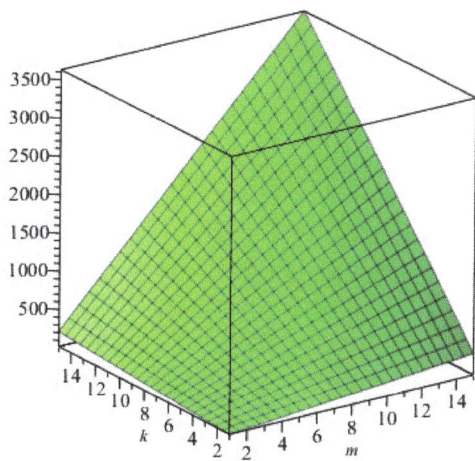

Figure 2. The graphically representation of total eccentricity index ζ of OX_n.

Table 3. Numerical computation of all indices for OX_n.

$[m,k]$	$\zeta(G)$	$avec(G)$	$M_1^*(G)$	$M_1^{**}(G)$	$M_2^*(G)$	$GA_4(G)$	$ABC_5(G)$
[1,1]	42	1.9	1416	2568	2014	112.5	315.4
[2,2]	162	3.5	4188	5478	4352	279.9	645.3
[3,3]	354	5.6	8304	10,523	9300	446.7	987.4
[4,4]	618	8.4	13,764	14,587	11,248	613.6	1125.6
[5,5]	956	10.5	16,898	16,325	13,654	842.3	1356.4
[6,6]	1242	14.5	19,652	19,876	16,324	1023.3	1586.7

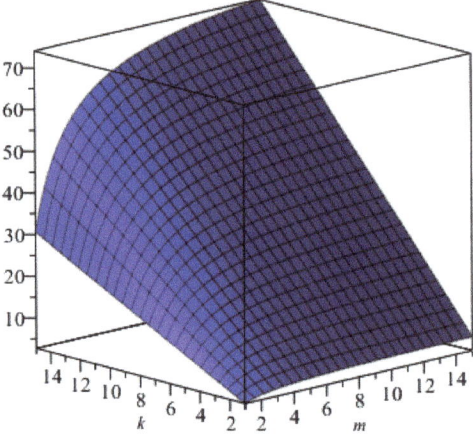

Figure 3. The graphically representation of the average eccentricity index *avec* of OX_n.

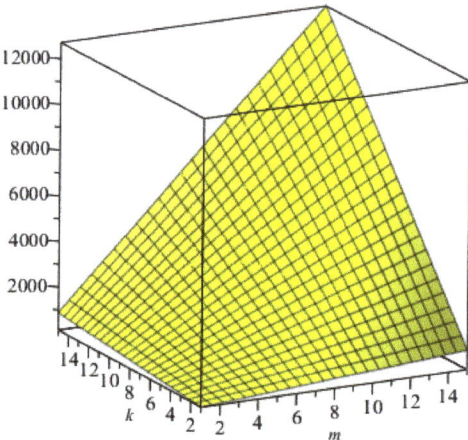

Figure 4. The graphically representation of the first Zagreb eccentricity index $M_1^*(OX_n)$.

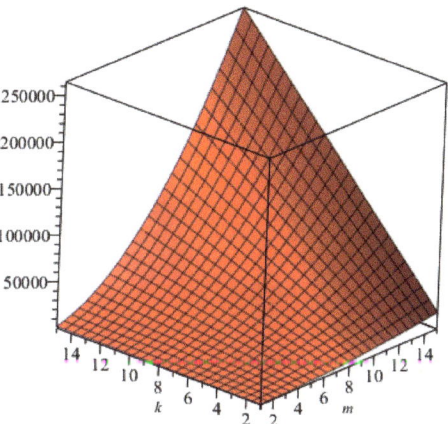

Figure 5. The graphically representation of the second Zagreb eccentricity index $M_1^{**}(OX_n)$.

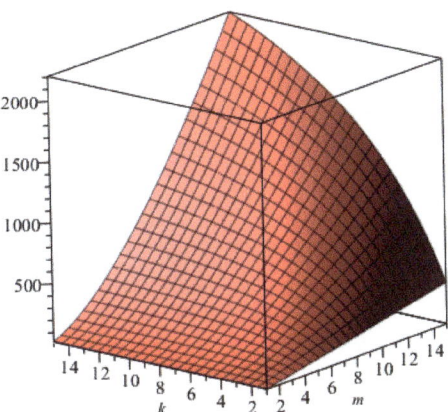

Figure 6. The graphically representation of the third Zagreb eccentricity index $M_1^{**}(OX_n)$.

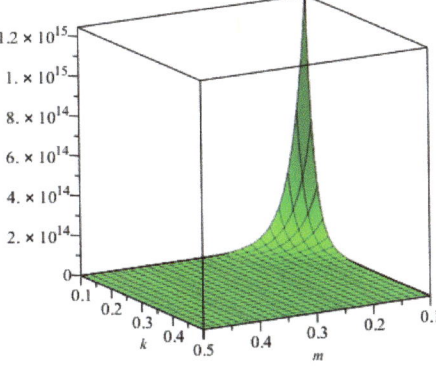

Figure 7. The graphically representation of the geometric-arithmetic index $GA_4(OX_n)$.

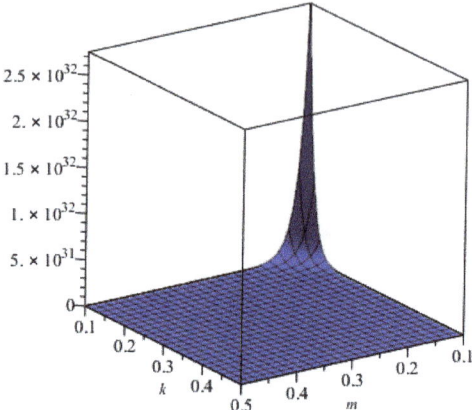

Figure 8. The graphically representation of the atom-bond connectivity index $ABC_5(OX_n)$.

6. Conclusions

In this paper, we computed the total eccentricity index $\zeta(OX_n)$, average eccentricity index $avec(OX_n)$, eccentricity-based Zagreb indices $M_1^*(OX_n)$, $M_1^{**}(OX_n)$ and $M_2^*(OX_n)$, atom-bond connectivity index $ABC_5(OX_n)$ and geometric arithmetic index $GA_4(OX_n)$ of the oxide network OX_n. So these indices are useful to analyzed the physico-chemical, pharmacological and toxicological properties of the oxide network OX_n.

Author Contributions: M.I. contribute for supervision, project administration, funding and analyzed the data curation. M.K.S. and A.Q.B. contribute for designing the experiments, validation, conceptualization and formal analysing. A.A.E.A. and D.A. contribute for performed experiments, resources, software and some computations. S.H.R. contribute for Investigation, Methodology and wrote the initial draft of the paper which were investigated and approved by M.I. and wrote the final draft. All authors read and approved the final version of the paper.

Acknowledgments: The authors are grateful to the anonymous referees for their valuable comments and suggestions that improved this paper. This research is supported by the Start-Up Research Grant 2016 of United Arab Emirates University (UAEU), Al Ain, United Arab Emirates via Grant No. G00002233, UPAR Grant of UAEU via Grant No. G00002590 and by the Summer Undergraduate Research Experience (SURE) plus 2017 research Grant via Grant No. G00002412.

Conflicts of Interest: The authors declare no conflict of interest.

References

1. Hayat, S.; Malik, M.A.; Imran, M. Computing topological indices of honeycomb derived networks. *Romanian J. Inf. Sci. Technol.* **2015**, *18*, 144–165.
2. Imran, M.; Ali, M.A.; Ahmad, S.; Siddiqui, M.K.; Baig, A.Q. Topological sharacterization of the symmetrical structure of bismuth tri-iodide. *Symmetry* **2018**, *10*, 201. [CrossRef]
3. Bie, R.J.; Siddiqui, M.K.; Razavi, R.; Taherkhani, M.; Najaf, M. Possibility of C_{38} and $Si_{19}Ge_{19}$ nanocages in anode of metal ion batteries: Computational examination. *Acta Chim. Slov.* **2018**, *65*, 303–311. [CrossRef] [PubMed]
4. Gao, W.; Siddiqui, M.K. Molecular descriptors of nanotube, oxide, silicate, and triangulene networks. *J. Chem.* **2017**, *2017*, 6540754. [CrossRef]
5. Farooq, R.; Malik, M.A. On some eccentricity based topological indices of nanostar dendrimers. 2018, in press.
6. Hinz, A.M.; Parisse, D. The Average Eccentricity of Sierpinski Graphs. *Graphs Comb.* **2012**, *5*, 671–686. [CrossRef]
7. Ilic, A. On the extremal properties of the average eccentricity. *Comput. Math. Appl.* **2012**, *64*, 2877–2885. [CrossRef]

8. Dankelmann, P.; Goddard, W.; Swart, C.S. The average eccentricity of a graph and its subgraphs. *Util. Math.* **2004**, *65*, 41–51.
9. Tang, Y.; Zhou, B. On average eccentricity. *MATCH Commun. Math. Comput. Chem.* **2012**, *67*, 405–423.
10. Ghorbani, M.; Khaki, A. A note on the fourth version of geometric-arithmetic index. *Optoelectron. Adv. Mater. Rapid Commun.* **2010**, *4*, 2212–2215.
11. Zhang, X.; Baig, A.Q.; Azhar, M.R.; Farahani, M.R.; Imran, M. The Average eccentricity and Eccentricity based Geometric-arithmetic index of tetra sheets. *Int. J. Pure Appl. Math.* **2017**, *117*, 467–479.
12. Farahani, M.R. Eccentricity version of atom bond connectivity index of benzenoid family $ABC_5(Hk)$. *World Appl. Sci. J. Chem.* **2013**, *21*, 1260–1265.
13. Imran, M.; Baig, A.Q.; Azhar, M.R.; Farahani, M.R.; Zhang, X. Eccentricity based geometric-arithmetic and atom-bond connectivity indices of copper oxide CuO. *Int. J. Pure Appl. Math.* **2017**, *117*, 481–502.
14. Gao, W.; Farahani, M.R.; Jamil, M.K. The eccentricity version of atom-bond connectivity index of linear polycene parallelogram benzoid $ABC_5(P(n,n))$. *Acta Chim. Slov.* **2016**, *63*, 376–379. [CrossRef] [PubMed]
15. Ghorbani, M.; Hosseinzadeh, M.A. A new version of Zagreb indices. *Filomat* **2012**, *6*, 93–100. [CrossRef]
16. Vukičević, D.; Graovac, A. Note on the comparison of the first and second normalized Zagreb eccentricity indices. *Acta Chim. Slov.* **2010**, *57*, 524–528.
17. Estrada, E.; Torres, L.; Rodríguez, L.; Gutman, I. An atom-bond connectivity inde. Modelling the enthalpy of formation of alkanes. *Indian J. Chem.* **1998**, *37*, 849–855.
18. Gao, W.; Siddiqui, M.K.; Naeem, M.; Rehman, N.A. Topological Characterization of Carbon Graphite and Crystal Cubic Carbon Structures. *Molecules* **2017**, *22*, 1496. [CrossRef] [PubMed]
19. Siddiqui, M.K.; Naeem, M.; Rahman, N.A.; Imran, M. Computing topological indicesof certain networks. *J. Optoelectron. Adv. Mater.* **2016**, *18*, 884–892.
20. Shao, Z.; Wu, P.; Zhang, X.; Dimitrov, D.; Liu, J. On the maximum ABC index of graphs with prescribed size and without pendent vertices. *IEEE Access* **2018**, *6*, 27604–27616. [CrossRef]
21. Siddiqui, M.K.; Imran, M.; Ahmad, A. On Zagreb indices, Zagreb polynomials of some nanostar dendrimers. *Appl. Math. Comput.* **2016**, *280*, 132–139. [CrossRef]
22. Shao, Z.; Wu, P.; Gao, Y.; Gutman, I.; Zhang, X. On the maximum ABC index of graphs without pendent vertices. *Appl. Math. Comput.* **2017**, *315*, 298–312. [CrossRef]
23. Baig, A.Q.; Imran, M.; Ali, H. On topological indices of poly oxide, poly silicate, DOX, and DSL networks. *Can. J. Chem.* **2015**, *93*, 730–739. [CrossRef]
24. Shao, Z.; Siddiqui, M.K.; Muhammad, M.H. Computing zagreb indices and zagreb polynomials for symmetrical nanotubes. *Symmetry* **2018**, *10*, 244. [CrossRef]
25. Gupta, S.; Singh, M.; Madan, A.K. Application of Graph Theory: Relationship of Eccentric Connectivity Index and Wiener's Index with Anti-inflammatory Activity. *J. Math. Anal. Appl.* **2002**, *266*, 259–268. [CrossRef]
26. Chartrand, G.; Zhang, P. *Introduction to Graph Theory*; McGraw-Hill Higher Education: New York, NY, USA, 2007.
27. Harris, J.M.; Hirst, J.L.; Mossinghoff, M.J. *Combinatorics and Graph Theory*; Springer Science and Business Media: Berlin/Heidelberg, Germany, 2008.

© 2018 by the authors. Licensee MDPI, Basel, Switzerland. This article is an open access article distributed under the terms and conditions of the Creative Commons Attribution (CC BY) license (http://creativecommons.org/licenses/by/4.0/).

MDPI AG
Grosspeteranlage 5
4052 Basel
Switzerland
Tel.: +41 61 683 77 34

Mathematics Editorial Office
E-mail: mathematics@mdpi.com
www.mdpi.com/journal/mathematics

Disclaimer/Publisher's Note: The statements, opinions and data contained in all publications are solely those of the individual author(s) and contributor(s) and not of MDPI and/or the editor(s). MDPI and/or the editor(s) disclaim responsibility for any injury to people or property resulting from any ideas, methods, instructions or products referred to in the content.

www.ingramcontent.com/pod-product-compliance
Lightning Source LLC
LaVergne TN
LVHW070434100526
838202LV00014B/1598